The Best Test Preparation for the

GED

GENERAL EDUCATIONAL DEVELOPMENT

Scott Cameron, M.S.
Science Department Chairperson
San Marino High School, San Marino, California

Janet G. Emmons, Ed.M.
Instructor of English
McCullough High School, The Woodlands, Texas

Linda Wiley Jackson, M.A.T.
English Department Chairperson
Raleigh-Egypt High School, Memphis, Tennessee

Mary Ann Kay, M.S.
Science Department Chairperson
Resurrection High School, Chicago, Illinois

Deloris K. Klug, M.A.
Science Department Chairperson
Westside High School, Anderson, South Carolina

Charles M. Mallek, M.A.
Social Studies Department Chairperson
Lakeview High School, St. Clair Shores, Michigan

Sandra A. Marona, Ed.M., M.A.
Reading Specialist
Agawam High School, Agawam, Massachusetts

June A. Niimi
Mathematics Department Chairperson
Pahoa High School, Pahoa, Hawaii

Joe D. Reed, Jr., M.S.
Science Department Chairperson
Big Spring High School, Big Spring, Texas

Thomasene W. Thomas, M.A.
Social Studies Department Chairperson
Lincoln High School, Port Arthur, Texas

Robert B. Truscott, M.A.
Former Assistant Director
Douglass/Cook College Writing Center
Rutgers University, New Brunswick, New Jersey

Robert E. Winstead, Ed.M.
Instructor of Mathematics
Burges High School, El Paso, Texas

 RESEARCH & EDUCATION ASSOCIATION
61 Ethel Road West • Piscataway, New Jersey 08854

The Best Test Preparation for the
GED (General Educational Development)

1997 PRINTING

Printed in the United States of America

Library of Congress Catalog Card Number 95-68124

International Standard Book Number 0-87891-869-8

Research & Education Association
61 Ethel Road West
Piscataway, New Jersey 08854

REA supports the effort to conserve and
protect environmental resources by
printing on recycled papers.

ACKNOWLEDGMENTS

Special recognition is extended to the following persons:

Dr. Max Fogiel, President, for his overall guidance which has brought this publication to completion

Stacey A. Daly, Managing Editor, for her management of the project and the editorial staff throughout each phase of the project

Jeffrey C. Turbitt, Revisions Editor, for his editorial contributions

Elizabeth Fili, Richard S. Gripp, Alexandra E. Sonshine, and Marianne Williams for their editorial contributions

CONTENTS

PREFACE
    About Research and Education Association vi
    GED Study Course Schedule vii

CHAPTER 1 • *Introduction* 1
    About This Book 2
    About the Test 2
    How to Use This Book 3
    Format for the GED 4
    About the Review Sections 6
    Scoring the Exam 7
    Requirements for Issuance of Certificate/Diploma 15
    Studying for the GED 21
    GED Test Taking Tips 21
    The Day of the Test 23

CHAPTER 2 • *Writing Skills Review* 25
    Part I Review 26
    Part II Review 94

CHAPTER 3 • *Social Studies Review* 115

CHAPTER 4 • *Science Review* 173

CHAPTER 5 • *Interpreting Literature and the Arts Review* 343

CHAPTER 6 • *Math Review* 387

THE PRACTICE TESTS

EXAM I 495
Answer Sheet 496
Exam I 501
Answer Key 589
Detailed Explanations of Answers 592

EXAM II 645
Answer Sheet 646
Exam II 651
Answer Key 738
Detailed Explanations of Answers 741

EXAM III 783
Answer Sheet 784
Exam III 789
Answer Key 878
Detailed Explanations of Answers 881

APPENDIX 927

INDEX 930

About Research and Education Association

Research and Education Association (REA) is an organization of educators, scientists, and engineers who specialize in various academic fields. REA was founded in 1959 for the purpose of disseminating the most recently developed scientific information to groups in industry, government, high schools, and universities. Since then, REA has become a successful and highly respected publisher of study aids, test preps, handbooks, and reference works.

REA's Test Preparation series extensively prepares students and professionals for the Medical College Admission Test (MCAT), the Graduate Record Examinations (GRE), the Graduate Management Admission Test (GMAT), the Scholastic Aptitude Test (SAT), the Test of English as a Foreign Language (TOEFL), the Advanced Placement Exams, as well as the Tests of General Educational Development (GED).

Whereas most test preparation books present few practice exams which bear little resemblance to the actual exams, REA's test preparation books present exams which accurately depict the official tests in degree of difficulty and in types of questions. REA's practice exams are always based on the most recently administered tests and include every type of question that can be expected on the actual tests.

REA's publications and educational materials are highly regarded for their significant contribution to the quest for excellence that characterizes today's educational goals. We continually receive an unprecedented amount of praise for our books from professionals, instructors, librarians, parents, and students. Our authors are as diverse as the subjects and fields represented in the books we publish. They are well known in their respective fields and serve on the faculties of universities and high schools throughout the United States.

GED STUDY
COURSE
SCHEDULE

GED Study Course Schedule

The following study course schedule allows for thorough preparation for the GED. Although it is designed for 12 weeks, it can be condensed into a six-week program if less time is available by combining two weeks into one. If you are not enrolled in a structured course, be sure to set aside enough time each day to study. Depending on your schedule, you may find it easier to study throughout the weekend. But no matter which study schedule works best for you, the more time you devote to studying for the GED, the more prepared and relaxed you will feel on the day of the exam.

Week	Activity
1	Read and study the introduction sections on studying for the GED on the following pages. Take Exam I to determine your strengths and weaknesses. You may wish to take one subject part of the test each day. For example, take the Writing Skills on Monday, Social Studies on Tuesday, Science on Wednesday, etc. Score each section by using the score chart found in the introduction. (You may need the help of a counselor or teacher to read your essay in order to score your essay.) You can then determine the subjects in which you will need to strengthen your skills. Compare your score to the average score needed to pass in your state found in the score chart information. If you should score lower than the average (around 35 – 40) on any particular subject, you will want to concentrate on that area as you study each review section in this book.
2	Study the Writing Skills Review: Part I. Be sure to complete every drill and study the list of commonly misspelled words.
3	Study the Writing Skills Review: Part II. Take the essay writing drill. Rework the essay until you believe it would receive a top score according to the qualifications found in this introduction in the scoring section, and in the review. You may want to request the help of a teacher or counselor to score your essay since the actual essay will be read by a reader.
4	Study the Social Studies Review. Be sure to complete all the drills.
5	Study the Science Review in Biology and Chemistry. Take all the drills.

Week	Activity
6	Study the Science Review in Earth Science and Physics. Take all the drills.
7	Study the Interpreting Literature and the Arts Review. Complete all the drills.
8	Study the Math Review in Arithmetic and Algebra. Complete all the drills.
9	Study the Math Review in Algebra and Geometry. Complete all the drills.
10	Take Exam II and after scoring your exam, review thoroughly all your incorrect answer explanations to determine your strengths and weaknesses.
11	Take Exam III and after scoring your exam, compare any improvement in comparison with the previously scored exam.
12	Determine your weaknesses based on Exam III and review thoroughly all your incorrect answer explanations. Then review the subjects in which you need to gain improvement by studying again the appropriate reviews.

▼

INTRODUCTION

Chapter 1

ABOUT THIS BOOK

This book will provide you with an accurate and complete representation of the Tests of General Educational Development (GED). The three sample tests are based on the most recently administered GED examinations. Our reviews are designed to prepare you for the types of questions you can expect to see when taking the actual test. You are allowed 7 hours and 35 minutes to complete each of the sample tests, which is the amount of time you will be given during the actual exam. (Don't panic! The actual exam is usually administered during two or three sittings over a period of two days. Check with your state's Department of Education for information on GED test centers, test times, and test dates.) The sample tests contain every type of question that you may expect to appear on the actual exam. Following each test you will find an answer key with detailed explanations which are designed to help you understand the test material.

About the Test

Who takes the test and what is it used for?

The GED is taken by people who did not complete their high school education and would like to obtain a state-issued high school diploma. A state-issued high school diploma is then obtained upon successful completion of the exam. A candidate may choose to take the GED to fulfill requirements for entrance into colleges or other schools, to further his employment opportunities, or even just for self-satisfaction. The GED is taken by nearly 700,000 people every year.

Who administers the test?

The GED is developed and administered by the GED Testing Service of the American Council on Education (ACE). Questions for the GED are created by writers and reviewers who are experienced in secondary or adult education. They follow standardized procedures, developed by the GED Testing Service, to ensure that the content and difficulty levels are appropriate. According to the American Council on Education, the writers and reviewers represent a wide variety of ethnic groups and are selected from many geographic areas. All questions are reviewed by a number of people, revised as necessary, and then are standardized based on a nationally selected sample of graduating high school seniors.

When and where is the test given?

The GED is administered on a regular basis in the United States and Canada. To accommodate all examinees, there are many versions of the exam, including administrations in English, French, Spanish, braille, large print, and audio tape recorded editions.

To receive information on upcoming administrations of the GED, contact your local high school, adult school, GED Testing Center, or the GED Testing Service at:

> 1-800-62 MY GED
> 1-800-626-9433, or
>
> General Educational Development
> GED Testing Service
> American Council on Education
> One Dupont Circle, N.W.
> Washington, D.C. 20036

How to Use This Book

What do I study first?

Before you do anything else, take one of the practice tests to help you determine what areas may cause you the most difficulty. Carefully going through the detailed explanations of answers will help you to understand what you are doing wrong. Once you have taken a practice test, you should first study the reviews which cover your problem areas. The reviews will cover the information you will need to know when taking the exam.

When you have done this, you should go back and study all of the remaining reviews and the test-taking tips which appear at the end of this introduction. They will be very useful in helping you brush up on your skills. Then, make sure you take the remaining two practice exams to further test yourself and become familiar with the format and procedures involved with taking the actual GED.

When should I start studying?

It is never too early for you to start studying for the GED—the earlier the better. You should start studying as soon as possible so that you will be able to learn more. Starting early will allow you the time necessary to strengthen your problem areas. Do not procrastinate! Last-minute studying and cramming is **not** an effective way to study since it does not allow you the time needed to learn the exam material.

Format for the GED

TEST	NUMBER OF QUESTIONS	MINUTES TO TAKE TEST	SUBJECT AREAS COVERED
TEST ONE: Writing Skills (two parts)	55	75	Part one deals with sentence structure, usage, and mechanics.
	Around 200 words	45	Part two is an essay.
TEST TWO: Social Studies	64	85	Areas include history, geography, economics, political science, and behavioral science.
TEST THREE: Science	66	95	Subjects covered are the life sciences (biology) and the physical sciences (earth science, physics, and chemistry).
TEST FOUR: Interpreting Literature and the Arts	45	65	Topics tested include popular literature, classical literature, and commentary.
TEST FIVE: Mathematics	56	90	Math areas covered include arithmetic (measurement, number relationships, data analysis), algebra, and geometry.

Total Testing Time: 7 hours, 35 minutes

All of the questions in the GED, with the exception of the essay, will be in multiple choice format. Each question will have five answers, numbered one through five, from which to choose. You should be aware of the amount of time you have to complete each section of the test, so that you do not waste too much time working on difficult questions, while neglecting to answer easy questions. Speed is very important. Using the practice tests will help you prepare for this task. Taking as many of the practice tests as possible, and making sure to time yourself, will help you become accustomed to the time constraints. Repeating this process will help you develop speed in answering the questions because you will become more familiar with the format.

First, make sure you know how much time you have to complete each section. Second, read the directions to each section so that you understand it completely. Third, you should become familiar with the five test areas covered on the GED. These tests include:

Test One: Writing Skills (Two parts)

Part One of the Writing Skills test consists of 55 questions which will ask you to read passages and then answer the questions that follow. You will have 75 minutes in which to complete this section. This test is composed of 35% sentence structure questions, 35% usage questions, and 30% spelling, punctuation, and capitalization questions. Approximately 50% of the questions on this test will deal with sentence correction and 35% with sentence revision, while 15% of the sentence structure and usage questions will deal with construction shift.

Part Two of the Writing Skills test is a 45-minute essay. Your essay must be written on the topic listed in your test booklet. You will be expected to follow all of the rules for sentence structure, usage, and mechanics in writing your essay.

Test Two: Social Studies

The Social Studies test has 64 multiple choice questions. You will have 85 minutes in which to answer questions based on a passage, graph, map, chart, or figure. The test consists of 25% history questions, 20% economics questions, 20% political science questions, 15% geography questions, and 20% behavioral science (anthropology, psychology, and sociology) questions. The test questions will deal 20% with evaluation, 30% with analysis, 30% with application, and 20% with comprehension.

Test Three: Science

The Science test is a 95-minute test consists of 66 questions. The questions on the test will be based on figures, charts, graphs, passages, and other written information. This test deals with 50% life sciences (biology) questions and 50% physical sciences (earth sciences, physics, and chemistry) questions. The test questions will deal 20% with evaluation, 30% with analysis, 30% with application, and 20% with comprehension.

Test Four: Interpreting Literature and the Arts

The Interpreting Literature and the Arts test is a 65-minute, 45-question test. The questions in this test are based on excerpts from poetry, essays, biographies, plays, critical reviews (of television, film, literature, dance, art, music, sculpture, and theater), and commentary. This test consists of 50% popular literature questions, 25% classical literature questions, and 25% commentary on literature and the arts questions. In this test, 60% of the questions will deal with comprehension, in which you will have to restate the ideas or information presented or summarize what you read. Application questions make up 15% of the questions and will ask you to draw your own conclusions, understand the effects or importance of the situation, or to identify the implications involved in the situation. The test also consists of 25% analysis questions which will ask you to define stylistic and structural techniques in terms of concept.

Test Five: Mathematics

The Mathematics test is a 90-minute test. The 56 questions on this test deal with 50% arithmetic, 30% algebra, and 20% geometry. The arithmetic questions are 30% measurement, 10% number relationships, and 10% data analysis. Approximately 30% to 40% of the questions on this test will ask you to solve a problem using proportion and ratio techniques, while 15% of the questions will ask you to identify a formula and then apply it to the problem.

About the Review Sections

Our reviews are written to help you understand the concepts behind the questions which will be asked on the actual GED. They will help you to prepare for the actual test by teaching you what you need to know. Each review is complete with drills which will help to reinforce the subject matter. The five review sections in this book correspond to the tests of the actual GED. By using the reviews in conjunction with the practice tests, you will be able to sharpen your skills and score well on the GED.

Writing Skills Test Review

This section reviews correct sentence structure, usage, spelling, punctuation, and capitalization, and includes drills to help reinforce these rules. Studying these rules will help you do well on both parts of the Writing Skills test. Also discussed in this review are essay writing techniques to aid you in developing a strong essay for Part II of the Writing Skills test.

Social Studies Test Review

This review provides a rundown of what you will need to know to pass the Social Studies test. Included are reviews of history, economics, political science, geography, and the behavioral sciences of anthropology, psychology, and sociology. Drills are also provided to help you enhance your skills to pass this test.

Science Test Review

Discussed in this review is everything you need to know to pass the Science test. Included are reviews and drills on biology, earth science, physics, and chemistry.

Interpreting Literature and the Arts Test Review

This review will help you become familiar with the type of material that you will encounter on the actual GED. The extensive reviews and drills cover writing forms including fiction, poetry, drama, essay, and commentary. Studying the Interpreting the Literature and the Arts test review will help you do well on this test.

Mathematics Test Review

The Math test review covers the basics of what you need to know to pass this test. Included are reviews and drills on arithmetic, algebra, and geometry.

Scoring the Exam

How is the GED scored?

When you receive your GED score report, it will contain six scores. Five individual scores will be reported, one for Parts One and Two of the Writing Skills test, one for the Social Studies test, one for the Science test, one for the Interpreting Literature and the Arts test, and one for the Mathematics test. The sixth score listed on the score report will be an average of the five individual test scores.

During the scoring process, an individual test is first given a raw score, which is your total number of correct answers. The raw score is then converted into a standard score, which ranges from a low of 20 to a high of 80. The standard score is what appears on your score report. Since each test has a different number of questions, raw scores must be converted into standard scores so that your performance on each of the individual tests may be accurately compared. Since various forms of the GED are administered during any one examination, the use of standard scores also corrects for changes in difficulty level between the different forms of the test. In other words, your score should be about the same no matter what form of the test you are administered.

How do I score my practice tests?

The first thing you must do to score your practice test is determine your number of correct answers for each test. This will give you your raw score (number of correct answers) for each test. Once you have determined your raw score for the individual tests, look at the chart which follows to determine your standard score.

Raw Score to Standard Score Conversion Chart

RAW SCORE (YOUR NUMBER OF CORRECT ANSWERS)

TEST ONE: Writing Skills (55 ques. & 1 essay)	TEST TWO: Social Studies (64 ques.)	TEST THREE: Science (66 ques.)	TEST FOUR: Interpreting Literature and the Arts (45 ques.)	TEST FIVE: Mathematics (56 ques.)	STANDARD SCORE
See table in following section entitled "How is my score obtained for the Writing Skills test?"	60–64	60–66	44–45	54–56	80
	59	58–59	40–43	50–53	75–79
	58	57	39	49	70–74
	56–57	55–56	38	48	65–69
	53–55	52–54	36–37	46–47	60–64
	48–52	47–51	34–35	43–45	55–59
	42–47	41–46	30–33	37–42	50–54
	33–41	33–40	24–29	30–36	45–49
	25–32	26–32	18–23	22–29	40–44
	18–24	18–25	13–17	16–21	35–39
	13–17	13–17	8–12	11–15	30–34
	10–12	10–12	6–7	9–10	25–29
	0–9	0–9	0–5	0–8	20–24

(The information in this chart is an approximation, since the actual scores change from each test administration.)

In the chart above, the five columns on the left show the complete range of raw scores that may be obtained. The column on the right shows every possible standard score that may be obtained. If, for example, you receive 49 correct answers on Test Three: Science, then your raw score is 49. Find the raw score column for Test Three: Science and find the score range which corresponds to your raw score. Then, look across to the standard score column and find the standard score which corresponds to your raw score. This is your standard score for the Science test. Repeat this process to find the standard scores for the other tests. Use the *Scoring Worksheet* at the end of this section to record your raw and standard scores.

How is my score obtained for the Writing Skills test?

In order to obtain your score for the Writing Skills test, your raw score for both Parts are combined to form one raw score. Then, the raw score is converted into a standard score to give you a single, composite score for this test. Generally, the multiple choice section of the Writing Skills test is weighed more heavily than the essay. The composite score will consist of 60 to 65 percent of the multiple choice section and 35 to 40 percent of the essay.

To find your score for the Writing Skills test, first determine your raw score for Part I, the multiple choice section. As mentioned before, your raw score will be the total number of correct answers for Part I. Once the raw score has been determined for Part I, record it in the *Scoring Worksheet* at the end of this section. Then go on to find the raw score for Part II, the essay.

Scoring your essay will require you to use the same technique used by the actual essay readers. A holistic method will be used to score your essay, in which two trained readers will read your paper and each assign it a score. The readers will judge your essay on its overall effectiveness and proper use of the rules of English, although they will not be keeping track of each and every mistake. Their overall impression of the essay will be the basis for your score.

Each essay will be graded using a six-point scale, with a score of six (6) being the highest and a score of one (1) being the lowest. The table below outlines what the reader will consider to be elements of an essay at each score level.

GED Essay Scores

Score of –6– An essay with a score of six will be extremely well organized. It will be concise and easy to understand. The topic will be effectively supported with examples that illustrate the point of the essay. Very few errors in the use of Standard Written English will be noted.

Score of –5– An essay with a score of five will be thoughtfully organized and present adequate support for the main idea. Some errors in the use of Standard Written English will appear; however, they will not be consistent.

Score of –4– An essay with a score of four is not extensively organized; however, the supporting details are somewhat effective. Errors in the use of Standard Written English appear, but they do not significantly detract from the essay.

Score of –3– An essay with a score of three will be underdeveloped, but will show some signs of planning and organization. The ideas used to support the main idea will often be weak and repetitive. There will be many errors in the use of Standard Written English.

Score of –2– An essay with a score of two will have very little structure. Ideas will be basically unorganized and will not be sufficient to support the essay. The use of Standard Written English will be very weak.

Score of –1– An essay with a score of one will have virtually no structure and the numerous errors in the use of Standard Written English will make the essay difficult to understand. The essay will not be developed and will have no apparent purpose.

Once each reader has assigned the essay a score, the two scores are added together, provided they do not differ by more than one point. A score between 2 and 12 will be obtained. This is your raw score.

In some cases, one reader will assign an essay a low score, while the other reader will assign the same essay a high score. When such discrepancies occur with the two scores differing by more than one point, a third reader is called in to score the essay. The three scores are averaged (to do this, add the three scores together and divide by 3), then the average is doubled and rounded off to the nearest whole number. In such a case, this number would be your raw score.

You may want to find two to three people who are willing to score your essay, in order to use the process described above to obtain a raw score. Should you decide to grade your own essay, assign the essay a score, using the *GED Essay Scores* chart, then double that number to determine the raw score. If you feel that your essay is between two scores (perhaps it is between a 4 and a 5 essay), add both numbers together to obtain your raw score (4 + 5 = 9). After determining your essay raw score, record the score in the *Scoring Worksheet*.

If you score your own essay, be objective! Most of us like to think that our work is excellent, but we must learn to see where there is room for improvement. On the other hand, some people have a tendency to automatically decide that their work is poor, when it may not be at all. Try to see your writing for what it is whether it is excellent, terrible, or average.

Now that you have a raw score for Parts I and II of the Writing Skills test, you can go on to find your standard score using the table below. On the left side of the table, the raw score range for the essay is given, while the raw score range for the multiple choice section is listed along the top. Find your essay raw score on the left side, then find your multiple choice raw score along the top. The point where these two scores intersect on the table represents your approximate standard score range.

TABLE 1
GED WRITING SKILLS TEST WEIGHTED COMPOSITE SCORE

Number of Multiple Choice Items Correct (Raw Score)

Total Essay Score	0	1	2	3	4	5	6	7	8	9	10	11	12	13	14	15	16	17	18	19	20	21	22	23	24	25
12	42	42	42	43	43	44	44	45	45	46	46	47	48	49	50	50	51	51	52	52	53	53	54	54	54	55
11	40	40	40	41	41	42	42	43	43	44	44	45	45	45	47	48	48	48	49	49	49	50	50	50	51	51
10	38	38	38	39	39	40	40	41	41	42	42	42	43	44	45	45	45	46	46	46	47	47	47	48	48	49
9	35	35	35	36	36	37	37	38	38	39	39	40	40	42	43	43	44	44	45	45	45	46	46	46	47	47
8	34	34	34	35	35	36	36	37	37	38	38	38	39	40	41	41	41	42	42	42	43	43	44	44	45	45
7	32	32	32	33	33	34	34	35	35	36	36	36	37	38	39	40	40	40	40	41	41	42	42	42	43	43
6	30	30	30	31	31	32	32	33	33	34	34	35	35	36	37	38	39	39	39	40	40	40	40	41	41	41
5	28	28	28	29	29	30	30	31	31	32	32	32	33	35	35	35	36	36	36	37	37	38	39	40	40	40
4	25	25	25	26	26	27	27	28	28	29	29	30	30	30	32	33	34	35	35	35	35	36	36	36	36	37
3	23	23	23	24	24	25	25	26	26	27	27	27	28	29	30	31	32	32	32	33	33	34	34	34	35	35
2	20	20	20	21	21	22	22	23	23	24	24	24	25	26	27	28	28	28	29	29	29	30	30	30	31	31

Note: Numbers in the body of the table represent standard scores for certain combinations of essay and multiple choice raw scores. The score scale represented in the table was obtained through the 1987 administration of the GED Writing Skills test to graduating high school seniors.

To find your standard score,

1. Locate your essay raw score along the left-hand side of the chart, labelled "Total Essay Score."
2. Then, locate your multiple choice raw score along the top of the chart, labelled "Number of Multiple Choice Items Correct (Raw Score)."
3. From your essay raw score, look across the column, and from your multiple choice raw score, look down the column. The number at which these two columns meet is your **standard score.**

TABLE 1 — Continued
GED WRITING SKILLS TEST WEIGHTED COMPOSITE SCORE

Number of Multiple Choice Items Correct (Raw Score)

Total Essay Score	26	27	28	29	30	31	32	33	34	35	36	37	38	39	40	41	42	43	44	45	46	47	48	49	50
12	55	55	56	56	56	57	57	58	58	59	59	60	60	61	62	64	66	67	68	70	72	74	76	78	80
11	51	52	52	52	53	53	54	54	55	55	56	56	57	58	58	59	60	61	62	64	66	68	70	72	74
10	49	50	50	50	51	51	52	52	53	53	54	54	55	55	56	56	57	57	58	60	62	64	66	68	70
9	47	48	48	49	49	50	50	50	51	51	52	52	53	53	54	55	55	56	57	59	61	63	65	67	69
8	45	46	46	46	47	47	47	48	49	49	50	50	51	51	51	52	52	53	54	56	58	60	62	64	66
7	44	44	45	45	45	46	46	47	47	48	48	49	49	50	50	50	51	51	52	54	56	58	60	62	64
6	42	42	42	43	43	43	44	44	45	45	46	46	47	47	48	49	50	50	51	53	55	57	59	61	63
5	40	40	41	41	41	42	42	42	43	43	44	44	45	45	46	46	47	47	48	50	52	54	56	58	60
4	37	37	38	38	38	39	39	40	40	41	41	42	42	43	43	44	45	45	46	48	50	52	54	56	58
3	35	35	36	36	36	37	37	37	38	38	39	39	40	40	41	41	42	42	43	45	47	49	51	53	55
2	31	32	32	32	33	33	34	34	35	35	36	36	37	37	38	39	40	40	41	43	45	47	49	51	53

Note: Numbers in the body of the table represent standard scores for certain combinations of essay and multiple choice raw scores. The score scale represented in the table was obtained through the 1987 administration of the GED Writing Skills test to graduating high school seniors.

To find your standard score,

1. Locate your essay raw score along the left-hand side of the chart, labelled "Total Essay Score."
2. Then, locate your multiple choice raw score along the top of the chart, labelled "Number of Multiple Choice Items Correct (Raw Score)."
3. From your essay raw score, look across the column, and from your multiple choice raw score, look down the column. The number at which these two columns meet is your **standard score.**

Scoring Worksheet

	Raw Score	Standard Score
Test One: Writing Skills		
Multiple Choice	_____	
Essay	_____	
Composite Score		_____
Test Two: Social Studies	_____	_____
Test Three: Science	_____	_____
Test Four: Interpreting Literature and the Arts	_____	_____
Test Five: Mathematics	_____	_____

What is a passing score for the GED?

Every state has its own requirements for what constitutes a passing score for the GED. Generally, each state will require that you obtain a certain score for each of the individual subject tests, and then also obtain a certain average (total) score, which is a combination of all of your individual scores.

Listed on the following pages are the current GED requirements for each of the fifty states, U.S. territories, and Canada. Also included are age and residency requirements, testing fee amounts, and the title of the certificate which you will be awarded. For further information, you should contact your state's Department of Education.

REQUIREMENTS FOR ISSUANCE OF CERTIFICATE/DIPLOMA

Location	Minimum Test Score	Minimum Age For Credential	Residency Requirement	Minimum Age For Testing	Testing Fee Per Battery	Title Of Credential
UNITED STATES						
Alabama	40 min & 45 avg	18[1]	30 days	18[1]	$25.00[2]	Cert. of H.S. Equiv.
Alaska	40 min & 45 avg	18[1]	resident	18[1]	max. $25.00	H.S. Dipl.
Arizona	40 min & 45 avg	18[1]	none	18[1]	max. $25.00[2]	H.S. Cert. of Equiv.
Arkansas	40 min & 45 avg	16	legal resident	16[1]	none	H.S. Dipl.
California	40 min & 45 avg	18[1]	resident	18[1]	varies	H.S. Equiv. Cert.
Colorado	40 min & 45 avg	17	resident[1]	17	$25.00-$40.00	H.S. Equiv. Cert.
Connecticut	40 min & 45 avg	17[1]	resident	17[1]	over 21, $13.00	H.S. Dipl.
Delaware	40 min & 45 avg	18	resident	18[1]	$25.00	St. Bd. of Ed. Endsmt.
Washington D. C.	40 min & 45 avg	18	resident[1]	18[1]	$20.00	H.S. Equiv. Cert.
Florida	40 min & 45 avg	18	legal resident	18[1]	$25.00	H.S. Dipl.
Georgia	40 min & 45 avg	18[1]	none	18[1]	$35.00	Gen. Educ. Dev. Diploma

[1] Jurisdictional requirements on exceptions and limitations.
[2] Jurisdictional requirements on credential and other fees.

Location	Minimum Test Score	Minimum Age For Credential	Residency Requirement	Minimum Age For Testing	Testing Fee Per Battery	Title Of Credential
Hawaii	40 min & 45 avg	17	resident[1]	17[1]	$20.00	Dept. of Ed. H.S. Dipl.
Idaho	40 min & 45 avg	18	resident	18[1]	varies	H.S. Equiv. Cert.
Illinois	40 min & 45 avg	18[1]	30 days	18[1]	$15.00[2]	H.S. Equiv. Cert.
Indiana	40 min & 45 avg	17[1]	30 days	17[1]	maximum $25.00	H.S. Dipl.
Iowa	40 min & 45 avg	17[1]	none	17[1]	$20.00[2]	H.S. Equiv. Dipl.
Kansas	40 min & 45 avg	16[1]	resident[1]	16[1]	$30.00	H. S. Dipl.
Kentucky	40 min & 45 avg	16	resident	16[1]	$25.00	H.S. Equiv. Dipl.
Louisiana	40 min & 45 avg	17[1]	resident[1]	17[1]	maximum $20.00	H.S. Equiv. Dipl.[1]
Maine	40 min & 45 avg	18[1]	none	18[1]	none[2]	H.S. Equiv. Dipl.
Maryland	40 min & 45 avg	16[1]	3 months	16	$18.00[2]	H.S. Dipl.
Massachusetts	40 min & 45 avg	19[1]	resident	19[1]	$40.00	H.S. Equiv. Cert.
Michigan	40 min & 45 avg	18[1]	30 days	16[1]	varies	H.S. Equiv. Cert.
Minnesota	40 min & 45 avg	19[1]	resident	19[1]	$40.00	Sec. Sch. Equiv. Cert.

[1] Jurisdictional requirements on exceptions and limitations.
[2] Jurisdictional requirements on credential and other fees.

Location	Minimum Test Score	Minimum Age For Credential	Residency Requirement	Minimum Age For Testing	Testing Fee Per Battery	Title Of Credential
Mississippi	40 min & 45 avg	17	30 days[1]	17[1]	$20.00	H.S. Equiv. Dipl.
Missouri	40 min & 45 avg	16[1]	resident[1]	16[1]	$20.00	Cert. of H.S. Equiv.
Montana	40 min & 45 avg	17[1]	resident[1]	17[1]	$18.00	H.S. Equiv. Cert.
Nebraska	40 min & 45 avg	18	30 days[1]	16[1]	$20.00–$30.00[2]	Dept. of Ed. H.S. Dipl.
Nevada	40 min & 45 avg	17	none	17	$25.00[2]	Cert. of H.S. Equiv.
New Hampshire	40 min & 45 avg	18	resident	18[1]	$40.00	Cert. of H.S. Equiv.
New Jersey	40 min & 45 avg	16[1]	resident	16[1]	$20.00	H.S. Dipl.
New Mexico	40 min & 45 avg	18[1]	resident	18[1]	varies[2]	H.S. Dipl.
New York	40 min & 45 avg	19[1]	1 month	19[1]	none	H.S. Equiv. Dipl.
North Carolina	40 min & 45 avg	16	resident[1]	16[1]	$7.50[2]	H.S. Dipl. Equiv.
North Dakota	40 min & 45 avg	18[1]	none	18[1]	varies	H.S. Equiv. Cert.
Ohio	40 min & 45 avg	19[1]	resident	19[1]	$42.00[1,2]	Cert. of H.S. Equiv.

[1] Jurisdictional requirements on exceptions and limitations.
[2] Jurisdictional requirements on credential and other fees.

Location	Minimum Test Score	Minimum Age For Credential	Residency Requirement	Minimum Age For Testing	Testing Fee Per Battery	Title Of Credential
Oklahoma	40 min & 45 avg	16[1]	resident	16[1]	varies[2]	Cert. of H.S. Equiv.
Oregon	40 min & 45 avg	18[1]	resident[1]	18[1]	varies[2]	Cert. of Gen. Ed. Dev.
Pennsylvania	40 min & 45 avg[1]	18[1]	resident[1]	18[1]	varies	Com. Sec. Sc. Dipl.
Rhode Island	40 min & 45 avg	16[1]	resident	16[1]	$15.00	H.S. Equiv. Dipl.
South Carolina	40 min & 45 avg	17	resident[1]	17[1]	varies	H.S. Equiv. Dipl.
South Dakota	40 min & 45 avg	18[1]	resident[1]	17[1]	maximum $20.00	H.S. Equiv. Cert.
Tennessee	40 min & 45 avg	18[1]	resident	18[1]	$20.00-$25.00	Equiv. H.S. Dipl.
Texas	40 min & 45 avg	18[1]	resident[1]	18[1]	varies[2]	Cert. of H.S. Equiv.
Utah	40 min & 45 avg	17[1]	resident[1]	17[1]	$25.00 and up	Cert. of Gen. Ed. Dev.
Vermont	40 min & 45 avg	16	none	16[1]	$25.00-$30.00	Sec. Sc. Equiv. Cert.
Virginia	40 min & 45 avg	18[1]	resident	18[1]	$25.00[2]	Com. Gen. Ed. Dev. Cert.
Washington	40 min & 45 avg	19[1]	resident	19[1]	$25.00	Cert. of Ed. Comp.
West Virginia	40 min & 45 avg	18[1]	30 days	18[1]	varies	H.S. Equiv. Dipl.

[1] Jurisdictional requirements on exceptions and limitations.
[2] Jurisdictional requirements on credential and other fees.

Location	Minimum Test Score	Minimum Age For Credential	Residency Requirement	Minimum Age For Testing	Testing Fee Per Battery	Title Of Credential
Wisconsin	40 min & 45 avg	18	voting resident	18[1]	varies	H.S. Equiv. Dipl.
Wyoming	40 min & 45 avg	18	resident[1]	17[1]	varies	H.S. Equiv. Cert.
CANADA - PROVINCES & TERRITORIES						
Alberta	45 min each test	18[1]	resident	18	$50.00	H.S. Equiv. Dipl.
British Columbia	45 min each test	19[1]	resident	19	$26.75	Sec. Sc. Equiv. Cert.
Manitoba	45 min each test	19[1]	resident	19	$22.00	H.S. Equiv. Dipl.
New Brunswick	45 min each test	19	resident	19	$10.00	H.S. Equiv. Cert.
Newfoundland	40 min & 45 avg	19[1]	resident	19	none	H.S. Equiv. Dipl.
Northwest Terr.	45 min each test	18[1]	6 months	18[1]	$5.00	H.S. Equiv. Cert.
Nova Scotia	45 min each test	19[1]	none	19	$20.00	H.S. Equiv. Dipl.
Prince Edward Is.	45 min each test	19[1]	resident	19[1]	$20.00	H.S. Equiv. Cert.
Saskatchewan	45 min each test[1]	19	resident	19[1]	$25.00	H.S. Equiv. Cert.

[1] Jurisdictional requirements on exceptions and limitations.
[2] Jurisdictional requirements on credential and other fees.

Location	Minimum Test Score	Minimum Age For Credential	Residency Requirement	Minimum Age For Testing	Testing Fee Per Battery	Title Of Credential
Yukon	45 min each test	19[1]	resident	19[1]	$25.00	Sec. Sc. Equiv. Cert.
U.S. TERRITORIES						
American Samoa	40 min & 45 avg	17	resident	17[1]	$20.00	H.S. Dipl. of Equiv.
Canal Zone	40 min & 45 avg	17	resident[1]	17	$38.00	Cert. of H.S. Equiv.
Guam	40 min & 45 avg	18	resident	18[1]	$10.00	H.S. Equiv. Dipl.
Kwajalein	40 min & 45 avg	18	resident	18	$27.50	H. S. Equiv. Dipl.
Mariana Islands	40 min & 45 avg	18[1]	30 days	18[1]	$5.00[2]	H.S. Equiv. Dipl.
Marshall Islands	40 min & 45 avg	17[1]	30 days	17	$7.50[2]	H.S. Equiv. Dipl.
Micronesia	40 min & 45 avg	18	resident	18[1]	$7.50[2]	H.S. Equiv. Cert.
Palau	40 min & 45 avg	16	Contact your local Dept. of Ed.	16[1]	$10.00	Cert. of Equiv.
Puerto Rico	40 min & 45 avg	18	resident	18	no charge	H.S. Equiv. Dipl.
Virgin Islands	40 min & 45 avg	18	none[1]	17	$20.00	H. S. Dipl.

[1] Jurisdictional requirements on exceptions and limitations.
[2] Jurisdictional requirements on credential and other fees.

Studying for the GED

It is important for you to choose the time and place for studying that works best for you. Some students may set aside a certain number of hours every morning to study, while others may choose to study at night before going to sleep. Other students may study during the day, while waiting in a line, or they may even study while eating lunch. Only you will be able to determine when and where your studying is most effective. The most important factor to keep in mind is consistency. Use your time wisely. Work out a study routine—and stick to it!

When you take the practice tests, try to make your practice conditions similar to actual testing conditions. Make sure you turn the television and radio off. Sit down at a quiet table which is free from distraction and **time yourself**! Afterwards, you should check each answer and thoroughly review the reasoning behind each question that you missed. You should not review too much at one time. Concentrate on each of your problem areas individually, until you feel comfortable with your ability in each of those areas.

Do not write in the margins and spaces of this book when practicing, since you will not be allowed to write in the test booklet when taking the actual test. Also, make sure you do not write anything on your answer sheet, except to mark the answer you choose. Make sure the question numbers correctly correspond to the question numbers on the answer sheet.

Keep track of your scores! You will be able to gauge your progress and discover general weaknesses in particular sections. You should carefully study the reviews that cover the areas which are causing you difficulty. This will help you build your skills in those areas.

GED Test Taking Tips

You may be unfamiliar with standardized tests, such as the GED. There are many ways for you to familiarize yourself with this type of examination. Listed below are points to help you become familiar with the GED, some of which may be applied to other standardized tests, as well.

How to Beat the Clock

Become comfortable with the standardized format. When you are practicing to take the GED, pretend that you are under the same time constraints as you would be during the test. Stay calm, pace yourself, and pay attention to the clock. Practice these techniques thoroughly. After simulating the test only a few times, you will boost your chances of doing well and you will be able to sit down for the actual GED much more confidently.

Become familiar with the directions. Make sure you read and understand the directions before you take the exam, so that you do not waste valuable testing time.

Know the format for each section before you actually take the test. (See the *Format for the GED* section of this introduction for more specific information on the format of the exam.) This will not only save you valuable time, but also ensure that you are familiar enough with the exam to avoid nervousness (and the mistakes that come from being nervous).

Work on the easier questions first. Mark the very difficult questions (in the test booklet, not on the answer sheet) and continue. **Remember, only correct answers will be counted in your score. You will not be penalized for guessing,** so when you have either answered or marked all of the questions, go back and answer any of the difficult questions that you may have skipped. If you find yourself working too long on one question, mark it and go on. Be sure that you are marking your answer in the space that corresponds to the number of the question in the test booklet.

Know how much time is allowed for each section. Remember that you are racing against the clock. This is why you should not spend too much time on a single question. Budget your time. Every question has the same value, whether it is difficult or easy, so it is important to move on if a question becomes too time consuming. Pace yourself and make sure to check your time periodically to make sure that you are moving at a good rate.

Should I guess?

If you don't know the answer to a question, guess! Eliminate answers that you know are wrong, and then pick the best answer from the ones that remain. Even if you can't eliminate any answers, guess anyway! Remember that there is no penalty for guessing, and only correct answers are counted. This means that you should never leave an answer choice blank. If you guess correctly, you will increase your number of correct answers, and if you guess wrong, you will not lose any points.

The Day of the Test

On the day of the test, you should wake up early (hopefully after a decent night's rest) and have a good breakfast. Make sure you dress comfortably, so that you are not distracted by being too hot or too cold while taking the exam. You should plan on arriving at the test center early. By being early, you will spare yourself the anxiety of being late for the test. It will also allow you to collect your thoughts and to relax before taking the exam.

Before you leave for the test center, make sure that you have **two** forms of identification. You will not be admitted to the test center without identification. Acceptable forms of identification include a driver's license, Social Security card, birth certificate, passport, and green card.

Make sure you bring at least two sharpened #2 pencils, with erasers, to the exam. You may want to wear a watch to the test center; however, only ordinary watches will be permitted. Watches with alarms, calculator functions, flashing lights, beeping sounds, etc., will not be allowed. In addition, neither food nor calculators will be allowed into the examination room.

During the Test

When you arrive at the test center, try to sit in a seat where you feel you will be comfortable. The GED is usually administered during two or three sittings, depending on your test center. No breaks are given during the exam. If you need to use the rest room, or if you become ill, you may leave the examination room, but you will not be allowed to make up any lost time.

Once you enter the test center, follow all of the rules and instructions given by the test supervisor. If you do not, you risk being dismissed from the examination or having your GED scores voided (they will not be scored).

When all of the test materials have been passed out, the test instructor will give you directions for filling out your answer sheet. You must fill out this sheet carefully since this information will be printed on your score report. Fill out your name exactly as it appears on your identification documents and admission ticket, unless otherwise instructed.

Make sure you do not write in your test booklet or on your answer sheet, except to fill in the circle corresponding to the answer you choose. Scratch paper will be provided. You will be marking your answers on side two of your answer sheet. Each numbered row will contain five circles corresponding to each answer choice for that question. Fill in the circle which corresponds to your answer darkly, completely, and in a neat manner. You can change your answer, but remember to completely erase your old answer. Only one answer should be marked. This is very important, as your answer sheet will be machine scored, and stray lines or unnecessary marks may cause the machine to score your answers incorrectly.

Only work on the test section on which the test instructor has instructed you to work. You should begin only when instructed to do so, and stop, immediately, when instructed to stop. Do not turn to the next section of the test until you are told to do so. When all of the sections have been completed, you should remain seated until all of the test materials have been collected.

▼
WRITING
SKILLS
REVIEW

Chapter 2

WRITING SKILLS: PART I REVIEW

I. WRITING I STRATEGIES

II. STANDARD WRITTEN ENGLISH

III. CAPITALIZATION

IV. PUNCTUATION

V. SPELLING AND WORD USAGE

Although we constantly come into contact with the English language, many people are still unfamiliar with the proper way to utilize this language. The Writing I section of the GED will test how well you understand and recognize correct standard written English. You will want to review the information we have provided for you in this section to ensure that you will do well on this section of the exam. Our review concentrates on the common errors that you should avoid in your writing and presents practice exercises in recognizing and correcting errors when they occur in the written language.

GED Writing I questions cover the areas of sentence structure, usage, and mechanics. The more familiar you are with correct standard written English, the better you will perform on the Writing I section of the GED. Our Review of Standard Written English represents various areas which will be covered in this test on the GED.

Along with this knowledge, speed and accuracy in answering the questions will have an effect upon your success on this section. Therefore, memorize the directions in order to save time and decrease your chances of making careless mistakes. Also, be sure to complete the practice drills which are included in the review, as they will help you to develop your skills.

I. WRITING I STRATEGIES

If you can determine that there is an error somewhere in the sentence, this is your plan of attack:

Sentence 1: **Many people say that their time spent in high school were the best time of their lives.**

What correction should be made to this sentence?

(1)   change the spelling of high school to highschool

(2)   change were to was

(3)   insert a comma after say

(4)   change lives to life

(5)   no correction is necessary

> **Step 1** Identify the part of the sentence in which you feel there is an error.

The part of the sentence which appears to be incorrect begins, "were the best time of their lives."

> **Step 2** Ask yourself if you can substitute the part in question with one of the answer choices.

The object of the verb "were" is "time" and is therefore incorrect. "Were" must be changed to "was" in order for the sentence to be correct due to the fact that "time" is a singular noun.

> **Step 3** Re-read the sentence with the answer choice you chose substituted for the part of the sentence in question. If it appears to be correct according to your knowledge of correct standard written English, this is your answer.

The sentence would then read:

Many people say that their time spent in high school was the best time of their lives.

If you cannot determine that there is an error somewhere in the sentence, this is your plan of attack:

Sentence 2: **Mr. Parker is <u>one of the professors who are teaching</u> students the importance of good grades and a good attitude.**

Which of the following is the best way to write the underlined portion of this sentence? If you think the original is the best way, choose option (1).

(1)   one of the professors who are teaching
(2)   one of the professors who is teaching
(3)   one of the professor that has taught
(4)   the professor that is to be teaching
(5)   the professor that taught

➤ **Step 1** Look at the answer choices to see what has been changed from the original sentence. This helps you to focus on the type of problem being tested in the question.

The changes that occur are related to the form of the verb **are** or the use of the phrase **one of**.

➤ **Step 2** Go back into the example sentence and try to find the error.

➤ **Step 3** Eliminate any answer choices that repeat the error that you have found.

➤ **Step 4** Eliminate any answer choices that are obviously incorrect.

Mr. Parker is the subject in this sentence. Since Mr. Parker is a singular noun, the verb "are," which is in the plural form, does not agree with the singular subject. "Are" must be changed to "is" in order to make the sentence correct. Therefore, answer choice (2) is correct. Answer choices (3), (4), and (5) are incorrect due to the improper use of the word "that."

➤ **ADDITIONAL HINTS**

- **Learn and understand the DIRECTIONS so you don't waste valuable time reading them on the day of the exam.**

- **Be sure to read the sentence exactly as it is written.**

- **Look for the most common errors in the sentence first. These are listed in the Review of Standard Written English.**

- Do not pay attention simply to the underlined words. The words that are not underlined can determine whether or not the underlined words are correct.

- If you still do not know the correct answer, try the shortest choice in the sentence first. Good writing tends to be concise.

- Do not waste time looking for errors that are not there—a correction may not be necessary.

- If all else fails, make an educated guess.

WRITING I TOPICS

The topics listed below should be reviewed in order to accurately answer the questions appearing on the Writing I section of the GED. See the Review of Standard Written English on the following pages.

SENTENCE STRUCTURE (35% of Test)

1. Sentence Fragments
2. Run-on Sentences
3. Comma Splices
4. Sentence Coordination
5. Use of the Subordinate Clause
6. Parallelism

USAGE (35% of Test)

1. Subject/Verb Agreement
2. Verb Tense
3. Pronouns

MECHANICS (30% of Test)

1. Capitalization
2. Punctuation
3. Spelling

II. REVIEW OF STANDARD WRITTEN ENGLISH

SUBJECT-VERB AGREEMENT

NO: The arrival of many friends promise good times.

Always remember to make the verb agree with the subject of the sentence. Be wary of the words that come between the subject and the verb. They may distract you.

YES: The **arrival** of many friends **promises** good times.

NO: Into the darkness stares her black cats.

Don't be fooled by sentences where the subject follows the verb. Be especially careful to determine the subject and make it agree with the verb.

YES: Into the darkness **stares** her black **cat**.

NO: Either the principal or the football coach usually attend the dance.

When singular subjects are joined by *either… or, neither… nor, or* or *nor,* the verb is also singular.

YES: Either the principal or the football **coach** usually **attends** the dance.

NO: Neither the cat nor the dogs is eating today.

If one of the subjects is plural and one is singular, make the verb agree with the subject nearest it.

YES: Neither the **cat** nor the **dogs are** eating today.

NO: Politics are a noun.

Remember that a word used as the title of a particular work, even if it is plural, requires a singular verb.

YES: Politics is a noun.

☞ Drill: Subject-Verb Agreement

DIRECTIONS: The following group of sentences may contain errors in subject-verb agreement. Make any necessary corrections.

1. Either her mother or her father usually drive her to school on rainy days.

2. There is, if I calculated right, two hundred dollars left in my bank account.

3. Mary, and her friends, was late for the test.

4. Economics are a major taught in many colleges.

5. The first years of high school is the most difficult.

6. Aristotle's *Poetics* have always been read widely.

7. The noise from all those fans were distracting.

8. Neither the chorus nor the actors knows their parts.

9. Each of us are going away for the weekend.

10. Neither the grass nor the flowers was growing well.

COMPARISON OF ADJECTIVES

NO: That was the most bravest thing he ever did.

Do not combine two superlatives.

YES: That was the **bravest** thing he ever did.

NO: Mary was more friendlier than Susan.

Do not combine two comparatives.

YES: Mary was friendlier than Susan.

NO: I can buy either the shirt or the scarf. The shirt is most expensive.

The comparative should be used when only two things are being compared.

YES: I can buy either the shirt or the scarf. The shirt is **more** expensive.

☞ Drill: Comparison of Adjectives

DIRECTIONS: In the following sentences, make the changes indicated in the parentheses. Also indicate if the comparative or superlative form is an adverb or an adjective.

1. He was sad to leave. (superlative)

2. She ran as fast as the others on the team. (comparative)

3. Throughout school, they were good in math. (superlative)

4. This class is as interesting as the European history class. (comparative)

5. He arrived as soon as I did. (comparative)

6. The test was as hard as we expected. (superlative)

7. He responded to the interviewer as candidly as Tom. (comparative)

8. The beggar had less possessions than she. (superlative)

9. That answer is perfectly correct. (superlative)

10. She read the part best. (comparative)

POSSESSIVE NOUNS

A common error to avoid is to write it's (the contraction for it is) for its (the possessive form) or vice versa.

Form the possessive singular of nouns by adding 's.

> Mary's book
>
> the Jones's family car
>
> the sun's rays
>
> my mother-in-law's suitcase

☞ Drill: Possessive Nouns

DIRECTIONS: The following group of sentences may contain errors in possession. Make any necessary corrections.

1. His suit, like James, was grey.

2. The president's adviser's past was investigated.

3. The pitcher's job is more difficult than the fielders.

4. The woman's cat's kittens were given away.

5. The majority leader of the House of Representatives' speech was well received.

6. The final plans of the Boy Scouts of America's meeting were made.

7. It was Susan, Ann, Joan and my idea.

8. The amateurs' life differs from the professionals.

9. That is Dr. White and her new house.

10. The play's ending satisfied the audience.

PREPOSITIONS

NO: She just couldn't start in to do her homework.

Do not overuse prepositions.

YES: She just couldn't start to do her homework.

☞ Drill: Prepositions

DIRECTIONS: The following group of sentences may contain prepositional errors. Make any necessary corrections.

1. Let's finish up the assignment.

2. He was interested and fascinated with physics.

3. She had learned of his life and his times through reading.

4. They were both repelled and driven toward the space creature.

5. Tell me on what he left it.

6. Let's go over to James' house tomorrow.

7. She always had an interest and an aptitude for science.

8. It took a long time to get at the problem.

9. She looked like her sister and her mother.

10. Her belief and dedication to the cause were total.

CONJUNCTIONS

NO: She loved him dearly but not his dog.

When using a conjunction, be sure that the sentence parts you are joining are in agreement.

YES: **She loved him dearly** but **she did not love his dog.**

NO: They complimented them both for their bravery and they thanked them for their kindness.

When using conjunctions, a common mistake that is made is to forget that each member of the pair must be followed by the same kind of construction.

YES: They both **complimented them for their bravery** and **thanked them for their kindness.**

NO: While I'm usually interested in Fellini movies, I'd rather not go tonight.

While refers to time and should not be used as a substitute for *although, and,* or *but.*

YES: **Although** I'm usually interested in Fellini movies, I'd rather not go tonight.

NO: We read in the paper where they are making great strides in DNA research.

Where refers to a place or location. Be careful not to use it when it does not have this meaning.

YES: We read in the paper **that** they are making great strides in DNA research.

☞ Drill: Conjunctions

<u>DIRECTIONS</u>: The following group of sentences may contain errors in the use of conjunctions. Make any necessary corrections.

1.   John's best assets are his personality and swimming ability.

2.   I heard on the radio where the play is closing this week.

3.   I was reading the paper and the phone rang.

4.   Susan ate vegetables often but not fruits.

5.   Please send me an answer to the question or opinions on the project.

6.   While I'm tired from the trip, I'll attend the concert tonight.

7.   Mary's goal is to study hard and pass the test.

8.   He produced the play while she directed it.

9.   A good essay is where the ideas are clearly articulated.

10.   The class wanted neither to read the book nor do the assignment.

MISPLACED MODIFIERS

NO: Harold watched the painter gaping in astonishment.

The dangling participle is an error that results in an unclear sentence. The participle should appear immediately before or after the subject of the sentence.

YES: Gaping in astonishment, Harold watched the painter.

NO: On correcting the test, his errors became apparent.

Many modifiers cause confusion when they are out of place.

YES: His errors became apparent when the test was corrected.

NO: Jane almost polished the plate until it shined.

Words such as *almost, only, just, even, nearly, hardly, not,* and *merely* must appear immediately before the word they modify or they will cause confusion.

YES: Jane polished the plate until it almost shined.

☞ Drill: Misplaced Modifiers

DIRECTIONS: The following group of sentences may contain misplaced modifiers. Make any necessary corrections.

1.   I saw a stray dog riding the bus this afternoon.

2.   The clothing was given to the poor in large packages.

3.   I found five dollars eating lunch in the park.

4.   We saw two girls riding bicycles from our car.

5.   Reading my book quietly, I jumped up when the car crashed.

6.   He ran the mile with a sprained ankle.

7.   The history majors only were affected by the new requirements.

8.   Running quickly to catch the bus, Susan's packages fell out of her arms onto the ground.

9.   He just asked the man directions to make sure.

10. He discovered a new route driving home.

PARALLEL STRUCTURE

NO: The janitor stopped, listened a moment, then he locked the door.

When ideas are similar, they should be expressed in similar forms. When elements of a sentence are similar, they too should appear in similar form.

YES: The janitor stopped, listened a moment, then locked the door.

☞ Drill: Parallel Structure

DIRECTIONS: The following group of sentences may contain errors in parallel structure. Make any necessary corrections.

1.   In the summer I usually like swimming and to water-ski.

2.   The professor explained the cause, effect, and the results.

3.   Mary read the book, studied the examples, and takes the test.

4.   Mark watched the way John started the car, and how he left the curb.

5.   They bought the house because of location and its affordability.

6.   The movie was interesting and had a lot of excitement.

7.   Shakespeare both wrote beautiful sonnets and complex plays.

8.   The painting is done either in watercolors or with oils.

9.   The lecturer spoke with seriousness and in a concerned tone.

10. Either we forget those plans, or accept their proposal.

RUN-ON SENTENCES

NO: It was a pleasant drive the sun was shining.

A run-on sentence is a sentence with too much in it. It usually contains two complete sentences separated by a comma, or two complete sentences merged together.

YES: It was a pleasant drive because the sun was shining.

NO: Talk softly, someone is listening.

Sometimes a writer will try to correct a run-on sentence by inserting a comma between the clauses, but this creates another error, a *comma splice*. The following examples illustrate various ways to correct the comma splice.

YES: Talk softly; someone is listening.

or

Talk softly, because someone is listening.

SENTENCE FRAGMENTS

NO: A tree as old as your father.

This is just the opposite of a run-on sentence. A sentence fragment does not have enough in it to make it a complete thought. It is usually missing a subject or a verb.

YES: The tree is as old as your father.

☞ Drill: Run-On Sentences/Sentence Fragments

DIRECTIONS: The following sentences may be either run-on sentences or sentence fragments. Make any necessary corrections.

1.   After the rain stopped.

2.   Mow the lawn, it is much too long.

3.   The settlement you reached it seems fair.

4.   When I read, especially at night. My eyes get tired.

5.   It was impossible to get through on the phone, the lines were down because of the storm.

6.   Is this the only problem? The leaky pipe?

7. Everyone saw the crime, no one is willing to come forth.

8. The weather was bad, she played in the rain.

9. Ellen paced the floor. Worrying about her economics final.

10. Their season was over, the team had lost the playoffs.

TENSE OF VERBS

Tense means time. Verbs have the ability to tell us not only what action is occurring, but also when it is occurring. The form of the verb changes to indicate when an action takes place.

NO: I swum two miles last week.

Do not confuse the past participle for the past tense.

YES: I **swam** two miles last week.

☞ Drill: Tense of Verbs

DIRECTIONS: For the following sentences, fill in the indicated form of the verb in parentheses.

1. I _____ fifty pages by tomorrow. (*to read, future*)

2. We _____ in the concert. (*to sing, past*)

3. He _____ class on Mondays and Wednesdays. (*to teach, present*)

4. You _____ the dress without permission. (*to take, past*)

5. It _____ once spring arrives. (*to grow, future*)

6. The bee _____ her while she was on vacation. (*to sting, past*)

7. He _____ many Broadway plays. (*to cast, past perfect*)

8. He _____ the plane tomorrow if the skies are clear. (*to fly, future progressive*)

9. They _____ furniture all afternoon. (*to choose, present perfect progressive*)

10. You _____ your ticket before the train arrived. (*to buy, past perfect progressive*)

STANDARD WRITTEN ENGLISH

ANSWER KEY

Drill: Subject-Verb Agreement

1. Either her mother or her father usually drives her to school on rainy days.

2. There are, if I calculated right, two hundred dollars left in my bank account.

3. Mary and her friends were late for the test.

4. Economics is a major taught in many colleges.

5. The first years of high school are the most difficult.

6. Aristotle's *Poetics* has always been read widely.

7. The noise from all those fans was distracting.

8. Neither the chorus nor the actors know their parts.

9. Each of us is going away for the weekend.

10. Neither the grass nor the flowers were growing well.

Drill: Comparison of Adjectives

1. He was **saddest** to leave. (adjective)

2. She ran **faster** than the others on the team. (adverb)

3. Throughout school, they were **the best** in math. (adjective)

4. This class is **more interesting** than European history class. (adjective)

5. He arrived **sooner** than I did. (adverb)

6. The test was the **hardest** we expected. (adjective)

7. He responded to the interviewer **more candidly** than Tom. (adverb)

8. This sentence (referring to "she") **cannot** be put in the superlative form.

9. The answer is **most perfectly** correct. (adverb)

10. She read the part **better**. (adjective)

Drill: Possessive Nouns

1. His suit, like James', was grey.
2. The past of the president's adviser was investigated.
3. The pitcher's job is more difficult than the fielders'.
4. The kittens of the woman's cat were given away.
5. The House of Representatives majority leader's speech was well received.
6. The final plans of the meeting of the Boy Scouts of America were made.
7. It was Susan's, Ann's, Joan's, and my idea.
8. The amateur's life differs from the life of the professional.
9. That is her and Dr. White's new house.
10. The ending of the play satisfied the audience.

Drill: Prepositions

1. Let's finish the assignment.
2. He was interested and fascinated by physics.
3. She had learned of his life and of his times through reading.
4. They were both repelled by and driven toward the space creature.
5. Tell me what he left it on.
6. Let's go to James' house tomorrow.
7. She always had an interest in and an aptitude for science.
8. It took a long time to get through the problem.
9. She looked like her sister and like her mother.
10. Her belief in and dedication to the cause were total.

Drill: Conjunctions

1. John's best assets are his personality and his swimming ability.
2. I heard on the radio that the play is closing this week.
3. I was reading the paper when the phone rang.
4. Susan often ate vegetables but not fruits.
5. Please send me either an answer to the questions or opinions on the project.
6. Although I'm tired from the trip, I'll attend the concert tonight.

7. Mary's goal is not only to study hard but also to pass the test.

8. He produced the play and she directed it.

9. A good essay is one in which the ideas are clearly articulated.

10. The class wanted neither to read the book nor to do the assignment.

Drill: Misplaced Modifiers

1. I saw a stray dog while I was riding the bus this afternoon.

2. The clothing was given in large packages to the poor.

3. I found five dollars while I was eating lunch in the park.

4. While we were in our car we saw two girls riding bicycles.

5. When the car crashed, I jumped up from quietly reading my book.

6. He ran the mile although his ankle was sprained.

7. Only the history majors were affected by the new requirements.

8. Susan's packages fell out of her arms onto the ground as she was running quickly to catch the bus.

9. He asked the man for directions just to make sure.

10. While driving home, he discovered a new route.

Drill: Parallel Structure

1. In the summer I usually like to swim and water-ski.

2. The professor explained the cause, the effect, and the results.

3. Mary read the book, studied the examples, and took the test.

4. Mark watched how John started the car, and how he left the curb.

5. They bought the house because of its location and its affordability.

6. The movie was both interesting and exciting.

7. Shakespeare wrote both (optional) beautiful sonnets and complex plays.

8. The painting is done with either watercolor or oils.

9. The lecturer spoke in a serious, concerned tone.

10. Either we forget those plans, or we accept their proposal.

Drill: Run-on Sentences/Sentence Fragments

1. Fragment: We went out after the rain stopped.

2. Run-on: Mow the lawn. It is much too long.

3. Run-on: The settlement you reached seems fair.

4.   Fragment: My eyes get tired when I read, especially at night.

5.   Run-on: It was impossible to get through on the phone, since the lines were down because of the storm.

6.   Fragment: Is the leaky pipe the only problem?

7.   Run-on: Everyone saw the crime, but no one is willing to come forth.

8.   Run-on: The weather was bad. She played in the rain.

9.   Fragment: Eileen paced the floor and worried about her economics final.

10. Run-on: The team had lost the playoffs; their season was over.

Drill: Tense of Verbs

1.   shall read
2.   sang
3.   teaches
4.   took
5.   will grow
6.   stung
7.   had cast
8.   will be flying
9.   have been choosing
10. had been buying

III. CAPITALIZATION

When a letter is capitalized, it calls special attention to itself. This attention should be for a good reason. There are standard uses for capital letters as well as much difference of opinion as to what should and should not be capitalized. In general, capitalize 1) all proper nouns, 2) the first word of a sentence, and 3) a direct quotation.

NAMES OF SHIPS, AIRCRAFT, SPACECRAFT, AND TRAINS:

Apollo 13	*Mariner IV*
DC-10	*S. S. United States*
Sputnik 11	*Boeing 707*

NAMES OF DEITIES:

God	*Jupiter*
Allah	*Holy Ghost*
Buddha	*Diana*
Jehovah	*Shiva*

GEOLOGICAL PERIODS:

Neolithic age	*Cenozoic era*
late Pleistocene times	*Age of Reptiles*
Ice Age	*Tertiary period*

NAMES OF ASTRONOMICAL BODIES:

Venus	*Big Dipper*
the Milky Way	*Halley's comet*
Ursa Major	*North Star*
Scorpio	*Deneb*
the Crab nebula	*Pleiades*

(Note that sun, moon and earth are not capitalized unless they are used with other astronomical terms that are capitalized.)

PERSONIFICATIONS:

Reliable Nature brought her promise of Spring.

Bring on Melancholy in his sad might.

Morning in the bowl of night has flung the stone/ that set the stars to flight.

HISTORICAL PERIODS:

the Middle Ages	*World War I*
Reign of Terror	*Great Depression*
Christian Era	*Roaring Twenties*
Age of Louis XIV	*Renaissance*

ORGANIZATIONS, ASSOCIATIONS, AND INSTITUTIONS:

Girl Scouts of America	*Kiwanis*
Young Men's Christian Association	*North Atlantic Treaty Organization*
New York Yankees	*League of Women Voters*
Smithsonian Institution	*Unitarian Church*
the Library of Congress	*Common Market*
the Illinois Central	*New York Philharmonic*
Franklin Glen High School	

GOVERNMENT AND JUDICIAL GROUPS:

New Jersey City Council	*Committee on Foreign Affairs*
Senate	*House of Commons*
Arkansas Supreme Court	*Parliament*
Peace Corps	*House of Representatives*
Municipal Court of Chicago	*Department of State*
Census Bureau	*Iowa Board of Education*
United States Court of Appeals	

A general term that accompanies a specific name is capitalized only if it follows the specific name. If it stands alone or comes before the specific name, it is put in lower case.

Washington State	*the state of Washington*
Senator Dixon	*the senator from Illinois*
Central Park	*the park*
Golden Gate Bridge	*the bridge*
President Andrew Jackson	*the president of the U.S.*
Pope John XXIII	*the pope*
Queen Elizabeth I	*the queen, Elizabeth I*
Tropic of Capricorn	*the tropics*
Glen Brook High School	*the high school in Glen Brook*
Monroe Doctrine	*the doctrine originated by Monroe*
the Milky Way Galaxy	*our galaxy the Milky Way*
the Mississippi River	*the river*
Easter Day	*the day we celebrated Easter*
Treaty of Versailles	*the treaty signed at Versailles*
Webster's Dictionary	*a dictionary by Webster*

Use a capital to start a sentence or a sentence fragment.

Our car would not start.

When will you leave? I need to know right away.

Never!

Let me in! Right now!

When a sentence appears within a sentence, start it with a capital.

The main question is, Where do we start?

We had only one concern: When would we eat?

My sister said, "I'll find the Monopoly set."

He answered, "We can only stay a few minutes."

In poetry, it is usual practice to capitalize the first word of each line even if the word comes in the middle of a sentence.

> *When I consider everything that grows*
> *Holds in perfection but a little moment,*
> *That this huge stage produceth naught but shows,*
> *Whereon the stars in secret influence comment.*
>
> — *William Shakespeare*

> *She dwells with Beauty — Beauty that must die;*
> *And Joy, whose hand is ever at his lips*
> *Bidding Adieu.*
>
> — *John Keats*

The most important words of titles are capitalized. Those words not capitalized are conjunctions (e.g., *and, or, but*), articles (e.g., *a, the, and*), and short prepositions (e.g., *of, on, by, for*). The first and last word of a title must always be capitalized.

A Man for All Seasons	*Crime and Punishment*
Of Mice and Men	"Let Me In"
Rise of the West	"What to Look For"
"Sonata in G-Minor"	"The Ever-Expanding West"
Strange Life of Ivan Osokin	"Rubaiyat of Omar Khayyam"
"All in the Family"	*Symphony No. 41*
"Ode to Billy Joe"	"Piano Concerto No. 5"

☞ Drill: Capitalization

DIRECTIONS: The following sentences contain errors in capitalization. Correct these sentences by making words capital where necessary, and other words lower case where necessary.

1. Where is the crab Nebula?

2. The girl scouts of America sell delicious cookies.

3. This year, senator Burns will run for re-election.

4. Barbara said, "let me know when you are off the phone."

5. beth's new car is a black dodge daytona which she purchased at the dodge dealer in new york city.

6. mike and jackie are both graduates of edison high school.

7. glaciers from the ice age still exist.

8. Today in class, the Professor lectured on the Neolithic Age.

9. sergeant bruce whisman of the united states marine corps is stationed in hawaii.

10. We will be spending easter day with our aunt clara who lives near the mississippi river.

11. Helen asked, "when will betty and Rich be returning from yellowstone park?"

12. our english teacher will be reviewing the first twenty pages of the book *of mice and men* with the class.

13. The case went as high as the United States court of appeals.

14. at the baseball game last night, the Los Angeles dodgers beat the New York yankees by Ten runs.

15. Eric asked the teacher, "do you have a Webster's dictionary?"

CAPITALIZATION

ANSWER KEY

Drill: Capitalization

1. Where is the Crab nebula?

2. The Girl Scouts of America sells delicious cookies.

3. This year, Senator Burns will run for re-election.

4. Barbara said, "Let me know when you are off the phone."

5. Beth's new car is a black Dodge Daytona which she purchased at the Dodge dealer in New York City.

6. Mike and Jackie are both graduates of Edison High School.

7. Glaciers from the Ice Age still exist.

8. Today in class, the professor lectured on the Neolithic age.

9. Sergeant Bruce Whisman of the United States Marine Corps is stationed in Hawaii.

10. We will be spending Easter Day with our Aunt Clara who lives near the Mississippi River.

11. Helen asked, "When will Betty and Rich be returning from Yellowstone Park?"

12. Our English teacher will be reviewing the first twenty pages of the book *Of Mice and Men* with the class.

13. The case went as high as the United States Court of Appeals.

14. At the baseball game last night, the Los Angeles Dodgers beat the New York Yankees by ten runs.

15. Eric asked the teacher, "Do you have a Webster's Dictionary?"

IV. PUNCTUATION

Try to read this paragraph:

take some more tea the march hare said to alice very earnestly ive had nothing yet alice replied in an offended tone so i cant take more you mean you cant take less said the hatter its very easy to take more than nothing lewis carroll

Now try again:

"Take some more tea," the March Hare said to Alice, very earnestly.

"I've had nothing yet," Alice replied in an offended tone, "so I can't take more."

"You mean you can't take less," said the Hatter, "it's very easy to take more than nothing."

—Lewis Carroll

This example illustrates how much punctuation helps the reader understand what the writer is trying to say. The most important role of punctuation is clarification.

In speech, words are accompanied by gesture, voice, tone, and rhythm that help convey a desired meaning. In writing, it is punctuation alone that must do the same job.

There are many rules about how to use the various punctuation marks. These are sometimes difficult to understand because they are described with so much grammatical terminology. Therefore, this discussion of punctuation will avoid as much terminology as possible. If you still find the rules confusing, and your method of punctuation is somewhat random, try to remember that most punctuation takes the place of pauses in speech.

Keeping this in mind, it is helpful to read your sentences aloud as you write; if you punctuate according to the pauses in your voice, you will do much better than if you put in your commas, periods, and dashes at random, or where they look good.

STOPS

There are three ways to end a sentence:
1. with a period
2. with a question mark
3. with an exclamation point

THE PERIOD

Periods end all sentences that are not questions or exclamations. In speech, the end of a sentence is indicated with a full pause. The period is the counterpart of this pause in writing:

Go get me my paper. I'm anxious to see the news.

Into each life some rain must fall. Last night some fell into mine.

The moon is round. The stars look small.

Mary and Janet welcomed the newcomer. She was noticeably happy.

When a question is intended as a suggestion and the listener is not expected to answer, or when a question is asked indirectly as part of a sentence, a period is also used:

Mimi wondered if the parade would ever end.

May we hear from you soon?

Will you please send the flowers you advertised.

We'll never know who the culprit was.

Periods also follow most abbreviations and contractions:

N.Y.	*Dr.*	*Jr.*	*Sr.*
etc.	*Jan.*	*Mrs.*	*Mr.*
Esq.	*cont.*	*A.M.*	*A.D.*

Periods (or parentheses) are also used after a letter or number in a series:

a.	*apples*	*1.*	*president*
b.	*oranges*	*2.*	*vice president*
c.	*pears*	*3.*	*secretary*

Errors to Avoid

Be sure to omit the period after a quotation mark preceded by a period. Only one stop is necessary to end a sentence:

She said, "Hold my hand." (no period after the final ")

"Don't go into the park until later."

"It's not my fault," he said. "She would have taken the car anyway."

After many abbreviations, particularly for organizations or agencies, no period is used (check your dictionary if in doubt):

AFL-CIO	*NAACP*	*GM*
FBI	*NATO*	*IBM*
TV	*UN*	*HEW*

THE QUESTION MARK

Use a question mark to end a direct question even if it is not in the form of a question. The question mark in writing is the same as the rising tone of voice used to indicate a question in speech. If you read the following two sentences aloud, you will see the difference in tone between a statement and a question composed of the same words.

Mary is here.

Mary is here?

Here are some more examples of correct use of question marks; pay special attention to the way they are used with other punctuation:

Where will we go next?

Would you like coffee or tea?

"Won't you," he asked "please lend me a hand?"

"Will they ever give us our freedom?" the prisoner asked.

"To be or not to be?" was the question asked by Hamlet.

Who asked "When?"

Question marks indicate a full stop and lend a different emphasis to a sentence than do commas. Compare these pairs of sentences:

Was the sonata by Beethoven? or Brahms? or Chopin?

Was the sonata by Beethoven, or Brahms, or Chopin?

Did they walk to the park? climb the small hill? take the bus to town? or go skating out back?

Did they walk to town, climb the small hill, take the bus to town, or go skating out back?

Sometimes question marks are placed in parentheses. This indicates doubt or uncertainty about the facts being reported:

The bombing started at 3:00 A.M. (?)

She said the dress cost 200,000 (?) dollars.

Harriet Stacher (18 (?)–1914) was well thought of in her time.

Hippocrates (460 (?)–(?) 377 B.C.) is said to be the father of modern medicine.

THE EXCLAMATON POINT

An exclamation point ends an emphatic statement. It should be used only to express strong emotions such as surprise, disbelief, or admiration. If it is used too often for mild expressions of emotion, it loses its effectiveness.

Let go of me!

Help! Fire!

It was a wonderful day!

What a beautiful woman she is!

Who shouted "Fire!" (notice no question mark is necessary)

Fantastic!

"Unbelievable!" she gasped. (notice no comma is necessary)

"You'll never win!" he cried.

Where else can I go! (The use of the exclamation point shows that this is a strong statement even though it is worded like a question.)

Avoid Overuse

The following is an example of the overuse of exclamation points:

Dear Susan,

I was so glad to see you last week! You looked better than ever! Our talk meant so much to me! I can hardly wait until we get together again! Could you believe how long it has been! Let's never let that happen again! Please write as soon as you get the chance! I can hardly wait to hear from you!

Your friend,

Nora

☞ Drill: Periods, Question Marks, Exclamation Points

<u>DIRECTIONS</u>: In the following sentences correctly supply periods, question marks, and exclamation points.

1. "Good gracious" she said "Didn't you know that I was coming"

2. Mr. Morgan works for the CIA

3. Alexander wondered if it was time to go

4. Leave me alone Can't you see that I'm busy

5. "How many boxes did you buy" asked Dr. Jones

6. "Be careful" he shouted "Didn't you see the car coming"

7. Impossible I have never seen anything like that before

8. Lynn asked if anyone had the time

9. What else can I do I lost all my money

10. Who cried "Help"

INTERJECTIONS

An interjection is a word or group of words used as an exclamation to express emotion. It need not be followed by an exclamation point. Often an interjection is followed by a comma (see "THE COMMA") if it is not very intense. Technically, the interjection has no grammatical relation to other words in the sentence, yet it is still considered a part of speech.

Examples:

Oh dear, I forgot my keys again.

Ah! Now do you understand?

Ouch! I didn't realize that the stove was hot.

Oh, excuse me. I didn't realize that you were next on line.

PAUSES

There are five ways to indicate a pause shorter than a period:
1. dash
2. colon
3. parentheses
4. semicolon
5. comma

THE DASH

Use the dash to indicate a sudden or unexpected break in the normal flow of the sentence. It can also be used in the place of parentheses or of commas if the meaning is clarified. Usually the dash gives the material it sets off special emphasis. (On a typewriter, two hyphens (--) indicate a dash.)

> *Could you — I hate to ask! — help me with these boxes?*

> *When we left town — a day never to be forgotten — they had a record snowfall.*

> *She said — we all heard it — "The safe is not locked."*

> *These are the three ladies — Mrs. Jackson, Miss Harris, and Ms. Forrester — you hoped to meet last week.*

> *The sight of the Andromeda Galaxy — especially when seen for the first time — is astounding.*

> *That day was the longest in her life — or so it seemed to her.*

A dash is often used to summarize a series of ideas that have already been expressed:

> *Freedom of speech, freedom to vote, and freedom of assembly — these are the cornerstones of democracy.*

> *Carbohydrates, fats, and proteins — these are the basic kinds of food we need.*

> *Jones, who first suggested we go; Marshall, who made all the arrangements; and Kline, who finally took us there — these were the three men I admired most for their courage.*

> *James, Howard, Marianne, Angela, Catherine — all were displeased with the decision of the teacher.*

The dash is also used to note the author of a quotation that is set off in the text:

> *Nothing is good or bad but thinking makes it so.*

> *— William Shakespeare*

> *Under every grief and pine*
> *Runs a joy with silken twine.*

> *— William Blake*

☞ Drill: Dashes

<u>DIRECTIONS</u>: Read the following sentences. What effect does the dash have on the writing, especially the tone and mood?

1.   Can you?—I would be ever so grateful—I'm having so much difficulty.

2.   Could it be—no it can't be—not after all these years.

3.   Time and patience—two simple words—yet why are they so hard for me to remember?

4.   Most of the paintings in the gallery—in fact all but one— were done in the l9th century.

5.   According to John Locke, these are man's inalienable rights—life, liberty, and property.

THE COLON

The colon (:) is the sign of a pause about midway in length between the semicolon and the period. It can often be replaced by a comma and sometimes by a period. Although used less frequently now than it was 50 to 75 years ago, the colon is still convenient to use, for it signals to the reader that more information is to come on the subject of concern. The colon can also create a slight dramatic tension.

It is used to introduce a word, phrase, or complete statement (clause) that emphasizes, illustrates, or exemplifies what has already been stated:

He had only one desire in life: to play baseball.

The weather that day was the most unusual I'd ever seen: It snowed and rained while the sun was still shining.

In his speech, the president surprised us by his final point: The conventional grading system would be replaced next year.

Jean thought of only two things the last half hour of the hike home: a bath and a bed.

Notice that the word following the colon can start with either a capital or a small letter. Use a capital letter if the word following the colon begins another complete sentence. But when the words following the colon are part of the sentence preceding the colon, use a small letter.

May I offer you a suggestion: Don't drive without your seatbelts fastened.

The thought continued to perplex him: Where will I go next ?

When introducing a series that illustrates or emphasizes what has already been stated, use the colon:

Only a few of the graduates were able to be there: Jamison, Mearns, Linkley, and Commoner.

> *For Omar Khayyam, a Persian poet, three things are necessary for a paradise on earth: a loaf of bread, a jug of wine, and his beloved.*

> *In the basement, he kept some equipment for his experiments: the test tubes, some chemical agents, three sunlamps, and the drill.*

Long quotes set off from the rest of the text by indentation rather than quotation marks are generally introduced with a colon:

> *The first line of Lincoln's Gettysburg address is familiar to most Americans:*

> > *Fourscore and seven years ago our fathers brought forth on this continent a new nation, conceived in liberty and dedicated to the proposition that all men are created equal.*

> *I quote from Shakespeare's Sonnets:*

> > *When I do count the clock that tells the time,*
> > *And see the brave day sunk in hideous night;*
> > *When I behold the violet past prime,*
> > *And sable curls all silver'd o'er with white...*

It is also customary to begin a business letter with a colon:

> *Dear Senator Jordan:*

> *To Whom It May Concern:*

> *Gentlemen:*

> *Dear Sir or Madam:*

But in informal letters, use a comma:

> *Dear Mary,*

> *Dear Father,*

The colon is also used in introducing a list:

> *Please send the following:*
> > *1. 50 index cards,*
> > *2. 4 typewriter ribbons,*
> > *3. 8 erasers.*

> *Prepare the recipe as follows:*
> > *1. Slice the oranges thinly.*
> > *2. Arrange them in a circle around the strawberries.*
> > *3. Pour the liqueur over both fruits.*

At least three ladies will have to be there to help:
1. *Mrs. Goldman, who will greet the guests;*
2. *Harriet Sacher, who will serve the lunch; and*
3. *my sister, who will do whatever else needs to be done.*

Finally, the colon is used between numbers when writing the time, between the volume and number or volume and page number of a journal, and also between the chapter and verse in the Bible.

4:30 P.M.

The Nation, 34:8

Genesis 5:18

THE SEMICOLON

Semicolons (;) are sometimes called mild periods. They indicate a pause midway in length between the comma and the colon. Writing that contains many semicolons is usually in a dignified, formal style. To use them correctly, it is necessary to be able to recognize main clauses — complete ideas. When two main clauses occur in a single sentence without a connecting word (*and, but, or, nor, for*), the appropriate mark of punctuation is the semicolon.

It is not a good idea for you to leave the country right now; you should actually try to stay as long as you possibly can.

Music lightens life; literature deepens it.

In the past, boy babies were often dressed in blue; girls in pink. ("were often dressed" is understood in the second part of the sentence.)

Can't you see it's no good to go on alone; we'll starve to death if we keep traveling this way much longer.

Burgundy and maroon are very similar colors; scarlet is altogether different.

Notice how the use of the comma, period, and semicolon each gives a sentence a slightly different meaning:

Music lightens life; literature deepens it.

Just as music lightens life, literature deepens it.

Music lightens life. Literature deepens it.

The semicolon lends a certain balance to writing that would otherwise be difficult to achieve. Nonetheless, you should be careful not to overuse it. A comma can just as well join parts of a sentence with two main ideas; the semicolon is particularly appropriate if there is a striking contrast in the two ideas expressed:

Ask not what your country can do for you; ask what you can do for your country.

It started out as an ordinary day; it ended being the most extraordinary of her life.

Our power to apprehend truth is limited; to seek it, limitless.

If any one of the following words or phrases are used to join together compound sentences, they are generally preceded by a semicolon:

then	*however*	*thus*	*furthermore*
hence	*indeed*	*so*	*consequently*
also	*that is*	*yet*	*nevertheless*
anyhow	*in addition*	*in fact*	*on the other hand*
likewise	*moreover*	*still*	*meanwhile*
instead	*besides*	*otherwise*	*in other words*
henceforth	*for example*	*therefore*	*at the same time*
even now			

For a long time, people thought that women were inferior to men; even now it is not an easy attitude to overcome.

Being clever and cynical, he succeeded in becoming president of the company; meanwhile his wife left him.

Cigarette smoking has never interested me; furthermore, I couldn't care less if anyone else smokes or not.

Some say Bach was the greatest composer of all time; yet he still managed to have an ordinary life in other ways: he and his wife had 20 children.

We left wishing we could have stayed much longer; in other words, they showed us a good time.

When a series of complicated items are listed or if there is internal punctuation in a series, the semicolon is sometimes used to make the meaning more clear:

You can use your new car for many things: to drive to town or to the country; to impress your friends and neighbors; to protect yourself from rain on a trip away from home; and to borrow against should you need money right away.

The scores from yesterday's games came in late last night: Pirates-6, Zoomers-3; Caterpillars-12, Steelys-8; Crashers-9, Links-8; and Greens-15, Uptowns-4.

In October a bag of potatoes cost 69¢; in December 99¢; in February $1.09; in April $1.39. I wonder if this inflation will ever stop.

The semicolon is placed outside quotation marks or parentheses, unless it is a part of the material enclosed in those marks.

I used to call him "my lord and master"; it made him laugh every time.

The weather was cold for that time of year (I was shivering wherever I went); nevertheless, we set out to hike to the top of that mountain.

☞ Drill: Colon and Semicolon

<u>DIRECTIONS</u>: Correctly place the colon and the semicolon in the following sentences.

1. I have only one thing to say don't do it.

2. They seemed compatible yet they did not get along.

3. She had only one goal in life to be a famous pianist.

4. He thought the problem was solved instead his solution proved to be entirely wrong.

5. By the end of the day there were only two things on her mind rest and relaxation.

6. Only a few members were able to attend the convention Henry, Karen, David, Mark, and Susan.

7. They were willing to accept the proposal he was not.

8. The art students were expected to supply the following brushes, paints, pallets, and pads.

9. The time is now the time is right.

10. The highest scores on the final exam are as follows Linda Jones 96 John Smith 94 Susan Green 90. These grades are unusually high they must have studied well.

PARENTHESES

To set off material that is only loosely connected to the central meaning of the sentence, use parentheses [( )]:

Most men (at least most that I know) like wine, women, and song, but have too much work and not enough time for such enjoyments.

On Tuesday evenings and Thursday afternoons (the times I don't have classes), the television programs are not too exciting.

Last year at Vale (we go there every year), the skiing was the best I've ever seen.

In New York (I've lived there all my life and ought to know), you have to have a license for a gun.

What must be done to think clearly and calmly (is it even possible?) and then make the decision?

Watch out for other punctuation when you use parentheses. Punctuation that refers to the material enclosed in the parentheses occurs inside the marks. Punctuation belonging to the rest of the sentence comes outside the parentheses.

I thought I knew the poem by heart (boy, was I wrong!).

For a long time (too long as far as I'm concerned), women were thought to be inferior to men.

We must always strive to tell the truth. (Are we even sure we know what truth is?)

When I first saw a rose (don't you think it's the most beautiful flower?), I thought it must be man-made.

☞ Drill: Parentheses

DIRECTIONS: Read the following sentences. What effect does the use of parentheses have on the writing? Also make any necessary corrections.

1. The choice (in my opinion,) was a good one.

2. Linda's comment ("Where did you get that dress")? wasn't intended to be sarcastic.

3. After today (and what a day it was!) I will begin to work harder.

4. Last summer in Cape Cod (this is the first year we went there,) we did a lot of sightseeing.

5. The first time I went driving (do you remember the day)?, I was so scared.

THE COMMA

Of all the marks of punctuation, the comma (,) has the most uses. Before you tackle the main principles that guide its usage, be sure that you have an elementary understanding of sentence structure. There are actually only a few rules and conventions to follow when using commas; the rest is common sense. The worst abuse of commas comes from those who overuse them, who place them illogically. If you are ever in doubt as to whether or not to use a comma, do not use it.

IN A SERIES

When more than one adjective (an adjective series) describes a noun, use a comma to separate and emphasize each adjective.

the long, dark passageway

another confusing, sleepless night

the bright, red dog

an elaborate, complex plan

the beautiful, starry night

the haunting, melodic sound

the old, grey, crumpled hat

In these instances, the comma takes the place of "and". To test if the comma is needed, try inserting "and" between the adjectives in question. If it is logical, you should use a comma. The following are examples of adjectives that describe an adjective-noun combination that has come to be thought of almost as one word. In such cases the adjective in front of the adjective-noun combination needs no comma.

a stately oak tree	*my worst report card*
an exceptional wine glass	*a borrowed record player*
a successful garage sale	*a porcelain dinner plate*

If you insert "and" between the adjectives in the above examples, it will not make sense.

The comma is also used to separate words, phrases, and whole ideas (clauses); it still takes the place of "and" when used this way:

an apple, a pear, a fig, and a banana

a lovely lady, an indecent dress, and many admirers

She lowered the shade, closed the curtain, turned off the light, and went to bed.

John, Frank, and my Uncle Harry all thought it was a questionable theory.

The only question that exists about the use of commas in a series is whether or not one should be used before the final item. Usually "and" or "or" precedes the final item, and many writers do not include the comma before the final "and" or "or." When first learning, however, it is advisable to use the comma because often its omission can be confusing; in such cases as these, for instance:

NO: *Would you like to shop at Sak's, Lord and Taylor's and Gimbels?*

NO: *He got on his horse, tracked a rabbit and a deer and rode on to Canton.*

NO: *We planned the trip with Mary and Harold, Susan, Dick and Joan, Gregory and Jean and Charles.* (Is it Gregory and Jean, or Jean and Charles, or Gregory and Jean and Charles?)

WITH A LONG INTRODUCTORY PHRASE

Usually if a phrase of more than five or six words precedes the subject at the beginning of a sentence, a comma is used to set it off.

After last night's fiasco at the disco, she couldn't bear the thought of looking at him again.

Whenever I try to talk about politics, my husband leaves the room.

When it comes to actual facts, every generation makes the same mistakes as the preceding one.

Provided you have said nothing, they will never guess who you are.

It is not necessary to use a comma with a short sentence:

In January she will go to Switzerland.

After I rest I'll feel better.

At Grandma's we had a big dinner.

During the day no one is home.

If an introductory phrase includes a verb form that is being used as another part of speech (a "verbal"), it must be followed by comma. Try to make sense of the following sentences without commas.

NO: *When eating Mary never looked up from her plate.*
       (When eating, Mary never looked up from her plate.)

NO: *Because of her desire to follow her faith in James wavered.*
       (Because of her desire to follow, her faith in James wavered.)

NO: *Having decided to leave Mary James wrote her a letter.*
       (Having decided to leave Mary, James wrote her a letter.)

Above all, common sense is the best guideline when trying to decide whether or not to use a comma after an introductory phrase. Does the comma make the meaning more clear? If it does, use it; if not, there is no reason to insert it.

TO SEPARATE SENTENCES WITH TWO MAIN IDEAS (COMPOUND SENTENCES)

To understand this use of the comma, you need to have studied sentence structure and be able to recognize compound sentences.

When a sentence contains more than two subjects and verbs (clauses) and the two clauses are joined by a connecting word (*and, but, or, yet, for, nor*), use a comma before the connecting word to show that another clause is coming.

I thought I knew the poem by heart, but he showed me three lines I had forgotten.

Are we really interested in helping the children, or are we more concerned with protecting our good names?

He is supposed to leave tomorrow, but who knows if he will be ready to go.

Jim knows you are disappointed, and he has known it for a long time.

If the two parts of the sentence are short and closely related, it is not necessary to use a comma:

He threw the ball and the dog ran after it.

Jane played the piano and Charles danced.

Errors to Avoid

Be careful not to confuse a sentence that has a compound verb and a single subject with a compound sentence. If the subject is the same for both verbs, there is no need for a comma:

NO: *Charles sent some flowers, and wrote a long letter explaining why he had not been able to come.*

NO: *Last Thursday we went to the concert with Julia, and afterwards dined at an old Italian restaurant.*

NO: *For the third time, the teacher explained that the literacy level of high school students was much lower than it had been in previous years, and, this time, wrote the statistics on the board for everyone to see.*

TO SET OFF INTERRUPTING MATERIAL

There are so many different kinds of interruptions that can occur in a sentence that a list of them all would be quite lengthy. In general, words and phrases that stop the flow of the sentence or are unnecessary for the main idea are set off by commas. Some examples are:

Abbreviations after names:

Did you invite John Paul, Jr., and his sister?

Martha Harris, Ph.D., will be the speaker tonight.

Interjections: An exclamation added without grammatical connection.

Oh, I'm so glad to see you.

I tried so hard, alas, to do it.

Hey, let me out of here.

No, I will not let you out.

Direct address:

Roy, won't you open the door for the dog?

I can't understand, mother, what you are trying to say.

May I ask, Mr. President, why you called us together?

Hey, lady, watch out for the car!

Tag questions: A question that repeats the helping verb in a negative phrase.

I'm really hungry, aren't you?

Jerry looks like his father, doesn't he?

You'll come early, won't you?

We are expected at nine, aren't we?

Mr. Jones can chair the meeting, can't he?

Geographical names and addresses:

The concert will be held in Chicago, Illinois, on August 12.

They visited Tours, France, last summer.

The letter was addressed to Ms. Marion Heartwell, 1881 Pine Lane, Palo Alto, California 95824.
(No comma is needed before the zip code because it is already clearly set off from the state name.

Transitional words and phrases:

On the other hand, I hope he gets better.

In addition, the phone rang six times this afternoon.

I'm, nevertheless, going to the beach on Sunday.

You'll find, therefore, no one is more loyal to me than you.

To tell the truth, I don't know what to believe.

Parenthetical words and phrases:

You will become, I believe, a great statesman.

We know, of course, that this is the only thing to do.

In fact, I planted corn last summer.

The Mannes affair was, to put it mildly, a surprise.

Bathing suits, generally speaking, are getting smaller.

Unusual Word Order:

The dress, new and crisp, hung in the closet. (Normal word order: The new, crisp dress hung in the closet.)

Intently, she stared out the window. (Normal word order: She stared intently out the window.)

NONRESTRICTIVE ELEMENTS (NOT ESSENTIAL TO THE MEANING)

Parts of a sentence that modify other parts are sometimes essential to the meaning of the sentence and sometimes not. When a modifying word or group of words is not vital to the meaning of the sentence, it is set off by commas. Since it does not restrict the meaning of the words it modifies, it is called "nonrestrictive." Modifiers that are essential to the meaning of the sentence are called "restrictive" and are not set off by commas. Compare the following pairs of sentences:

The girl who wrote the story is my sister. (essential)

My sister, the girl who wrote the story, has always been drawn to adventure. (nonessential)

John Milton's famous poem "Paradise Lost" tells a remarkable story. (essential — Milton has written other poems)

Dante's great work, "The Divine Comedy", marked the beginning of the Renaissance and the end of the Dark Ages. (nonessential — Dante wrote only one great work)

The cup that is on the piano is the one I want. (essential)

The cup, which my brother gave me last year, is on the piano. (nonessential)

My parakeet Simian has an extensive vocabulary. (essential — because there are no commas, the writer must have more than one parakeet)

My parakeet, Simian, has an extensive vocabulary. (nonessential — the writer must have only one parakeet whose name is Simian)

The people who arrived late were not seated. (essential)

George, who arrived late, was not seated. (nonessential)

She always listened to her sister Jean. (essential — she must have more than one sister)

She always listened to her husband, Jack. (nonessential — obviously, she has only one husband)

TO SET OFF DIRECT QUOTATIONS

Most direct quotes or quoted materials are set off from the rest of the sentence by commas:

"Please read your part more loudly," the director insisted.

"I won't know what to do," said Michael, "if you leave me now."

The teacher said sternly, "I will not dismiss this class until I have silence."

Mark looked up from his work, smiled, and said, "We'll be with you in a moment."

Be careful not to set off indirect quotations or quotes that are used as subjects or complements:

> *"To be or not to be" is the famous beginning of a soliloquy in Shakespeare's* **Hamlet.** *(subject)*

> *Back then my favorite song was "A Summer Place." (complement)*

> *She said she would never come back. (indirect quote)*

> *"Place two tablespoons of chocolate in this pan" were her first words to her apprentice in the kitchen. (subject)*

TO SET OFF CONTRASTING ELEMENTS

> *Her intelligence,* **not her beauty,** *got her the job.*

> *Your plan will take you further from,* **rather than closer to,** *your destination.*

> *It was a reasonable,* **though not appealing,** *idea.*

> *He wanted glory,* **but found happiness instead.**

> *James wanted an active,* **not a passive,** *partner.*

IN DATES

(Both forms of the date are acceptable.)

> *She will arrive on April 6, 1981.*

> *He left on 5 December 1980.*

> *In January, 1967, he handed in his resignation.*

> *In January 1967 he handed in his resignation.*

☞ Drill: Commas

<u>DIRECTIONS</u>: In the following sentences insert commas wherever necessary. You may also want to note the reason for your choice.

1. However I am willing to reconsider.

2. She descended the long winding staircase.

3. Whenever I practice the violin my family closes the windows.

4. While driving Francis never took his eyes off the road.

5. The car which I bought last year is in the garage.

6. "Answer the door" said his mother loudly.

7. Miss can I ask you for the time?

8. He was after all an ex-convict.

9. I'm so bored aren't you?

10. The old tall shady tree is wonderful during the summer.

11. George Gary and Bill were on line early this morning. They bought their tickets read the newspaper and spoke for a while.

12. The author James Grey was awarded the prize.

13. She attended school in London England last year.

14. They said they would do the job.

15. His weight not his height prevented him from competing in the race.

16. The family who won the lottery lives in New Jersey.

17. She got in the car turned on the ignition and left the curb.

18. Incidentally he called last night.

19. The kitten small and cute was adopted by the Brown family.

20. Mary did you see James Jr. at the party last night?

21. Lisa saw the mailman and gave him the letter.

22. Last night I finished my essay and started on my next assignment.

23. Really I can't believe that is the truth.

24. We thought it was time to leave but we arrived early.

25. Monday she will leave for Boston.

26. After he got home he read a magazine ate dinner and left for the movies.

27. If you pass the test you will graduate.

28. When she decided to leave everyone was disappointed.

29. Hey John it's time to go.

30. He seemed wrong for the part yet he turned out to be the best actor in the production.

☞ Drill: Mechanics

<u>DIRECTIONS</u>: All of the needed punctuation and other aspects of mechanics have been omitted from the following passage. In making the necessary corrections there will often be more than one way of correcting the error. Therefore, try taking into account the mood and tone of the writing and the overall coherence of the piece when punctuating the passage.

my sister amy had finally finished packing for college at about 11 am what a day it was as usual she had overpacked but this was clearly an understatement standing in the hallway were the following 7 large blue suitcases 3 borrowed trunks 4 old bulging macys shopping bags and 2 duffel bags but im going halfway across the united states how many times do you think ill be coming home she asked once every 5 years at christmas time i guessed i do hope youll write seriously do you know the difference between the words pack and hoard i said amy laughed self-consciously civilization does exist in chicago illinois i added trust me it really does really remarked amy with her own personal brand of sarcasm after all its only the 1980s its well known that 3 4 s of chicago is still unsettled territory i turned away in disgust it was useless

i went to help amy with her baggage picking up the large over stuffed green duffel bag i screamed whats in here is this a 50 or 100 pound bag you have got to be kidding i added she had filled the entire bag with books i knew shed want to take a couple of her favorite books and magazines albert camus the stranger charles dickens great expectations shakespeares king lear copies of keats and ts eliots best poems some national geographics but i realized i was all wrong instead she had packed 30 copies of tolstoys war and peace or so it seemed on her book shelf remained 1 lone copy of websters new collegiate dictionary in fact it was an extra one she had received it for her birthday last year i believe the rest of the move was sadly repetitious i realized amy was nuts

i wasnt about to reason with her i was tired it was futile there was no time meanwhile amy was totally calm and relaxed as she went through the radio stations finally settling on wnbc as she listened to the beatles hey jude i seemingly all powerful carried the last trunk out the door the plane a 747 was scheduled to leave at 12 oclock we were 10 minutes off schedule when we arrived at kennedy airport furthermore i had to pay a $5.00 surcharge for the extra baggage amy said she only had large bills as she was about to board the plane after 101 good byes i handed her a package as if she really needed anything else its a green pull over sweater just like mine i said tearfully oh you really shouldn't have please take it back amy replied theres no time for humility your plane is about to take off i said really you should keep it yours is already on the plane along with a few other things it took me a few moments to realize what she meant then i said one last final good bye to amy my ex sister

PUNCTUATION

ANSWER KEY

Drill: Periods, Question Marks, Exclamation Points

1. "Good gracious!" she said. "Didn't you know that I was coming?"
2. Mr. Morgan works for the CIA.
3. Alexander wondered if it was time to go.
4. Leave me alone! Can't you see that I'm busy?
5. "How many boxes did you buy?" asked Dr. Jones.
6. "Be careful!" he shouted. "Didn't you see that car coming?"
7. Impossible! I have never seen anything like that before.
8. Lynn asked if anyone had the time.
9. What else can I do? I lost all my money.
10. Who cried "Help!"

Drill: Dashes

1. The use of the dash makes the sentence more urgent.
2. The use of the dash helps to convey a feeling of disbelief.
3. The words set off by dashes emphasize and modify the key words, "Time and patience."
4. The dashes help to emphasize and clarify the subject.
5. The dash is used to set off specifics.

Drill: Colon and Semicolon

1. I have only one thing to say: don't do it.
2. They seemed compatible; yet they did not get along.
3. She had only one goal in life: to be a famous pianist.
4. He thought the problem was solved; instead, his solution proved to be entirely wrong.
5. By the end of the day there were only two things on her mind: rest and relaxation.

6. Only a few members were able to attend the convention: Henry, Karen, David, Mark, and Susan.

7. They were willing to accept the proposal; he was not.

8. The art students were expected to supply the following: brushes, paints, pallets, and pads.

9. The time is now: the time is right.

10 . The highest scores on the final exam are as follows: Linda Jones, 96; John Smith, 94; Susan Green, 90. These grades are unusually high: they must have studied well.

Drill: Parentheses

1. The choice (in my opinion) was a good one. The comma in the example is unnecessary.

    The choice, in my opinion, was a good one. The parentheses are unnecessary in the example. "In my opinion" is not very necessary, since the statements made in writing are usually considered to be the author's, unless otherwise indicated.

2. Linda's comment ("where did you get that dress?") wasn't intended to be sarcastic. The parentheses are a clear, effective method for containing a quote.

3. The parentheses properly set off material that is loosely connected to the central meaning of the sentence.

4. Last summer in Cape Cod (that was the first year we went there), we did a lot of sightseeing. The parentheses effectively contain the additional information.

5. The first time I went driving (do you remember the day?), I was so scared. The parentheses smoothly incorporate an important aside from the speaker.

Drill: Commas

1. However, I am willing to reconsider.
    Reason: " However" is a transitional word and requires a comma after it.

2. She descended the long, winding staircase.
    Reason: A comma is used in a series to emphasize each adjective.

3. Whenever I practice my violin, my family closes the windows.
    Reason: Use a comma after a long introductory phrase.

4. While driving, Francis never took his eyes off the road.
    Reason: When the introductory phrase includes a "verbal," a comma is necessary.

5. The car, which I bought last year, is in the garage.
    Reason: The modifying group of words ("which I bought last year") is not vital to the meaning of the sentence and, therefore, is set off by commas.

6. "Answer the door," his mother said loudly.
    Reason: Use a comma to set off direct quotations.

7. Miss, can I ask you for the time?
    Reason: Use a comma to set off direct address.

8. He was, after all, an ex-convict.
    Reason: Use commas to set off parenthetical words and phrasing.

9. I'm so bored, aren't you?
    Reason: Use a comma to set off tag questions.

10. The old, tall, shady tree is wonderful during the summer.
    Reason: When an adjective series describes a noun, use a comma to separate and emphasize each adjective.

11. George, Gary, and Bill were on line early this morning. They bought their tickets, read the newspaper, and spoke for a while.
    Reason: (For both sentences) use a comma to separate words, phrases, and whole ideas (clauses).

12. The author, James Grey, was awarded the prize.
    Reason: Use commas to set off nonrestrictive words.

13. She attended school in London, England, last year.
    Reason: Use commas to set off geographical names.

14. No correction necessary.

15. His weight, not his height, prevented him from competing in the race.
    Reason: Use commas to set off contrasting elements.

16. No correction necessary.

17. She got in the car, turned on the ignition, and left the curb.
    Reason: A comma is used to separate words, phrases, and whole ideas.

18. Incidentally, he called last night.
    Reason: Use a comma to set off parenthetical words and phrases.

19. The kitten, small and cute, was adopted by the Brown family.
    Reason: Use commas to set off nonrestrictive elements.

20. Mary, did you see James, Jr., at the party last night?
    Reason: 1. Use a comma to set off direct address. 2. Use a comma to set off abbreviations after names.

21. No change necessary.

22. No change necessary.

23. Really, I can't believe that is the truth.
    Reason: Use a comma to set off an interjection.

24. We thought it was time to leave, but we arrived early.
    Reason: Use a comma to set off sentences with two main ideas.

25. Monday, she will leave for Boston.
    Reason: Use a comma to set off parenthetical words and phrases.

26. After he got home he read a magazine, ate dinner, and left for the movies.
    Reason: The comma is used to separate words, phrases, and clauses.

27. No correction necessary.

28. When she decided to leave, everyone was disappointed.
    Reason: Use a comma to set off a long introductory phrase.

29. Hey, John, it's time to go.
    Reason: Use commas to set off direct address.

30. He seemed wrong for the part, yet he turned out to be the best actor in the production.
    Reason: Use a comma to separate sentences with two main ideas.

Drill: Mechanics

My sister, Amy, had finally finished packing for college at about eleven A.M. What a day it was! As usual, she had over-packed—but this is an understatement. Standing in the hallway were the following: seven large, blue suitcases; three borrowed trunks; four old, bulging Macy's shopping bags; and two duffel bags.

"But I'm going halfway across the United States! How many times do you think I'll be coming home?" she asked.

"Once every five years at Christmas time?" I guessed.

"I hope you'll write," she said.

"Seriously, do you know the difference between the words 'pack' and 'hoard'?" I asked. Amy laughed self-consciously.

"Civilization does exist in Chicago, Illinois," I added. "Trust me; it really does."

"Really?" remarked Amy, with her own personal brand of sarcasm. "After all, it's only the nineteen-nineties: It's well-known that three-fourths of Chicago is still unsettled territory."

I turned away in disgust. It was useless.

I went to help Amy with her baggage. Picking up the large, overstuffed, green duffel bag, I screamed, "What's in here? Is this a fifty-, or a hundred-pound bag? You have got to be kidding," I added.

She had filled the entire bag with books and magazines. I knew she would want to take a few of her favorites—*The Stranger*, by Albert Camus; *Great Expectations*, by Charles Dickens, *King Lear*, by William Shakespeare; copies of Keat's and T.S. Eliot's best poems; some copies of *National Geographic*—but I realized I was all wrong; instead, she had packed thirty copies of Tolstoy's *War and Peace*, or so it seemed. One lone copy of *Webster's New Collegiate Dictionary* remained on her bookshelf; in fact, it was an extra one she had received for her birthday last year. I believe the rest of the move was sadly repetitious. I realized Amy was nuts.

I wasn't about to reason with her: I was tired, it was futile, and there was no time. Meanwhile, Amy was totally calm and relaxed as she went through the radio stations. She finally settled on WNBC, and she listened to the Beatles' "Hey Jude". I, seemingly all-powerful, carried the last trunk out the door.

The plane, a 747, was scheduled to leave at noon. We were ten minutes off schedule when we arrived at Kennedy airport; furthermore, I had to pay a five-dollar surcharge for the extra baggage: Amy said she only had large bills. As she was about to board the plane (after one hundred and one good-byes), I handed her a package—as if she really needed anything else!

"It's a green pullover sweater—just like mine," I said tearfully.

"Oh, you really shouldn't have. Please take it back," Amy replied.

"There's no time for humility: your plane is about to take off," I said.

"Really, you should keep it! Yours is already on the plane—along with a few other things."

It took me a few moments to realize what she meant; then I said one last, final good-bye to Amy, my ex-sister.

V. SPELLING AND WORD USAGE

GED FREQUENTLY MISSPELLED WORDS

The following list of words are frequently misspelled words, and they are also words which may appear on the GED test. Study the spelling of each word by having a friend or counselor drill you on the words. Then mark down the words which you misspelled and study those select ones again. Be sure to take all the drills which follow the list of words. This will increase your accuracy in spelling.

a lot	address	already
ability	addressed	although
absence	adequate	altogether
absent	advantage	always
abundance	advantageous	amateur
accept	advertise	American
acceptable	advertisement	among
accident	advice	amount
accommodate	advisable	analysis
accompanied	advise	analyze
accomplish	advisor	angel
accumulation	aerial	angle
accuse	affect	annual
accustomed	affectionate	another
ache	again	answer
achieve	against	antiseptic
achievement	aggravate	anxious
acknowledge	aggressive	apologize
acquaintance	agree	apparatus
acquainted	aisle	apparent
acquire	all right	appear
across	almost	appearance

appetite	avenue	burial
application	awful	buried
apply	awkward	bury
appreciate	bachelor	bushes
appreciation	balance	business
approach	balloon	cafeteria
appropriate	bargain	calculator
approval	basic	calendar
approve	beautiful	campaign
approximate	because	capital
argue	become	capitol
arguing	before	captain
argument	beginning	career
arouse	being	careful
arrange	believe	careless
arrangement	benefit	carriage
article	benefited	carrying
artificial	between	category
ascend	bicycle	ceiling
assistance	board	cemetery
assistant	bored	cereal
associate	borrow	certain
association	bottle	changeable
attempt	bottom	characteristic
attendance	boundary	charity
attention	brake	chief
audience	breadth	choose
August	breath	chose
author	breathe	cigarette
automobile	brilliant	circumstance
autumn	building	citizen
auxiliary	bulletin	clothes
available	bureau	clothing

coarse
coffee
collect
college
column
comedy
comfortable
commitment
committed
committee
communicate
company
comparative
compel
competent
competition
compliment
conceal
conceit
conceivable
conceive
concentration
conception
condition
conference
confident
congratulate
conquer
conscience
conscientious
conscious
consequence
consequently

considerable
consistency
consistent
continual
continuous
controlled
controversy
convenience
convenient
conversation
corporal
corroborate
council
counsel
counselor
courage
courageous
course
courteous
courtesy
criticism
criticize
crystal
curiosity
cylinder
daily
daughter
daybreak
death
deceive
December
deception
decide

decision
decisive
deed
definite
delicious
dependent
deposit
derelict
descend
descent
describe
description
desert
desirable
despair
desperate
dessert
destruction
determine
develop
development
device
dictator
died
difference
different
dilemma
dinner
direction
disappear
disappoint
disappointment
disapproval

disapprove	emphasize	explanation
disastrous	enclosure	extreme
discipline	encouraging	facility
discover	endeavor	factory
discriminate	engineer	familiar
disease	English	fascinate
dissatisfied	enormous	fascinating
dissection	enough	fatigue
dissipate	entrance	February
distance	envelope	financial
distinction	environment	financier
division	equipment	flourish
doctor	equipped	forcibly
dollar	especially	forehead
doubt	essential	foreign
dozen	evening	formal
earnest	evident	former
easy	exaggerate	fortunate
ecstasy	exaggeration	fourteen
ecstatic	examine	fourth
education	exceed	frequent
effect	excellent	friend
efficiency	except	frightening
efficient	exceptional	fundamental
eight	exercise	further
either	exhausted	gallon
eligibility	exhaustion	garden
eligible	exhilaration	gardener
eliminate	existence	general
embarrass	exorbitant	genius
embarrassment	expense	government
emergency	experience	governor
emphasis	experiment	grammar

grateful	incidental	jealous
great	increase	judgment
grievance	independence	journal
grievous	independent	kindergarten
grocery	indispensable	kitchen
guarantee	inevitable	knew
guess	influence	knock
guidance	influential	know
half	initiate	knowledge
hammer	innocence	labor
handkerchief	inoculate	laboratory
happiness	inquiry	laid
healthy	insistent	language
heard	instead	later
heavy	instinct	latter
height	integrity	laugh
heroes	intellectual	leisure
heroine	intelligence	length
hideous	intercede	lesson
himself	interest	library
hoarse	interfere	license
holiday	interference	light
hopeless	interpreted	lightning
hospital	interrupt	likelihood
humorous	invitation	likely
hurried	irrelevant	literal
hurrying	irresistible	literature
ignorance	irritable	livelihood
imaginary	island	loaf
imbecile	its	loneliness
imitation	it's	loose
immediately	itself	lose
immigrant	January	losing

loyal	narrative	oscillate
loyalty	natural	ought
magazine	necessary	ounce
maintenance	needle	overcoat
maneuver	negligence	paid
marriage	neighbor	pamphlet
married	neither	panicky
marry	newspaper	parallel
match	newsstand	parallelism
material	niece	particular
mathematics	noticeable	partner
measure	o'clock	pastime
medicine	obedient	patience
million	obstacle	peace
miniature	occasion	peaceable
minimum	occasional	pear
miracle	occur	peculiar
miscellaneous	occurred	pencil
mischief	occurrence	people
mischievous	ocean	perceive
misspelled	offer	perception
mistake	often	perfect
momentous	omission	perform
monkey	omit	performance
monotonous	once	perhaps
moral	operate	period
morale	opinion	permanence
mortgage	opportune	permanent
mountain	opportunity	perpendicular
mournful	optimist	perseverance
muscle	optimistic	persevere
mysterious	origin	persistent
mystery	original	personal

personality	preferential	quart
personnel	preferred	quarter
persuade	prejudice	quiet
persuasion	preparation	quite
pertain	prepare	raise
picture	prescription	realistic
piece	presence	realize
plain	president	reason
playwright	prevalent	rebellion
pleasant	primitive	recede
please	principal	receipt
pleasure	principle	receive
pocket	privilege	recipe
poison	probably	recognize
policeman	procedure	recommend
political	proceed	recuperate
population	produce	referred
portrayal	professional	rehearsal
positive	professor	reign
possess	profitable	relevant
possession	prominent	relieve
possessive	promise	remedy
possible	pronounce	renovate
post office	pronunciation	repeat
potatoes	propeller	repetition
practical	prophet	representative
prairie	prospect	requirements
precede	psychology	resemblance
preceding	pursue	resistance
precise	pursuit	resource
predictable	quality	respectability
prefer	quantity	responsibility
preference	quarreling	restaurant

rhythm	significant	surprise
rhythmical	similar	suspense
ridiculous	similarity	sweat
right	sincerely	sweet
role	site	syllable
roll	soldier	symmetrical
roommate	solemn	sympathy
sandwich	sophomore	synonym
Saturday	soul	technical
scarcely	source	telegram
scene	souvenir	telephone
schedule	special	temperament
science	specified	temperature
scientific	specimen	tenant
scissors	speech	tendency
season	stationary	tenement
secretary	stationery	therefore
seize	statue	thorough
seminar	stockings	through
sense	stomach	title
separate	straight	together
service	strength	tomorrow
several	strenuous	tongue
severely	stretch	toward
shepherd	striking	tragedy
sheriff	studying	transferred
shining	substantial	treasury
shoulder	succeed	tremendous
shriek	successful	tries
siege	sudden	truly
sight	superintendent	twelfth
signal	suppress	twelve
significance	surely	tyranny

undoubtedly	vengeance	weather
United States	versatile	Wednesday
university	vicinity	week
unnecessary	vicious	weigh
unusual	view	weird
useful	village	whether
usual	villain	which
vacuum	visitor	while
valley	voice	whole
valuable	volume	wholly
variety	waist	whose
vegetable	weak	wretched
vein	wear	

☞ Drill: Spelling

<u>DIRECTIONS</u>: Indicate if the word is spelled correctly or incorrectly. If you believe the word is misspelled, then spell it correctly in the space provided.

1. alot _____
2. abcent _____
3. axident _____
4. adviseable _____
5. agressive _____
6. angel _____
7. appropriate _____
8. arangement _____
9. auful _____
10. awkward _____
11. bargen _____
12. beautiful _____

13. beggining _____
14. benifit _____
15. breathe _____
16. bisness _____
17. cafeteria _____
18. capten _____
19. category _____
20. cheif _____
21. congradulate _____
22. coffee _____
23. compitition _____
24. concientious _____

25. controled	_____	52. hapiness	_____
26. courage	_____	53. heroes	_____
27. curteous	_____	54. humurous	_____
28. curiosity	_____	55. imaginery	_____
29. day break	_____	56. independent	_____
30. decition	_____	57. innoculate	_____
31. delishious	_____	58. intelligence	_____
32. desend	_____	59. itself	_____
33. desperate	_____	60. gellous	_____
34. develope	_____	61. kindergartan	_____
35. diferent	_____	62. knowlege	_____
36. disappoint	_____	63. leson	_____
37. dizease	_____	64. liklihood	_____
38. distence	_____	65. loyal	_____
39. estatic	_____	66. mariage	_____
40. eliminate	_____	67. miscellaneous	_____
41. english	_____	68. mispelled	_____
42. exagerate	_____	69. muscle	_____
43. exhaustion	_____	70. news stand	_____
44. exorbitant	_____	71. ocassion	_____
45. experence	_____	72. omition	_____
46. fasinating	_____	73. oporttunity	_____
47. forehead	_____	74. opinion	_____
48. foreteen	_____	75. osillate	_____
49. friend	_____	76. paralelism	_____
50. goverment	_____	77. pencil	_____
51. guess	_____	78. perserverence	_____

79. persuede _____
80. playright _____
81. poison _____
82. posses _____
83. potatos _____
84. predictible _____
85. priviledge _____
86. persue _____
87. pronounciation _____
88. psychology _____
89. quarel _____
90. quarter _____
91. rebelion _____
92. recipe _____
93. reccomend _____
94. repeat _____
95. respectibility _____
96. rythm _____
97. scedual _____

98. seasin _____
99. separate _____
100. shepheard _____
101. siege _____
102. similiar _____
103. sophmore _____
104. stomack _____
105. successful _____
106. sinonim _____
107. technical _____
108. temperiture _____
109. title _____
110. undoubtedley _____
111. vacume _____
112. vengeance _____
113. visiter _____
114. Wensday _____
115. wretched _____

☞ Drill: Homophone

DIRECTIONS: A homophone is a word that sounds the same as another word, but which has a different meaning. The following sentences have a pair or pairs of homophones in parentheses. Circle the word you believe is used correctly in the sentence.

1. Mary was so (board,bored) with the lecture that she almost fell asleep.

2. Washington, D.C. is the (capitol,capital) of the United States.

3. The cement felt (coarse,course) against his (bear,bare) feet.

4. You should (council,counsel) Harry on his inappropriate behavior.

5. I had (two, too) ice cream (sundaes,sundays) for (desert,dessert) after lunch and now I can't eat a thing for (dinner,diner).

6. Ruby will graduate (fourth,forth) in her class.

7. You (great,grate) the cheese and I'll slice the tomatoes.

8. I would like to learn how to ride a (horse,hoarse).

9. The cat fed (it's,its) kittens.

10. The bride wanted to (where,wear) something old and something (knew,new).

11. Was there ever a time when (there,their) was (piece,peace) in the world?

12. I saw a good (sale,sail) on a (pear,pair) of shoes.

13. Someday, I will become a pilot of a (plane,plain).

14. Please put some more mustard on that hotdog (roll,role).

15. The (site,sight) of the conference was in a great location near the beach.

16. The (soul,sole) of my sneaker is wearing away.

17. (Where,Wear) will you be tonight?

18. That interview was really a (waist,waste) of time.

19. That virus made me feel so (weak,week).

20. (Whether,Weather) or not he wants to pursue his career for a lifetime is up to him.

21. I would like to (weigh, way) myself on the scale but I am afraid I did not (lose,loose) any pounds.

22. (Here,Hear) today, gone tomorrow.

23. (Which,witch) way did he go, George?

24. There's a (hole,whole) in the bucket.

25. (Who's, Whose) turn is it anyway?

☞ Drill: Usage and Sentence Correction

DIRECTIONS: In each of the following sentences, some part or all of the sentence is underlined. Below each sentence you will find five ways of phrasing the underlined part. Select the answer that produces the most effective sentence, one that is clear and exact, without awkwardness or ambiguity. In choosing answers, follow the requirements of standard written English. Choose the answer that best expresses the meaning of the original sentence.

Answer (1) is always the same as the underlined part. Choose answer (1) if you think the original sentence needs no revision.

EXAMPLE:

The children swam in the lake all day <u>and that is because it was so hot.</u>
- (1)   and that is because it was so hot.
- (2)   when it was so hot.
- (3)   since it was so hot.
- (4)   which is why it was so hot.
- (5)   at the time when it was so hot.

① ② ⬤ ④ ⑤

---

1.   When a customer requested whole wheat instead of white bread, <u>it was a simple matter to substitute it for them.</u>

- (1)   it was a simple matter to substitute it for them.
- (2)   it was simple to substitute it.
- (3)   a simple matter it was to make the substitution.
- (4)   substitution was made a simple matter for him or her.
- (5)   it was easy to serve it to him or her.

2.   That some serious cuts would have to be made in the city's budget <u>was evident to most everyone on the city council.</u>

- (1)   was evident to most everyone on the city council.
- (2)   was in evidence to most all on the city council.
- (3)   was evident to almost everyone on the city council.
- (4)   was evidenced by most everyone on the city council.
- (5)   was evidencing to almost everyone on the city council.

3.   The train roared into town <u>with a whistle so ear-shattering so as to frighten</u> the waiting cattle.

- (1)   with a whistle so ear-shattering so as to frighten
- (2)   with as ear-shattering and frightening a whistle
- (3)   with a whistle so ear-shattering that it frightened

      (4)   with an ear-shattering whistle and to frighten

      (5)   with an ear-shattering and frightening whistle

4.   <u>This kind of a problem</u> requires a knowledge of the tensile strength of steel.

      (1)   This kind of a problem   (4)   Those kinds of problems

      (2)   These kinds of a problem   (5)   This kind of problem

      (3)   These kind of problems

5.   <u>The child who was the winner's voice had an incredulous tone.</u>

      (1)   The child who was the winner's voice had an incredulous tone.

      (2)   The child winner's voice had an incredulous tone.

      (3)   The winner's child's voice had an incredulous tone.

      (4)   The voice of the winner's child had an incredulous tone.

      (5)   Winning excited the child's voice to sound incredulous.

6.   <u>This morning's meeting having gone well</u> because Mrs. Chen was prepared with information to answer all our questions.

      (1)   This morning's meeting having gone well

      (2)   This morning's meeting having gone good

      (3)   The meeting of this morning went good

      (4)   This morning's meeting went well

      (5)   This meeting in the morning going well

7.   <u>If you would have called me,</u> I could have told you about the book-signing party at Swift's Restaurant.

      (1)   If you would have called me

      (2)   If you had called me

      (3)   When calling me

      (4)   In order to call me

      (5)   During our phone conversation

8.   <u>During the summer, Lydia developed her skill in both diving and swimming.</u>

      (1)   During the summer, Lydia developed her skill in both diving and swimming.

      (2)   During the summer, Lydia's skill was developed in both diving and swimming.

(3) Lydia, during the summer, developed both her skill in diving and swimming.

(4) Lydia both developing her skill in diving and in swimming during the summer.

(5) Both in diving and swimming Lydia developed her skill during the summer.

9. In order to keep track of his costs, a detailed diary was kept by the salesman for his automobile expenses.

(1) costs, a detailed diary was kept by the salesman for his automobile expenses.

(2) costs; a detailed diary was kept by the salesman for his automobile expenses.

(3) automobile expenses, the salesman kept a detailed diary.

(4) expenses for his automobile, a detailed costs diary was kept by the salesman.

(5) automobile expenses, the salesman kept a detailed diary of costs.

10. After the hurricane, we were told to leave the tree laying on the house until an insurance inspector could assess the damage.

(1) to leave the tree laying

(2) to leave the tree lay

(3) about leaving the tree to lay

(4) about leaving the tree lying

(5) to leave the tree lying

11. Practicing his manners for the economic conference. Lincoln Fagbemi arrived at the hospitality training session.

(1) Practicing his manners for the economic conference, Lincoln Fagbemi arrived

(2) In order of arriving at good manners for the economic conference, Lincoln Fagbemi practiced

(3) Because of arriving at good manners for the economic conference, Lincoln Fagbemi practiced

(4) To practice his manners for the economic conference, Lincoln Fagbemi arrived

(5) When practicing his manners for the economic conference, Lincoln Fagbemi arrived

12. It's the same charm and politeness he <u>plans to extend to</u> conference visitors who ride in his cab.
    (1) plans to extend to
    (2) plans on extending for
    (3) plans in extending in
    (4) is planning for extension to
    (5) will plan at extensions of

13. The judges at state competition all agreed that our one-act play performance <u>was crisp, witty, and the entire cast appeared to be very mature in their interpretation.</u>

    (1) was crisp, witty, and the entire cast appeared to be very mature in their interpretation.
    (2) was very crisp, very witty, and very mature was the cast's interpretation.
    (3) seemed crisp and witty and mature in the cast's interpretations.
    (4) appeared to be crisp and witty, and the cast was very mature.
    (5) was crisp, witty, and mature.

14. <u>Such of his songs as was sentimental and romantic were successful.</u>

    (1) Such of his songs as was sentimental and romantic were successful.
    (2) Such of his songs, sentimental and romantic, were successful.
    (3) His songs such as were sentimental, romantic, and successful.
    (4) His sentimental and romantic songs were successful.
    (5) His songs were successful and romantic.

15. Because the two top contestants are so evenly matched, <u>it is difficult for me deciding which one to receive the trophy.</u>

    (1) it is difficult for me deciding which one to receive the trophy.
    (2) it is difficult for me deciding which to give the trophy to.
    (3) it is difficult for me to decide to whom to give the trophy.
    (4) I am having difficulty deciding who should receive the trophy.
    (5) I am having difficulty deciding whom should receive the trophy.

SPELLING AND WORD USAGE

ANSWER KEY

Drill: Spelling

1. Incorrect. a lot
2. Incorrect. absent
3. Incorrect. accident
4. Incorrect. advisable
5. Incorrect. aggressive
6. Correct. angel
7. Correct. appropriate
8. Incorrect. arrangement
9. Incorrect. awful
10. Correct. awkward
11. Incorrect. bargain
12. Correct. beautiful
13. Incorrect. beginning
14. Incorrect. benefit
15. Correct. breathe
16. Incorrect. business
17. Correct. cafeteria
18. Incorrect. captain
19. Correct. category
20. Incorrect. chief
21. Incorrect. congratulate
22. Correct. coffee
23. Incorrect. competition
24. Incorrect. conscientious
25. Incorrect. controlled
26. Correct. courage
27. Incorrect. courteous
28. Correct. curiosity
29. Incorrect. daybreak
30. Incorrect. decision
31. Incorrect. delicious
32. Incorrect. descend
33. Correct. desperate
34. Incorrect. develop
35. Incorrect. different
36. Correct. disappoint
37. Incorrect. disease
38. Incorrect. distance
39. Incorrect. ecstatic
40. Correct. eliminate
41. Incorrect. English
42. Incorrect. exaggerate
43. Correct. exhaustion
44. Correct. exorbitant
45. Incorrect. experience
46. Incorrect. fascinating
47. Correct. forehead
48. Incorrect. fourteen
49. Correct. friend
50. Incorrect. government
51. Correct. guess
52. Incorrect. happiness

53.	Correct. heroes	85.	Incorrect. privilege
54.	Incorrect. humorous	86.	Incorrect. pursue
55.	Incorrect. imaginary	87.	Incorrect. pronunciation
56.	Correct. independent	88.	Correct. psychology
57.	Incorrect. inoculate	89.	Incorrect. quarrel
58.	Correct. intelligence	90.	Correct. quarter
59.	Correct. itself	91.	Incorrect. rebellion
60.	Incorrect. jealous	92.	Correct. recipe
61.	Incorrect. kindergarten	93.	Incorrect. recommend
62.	Incorrect. knowledge	94.	Correct. repeat
63.	Incorrect. lesson	95.	Incorrect. respectability
64.	Incorrect. likelihood	96.	Incorrect. rhythm
65.	Correct. loyal	97.	Incorrect. schedule
66.	Incorrect. marriage	98.	Incorrect. season
67.	Correct. miscellaneous	99.	Correct. separate
68.	Incorrect. misspelled	100.	Incorrect. shepherd
69.	Correct. muscle	101.	Correct. siege
70.	Incorrect. newsstand	102.	Incorrect. similar
71.	Incorrect. occasion	103.	Incorrect. sophomore
72.	Incorrect. omission	104.	Incorrect. stomach
73.	Incorrect. opportunity	105.	Correct. successful
74.	Correct. opinion	106.	Incorrect. synonym
75.	Incorrect. oscillate	107.	Correct. technical
76.	Incorrect. parallelism	108.	Incorrect. temperature
77.	Correct. pencil	109.	Correct. title
78.	Incorrect. perseverance	110.	Incorrect. undoubtedly
79.	Incorrect. persuade	111.	Incorrect. vacuum
80.	Incorrect. playwright	112.	Correct. vengeance
81.	Correct. poison	113.	Incorrect. visitor
82.	Incorrect. possess	114.	Incorrect. Wednesday
83.	Incorrect. potatoes	115.	Correct. wretched
84.	Incorrect. predictable		

Drill: Homophones

1.	bored	14.	roll
2.	capital	15.	site
3.	coarse	16.	sole
4.	counsel	17.	Where
5.	sundaes; dessert; dinner	18.	waste
6.	fourth	19.	weak
7.	grate	20.	Whether
8.	horse	21.	weigh; lose
9.	its	22.	Here
10.	wear; new	23.	Which
11.	there; peace	24.	hole
12.	sale; pair	25.	Whose
13.	plane		

Drill: Usage and Sentence Correction

1.	(1)	5.	(2)	9.	(3)	13.	(5)
2.	(3)	6.	(4)	10.	(5)	14.	(4)
3.	(3)	7.	(2)	11.	(4)	15.	(4)
4.	(5)	8.	(1)	12.	(1)		

WRITING SKILLS: PART II REVIEW

I. THE ESSAY TEST

II. WHY ESSAYS EXIST

III. ESSAY STRATEGIES

IV. PRE-WRITING/PLANNING TIME

V. WRITING YOUR ROUGH DRAFT

VI. REVISING, EDITING, AND PROOFREADING

I. THE ESSAY TEST

This review is meant to help you become familiar with the skills you will need to pass Part Two of the Writing Skills Test. This section of the GED will ask you to produce ideas, rather than to analyze ideas. Our review will guide you through a step-by-step process of how to write your essay, from writing strategies to budgeting your time during the exam. Even if you feel that you are a good writer, you should still use this review as it will help you become familiar with the type of essay you will be expected to write. By reading through this review and going through the included drills, you will increase your chances of doing well on this section of the test.

As you begin reading each section of this review, try not to become frustrated if you feel that you are not a good writer. The strategies included are provided to help you write an essay which is to the point, easily understood, properly structured, well supported, and correct according to the rules of grammar. You will not be expected to write a best-selling book in order to pass this test. Remember, the more you practice the strategies provided in this review, the easier it will be for you to write a passing essay.

WRITING SKILLS: PART II TOPICS

Part II of the Writing Skills Test will require you to be familiar with various aspects of good writing, all of which are listed below. The topics covered in the Writing Skills: Part I review are also necessary elements of good writing. For a comprehensive review on writing skills, you should study both the Writing Skills: Part I review, which proceeds this review, and the Writing Skills: Part II review, which follows.

EVIDENCE OF THOUGHTFUL WRITING

1. Planning (definite purpose, is structured, and is supported)
2. Drafting
3. Revising
4. Proofreading

CORRECT USE OF STANDARD WRITTEN ENGLISH

1. Spelling
2. Punctuation
3. Grammar
4. Word Choice
5. Sentence Structure

You must realize that your essay will not be scored on each of these skills directly. The person reading your essay will be grading it based on his or her overall impression of how you applied all of these skills to your essay.

II. WHY ESSAYS EXIST

People write essays for many reasons, and not just to complete tests. Some of our best thinkers have written essays which we continue to read from generation to generation. Essays offer the reader a logical, coherent, and imaginative written composition showing the nature or consequences of a single controlling idea considered from the writer's unique point of view. Writers use essays to communicate their opinion or position on a topic to readers who are not present at that time. Writers use essays to help their readers understand or learn about something that readers should or might want to know or do. Essays always express more or less directly the author's opinion, belief, position, or knowledge (backed by evidence) about the idea or object in question.

III. ESSAY STRATEGIES

All of an essay's organizational strategies may be used to aid an argument in writing. The author offers reasons and/or evidence so an audience will be inclined to believe the position the author presents about the idea under discussion. Writers use seven basic strategies to organize information and ideas in essays to help prove their point (thesis). All of these strategies may be useful to you in arguing an idea, in persuading a reader to see the issue your way. Essays may:

(1)   show how a **process** or a procedure does or should work step by step in time;

(2)   **compare or contrast** two or more things or ideas to show important differences or similarities;

(3)   **identify a problem** and then explain how to solve it;

(4)   **analyze** into its components, or **classify** by its types or categories, an idea or thing to show how it is put together, how it works, or how it is designed;

(5)   **explain** why something happens to produce a particular result or set of results;

(6)   **describe** the particular individual characteristics, beauty, features, of a place, person(s), time, or idea; or

(7)   **define** what a thing is or what an idea means.

In a given essay, one pattern tends to dominate the discussion, depending on the object or idea in question. (For example, I might use **description** and **explanation** in order **to define** the varied meanings of "love.")

COMPOSING YOUR ESSAY: USING THE WRITING PROCESS

Most people wrongly think that writers just sit down and churn out wonderful essays or poems in one sitting, in a flash of genius and inspiration. This is not true! Writers use the writing process from start to finish to help them develop a well-composed document. If you do not **reflect** on your composition in stages and make changes as you develop it, you will not see all the problems or errors in it. Don't try to write an essay all at one time and then leave the room. Stay and look through it. Reflect upon it using the writing process in the following way.

The writing process has about four or five steps: (1) pre-writing or planning time, (2) rough drafting, (3) organizing and revising the ideas (not the words or sentences themselves), (4) polishing or editing (making sure sentences themselves are sentences, that the words you use are the right words, and that the spelling and punctuation are correct), and (5) proofreading to make sure no littel mistakes are left (like the misspelling of the word "little" here).

Using this process does not mean that you have to write five drafts. No way! You should write one draft (stages 1 and 2), leaving space for corrections; e.g., writing on every other line, and then working on the existing draft through the rest of the stages (3 through 5). If time allows, you may want to do the whole process on scrap paper and then copy the finished product onto the allotted test paper. But if you do copy it, make sure you proofread your copy to see if while transcribing it you left anything out or said a word twice twice (or something silly like that mistake).

Since you have forty-five minutes for this test, you might allocate your time for all these steps in a manner similar to the following:

1) Pre-writing planning: 5 minutes

2) Rough Draft: 15 minutes

3) Organizing, paragraphing: 10 minutes

4) Polishing, editing: 5–10 minutes

5) Proofreading: 2–5 minutes

If you have more time or less time, adjust this schedule proportionately. Practice this making sure to have someone time you — someone who can keep you concentrating on this task until you're done.

IV. PRE-WRITING/ PLANNING TIME

Read the essay question and **decide on your purpose**: Do you want to persuade your reader? Or, do you want to explain something?

Sample: "Television is bad for people." Do you agree or disagree with this statement?

Decide. Take a stand. Don't be wishy-washy. Write the statement of your position:

Sample: I agree that television is bad for people.

Or: Television is an excellent learning tool and is good for most people.

One of these is your thesis, depending on your point of view.

CONSIDER YOUR AUDIENCE

The writer's responsibility is to write clearly, honestly, and cleanly for the reader's sake. Essays would be pointless without an audience. Why write an essay if no one wants or needs to read it? Why add evidence, organize your ideas, or correct bad grammar? The reason to do any of these things is because someone out there needs to understand what you mean or say. What would the audience need to know in order to believe you or to come over to your position? Imagine someone you know (visualize her — name him) listening to you declare your position or opinion and then saying, "Oh, yeah? Prove it!" Don't you know someone like that? Sure you do. It's the wiseguy, your history teacher. These are the people — write to them. When you write your essay, make sure to answer the following questions so that you will not be confronted with a person who says, "Prove it!"

What evidence do you need to prove your idea to this skeptic?

What would s/he disagree with you about?

What does s/he share with you as common knowledge? What does s/he need to be told by you?

CONTROL YOUR POINT OF VIEW.

People may write essays from one of three points of view, depending upon whom the audience is for the essay. The points of view below are discussed from Informal ⟶ Formal.

1) Subjective/Personal Point of View:

"I think
"I believe } cars are more trouble than they are worth."
"I feel

2) Second Person (We... You; I... You): "If **you** own a car, **you** will soon find out that it is more trouble than it is worth."

3) Third Person Point of View: (focuses on the idea, not what "I" think of it): "**Cars** are more trouble than **they** are worth."

Stick with one, or another; don't switch your "point of view" in the middle. Any one is OK.

CONSIDER YOUR EVIDENCE

During the pre-writing stage, jot down a few phrases that show ideas and examples which support your point of view. Do this quickly on a separate piece of paper, spending no more than **5 minutes** on the task. Don't try to outline, just **list things** you think may be important to discuss. After you have listed several ideas, pick at least three to five things you want or need to discuss and number them in the order of importance to prove your point.

V. WRITING YOUR ROUGH DRAFT

Spend about **twenty minutes** writing your **rough draft**. Looking over at your pre-writing list, write down the ideas you think will be most useful in proving your point in the order you think is the best to convince the reader. Be sure to **use real evidence** from life experiences or knowledge to support what you say. It is not necessary to draw evidence from books. Look into your own life — it will do fine.

For example, do not just write, "Cars are more trouble to fix than bicycles," and then not show evidence to support your claim. Give **examples** of what you mean: "**For example**, my father's Buick needs two hundred parts to make one brake work, but the brakes on my bicycle consist only of four pieces, and I can replace those myself." Write naturally and quickly. Don't worry too much at this point about paragraphing, spelling, punctuation — just write down what you think or want to say in the order of your list.

WRITING PARAGRAPHS

In the examples below, two paragraphs are offered as exhibits. One is an example of a paragraph without concrete evidence, and the other is an example of a paragraph with evidence for the idea. Study each. Note the topic sentence (T) and how that sentence is or is not supported with evidence.

Paragraphing with evidence:

(T) Television is bad for people. **Watching television takes time away from other things.** Programs on television are often stupid and depict crimes that people later copy. Television takes time away from loved ones, and it often becomes addictive. So, television is bad for people because it is no good.

In this example, the author has not given any concrete evidence for any of the good ideas presented. S/he just declares his/her ideas to be so. However, any one of the sentences above might make a good opening sentence for a whole paragraph. Take the second sentence, for example:

Watching television takes time away from other things. (first piece of evidence) For example, all those hours people spend sitting in front of the tube, they could be working on building a chair or fixing the roof. **(second piece of evidence)** Maybe the laundry needs to be done, but because people watch television, they may end up not having time to do it. Then Monday comes around again and they have no socks to wear to work — all because they couldn't stand to miss that episode of "All in the Family." **(third piece of evidence)** Someone could be writing a letter to a friend in Boston who hasn't been heard from or written to for months. **(fourth piece of evidence)** Or maybe someone misses the opportunity to take in a beautiful day in the park because s/he had to see "Dallas." They'll repeat "Dallas," but this beautiful day only comes around once. Watching television definitely keeps people from getting things done.

Always supply evidence. Three examples or illustrations of your idea per paragraph is a useful number. Four is OK, but stop there. Don't go on and on about a single point. You don't have time. A typical test essay, then, should have about five paragraphs. It should be broken like this:

Introduction: A paragraph which shows your point of view (thesis) about an issue and introduces your position with three general ideas which support this thesis.

Development: Three middle paragraphs which prove your position from different angles, using evidence from real life and knowledge. Each paragraph of these paragraphs should support each of the three ideas you started out with in Paragraph 1.

Conclusion: The last paragraph, which sums up your position and adds one final reminder of what the issue was and perhaps points to a solution.

"So, television takes away from the quality of life and is therefore bad for human beings. We should be watching the sun, the sky, the birds, and each other, not the 'boob tube.'"

Write a paragraph below using this sentence for your focus: (Have someone read it and comment critically on it when you are done.)

"Television takes valuable time away from our loved ones."

TRANSITIONS

To help the reader follow the flow of your ideas, and to help unify the essay, use transitions to show the connections among your ideas. You may use transitions either at the beginnings of paragraphs, or you may use them to show the connections among ideas within a single paragraph.

Here are some typical transitional words and phrases.

Linking similar ideas

again	*for example*	*likewise*
also	*for instance*	*moreover*
and	*further*	*nor*
another	*furthermore*	*of course*
besides	*in addition*	*similarly*
equally important	*in like manner*	*too*

Linking dissimilar/contradictory ideas

although	*however*	*otherwise*
and yet	*in spite of*	*provided that*
as if	*instead*	*still*
but	*nevertheless*	*yet*

conversely	*on the contrary*
even if	*on the other hand*

Indicating cause, purpose, result

as	*for*	*so*
as a result	*for this reason*	*then*
because	*hence*	*therefore*
consequently	*since*	*thus*

Indicating time or position

above	*before*	*meanwhile*
across	*beyond*	*next*
afterwards	*eventually*	*presently*
around	*finally*	*second*
at once	*first*	*thereafter*
at the present time	*here*	*thereupon*

Indicating an example or summary

as a result	*in any event*	*in short*
as I have said	*in brief*	*on the whole*
for example	*in conclusion*	*to sum up*
for instance	*in fact*	
in any case	*in other words*	

☞ Drill: Writing

DIRECTIONS: Each of the following phrases or sentences is incorrect. Determine what is wrong with each item and correct it in the space provided.

1. About the television.

2. I like television and I think people should watch it television is good because it is so real I think many people would die without it.

3. In my opinion, I believe that in order to be able to understand this issue many hours and a lot of time must be devoted to comprehending what

the message is that the writer is trying to communicate with ideas due to the fact that s/he is so involved with them.

4. While waiting for the check, the doorbell rang in the living room.

5. I like eating fish and to go to the shore.

6. I bought a computer and some word processing software which was frightening.

7. We cannot reimburse you for moving boats over 14 feet.

8. We could of been contenders in the contest, but the sweep of events make us losers in the end.

9. I like ducks, however, I prefer swans.

10. In the long run, the most important thing is not to be effected by the affects of television commercials.

VI. REVISING, EDITING, AND PROOFREADING

REVISE AND ORGANIZE THE PARAGRAPHS

The unit of work for revising is "the paragraph." After you have written what you want to say based on your pre-writing list, spend about **ten minutes** revising your draft, looking to see if you need to indent for paragraphs anywhere. If you do, make a little proofreader's mark (¶) to indicate that you think a paragraph should begin at that point. Check to see if you want to add anything that would make your point of view more convincing. Be sure to supply useful transitions to keep up the flow of your ideas. If you don't have room on the paper, or if your new paragraph shows up out of order, add that paragraph and indicate with a number or some other mark where you want it go. Check to make sure that you provide examples and illustrate your statements.

POLISHING AND EDITING THE ESSAY SENTENCES

If the unit of work for revising is the paragraph, the unit of work for editing is the sentence. In **the last 5 to 10 minutes**, check your paper for mistakes by editing.

Polishing Checklist:

- Are all your sentences really sentences, or have you written some fragments or run-on sentences?

- Are you using your vocabulary correctly?

- Have you used some inappropriate words that you would never use with your history teacher?

- Did you leave out punctuation anywhere? Did you capitalize correctly? Did you check for commas, periods, and quotation marks?

Be sure to **read every word** during this time and make corrections as you go. To help you recognize what you should look for in polishing and editing, refer to the Writing I Review in this book.

PROOFREADING

In the last two or three minutes, read your paper, word for word, forward and then backward from the end to the beginning. Read it out loud if possible, but read it! By doing so, you will notice a certain number of errors that you may have missed by having red forward only. For example, read the sentence before this one backward, starting with "only," and see if you spot any more errors than you read the first time.

☞ Drill: Essay Writing

Give yourself 45 minutes to write an essay on the topic below, using the lined space provided and making sure to time yourself. Write only on the topic provided. Write legibly, use a ball-point pen, and budget your space so you do not run out of room to write. (Remember to use the strategies which you learned in this review.)

Television often causes the viewer to lose reality and become completely passive and unaware. Like other addictions, television provides a pleasurable escape route from action to inaction.

Is this statement true or false? Do you feel that television's effects are good or bad? Respond to this statement in an essay of approximately two hundred words, making sure to support your view with examples using your own past experiences or knowledge of other people's experiences.

WRITING SKILLS, Part II REVIEW

Write your essay on these lined pages.

WRITING II

ANSWER KEY

DRILL: Writing

Since more than one answer may be obtained for each item, we will only identify what errors are present in each phrase and sentence rather than provide a single correct sentence among various correct answers.

1. This sentence is a fragment; it has no subject or verb to complete it.

2. This is a run-on sentence. It has many subject and verb units not correctly separated by punctuation.

3. This is a wordy sentence. It should be rewritten as a single short sentence.

4. This is an example of a dangling modifier. Reading this sentence, one would think that the doorbell works for a living, i.e., who was really waiting for the check?

5. This sentence does not link up the phrases that begin "eating…" and "to go…." They are not parallel.

6. This sentence suggests that either or both the computer or the software is frightening. Which is it? The reader cannot be sure because s/he cannot tell to which word the word "which" refers.

7. This sentence is confusing because the meaning of "14 feet" is ambiguous. Does the writer mean 14-foot long boats? Surely, moving boats over a distance of 14 feet is not such a costly proposition.

8. This sentence has two major flaws:

    (1) The phrase "could of" should be "could have." "Of" is never part of a verb.

    (2) In the second half, "make" should be "makes" to agree with the real subject, "sweep."

    The trouble is the writer probably thought "events" was the subject as s/he wrote the sentence.

9. This sentence is incorrectly punctuated with commas. It is actually two sentences on either side of the "however." Consequently, a semicolon [;] could be placed after "ducks." You can also use a

period [.] to separate the two sentences, or you can replace "however" with "but" and leave the commas as they appear.

10. Which "effect" word is correct? Neither. Make sure you use the right words in the right place. For example, don't write "red" for "read," or "there" for "their."

ESSAY I

In the past thirty years, television has become a very popular pastime for almost everyone. From the time the mother places the baby in his jumpseat in front of the television so that she can relax and have a second cup of coffee until the time the senior citizen in the retirement home watches Vanna White turn the letters on "Wheel of Fortune," Americans spend endless hours in front of the "boob tube." I believe that television can become an addiction that provides an escape from the problems of the world and from facing responsibility for your own life.

When my mother was a little girl, what did children do to entertain themselves? They played. Their games usually involved social interaction with other children as well as imaginatively creating entertainment for themselves. They also developed hobbies like woodworking and sewing. Today, few children really know how to play with each other or entertain themselves. Instead, they sit in front of the television, glued to cartoons that are senseless and often violent. Even if they watch educational programs like "Sesame Street," they don't really have to do anything but watch and listen to what the answer to the question is.

Teenagers, also, use television as a way of avoiding doing things that will help them mature. How many kids do much homework anymore? Why not? Because they work part-time jobs and come home from work tired and relax in front of the television. Even if they watch a controversial program about some problem in the world like AIDS or the war in the Middle East, they don't usually do anything about it.

In addition, young mothers use television to escape their problems. The terrible woes of the people on the soap operas make their problems seem less important. This means that they don't need to solve their own problems.

Although it may seem as if television is really great for older people, I think even my grandma would have more fun if she had more interests rather than just watching quiz shows. I know she has blotted out the "real world" when she expects us to act like the Cosby kids when she comes to visit.

In conclusion, I believe that television really can become an addiction that allows people of all ages to avoid facing their own problems and lose themselves in the problems of other people.

Analysis of Essay I

This essay scores between 6 and 5. The writer appears largely in control of the discussion and the mechanics of writing.

In the past thirty years, television has become a very popular pastime for almost everyone. From the time the mother places the baby in his jumpseat in front of the television so that she can relax and have a second cup of coffee until the time the senior citizen in the retirement home watches Vanna White turn the letters on "Wheel of Fortune," Americans spend endless hours in front of the "boob tube." [1—I believe that television can become an addiction that provides an escape from the problems of the world and from facing responsibility for your own life.]

> 1. The essay has a traditional structure; the first paragraph introduces the topic, even suggesting the organization of the essay. This last sentence states the writer's thesis clearly.

[2—When my mother was a little girl, what did children do to entertain themselves? They played.] Their games usually involved social interaction with other children as well as imaginatively creating entertainment for themselves. [3—They also developed hobbies like woodworking and sewing.] Today, few children really know how to play with each other or entertain themselves. Instead, they sit in front of the television, glued to cartoons that are senseless and often violent. Even if they watch educational programs like "Sesame Street," they don't really have to do anything but watch and listen to what the answer to the question is.

> 2. Each of the following paragraphs has a clear topic sentence. Here, it is in the form of a question which the writer immediately answers. The reader feels as though s/he is really taking part in the writer's thought process.
>
> 3. The writer's consistent use of specific, concrete evidence supports the general ideas effectively. Readers begin to feel convinced of the writer's opinion (thesis).

[4—Teenagers, also, use television as a way of avoiding doing things that will help them mature. How many kids do much homework anymore? Why not? Because they work part-time jobs and come home from work tired and relax in front of the television. Even if they watch a controversial program about some problem in the world like AIDS or the war in the Middle East, they don't usually do anything about it.]

> 4. This paragraph explores a new, interesting angle in support of the thesis.

[5—In addition,] young mothers use television to escape their problems. The terrible woes of the people on the soap operas make their problems seem less important. This means that they don't need to solve their own problems.

> 5. Effective transitions keep the flow of ideas going for the reader.

[6—Although it may seem as if television is really great for older people, I think even my grandma would have more fun if she had more interests rather than just watching quiz shows.] I know she has blotted out the "real world" when she expects us to act like the Cosby kids when she comes to visit.

> 6. Varied sentence structure helps create emphasis and changes the pace for the reader, helping to relieve monotony of tone and to keep the writing interesting.

[7—In conclusion, I believe that television really can become an addiction that allows people of all ages to avoid facing their own problems and lose themselves in the problems of other people.]

> 7. The concluding paragraph, although only one sentence long, restates the main idea. The writer may have run out of time and so could not write more, but at least s/he rounded out the thesis with a clear control of the main idea.

ESSAY II

I do not agree with the given statement. I think that instead of being bad for people, television not only does not blot out the real world but, instead, gives the person watching it a chance to experience the real world, even places he can't possibly go and may never get a chance to go.

For instance, I've learned a lot about the Vietnam War by watching TV. For a while, I heard things about it, about how some of the veterans didn't feel as if they were welcomed right when they came back from that war. I didn't understand what was the matter. Then they built a special memorial in Washington for the veterans that didn't come back. Since then, I have seen a lot of programs that showed what went on in Vietnam, and I've heard Vietnam vets talk about what happened to them. I think that that war has became very real to me because of TV.

Television educates us about the dangers of growing up in America today. I've seen good programs about the dangers of using drugs, about teenage pregnancy and what happens if you try to keep the baby, about eating too much cholesterol (That doesn't matter to me yet, but my dad needs to watch that!), and also anorexia. These are things we all need to know about, and TV has told about them so we know what to do.

I really am convinced that television brings the real world into your house. I think us kids today know a lot more about the real world than our grandparents did who grew up without television.

Analysis of Essay II

This essay scores between 4 and 3. The writer appears to have good control over the discussion and fairly good control over grammar and mechanics.

I do not agree with the given statement. [1—I think that instead of being bad for people, television not only does not blot out the real world but, instead, gives the person watching it a chance to experience the real world, even places he can't possibly go and may never get a chance to go.]

> 1. The writer takes one position and develops it. The first paragraph provides a clear introduction, and paragraphs two and three below develop this thesis.

[2—For instance, I've learned a lot about the Vietnam War by watching TV.] For a while, I heard things about it, about how some of the veterans didn't feel as if they were welcomed right when they came back from that war. I didn't understand what was the matter. Then they built a special memorial in Washington for the veterans that didn't come back. Since then, I have seen a lot of programs that showed what went on in Vietnam, and I've heard Vietnam vets talk about what happened to them. [3—I think that that war has became very real to me because of TV.]

> 2. This generalized example is not supported with specific evidence. The lack of specifics pulls this essay down.
>
> 3. Occasional weak sentence structure and a failure to proofread effectively take the essay down another step because the style and mechanics appear to be only fairly under control.

Television educates us about the dangers of growing up in America today. I've seen good programs about the dangers of using drugs, about teenage pregnancy and what happens if you try to keep the baby, about eating too much cholesterol (That doesn't matter to me yet, but my dad needs to watch that!), and also anorexia. These are things we all need to know about, and TV has told about them so we know what to do.

[5—I really am convinced that television brings the real world into your house. I think us [4—kids] today know a lot more about the real world than our grandparents did who grew up without television.]

> 4. The occasional use of slang such as this makes the writer's style inconsistent and less literate than it could be.
>
> 5. This last paragraph concludes, but weakly, and seems to wander off onto a possible new area of discussion not called for by the thesis.

ESSAY III

On the one hand, I think television is bad, But it also does some good things for all of us. For instants, my little sister thought she wanted to be a policeman until she saw Cagney and Lacey. Then she learned how dangerous it is and now she wants to be an astronaut. I guess she didn't watch the Challenger explode often enough to scare her out of that.

But the bad thing about television programs are the ideas it puts in kids heads. Like violent things happen on television, and little kids see it and don't know that other people hurt when they are hit, battered up, beat. shot, ect. Then the kids go out and try to knock their friends around and think if they are strong and handsome that they can get their own way whatever happens. Even parents sometimes have trouble controling their own kids because of too much TV. Of course that's partly because the parents watch too much too when they should of been taking care of the kids they necklected them watching television.

So I think that television has both it's good and it's bad points. I'd hate to see us get rid of it all together, but I wonder if I'll let my kids watch it when I have them. It sometimes puts bad ideas in their heads.

Analysis of Essay III

This essay scores between 2 and 1. The writer appears largely out of control of both the controlling idea, evidence to support the opinions expressed, and the grammar and mechanics of English itself.

[1—On the one hand, I think television is [2—bad], But it also does some good things for all of us. For [3—instants], my little sister thought she wanted to be a policeman until she saw Cagney and Lacey. Then she learned how dangerous it is and now she wants to be an astronaut. I guess she didn't watch the Challenger explode often enough to scare her out of that.]

1. The writer's failure to take one opinion (thesis) and clearly develop it weakens the whole essay. Some specific examples are attempted, but the details in this paragraph would be better stated in later paragraphs.

2. Punctuation errors plague the essay and help the writer appear illiterate to the reader.

3. Poor spelling contributes to a sloppy, illiterate appearance.

[5—[4—But the bad thing about television programs are the ideas it puts in kids heads.] Like violent things happen on television, and little kids see it and don't know that other people hurt when they are hit, battered up, beat. shot, etc. Then the kids go out and try to knock their friends around and think if they are strong and handsome that they can get their own way whatever happens. Even parents sometimes have trouble controling their own kids because of too much TV. [6—Of course that's partly because the parents watch too much too when they should of been taking care of the kids they necklected them watching television.]]

4. Weak subject/verb agreement makes this sentence sound careless to the reader .

5. The lack of specificity forces the writer to blend what should be at least two paragraphs into one. The writer comes across as rambling and as not having thought through the ideas.

6. Persistent spelling and grammatical errors ("should of" instead of "should have") point to a writer who is out of control of his medium—language. This exasperates the reader and drives him or her away.

[8—So I think that television has both [7—it's] good and it's bad points. I'd hate to see us get rid of it all together, but I wonder if I'll let my kids watch it when I have them. It sometimes puts bad ideas in their heads.]

7. A typical apostrophe error that only the careless or rushed would let get by them.

8. In this weak "conclusion," the writer doesn't take a clear stand, plays it safe, probably hoping that a risk-free wishy-washy ending will go well with the teachers reading this. That is a big mistake. Stick to your guns! The stronger your stand, the better your chances. But prove what you claim.

SOCIAL STUDIES REVIEW

Chapter 3

SOCIAL STUDIES REVIEW

I.   SOCIAL STUDIES TOPICS

II. U.S. HISTORY

III. ECONOMICS

IV. POLITICAL SCIENCE

V.   GEOGRAPHY

VI. BEHAVIORAL SCIENCE

The following review has been created to help you become familiar with the types of questions you will encounter in the Social Studies section of the GED. Prior knowledge of the subjects tested is not necessary in order for you to do well on this exam. This test will require you to read a passage and/or interpret information from a graph, map, or chart, and then answer questions based on this information. Our review concentrates on presenting passages and questions similar to those appearing on the GED. By studying this review, you can familiarize yourself with the type of vocabulary which will appear on the test, as well as the content covered.

I. SOCIAL STUDIES TOPICS

The table below represents the areas covered in the Social Studies test. You should review these topics in order to accurately answer the questions appearing in this section.

HISTORY (25% of Test)

1. North American Native People
2. The New World and the New Nation
3. Growth and Change
4. Industrialization
5. Crisis and Reform
6. The United States as a World Power
7. Challenges of the Modern World

ECONOMICS (20% of Test)

1. Scarcity
2. Economic Systems: Capitalism, Communism, Socialism
3. Free Enterprise
4. Production
5. The Consumer
6. Financial Institutions
7. Government and the Economy
8. The Economy
9. Labor and the Economy
10. Foreign Trade

POLITICAL SCIENCE (20% of Test)

1. Political Systems
2. The U.S. Political System

GEOGRAPHY (15% of Test)

1. Basic Principles
2. Regions of the U.S.
3. Themes and Issues in the U.S.
4. Cultural regions
5. Utilizing World Resources

BEHAVIORAL SCIENCE (20% of Test)

1. Anthropology
2. Psychology
3. Sociology

The more familiar you are with the format of the Social Studies test, the better you will perform. Our review will present you with maps, charts, graphs, and various passages similar to those found on the actual test. You will be asked to answer questions based on the information given. Although you may feel that you are well prepared for this test, you should still read this review to brush up on your skills, and develop speed and accuracy in answering the questions. Also, make sure to memorize the directions to this section, so that valuable time is not wasted.

II. U.S. HISTORY

THE NEW WORLD

In 1606, three ships, the *Discovery*, *Godspeed*, and *Susan Constant*, left England with over 100 passengers aboard. The ships arrived in Jamestown, Virginia, in 1607 with people of various professions, such as doctors, bricklayers, carpenters, and farmers, among others.

The name Virginia was chosen because Queen Elizabeth I of England, who died in 1603, was known as the "Virgin Queen." Thick forests loomed everywhere in the new colony. Farms were begun only after a wilderness of trees and brush had been cleared. Times were indeed hard for the first colonists, but despite the hardships new settlers continued to make the long and arduous journey to the new land.

Many settlers of all nationalities settled in the colonies after 1607. A steady stream of French, Swedish, Portuguese, Dutch, English, and other nationalities settled up and down the eastern seaboard between 1607 and 1776. In 1619, the first 20 black immigrants arrived in Jamestown, and they accumulated land and did quite well despite the inevitable hardships of getting established in the new world. (Slavery came about 40 years later.)

The first law-making governmental structure in the new world was called the Virginia House of Burgesses. In 1619, two men from each of the eleven settlements made up the first representative Congress in Virginia. This bold step of setting up a representative government in 1619, in Virginia, served as a landmark achievement which other colonies emulated.

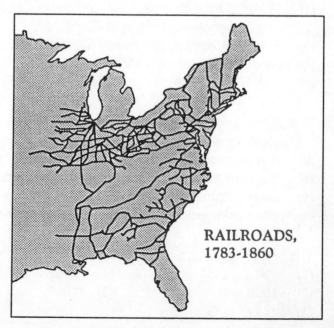

RAILROADS, 1783-1860

☞ Drill: The New World

<u>DIRECTIONS</u>: The following questions are based on the passage above. Read each question and choose the correct answer.

1. One of the conclusions that we can draw from the passage is that
   (1) thick forests of trees made it difficult to start farms in colonial Virginia.
   (2) thick forests of trees made it easy to get farms started.
   (3) new settlers stopped coming to the New World.
   (4) life was easy in colonial Virginia.
   (5) Queen Elizabeth I of England was alive when the first settlers founded Jamestown, Virginia.

2. One conclusion that can be drawn is that
   (1) each ship had over 100 passengers aboard.
   (2) most people went to the New World for adventure.
   (3) a variety of skilled people went to the new world in order to build houses, plant farms, and to take care of the sick.
   (4) the *Discovery, Godspeed*, and *Susan Constant* were forts in Virginia.
   (5) the *Discovery, Godspeed*, and *Susan Constant* were lakes in Virginia.

3. The three ships that landed in Jamestown, Virginia, were
   (1) *Susan Constant, Discovery*, and *Virgin Queen*.
   (2) *Susan Constant, Pinta*, and *Godspeed*.
   (3) *Pinta, Godspeed*, and *Susan Constant*.
   (4) *Nina, Pinta*, and *Santa Maria*.
   (5) *Discovery, Godspeed*, and *Susan Constant*.

4. The main idea of the passage is that
   (1) black immigrants settled in the country in 1619.
   (2) many nationalities settled in America after 1607.
   (3) the English were the first settlers in the New World.
   (4) slavery came about 40 years after 1619.
   (5) other colonies also settled on the Eastern seaboard.

5. The first colony was established in
   (1) 1607.   (4) 1492.
   (2) 1620.   (5) 1916.
   (3) 1619.

6. Which of the following statements is an opinion?
    (1) Twenty-two members made up the first representative Congress.
    (2) In 1619, the Virginia House of Burgesses was established.
    (3) Only men were elected to the representative assembly.
    (4) Eleven settlements were represented.
    (5) The setting up of the Virginia House of Burgesses was a landmark achievement.

7. In which colony did the House of Burgesses begin?
    (1) Maryland   (4) South Carolina
    (2) Virginia   (5) Rhode Island
    (3) Massachusetts

8. According to the map, which of the following statements is most correct?
    (1) The South had the most extensively developed railroad system.
    (2) The transportation system ran primarily east-west.
    (3) The West had a poorly developed transportation system.
    (4) The South depended upon canals for transportation.
    (5) The United States had developed few railroad lines prior to 1860.

THE INDUSTRIAL REVOLUTION

The industrial revolution began with inventions such as the flying shuttle of 1733, the spinning jenny of 1764, the water frame of 1769, the power loom of 1785, and the cotton gin of 1793. In 1784, wrought iron was made from pig iron, and in 1785, the cotton mill was first operated by steam power. These inventions, among others, made it much easier for products to be produced at a much faster pace.

The industrial revolution continues to play a major role today in many parts of the world. Computers have revolutionized the way that goods are produced. An example of this would be in the making of garments. There are sewing machines on the market today that can be programmed to actually make a garment to exact proportions and specifications.

The industrial revolution, which introduced machine labor, began in England around 1760 and changed the face of America and Europe. A shift in population from the rural areas to the cities began as new technology provided more and more jobs. Some of the inventions that fueled the industrial revolution were the cotton gin, the spinning jenny, the power loom, the steamboat, Morse's telegraph, and others.

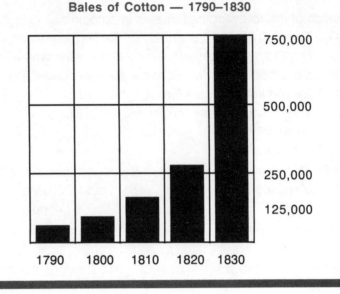

Bales of Cotton — 1790–1830

750,000

500,000

250,000

125,000

1790   1800   1810   1820   1830

🖝 Drill: The Industrial Revolution

DIRECTIONS: The following questions are based on the information above. Read each question and choose the correct answer.

9.   Based on the passage, which of the following is the best example of a new invention being used to change the way things were made in the 1700s?
   (1)   The assembly line being introduced
   (2)   Oxen being used to plow fields
   (3)   Shoes being made by hand by a cobbler
   (4)   Fabric being made with a machine in a mill instead of by hand
   (5)   Furniture being carved by hand

10.   The new industrial revolution is continuing because of the advent of
   (1)   computers.   (4)   knitting needles.
   (2)   the spinning jenny.   (5)   the stock market.
   (3)   the loom.

11.   Which of the following statements expresses an opinion rather than a fact?
   (1)   Computers can improve productivity.
   (2)   Computers are difficult to operate.
   (3)   Computers are used only in America.
   (4)   Computers are not a part of the industrial revolution.
   (5)   Computers can be programmed for specific tasks.

12. One profession that was least likely to flourish during the industrial revolution was the
    (1) factory worker.
    (2) steamboat captain.
    (3) city housing worker.
    (4) telegraph operator.
    (5) farmer.

13. The industrial revolution began in
    (1) America.
    (2) England.
    (3) France.
    (4) Germany.
    (5) Japan.

14. An invention that was not a part of the industrial revolution was the
    (1) cotton gin.
    (2) radio.
    (3) telegraph.
    (4) steamboat.
    (5) power loom.

15. According to the graph, how many bales of cotton were produced in 1830?
    (1) 200,000
    (2) 500,000
    (3) 750,000
    (4) 50,000
    (5) 75,000

16. In what year was more cotton produced than in 1830?
    (1) 1790
    (2) 1800
    (3) 1830
    (4) All of the above.
    (5) None of the above.

THE CIVIL WAR

The Civil War, which started in 1861 and ended in 1865, was the bloodiest war in all of U.S. history. It tore the country apart and, in some instances, pitted brother against brother. The war was fought over political and social differences between the Union and Confederacy. The war essentially brought down the tragic institution of slavery. To this day, the scars of the Civil War are evident in American society.

At the beginning of the hostilities between the North and South, the states of South Carolina, Georgia, Florida, Alabama, Mississippi, Texas, Louisiana, North Carolina, Arkansas, Tennessee, and eventually Virginia, decided to secede from the Union.

After the Civil War ended and the Union forces were victorious, there remained monumental tasks that had to be tackled in reuniting the country. Some states were not admitted to the Union until the Fourteenth and Fifteenth Amendments, granting citizenship rights and the right to vote to blacks, were approved. As a result of the new freedoms, black men became office holders in the deep South between 1868 and 1877.

☞ Drill: The Civil War

DIRECTIONS: The following questions are based on the passage above. Read each question and choose the correct answer.

17. The Civil War began in
    (1) 1865.   (4) 1861.
    (2) 1860.   (5) 1862.
    (3) 1866.

18. A civil war means a war that is fought
    (1) between citizens of the same country.
    (2) between two or more countries.
    (3) between the army ground forces and naval forces.
    (4) between adjacent countries.
    (5) between allied countries.

19. Secede may be defined as
    (1) to leave or get out of.
    (2) to become an ally of another country.
    (3) to make peace.
    (4) to become successful.
    (5) to stay behind or remain.

20. One result of the ratification of the Fourteenth and Fifteenth Amendments was the
    (1) ratification of the Congressional Plan of Reconstruction.
    (2) end of Reconstruction.
    (3) election of blacks to political office.
    (4) Civil War.
    (5) the assassination of Abraham Lincoln.

THE ELECTION OF 1912

The election of 1912 was one of the most dramatic in American history. President Taft's inability to maintain party harmony led Theodore Roosevelt to return to national politics. When denied the Republican nomination, Roosevelt and his supporters formed the Progressive Party (Bull Moose) and nominated Roosevelt for president and Hiram Johnson (California) for vice president on a political platform nicknamed "The New Nationalism." It called for stricter regulation of large corporations; creation of a tariff commission; women's suffrage; minimum wages and benefits; direct election of senators; initiative, referendum and recall; presidential primaries; and prohibition of child labor. Roosevelt also called for a Federal Trade Commission to regulate the broader economy, a stronger executive, and more government planning. Theodore Roosevelt did not see big business as evil, but as a permanent development that was necessary in a modern economy.

☞ Drill: The Election of 1912

<u>DIRECTIONS</u>: The following questions are based on the passage above. Read each question and choose the correct answer.

21. The Progressive movement started in
    (1) 1914.   (4) 1965.
    (2) 1912.   (5) 1913.
    (3) 1915.

22. Which was **not** a part of Theodore Roosevelt's political platform in 1912?
    (1) The formation of the "Bull Moose" party
    (2) A stronger chief executive
    (3) Annexation of Cuba
    (4) Minimum wages
    (5) Women's suffrage

THE GREAT DEPRESSION

The Great Depression began in 1929 with the crash of the stock market. This brought on a period of approximately twenty-five percent unemployment and very bleak times for millions of people. Banks closed and many people lost all of their savings.

Long soup lines in cities became a common sight. It became extremely difficult for families to get by without some government assistance.

Franklin Roosevelt was elected to the Presidency in 1932 during the Great Depression. He had many "new deal" ideas about how to turn the economy around. Many work programs were instituted, such as the Works Progress Administration (WPA) and the Civilian Conservation Corps (CCC). Such programs put large numbers of people to work on public projects. The government became their employer. Congress also passed a social security law in 1935 at the urging of President Roosevelt.

☞ Drill: The Great Depression

DIRECTIONS: The following questions are based on the passage above. Read each question and choose the correct answer.

23. One of the conclusions that can be drawn from the above passage is that
    (1) many businesses failed for lack of customers during the Great Depression.
    (2) many people did not want to work.
    (3) employment was high.
    (4) few people lived in the city.
    (5) many people left the country.

24. The Great Depression started because of
    (1) the stock market crash of 1929.
    (2) runaway inflation.
    (3) a migration of people from the farm to the city.
    (4) adverse economic conditions in foreign countries.
    (5) Roosevelt's "new deal" ideas.

25. Which of the following statements is an example of a "new deal" program?
    (1) Changing the laws governing the states
    (2) Recruits being drafted into the armed forces
    (3) Volunteers working in soup kitchens
    (4) Politicians making speeches
    (5) Masses of people being hired by the government to build and repair bridges and highways

26. In the above passage, one of the conclusions that can be drawn is that
    (1) the government had little to do with ending the depression.
    (2) President Roosevelt helped to bring the country out of the depression.
    (3) the depression ended before President Roosevelt took office.
    (4) the depression did not cause many hardships.
    (5) Roosevelt was a very popular president.

THE POPULATION

Comparison of Population in Selected Cities in the United States – 1988

City	Population
New York	7,352,700
Los Angeles	3,352,710
Chicago	2,977,520
Houston	1,698,090
Philadelphia	1,647,000
San Diego	1,070,310

Demographic Statistics of Selected States in the United States – 1989

State	Population	Approx. Pop. Density	Land Area Sq. Mi.	Per Capita Income
Virginia	6,098,000	149	39,704	$16,399
Rhode Island	998,000	823	1,055	$18,061
Massachusetts	5,913,000	713	7,824	$22,196
Georgia	6,436,000	109	58,056	$16,188
New York	17,950,000	366	47,377	$20,540

☞ Drill: The Population

DIRECTIONS: The following questions are based on the graph above. Read each question and choose the correct answer.

27. How many cities listed above have populations less than 3 million?
    (1) 3   (4) 1
    (2) 5   (5) 2
    (3) 4

28. Which state has the second smallest population of the states listed?
    (1) Georgia
    (2) New York
    (3) Rhode Island
    (4) Virginia
    (5) Massachusetts

29. Of the states listed, which state has the highest population density (number of people per square mile)?
    (1) Rhode Island
    (2) Virginia
    (3) Massachusetts
    (4) New York
    (5) Georgia

30. The state with the third highest per capita income is
    (1) Virginia.
    (2) Rhode Island.
    (3) Massachusetts.
    (4) Georgia.
    (5) New York.

U.S. HISTORY

ANSWER KEY

Drill: The New World

1.	(1)	3.	(5)	5.	(1)	7.	(2)
2.	(3)	4.	(2)	6.	(5)	8.	(2)

Drill: The Industrial Revolution

9.	(4)	11.	(2)	13.	(2)	15.	(3)
10.	(1)	12.	(5)	14.	(2)	16.	(5)

Drill: The Civil War

17.	(4)	18.	(1)	19.	(1)	20.	(3)

Drill: The Election of 1912

21.	(2)	22.	(3)

Drill: The Great Depression

23.	(1)	24.	(1)	25.	(5)	26.	(2)

Drill: The Population

27.	(3)	28.	(5)	29.	(1)	30.	(2)

III. ECONOMICS

THE IMPORTANCE OF ECONOMICS

A study of economics is crucial to the fiscal well-being of a nation and can be defined as the effectiveness with which people use limited resources to meet unlimited wants. Macroeconomics is a study of looking at the economy as a whole. Microeconomics is a method of looking at the economy in small units or parts. Economics, as a formalized discipline, is a little over two hundred years old. Adam Smith, the father of economics, paved the way in 1776 with the writing of his book, *The Wealth of Nations*.

Adam Smith's *The Wealth of Nations* served as the impetus for synthesizing the various elements of the industrial society into the discipline of economics. He believed that the free market system inherently works to produce the best products in the most efficient manner possible. He felt that the competitors who were less efficient would be driven out of business. Adam Smith also espoused *laissez-faire* economics, which means that the free market system should be unrestricted by government controls.

The reality of making choices in economics is very meaningful. One makes many choices on a daily basis. Earning and spending money and deciding how to spend your time are all involved in daily decision making. Suppose, for example, you had decided to go to college and had applied and been accepted to several schools. The choice you make will depend on several factors, such as tuition, courses offered, and distance from home.

Scarcity is the reason that choices have to be made. Since there is a limited supply of goods and services, it is very important to make the right choices.

Every decision you make has an opportunity cost. An opportunity cost of a good refers to the good or service you had to forego in order to choose another. When you choose one item or service over another, it costs you the one you did not choose.

☞ Drill: The Importance of Economics

DIRECTIONS: The following questions are based on the passage above. Read each question, then choose the correct answer.

1. Economics as a scholarly discipline can be traced back to about
    (1)   the American Revolutionary War.
    (2)   the Roaring Twenties.
    (3)   the Sixties.
    (4)   the Classical Age.
    (5)   the Civil War.

2. The study of how people use limited natural resources to meet unlimited wants is
    (1)   political science.   (4)   microeconomics.
    (2)   economics.   (5)   sociology.
    (3)   macroeconomics.

3. A method of looking at individual parts of the economy is
    (1)   macroeconomics.   (4)   technology.
    (2)   scarcity.   (5)   fiscal well-being.
    (3)   microeconomics.

4. *Laissez-faire* stated that there should be
    (1)   government controls in business.
    (2)   no government controls in the free market system.
    (3)   competition in all businesses.
    (4)   pacts between labor and the government.
    (5)   state-owned factories.

5. According to the passage above, which is an example of *laissez-faire*?
    (1)   State-run trash collection
    (2)   Government-subsidized hospital care
    (3)   The government's dismantling of Bell Telephone
    (4)   Privately run stock market
    (5)   Public transportation systems

6. The cost of tuition will be one of the factors considered in
    (1)   choosing a college.
    (2)   deciding on a major field of study.
    (3)   buying a car.
    (4)   moving.
    (5)   making a decision.

7. Economic decisions
    (1)   do not affect most people.

(2)   are made only in the government.
(3)   are easy decisions to make.
(4)   must be made by everyone.
(5)   are only made by college graduates.

8.   Scarcity is
       (1)   a limited supply of goods and services.
       (2)   an economic unreality.
       (3)   pluralism.
       (4)   opportunity cost.
       (5)   the supply of goods and services.

9.   When you forego one good or service in favor of another, this is known
       as
       (1)   relative scarcity.   (4)   decision making.
       (2)   economizing.   (5)   favoritism.
       (3)   opportunity cost.

BUSINESS

The factors of production are essential to producing and distributing goods and services. The three primary factors of production are land, labor, and capital. The two secondary factors of production are entrepreneurship and technology. Land includes the soil and all natural resources. Labor is defined as the physical and mental effort used to produce goods and services. Capital, as a factor of production, refers to the tools and equipment used in making goods and services. Entrepreneurship is defined as directing and managing a business. Technology means the application of knowledge and skills to production.

A market system is the method of producing and distributing goods and services as a result of individuals making decisions in the market place.

A command economy is defined as one wherein all decisions of an economic nature are in the hands of the government. A mixed economy is one in which some industries are government regulated and co-exist along with free markets.

The three major kinds of business organizations are sole proprietorship, partnership, and corporation. A sole proprietorship is owned by one person. Some advantages of a sole proprietorship are: all decisions are made by one person, all profits go to the owner, and the owner is the sole boss. Some disadvantages of a sole proprietorship are: the owner is liable for all debts, business expertise is limited to one person, and limited capital. A partnership is composed of two or more persons. The advantages of a partnership are: more than one person can offer ideas, more capital, and any liability is spread among partners. Some disadvantages are: if one person leaves the partnership, the company dissolves, partners are responsible for all debts of the business, and profits must be divided. In a corporation, the organization is set up as an artificial individual which pays income taxes. The advantages are: increased capital, increased managerial ability, and limited liability. The disadvantages of the corporation are: increased taxes, unwieldy size, and government restrictions.

☞ Drill: Business

DIRECTIONS: The following questions are based on the passage above. Read each question, then choose the correct answer.

10. The three primary factors of production are
    (1) land, labor, and technology.
    (2) labor, capital, and entrepreneurship.
    (3) land, labor, and capital.
    (4) technology, capital, and land.
    (5) labor, capital, and technology.

11. Entrepreneurship is defined as
    (1) directing and managing a business.
    (2) a circular flow of activity.
    (3) a production unit.
    (4) an economic model.
    (5) a supply-based system.

12. A market economy is one in which
    (1) decisions about production and distribution are made by individuals.
    (2) supply and demand are equal.
    (3) supply is larger than demand.
    (4) supply is always up.
    (5) all decisions are made by the government.

13. The three major kinds of businesses are
    (1) cooperative, corporation, and partnership.

    (2)   partnership, coalition, and sole proprietorship.
    (3)   corporation, sole proprietorship, and partnership.
    (4)   sole proprietorship, coalition, and corporation.
    (5)   coalition, corporation, and cooperative.

14.   One advantage of a corporation is
    (1)   increased capital.   (4)   government restrictions.
    (2)   unlimited liability.   (5)   increased profits.
    (3)   double taxation.

15.   One disadvantage of a sole proprietorship is
    (1)   limited liability.
    (2)   increased managerial ability.
    (3)   limited capital.
    (4)   lack of restrictions.
    (5)   decreased profits.

16.   A partnership is composed of
    (1)   one owner.   (4)   no more than two owners.
    (2)   two or more owners.   (5)   three owners only.
    (3)   not less than ten owners.

INSURANCE

The Federal Reserve System, established in 1913, regulates the banking industry. It is mandatory that all national banks be members of the Federal Reserve System.

There are a dozen Federal Reserve districts located in San Francisco, Kansas City, Dallas, Chicago, Minneapolis, St. Louis, Atlanta, Richmond, Philadelphia, New York, Cleveland, and Boston. The Federal Reserve Bank in each district is owned by the member banks in that district.

Authorized by Congress in 1933, the Federal Deposit Insurance Corporation (FDIC) insures depositors' money. All national banks must also belong to the FDIC as well as to the Federal Reserve System. At this time, deposits are guaranteed by the FDIC for up to $100,000.

Insurance is a means of sharing risk. There are many types of insurance policies, including term insurance and whole insurance. Term insurance is paid for a certain period of time and then renewed. Whole, or straight life, insurance is paid for a lifetime. The premiums for whole insurance are usually small. Limited payment life insurance means the policyholder pays the insurance for a limited number of years and then the policy is paid up for life.

Endowment policies are used basically as a savings plan as well as insurance protection. The endowment policies provide funds for college and also additional income when a policyholder retires.

☞ Drill: Insurance

DIRECTIONS: The following questions are based on the passage above. Read each question, then choose the correct answer.

17. The Federal Reserve System is made up of
    (1) twenty Federal Reserve districts.
    (2) five Federal Reserve districts.
    (3) fourteen Federal Reserve districts.
    (4) twelve Federal Reserve districts.
    (5) nine Federal Reserve districts.

18. A conclusion that can be drawn from the above passage is
    (1) that a depositor's money up to $100,000 is safe in a bank if it is a member of the FDIC.
    (2) that every bank is a member of the FDIC.
    (3) that deposits of $200,000 are guaranteed by the FDIC.
    (4) that all state banks are members of the FDIC.
    (5) that anyone can withdraw $100,000 from the FDIC.

19. The Federal Reserve Banks are
    (1) located only on the East Coast.
    (2) spread throughout the United States.
    (3) located only on the West Coast.
    (4) found in all fifty states.
    (5) found only in coastal cities.

20. Congress established the Federal Deposit Insurance Corporation in
    (1) 1935.   (4) 1933.
    (2) 1920.   (5) 1913.
    (3) 1965.

21. A straight life policy is
    (1) paid over a lifetime.
    (2) paid for a limited period of time.
    (3) a savings policy.
    (4) very expensive.
    (5) usually reserved for married couples.

22. A term insurance policy is
    (1) paid for a lifetime.
    (2) paid for a certain number of years.
    (3) a hospitalization policy.
    (4) a savings.
    (5) for college tuition.

TAXES

Some of the different kinds of taxes that are paid to the federal government are excise taxes on the sale of goods like cigarettes, liquor, and gasoline. Other types of taxes include income taxes, corporate income taxes, and payroll taxes which are social security taxes.

An excise tax is also called a regressive tax because the tax is the same for everyone, while the income tax is called a progressive tax because it is prorated according to income.

☞ Drill: Taxes

DIRECTIONS: The following questions are based on the passage above. Read each question, then choose the correct answer.

23. The tax one has to pay on gasoline is
    (1) an excise tax.   (4) a payroll tax.
    (2) an income tax.   (5) an expensive tax.
    (3) a corporate tax.

24. One conclusion that can be drawn from the above passage is that
    (1) the federal government's expenses are so large that it needs taxes from many sources.
    (2) the deferral government has a balanced budget.
    (3) everyone pays the same taxes.
    (4) taxes are not necessary.
    (5) the federal government taxes everything.

25. A progressive tax is
     (1)   aimed solely at the middle class.
     (2)   the same as an excise tax.
     (3)   put on products.
     (4)   the same for everyone.
     (5)   based on earnings.

INFLATION

Inflation is a rise in the general level of prices.

Deflation is a decline in the general level of prices.

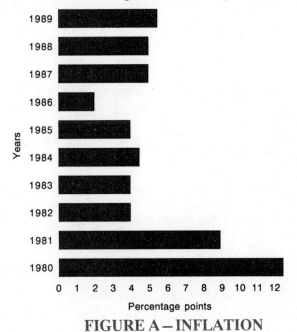

FIGURE A – INFLATION

Year	Total Bank Failures	Year	Total Bank Failures
1980	10	1985	120
1981	10	1986	138
1982	42	1987	184
1983	48	1988	200
1984	79	1989	208

FIGURE B – BANK FAILURES 1980–89

Banks have been deregulated since 1980 when the Depository Institutions Deregulation and Monetary Control Act was passed. Ceilings on interest rates were removed.

Formula for Calculating the Time it Will Take for Prices to Double

$$\frac{70}{\text{Annual rate of inflation}} = \text{Years it will take for prices to double}$$

FIGURE C

☞ Drill: Inflation

<u>DIRECTIONS</u>: The following questions are based on the information above. Read each question then choose the correct answer.

Questions 26 through 28 are based on Figure A.

26. What three years had the same inflation rate?
    (1) 1988, 1989, 1980   (4) 1986, 1981, 1980
    (2) 1981, 1985, 1987   (5) 1980, 1985, 1988
    (3) 1982, 1983, 1985

27. What year experienced the lowest inflation rate?
    (1) 1989   (4) 1986
    (2) 1981   (5) 1985
    (3) 1984

28. What year had the second highest inflation rate?
    (1) 1984   (4) 1980
    (2) 1989   (5) 1981
    (3) 1986

Questions 29 through 31 are based on Figure B.

29. Based on the above statistics, the conclusion can be drawn that
    (1) banks made riskier investments after 1980.
    (2) all banks were on sound financial footing.
    (3) there was a growth of banks.
    (4) all banks are covered by the Federal Deposit Insurance Corporation.
    (5) deregulation was a success.

30. The biggest jump in bank failures took place from
    (1) 1983–84.   (4) 1988–89.
    (2) 1984–85.   (5) 1986–87.
    (3) 1982–83.

31. Which year had the fourth highest number of bank failures?
    (1) 1988   (4) 1983
    (2) 1982   (5) 1987
    (3) 1986

Questions 32 and 33 are based on Figure C.

32. If the inflation rate is 10%, how many years will it take for prices to double?
    (1) 10 years   (4) 7 years
    (2) 20 years   (5) 8 years
    (3) 5 years

33. If the inflation rate is 7%, how many years will it take for prices to double?
    (1) 5 years   (4) 15 years
    (2) 12 years   (5) 10 years
    (3) 7 years

ECONOMICS

ANSWER KEY

Drill: The Importance of Economics

1.	(1)	4.	(2)	7.	(4)
2.	(2)	5.	(4)	8.	(1)
3.	(3)	6.	(1)	9.	(3)

Drill: Business

10.	(3)	12.	(1)	14.	(1)	16.	(2)
11.	(1)	13.	(3)	15.	(3)		

Drill: Insurance

17.	(4)	19.	(2)	21.	(1)
18.	(1)	20.	(4)	22.	(2)

Drill: Taxes

23.	(1)	24.	(1)	25.	(5)

Drill: Inflation

26.	(3)	28.	(5)	30.	(5)	32.	(4)
27.	(4)	29.	(1)	31.	(3)	33.	(5)

IV. POLITICAL SCIENCE

THE CONSTITUTION

The Constitution of the United States was written in 1787 and by June 1788, at least nine states had approved it. The great document has stood the test of time and is as contemporary now as it was when it was written, over 200 years ago. It is the chief law of the land.

The Constitution requires three main branches of government: the executive, legislative, and judicial branches. It has a checks and balances system which keeps any one branch from becoming too powerful.

The Constitution may be amended when changes or additions are needed. So far, there are twenty-six amendments to the Constitution. The first ten amendments are called the Bill of Rights and were added in 1791.

The first four amendments are listed:

Amendment I — protects the basic freedoms of religion, speech, press, the right to assemble, and the right to petition.

Amendment II — gives people the right to bear arms.

Amendment III — forbids any soldier from being lodged in a citizen's home during peace time.

Amendment IV — states that there shall not be unreasonable search or seizure of person's property without a warrant.

☞ Drill: The Constitution

DIRECTIONS: The following questions are based on the passage above. Read each question, then choose the correct answer.

1. The Constitution of the United States is
    (1) the chief law of the land.   (4) no longer being used.
    (2) written in 1687.   (5) becoming too powerful.
    (3) not very flexible.

2. The government outlined by the Constitution has
   (1) two branches. (4) no real branches.
   (2) three branches. (5) one branch.
   (3) four branches

3. An example of freedom of speech is
   (1) speaking before a city council meeting.
   (2) making a speech to an audience.
   (3) disagreeing with proposed legislation.
   (4) All of the above.
   (5) None of the above.

4. The four basic freedoms are contained in
   (1) the Second Amendment. (4) the Fourth Amendment.
   (2) the Third Amendment. (5) the Eighth Amendment.
   (3) the First Amendment.

5. The first ten amendments are called
   (1) the basic freedoms. (4) the Civil Liberties Amendments.
   (2) the basic amendments. (5) the Constitution.
   (3) the Bill of Rights.

THE PRESIDENCY

The President is the head of the executive branch. He has to carry out the laws of the land. The President is elected every four years and can be elected for two four year terms.

Although he has many powers, the President must consult with Congress before declaring war on another country. The President has the power to recommend legislation to Congress. The President has certain bills passed in order to carry out the agenda he has set forth. He sometimes calls key members of both Houses to the White House to try to persuade them to pass legislation that he favors.

Any person running for President has to be at least thirty-five years old and be a natural born citizen of the United States. He or she also must have resided in the country for fourteen years prior to being elected.

☞ Drill: The Presidency

<u>DIRECTIONS</u>: The following questions are based on the passage above. Read each question, then choose the correct answer.

6. The office of the President falls under which branch of government?
    (1) Executive Branch   (4) Political Branch
    (2) Legislative Branch   (5) Republican Branch
    (3) Judicial Branch

7. Which of the following statements is a fact?
    (1) The President is the head of the executive branch.
    (2) The President is the most powerful man in the world.
    (3) The President is elected every two years.
    (4) The President is able to be elected for four years.
    (5) The President can declare war on his own.

8. Which of the following is incorrect?
    (1) The President has an agenda.
    (2) The President can recommend legislation to Congress.
    (3) The President never tries to sway House members' votes.
    (4) The President favors certain bills.
    (5) The President often persuades Congress to vote a certain way.

9. A candidate for the presidency must be at least
    (1) 35 years old.   (4) 30 years old.
    (2) 25 years old.   (5) 21 years old.
    (3) 40 years old.

GOVERNMENT

The United States Congress is composed of two houses: the House of Representatives and the Senate. The House is composed of 435 members. The Senate is composed of 100 members. This august body is a part of the legislative branch. The members of the Senate must be at least 30 years old and a citizen of the United States at least nine years prior to being elected. The members of the House must be at least 25 years old and a citizen of the United States for at least seven years.

Bills introduced in the Senate and the House of Representatives are recommended by citizens, the President, or the congressmen themselves. If the bill is passed by both houses of Congress, it is sent to the President for his signature. He may sign the bill or veto the bill or use the pocket veto (the bill remains on the President's desk for ten days). If he vetoes the bill, it goes back to the house from which it originated. If both Houses have a two-thirds majority voting for the bill, the President's veto is overridden.

The Senate has the following specific powers: to approve appointments made by the President; to ratify treaties; to try cases of impeachment. The House has the following specific powers: create bills to raise money for the government; elect the President from the top three candidates if neither gets a majority of the electoral college votes; bring charges of impeachment.

Congress has the power to promote the progress of science and useful arts by securing the authors and inventors exclusive right to their respective writings and discoveries for limited times. Congress has the power to regulate commerce with foreign nations and among the several states. It also has the power to borrow on the credit of the United States.

The judicial branch of the government is composed of federal courts and judges. The Supreme Court is composed of nine justices and is the supreme law of the land. There are eleven United States Courts of Appeals and almost 100 United States District Courts.

The Supreme Court has original jurisdiction in two kinds of cases: cases in which a state is one of the parties involved and cases where ambassadors or other foreign officials are involved.

A unicameral legislature's body consists of one house. (The only example is the Nebraska state legislature.) A bicameral legislature's body consists of two houses.

All states have patterned their legislatures after the United States Congress. Each state has three branches of government and has a system of checks and balances.

All states have a governor who is the head of the state executive branch.

Most states have divisions of local governments called counties. Louisiana called its divisions parishes. Some of the county officials are: a treasurer, a county auditor, a district attorney, a sheriff, and others.

Three kinds of city governments are in existence in this country. They are the commission, council-manager, and mayor-council systems.

In a weak mayor-council system, the council makes most of the major decisions. In a strong mayor-council system, the mayor has many important powers, including the power to veto acts passed by the council. Most large cities have the strong mayor-council system whose mayor works full time.

☞ Drill: Government

DIRECTIONS: The following questions are based on the passage above. Read each question, then choose the correct answer.

10. The legislative branch is composed of
    (1)   the House of Representatives and the Senate.
    (2)   the President.
    (3)   the judges.
    (4)   the President and judges.
    (5)   Congress and the President.

11. The Senate is composed of
    (1)   100 members.   (4)   101 members.
    (2)   435 members.   (5)   50 members.
    (3)   200 members.

12. A candidate for the Senate must be at least
    (1)   30 years old.   (4)   18 years old.
    (2)   25 years old.   (5)   21 years old.
    (3)   40 years old.

13. A candidate for the House of Representatives must be a citizen of the United States for at least
    (1)   five years prior to election.
    (2)   seven years prior to election.
    (3)   nine years prior to election.
    (4)   five months prior to election.
    (5)   nine weeks prior to election.

14. A bill can be recommended for consideration by
    (1)   the President.   (4)   All of the above.
    (2)   a citizen.   (5)   None of the above.
    (3)   a congressman.

15. If the President vetoes a bill, it will still become law if
    (1) two-thirds of the members of the Senate and the House vote to override this veto.
    (2) three-fourths of the members of the Senate and the House vote to override his veto.
    (3) one house votes to override his veto.
    (4) neither house votes to override his veto.
    (5) both houses unanimously vote to override his veto.

16. The word veto means to
    (1) accept.
    (2) reject.
    (3) compromise.
    (4) override.
    (5) change.

17. An example of an event that would fall under the powers of the Senate is
    (1) introducing a bill to raise money.
    (2) bringing charges of impeachment.
    (3) electing a President if neither of the candidates receives a majority of electoral votes.
    (4) approving an appointee to a cabinet position.
    (5) appointing a new President in the event of the death of the President.

18. An example of an event that would fall under the powers of the House of Representatives is
    (1) ratifying treaties.
    (2) confirming an appointment to the Supreme Court.
    (3) bringing charges of impeachment.
    (4) electing the Vice President if there is a tie in the voting in the electoral college for the top candidate.
    (5) declaring official holidays.

19. Which of the following is an example of the power of Congress to promote science and art by giving authors and inventors the exclusive use of their product for a specified period of time?
    (1) A speech made to a public audience
    (2) An essay written for a class project
    (3) The invention of a new way to do something
    (4) The singing of a solo on a musical program
    (5) Controlling a Broadway musical

20. Which of the following is an example of the power of Congress to regulate commerce with foreign nations?
    (1) Senate proposal to limit the number of foreign-made goods coming into the U.S.
    (2) The limitation of the number of farms in existence
    (3) The growth of the gross national product
    (4) Subsidies for farmers
    (5) Declare war on another country

21. The Supreme Court is comprised of
    (1) eight justices.
    (2) nine justices.
    (3) seven justices.
    (4) five justices.
    (5) one justice.

22. The judicial branch is made up of
    (1) federal courts and judges.
    (2) the lower courts only.
    (3) the House of Representatives and the Senate.
    (4) the President.
    (5) the Supreme Court only.

23. In which one of the following cases would original jurisdiction be in the Supreme Court?
    (1) An ambassador from another country has violated a civil law
    (2) A citizen has a dispute with a neighbor
    (3) A newspaper slanders one of the politicians in the community
    (4) A mayor is involved
    (5) None of the above.

24. All of the following states have a bicameral legislature except
    (1) Texas.
    (2) Louisiana.
    (3) Massachusetts.
    (4) Nebraska.
    (5) New York.

25. Each state has
    (1) three branches of government.
    (2) one branch of government.
    (3) two branches of government.
    (4) different numbers of branches of government.
    (5) three executive branches of government.

26. In most states, divisions of local governments are called
    (1) counties.
    (2) states.
    (3) boards.
    (4) auditors.
    (5) sheriffs.

27. In Louisiana, the local division is called a
    (1) county.
    (2) parish.
    (3) board.
    (4) township.
    (5) territory.

28. A strong mayor-council system gives many powers to the
    (1) council.
    (2) cities.
    (3) state.
    (4) country.
    (5) mayor.

POLITICAL SCIENCE

ANSWER KEY

Drill: The Constitution

1.	(1)	3.	(4)	5.	(3)
2.	(2)	4.	(3)		

Drill: The Presidency

6.	(1)	7.	(1)	8.	(3)	9.	(1)

Drill: Government

10.	(1)	15.	(1)	20.	(1)	25.	(1)
11.	(1)	16.	(2)	21.	(2)	26.	(1)
12.	(1)	17.	(4)	22.	(1)	27.	(2)
13.	(2)	18.	(3)	23.	(1)	28.	(5)
14.	(4)	19.	(3)	24.	(4)		

V. GEOGRAPHY

UNITED STATES

STATE	Student Dropout Rate
Connecticut	17.8%
Iowa	13.1%
Massachusetts	30.1%
Michigan	27.1%
Missouri	24.5%
New York	33.7%
Tennessee	31.4%
Texas	35.1%
Wisconsin	16.7%

FIGURE A — Student Dropout Rate — 1988 (Selected States)

San Diego, California	1,070,310
Omaha, Nebraska	353,170
Baltimore, Maryland	751,400
Houston, Texas	1,698,090
Boston, Massachusetts	577,830
New York City, New York	7,352,700

FIGURE B — U.S. City Populations — 1988 (Selected Cities)

Year	Population	Year	Population
1860	31,443,321	1930	123,202,624
1870	38,558,371	1940	132,164,569
1880	50,189,209	1950	151,325,798
1890	62,979,766	1960	179,323,175
1900	76,212,168	1970	203,302,031
1910	92,228,496	1980	226,547,082
1920	106,021,537		

FIGURE C — Population of the United States

There are many sources of energy in the United States that are being developed to lessen the country's dependence on foreign oil. Some of these sources are solar energy, nuclear energy, gasohol, fossil fuels, and others. With the development of these sources of energy, more jobs will be made available and our economy will not be afflicted by adverse situations in oil-rich countries.

The United States is a relatively young country made up of immigrants from all over the world. This country serves as a leader of the free world and has many allies around the world.

It has helped many countries that needed financial help to rebuild their countries and continues to play an important part in world affairs.

The Middle Atlantic states, which include New York, West Virginia, Delaware, Maryland, New Jersey, and Pennsylvania, are a hub of activity. This area is highly industrialized and includes a skilled work force. The financial center of the nation is found in New York and cultural activities of all kinds are found in this area.

The states of North Dakota, South Dakota, Nebraska, Kansas, Minnesota, Iowa, Missouri, Wisconsin, Illinois, Michigan, Indiana, and Ohio make up the Plains states. This area is also referred to as the Midwest Region of the United States. It is known as a great agricultural region. Some of the crops grown are wheat, corn, and oats.

The Plains states are highly industrialized. The location near waterways and the close proximity to coal and iron deposits have made it relatively easy for industries to develop. Skilled laborers are available and are necessary to work in manufacturing plants.

The South includes the following states: Texas, Oklahoma, Louisiana, Arkansas, Mississippi, Alabama, Florida, Georgia, South Carolina, North Carolina, Tennessee, Kentucky, and Virginia. This area is known for its relatively mild weather and good, rich soil. Agriculture and oil are two of the most important industries in the South. Some of the crops grown are cotton, corn, tobacco, peanuts, and rice. Cattle raising is also very important in some of these states. Five of these states border on the Gulf of Mexico.

Texas is the second largest state. It is composed of 267,000 square miles and 254 counties. It is broken up into many large physical regions such as piney woods, post oak belt, plains, rolling prairie, high plains, valley, coastal prairie, and West Texas. The population of Texas as of the 1980 census is

14,225,513. Texas is, without a doubt, one of the most beautiful states in the United States.

The Pacific states include Washington, Oregon, and California. California has the largest population of any state in the United States. It is known for its agriculture and leads all other states in this regard. Oregon and Washington also are known for farming. All three states also have very developed industries.

Some of the major cities located in the Pacific states are Seattle, Spokane, Portland, Olympia, San Francisco, Los Angeles, Salem, and San Diego. There are many interesting places to visit in this area and thus tourism is a major industry.

The Mountain states are Montana, Idaho, Wyoming, Nevada, Utah, Colorado, Arizona, and New Mexico. These states are sparsely populated, even though the combined square mileage is over 800,000. The Rocky Mountains stretch through this area and most people feel they are a beautiful sight to behold.

The New England states include Maine, Massachusetts, New Hampshire, Vermont, Rhode Island, and Connecticut. Territorially, this is a very small region. The total size is about 67,000 square miles. The main industries in this area are fishing, shipping, manufacturing, and dairy farming.

☞ Drill: United States

DIRECTIONS: The following questions are based on the information above. Read each question, then choose the correct answer.

Questions 1 and 2 are based on Figure A.

1. Of the states listed in the first chart, which state has the lowest dropout rate?

    (1) Wisconsin   (4) Michigan
    (2) New York   (5) Iowa
    (3) Connecticut

2. Of the states listed, which two states have the highest dropout rates?

    (1) Tennessee and Massachusetts
    (2) New York and Massachusetts
    (3) Michigan and Texas

(4)   New York and Texas

(5)   Iowa and Missouri

Questions 3 and 4 are based on Figure B.

3.   Which city has the third largest population?
  (1)   Houston   (4)   San Diego
  (2)   Boston   (5)   Baltimore
  (3)   Omaha

4.   Arrange the following five cities in order of their population, placing the city with the largest population first, etc.

  Baltimore, New York, Houston, San Diego, Boston

  (1)   New York, Boston, Baltimore, San Diego, Houston
  (2)   Baltimore, New York, Houston, San Diego, Boston
  (3)   Houston, Baltimore, Boston, New York, San Diego
  (4)   San Diego, Boston, Baltimore, New York, Houston
  (5)   New York, Houston, San Diego, Baltimore, Boston

Questions 5 through 7 are based on Figure C.

5.   What was the United States population in 1910?
  (1)   151,325,798   (4)   92,228,496
  (2)   203,302,031   (5)   151,325,798
  (3)   50,189,209

6.   How much did the population increase between 1970 and 1980?
  (1)   By approximately 20,000
  (2)   By approximately 200,000
  (3)   By approximately 2,000,000
  (4)   By approximately 20,000,000
  (5)   By approximately 200,000,000

7.   The population of the United States has
  (1)   steadily declined.
  (2)   remained about the same.
  (3)   dropped markedly.
  (4)   fluctuated widely.
  (5)   steadily increased.

Questions 8 through 21 are based on the passage.

8. Which of the following statements is based on fact?
   (1) Texas has many diverse physical regions.
   (2) Texas weather is ideal most of the time.
   (3) Texas is an extremely beautiful state.
   (4) Dallas is the nicest city in Texas.
   (5) Texas is too diverse.

9. According to the passage, why is it necessary to develop alternative sources of energy in the United States?
   (1) The economy in this country will not be adversely affected by conditions elsewhere.
   (2) Technology is available to do the job.
   (3) More jobs will be provided.
   (4) All of the above.
   (5) None of the above.

10. The main idea in the energy passage is that
    (1) there are different sources of energy being developed in the United States.
    (2) jobs are plentiful in the United States.
    (3) solar energy is very clean.
    (4) All of the above.
    (5) None of the above.

11. The United States
    (1) is one of the oldest countries in the world.
    (2) is a young country by comparison.
    (3) is located in South America.
    (4) is the only country in North America.
    (5) is located entirely on the North American continent.

12. One conclusion that can be drawn from the passage is that
    (1) an unskilled work force is necessary for an area to become industrialized.
    (2) cultural activities are necessary for a city or state to thrive.
    (3) highly industrialized areas are found only on the East Coast.
    (4) cultural activities are only found in New York.
    (5) the financial center of the United States can be found in the region of Middle Atlantic states.

13. One reason for the growth of industry in the Plains states is
     (1) its location near waterways and coal and iron deposits.
     (2) the rolling plains.
     (3) the mild climate.
     (4) the unskilled workforce.
     (5) its proximity to the nation's financial center.

14. The area of the South includes
     (1) 13 states.   (4) 10 states.
     (2) 5 states.   (5) 9 states.
     (3) 12 states.

15. Most of the states in the South border on
     (1) the Atlantic Ocean.   (4) the Indian Ocean.
     (2) the Gulf of Mexico.   (5) Lake Michigan.
     (3) the Pacific Ocean.

16. Two of the main industries of the South are
     (1) oil and agriculture.   (4) oil and cattle raising.
     (2) oil and mining.   (5) cotton and corn.
     (3) agriculture and fishing.

17. The Pacific states have one thing in common. They are
     (1) farming centers.
     (2) extremely cold in the winter.
     (3) located in the Southwest.
     (4) not highly populated.
     (5) prone to natural disasters.

18. One of the major industries in the Pacific states is
     (1) auto manufacturing.   (4) travel.
     (2) tourism.   (5) airline.
     (3) oil refining.

19. The mountain range that stretches throughout the Mountain states are
     the
     (1) Appalachian Mountains.   (4) None of the above.
     (2) Rocky Mountains.   (5) All of the above.
     (3) Himalayan Mountains.

20. The Mountain states do not include
    (1) Arizona.   (4) Idaho.
    (2) New Mexico.   (5) Nevada.
    (3) Louisiana.

21. Which of the two industries listed are very important in New England?
    (1) Dairy farming and shipping
    (2) Oil refining and shipping
    (3) Shipping and farming
    (4) Oil refining and farming
    (5) Fishing and oil refining

MEXICO

Mexico borders the United States on the south and has about 88,000,000 people. The land area is about 762,000 square miles. The capital is Mexico City. Some of the chief crops are coffee, cotton, corn, sugar cane, and rice.

Mexico has an abundance of natural resources, such as oil, gold, silver, and natural gas. Textiles, steel production, tourism, and petroleum are the major industries in Mexico.

☞ Drill: Mexico

DIRECTIONS: The following questions are based on the previous passage. Read each question, then choose the correct answer.

22. Mexico borders the United States on the
    (1) north.   (4) south.
    (2) east.   (5) southeast.
    (3) west.

23. The population of Mexico is about
    (1) 8 billion people.   (4) 18 million people.
    (2) 80 million people.   (5) 80 hundred thousand people.
    (3) 88 million people.

24. Mexico has an abundance of
    (1) oil and gold.   (4) diamonds and natural gas.
    (2) natural gas and nickel.   (5) oil and diamonds.
    (3) nickel and diamonds.

CANADA

Canada is the United States neighbor to the north. It includes the second largest territory in the world. The current population is about 27 million people. The capital of Canada is Ottawa.

The United States and Canada are two sprawling countries that make up North America. Each country is an industrial giant and provides a very high standard of living for its population. The population of the United States is about nine or ten times larger than that of Canada.

The United States and Canada have large supplies of natural resources. In the United States, the minerals include coal, copper, gold, nickel, silver, zinc, and others. In Canada, the minerals found are nickel, gold, lead, silver, zinc, and others.

☞ Drill: Canada

DIRECTIONS: The following questions are based on the passage above. Read each question, then choose the correct answer.

25. Canada
    (1)   is the largest country in the world.
    (2)   is located to the south of the United States.
    (3)   includes the second largest territory in the world.
    (4)   is a part of the United States.
    (5)   is the capital is Ohio.

26. The population of Canada is near
    (1)   25,000,000.   (4)   127,000,000.
    (2)   7,000,000.   (5)   2,700,000.
    (3)   27,000,000.

27. Based on the above passage, the conclusion that can be drawn is that
    (1)   the United States produces and consumes far more than Canada.
    (2)   Canada's population is larger than that of the United States.
    (3)   the standard of living in Canada is higher than that in the United States.
    (4)   the climate in the United States is better than the climate in Canada.
    (5)   All of the above.

28. The main idea of the third paragraph is
    (1) Canada has a large supply of natural resources.
    (2) the United States has a large supply of natural resources.
    (3) the United States and Canada have large quantities of natural resources.
    (4) the United States is the largest producer of coal.
    (5) Canada is the largest producer of lead.

MAPS

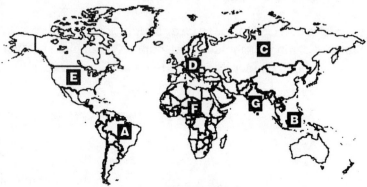

FIGURE A

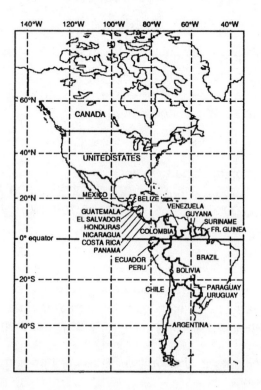

FIGURE B

FIGURE C — Election of 1868

☞ Drill: Maps

<u>DIRECTIONS</u>: The following questions are based on the maps above. Read each question, then choose the correct answer.

Questions 29 through 31 are based on Figure A.

29. Using Figure A choose which letter represents the continent of North America.
    (1) A   (4) D
    (2) B   (5) E
    (3) C

30. The area marked as letter "F" on Figure A represents the continent of
    (1) North America.   (4) Africa.
    (2) South America.   (5) Antarctica.
    (3) Europe.

31. Which continent is not shown on Figure A?
    (1) North America.   (4) South America.
    (2) Antarctica.   (5) Asia.
    (3) Europe.

Questions 32 and 33 are based on Figure B.

32. Using Figure B, which country can be found at the intersection of the coordinates 20 degrees North, 100 degrees West?
    - (1) Paraguay
    - (2) United States
    - (3) Mexico
    - (4) Panama
    - (5) Nicaragua

33. Which of the following countries, on Figure B, is not bordered by an ocean?
    - (1) Bolivia
    - (2) Peru
    - (3) Chile
    - (4) Costa Rica
    - (5) Canada

Questions 34 and 35 are based on Figure C.

34. According to Figure C, which of the following had achieved statehood by 1868?
    - (1) Montana
    - (2) Oregon
    - (3) Washington
    - (4) Arizona
    - (5) New Mexico

35. According to Figure C, which state was bordered by three territories in 1868?
    - (1) Texas
    - (2) Oregon
    - (3) California
    - (4) New York
    - (5) Nevada

SOUTH AND CENTRAL AMERICA

Selected South American Countries

Country	Population	Square Miles
Argentina	32,291,000	1,065,189
Brazil	153,771,000	3,286,470
Chile	13,000,000	292,257
Venezuela	29,753,000	352,143
Ecuador	10,506,000	109,483

Central America is the connecting point between North and South America. The countries in Central America have an extremely long coastline. The main industry of this area is agriculture, and most people who live in this area are extremely poor. Bananas, coffee, and corn are some of their chief crops.

The seven nations that make up Central America are Belize, Guatemala, Honduras, El Salvador, Panama, Costa Rica, and Nicaragua.

☞ Drill: South and Central America

DIRECTIONS: The following questions are based on the passage above. Read each question, then choose the correct answer.

36. Which two countries have the closest population?
    (1) Chile and Ecuador
    (2) Brazil and Chile
    (3) Argentina and Ecuador
    (4) Brazil and Chile
    (5) Venezuela and Argentina

37. Which country is the largest in both population and square miles?
    (1) Ecuador
    (2) Brazil
    (3) Venezuela
    (4) Argentina
    (5) Chile

38. One of the chief crops in Central America is
    (1) wheat.
    (2) bananas.
    (3) barley.
    (4) rice.
    (5) beans.

39. The number of countries in Central America is
    (1) six.
    (2) two.
    (3) seven.
    (4) five.
    (5) eight.

CLIMATE AND WEATHER

Weather and climate conditions affect the way of life for people everywhere and in a variety of ways. A definition of weather refers to day-to-day conditions, such as how hot or cold it is or how dry or humid. Climate refers to the overall condition of the atmosphere over a period of time.

☞ Drill: Climate and Weather

DIRECTIONS: The following questions are based on the passage above. Read each question, then choose the correct answer.

40. Which of the following is an example of weather?
     (1)   A forecast of rain
     (2)   Tropical rain forest conditions
     (3)   Tropical rain forest
     (4)   Ice in the Arctic
     (5)   Seasons in New England

41. Which of the following is an example of climate?
     (1)   Changes in the temperature from time to time
     (2)   Long, extended periods of little or no rainfall in certain areas
     (3)   A forecast of sunshine
     (4)   An electrical storm
     (5)   A temporary drought

GEOGRAPHY

ANSWER KEY

Drill: United States

1.	(5)	7.	(5)	13.	(1)	19.	(2)
2.	(4)	8.	(1)	14.	(1)	20.	(3)
3.	(4)	9.	(3)	15.	(2)	21.	(1)
4.	(5)	10.	(1)	16.	(1)		
5.	(4)	11.	(2)	17.	(1)		
6.	(4)	12.	(5)	18.	(2)		

Drill: Mexico

22.	(4)	23.	(3)	24.	(1)

Drill: Canada

25.	(3)	26.	(3)	27.	(1)	28.	(3)

Drill: Maps

29.	(5)	31.	(2)	33.	(1)	35.	(5)
30.	(4)	32.	(3)	34.	(2)		

Drill: South and Central America

36.	(1)	37.	(2)	38.	(2)	39.	(3)

Drill: Climate and Weather

40.	(2)	41.	(2)

VI. BEHAVIORAL SCIENCE

SOCIOLOGY AND THE FAMILY

The ideas and beliefs about right and wrong make up the values of a community or society. These values are learned through the major institutions in our society which are the homes, school, church, government, and an economic system. These institutions may vary from society to society, but they serve as a means to meet the basic needs of society.

An extended family consists of the nuclear family plus other relatives, such as the grandparents and uncles and aunts. A nuclear family consists of the parents and children.

The traditional family has undergone many changes over the past few years. The extended family is disappearing and single parent households are on the increase because of many factors such as high divorce rates, etc.

☞ Drill: Sociology and the Family

DIRECTIONS: The following questions are based on the passage above. Read each question, then choose the correct answer.

1. One conclusion that can be drawn from the passage above is
   (1) that various societal institutions are absolutely necessary to enable its inhabitants to fulfill basic needs.
   (2) that societies are alike.
   (3) that some societies are better than others.
   (4) that some societies never change.
   (5) that all societies are unnecessary.

2. Values are
   (1) an inborn trait.
   (2) taught in only one institution.
   (3) the same in every society.
   (4) learned.
   (5) hard to determine.

3. Which is the example of a nuclear family?
   (1) A mother, grandmother, and two children
   (2) A grandmother and her two grandchildren

(3)   A visiting cousin, a grandfather, and grandson

(4)   An uncle, an aunt, a mother and father and their son

(5)   A mother, father, and child

4.   Extended family members that live in separate dwellings
   (1)   must be related.
   (2)   are all friends.
   (3)   are increasing.
   (4)   live in a single dwelling.
   (5)   must have the same grandparents.

5.   Why is the extended family disappearing?
   (1)   People are getting married at a younger age.
   (2)   The threat of nuclear war makes people decide to have smaller families.
   (3)   Relatives cannot get along for an extended period of time.
   (4)   People are getting divorced more often and families split up.
   (5)   None of the above.

STATUS AND RELATIONSHIPS

Status is the supposed position of one in a group with a particular position in a group. Status can be measured on a range from low to high, with low being the least important and high being the most important.

Primary groups, such as families, close friends, and social clubs are closely knit and very supportive. Secondary groups are made up of a collection of persons that are loosely knit and are so grouped for meeting an objective, such as classes, panels, and forums.

Single-parent families are growing at a very high rate. Most of the single-parent families are headed by women. This group represents over 26% of the families nationwide. A single-parent family is one that includes dependent children and is headed by a single adult.

There are over five billion people in the world today. The populations of developing countries are growing at a rapid clip. In some of the industrial nations, the populations are declining. In some areas where there is a high population density, there are problems of attaining adequate housing, food, and medical care.

The fastest growing group in the U.S. is the over-65-year-old group. This phenomenon is sometimes referred to as the graying of America. Some of the problems this age group encounters are inadequate income, poor medical care, and loneliness.

☞ Drill: Status and Relationships

DIRECTIONS: The following questions are based on the passage above. Read each question, then choose the correct answer.

6. Which of the following is an example of status?
    (1) Being a top executive in a major company
    (2) Buying a dress
    (3) Attending elementary school
    (4) Playing the piano
    (5) Being part of the student body

7. Which of the following is an example of a status symbol?
    (1) An expensive car
    (2) Someone attending elementary school
    (3) Someone wearing clothes
    (4) Someone living in a condo
    (5) Inner peace

8. One conclusion that can be drawn from the above passage is that
    (1) each person is a part of a secondary group.
    (2) each person is a part of a primary group.
    (3) primary groups are not close.
    (4) secondary groups are close.
    (5) no one can be a part of both groups.

9. Families are an example of
    (1) secondary groups.
    (2) primary groups.
    (3) primary and secondary groups.
    (4) reference groups and secondary groups.
    (5) a larger group of loose-knit acquaintances.

10. The main idea of the third paragraph is
    (1) that single-parent families are on the increase.
    (2) that single-parent families are on the decrease.
    (3) that most single-parent families are headed by men.

(4)   that single-parent households remain about the same.

(5)   it is hard to be a single parent.

11.   One inference that can be drawn from the fourth paragraph is that
(1)   technology is not widely used in the developing countries.
(2)   only industrialized nations are able to keep the birth rate under control.
(3)   in most developing countries the birth rate is stable.
(4)   everyone has adequate food, shelter, and clothing.
(5)   the less industrialized the country, the better the living conditions.

12.   There are over
(1)   five million people in the world.
(2)   fifteen million people in the world.
(3)   five billion people in the world.
(4)   fifty billion people in the world.
(5)   five hundred billion people in the world.

13.   Two of the problems plaguing the over-65-year-old group are
(1)   inadequate medical care and lack of entertainment.
(2)   loneliness and inadequate income.
(3)   lack of schooling and poor medical care.
(4)   arthritis and inadequate income.
(5)   loss of memory and poor medical care.

14.   One conclusion that can be drawn from the fifth paragraph is that
(1)   the field of geriatrics (science dealing with treatment of older patients) is growing.
(2)   the gross national product is declining.
(3)   adequate housing is easy to find.
(4)   older Americans are highly respected.
(5)   older people do not experience problems.

TRENDS AND VALUES

1930	41%	1970	91%
1950	63%	1980	96%
1960	78%		

FIGURE A — Percentage of Households with Telephones
in the United States

1970	–	3.58	1986	–	3.21
1975	–	3.54	1987	–	3.19
1980	–	3.29	1988	–	3.17
1985	–	3.23			

FIGURE B — Average Family Size — 1970–88

Monogamy means that a man or woman can be married to only one person at any one time. *Polygamy* is the practice whereby a person may have more than one mate at a time. (Polygamy is not legal in the United States.) *Polygyny* is the practice of a man having more than one wife. (Polygyny is not legal in the United States.) *Polyandry* is the practice of a woman having more than one husband. (Polyandry is not legal in the United States.)

The standards of conduct in a society are dependent on the values taught to young people at a very early age and are followed for a lifetime. The idea of right and wrong has to be taught. Values are the accepted behavior that is considered correct by society.

☞ Drill: Trends and Values

DIRECTIONS: The following questions are based on the information above. Read each question, then choose the correct answer.

Questions 15 and 16 are based on Figure A.

15. In what year was the second largest percentage of telephones used in households?
    (1) 1930   (4) 1950
    (2) 1970   (5) 1980
    (3) 1960

16. From the information in the chart, what can you most likely conclude about the percentage of telephones used in households today?
    (1) The percentage has gone up.
    (2) The percentage has dropped steadily since 1980.
    (3) Most people own more than one telephone.
    (4) People are using telephones less.
    (5) Nothing can be concluded.

Questions 17 through 20 are based on Figure B.

17. What was the average family size in 1985?
    (1) 3.29   (4) 4.23
    (2) 3.21   (5) 3.23
    (3) 3.17

18. What was the average family size in 1970?
    (1) 3.17   (4) 3.21
    (2) 3.19   (5) 3.18
    (3) 3.58

19. In what year was the average family size 3.17?
    (1) 1970   (2) 1980
    (3) 1985   (4) 1986
    (5) 1988

20. What conclusion can be drawn from the above information?
    (1) The average family size is getting larger.
    (2) The average family size is getting smaller each year.
    (3) The average family size is not growing at all.
    (4) The average family size is larger in some parts of the country than in others.
    (5) It is difficult to have an even number of family members.

Questions 21 and 22 are based on the passage.

21. In America, the system of marriage is
    (1) monogamy.   (4) polygyny.
    (2) polygamy.   (5) monotonous.
    (3) polyandry.

22. Values
    (1) are inborn.   (4) are forgotten.
    (2) must be taught.   (5) must be memorized.
    (3) become outdated.

PSYCHOLOGY

Group psychology is an interacting of people in small groups. The groups meet together to work through problems. The group may last for a specific time or may go on indefinitely.

The discussion concerning which is more important, environment or heredity, in the development of the person has never been resolved. Certainly, it is known that environment plays a major role in one's development, but heredity, one's innate ability, is also very important. However, research shows that there is no consensus.

Id, according to Freud, is the basic human personality and operates based on biological tendencies. *Ego*, according to Freud, is the capacity of the person to think and act. The *superego* acts as the internal conscience or moral guidepost of the individual.

☞ Drill: Psychology

DIRECTIONS: The following questions are based on the passage. Read each question, then choose the correct answer.

23.   Group psychology means that
      (1)   one person addresses the group.
      (2)   the group has to be limited to no more than five persons.
      (3)   a group of any number will meet to interact with one another.
      (4)   everyone in the group is a psychiatrist.
      (5)   society causes a person's problems.

24.   The idea of which is more important, the heredity of a person or his/her environment, has
      (1)   never been resolved.   (4)   proven to be neither.
      (2)   proven to be heredity.   (5)   become less important.
      (3)   proven to be environment.

25.   Which of the following would be an example of the superego?
      (1)   Treating everyone with respect
      (2)   Writing a short story
      (3)   Visiting relatives
      (4)   Laughing out loud
      (5)   The ability to add and subtract

BEHAVIORAL SCIENCE

ANSWER KEY

Drill: Sociology and the Family
1. (1)   3. (5)   5. (4)
2. (4)   4. (1)

Drill: Status and Relationships
6. (1)   9. (2)   12. (3)
7. (1)   10. (1)   13. (2)
8. (2)   11. (1)   14. (1)

Drill: Trends and Values
15. (2)   17. (5)   19. (5)   21. (1)
16. (1)   18. (3)   20. (2)   22. (2)

Drill: Psychology
23. (3)   24. (1)   25. (1)

SCIENCE
REVIEW

Chapter 4

SCIENCE REVIEW

I. STRATEGIES FOR SCIENCE SECTIONS

II. BIOLOGY

III. CHEMISTRY

IV. EARTH SCIENCE

V. PHYSICS

Your first step in preparing for the GED science sections is to study our science review. Included are hints to help you quickly and accurately answer the questions which will appear in this test. Remember that the more you know about science, the more accurately you will be able to answer the questions. By studying the science review and our hints, you will greatly increase your chances of achieving a passing score on the GED Science Test.

GED science problems test your basic knowledge of life sciences and physical sciences. In order to accurately answer the science sections of the GED, the following topics should be reviewed.

LIFE SCIENCES (50% of Test)

1. Biology

PHYSICAL SCIENCES (50% of Test)

1. Earth Science
2. Physics
3. Chemistry

The more familiar you are with the topics that will appear on this section of the test, the more likely you are to do well. Our review covers only the topics which will appear on the test. Since the GED presents concepts with which you should already be familiar, a review of the topics presented may be all that is needed in preparation for this test.

Make sure to memorize the directions for this section of the test, as speed and accuracy are just as important as knowledge of the subject matter. Even if you are sure you know all of the information provided in our review, still complete the included drills. These drills will help you become accustomed to the types of questions presented on this test, as well as sharpen your overall thinking skills.

I. STRATEGIES FOR SCIENCE SECTIONS

➤ Step 1 | Carefully read the passage, graph, chart, figure, and/or other information on which the questions are based. Then read the first question.

➤ Step 2 | Make sure you clearly understand what the question is asking. Misinterpreting a question will cost you time and points. Scan the passage, graph, chart, or figure again to make sure the answer is accurately based upon this given information.

If you know the answer to the question, this is your plan of attack:

> ➤ Step 3 | Quickly find your answer among the answer choices, making sure to fill in the circle correctly corresponding to your answer.

If you do not know the answer to the question, this is your plan of attack:

> ➤ Step 3 | Use the process of elimination, based on the following hints, to narrow down the answer choices. Then, make an educated guess.

> ➤ ADDITIONAL HINTS

- **If a word is unfamiliar to you, try to figure out its meaning from the context in which it is used.**

- **When a question asks you to apply an unfamiliar idea or principle, try to apply it to a familiar situation first. Next, apply the principle, in the same manner, to the given question. This often aids in the understanding of the problem.**

- **Often, when an answer choice repeats information from a passage, it is a trick. Be sure to read all of the choices before making a hasty decision.**

- **Although the answer you choose may seem logical and correct, make sure it is supported by the given information.**

II. BIOLOGY

A. THEMES AND GENERAL VOCABULARY

Biology is an independent set of explanatory concepts. Thus, we describe biology as the study of living organisms/things.

A hypothesis is very tentative and is something to be proven; it is only tentatively held and must be checked out fully and possibly proven. A hypothesis is an educated guess.

There are many fields of study in the biological sciences. Zoology, for example, is the study of animal life. Botany is the study of plant life; ecology is the study of the relationship of living things to their environment; embryology is the study of embryos; anatomy is the study of structures of the body; physiology is the study of the functions of the body; genetics is the study of heredity; cytology is the study of the cell; histology is the study of tissues; and bacteriology is the study of bacteria and/or one-celled plant life.

☞ Drill: Themes and General Vocabulary

DIRECTIONS: Carefully read and answer each of the following questions which are based on the information which you have just read.

1. Biology is the study of
    (1) life.
    (2) living things.
    (3) explanatory concepts.
    (4) All of the above.
    (5) None of the above.

2. A hypothesis explains and relates
    (1) conclusions.
    (2) facts.
    (3) theories.
    (4) guesses.
    (5) myths.

3. A hypothesis that has survived a number of independent tests becomes a
    (1) law.
    (2) fact.
    (3) theory.
    (4) principle.
    (5) strong guess.

B. THE CELL

The cell is the basic structure of all living things. This is the foundation of the cell theory. Some cells are total living organisms while other cells are the basic units of structure of other living things. All cells reproduce from identical cells by reproduction. Sex cells reproduce by meiosis while somatic cells (autosomes or body cells) reproduce by mitosis.

Cells are of two types: prokaryotic or eukaryotic. Prokaryotes are cells that do not have a nuclear membrane or a membrane surrounding its organelles. Bacteria and blue-green bacteria are examples of prokaryotes. Eukaryote refers to most cells making up all other living organisms.

A generalized cell will contain:
1.   a cell membrane which is a double layer of lipids that surrounds the cell, thus acting as a "gatekeeper," controlling what moves into and out of the cell.
2.   a nucleus which is separated from the cytoplasm by a thickened membrane that is more selective than the cell membrane.
3.   cytoplasm, the gel-like material that surrounds and protects by cushioning the organelles. It also contains all the chemicals for that particular cell to carry out its living activities.

Depending upon the kind of cell and the function of the cell, any cell can contain any number of the following organelles:
1.   Mitochondria: the powerhouse of the cell. It is the site where energy is obtained from food consumed and made available for the cell's use.
2.   Chloroplast: the site of photosynthesis.
3.   Plastids: store chlorophyll for use by the chloroplasts.
4.   Lysosomes: carry out digestive functions and store digestive enzymes as needed by the cell.
5.   Smooth endoplasmic reticulum: does not have ribosomes attached and is the transportation system of the cell.
6.   Rough endoplasmic reticulum: has ribosomes attached and also carries out cell transportation but mainly of necessary protein materials needed by the cell.
7.   Golgi apparatus: manufacture, synthesize, store, and distribute hormone and enzyme materials needed by the cell.
8.   Peroxisomes: manufacture, store and secrete oxidation enzymes needed by the cell.
9.   Vacuoles: spaces that act as a vacuum cleaner to rid the cell of

wastes and water. Also, when not cleaning the cell, the vacuole will act as a storehouse for chemicals and compounds needed by the cell.

10. Basal bodies: structures that clean the cell.

11. Cell wall: a tough outer membrane that supports and protects the plant cell.

12. Centrioles: rod-shaped structures responsible for animal cell reproduction.

13. Nucleolus: the center of the nucleus that resembles a golf ball and houses the genes, chromosomes, and their needed materials.

14. Chromosomes: hereditary structures that contain the genes which determine the hereditary information contained in the cell.

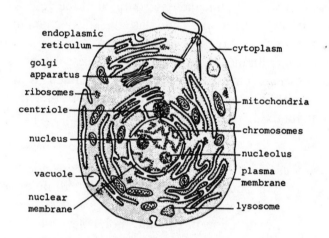

Typical Animal Cell

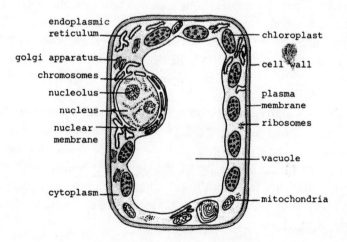

Typical Plant Cell

Cells maintain a balance or working equilibrium that is optimum for their needs. This balance, obtained by this internal control, is called homeostasis. This accounts for all movement into and out of the cell. Though the cell can adjust to a wide range of environmental needs and amounts, there is a limit to how much and how often it can adjust.

To understand homeostasis, one must understand how molecules move by osmosis and diffusion. When molecular movement has met needed concentrations of materials on either side of the cell membrane, the state of equilibrium exists. It is in this state that the cell operates most efficiently.

Materials move into and out of the cell either by active transport, passive transport, endocytosis, phagocytosis, or exocytosis. The exact method used depends on the type, function, and environment of the cell. A cell exists in a constantly changing environment and has constantly changing needs which must be met in order to stay alive and function. All transport occurs over a semipermeable membrane. Turgor pressure is necessary for the cell to adjust to its needs and environment. This pressure determines the amount of water maintained inside the cell to counterbalance the environment outside the cell. It is by the maintaining of this pressure that all transportation needed in the cell is determined.

Proteins are used by the cell or organism to provide energy, general maintenance, growth, and reproduction functions. All living material needs carbon, nitrogen, hydrogen, and oxygen to survive. Also, these elements are essential for the construction of organic molecules that constitute what it means to be "living." Only protein will supply the necessary nitrogen for life within a cell or organism. Protein degradation is the process by which proteins are broken down into the smallest units, called amino acids. Then, the amino acids are reconstructed into peptide chains (by the process of protein synthesis) that can be used by cell organelles or other materials as needed by the cell. This process of combining amino acids to produce peptide chains to reconstruct proteins is called protein synthesis.

Reproduction is a process that is necessary for life to continue. Reproduction is the process the organism or cell utilizes to create an offspring like itself. Reproduction can be asexual or sexual. Asexual reproduction occurs when one split produces a carbon-copy of the cell itself. Asexual processes are called fission, budding, fragmentation, regeneration, conjugation, or sporulation. The asexual methods of reproduction are used by one-cell organisms or lower life organisms.

Mitosis is the division of a body cell. The division or reproduction is for the purpose of maintaining life as a productive and efficient organism. Meiosis is the division of sex cells, namely, production of the egg or the sperm. Meiosis is a double process like mitosis.

CELL DIVISION

MITOSIS

Mitosis is a form of cell division whereby each of two daughter nuclei receives the same chromosome complement as the parent nucleus. All kinds of asexual reproduction are carried out by mitosis; it is also responsible for growth, regeneration, and cell replacement in multicellular organisms.

Interphase — Interphase is no longer called the resting phase because a great deal of activity occurs during this phase. In the cytoplasm, oxidation and synthesis reactions take place. In the nucleus, DNA replicates itself and forms messenger RNA, transfer RNA and ribosomal RNA.

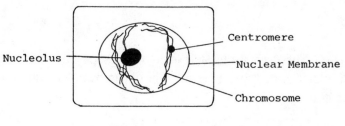

Interphase

Prophase — Chromatids shorten and thicken during this stage of mitosis. The nucleoli disappear and the nuclear membrane breaks down and disappears as well. Spindle fibers begin to form. In an animal cell, there is also division of the centrosome and centrioles.

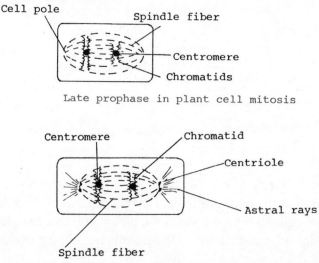

Late prophase in plant cell mitosis

Prophase in animal cell mitosis

Metaphase — During this phase, each chromosome moves to the equator, or middle of the spindle. The paired chromosomes attach to the spindle at the centromere.

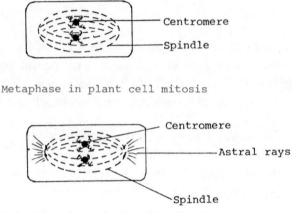

Metaphase in plant cell mitosis

Metaphase in animal cell mitosis

Anaphase — Anaphase is characterized by the separation of sister chromatids into a single-stranded chromosome. The chromosomes migrate to opposite poles of the cell.

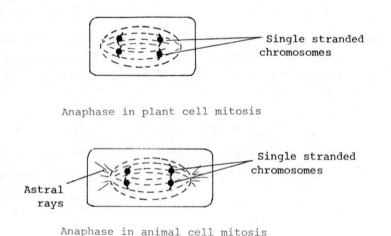

Anaphase in plant cell mitosis

Anaphase in animal cell mitosis

Telophase — During telophase, the chromosomes begin to uncoil and the nucleoli as well as the nuclear membrane reappear. In plant cells, a cell plate appears at the equator which divides the parent cell into two daughter cells. In animal cells, an invagination of the plasma membrane divides the parent cell.

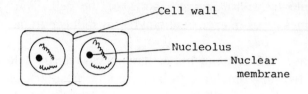

Late telophase in animal cell

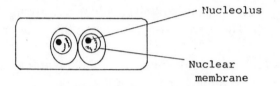

Late telophase in plant cell

MEIOSIS

Meiosis consists of two successive cell divisions with only one duplication of chromosomes. This results in daughter cells with a haploid number of chromosomes or one-half of the chromosome number in the original cell. This process occurs during the formation of gametes and in spore formation in plants.

Spermatogenesis — This process results in sperm cell formation with four immature sperm cells with a haploid number of chromosomes.

Oogenesis — This process results in egg cell formation with only one immature egg cell with a haploid number of chromosomes, which becomes mature and larger as yolk forms within the cell.

FIRST MEIOTIC DIVISION

Interphase I — Chromosome duplication begins to occur during this phase.

Prophase I — During this phase, the chromosomes shorten and thicken and synapsis occurs with pairing of homologous chromosomes. Crossing-over between non-sister chromatids will also occur. The centrioles will migrate to opposite poles and the nucleolus and nuclear membrane begin to dissolve.

Metaphase I — The tetrads, composed of two doubled homologous chromosomes, migrate to the equatorial plane during Metaphase I.

Anaphase I — During this stage, the paired homologous chromosomes separate and move to opposite poles of the cell. Thus, the number of chromosomes types in each resultant cell is reduced to the haploid number.

Telophase I — Cytopolasmic division occurs during telophase I. The formation of two new nuclei with half the chromosomes of the original cell occurs.

Prophase II — The centrioles that had migrated to each pole of the parental cell, now incorporated in each haploid daughter cell, divide, and a new spindle forms in each cell. The chromosomes move to the equator.

MetaphaseII — The chromosomes are lined up at the equator of the new spindle, which is at right angles to the old spindle.

AnaphaseII — The centromeres divide and the daughter chromatids, now chromosomes, separate and move to opposite poles.

Telophase II — Cytoplasmic division occurs. The chromosomes gradually return to the dispersed form and a nuclear membrane forms.

A living organism could be called a chemical factory. More chemical activity is carried on inside the cell or inside the living organism than any other place. Chemical bonds are broken, constructed and reconstructed in a continuous operation. Chemical reactions occur simultaneously throughout the organism so that life will be an ongoing process. Carbohydrates, starches, lipids, proteins, water, and nucleic acids are the chemicals (organic molecules) and compounds that are basic to all life.

DNA was discovered in 1869. It was not until the development of the electron microscope in the mid-1940s that scientists gained a true realization of the functioning of DNA.

DNA (deoxyribonucleic acid) is the basic chemical of life. It is a giant molecule made of four different nitrogenous bases (adenine, guanine, cytosine, thymine), phosphate groups, and 5- carbon sugars that collectively are called a nucleotide. It is a self-duplicating molecule that is in a double helix (spiral staircase appearance). It is found inside the nucleus of the cell. It contains the directions, or "blueprints," for the making of all the proteins that a cell needs. Proteins play a major role in cell metabolism and are the basic building blocks of a cell. DNA is the controller of heredity and all life activities of the cell. Its function is linked to the functioning of a companion chemical called RNA (ribonucleic acid).

Ribonucleic acid differs from DNA in that uracil replaces thymine as a

The Chemical Composition of DNA:

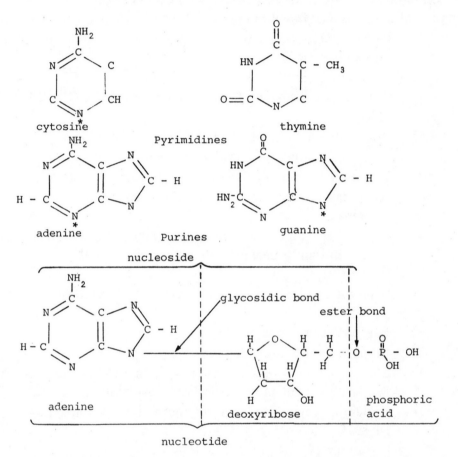

* = site of attachment to deoxyribose

Structural formulas of purines (adenine and guanine), pyrimidines (thymine and cytosine), and a nucleotide.

nitrogenous base, and the sugar bond used by RNA has one less oxygen present. Also, RNA is a straight chain. The genetic information in DNA is carried out of the nucleus by what is called messenger RNA (mRNA). Protein synthesis is carried out in the cytoplasm of the cell by transfer RNA (tRNA) using ribosomes composed of ribosomal RNA and proteins.

The DNA acts as an interpreter or decoder for the many chemical messages that are carried through the cell as a part of the life activities. The DNA cannot leave the nucleus and, therefore, must have a messenger and translator working directly with it. In addition, the tRNA picks up and delivers necessary amino acids to complete the needed activity. This process enables the cell to carry out digestion, oxidation, assimilation, synthesis, and other necessary cell activities.

The basic functions of life comprising total cell metabolism are:
1. Ingestion: taking in of food.
2. Digestion: breaking down of food by enzymes to simpler, soluble forms.
3. Secretion: formation of useful substances.
4. Absorption: diffusion of dissolved material through cell membranes.
5. Respiration: release of energy by oxidation of food.
6. Excretion: getting rid of wastes of the cells.
7. Transportation: circulation of materials throughout the organism.
8. Assimilation: formation of more protoplasm, resulting in growth and repair.
9. Regulation: maintaining stability of organism's chemical makeup under constantly changing internal and external environment (homeostasis).
10. Synthesis: building up of complex molecules from simple compounds.
11. Reproduction: production of more living individuals.
12. Irritability: response to stimuli.
13. Movement: the ability to change position. In some rare cases, as in plants, movement is coupled with irritability.
14. Bioluminescence: production of internal light within some organisms.

Photosynthesis is a process that occurs within all plant cells which supply all of the carbohydrates used by both plants and animals. Not only are essential organic compounds formed, but needed water and oxygen are given off as by-products in this autotrophic nutrition process.

Chloroplasts absorb light energy from the sun. Carbon dioxide and water are present as raw materials at the chloroplast manufacturing site.

An overall chemical description of photosynthesis is the equation

$$6\ CO_2 + 6\ H_2O \xrightarrow[\text{chlorophyll}]{\text{light}} C_6H_{12}O_6 + 6\ O_2$$

Photosynthesis is a two-step process involving light reactions and dark reactions. In the light reaction process, light must be present along with chlorophyll to start the chemical reaction. Carbon dioxide and water are broken down into free atoms. Then the dark reaction can happen. Light is not necessary for this chemical reaction to occur. Carbon, acting as a centerpiece, joins with oxygen and hydrogen to form carbohydrates. Water and unused oxygen are given off as waste products.

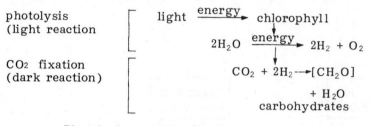

Photolysis and CO_2 fixation

Cellular respiration is the process by which the cell or organism gets energy for all of its activities. It is through this respiration process that chemical energy is released. This process occurs in the mitochondria through a series of steps.

Step 1
      Glucose (6 carbons)
  ATP
  ADP

Step 2
      Glucose Phosphate (6 carbons)

      Sugar Phosphate (6 carbons)
  ATP
  ADP

Step 3
      Sugar Diphosphate (6 carbons)

      2 PGAL (3 carbons each)

Step 4
  4 ADP   2NAD
  4 ATP   2 NADH$_2$
    2 Molecules of pyruvic acid (3 carbons each)

The steps are summarized as follows:

Step 1 - Activation of glucose

Step 2 - Formation of sugar diphosphate

Step 3 - Formation and oxidation of PGAL, phosphoglyceraldehyde

Step 4 - Formation of pyruvic acid ($C_3H_4O_3$)
    Net gain of two ATP molecules

Cellular respiration can be either aerobic or anaerobic. In aerobic respiration, release of energy from organic compounds occurs in the presence of oxygen. The oxidation, or process of breaking down and releasing energy, is stimulated by enzymes and acids present in and around the mitochondria. In anaerobic respiration, there is no oxygen present and it must occur by a fermentation process. Lactic acid is produced as a by-product of this process. Lactic acid in muscles results in muscle fatigue and soreness.

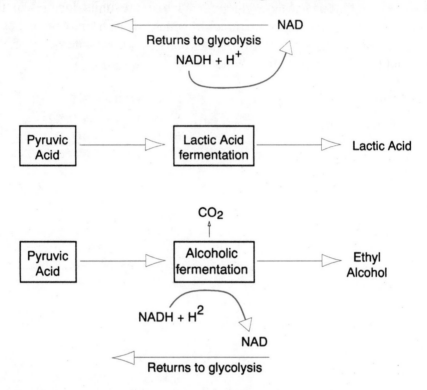

Everyone is aware of how offspring will resemble their parents. Yet, the offspring may have traits that are not present in either parent. In 1857, Gregor Mendel developed his Laws of Genetics after seven years of studying the garden green pea. Mendel's Laws of Genetics are:

1. Law of Dominance: Every organism receives a trait from the mother and a trait from the father. One trait may have dominance over the other and mask the recessive trait to keep it from showing in the offspring. Dominant traits are normally the darker, heavier, or larger of the two traits.

2. Law of Segregation and Recombinant: Genes separate into single units at the time the egg and sperm unite. Each character links with a like character to form a gene. It is segregation that assures each parent contributes equally to the offspring.

3. Law of Independent Assortment: Each unit or character for a trait is independently distributed to link with a like gene to form another pair. There is no pattern to their separation and rejoining to form the genes for the potential offspring. Genes on separate chromosomes are inherited independently.

In 1900, Walter Sutton began further studies based on Mendel's studies. Sutton compared the behavior of the chromosomes to the principles of inheritance. He confirmed all that Gregor Mendel had formulated. Sutton learned that the "factors" Mendel referred to were units located in the chromosomes. Sutton named these factors "genes." The chromosomal theory of inheritance, established by Sutton, states that genes are located on chromosomes and forms the basis for the study of genetics.

The Sutton Law was followed by the Hardy-Weinberg Law, which was based on population studies. The law states that in a population at equilibrium, both genes and genotypic frequencies remain constant from generation to generation. Each trait, whether dominant or recessive, has an equal chance to exert its influence.

Basic Language of Genetics:

1. A gene is the part of a chromosome that codes for a certain hereditary trait.
2. A chromosome is a rod-shaped body formed from the genes found in the cell nucleus.
3. A genotype is the genetic makeup of an organism or the set of genes that it possesses. This is always expressed in capital letters to express dominant traits or small letters to express recessive traits.
4. The phenotype is the outward visible appearance or expression of gene action. It is the hereditary makeup of an organism that we see or measure.
5. Homologous chromosomes are chromosomes bearing genes for the same characters.
6. A homozygous trait is an identical pair of alleles on homologous chromosomes for any given trait.
7. A heterozygous trait is a mixed pair of alleles on homologous chromosomes for any given trait.
8. Hybrid refers to an organism carrying unlike genes for certain traits. This is a preferred trait when breeding for the "best of both" traits.
9. Mutation is a sudden appearance of a new trait or variation which is inherited.
10. Lethal means deadly. This trait will cause death of the organism.

Each gene has a particular location on a chromosome (allele). Genes carried on the X chromosome are called sex-linked genes. Males carrying a recessive allele on their single X chromosome express a recessive phenotype.

Females must carry recessive alleles on both X chromosomes to express a recessive phenotype.

Mutations can affect either chromosomes or individual genes. Chromo-somal aberrations like mutations occur in reproductive cells and may be passed on to the offspring. Nondisjunction of the chromosomes results in gametes that have too few or too many chromosomes. In polyploidy, organisms have an extra set of chromosomes. In the disease called trisomy 21, or Down's Syndrome, a person has an extra twenty-first chromosome. Gene mutations occur due to a change in the DNA sequence for that particular gene at that particular time. A mutated gene does not give correct directions for protein synthesis and normally harms the organism. There are a few mutations that have proven to be beneficial, however.

The Punnett Square is a method used to predict the probable outcome of a particular genetic cross. This testcross will help determine information about an organism or potential organism. Study the basis crosses worked out below.

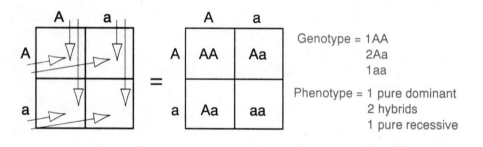

☞ Drill: The Cell

DIRECTIONS: Carefully read and answer each of the following questions which are based on the information which you have just read.

4. How do body cells, such as muscle or bone cells, reproduce?
    (1) Osmosis   (4) Meiosis
    (2) Mitosis   (5) Spore formation
    (3) Diffusion

5. Which of the following is part of the cell theory?
    (1) All cells are eukaryotes.   (4) All cells come from other cells.
    (2) All cells are prokaryotes.   (5) All cells undergo meiosis.
    (3) All cells have nuclei.

6. According to the cell theory,
   (1) all living things are composed of cells.
   (2) the number of cells in an organism is set before birth.
   (3) cell activity is controlled by the nucleus.
   (4) cells can be neither created or destroyed.
   (5) eukaryotic cells have a cell wall for protection.

7. Prokaryotic cells have no
   (1) need for energy.
   (2) metabolism.
   (3) DNA.
   (4) cell membrane.
   (5) membrane to separate nuclear components from the rest of the cell.

8. Most living cells are
   (1) prokaryotes.   (4) pentokaryotes.
   (2) eukaryotes.   (5) sex cells.
   (3) cellokaryotes.

9. Which cellular component is responsible for the regulation of exchanges of substances between a cell and its environment?
   (1) The endoplasmic reticulum
   (2) The cell nucleus
   (3) The cytoplasm
   (4) The cell membrane
   (5) The nuclear membrane

10. Which of the cellular components contains all of the cell except the nucleus and possesses substances for functioning organelles?
    (1) Cytoplasm   (4) Vacuole
    (2) Cell membrane   (5) Mitochondria
    (3) Nucleus

11. Which of the following is a cytoplasmic structure attached to the endoplasmic reticulum?
    (1) Plastid   (4) Ribosome
    (2) Mitochondria   (5) Chromosome
    (3) Lysosome

12. Which of the following is a cytoplasmic organelle associated with cellular digestion?
    (1) Plastid
    (2) Mitochondria
    (3) Lysosome
    (4) Golgi bodies
    (5) Stomach

13. Golgi apparatus are most common in
    (1) glandular tissue.
    (2) nervous tissue.
    (3) muscle tissue.
    (4) blood tissue.
    (5) striated tissue.

14. An organelle associated with protein synthesis is
    (1) plastids.
    (2) Golgi apparatus.
    (3) mitochondria.
    (4) ribosome.
    (5) nucleolus.

15. Diffusion of particles across a semipermeable membrane
    (1) is called osmosis.
    (2) always involves carriers.
    (3) results in dynamic equilibrium.
    (4) occurs from lesser to greater concentrations.
    (5) is not strictly controlled.

16. Maintaining a balanced internal control is called
    (1) homeostasis.
    (2) osmosis.
    (3) diffusion.
    (4) movement.
    (5) pump balance.

17. Osmosis and diffusion are processes that are used in homeostasis. They serve the purpose of
    (1) meeting a need of nutrition for the cell.
    (2) protein synthesis.
    (3) establishing a state of equilibrium.
    (4) using energy.
    (5) moving the cell through a solution.

18. The pressure that plant cells exert against cell walls is called
    (1) osmotic pressure.
    (2) isotonic pressure.
    (3) turgor pressure.
    (4) wall pressure.
    (5) exocytosis.

19. Even though glucose concentration is higher in our liver cells than in our bloodstream, glucose will still move into our liver by
    (1) facilitated diffusion.   (4) endocytosis.
    (2) active transport.   (5) osmosis.
    (3) osmotic pressure.

20. Which type of transport requires energy from the breakdown of ATP?
    (1) Active transport   (4) Osmosis
    (2) Bulk flow   (5) Exocytosis
    (3) Facilitated diffusion

21. An organic molecule is any molecule
    (1) containing carbon.   (4) containing zinc.
    (2) containing phosphorus.   (5) that is naturally grown.
    (3) found in dead organisms.

22. One kind of organic molecule is a
    (1) protein.   (4) All of the above.
    (2) carbohydrate.   (5) None of the above is organic.
    (3) lipid.

23. The type of organic molecule that is the basic structure of protein is
    (1) glucose.   (4) glycerol.
    (2) amino acid.   (5) carbohydrate.
    (3) starch.

24. Asexual reproduction produces offspring
    (1) with the same features.
    (2) with most of the same features.
    (3) with one of the parent features.
    (4) with adapted features.
    (5) that vary in genotype and size.

25. Sexual reproduction involves
    (1) mitosis.   (4) All of the above.
    (2) fission.   (5) None of the above.
    (3) chromosomes from each parent.

26. Formation of chains of yeast cells is an example of
    (1) conjugation.   (4) budding.
    (2) fragmentation.   (5) polymerization.
    (3) fission.

27. Mitosis results in
    (1)   offspring cells exactly like the parent cell.
    (2)   offspring cells different from the parent cell.
    (3)   new combinations of father cells.
    (4)   new combinations of mother cells.
    (5)   a smaller number of cells.

28. Meiosis produces
    (1)   zygotes.   (4)   sex cells.
    (2)   gametes.   (5)   2 and 4
    (3)   body cells.

29. Meiosis produces
    (1)   two genes for each trait joined together.
    (2)   two genes for each trait separated.
    (3)   only female traits.
    (4)   only male traits.
    (5)   a zygote with two genes for each trait.

30. The breaking of chemical bonds
    (1)   ends life.
    (2)   is an ongoing process.
    (3)   does not occur simultaneously.
    (4)   has no effect on life.
    (5)   may be painful to an organism.

31. The greatest amount of chemical activity is found
    (1)   inside the cell.   (4)   at birth.
    (2)   outside the cell.   (5)   during cell fusion.
    (3)   at death.

32. A DNA nucleotide is named on the basis of its
    (1)   base.   (4)   shape.
    (2)   phosphate.   (5)   rate of mutation.
    (3)   sugar.

33. DNA is found in the
    (1)   cytoplasm.   (4)   ribosome.
    (2)   nucleus.   (5)   2 and 3
    (3)   mitochondria.

34. The sequence of the DNA sets up a(n)
    (1) electrochemical reaction.
    (2) blueprint for supplying cells with protein.
    (3) way to convert DNA to carbohydrates.
    (4) mutation.
    (5) method for analyzing the number of hydroxyl groups on the 2' carbon.

35. RNA contains
    (1) uracil.
    (2) deoxyribose phosphate.
    (3) thymine.
    (4) proteins.
    (5) a dideoxyribose sugar.

36. A particular tRNA molecule attaches to a particular
    (1) amino acid.   (4) nucleotide.
    (2) gene.   (5) rRNA.
    (3) protein.

37. Genetic information that needs to move out of the nucleus can not leave by way of the DNA. Therefore, it is carried out by the
    (1) tRNA.   (4) mRNA.
    (2) mDNA.   (5) mPNA.
    (3) tDNA.

38. The RNA molecule that transcribes (receives information) from DNA and carries the information to code for a particular protein chain is called
    (1) hRNA.   (4) sRNA.
    (2) mRNA.   (5) DNA.
    (3) tRNA.

39. The interpretations of DNA enable the cell to
    (1) carry out living processes.   (4) direct its own death.
    (2) grow to an infinite size.   (5) develop a brain.
    (3) leave the nucleus.

40. During cellular respiration, energy is transferred from
    (1) ATP to glucose.   (4) glucose to CO_2.
    (2) enzymes to CO_2.   (5) CO_2 to O_2.
    (3) glucose to ATP.

41. The working and functioning of a cell is called
    (1) cell metabolism.   (4) cell oxidation.
    (2) cell catabolism.   (5) cell anabolism.
    (3) cell reduction.

42. Movement within a cell is its ability to
    (1) stir its cytoplasm.
    (2) move from place to place.
    (3) respond to irritability.
    (4) respond to sound.
    (5) oxygenate its blood.

43. Photosynthesis supplies the major portion of
    (1) proteins.   (4) amino acids.
    (2) lipids.   (5) light.
    (3) carbohydrates.

44. During photosynthesis, light energy is trapped by
    (1) sugar.   (4) carbon dioxide.
    (2) water.   (5) leaf stomata.
    (3) chlorophyll.

45. The structural unit of photosynthesis is the
    (1) chloroplast.   (4) matrix.
    (2) stroma.   (5) mitochondriam.
    (3) cristae.

46. When water is split to provide raw ingredients for the chemical process of photosynthesis,
    (1) oxygen is freed.   (4) carbon is freed.
    (2) hydrogen is freed.   (5) carbon dioxide is freed.
    (3) nitrogen is freed.

47. Cells release energy by a process called
    (1) breathing.   (4) photosynthesis.
    (2) metabolism.   (5) exocytosis.
    (3) respiration.

48. Cell respiration is responsible for supplying the cell with needed
    (1) energy.   (4) protein.
    (2) nutrition.   (5) reproductive structures.
    (3) water.

49. Anaerobic respiration in humans is commonly carried out in the
    _____ tissue.
    (1) heart   (4) muscle
    (2) liver   (5) kidney
    (3) brain

50. The passing of traits from parents to offspring is called
    (1) genetic.   (4) maturation.
    (2) heredity.   (5) DNA transcription.
    (3) development.

51. The principle of independent assortment requires the observation of
    (1) one contrasting trait.
    (2) at least two contrasting traits.
    (3) one contrasting trait in two different plants.
    (4) the same trait tested twice in one plant.
    (5) one trait tested for four generations.

52. The process that enables the principle of segregation to occur is known
    as
    (1) meiosis.   (4) growth.
    (2) mitosis.   (5) fusion.
    (3) development.

53. Which pair of terms are most identical in meaning?
    (1) Chromosomes and genes
    (2) DNA and mitosis
    (3) Protein and ribosomal RNA
    (4) Mendel's "factors" and chromosomes
    (5) Genes and Mendel's "factors"

54. What happens to traits as a population grows?
    (1) Most recessive traits quickly become extinct.
    (2) Dominant traits combine to form a trait exhibiting hyperdominance.
    (3) Fluctuations in genotypic frequencies do not occur.
    (4) Dominant traits will permanently mask recessive traits in all future
        generations.
    (5) The Hardy-Weinberg Law no longer is applicable.

55. A change in the genetic coding is called
    (1) an anticodon.   (2) a procodon.

(3)   lethal.   (4)   a mutation.
(5)   an evolving gene.

56.   The phenotype of an organism
      (1)   represents its genetic composition.
      (2)   is all the traits that are actually expressed.
      (3)   occurs only in dominant pure organisms.
      (4)   cannot be observed.
      (5)   is equivalent to the genotype.

57.   A hybrid organism would have a genotype of
      (1)   Aa.   (4)   AaA.
      (2)   AA.   (5)   AAbb.
      (3)   aa.

58.   Each gene has a particular location on a chromosome. This seat, or
      location, is called a(n)
      (1)   autosome.   (4)   chromosome.
      (2)   gene locus.   (5)   allele.
      (3)   gene.

59.   A trait that is carried on the X chromosome and has no allele on the Y
      chromosome is considered
      (1)   normal autosomal.   (4)   sex-influenced.
      (2)   mutation.   (5)   female.
      (3)   sex-linked.

60.   The failure of a chromosome pair to separate during meiosis or mitosis
      is called
      (1)   sex-linked.   (4)   polysomy.
      (2)   mutation.   (5)   Down's Syndrome.
      (3)   nondisjunction.

61.   Trisomy 21, a genetic defect whereby an organism has an extra twenty-
      first chromosome, is a
      (1)   defect caused by a mutation of one base pair.
      (2)   correctable defect.
      (3)   case where the extra chromosome takes the place of chromo-
            some 22.
      (4)   sex-linked trait seen only in males.
      (5)   nondisjunctive genetic trait.

62. A testcross results in all the offspring being one color. We can predict that parent was
    (1) inbred.
    (2) hybrid.
    (3) impure.
    (4) homozygous.
    (5) heterozygous.

63. Lobed ears are dominant over attached ears as a human trait. What would the predicted results be if two hybrid lobed ear parents mated?
    (1) 4 lobed
    (2) 3 lobed, 1 attached
    (3) 2 lobed, 2 attached
    (4) 1 lobed, 1 attached, 2 split
    (5) 4 attached

C. BREAKING THE CODE OF LIFE

More is being learned about the code of life that is locked into the DNA of every cell. Every living organism has its own unique pattern of DNA that accounts for the individualism in each organism. Prior to mitosis or meiois occurring within the cell, that is the reason for organisms to grow, develop, and reproduce, so replication of the DNA must occur. In this process, DNA unspirals, unzips, and separates, and new strands of DNA are constructed from nucleotides present in the nucleus. Then the process of cell division may occur. This occurrence is what holds the code of life. Never is the code altered in any replication that totally alters the organism. Although this may be the key to answering questions about cancer and other life-threatening diseases that affect certain organisms, much research still needs to be done.

☞ Drill: Breaking the Code of Life

DIRECTIONS: Carefully read and answer each of the following questions which are based on the information which you have just read.

64. A nucleotide consists of
    (1) a sugar, a protein, and uracil.
    (2) a sugar, a phosphate group, and a nitrogenous base.
    (3) a starch, a nitrogenous base, and a sugar.
    (4) a protein, a starch, and a sugar.
    (5) a nucleus and a sugar.

65. The process by which DNA copies itself is called
    (1) transcription.
    (2) replication.

(3)   nucleotide.   (4)   codon.
(5)   translation.

66.   It has been determined that chromosomes are made of genes, and
      genes are composed of
      (1)   DNA.   (4)   DNA and lipoproteins.
      (2)   DNA and carbohydrates. (5)   amino acids.
      (3)   DNA and starches.

D. EVOLUTION OF ORGANISMS

Several theories have been formulated on how life evolves. One such theory was proposed by Jean Lamarck in 1809 when he proposed that an organism evolves in response to its environment by acquiring a trait which would adapt them to live in its changing environment. For instance, if a giraffe's neck was too short, by the constant stretching during the parent's life, offspring would be born with longer necks.

In 1859, Darwin formulated his theory in his book called *The Origin of Species*. The book supported the theory of evolution but gave a completely different twist to the evolution idea. After studying many plants and animals, Darwin concluded that no two organisms are exactly alike, but instead differ in size, shape, color, etc., and that these traits are inherited from the parents to the offspring and not acquired. Individuals who inherit adaptive traits have a greater chance for survival. Thus, Darwin called his theory natural selection.

Evidence that supports evolutionary theories includes adaptations to the environment, homologous organs, vestigial organs, similarity of embryonic development, similarity of nucleic acids, and similar protein structure. With the groundwork laid by Lamarck and Darwin, modern evolutionists include speciation, adaptive radiation, convergent evolution, divergent evolution, and population genetics as phenomena that support evolutionary theory.

Over time, there have been marked changes in atmospheric content, climate, and environment. If a species did not have the necessary adaptive traits to change with the external changes, the species became extinct.

Fossils are evidence of living things that existed long ago. The most common fossils are found in sedimentary rock that can be dated by using radioactive isotopes to measure the amount of carbon in the remains. This amount determines a close approximation to the exact age of the fossil remains.

It is proposed by evolutionary theory that each era is briefly marked by rapid adaptive radiation normally followed by mass extinction that ended each era. Stanley Miller provided evidence that life-supporting molecules arose under abiotic conditions. He produced the exact atmosphere that was thought to have first existed and showed how heterotrophs used the available organic substances for food.

Geological evolution is as follows:

Precambrian Era	unicellular organisms originated
Paleozoic Era	multicellular animals and fern-like plants originated
Mesozoic Era	birds, mammals, reptiles, and flowering plants originated
Cenozoic Era	radiation of birds, mammals, reptiles, and flowering plants occurred

☞ Drill: Evolution of Organisms

DIRECTIONS: Carefully read and answer each of the following questions which are based on the information which you have just read.

67. According to Lamarck,
    (1) evolution was slow.
    (2) organisms passed acquired traits to offspring.
    (3) evolution was a mutation.
    (4) each organism adapted quickly to survive.
    (5) giraffes with short necks can stretch and never produce long-necked offspring.

68. After long study, Darwin proposed that
    (1) acquired traits are passed.
    (2) all organisms are alike.
    (3) no two organisms are exactly alike.
    (4) all organisms will reproduce.
    (5) an organism with a long lifetime will evolve mostly during its youth.

69. Natural selection is a process by which
    (1) organisms compete for food.
    (2) organisms with traits well-suited to the environment will survive and reproduce.

(3)   acquired traits will be passed on from parent to offspring.

(4)   the phenomenon of mutation kills all organisms it afflicts.

(5)   animals choose to eat only those foods which are non-toxic.

70.   The general effect of migration upon the Hardy-Weinberg principle is
(1)   to increase the differences in populations.
(2)   to cause mutations.
(3)   to reduce differences in populations by mixing genes.
(4)   to discourage the movement of organisms into or out of a population.
(5)   to eliminate recessive alleles from a population.

71.   A group of the same species living in the same place at the same time that is genetically studied is an example of
(1)   community study.   (4)   a genealogical study.
(2)   ecosystem genetics.   (5)   niche work.
(3)   population genetics.

72.   The type of evolution that explains the polar bear and the brown bear is called
(1)   divergent evolution.   (4)   disruptive evolution.
(2)   convergent evolution.   (5)   convolution.
(3)   directional evolution.

73.   Extinction refers to an organism's
(1)   parents dying before it is born.
(2)   species dying out.
(3)   death.
(4)   parents deciding again to have offspring.
(5)   escape from an environment by migrating.

74.   Fossils are
(1)   remains found in sedimentary rock.
(2)   dried organisms.
(3)   old animals still around.
(4)   something that is old.
(5)   perfectly preserved animals that died during a narrow time period of the earth's history.

75.   What simple components were combined in Miller's experiment to find biologically important molecules?
(1)   DNA, RNA, and protein

    (2)   Ammonia, methane, water, and hydrogen
    (3)   Purines and pyrimidines
    (4)   Oxygen, hydrogen, and chlorophyll extract
    (5)   Urea and lactic acid

76.   An era is
    (1)   a period of evolutionary time.
    (2)   an evolution theory.
    (3)   a short period of time filled with rapid changes.
    (4)   a period of time something lived.
    (5)   usually about 20 years in length.

77.   Man probably first evolved during the
    (1)   Mesozoic Era.   (4)   Cenozoic Era.
    (2)   Precambrian Era.   (5)   era following the Cenozoic Era.
    (3)   Paleozoic Era.

78.   Geological evolution began with the
    (1)   Precambrian Era.
    (2)   unicellular organisms living on land.
    (3)   multicellular organisms living in water.
    (4)   Paleozoic Era.
    (5)   Cenozoic Era.

E. CLASSIFICATION

Classification is a method of organizing information based on similarities. Aristotle was the first scientist to attempt to classify living things by grouping them into two major groups — plants or animals. Then they were divided into three major sub-groups as to their habitat — land, water, or air. Since Aristotle's first attempt at classification, man has used various systems of classifying living things in an effort to identify them. With so many languages and word meanings, a standard language had to be developed so that the use of common names in each language could be avoided. Thus, scientists began to use the genus and species names as this would be a consistent language in any nation. This classification system is called binomial nomenclature.

The levels of classification from largest to smallest are kingdom, phylum class, order, family, genus, and species. All living organisms are classified into one of five kingdoms to start the identifying procedure. Then the organism will be studied, compared to specific requirements, and placed in an appropriate level until a species is finally established. The biological name would be the genus and species.

A classification key can be used as an aid to identify organisms. It uses an organism's general characteristics and special features to find its appropriate placement. (Study the following mini-key.)

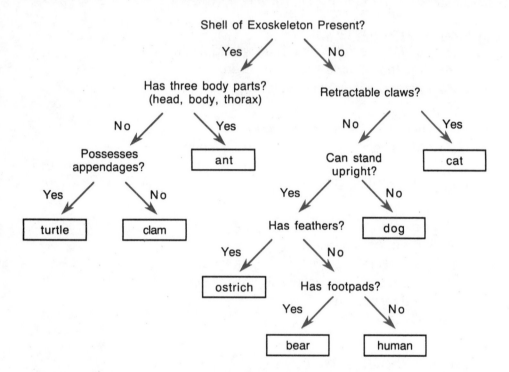

Often, as seen throughout time, organisms change in order to survive. Natural selection causes all species to adapt to changing environmental conditions. This change is called adaptation. The organisms change to adapt to their new environments and through time they evolve into entirely different organisms. This is called speciation.

MONERAN KINGDOM

Bacteria and blue-green bacteria

Characteristics: prokaryotes, microscopic, lives as a single cell or in colonies in water, autotrophic, few heterotrophic

Structures: flagella, capsules

Functions:: food getting, respiration, reproduction

Systems: none

Growth: cell membrane and availability of food set growth limit

Reproduction Method: binary fission

PROTISTAE KINGDOM

Animal-like organism, distinguished by method of locomotion

Characteristics: eukaryotes, mainly microscopic, single-celled or multi-cellular; some autotrophic and many heterotrophic

Structures: cilia, flagella, cell organelles membrane bound, photosynthetic

Functions: organelles function as organ systems

Systems: none

Growth: cell membrane and availability of food set growth limit

Reproduction Method: asexual or sexual

FUNGI KINGDOM

Characteristics: eukaryotes, mainly multicellular, parasitic, symbiotic, mycorrhizae

Structures: root-like, caps, filaments, reproductive

Functions: digestive-like, respiration, reproductive

Systems: beginning to develop

Growth: based on food source and availability

Reproduction Method: asexual, sexual

PLANTAE KINGDOM

Characteristics: eukaryotes, multicellular, nonmotile, autotrophic

Structures: cellulose cell walls

Functions: based on cell and tissue chemistry

Systems: all present and functioning

Growth: based on hormone action

Reproduction Method: asexual, sexual by spores, seeds, flowers, and cones

ANIMALAE KINGDOM

Characteristics: eukaryotes, multicellular, heterotrophic, most are motile at some point in lifetime

Structures: all present and unique to organism

Functions: based on nutrition, cell and tissue chemistry, and individual demands

Systems: all present and functioning

Growth: based on hormone action and nutrition

Reproduction Method: asexual, sexual

☞ Drill: Classification

DIRECTIONS: Carefully read and answer each of the following questions which are based on the information which you have just read.

79. Aristotle would have classified which two organisms in the same grouping?
    (1) Ferns and feathered birds
    (2) Algae and whales
    (3) Roses and mushrooms
    (4) Cats and carnations
    (5) Dogs and dandelions

80. The practice of giving organisms two names is known as
    (1) binomial nomenclature.   (4) binomial species.
    (2) common name.   (5) Arabic numerals.
    (3) family name.

81. Which of the following do modern taxonomists study to determine relationships among organisms?
    (1) Chromosome structure   (2) Embryology

(3)   Biochemical similarities   (4)   All of the above.
(5)   None of the above.

82.   A human being is known as *Homo sapiens*. Its species name is
(1)   man.   (4)   sapiens.
(2)   human.   (5)   Mammalia.
(3)   Homo.

83.   To use a classification key, one must
(1)   study structures and features of organisms.
(2)   be able to see well.
(3)   know a lot about plants.
(4)   study many books.
(5)   memorize the names used in binomial nomenclature.

84.   Organisms change to adapt to their new environments and through
       time they evolve into entirely different organisms. This process is called
(1)   specialization.   (4)   convergent evolution.
(2)   speciation.   (5)   divergent evolution.
(3)   special evolution.

85.   Monerans do not have a true nucleus or membrane-bound organelles;
       therefore they are called
(1)   eukaryotes.   (4)   nokaryotes.
(2)   cokaryotes.   (5)   anucleotic.
(3)   prokaryotes.

86.   Autotrophic bacteria
(1)   depend on other organisms for food.
(2)   depend on other organisms for nitrogen.
(3)   always need oxygen.
(4)   produce their own food.
(5)   are parasitic.

87.   Protozoa are mostly heterotrophic. This means they
(1)   produce their own food.
(2)   obtain energy by feeding on other organisms.
(3)   are harmful to prokaryotes.
(4)   require sunlight constantly.
(5)   eat various sources of food (originating from plants and animals).

88. Protozoans are classified by their method of
    (1) reproduction.   (4) food-getting.
    (2) growth.   (5) protein synthesis.
    (3) locomotion.

89. An example of a fungus is
    (1) mushroom.   (4) All of the above.
    (2) bread mold.   (5) None of the above.
    (3) penicillum.

90. Most fungi spread through the world by
    (1) air.   (4) organisms.
    (2) water.   (5) moving by the use of cilia.
    (3) spores.

91. One cellular characteristic that results in plant and animal differences
    is
    (1) plants have cellulose-filled cell walls.
    (2) plants are autotrophic.
    (3) plants have roots.
    (4) plants are green.
    (5) plants bend towards light.

92. Plants are unique in that their growth is based on
    (1) water.   (4) enzyme action.
    (2) food.   (5) exercise.
    (3) hormone action.

93. To be classified an animal, an organism must
    (1) have a cell membrane.
    (2) have hormone functions.
    (3) be motile at some point in life.
    (4) reproduce at some point in life.
    (5) eat meat.

94. Most organisms classified as animals reproduce
    (1) asexually.
    (2) sexually.
    (3) by a combination of asexual and sexual.
    (4) once a year.
    (5) by the fission of sperm with an ovary.

F. HUMAN SYSTEMS BIOLOGY

DIGESTIVE SYSTEM

The digestive system is responsible for both mechanical and chemical digestion that break down food into molecules so they can move into the cell and be used for the living process. The mouth, teeth, and tongue begin the chemical digestion by mechanically breaking down the food through the chewing process and the addition of saliva. The enzyme amylase breaks down carbohydrates and starts the breakdown of starches. Food moves from the mouth to the stomach by way of the esophagus. In the stomach, other digestive enzymes and hydrochloric acid begin the breakdown of proteins. The stomach churns and mixes the food. Food, now in a liquid-like state, moves from the stomach into the small intestine, where it is absorbed through the villa into the bloodstream where it is delivered and assimilated by the cells of the body. Waste materials and unused food are carried back to the large intestine where they mix with roughage and water. The undigested materials are excreted from the body.

CIRCULATORY SYSTEM

The circulatory system is composed of the heart, arteries, veins, red blood cells, white blood cells, antibodies, thrombin, water, and plasma. A four-chambered heart, controlled by the pacemaker, rhythmically controls the pumping action by alternating contractions of the atria and ventricles. Blood circulates through the body in two loops — arteries carrying oxygenated blood away from the heart to all parts of the body, and veins returning deoxygenated blood to the heart and lungs to be reoxygenated. An auxiliary portion is the lymphatic system, which drains excess tissue fluids back into the circulatory system along with white blood cells that destroy harmful microorganisms.

SKELETAL SYSTEM

The skeleton is the basic framework of the human body and is made of connective tissue — bones and cartilage. Bone is living tissue with vitamins, collagen, and minerals to give it strength and hardness. The process by which the bones harden is called ossification. Bones are joined by cartilage at joints. Joints are classified as to the amount of movement they allow: stationary (skull), hinge (elbow), or ball and socket (hip).

MUSCULAR SYSTEM

Three human muscle types are skeletal, cardiac, and smooth. All muscle tissue exerts force when it contracts; therefore, muscles are responsible for all movement of the body, voluntary or involuntary. Energy for all movement is derived from an ample supply of mitochondria in the muscle cell. ATP, a high level energy carrier, is produced by the mitochondria for use by other cells and tissue parts during movement or exercise. Muscles are paired to accomplish full movement. Each contracting muscle will be paired with an antagonistic muscle, and tendons attach paired muscle groups to bones to complete the movement action. The skeletal muscles make up this grouping of muscles and are mainly voluntary.

Cardiac muscle is found only in the heart. The heart is the strongest muscle of the body. It is responsible for keeping the blood flowing through the circulatory system at a given pressure. The cardiac muscle is an involuntary muscle.

Smooth muscles are found in the linings of the body such as the digestive system and internal organs. They are generally involuntary muscles.

NERVOUS SYSTEM

The basic unit of the nervous system is the neuron (nerve cell). Its structure allows electrochemical signals to travel across synapses to activate muscles, glands, or organ tissue. The nervous system is divided into two parts. One part, the central nervous system, includes the brain, spinal cord, and the peripheral nervous system, which is a vast network of nerves that totally connect all parts of the body. Receptors located in sense organs and in the skin send information along the sensory neurons to the spinal cord and then to the brain where the information is chemically interpreted, causing a motor response.

RESPIRATORY SYSTEM

Respiration involves actions started by nerves stimulating muscles and bones to mechanically enlarge the respiratory cavity of the body. The breathing rate is controlled by nerves originating in the brain based on carbon dioxide content. The human nasal passages are adapted to clean, moisten, and warm the air before it enters the lungs by way of the trachea and bronchi. The lungs are made up of many tiny air sacs called alveoli that are found at the end of the bronchiole in clusters. The exchange of gases between the lungs and circulatory system occurs in the alveoli.

EXCRETORY SYSTEM

The excretory system is made up of the kidney, bladder, connecting tubes, and capillaries joined to the kidney. Urine is collected by structures in the kidney called nephrons. From the nephrons, the liquid wastes are collected and stored in the bladder. Urine leaves the body through the urethra.

ENDOCRINE SYSTEM

The endocrine system produces hormones which travel by way of the bloodstream to specific target cells. The manner in which the hormone acts on the target cells depends on whether it is a protein or steroid. Each will cause a feedback, which is one way to regulate hormones secreted into the body. Homeostasis depends on the actions of the nervous and endocrine systems. Organs, like the kidney, function based on endocrine stimulation.

INTEGUMENTARY SYSTEM

The integumentary covering of the body is called the skin. Skin consists of two layers, the epidermis and the dermis. Skin protects the body, rids the body of mineral salts and wastes, regulates body temperature, and picks up environmental signals. The skin is the bonding or holding agent that keeps the body intact and functioning. Also part of the integumentary system are the hair and nails.

IMMUNITY AND DISEASES

IMPORTANT LYMPHATIC ORGANS
— A defense against Pathogens

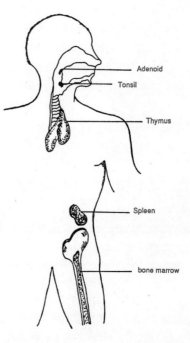

Adenoids and Tonsils — Organs that filter out antigens (substances, such as viruses, which stimulate antibody synthesis) that enter the body via the upper-respiratory and gastro-intenstinal tracts.

Thymus — Produces cells that eventually become what are called peripheral T cells, which possess surface receptors for antigens.

Bone Marrow — Produces blood-forming stem cells.

Spleen — Has three functions:

(1) Can mount an immune response to antigens in the blood stream.

(2) Scavanges old red blood cells.

(3) reserve site for making blood forming stem cells.

DISORDERS OF THE IMMUNE SYSTEM

Lupus — People develop immune reactions to their own nucleic acids.

Allergies — People become hypersensitive to environmental substances, called allergens.

AIDS (Acquired Immune Deficiency Syndrome) —

(1) People have reduced numbers of helper T cells.

(2) People may not be able to form antibodies against diseases like pneumonia.

☞ Drill: Human Systems Biology

DIRECTIONS: Carefully read and answer each of the following questions which are based on the information which you have just read.

95. Food is broken down into essential nutrients in the
    (1) digestive system.
    (2) circulatory system.
    (3) skeletal system.
    (4) nervous system.
    (5) oral cavity.

96. Although humans can not digest cellulose, the fiber helps us by
    (1) providing antibiotic activity in the intestines.
    (2) stimulating muscle action in the digestive system.
    (3) providing a padding medium.
    (4) providing energy for the digestive system.
    (5) expanding so that the stomach feels extremely full.

97. Mechanical digestion involves
    (1) converting food particles into molecules.
    (2) building usable food molecules.
    (3) obtaining food.
    (4) tearing and grinding food into small bits.
    (5) using tools, such as blenders, to break down food.

98. The circulatory system is responsible for all of the following except
    (1) the distribution of oxygen.
    (2) carrying nutrients.
    (3) providing for natural defenses of the body.
    (4) removing urea from the body.
    (5) stopping the flow of blood after an injury.

99. Vessels that carry deoxygenated blood to the heart are called the
    (1) arteries.
    (2) veins.
    (3) capillaries.
    (4) vesicles.
    (5) aorta and vena cava.

100. Minerals normally found in bone tissue are
    (1) iron and mercury.
    (2) calcium and iron.
    (3) iron only.
    (4) strontium and phosphorus.
    (5) calcium and strontium.

101. During the process of ossification,
    (1) calcium is lost from bone tissue.
    (2) phosphorus is lost from bones.
    (3) bones are changed to cartilage.
    (4) cartilage is changed to bone.
    (5) bones may fracture easily.

102. The type of muscle tissue found in the walls of many internal organs is identified as
    (1) striated.
    (2) voluntary.
    (3) smooth.
    (4) skeletal.
    (5) cardiac.

103. The point where two bones meet is called
    (1) point of connection.
    (2) joint.
    (3) point of insertion.
    (4) growth plane.
    (5) cartilage.

104. The central nervous system consists of
    (1) the brain and spinal cord.
    (2) spinal nerves only.
    (3) the medulla and cerebrum.
    (4) the cerebrum and spinal column.
    (5) the brain and skin.

105. The junction where an impulse travels from one neuron to another is
    called the
    (1)   synapse.   (4)   affector node.
    (2)   stimuli.   (5)   nervous system.
    (3)   nerve message.

106. The actual exchange of gases occurs at the
    (1)   trachea.   (4)   bronchioles.
    (2)   nostrils.   (5)   bronchi.
    (3)   alveoli.

107. The breathing center of the brain is sensitive to
    (1)   the concentrations of oxygen.
    (2)   contractions of carbon dioxide in body cells.
    (3)   the amount of oxygen in the blood.
    (4)   the concentration of carbon dioxide in the blood.
    (5)   pollutants in the carbon dioxide we breathe.

108. Maintenance of the body's fluid and chemical balance is dependent
    upon the proper functioning of the
    (1)   digestive system.   (4)   circulatory system.
    (2)   excretory system.   (5)   skeletal system.
    (3)   nervous system.

109. Metabolic wastes include all of the following except
    (1)   water.   (4)   feces.
    (2)   urea.   (5)   None of the above.
    (3)   carbon dioxide.

110. Chemical messengers called hormones are found in the
    (1)   endocrine system.   (4)   integumentary system
    (2)   digestive system.   (5)   skeletal system.
    (3)   nervous system.

111. Homeostasis depends primarily on the actions of the
    (1)   nervous and endocrine systems.
    (2)   nervous and muscular systems.
    (3)   digestive and nervous systems.
    (4)   circulatory and nervous systems.
    (5)   endocrine and digestive systems.

112. Skin, hair, and nails are part of the
    (1)   skeletal system.   (4)   endocrine system.
    (2)   circulatory system.   (5)   nervous system.
    (3)   integumentary system.

113. Skin protects the body and
    (1)   rids the body of mineral salts and wastes.
    (2)   regulates body temperature.
    (3)   picks up environmental signals.
    (4)   All of the above.
    (5)   None of the above.

114. Infectious diseases are caused by
    (1)   bacteria, fungi, and protozoans.
    (2)   bacteria only.
    (3)   fungi only.
    (4)   protozoans only.
    (5)   antibodies.

115. The only group of diseases or disorders for which there are no known
     cures is the group that includes
    (1)   infectious diseases.   (4)   STDs.
    (2)   degenerative diseases.   (5)   psychological disorders.
    (3)   genetic disorders.

G. ECOLOGY

Ecology can be defined as the study of interactions between groups of organisms and their environment. Groups are referred to as populations. Ecology is the basis of all life and all support systems of life. It is made up of chains — the food chain, carbon/oxygen chain, energy chain, and water chain. It is through the linking of the chains that life continues. Each organism has a specific habitat in an ecosystem carrying out a specific role (niche).

Ecology and behavior are closely linked. It is because of learned and innate behaviors that that organisms are equipped to meet the ever-changing environmental demands and the interactions with other living organisms.

Life on earth exists in a thin layer known as the biosphere. The land, air, and water that make up the biosphere each have their own areas where life exists. The land, or terrestrial, biomes are determined mainly by climate. Water, or aquatic, biomes are classified as freshwater or marine, depending upon the amount of salt (salinity) in the water. Marine life occurs in various zones depending on depth, temperature, and light intensity. Freshwater abiotic factors are depth, turbidity, temperature, and light intensity. Estuaries are mixtures of salt and fresh water. They are more protected than the ocean, but more nutrient-rich than rivers and support a wide variety of species.

The size of a population at a given time is determined by its growth rate. Growth rate is determined by the factors of birth rate, immigration, death rate, and emigration. Other factors like natural disasters, availability of food, and disease also independently affect population. Environmental resistance to increased population often depends on population density. Crowding of organisms can reduce nutrients, spread disease, and interfere with reproduction. Competition for an environment's limited resources occurs between members of a population (intraspecific competition) and between different species in an area (interspecific competition). Competition also limits population size.

Humans are unique in their ability to modify the carrying capacity of their environment to be favorable for population growth. Most scientists agree that it is only a matter of time before humans will be unable to increase the earth's carrying capacity any further. At that time, the birth rate must decrease and the death rate must increase to balance population growth.

Natural resources are necessary for human survival and the making of necessary products. The natural resources are water, soil, air, wildlife, and forests. Problems that are now being faced are related to erosion, soil depletion, species extinction, deforestation, desertification, and water shortages. Efforts to reverse these problems and their environmental damages are found in the planned programs of reforestation, captive breeding, biological harvesting, or planned farming through efficient plowing and planting procedures.

Pollution is damaging both the ecosystems and living organisms. Air, water, soil, and food resources are being affected by pollution. Pollutants include automobile exhaust, fertilizers, pesticides, industrial wastes, radioactive wastes, and most of all, household wastes. The growing population and modern conveniences greatly contribute to this insurmountable problem. Government regulations, community efforts, and changes in the habits of industries and individuals are necessary to solve pollution problems .

☞ Drill: Ecology

DIRECTIONS: Carefully read and answer each of the following questions which are based on the information which you have just read.

116. The areas of earth where life exists collectively is called
    (1) the ecosystem.   (4) an ecosystem.
    (2) a biome.   (5) a niche.
    (3) a biosphere.

117. An organism's niche is composed of
    (1) what he eats.   (4) All of the above.
    (2) how he sleeps.   (5) None of the above.
    (3) how he reproduces.

118. Learned and innate behaviors function to
    (1) allow flexibility to meet environmental changes.
    (2) allow interactions with other living organisms.
    (3) choose lifestyles.
    (4) Both 1 and 2.
    (5) Both 1 and 3.

119. The abiotic parts of an ecosystem include
    (1) bacteria.   (4) temperature.
    (2) plants.   (5) algae.
    (3) animals.

120. The biotic potential of a population is
    (1) the rate at which a population would reproduce if every individual lived.
    (2) the rate at which a population would die.
    (3) the rate at which a population would over-populate.
    (4) None of the above.
    (5) All of the above.

121. All of the following are limiting factors except
    (1) habitat.   (4) population density.
    (2) food.   (5) shelter.
    (3) water.

122. The carrying capacity means the ability
     - (1) to carry a load.
     - (2) to support life.
     - (3) to support offspring.
     - (4) to supply occupations.
     - (5) to hold a very heavy weight.

123. Cities near the ocean may meet their demands for water by using a procedure called
     - (1) water recovery.
     - (2) desalination.
     - (3) irrigation.
     - (4) water recycling.
     - (5) beach cleaning.

124. A substance that is nonbiodegradable is
     - (1) paper waste.
     - (2) plastic.
     - (3) wood.
     - (4) food waste.
     - (5) an aluminum can.

125. The ecosystem and living organisms are being damaged by
     - (1) changing environmental conditions.
     - (2) pollution.
     - (3) pesticides.
     - (4) acid rain.
     - (5) All of the above.

BIOLOGY

ANSWER KEY

Drill: Themes and General Vocabulary

1. (4)   2. (2)   3. (3)

Drill: The Cell

4. (2)	19. (2)	34. (2)	49. (4)
5. (4)	20. (1)	35. (1)	50. (2)
6. (1)	21. (1)	36. (1)	51. (2)
7. (5)	22. (4)	37. (4)	52. (1)
8. (2)	23. (2)	38. (2)	53. (5)
9. (4)	24. (1)	39. (1)	54. (3)
10. (1)	25. (3)	40. (3)	55. (4)
11. (4)	26. (4)	41. (1)	56. (2)
12. (3)	27. (1)	42. (3)	57. (1)
13. (1)	28. (5)	43. (3)	58. (2)
14. (4)	29. (2)	44. (3)	59. (3)
15. (3)	30. (2)	45. (1)	60. (3)
16. (1)	31. (1)	46. (1)	61. (5)
17. (3)	32. (1)	47. (3)	62. (4)
18. (3)	33. (5)	48. (1)	63. (2)

Drill: Breaking the Code of Life

64. (2)   65. (2)   66. (1)

Drill: Evolution of Organisms

67. (2)	70. (3)	73. (2)	76. (1)
68. (3)	71. (3)	74. (1)	77. (4)
69. (2)	72. (1)	75. (2)	78. (1)

Drill: Classification

79. (3)	83. (1)	87. (2)	91. (1)
80. (1)	84. (2)	88. (3)	92. (3)
81. (4)	85. (3)	89. (4)	93. (3)
82. (4)	86. (4)	90. (3)	94. (2)

Drill: Human Systems Biology

95. (1)	101. (4)	107. (4)	113. (4)
96. (2)	102. (3)	108. (2)	114. (1)
97. (4)	103. (2)	109. (4)	115. (3)
98. (4)	104. (1)	110. (1)	
99. (2)	105. (1)	111. (1)	
100. (2)	106. (3)	112. (3)	

Drill: Ecology

116. (3)	119. (4)	122. (2)	125. (5)
117. (4)	120. (1)	123. (2)	
118. (4)	121. (4)	124. (2)	

III. CHEMISTRY

A. INTRODUCTION TO CHEMISTRY

Chemistry is one of the oldest branches of science. The study of chemistry can be traced back as far as the Babylonian Period. The field of chemistry seeks to transform one molecule into another to tailor or refine such chemicals as plastics, drugs, food technology, fuels, and dyes. Out of these raw materials, countless products required to meet our needs of daily living can be manufactured. Chemistry is defined as the study of the composition and behavior of elements in combination with each other.

Chemistry began to grow as knowledge spread about the atomic theory proposed by Thomas Dalton about 1807. He advocated that all matter is composed of small indivisible particles which he named "atoms" and described as little round balls. He believed these particles could combine with one another in many forms to produce all possible substances. It was remarkable how close his theory was to being correct considering the lack of experimental techniques available at that time. He was correct in stating that atoms join together to form complex substances. Dalton was incorrect in his assumption that all atoms are alike.

A great growth was experienced in the field of chemistry after the discovery of the group-forming pattern by D. L. Mendeleev in 1896. With the newly acquired information, a listing of all of the known chemical elements was placed on a chart in the order of their increasing atomic weights and number of energy levels. This charted information was the first periodic table.

As information in the field of chemistry grew, studies branched into the areas of organic chemistry and inorganic chemistry. Organic chemistry deals with the carbon compounds while inorganic chemistry deals with all the other elements and compounds.

The field of chemistry has vastly expanded based on the study of the atomic structure of elements and their behavior. Atomic structure is related to the properties and arrangement of elements in the periodic chart. The elements are classified into groups, periods, and families. It is from these groupings that matter is classified and its behavior is studied based on the ability of an element to combine or react with other elements. The study of the behavior of matter is based on properties of the elements and their ability to combine through the transfer and sharing of electrons to form compounds and other matter. This is commonly referred to as the process of bonding.

Every element has its own letter symbol. With these letter symbols and atomic numbers used together correctly, one can construct a formula. The formulas can be combined to show the composition of compounds, reactions between elements, chemical equilibrium, and oxidation and reaction rates. This is accomplished by the process of balancing equations.

It is necessary that everyone understands the basics of chemistry since our lives are centered around this subject. Also, how far we can progress is based on our ability to understand chemical concepts and apply them to our everyday life.

☞ Drill: Introduction to Chemistry

DIRECTIONS: Carefully read and answer each of the following questions which are based on the information which you have just read.

1. Which one of the following is NOT the job of a chemist?
    (1) Changing one material into another
    (2) Turning raw materials into products
    (3) Selling new chemicals
    (4) Refining materials
    (5) Studying the behavior of elements

2. In making bread, a mixture of flour, water, and yeast are baked in an oven. The raw materials of bread baking are
    (1) an oven.   (4) yeast and flour.
    (2) water, flour, and yeast.   (5) yeast and an oven.
    (3) water, flour, and an oven.

3. Which one of the following is a synthetic food?
    (1) An apple
    (2) Water
    (3) A cherry pie made of flour, fruit, sugar, and fat
    (4) A diet supplement made of wheat protein, BHT, artificial colors, and other ingredients
    (5) Tofu, made of soybeans, sea salt, and water

4. The atomic theory states that all matter is composed of
   (1) carbon.
   (2) atoms.
   (3) molecules.
   (4) compounds.
   (5) complex substances.

5. According to Dalton's theory, which of the following is NOT assumed?
   (1) Atoms can be broken into subatomic particles
   (2) All matter is made of atoms
   (3) Atoms are round
   (4) Atoms can join together
   (5) Atoms of the same substance are identical

6. Dalton was incorrect in some assumptions concerning the atom. This error can be based on his experimentation technique. One incorrect assumption was
   (1) all atoms are alike.
   (2) all atoms are not alike.
   (3) some atoms are more alike than others.
   (4) atoms are not found everywhere.
   (5) atoms can combine with each other.

7. In the periodic table, elements increase in
   (1) both mass and number of energy levels.
   (2) mass only.
   (3) number of energy levels.
   (4) atomic structure.
   (5) mass number at energy levels.

8. Mendeleev discovered there was a pattern when one started to arrange elements based on their
   (1) name.
   (2) atomic weights.
   (3) particulate composition.
   (4) period.
   (5) melting point.

9. An element near the bottom of the periodic table would have
   (1) electrons in low energy levels only and low atomic weight.
   (2) electrons in high energy levels and low atomic weight.
   (3) electrons in high energy levels and high atomic weight.
   (4) one energy level and high atomic weight.
   (5) no energy levels and low atomic weight.

10. Organic differs from inorganic in that the organic
    (1) contains only one distinguishable phase.
    (2) contains no specific elements.
    (3) is uniform.
    (4) deals with carbon compounds.
    (5) deals with naturally occurring compounds.

11. In the following formulas, the symbol "C" indicates carbon. Which formulas represent organic compounds?
    a. H_2O b. C_2H_2 c. H_2O_2 d. $C_6H_{12}O_6$
    (1) a only   (4) b and d
    (2) b only   (5) d only
    (3) a and c

12. Which is the most likely reason why organic and inorganic chemistry have become separate studies?
    (1) Fights among chemists
    (2) Lack of lab space
    (3) Chemical knowledge is too great for one person to master it all
    (4) Salaries are better for chemists who specialize
    (5) Schools prefer organic chemists

13. The study of matter is based on
    (1) evaluating properties of one element.
    (2) evaluating types and abilities of properties of one element.
    (3) the ability to transfer through the sharing of electrons.
    (4) the ability to transfer through the sharing of neutrons.
    (5) elements that cannot bond.

14. The sharing of electrons or transfer of electrons is called
    (1) bonding.   (4) effect of gravity.
    (2) transference.   (5) kinetic flow.
    (3) boiling.

15. Matter is group-based on its ability to
    (1) react with itself in the presence of other elements.
    (2) be studied.
    (3) react and combine with other elements.
    (4) change.
    (5) bond irreversibly with other elements.

16. Bonding is the process by which atoms
    (1) behave in the presence of heat.
    (2) only transfer electrons.
    (3) only share electrons.
    (4) either share or transfer electrons.
    (5) share and transfer properties.

17. When one balances a chemical equation, they are showing
    (1) combination of compounds.
    (2) equilibrium.
    (3) oxidation and reaction rates.
    (4) reactions between different elements.
    (5) All of the above.

18. Equilibrium can be expressed as the point at which
    (1) all the chemicals present stop reacting.
    (2) the chemicals start to react.
    (3) the chemical reactants are used up.
    (4) the products react together at the same rate as the reactants.
    (5) the reactants are chemically reacting at maximum velocity.

19. For a chemical equilibrium involving gaseous reactants and products, an increase in pressure
    (1) always displaces the equilibrium in the direction in which the number of molecules decrease.
    (2) displaces the equilibrium to form more of the reactants.
    (3) displaces the equilibrium to form more of the products.
    (4) has no effect on the equilibrium.
    (5) leads to extremely rapid formation of reactant molecules.

20. Formulas can be combined to show the composition of
    (1) compounds.   (4) reactions.
    (2) atomic numbers.   (5) oxidation and reduction rates.
    (3) symbols.

21. A chemical formula is constructed by correctly combining
    (1) compounds.   (4) equilibrium.
    (2) elements.   (5) symbols and atomic numbers.
    (3) symbols.

22. Every element has its own
    (1) symbol.
    (2) color.
    (3) emblem.
    (4) insignia.
    (5) six-digit serial number.

23. Chemistry is a study that
    (1) only deals with mixing chemicals.
    (2) only shows reactions.
    (3) only relates to electrons and protons.
    (4) deals with everyday life.
    (5) does not affect biology.

B. STRUCTURE OF MATTER

Matter is anything that occupies space and has mass. Matter resists changes in motion. It takes force to accelerate matter. There are four states of matter — solid, liquid, gas, and a fourth state called the plasma state. This state only exists at extremely high temperatures, such as those found on the sun. Plasma consists of high-energy, electrically charged particles. Plasma is created when a fluorescent lamp is turned on. Most of the matter in the universe is in the plasma state.

The structure of matter depends on the number and types of atoms that combine or react to form the matter. Matter is measured by the force with which gravity pulls on the mass toward the center of the earth. Matter can also be measured by its capacity for doing work, or the energy that it contains. This energy can be either activation, potential, or kinetic energy. Activation energy is that energy necessary to start a reaction. Potential energy is stored energy, while kinetic energy is the energy that matter possesses due to motion.

It can be shown experimentally that potential energy can be transformed into kinetic energy without any energy loss. This is an illustration of the Law of Conservation of Matter or Energy, which states that under ordinary conditions, matter or energy can neither be created nor destroyed but can be converted from one form to another.

One method of classifying matter is to find out if it is a substance or a mixture of substances. If a substance is composed of only one kind of atom, it is an element. If the substance is composed of two or more kinds of atoms, the matter can be a mixture or a compound, depending on how the atoms are joined and react to each other under normal conditions.

Mixtures do not follow the law of definite proportions, which means that the two substances can be mixed in almost any proportion. Thus, the properties of a mixture vary with composition. If the substances in a mixture are spread out evenly, it is considered to be a homogeneous mixture. If the substances in a mixture are not spread out evenly, it is considered to be a heterogeneous mixture. Vinegar is a homogeneous mixture as the substances are spread out evenly throughout. A homogeneous mixture can be called a solution. Other solutions include seawater, soft drinks, tea, or milk.

A suspension is a heterogeneous mixture in which the particles are large enough to be seen by a microscope or the eye. These particles are affected by gravity and may settle out of the mixture. The particles can be temporarily suspended again by shaking. The mixing of water and pepper is an example of a suspension. Stirring up the bottom of a river will produce a suspension. With time, the action of gravity on the sand and soil will cause the particles to settle back to the bottom of the river.

If particles of a mixture are larger than those found in a solution, yet smaller than particles found in a suspension, the mixture is referred to as a colloid. Colloidal particles appear to be evenly distributed and they will not settle out. The small size of the particles causes gravity to have less of an effect. Thus, there is less possibility of settling out caused by gravity.

All matter can be identified as having either physical or chemical properties. A physical property is a characteristic of matter that can be observed without changing the makeup of the substance. Boiling points and freezing points are examples of physical properties. Other physical properties are color, odor, hardness, density, and the ability to conduct heat or electricity. Physical properties can be used to separate mixtures. A mixture of iron and sand can be separated by a magnet. Iron is magnetic. Sand is not, and thus they can be separated with ease.

A physical change occurs when matter changes in size, shape, color, or state. A physical change does not change the chemical composition of a substance. When a glass breaks, the size and shape of the glass change, but the chemical makeup remains the same no matter in how many pieces the glass might exist.

A chemical property is a characteristic that determines how a substance reacts to form other substances. Chemical properties are determined by chemical changes. When a chemical change occurs, the substance seldom will, if ever, return to its original state. For example, iron will rust in the presence of water and oxygen. Rusting is an example of the chemical property known as corrosion. Corrosion occurs when metals are destroyed as they combine chemically with other substances.

In a chemical change, a substance is changed to a new substance which has different properties. Chemical changes may release thermal energy, light, or electricity. Some chemical changes need energy. All changes, chemical and physical, involve an energy change of some kind. Many compounds are formed from elements by chemical changes. In the same respect, many compounds are broken down by a chemical change.

When wood burns, heat is given off and a small amount of ashes is left. The substance of the wood has changed. Wood is made of carbon, hydrogen, and oxygen. When wood burns, the elements unite with atmospheric oxygen resulting in the formation of carbon dioxide and water. Also, carbon is the element of the ash substance that remains. This is a chemical change as energy is used to bring about the change and heat (an energy form) is given off; other compounds have been formed and the elements can never return to the state of wood (unless they again become integrated into the growth of a tree).

☞ Drill: Structure of Matter

DIRECTIONS: Carefully read and answer each of the following questions which are based on the information which you have just read.

24. Anything that takes up space, has mass, and resists change is called
    (1) a solid.   (4) matter.
    (2) a liquid.   (5) energy.
    (3) plasma.

25. The particles of a compound are most strongly held together when it is in the state of a
    (1) solid.   (4) plasma.
    (2) liquid.   (5) gel.
    (3) gas.

26. A scientist discovers a substance that possesses a high temperature under normal conditions. The substance is most likely
    (1) liquid.   (4) gas.
    (2) plasma.   (5) not matter.
    (3) solid.

27. Matter can be measured
    (1) by its capacity to do work.
    (2) by the energy that it could contain.
    (3) by the energy that it did contain.
    (4) by its constant movement.
    (5) by counting the number of atoms which make up the matter.

28. Activation energy is
    (1) the energy necessary to move an object.
    (2) the energy necessary to cause motion.
    (3) the energy that measures an activity.
    (4) the energy necessary to start a reaction.
    (5) the energy needed to keep a reaction under control.

29. Potential energy is possessed by
    (1) a book on a high shelf.   (4) an electric generator.
    (2) a bullet in motion.   (5) X-rays.
    (3) a hot wire.

30. A substance which cannot be further decomposed by ordinary chemi-
    cal means is
    (1) water.   (4) copper.
    (2) air.   (5) wood.
    (3) sugar.

31. When 30 grams of mercury are heated with oxygen, the mercury unites
    with 3 grams of oxygen to form 33 grams of mercuric oxide. This
    reaction illustrates
    (1) the fact that the elements always combine.
    (2) a nuclear transformation.
    (3) the Law of Conservation of Matter.
    (4) the formation of mixtures.
    (5) the reduction of mercury to mercuric oxide.

32. The Law of Conservation of Energy states that
    (1) either energy or mass may be destroyed.
    (2) energy may neither be created nor destroyed.
    (3) energy can be converted to only one form.
    (4) energy may either be created or destroyed.
    (5) energy must be maintained in one form.

33. A substance composed of two or more elements that are chemically united is called
    (1) an isotope.
    (2) a compound.
    (3) an element.
    (4) a mixture.
    (5) a solution.

34. A can of baking powder carries the ingredient statement, "cornstarch, sodium bicarbonate, calcium acid phosphate, and sodium aluminum sulfate." This baking powder is
    (1) a compound.
    (2) a mixture.
    (3) a mixture or a compound.
    (4) a mixture or an atom.
    (5) a complex element.

35. Which one of the following is not an element?
    (1) Aluminum
    (2) Water
    (3) Tin
    (4) Oxygen
    (5) Gold

36. All solutions
    (1) contain water.
    (2) are liquids.
    (3) contain dissolved molecules.
    (4) are heterogeneous.
    (5) contain electrolytes.

37. If a sample of a material contains oxygenated water and dissolved salt, the sample is what type of mixture?
    (1) A compound
    (2) A substance
    (3) An element
    (4) A proportional mixture
    (5) Homogeneous

38. A heterogeneous mixture is
    I.   a type of matter
    II. a pure substance
    III. a type of mixture
    IV. a solution

    (1) I, II, III, IV
    (2) I, III, IV
    (3) I only
    (4) III, IV
    (5) I, III

39. A certain material contains three kinds of matter and has properties that vary from one point in the material to another. The material should be classified as
    (1) an element.
    (2) a mixture.
    (3) a liquid.
    (4) a solid.
    (5) a compound.

40. Suspensions can be reproduced by
    (1) shaking.
    (2) mixing.
    (3) stirring.
    (4) All of the above.
    (5) None of the above.

41. A suspension will have solid particles to settle out after a period of time due to
    (1) chemical action.
    (2) heat.
    (3) gravity.
    (4) continuous agitation during settling.
    (5) a change in the solubility of the particles.

42. If particles can be suspended for a short period of time by stirring, the mixture is called a
    (1) suspension.
    (2) colloid.
    (3) compound.
    (4) chemical solution.
    (5) whirlpool.

43. A dessert that is a colloid is
    (1) pie.
    (2) gelatin.
    (3) pudding.
    (4) ice cream.
    (5) chocolate cake.

44. A mixture is noted to have suspended particles evenly dispersed throughout and there is no evidence of sedimentation. This mixture is referred to as a
    (1) suspension.
    (2) homogeneous compound.
    (3) mixture.
    (4) colloid.
    (5) solution.

45. The properties that can be used to separate mixtures are
    (1) chemical.
    (2) acid.
    (3) alkaline.
    (4) physical.
    (5) unstable.

46. The ability to conduct electricity is
    (1) a chemical property.
    (2) a physical change.
    (3) a chemical change.
    (4) a physical property.
    (5) a biological property only.

47. A physical property is
    (1) an observable fact.
    (2) a characteristic of matter that can be observed without changing the makeup of the substance.
    (3) a characteristic of matter that cannot be observed without changing the makeup of the substance.
    (4) not useful for separating two substances.
    (5) based on the physical shape of the substance being analyzed.

48. Which of the following involves a physical change?
    (1) The melting of wax
    (2) The corroding of iron
    (3) The breaking of glass
    (4) The burning of wood
    (5) The breaking of bonds between sodium and chloride in table salt

49. A student observes that when a solid is heated in contact with air and remains hot, a liquid is formed. He may reasonably conclude that
    (1) a chemical change took place.
    (2) a physical change took place.
    (3) both physical and chemical changes took place.
    (4) no decision can be made concerning the change that occurred from this single observation.
    (5) the air is causing the liquid to remain hot.

50. Jon watches a match burn. Which of the following is true?
    (1) This is a chemical change because chemical properties of the match are unchanged.
    (2) This is a chemical change because burning is a chemical reaction.
    (3) This is a physical change because chemical properties of the match are unchanged.
    (4) This is neither a chemical nor a physical change.
    (5) This is both a chemical and physical change.

51. Chemical action may involve all of the following except
    (1) combining of atoms of the elements to form a molecule.
    (2) separation of the molecules in a mixture.
    (3) breaking down compounds into elements.
    (4) reacting a compound and an element to form an element and a new compound.
    (5) None of the above.

52. All chemical changes involve
    (1) a decreased stability in a solution.
    (2) an increased stability in a solution.
    (3) breaking of bonds and forming new ones.
    (4) formation of ion reactants.
    (5) a change of state.

53. When a chemical change takes place, a new _____ is always formed.
    (1) substance
    (2) element
    (3) mixture
    (4) solution
    (5) colloid

54. When an ice cube melts to form water, this change is an example of
    (1) a chemical change, because water is not the same material as ice.
    (2) a chemical change, because heat is needed to make it happen.
    (3) a physical change.
    (4) forming a solution.
    (5) creating a gas.

55. Which of the following involves a chemical change?
    (1) The rusting of iron
    (2) The breaking of glass
    (3) The evaporation of water
    (4) The melting of ice
    (5) An ice cube floating in a glass of water

56. A chemical change may involve all of the following except
    (1) combining of atoms of elements to form compounds.
    (2) the separation of the molecules in a mixture.
    (3) breaking down of compounds into elements.
    (4) reacting a compound and an element to form a new compound and a new element.
    (5) burning a piece of paper.

57. An example of a chemical change is
    (1) breaking of a glass bottle.
    (2) sawing of a piece of wood.
    (3) burning of wood.
    (4) melting of an ice cube.
    (5) crushing a boulder into pebbles.

58. In a chemical reaction like burning wood,
    (1) heat is given off.
    (4) heat is a useless by-product.
    (2) no heat is given off.
    (5) oxygen is liberated.
    (3) heat is absorbed.

C. SIMPLE EQUATIONS SHOWING STRUCTURE OF MATTER

Matter can be identified not only by name, but by the way the element fits together with other elements to form matter. It is important for one to know if the proposed combination actually exists. For example, no chemist has ever been able to prepare hydrogen nitrate. Additionally, in making combinations, one must have a positive and a negative component. Generally speaking, metals are positive components, while nonmetals are negative components (with the exception of ammonia and radicals). When elements combine in varying proportions, prefixes are used for the naming of the compound and for formula writing. Mono- means one, bi- or di- means two, tri- means three, tetra- means four, pent- means five, and so on. Common suffixes and meanings are -ide (for naming monatomic anions), -ous (for the ion with the lower charge), and -ic (for the ion with the higher charge).

☞ Drill: Simple Equations Showing Structure of Matter

DIRECTIONS: Carefully read and answer each of the following questions which are based on the information which you have just read.

59. A scientist combines hydrogen, oxygen, and sodium to make a compound. Which of these four substances is the name of the compound?
    (1) Hydrogen
    (4) Sodium
    (2) Lye
    (5) Table salt
    (3) Oxygen

60. The formula for ferrous chloride or iron (II) chloride is
    (1) $FeCl_2$
    (4) $2FeCl$
    (2) $2FeCl_2$
    (5) $FeCl$
    (3) Fe_2Cl

61. When hydrogen is burned with oxygen, water is produced. This can be written

(1) $H_2 + O_2 \rightarrow HO$
(2) $H_2 + O \rightarrow H_2O$
(3) $2H + O_2 \rightarrow HO$
(4) $H_2 + O \rightarrow H_3O$
(5) $2H_2 + O_2 \rightarrow 2H_2O$

62. Which of the following is classified as a monatomic element?
(1) Water
(2) Milk
(3) Benzene
(4) Helium
(5) Bicarbonate

D. PERIODICITY OF ELEMENTS

The latter half of the 19th century brought about the updating of the Periodic Law: the properties of the elements are periodic functions of their atomic numbers. Atomic numbers represent the number of protons and also the number of electrons in a neutral atom. The electron structures of the atoms provide information showing the properties of the elements. Vertical columns represent the chemical families while horizontal columns represent the period or row. Proceeding across a row, the ability to hold electrons decreases. For example, lithium is the most metallic while fluorine is the least metallic. Study the Periodic Table which appears in the appendix of this book.

Some atoms tend to join with other atoms, while others will show no tendency to join with like atoms or like elements. The results of this tendency or attraction of the atoms involved in joining is called a chemical bond. When atoms combine to form new molecules, there is a shifting or transfer of valence electrons found in the outer shell of each atom. This usually results in the completing of outer shells by each atom. A more stable compound or form is achieved by the gaining, losing, or sharing of pairs of electrons. In forming chemical bonds, there is a release of energy or an absorption of energy. The bonds can be ionic, covalent, or metallic.

The kinetic model explains the forces between molecules and the energy they possess in three basic assumptions:

1. All matter is composed of extremely small particles.

2. The particles making up all matter are in constant motion.

3. When these particles collide with each other or with the walls of the container, there is no loss of energy.

☞ Drill: Periodicity of Elements

DIRECTIONS: Carefully read and answer each of the following questions which are based on the information which you have just read.

63. Metallic ions are _____ their corresponding atoms.
    (1) smaller than   (4) heavier than
    (2) the same size as   (5) darker in color than
    (3) larger than

64. In a horizontal (series) row, the ionization energy tends to _____ with increasing atomic number.
    (1) increase   (4) increase in frequency
    (2) decrease   (5) become kinetic
    (3) remain constant

65. Molecular mass and formula mass are similar because both represent the mass of the smallest
    (1) atom that makes up the element.
    (2) element that combines to form a molecule.
    (3) unit that makes up a compound.
    (4) ion that makes up an atom.
    (5) formula that makes up an equation.

66. The tendency or attraction of the atoms involved in joining is called a(n)
    (1) covalent bond.   (4) stable bond.
    (2) metallic bond.   (5) ionic bond.
    (3) chemical bond.

67. A more stable compound is achieved when atoms
    (1) gain electrons to fill their outer shell.
    (2) share pairs of electrons.
    (3) absorb energy.
    (4) Both 1 and 2.
    (5) 1, 2, and 3.

68. When an ionic bond occurs between two atoms,
    (1) the forces of repulsion are greater than the forces of attraction.
    (2) a pair of electrons join or are simultaneously attracted.
    (3) an increase in energy results.

(4)   the atoms become unstable.

(5)   two cations are attracted and bond together.

69.   The kinetic model implies that oxygen molecules would have _____ average kinetic energy than/as hydrogen molecules at the same temperature.

(1)   higher   (4)   not the same

(2)   the same   (5)   sixteen times the

(3)   lower

70.   According to the kinetic model, matter is not made of

(1)   atoms.

(2)   extremely small particles.

(3)   atoms in constant motion.

(4)   particles moving without collisions.

(5)   atoms that do not lose energy during rebounding.

71.   Under ideal gas circumstances, when atoms collide together

(1)   there is no energy loss.

(2)   there is an energy gain.

(3)   there is energy exchanged.

(4)   there is no source of comparison.

(5)   they will stick together.

E. BEHAVIOR OF MATTER

The behavior and classification of matter is dependent upon the electron attraction and interaction of electrons forming the matter. When atoms react with one another, it is the electrons that are involved in bonding, whether it be ion or covalent.

All reactions need to receive a certain amount of energy before they can start. The amount of energy needed or received to start the chemical reaction is called activation energy. Some reactions require so little energy that it can be absorbed from the surroundings. This is called a spontaneous reaction which takes place with so little energy that it seems as if no energy was needed. A reaction that gives off energy is called an exothermic reaction. A reaction that absorbs energy is called an endothermic reaction. Combustion is a decomposition reaction. A catalyst can be added to a chemical reaction to control the reaction rate.

ACIDS

Acid properties are:

1. Water solutions of acids conduct electricity.

2. Acids will react actively with metals.

3. Acids will change blue litmus to pink.

4. Acids will react with bases resulting in both a loss of water and leaving a salt (neutralization).

5. Weak acid solutions taste sour.

6. Acids react with carbonates to release carbon dioxide.

BASES

Bases properties are:

1. Bases are conductors of electricity in strong solutions.

2. Bases change red litmus paper blue.

3. Bases react with acids to neutralize each other and to form a salt and water.

4. Bases react with fats to form a class of compounds called soaps.

5. Bases feel slippery and strong solutions are caustic to the skin.

SALTS

A salt is an ionic compound containing positive ions other than hydrogen and a negative ion other than hydroxide ions. It is usually formed by neutralization when certain acids and bases are combined and form water and salt as the products.

A formula is a sort of road map, or a detailed description, of how something is organized or produced. A formula will not reveal the hidden structures of substances. In some reactions, no product is formed at completion, or reactants and products may react both ways. The reaction is said to have reached equilibrium when the rate of the forward reaction is equal to the rate of the reverse reaction. Factors that affect chemical equilibrium are changing concentration, temperature, and pressure.

Reactions that do not occur spontaneously can be forced by an external supply of energy. This is called an electrolytic reaction. Many chemicals and useful products are produced in this manner. Electroplating, electrolysis of water or salts, and the cathode functioning of a battery all are examples of electro-chemistry.

Simple electrochemical cells, in which electrons produced by the oxidation of zinc atoms are transferred through an external circuit into a copper solution, are called galvanic cells or voltaic cells. All electrochemical cells have the same general components: an oxidation half-cell, a reduction half-cell, and a means of separation so that the electrons produced by the oxidation reaction can be supplied through an external circuit into the reduction reaction. The voltage of the cell is the net voltage or potential voltage of two half-cell reactions. Lead storage cells contain a series of lead grids separated by an insulating material. The grids are alternately filled with spongy lead and lead dioxide that compose what are called dry cells. As long as the grids remain intact, the cell will deliver about two volts of electric current.

☞ Drill: Behavior of Matter

DIRECTIONS: Carefully read and answer each of the following questions which are based on the information which you have just read.

72. The behavior of matter is dependent upon
    (1)   the proton attraction.   (4)   the ion attraction.
    (2)   the neutron attraction.   (5)   covalent interactions.
    (3)   the electron attraction.

73. The addition of a catalyst to a reaction
    (1)   changes the chemicals.
    (2)   changes the temperature.
    (3)   changes the rate of reaction.
    (4)   changes the ingredients of the reaction.
    (5)   can make previously impossible reactions work.

74. In a(n) _____ reaction, the products are lower in energy than the reactants.
    (1)   exothermic   (4)   chemothermic
    (2)   endothermic   (5)   mesothermic
    (3)   isothermica

75. Which of the following reactions is considered to be spontaneous?
    (1)   The conversion of copper to gold
    (2)   The conversion of water to steam
    (3)   The conversion of carbon dioxide to methane
    (4)   The conversion of hydrogen and oxygen to form water
    (5)   The conversion of iron to its oxide

76. Combustion is a(n)
    (1) reaction where things are broken down to products with less potential energy.
    (2) reaction where things are combined together to form a more complex product.
    (3) endothermic reaction.
    (4) exothermic reaction.
    (5) reaction characterized by lack of energy transfer.

77. A lemon has a sour taste because
    (1) all fruits are sour.
    (2) it contains a base.
    (3) it contains an acid.
    (4) it does not contain sugar.
    (5) carbon dioxide is being released.

78. Soap has as an ingredient what kind of a substance?
    (1) Acid
    (2) Base
    (3) Salt
    (4) Neutralized ion
    (5) Caustic

79. A student determines that an unknown substance conducts electricity, tastes sour, and reacts with another substance to produce a salt. Most likely, the substance is a
    (1) base.
    (2) acid.
    (3) catalyst.
    (4) solution.
    (5) salt.

80. A salt derived from a strong base and a weak acid will undergo hydrolysis and give a solution that will be
    (1) basic.
    (2) acidic.
    (3) neutral.
    (4) volatile.
    (5) caustic.

81. A formula will
    (1) describe the organization and composition of a substance.
    (2) tell the rate of the chemical reaction.
    (3) construct hidden structures.
    (4) show when equilibrium is reached.
    (5) describe the physical properties of each element involved.

82. Equilibrium can be expressed as the point at which
    (1) all the chemicals present stop reacting.
    (2) the chemicals start reacting.

(3) the chemical reactants are used up.
(4) the products react together at the same rate as the reactants.
(5) the number of reactant molecules equals the number of product molecules.

83. In a chemical reaction at equilibrium, which of the following changes would always increase the concentration of the product?
(1) Add a catalyst
(2) Increase pressure
(3) Increase temperature
(4) Increase concentration of reactant
(5) Decrease pressure

84. Which of the following objects are made by the process of electroplating?
I. silver-plated spoon
II. chromium-plated automobile bumper
III. radioactive carbon

(1) I, II, III   (4) II only
(2) II, III   (5) I, II
(3) I only

85. Which one of the following metals does not undergo corrosion and thus does not need to be electroplated?
(1) iron   (4) nickel
(2) aluminum   (5) gold
(3) copper

86. A galvanic cell has a porous barrier between the half-cell on the left and the half-cell on the right in order to
(1) halt the movement of ions.
(2) allow the two solutions to mix completely.
(3) preserve the strong acid nature of the solutions.
(4) allow movement of ions for preserving neutrality.
(5) measure the quantity of current.

87. A galvanic cell
(1) produces an electrical current that can be used to perform work.
(2) is very different from a flashlight battery.
(3) converts chemical energy to electrical energy.
(4) 1, 2, and 3
(5) 1 and 3

F. SOLUTIONS

Forces of attraction between particles produce a solution. One must mix a solute and a solvent to produce a solution. The particles making up each have certain forces of attraction that produce bonds. The bonds produced by these forces of attraction will determine the solubility of the solute. Temperature also affects the solubility of a solution. If the solution is made of gases, the solubility will be affected by pressure. Pressure does not affect the solubility of solids and liquids. If no more solute can be dissolved in the solvent, the solution is said to be saturated. In an unsaturated solution, more solute can be added to the solvent, while in a supersaturated solution, the solution is holding more dissolved solute than normal at that given temperature.

Matter exists as a substance or a mixture. If a substance is made of only one kind of atom, it is an element. If it is made of two or more kinds of atoms in a definite grouping, it is a compound. A compound always occurs in a definite composition based on the Law of Definite Composition, which states, "A compound is composed of two or more elements chemically combined in a definite ratio by weight." Compounds always have a fixed composition and will be classified as ionic or covalent depending on the type of bonding that occurs when the atoms are combined. The ability to combine is dependent upon the valence of the atom or element. An ionic compound contains ionic bonds — a force of attraction between oppositely charged ions. A covalent compound is a compound that is composed of covalent bonds — a bond in which the electrons are shared between atoms. When a compound is formed, the elements or atoms making up the compound lose their properties and take on the properties of the compound formed.

It is important to remember that the gain of electrons is reduction, and the loss of electrons is oxidation. The oxidation number of a bonded atom is the number of electrons gained, lost, or shared in a chemical reaction. The metal elements that lose electrons easily and become positive ions are placed high in the electromotive series.

The metal elements that lose electrons with greater difficulty are placed lower on the periodic chart. The energy required to remove electrons from metallic atoms can be assigned numeral values called electrode potentials. Binary compounds are named by changing the name of the element that has the negative oxidation number to end in -ide.

The rate of the reaction is defined as the quantity of product formed in some stated interval or the rate at which the reaction will take place. The rate of the chemical reaction can be defined in terms of the change in concentration of any species in the reaction with respect to time. The rate of the reaction can be determined by measuring how fast the product is formed after the reactants are mixed, or how many moles are formed per second. Also, increase in temperature will increase frequency of molecular collision and increase rate of reaction. Activation energy is necessary to produce enough energy to break or weaken bonds before new bonds can be formed. Some reactions produce energy in the formation of new compounds or the products have more energy than the reactants (exothermic reactions) while other reactants need a greater amount of energy than the activation energy (endothermic reactions). The study of reaction rate factors is called chemical kinetics.

☞ Drill: Solutions

DIRECTIONS: Carefully read and answer each of the following questions which are based on the information which you have just read.

88. Solution rate of a solid solute dissolving in a liquid solvent may be increased by
    (1) changing the temperature.   (4) All of the above.
    (2) stirring the solution.   (5) None of the above.
    (3) shaking the solution.

89. A solution can be both
    (1) diluted and concentrated simultaneously.
    (2) saturated yet diluted simultaneously.
    (3) saturated and unsaturated simultaneously.
    (4) supersaturated and saturated simultaneously.
    (5) acidic and neutral simultaneously.

90. The solubility of a solute must indicate
    (1) the temperature of the solution.
    (2) the quantity of solute.
    (3) the quantity of solvent.
    (4) All of the above.
    (5) None of the above.

91. The most common solvent is
    (1) alcohol.   (4) an acid.
    (2) benzene.   (5) acetone.
    (3) water.

92. The ability to combine is dependent upon the _____ of the atom or element.
    - (1) valence
    - (2) molecular count
    - (3) atomic number
    - (4) atomic mass
    - (5) proton number

93. The Law of Definite Composition is based on definite composition by
    - (1) weight.
    - (2) volume.
    - (3) density.
    - (4) specific weight.
    - (5) temperature.

94. Which of the following substances are joined by ionic bonds?
    - (1) O_2
    - (2) NaCl
    - (3) formaldehyde
    - (4) Cl_2
    - (5) Na_2

95. The number of bonds formed by an atom is most closely associated with
    - (1) its atomic weight.
    - (2) the number of electrons in the atom.
    - (3) the number of electron shells.
    - (4) the number of electrons in the outer shell.
    - (5) the number of electrons in the innermost shell.

96. A binary compound can be identified by the ____ ending.
    - (1) -ous
    - (2) -ide
    - (3) -ic
    - (4) -ion
    - (5) -ate

97. A reduction reaction always involves the
    - (1) loss of electrons.
    - (2) gain of electrons.
    - (3) addition of oxygen.
    - (4) removal of oxygen.
    - (5) gain of electrons and protons.

98. Which of the following formulas shows a naturally occurring reduction?
    - (1) $Fe^{+2} \rightarrow Fe^{+3} + e-$
    - (2) $Mg \rightarrow Mg^{+2} + 2e-$
    - (3) $Fe^{+2} + e- \rightarrow Fe^{+1}$
    - (4) $Fe^{+3} + e- \rightarrow Fe^{+2}$
    - (5) $Mg + e- \rightarrow Mg^{-1}$

99. An ion with an oxidation number of 3+ can combine with three identical ions, each having an oxidation number of
    (1) 1+   (4) 3-
    (2) 1-   (5) 2+
    (3) 3+

100. In a(n) _____ reaction, the products are lower in energy than the reactants.
    (1) endothermic   (4) exothermic
    (2) moles   (5) kinetic
    (3) chemical

101. When the energy released by the products of a reaction is greater than the energy of activation,
    (1) the reaction stops.
    (2) the reaction is exothermic.
    (3) the reaction always forms products.
    (4) the product is unstable.
    (5) the reaction needs excessive heat to begin.

102. The effect of an increase in temperature on a chemical reaction is to increase the
    (1) energy of activation.
    (2) concentration of reactants.
    (3) frequency of collision.
    (4) potential energy barrier.
    (5) heat of formation.

103. Chemical action may involve all of the following except
    (1) combining of atoms of elements to form a molecule.
    (2) separation of the molecules in a mixture.
    (3) breaking down compounds into elements.
    (4) reacting a compound and an element to form a new compound and a new element.
    (5) combusting a compound to form a new substance.

CHEMISTRY

ANSWER KEY

Drill: Introduction to Chemistry

1.	(3)	7.	(1)	13.	(3)	19.	(1)
2.	(2)	8.	(2)	14.	(1)	20.	(1)
3.	(4)	9.	(3)	15.	(3)	21.	(5)
4.	(2)	10.	(4)	16.	(4)	22.	(1)
5.	(1)	11.	(4)	17.	(5)	23.	(4)
6.	(1)	12.	(3)	18.	(4)		

Drill: Structure of Matter

24.	(4)	33.	(2)	42.	(1)	51.	(2)
25.	(1)	34.	(2)	43.	(2)	52.	(3)
26.	(2)	35.	(2)	44.	(4)	53.	(1)
27.	(1)	36.	(3)	45.	(4)	54.	(3)
28.	(4)	37.	(5)	46.	(4)	55.	(1)
29.	(1)	38.	(5)	47.	(2)	56.	(2)
30.	(4)	39.	(2)	48.	(3)	57.	(3)
31.	(3)	40.	(4)	49.	(2)	58.	(1)
32.	(2)	41.	(3)	50.	(2)		

Drill: Simple Equations Showing Structure of Matter

59.	(2)	60.	(1)	61.	(5)	62.	(4)

Drill: Periodicity of Elements

63.	(1)	66.	(3)	69.	(2)	71.	(1)
64.	(2)	67.	(4)	70.	(4)		
65.	(3)	68.	(2)				

Drill: Behavior of Matter

72.	(3)	76.	(1)	80.	(1)	84.	(5)
73.	(3)	77.	(3)	81.	(1)	85.	(5)
74.	(1)	78.	(2)	82.	(4)	86.	(4)
75.	(5)	79.	(2)	83.	(4)	87.	(5)

Drill: Solutions

88. (4)	92. (1)	96. (2)	100. (4)
89. (2)	93. (4)	97. (2)	101. (2)
90. (4)	94. (2)	98. (4)	102. (3)
91. (3)	95. (4)	99. (2)	103. (2)

IV. EARTH SCIENCE

A. ASPECTS OF EARTH SCIENCE

An understanding of the beginnings of the solar system and the Earth's development is essential to environmental survival. This understanding is filled with curiosity, and may be the price of environmental survival. A lack of curiosity and understanding may signal the environment's demise.

1. THEORIES

Hipparchus, in 150 B.C., determined the distance of the moon based on his calculations on the Earth's diameter. The Greeks added to the study of astronomy by determining that an eclipse was caused by the Earth passing between the sun and the moon, and, the sun was at the center of the solar system. These and other basic studies concerning the sun, moon, planets, galaxies, and solar system have led to questions like, "Does the universe go on forever? Where does it all end? Is space infinite?" It is because of such challenging questions that astronomy has developed into an exact science.

The theory developed by Sir Isaac Newton is in direct opposition to the theory developed by Albert Einstein. Newton stated that a planet moves around the sun because of the gravitational force exerted by the sun. This theory holds true if one is studying the velocities of small objects compared to light. Einstein's theory of relativity states that the planet chooses the shortest possible path throughout the four-dimensional world which is defined by the presence of the sun. According to this theory, if you left home and walked in a straight line, you would eventually return home. Both these theories were inventions by human minds and have been used to create many of our scientific explanations (theories). New theories will show weaknesses and limitations to each theory.

Most scientists tend to believe the theory stating the solar system probably developed as a nebula (cloud of gas and dust) that once swirled around the sun and slowly flattened out. Sections of the cloud began to spin like eddies in a stream, collecting gases and dust and causing the sections to grow and form planets. They slowly developed into spinning planets that now travel around the sun.

The Earth's possession of an atmosphere is a strong point against the theory that any of the planets in the solar system originated from some catastrophic accident such as a near-collision between another sun and ours.

This theory, widely known as the Big Bang Theory, generally states that there was a collision between the sun and an exploding star. Most of the material lost from this collision escaped into space, and based on the size of the gaseous mass and its gravitational attraction to the sun, established our solar system. Temperature factors and the study of gravity are used to dispel the collision theory sometimes referred to as the Big Bang Theory.

In the early 1700s, Abraham Werner presented his theory that an ocean once covered the Earth. The chemicals in the water slowly settled to the bottom of the water where they formed granite and other forms of rock layers. The Earth was completely formed with the settling of the water and no other changes occurred. All life, according to Werner, began with the settling of the water and the formation of the Earth.

The Hutton Theory of 1785 claimed that the Earth was gradually changing and would continue to change in the same ways. According to Hutton, these changes could be used to explain the past. He died before he could get other scientists to accept his ideas, yet after his death and publication of his ideas, they became a leading guide for the geological thinkers.

The Creation Theory with which we are most familiar is that given in the first chapters of Genesis. Various attempts have been made to work out the date of the creation on the basis of the data given in the Bible and the date of creation has been set at 3760 B.C. The creation, as explained in Genesis, is accepted by some people as the formation of the Earth and the origin of life.

Battle lines have been drawn. One theorist will research and develop a possible strategy for solving the age-old question, only for another theorist to come along and find a flaw in that research and then develop a new theory. Thus new theories are constantly developed. Each theory developed is viewed in a manner to gain an understanding of the information presented pertaining to the Earth's formation for the purpose of survival and prosperity of the universe.

2. SOLAR SYSTEM

The solar system includes the sun, nine planets with their moons, asteroids, meteoroids, comets, interplanetary dust, and interplanetary plasma that is circular in shape. The sun is the center of the solar system with a mass 750 times greater than that of all of the planets combined. The planets rotate around the sun with Mercury being the closest to and Pluto being the farthest from the sun. The terrestrial (earth-like) planets — Mercury, Venus, Mars, and the Earth — are composed chiefly of iron and rock. These planets are smallest in comparison to the four largest planets, Jupiter, Saturn, Uranus, and Neptune, which are called the Major planets. They are composed chiefly of hydrogen, helium, ammonia, and methane. Pluto is believed to be less than one-fifth the size of Earth, which makes it smaller than our moon.

Asteroids or planetoids are small, irregularly-shaped objects orbiting between Jupiter and Mars. Meteoroids are chunks of iron resulting from collisions between asteroids. Comets are round heads consisting of dust particles mixed with frozen water, frozen methane, and frozen ammonia, and a tail made of dust and gases escaping from the head.

3. METEORS AND METEORITES

A meteor is a metallic or stony mass belonging to the solar system that is hurtled into the Earth's atmosphere. The meteor cannot be seen until it enters the atmosphere, at which time the friction with the air makes it glow and shine for only a few seconds as it falls to the Earth. Thus, it is called a falling, or shooting, star.

Meteorites seldom do damage, yet they have devastating potentiality. Meteorites are pieces of extraterrestrial matter that are studied to determine the origins of the universe and the solar system. Meteorites make up only a tiny fraction of the matter falling into the Earth's atmosphere from space. They sometimes explode into fragments with a noise that can be heard for many miles when they strike the surface of the Earth.

4. STARS

When you look at the sky, you see only a tiny part of the universe consisting mainly of stars, clouds of dust, and the solar system. Astronomers study the brightness and color of the stars. Brightness indicates the mass of the stars, while the color indicates the temperature of the star's surface. The distance is difficult to determine as most stars are so far away. Stars have been studied as early as 3000 B.C.; yet, they still remain a mystery.

Stars and star groupings (constellations) are used as compasses at night, as a navigational aid, as a basis for astrology, for study, and for viewing at the planetarium. What appears as movement of the stars and the nearly 80 constellations is actually the spinning and placement of the Earth. Seasonally and yearly, the constellations that can be seen will differ, causing the sky to appear to move west during the year.

5. GALAXIES

Galaxies are groups or systems of stars located millions to billions of lightyears from Earth. Sometimes called stellar universes, galaxies include billions of stars, and are classified as to their appearance. Irregular systems have no special form or symmetry. The spiral system resembles a large pinwheel with arms extending from the dense central core. Elliptical systems appear round without the spiral arms.

Our solar system is in the Milky Way Galaxy. The Milky Way is a spiral galaxy and is held together by gravity. It slowly rotates, with its spiral arms turning once in about 200 million years. The Milky Way contains clouds of gas, dust, and millions or billions of star clusters which form their own distinct patterns. Bands of stars making-up the spiral arms of our galaxy can be seen in the night sky. The Andromeda Nebula Galaxy, first studied in 1612, resembles the Milky Way. It is the nearest galaxy that northern hemisphere observers can see.

In the past few decades, radio astronomy has played a great role in studying celestial objects. In 1959, the first quasar was discovered. It was noticed that some sources of celestial radio waves appeared to be point-like — "quasi-stellar" — instead of looking like radio waves emitted by galaxies. These "quasi-stellar radio sources," or quasars as they are known, give off radio waves and light at a rate over 100,000 billion times as fast as the sun. Quasars appear to be far smaller than ordinary galaxies, and are believed by some astronomers to be the core of violently exploding galaxies. Quasars appear to be among the most distant objects in the universe. Today, astronomers have identified over 1,000 quasars.

☞ Drill: Aspects of Earth Science

DIRECTIONS: Carefully read and answer each of the following questions which are based on the information which you have just read.

1. When the Earth passes between the sun and the moon, this causes the occurrence of a(n)
    (1) phase.
    (2) ellipse.
    (3) darkness.
    (4) eclipse.
    (5) None of the above.

2. The first to study astronomy was/were

(1) Hipparchus.   (4) Plato.

(2) Greeks.   (5) All of the above.

(3) Aristotle.

3. The survival of planet Earth could possibly be based on the study of the
    (1) eclipse occurrences.
    (2) sun and moon relationships.
    (3) solar system.
    (4) galaxies.
    (5) the moon.

4. A theory can be defined as
    (1) an educated guess.
    (2) an invention of the human mind.
    (3) a possible idea that would lead to scientific explanation.
    (4) a scientific explanation.
    (5) a fact.

5. "Planets move around the sun because of the gravitational force exerted by the sun" is part of which scientist's theory?
    (1) Aristotle   (4) Hipparchus
    (2) Newton   (5) Copernicus
    (3) Einstein

6. A planet chooses its shortest path through a four-dimensional world which is defined by the presence of the sun would be the theory of which scientist?
    (1) Aristotle   (4) Hipparchus
    (2) Newton   (5) Copernicus
    (3) Einstein

7. Possibly, a planet could have begun as
    (1) a nebula.
    (2) eddies.
    (3) a collection of gases.
    (4) a spinning dust collection.
    (5) a galaxy

8. The difference between a nebula and an eddy would be their
    (1) shape.
    (2) movement.

(3)   shape and movement.

(4)   type of gas forming mass.

(5)   None of the above.

9.   The Big Bang Theory describes a collision between an exploding star and (the)

(1)   solar system.   (4)   lost terrestrial material.

(2)   a galaxy.   (5)   sun.

(3)   another planet.

10.   The factors that dispel the collision theory are

(1)   escape of dust and gases.

(2)   the study of gravity and speed the planets are traveling.

(3)   temperature and gaseous mass.

(4)   temperature and Earth's atmosphere.

(5)   All of the above.

11.   What was formed from the masses that were knocked loose at the time of the collision?

(1)   Planets   (4)   Other stars

(2)   Solar system   (5)   Moons

(3)   Sun

12.   The type of rock formed on the ocean's floor is

(1)   granite.   (4)   marble.

(2)   limestone.   (5)   conglomerate.

(3)   phosphate.

13.   _____ developed the theory stating that the ocean covered the entire Earth.

(1)   Benjamin Warner   (4)   Alexander Bell

(2)   Joseph Copernicus   (5)   None of the above.

(3)   Abraham Werner

14.   The theory that all life began with the settling of the water was formulated in the

(1)   1940s.   (4)   1800s.

(2)   1850s   (5)   1700s.

(3)   1650s.

15.   According to Hutton, changes would be explained by the

(1) past.

(4) social attitudes.

(2) present.

(5) None of the above.

(3) future.

16. Hutton's theory stated
    (1) how to explain the past.
    (2) how the sun and moon were the same.
    (3) how the Earth was gradually changing and would cease the gradual changing.
    (4) how the Earth was gradually changing and would continue to change in the same ways.
    (5) that the Earth is not changing.

17. Hutton _____ before he was able to get his fellow scientists to accept his ideas.
    (1) left the scientific field
    (4) disappeared
    (2) was institutionalized
    (5) quit
    (3) died

18. The Creation Theory is based on the
    (1) findings on the bottom of the ocean.
    (2) first chapter of Genesis.
    (3) first chapter of Matthew.
    (4) first happenings on Earth.
    (5) Adam and Eve.

19. According to the Creation Theory, the beginning of the Earth was
    (1) 1796 B.C.
    (4) 2796 B.C.
    (2) 3706 B.C.
    (5) 1 B.C.
    (3) 3760 B.C.

20. Various attempts have been made to establish the correct order of beginnings based on
    (1) data in the Bible.
    (4) dates in the Koran.
    (2) data in the Koran.
    (5) data and dates in the Koran.
    (3) dates in the Bible.

21. Theories are developed for the purpose of
    (1) further discussion and experimentation.
    (2) gaining an understanding of information for survival.
    (3) momentary gains.

(4)   solving world peace.

(5)   settling disputes.

22.   The major battle is
    (1)   which strategy is most correct.
    (2)   which research is best developed.
    (3)   which theory is best presented.
    (4)   which strategy solves the problem.
    (5)   None of the above.

23.   When considering evolution and change, survival and prosperity of the universe is the basis for
    (1)   all theories.   (4)   all debates.
    (2)   all experimentations.   (5)   All of the above.
    (3)   all research.

24.   Galaxies are groups or systems of
    (1)   moons.   (4)   rockets.
    (2)   stars.   (5)   asteroids.
    (3)   planets.

25.   The Earth is a planet in the galaxy called the
    (1)   Quasar.   (4)   Solar System.
    (2)   Orion.   (5)   Milky Way.
    (3)   Nebula.

26.   Galaxies are located _____ of light years from the Earth.
    (1)   hundreds   (4)   trillions
    (2)   thousands   (5)   tens
    (3)   billions

27.   Elliptical systems appear to lack spiral arms but possess
    (1)   round bodies.   (4)   rectangular bodies.
    (2)   square bodies.   (5)   oval bodies.
    (3)   triangular bodies.

28.   The Earth is a
    (1)   galaxy.   (4)   moon.
    (2)   planet.   (5)   satellite.
    (3)   star.

29. The band of starlight coming from our own galaxy forms the
    - (1) sun.
    - (2) moon.
    - (3) spiral arms.
    - (4) Milky Way.
    - (5) planets.

30. Located in the center of the solar system is the
    - (1) earth.
    - (2) moon.
    - (3) sun.
    - (4) comet.
    - (5) Orion Nebula.

31. The Milky Way is a(n)
    - (1) elliptical galaxy.
    - (2) flattened galaxy.
    - (3) spiral galaxy.
    - (4) pinwheel galaxy.
    - (5) round galaxy.

32. The Milky Way contains
    - (1) clusters of stars forming their own distinct pattern.
    - (2) clusters of dust forming their own distinct pattern.
    - (3) clusters of planetoids forming their own distinct pattern.
    - (4) clusters of comets forming their own distinct pattern.
    - (5) clusters of meteors forming their own distince pattern.

33. The galaxy that is closest in resemblance to the Milky Way is
    - (1) Quasar.
    - (2) Nebula.
    - (3) Earth.
    - (4) Andromeda.
    - (5) Orion.

34. The discovery of quasars has been aided by
    - (1) radio astronomy.
    - (2) telescopes.
    - (3) light waves.
    - (4) clouds of gas.
    - (5) Star clusters.

35. The first quasar was located in 1959. Since that date, scientists have located more than _____ quasars.
    - (1) 20,000
    - (2) 1,000
    - (3) 1,959
    - (4) 100,000
    - (5) 100

36. A star's mass is indicated by its
    - (1) color.
    - (2) surface.
    - (3) distance.
    - (4) brightness.
    - (5) density.

37. The temperature of a star is indicated by its
    (1) surface.
    (4) brightness.
    (2) mass.
    (5) density.
    (3) color.

38. A person who studies the stars is called a(n)
    (1) astrologer.
    (4) star searcher.
    (2) astronomer.
    (5) astrologist.
    (3) astrophysicist.

39. A group of stars is called a(n)
    (1) compass.
    (2) navigational instrument aid.
    (3) consolation.
    (4) constellation.
    (5) installation.

40. What appears as star movement is actually
    (1) spinning and placement of the Earth.
    (2) spinning and placement of the sun.
    (3) spinning and placement of the moon.
    (4) spinning and placement of the star grouping.
    (5) None of the above.

41. The place where stars are viewed and studied is called the
    (1) atmosphere.
    (4) planetoid.
    (2) laboratory.
    (5) telescope.
    (3) planetarium.

42. Upon entering the atmosphere, metallic masses glow due to friction with the atmosphere and cause the mass to glow; hence, we are able to see a(n)
    (1) sun.
    (4) star.
    (2) meteor.
    (5) eclipse
    (3) moon.

43. A meteor is
    (1) a comet.
    (4) glowing air.
    (2) a star falling.
    (5) a metallic mass.
    (3) a falling comet.

44. A meteor is sometimes called a
    (1) falling comet.   (4) failing sun.
    (2) falling sun.   (5) exploding star.
    (3) shooting star.

45. A meteor will glow for
    (1) a few days.   (4) a month.
    (2) a few hours.   (5) years.
    (3) a few seconds.

46. Damage to the Earth by meteorites occurs
    (1) at the changing of the moon.
    (2) at times of devastation.
    (3) seldomly, but could be devastating.
    (4) at changing of the seasons.
    (5) during hail storms.

47. To determine the origins of the universe and the solar system, one could study
    (1) mentors.   (4) mentalities.
    (2) meteorites.   (5) oceans.
    (3) cometrites.

48. Meteorites are
    (1) extrametal matter.
    (2) fractions of moon beams.
    (3) extraterrestrial matter.
    (4) fractions of sun beams.
    (5) satellites.

49. The Earth-like planets are made up of
    (1) lava and stone.   (4) hydrogen and methane.
    (2) tin and copper.   (5) oxygen and carbon dioxide.
    (3) iron and rock.

50. The sun has a mass of 750 times greater than
    (1) all terrestrial planets.
    (2) the four largest planets.
    (3) the Earth, moon, and sun combined.
    (4) all planets combined.
    (5) Mercury.

51. Which planet is the farthest from the sun?
    - (1) Earth
    - (2) Mars
    - (3) Saturn
    - (4) Jupiter
    - (5) Pluto

52. Which planet is the closest to the sun?
    - (1) Earth
    - (2) Mars
    - (3) Mercury
    - (4) Pluto
    - (5) None of the above.

53. Which of the following planets is the largest?
    - (1) Earth
    - (2) Mars
    - (3) Saturn
    - (4) Pluto
    - (5) Moon

54. Asteroids are irregularly-shaped objects orbiting between Jupiter and Mars that are _____ in size.
    - (1) tiny
    - (2) large
    - (3) small
    - (4) medium
    - (5) planet-like

55. Meteoroids are chunks of iron resulting from collisions between
    - (1) asteroids.
    - (2) comets.
    - (3) planetoids.
    - (4) stars.
    - (5) meteorites.

56. Asteroids orbit between
    - (1) Neptune and Venus.
    - (2) Jupiter and Mars.
    - (3) Mars and Venus.
    - (4) Neptune and Jupiter.
    - (5) Earth and the moon.

B. PHYSICS AND CHEMISTRY OF THE EARTH

1. PHYSICAL PROPERTIES

The Earth has three motions: it spins like a top, moves in the spinning motion around the sun, while moving through the Milky Way with the rest of the solar system. The Earth spins around on its axis, an imaginary line that connects the North and South poles at either end of the planet Earth. The spinning motion has a path it follows around the sun (orbit), making the sun seem to move from east to west and causing the occurrences of day and night.

The Earth has only one moon. The sun's gravity acts on both the Earth and the moon, causing the moon to travel in an oval-like orbit around the Earth. Because of this movement, we have the seasons of spring, summer, fall, and winter. The seasons are a result of the tilting of the Earth on its axis, movement, and position of the moon in relation to the sun.

2. CHEMICAL COMPOSITION

The Earth's surface is about 70% water, with most of the water being oceans with depths extending to 12,450 feet. The land surface makes up the remaining 30% and extends an average of 2,757 feet above the division of land and water. The highest peak is Mount Everest in Asia at 29,028 feet above sea level. Oceans, lakes, rivers, and all other bodies of water and ice make up a part of the Earth called the hydrosphere. Land bodies surrounded by water make up the continents. Together, land and water surfaces that support life are called the biosphere.

The chemical composition of the Earth is 46.6% oxygen, 27.72% silicon, 8.13% aluminum, 5.0% iron, 3.60% calcium, 2.83% sodium, 2.59% potassium, 2.09% magnesium, 0.44% titanium, and all other elements total 1.0%. A geologist is a person who studies the Earth and its contents. It is through the work of geologists that the chemical composition of the Earth has been established.

3. ROCKS

The hard, solid part of the Earth's surface is called rock. Rock may be exposed from its soil cover when highways are cut through hillsides or mountain regions. River channels or shorelines frequently cut through rock beds. Some mountain chains expose rock beds when weathering exposes the rock base. Rocks are useful in many ways as granite (igneous), marble (metamorphic), or limestone (sedimentary) can be used in buildings, dams, highways, or the making of cement. Metals like aluminum, iron, lead, and tin are removed from rock that is called ore.

4. MINERALS

Minerals are the most common form of solid material found in the Earth's crust. Even soil contains bits of minerals that have broken away from its rock source. Minerals are dug from the Earth and are used to make a variety of products. To be considered a mineral, the element must be found in nature and never have been a part of any living organism. Atoms making up the element or substance must be arranged in regular patterns to form crystals and must have the same chemical makeup as the area where it is found.

5. ORES

Ores are mineral deposits high enough in an element content that it would be economically feasible to be mined and sold for a profit. Ore deposits are located from geological knowledge about crustal movements and ore formations along with sophisticated instruments and a lot of luck. Once the ore has been located, the mining process is based on the most economical method to remove the highest amount of the mineral from the rock with the least amount of environmental damage. Processes include leaching or separating the mineral from the rock by heat, brine solutions, evaporation of seawater, or chemically removing the metal from the ore.

6. EARTH'S MAGNETISM

Imaginary lines curve from the North pole to the South pole, making up the Earth's magnetic field. The Earth acts as though its center is a large magnet. These imaginary lines aid the compass needle to determine directions based on the Earth's natural magnetic field. Scientists are not sure what produces the enormous currents that are deep within the Earth and responsible for the Earth's magnetic fields.

☞ Drill: Physics and Chemistry of the Earth

DIRECTIONS: Carefully read and answer each of the following questions which are based on the information which you have just read.

57. The Earth spins around on its
    (1) equator.   (4) orbit.
    (2) poles.   (5) rotation.
    (3) axis.

58. An axis is
    (1) a definite line.
    (2) a connecting line at the equator.
    (3) a connecting line between the poles.
    (4) a connecting line between orbits.
    (5) a pole.

59. The Earth has
    (1) no moon.   (4) four moons.
    (2) two moons.   (5) one moon.
    (3) three moons.

60. An orbit is the
    (1) spinning motion of the Earth.
    (2) axis of the Earth.
    (3) movement and position of the Earth around the sun.
    (4) gravity action of the Earth.
    (5) time of year.

61. The percentage of the Earth's surface that is water is
    (1) 30%.   (4) 90%.
    (2) 50%.   (5) 25%.
    (3) 70%.

62. The highest point in the world is located in
    (1) North America.   (4) Africa.
    (2) Europe.   (5) Antarctica.
    (3) Asia.

63. The highest altitude on Earth is Mount Everest, which is
    (1) 28,028 ft. above sea level.
    (2) 29,028 ft. above sea level.
    (3) 29,208 ft. above sea level.
    (4) 28,208 ft. above sea level.
    (5) 20,928 ft. above sea level.

64. The hydrosphere is
    (1) land surrounded by bodies of water.
    (2) areas of atmosphere with water present.
    (3) oceans, land, and lakes.
    (4) oceans, lakes, and rivers, and all other bodies of water and ice.
    (5) where glaciers are present.

65. The biosphere is
    (1) land and water surfaces that support life.
    (2) land that supports life.
    (3) living parts of the atmosphere.
    (4) water surfaces that support life.
    (5) the highest level of the atmosphere.

66. How much greater is the Earth's oxygen content compared to silicon content?

(1) 18.8%   (4) 8.9%
(2) 19.8%   (5) 18.88%
(3) 21.1%

67. A geologist is a person who studies
(1) geography.   (4) chemical composition.
(2) rocks only.   (5) soil.
(3) gaseous composition.

68. The element that makes up the greater percentage of the Earth's atmosphere is
(1) oxygen.   (4) magnesium.
(2) silicon.   (5) carbon dioxide.
(3) calcium.

69. The solid part of the Earth is called
(1) ore.   (4) metals.
(2) rock.   (5) air.
(3) highways.

70. Igneous rock forms are commonly called
(1) marble.   (4) cement.
(2) limestone.   (5) stalagmites.
(3) granite.

71. Metamorphic rock forms are commonly called
(1) cement.   (4) limestone
(2) iron.   (5) sandstone.
(3) marble.

72. The sedimentary rock forms are commonly called
(1) limestone.   (4) cement.
(2) granite.   (5) conglomerate.
(3) marble.

73. Minerals are found
(1) in the atmosphere.   (4) only in your body.
(2) in the Earth's crust.   (5) None of the above.
(3) at the ocean bottom.

74. To be considered a mineral, the substance must never have been a part of a living organism and must be found in
    (1) water.
    (2) rock.
    (3) ore.
    (4) nature.
    (5) sand.

75. Elements are made up of
    (1) atoms.
    (2) particles.
    (3) minerals.
    (4) soil.
    (5) elementary.

76. Minerals are the most common form of _____ found in the Earth's crust.
    (1) aquatic material
    (2) solid material
    (3) living organisms
    (4) soil material
    (5) All of the above.

77. Ores are
    (1) minerals beneath Earth's surface.
    (2) mineral deposits high enough in element content to be profitable to dig.
    (3) materials that are removed from minerals.
    (4) mineral deposits low in element content.
    (5) used in water.

78. One process used to separate mineral from rock is
    (1) heating the rock.
    (2) chemical evaporation.
    (3) environmental leaching.
    (4) boiling seawater.
    (5) freezing the rock.

79. Mineral deposits are located by studying
    (1) mining areas.
    (2) crustal movements.
    (3) geographical rises.
    (4) ocean beds.
    (5) volcanic eruptions.

80. The Earth acts as though its center is a large
    (1) rock.
    (2) black hole.
    (3) magnet.
    (4) curve.
    (5) empty space.

81. Imaginary lines curve from
    - (1)   east to west.
    - (2)   north to east.
    - (3)   north to west.
    - (4)   south to east.
    - (5)   north to south.

82. The cause of the Earth's magnetic field is
    - (1)   enormous currents.
    - (2)   space satellites.
    - (3)   a lost secret.
    - (4)   in the Earth's crust.
    - (5)   unknown.

C. EVOLUTION AND CRUSTAL PROCESS

1. CHANGING OF THE EARTH

The moon's gravitational pull produces tides both in the ocean and in the Earth's solid crust. Throughout time, slow evolutionary changes have taken place and continue to take place. As shorelines are inched away in one location, mud and silt build up in other areas, adding to the land surface. With all these changes occurring slowly over long periods of time, little difference can be recorded as to variations in land or water surfaces of the Earth.

2. CONTINENTAL DRIFTS

The continental shelves are zones of relatively shallow portions of the continent extending out under the oceans. The continental shelves or edges are a part of the continent they adjoin and the edge of the shelf is the true boundary of the continent. The continental shelf is not a small area. In some areas, they may contain the same area as the size of the Soviet Union under the waters of the ocean. The shelves were formed eighteen to twenty thousand years ago due to the melting of the glaciers, along with time, wave-cutting terraces, erosion and sedimentation all part of the formation explanation. At the edge of the shelf, the continental slope leads downward to the deep ocean. At the bottom of the slope, an area of deposition called the continental rise may form a gentler slope. Other features included in the continental margin are trenches, ridges, and submarine canyons. A reef is a rocky or coral elevation dangerous to the surface navigation which may or may not be uncovered by water. A rocky reef is always detached from shore; a coral reef may or may not be connected to the shoreline.

3. NATURE'S RECYCLING

Nature's method of recycling is evident through many processes. Some processes are the water cycle, carbon cycle, oxygen cycle, and energy cycle as demonstrated by prey and predators. These concepts are explained through the following drawings.

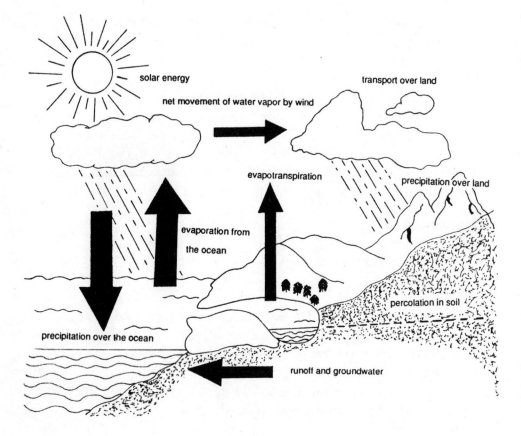

The Hydrologic (Water) Cycle

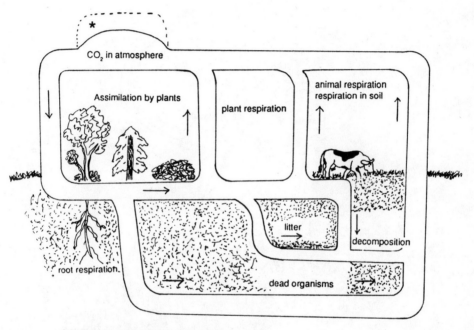

* A seasonal change in atmospheric CO_2 levels is
caused by variations in the distribution of vegetation on
the earth.

Carbon Cycle

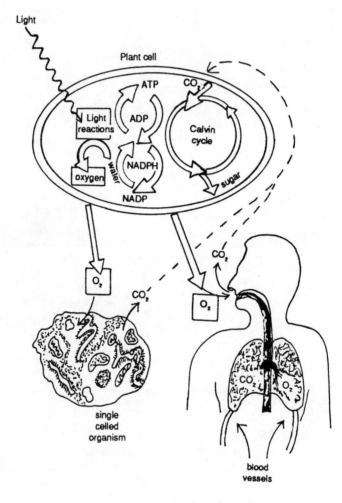

Light

Plant cell

ATP

ADP

Light reactions

Calvin cycle

NADPH

oxygen

water

NADP

sugar

CO₂

O₂

CO₂

single
celled
organism

CO₂

O₂

CO₂

O₂

blood
vessels

Oxygen Cycle

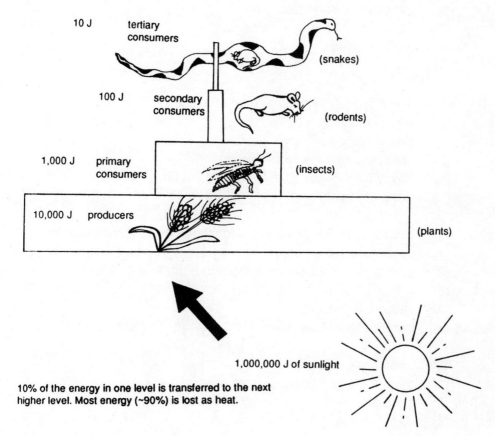

10 J   tertiary
        consumers   (snakes)

    100 J   secondary
             consumers   (rodents)

1,000 J   primary
           consumers   (insects)

10,000 J   producers   (plants)

1,000,000 J of sunlight

10% of the energy in one level is transferred to the next
higher level. Most energy (~90%) is lost as heat.

Energy Cycle

☞ Drill: Evolution and Crustal Process

DIRECTIONS: Carefully read and answer each of the following questions which are based on the information which you have just read.

83. The moon's gravitational pull produces the
    (1) tides.
    (2) solid crustal surfaces.
    (3) movement of surface water.
    (4) shore build-up.
    (5) weather.

84. Throughout time, changes have taken place
    (1) slowly and stopped.
    (2) slowly and continually.
    (3) slowly along the shores.
    (4) slowly throughout different periods of time.
    (5) None of the above.

85. The shifting of the Earth's surface locations gives some proof to
    (1) evolutionary changes.
    (2) land changes which will bring about the end of time.
    (3) shore build-up.
    (4) shore erosion.
    (5) the Big Bang Theory.

86. Shorelines are made of
    (1) mud and silt.   (4) silt and soil.
    (2) sand and mud.   (5) sand and snow.
    (3) rock and silt.

87. Terracing, erosion, and sedimentation are responsible for forming the
    (1) continental rise.   (4) continental margin.
    (2) continental slope.   (5) None of the above.
    (3) continental shelf.

88. An area that is always detached from a shore would be a
    (1) peninsula.   (4) marginal reef.
    (2) coral reef.   (5) rocky reef.
    (3) barrier reef.

89. A shelf that leads downward is called a
    (1) continental drop.
    (2) continental reef.
    (3) continental slope.
    (4) continental margin.
    (5) All of the above.

90. When compared, the water cycle, carbon cycle, oxygen cycle, and energy cycle have
    (1) only a few minor differences.
    (2) only one major difference.
    (3) nothing that can be compared among the four cycles.
    (4) evidence of recycling.
    (5) many major problems.

91. All, except the _____ cycle, use various forms of life.
    (1) energy
    (2) oxygen
    (3) carbon
    (4) rinse
    (5) water

92. The two cycles that involve gaseous exchanges are
    (1) carbon and energy.
    (2) energy and oxygen.
    (3) carbon and water.
    (4) oxygen and carbon.
    (5) oxygen and water.

D. SURFACE PROCESSES

1. ATMOSPHERE

Air, an odorless and colorless gas, surrounds the Earth and extends approximately 1,000 miles above the surface of the Earth. This is called the atmosphere. It is made up of 78% nitrogen and 21% oxygen; the remaining 1% consists mainly of argon, water vapor, dust particles, and other gases. Cloud formations float in the lowest portion of the atmosphere, called the troposphere. Weather occurrences are formed in the troposphere. It is also the more dense portion of the atmosphere, followed by the stratosphere, mesosphere and exosphere.

The ionosphere is a belt of radiation surrounding the Earth. Outside the atmosphere, in what used to be considered "empty" space, man's satellites in 1958 disclosed the existence of magnetism. The aurora borealis or "northern dawn/lights" is a beautiful display of moving, colored streamers or folds of light. Its counterpart in the Antarctic is the aurora australis, or "southern dawn/lights," both connected to the Earth's magnetic field or lines of force. During magnetic storms, aurora borealis can be seen as far south as Boston and New York.

2. WATER

The most important source of sediment is Earth and rock material carried to the sea by rivers and streams; the same materials may also have been transported by glaciers and winds. Other sources are volcanic ash and lava, shells and skeletons of organisms, chemical precipitates formed in seawater, and particles from outer space.

Water is a most unusual substance because it exists on the surface of the Earth in its three physical states: ice, water, and water vapor. There are other substances that might exist in a solid and liquid or gaseous state at temperatures normally found at the Earth's surface, but there are fewer substances which occur in all three states.

Water is odorless, tasteless, and colorless. It is the only substance known to exist in a natural state as a solid, liquid, or gas on the surface of the Earth. It is a universal solvent. Water does not corrode, rust, burn, or separate into its components easily. It is chemically indestructible. It can corrode almost any metal and erode the most solid rock. A unique property of water is that it expands and floats on water when frozen or in the solid state. Water has a freezing point of 0°C and a boiling point of 100°C. Water has the capacity for absorbing great quantities of heat with relatively little increase in temperature. When distilled, water is a poor conductor of electricity but when salt is added, it is a good conductor of electricity.

Sunlight is the source of energy for temperature change, evaporation, and currents for water movement through the atmosphere. Sunlight controls the rate of photosynthesis for all marine plants, which are directly or indirectly the source of food for all marine animals. Migration, breeding, and other behaviors of marine animals are affected by light.

Water, as the ocean or sea, is blue because of the molecular scattering of the sunlight. Blue light, being of short wavelength, is scattered more effectively than light of longer wave lengths. Variations in color may be caused by particles suspended in the water, water depth, cloud cover, temperature, and other variable factors. Heavy concentrations of dissolved materials cause a yellowish hue, while algae will cause the water to look green. Heavy populations of plant and animal materials will cause the water to look brown.

3. WEATHERING

Weathering is the natural wearing away of rock or soil due to chemical or physical actions on these Earth surfaces. This occurs very slowly over a long period of time. Through chemical weathering, rocks break down as oxygen, carbon dioxide, and water vapor react with rock until it is finally changed into soil. Physical weathering occurs in dry regions by the wind action constantly wearing away the surface of the rock.

4. EROSION

The first concept of erosion was that natural weathering that we call erosion led to the formation of mountains and mountain chains. The main causes of erosion are air and/or water movement across rock or soil, changes in the temperature, or any combination of these factors. Chemical erosion can occur as carbon dioxide and water vapor are removed from dead organic matter. These are all natural forms of erosion. Man can cause erosion with poor crop-planting procedures, lack of crop rotation, and the cutting of trees without planning or replacement.

5. TEMPERATURE

Temperature is controlled by the position of the Earth on its axis and its distance from the sun at rotation. At the equator, the air would be warmest and always pushing upward while cold air would be flowing in to be warmed. The constant changing of air will cause changes in the temperature.

6. PRESSURE

Air pressure also plays an important role in the movement of air and the changing of air temperatures and weather changes. Next to the equator, a low pressure cell is formed because the air is warmer, lighter, and moving upward. The low pressure is a result of the molecules of air being further apart. The colder air has closer air molecules; thus, a high pressure cell is formed. Extreme weather conditions, such as flooding, may result when both low cells and high cells occupy the same air space.

7. CLIMATE

Climate is the usual weather that occurs in a general area over a period of time. The study of climate is called climatology. When referring to climate, one takes into consideration air temperature, wind speed, sunshine, humidity, amount of precipitation, air pressure, and general geographic conditions.

Climate has a direct effect upon living organisms and the type(s) of life that can exist in the region being considered. Climate also affects our method of transportation, outdoor activities, choices for employment, type of clothing, type of housing, and food naturally available or that can be grown.

8. ALTERNATE ENERGY FORMS

About 90% of today's energy is supplied from fossil fuels as crude oil, natural gas, and coal. These materials are a result of nature providing such supplies for man's use. Thus, these are considered our nonrenewable resources as they cannot be replaced after they have been used. With conservation and suitable alternate energy sources, our natural resources will last longer and these fossil fuels can be usable for many more years. Alternate energy sources include methanol, ethanol, wood and wood wastes, garbage and plant material, corn, other grains, solar energy, photovoltaic cells, hydroelectricity, nuclear power, wind energy (windmills), tidal energy, geothermal energy (geysers), and fusion using nuclear waste materials.

☞ Drill: Surface Processes

DIRECTIONS: Carefully read and answer each of the following questions which are based on the information which you have just read.

93. The atmosphere is partially made up of
    (1) 78% oxygen.   (4) 1% nitrogen.
    (2) 78% carbon dioxide.   (5) 78% nitrogen.
    (3) 21% argon.

94. Cloud formations float in the lowest portion of the atmosphere, called the
    (1) stratosphere.   (4) exosphere.
    (2) mesophere.   (5) ozone layer.
    (3) troposphere.

95. An odorless, colorless gas that surrounds the Earth is commonly called
    (1) nitrogen.   (4) air.
    (2) oxygen.   (5) carbon dioxide.
    (3) argon.

96. A belt of radiation surrounding the Earth is called the

(1)   stratosphere.   (4)   mesophere.
(2)   ionosphere.   (5)   ozone layer.
(3)   trophosphere.

97.   Aurora borealis, the beautiful display of colored streamers, is commonly called
(1)   southern lights.   (4)   eastern lights.
(2)   western lights.   (5)   None of the above.
(3)   northern lights.

98.   The aurora australis is seen in the
(1)   Arctic region.   (4)   northern region.
(2)   Antarctic region.   (5)   eastern region.
(3)   southern region.

99.   Sediment is transported by
(1)   oceans and trees.   (4)   earth and rock.
(2)   rivers and streams.   (5)   wind.
(3)   lava and streams.

100.   Sediment can be formed from
(1)   water and snow.
(2)   snails.
(3)   shells and skeletons of organisms.
(4)   volcanic ash and rock from Mars.
(5)   dirt.

101.   One of the few substances that can exist in all three states is
(1)   nitrogen.   (4)   oxygen.
(2)   sediment.   (5)   water.
(3)   soil.

102.   The three physical states matter can exist in are
(1)   solid, liquid, and gas.   (4)   soil, liquid, and gas.
(2)   solid, gas, and water.   (5)   solid, liquid, and air.
(3)   solid, liquid, and oxygen.

103.   Water can corrode and erode
(1)   any solid.   (4)   when distilled.
(2)   the most solid rock.   (5)   All of the above.
(3)   only metals.

104. Water can
    (1) corrode, rust, burn, and separate.
    (2) freeze at 100°C.
    (3) be destroyed by chemical means.
    (4) expand and float.
    (5) boil at 32°F.

105. When salt water is distilled, it
    (1) is a poor conductor of electricity.
    (2) is doubled in power to conduct electricity.
    (3) is a very good conductor of electricity.
    (4) is not able to conduct electricity.
    (5) converts electricity into stored energy.

106. Temperature change, rate of photosynthesis, and migration are all
    (1) affected by sunlight.
    (2) least affected by sunlight.
    (3) most affected by sunlight.
    (4) not controlled by sunlight.
    (5) not affected by sunlight.

107. The source of evaporation is the
    (1) movement of air.   (4) currents.
    (2) atmosphere.   (5) ozone.
    (3) sunlight.

108. An indirect source of food for all marine plants is
    (1) temperature changes.
    (2) sunlight.
    (3) breeding.
    (4) migration behaviors of aquatic life.
    (5) water.

109. Marine animal behavior is greatly affected by
    (1) water movement.   (4) migration.
    (2) sunlight.   (5) warm weather.
    (3) photosynthesis.

110. According to the passage, water, as in the ocean or sea, is
    (1) blue-green.   (4) blue.
    (2) red-brown.   (5) green.
    (3) yellowish.

111. Water displays a blue color because of
    (1) scattered sunlight.
    (2) heavy plant growth.
    (3) organic material in water.
    (4) lack of organic material in water and presence of inorganics.
    (5) dyes.

112. A control of water color is the
    (1) population present.
    (2) amount of oxygen.
    (3) types of minerals present.
    (4) lack of water movement.
    (5) level of pollution.

113. The natural wearing away of rock or soil due to chemical or physical actions is called
    (1) weather.
    (2) weathering.
    (3) erosion.
    (4) corrosion.
    (5) fading.

114. Rocks break down as oxygen, carbon dioxide, and water vapor due to
    (1) physical weathering.
    (2) chemical weather.
    (3) physical weather.
    (4) chemical weathering.
    (5) None of the above.

115. Physical weathering occurs in
    (1) wet, windy regions.
    (2) dry, windy regions.
    (3) dry, cold regions.
    (4) dry, hot regions.
    (5) dry, stagnant regions.

116. Man can control erosion by
    (1) adding chemicals to the soil.
    (2) cutting trees and clearing land.
    (3) rotating crops.
    (4) removing dead organic matter.
    (5) never rotating crops.

117. Erosion actually
    (1) destroys the Earth.
    (2) does not affect the Earth.
    (3) leads to forest growth.
    (4) only occurs with water movement.
    (5) creates soil.

118. Erosion is a form of natural weathering that
     (1)   led to the forming of mountain chains.
     (2)   formed only a few mountains out west.
     (3)   was proven false.
     (4)   is caused by chemical, physical, and psychological means.
     (5)   has no important impact on the environment.

119. Temperature is controlled by
     (1)   weather.   (4)   pressure.
     (2)   position of the axis.   (5)   the sun.
     (3)   time.

120. One of the factors that causes a change in temperature is
     (1)   time.   (4)   rainy weather.
     (2)   changing air currents.   (5)   the moon.
     (3)   wind blowing hard.

121. Air is the warmest at the
     (1)   North pole.   (4)   axis.
     (2)   South pole.   (5)   equator.
     (3)   poles.

122. Air temperature, movement of air, and weather changes are all affected
     by
     (1)   air pressure.   (4)   high pressure cells.
     (2)   low pressure only.   (5)   clouds.
     (3)   high pressure only.

123. Colder air has close air molecules that form a
     (1)   low pressure cell.   (4)   dry condition.
     (2)   high pressure cell.   (5)   None of the above.
     (3)   flooding condition.

124. Warmer air has molecules of air that are far apart. Therefore, it
     produces
     (1)   a low pressure cell.   (4)   dry conditions.
     (2)   a high pressure cell.   (5)   not conditions.
     (3)   rainy weather.

125. A low pressure cell is the result of the molecules
     (1)   blowing upward.   (2)   being close together.

(3)   being far apart.   (4)   bouncing up and down.
(5)   blowing downward.

126. Usual weather that occurs in a general area is called
   (1)   rain.   (4)   conditions.
   (2)   snow.   (5)   stability.
   (3)   climate.

127. The study of climate is called
   (1)   air temperature.   (4)   astrology.
   (2)   geography.   (5)   meterology.
   (3)   climatology.

128. Climate affects all of the following except:
   (1)   number of human chromosomes.
   (2)   transportation.
   (3)   organisms.
   (4)   outdoor activities.
   (5)   living conditions.

129. An alternate energy source is
   (1)   crude oil.   (4)   coal.
   (2)   ethanol.   (5)   methanol.
   (3)   natural gas.

130. Fossil fuels are considered to be nonrenewable because
   (1)   they are easily and quickly replaced.
   (2)   they can be replaced within a normal lifetime.
   (3)   they can never be replaced.
   (4)   they can be replaced with an alternate energy source.
   (5)   they do not need to be renewed because they are abundant.

131. A geyser is considered
   (1)   wind energy.   (4)   nuclear energy.
   (2)   solar energy.   (5)   hydrolic energy.
   (3)   geothermal energy.

132. Crude oil, natural gas, and coal are called
   (1)   nuclear energy sources.
   (2)   alternate energy sources.
   (3)   natural sources.

    (4)   renewable energy sources.

    (5)   fossil fuel sources.

133. Conservation of nonrenewable energy sources means
    (1)   not using fossil fuels.
    (2)   using less fossil fuels.
    (3)   using all fossil fuels as they are found.
    (4)   recycling fossil fuels.
    (5)   None of the above.

E. EARTH'S HAZARDS AND RESOURCES

1. EARTHQUAKES

Earthquakes are vibrations due to the movements within and beneath the Earth's crust. They occur as a result of faulting or other structural processes happening as a result of a strain on the rocks at the edge of the crust. A long series of quakes with none being greater than the others is called an Earth swarm and occurs near volcanic regions. Imperial Valley, California, is known for having Earth swarms. Earth tremors are vibrations of low intensity and can be felt only by those located directly over the affected area.

Earthquake intensity is measured on a scale from 0 to 9, where each number represents an energy release ten times that of the number. This energy release is measured by the "Richter Scale" as it was introduced by Charles F. Richter in 1935. Richter was an American seismologist. About 80% of Earthquake energy is released in the areas bordering the vast Pacific Ocean, with 15% released in an east-west band across the Mediterranean. The remaining 5% occur sporadically throughout the remaining parts of the world bordering large bodies of water.

2. VOLCANOES

Volcanoes are a natural phenomenon with their effects confined to a small area. About 500 volcanoes are known to have been active, with two-thirds of them in the Pacific Ocean area. Modern research into volcanoes and their role in forming much of the Earth's crust began with the French geologist Jean Etienne Guettard in the mid-eighteenth century.

Volcanoes discharge a large amount of carbon dioxide into the air; the weathering of rocks utilizes carbon dioxide. This presents a pair of mechanisms for possible long-term climatic changes. A period of greater than normal volcanic action might initiate a warming of the Earth. The mountains built by the volcanic ash might expose large areas of new and unweathered rock to the air, which will lower the carbon dioxide levels, thus reducing the atmospheric temperature.

3. OCEANS

It is estimated the world's oceans extend over 328 million cubic miles with the greatest depth being 36,198 feet off the coast of Guam. The deepest of all oceans is the Pacific Ocean, averaging 14,048 feet, and the most shallow is the Baltic Sea at 180.4 feet deep. Sedimentary rock at the bottom of the oceans has been dated at 3 billion years old with the water dated at 4 billion years old.

The oceans supply man with a means of transportation, habitat for aquatic life that is used for food, a source of minerals, and a means of weather control. Also, the ocean offers various sources of energy for consumption and use in the future. Presently, oil and gas are being derived from the ocean as sources of energy. Much research is presently being conducted as to the feasibility of waves or water of the ocean being used to produce power. Also, the ocean is being used to simulate islands of lush plant growth to increase the photosynthesis process as a possible way to reduce the depletion of the ozone layer.

4. HOT SPRINGS

Hot springs are naturally occurring bodies of water that are warmer than their surrounding air. Hot springs (thermal springs) occur in regions of faulted or folded rock due to volcanic action. The water that comes from underground where the rocks are hot will produce hot water that rises to the Earth's surface in the form of a spring. Not all hot springs are a direct result of volcanoes, but are produced by geysers.

5. MIGRATION

Migration is the movement of people or animals from one area to another area. Migration occurs because of seasonal changes, wars, famines, floods, volcanic eruptions, weather, and other natural disasters for the purpose of survival. Migration practices began with prehistoric man. Little is known about the pattern of movement or why migrations took place. It is believed the first migrations were to escape the spread of the great glaciers and ice sheets. The most common application of migration is that of birds and other animals moving to survive winters or for the purpose of reproduction as illustrated by the salmon moving into the colder waters.

6. FLOODING

Flooding is the natural occurrence of an extremely large amount of water flowing into a given area faster than it can leave the area. As a result, the stream, lake, or river will overflow its natural level. Estuary zones and sand dunes are natural flood control devices. Man-made devices include dams and sandbagging to control flood waters. The control of flood waters is important to the survival of coastal habitats for wading marsh birds, birds of prey, migratory birds, water fowl, and other aquatic life, as well as man.

7. WATER BASED FORMATIONS

The commonly seen waves on the surface of water are caused principally by wind. When a breeze blows over calm water, it forms small ripples or capillary waves. As the wind speed increases, larger, more visible gravity waves are formed. When the wind reaches high speeds, whitecaps are formed. However, submarine Earthquakes, volcanic eruptions, and tides also cause waves. Waves will always break parallel to the shoreline.

The tide is the continuous cycle of alternating rise and fall of the sea level observed along the coastlines and bodies of water connected to the sea. On most coastlines, the cycle occurs about every 12 hours. Along the Gulf coastline, a tidal cycle can occur about every 24–25 hours. The rise and fall of sea level observed along coastlines is produced by waves of extreme length; high water is the crest of the wave; low water is the trough. Tides can be predicted once observations have been mathematically related to the positions of Earth, moon, and sun. Tides are caused by the gravitational interaction between the sun, moon, and Earth. The moon exercises the greatest influence on our tide; although its mass is much less than the sun's, it is closer to the Earth and its tide-producing effect is more than twice as great.

The maximum height reached by a rising tide is called high water. This is due solely to the periodic tidal force, but at times, the meteorological effects of severe storms or strong winds may be superimposed on the normal tide to produce high water.

Low water is the minimum height reached by a falling tide. Usually this is due solely to the influence of a periodic tidal force, but sometimes the influence of severe storms or strong winds may be superimposed on the normal tide to produce low water.

Tides are classified as semidiurnal, diurnal, and mixed. Areas having semidiurnal tides have two high waters and two low waters each day; this is the most common type. Diurnal tides consist of one high water and one low water each day. Tides are classified as mixed when they are diurnal on some days and semidiurnal on others.

Hurricanes occur when the atmospheric conditions, tail movements, winds, and pressure change severely. Hurricanes begin with winds moving in a circular motion over bodies of water, picking up both speed and rainy weather conditions. When a hurricane approaches a coastline, the sea level will go 20 feet above normal tide level. The months of June through November are considered hurricane season. August, September, and October normally have more hurricanes documented than any other months with September having the greatest number of hurricanes. May and December, on rare occasions, have logged hurricanes. Hurricanes can cause both property damage and personal damage when they move from the water to land surfaces with a tornado resulting from its wind force as it moves further inland.

A typhoon is a severe storm over the oceans that is made of rain, wind, and water and will affect tidal movements of shorelines of islands near their occurrences.

Currents are water movements in horizontal or vertical flow occurring at differing depths of the water. Currents stabilize the climate of adjacent land areas, preventing extremes of temperatures. Currents are also influenced/ affected by the moon and its position relative to the equator.

Density differences may produce both horizontal and vertical movement of water, causing modifications to the wind-driven surface currents. Water tends to flow from an area of low density to an area of high density. Water may tend to become of greater density as the temperature decreases.

Fog is a hydrometer which consists of a visible collection of minute water droplets suspended in the atmosphere near the Earth's surface. It will interfere with the ability to see at a distance over the area that it covers. It is caused by atmospheric humidity and a warm temperature layer being transported over a cold body of water or land surface.

8. ECONOMICS OF EARTH'S RESOURCES

Conservation is the protection and wise management of Earth's resources or natural resources, for the benefit of not only man, but all living things. Without wise practices of conservation and concern for the quality of the environment, all natural resources necessary for life, such as air, animals, energy, minerals, plants, soil, water, and other elemental forms would be damaged, wasted, or destroyed. With greater conservation enforcement, the cost of living will be lower for everyone and more ideal surroundings will be present. The Earth not only has limited resources, but the demands are greater as populations increase, which means there must be a wiser use of Earth's resources if they are to last as long as man or if man is to survive. The cost of man's poor resource management can be life itself.

☞ Drill: Earth's Hazards and Resources

DIRECTIONS: Carefully read and answer each of the following questions which are based on the information which you have just read.

134. Vibrations due to movements within and beneath the Earth's crust are called
    (1) shifting plates.   (4) fault lines.
    (2) volcanic eruptions.   (5) seismic encounters.
    (3) earthquakes.

135. Earth swarms are
    (1) a long series of quakes with none being greater than the others.
    (2) a group of quakes which occur at the same time.
    (3) large tidal waves that occur because of an Earthquake.
    (4) bees which form colonies along the fault line.
    (5) aftershocks.

136. Imperial Valley, California, is known for having
    (1) Earth swarms.   (4) Earthquakes.
    (2) Earth trimmers.   (5) None of the above.
    (3) volcanic regions.

137. If vibrations are felt directly over the area affected, then one has experienced a(n)
    (1) volcano.   (4) Earth trimmer.
    (2) Earthquake.   (5) Earth tremor.
    (3) Earth swarm.

138. Earthquake intensity is measured on a scale called the
    (1) Friction Scale.   (4) Pitcher Scale.
    (2) Vibration Scale.   (5) Pitch Scale.
    (3) Richter Scale.

139. _____ % of the energy of earthquakes is released in areas bordering the vast Pacific Ocean.
    (1) 8   (4) .8
    (2) 18   (5) 81
    (3) 80

140. Earthquakes are measured on a scale of
    (1) 0-9.   (4) 0-1000.
    (2) 1-10.   (5) 1-5
    (3) 10-100.

141. The Richter Scale was introduced in
    (1) 1934.   (4) 1955.
    (2) 1844.   (5) 1975.
    (3) 1935.

142. Two-thirds of all known active volcanos have occurred in the
    (1) Atlantic Ocean.   (4) Red Sea.
    (2) Pacific Ocean.   (5) Baltic Sea.
    (3) Gulf of Mexico.

143. The number of known active volcanoes is about
    (1) 700.   (4) 600.
    (2) 900.   (5) 400.
    (3) 500.

144. Modern research of volcanoes was begun by Jean Etienne Guettard in the mid-eighteenth century as he analyzed volcanoes' role in
    (1) forming much of the Earth's crust.
    (2) forming the plates the Earth now rests on.
    (3) formation of Earth from atmospheric wastes.
    (4) rock formations.
    (5) changes in the atmosphere.

145. Volcanoes discharge a large amount of
    (1) random types of gas.   (4) carbon dioxide.
    (2) acids.   (5) mud.
    (3) oxygen.

146. A period of greater than normal volcanic action might
    (1) lower carbon dioxide levels, thus reducing temperature.

    (2)   lower carbon dioxide levels, thus raising temperature.

    (3)   warm the Earth immediately and for an extended period.

    (4)   initiate a warming of the Earth.

    (5)   cool the Earth.

147. Mountains built by volcanic ash might expose large areas of new and unweathered rock to the air, causing
    (1)   a warming of the Earth for an extended period.
    (2)   an increase in the carbon dioxide levels, thus raising the temperature.
    (3)   a decrease in the carbon dioxide levels, thus lowering temperature.
    (4)   a rise in carbon dioxide levels, thus lowering temperature.
    (5)   All of the above.

148. It is estimated that the world's oceans extend over
    (1)   323 cubic million miles.   (4)   328 million cubic miles.
    (2)   328 million miles.   (5)   328 cubic miles.
    (3)   323 million miles.

149. The trench with the greatest depth is located off the coast of
    (1)   Cuba.   (4)   Guatemala.
    (2)   Asia.   (5)   Iraq.
    (3)   Guam.

150. The deepest of the oceans is the
    (1)   Indian Ocean.   (4)   Baltic Ocean.
    (2)   Pacific Ocean.   (5)   North Sea.
    (3)   Atlantic Ocean.

151. Water in the ocean dates about
    (1)   4 million years old.   (4)   4 thousand years old.
    (2)   4 billion years old.   (5)   4 hundred thousand years old.
    (3)   4 trillion years old.

152. 180.4 feet measurement is the most shallow of the oceans. This is the depth of the
    (1)   Baltic Sea.   (4)   Arctic Ocean.
    (2)   Baltic Ocean.   (5)   Pacific Ocean.
    (3)   Atlantic Ocean.

153. Presently oil and _____ are being derived from the ocean as sources of energy.
    (1) minerals
    (2) hydroelectric power
    (3) gas
    (4) food
    (5) fish

154. The oceans supply man with a variety of things, including
    (1) a place for water sports.
    (2) a natural site for photosynthesis.
    (3) a means of transportation.
    (4) All of the above.
    (5) None of the above.

155. The ocean can be of assistance to the maintaining of the ozone layer by
    (1) being a breeding area for more fish.
    (2) being a site of increased photosynthesis.
    (3) acting as a weather controller.
    (4) decreasing evaporation processes.
    (5) creating ozone.

156. Hot springs are
    (1) located in Mississippi.
    (2) man-made bodies of water.
    (3) located only in mountainous areas.
    (4) naturally occurring bodies of water.
    (5) found in arid areas.

157. Hot springs occur mainly
    (1) in colder regions of the nation.
    (2) in warmer regions of the nation.
    (3) in faulted or folded rock and tornado regions.
    (4) in faulted or folded rock and volcanic regions.
    (5) All of the above.

158. Some hot springs are produced by
    (1) wheezers.
    (2) underground seepages.
    (3) geysers.
    (4) naturally occurring water rocks.
    (5) whirlpools.

159. Migration occurs because of
    (1)   famines.
    (2)   the need for cold weather.
    (3)   the need to escape cavemen.
    (4)   the need to develop a pattern of movement to be studied.
    (5)   the need to escape floods.

160. The most common animal that practices migration is the
    (1)   buffalo.   (4)   bird.
    (2)   crane.   (5)   elephant.
    (3)   cow.

161. Migration is the
    (1)   movement of a family from house to house.
    (2)   movement of people or animals from one area to another.
    (3)   movement of birds to reproduce.
    (4)   movement of people to room together.
    (5)   None of the above.

162. One natural flood control device is the
    (1)   man-made dam.   (4)   sand dune.
    (2)   sandbagged river.   (5)   beaver.
    (3)   flood gate.

163. The control of flood waters is important for the
    (1)   a survival of coastal habitats.
    (2)   survival of wading birds.
    (3)   providing of recreational areas.
    (4)   All of the above.
    (5)   None of the above.

164. An extremely large amount of water flowing into a given area faster than it can leave the area describes a
    (1)   tornado.   (4)   flood.
    (2)   hurricane.   (5)   tidal wave.
    (3)   volcano.

165. Capillary waves occur in
    (1)   the ocean.   (4)   all types of water.
    (2)   the sea.   (5)   sequences of five.
    (3)   a pond.

166. Whitecaps usually begin to occur when the wind speed is
    - (1) high speed.
    - (2) medium speed.
    - (3) slow speed.
    - (4) varying.
    - (5) diminishing.

167. Waves are normally caused by
    - (1) the moon.
    - (2) the sun.
    - (3) the Earth's rotation.
    - (4) the current.
    - (5) the wind.

168. Tides are caused by
    - (1) the moon.
    - (2) the Earth.
    - (3) the sun.
    - (4) All of the above.
    - (5) None of the above.

169. The continuous cycle of alternating rise and fall of the sea level observed along the coastlines and bodies of water connected to the sea is called
    - (1) the tide.
    - (2) moon exercises.
    - (3) sun exercises.
    - (4) a waterfall.
    - (5) a tidal wave.

170. A tidal cycle along the Gulf coastline will occur about every
    - (1) 12 hours.
    - (2) 24 hours.
    - (3) 28 hours.
    - (4) 36 hours.
    - (5) 6 hours.

171. Tides are caused by the gravitational interaction between the sun, moon, and
    - (1) Mars.
    - (2) the oceans.
    - (3) the mountains.
    - (4) Earth.
    - (5) Jupiter.

172. Low water is the
    - (1) trough.
    - (2) crest of the wave.
    - (3) lowest tidal cycle.
    - (4) bottom of the water.
    - (5) crest.

173. The maximum height reached by a rising tide is called
    - (1) low water.
    - (2) high water.
    - (3) flood.
    - (4) hurricane.
    - (5) peak.

174. The minimum height water can reach during the falling tide is called the
    (1) high water.   (4) forced water.
    (2) cold water.   (5) trough.
    (3) low water.

175. Tides are classified as
    (1) one high and low water.
    (2) two high and one low water.
    (3) semidiurnal.
    (4) antidiurnal.
    (5) diurnal.

176. Mixed tides are
    (1) those that change from day to day.
    (2) either diurnal or semidiurnal.
    (3) semidiurnals only in certain areas.
    (4) seasonal changes of tides.
    (5) None of the above.

177. Tides are classified as diurnal if they are composed of
    (1) two high waters and two low waters.
    (2) one high water and one low water.
    (3) one high water and two low waters.
    (4) two high waters and one low water.
    (5) All of the above.

178. Hurricanes occur when
    (1) atmospheric conditions change slowly.
    (2) severe climate changes occur at the poles.
    (3) the sky changes color.
    (4) atmosphere and pressure change is severe.
    (5) the weather turns cold.

179. Hurricanes occur over
    (1) land.   (4) water and land.
    (2) water.   (5) the polar caps only.
    (3) land during the day.

180. August, September, and October normally have more hurricanes documented than any other months with
    (1) September having the greatest number of hurricanes.

(2)   August having the greatest number of hurricanes.

(3)   October having the greatest number of hurricanes.

(4)   August and October having the greatest number of hurricanes.

(5)   all three months having the same approximate number of hurri-
       canes.

181. A typhoon is a severe storm that occurs over
    (1)   bodies of water making up rivers.
    (2)   bodies of land and water.
    (3)   bodies of land.
    (4)   bodies of water making up oceans.
    (5)   the polar ice caps.

182. According to the passage, rain, wind, and water make up
    (1)   tornadoes.   (4)   severe storms.
    (2)   volcanoes.   (5)   blizzards.
    (3)   typhoons.

183. Currents prevent extremes of temperature by
    (1)   eroding the land.
    (2)   stabilizing the climate over water areas.
    (3)   stabilizing the climate over land areas.
    (4)   wind movement.
    (5)   None of the above.

184. Currents are influenced by the
    (1)   moon and planets.   (4)   sun and gravity.
    (2)   sun and wind.   (5)   moon and equator.
    (3)   sun.

185. Currents are
    (1)   movements in horizontal or vertical flow occurring at all depths.
    (2)   movements in a horizontal flow occurring at all depths.
    (3)   movements in a vertical flow occurring at all depths.
    (4)   movements in horizontal or vertical flow occurring at one certain
           depth.
    (5)   movements in a vertical flow occurring at shallow depths.

186. Differences in density may be produced
    (1)   by horizontal movements of water.
    (2)   by vertical movements of water.

(3)   both by vertical and horizontal movements of water.
(4)   both by horizontal and vertical movements of air.
(5)   the magnetic field.

187. A decrease in temperature will cause the density of water to
(1)   be cut in half.   (4)   weaken.
(2)   decrease.   (5)   increase.
(3)   remain the same.

188. Water tends to flow from an area of
(1)   low density to high density.   (4)   hotness to coldness.
(2)   high density to low density.   (5)   None of the above.
(3)   coldness to hotness.

189. Fog will interfere with one's ability to
(1)   see over a small area.   (4)   see large moving objects.
(2)   see at a distance.   (5)   see anything.
(3)   see colors.

190. Fog is
(1)   the same as smog.
(2)   caused when cold air moves over warm air.
(3)   a collection of minute water droplets.
(4)   extremely rare on Earth.
(5)   associated with a tornado.

191. Fog is also called a
(1)   geyser.   (4)   hydrometer.
(2)   hydrotherapy.   (5)   black cloud.
(3)   fallen cloud.

192. Conservation is
(1)   protection and wise use of animals.
(2)   protection and wise use of all Earth's resources.
(3)   protection and wise use of some of the Earth's resources.
(4)   management of natural resources only.
(5)   the using up of all resources.

193. Conservation is concerned with the following:
(1)   air, food, water, and heat.
(2)   air, minerals, gas, and oil.

(3)　food, water, oil, and gas.

(4)　None of the above.

(5)　All of the above.

194. The cost of living will be lower for everyone and more ideal surroundings will be present

(1)　with legislation to get better conservation laws.

(2)　with or without conservation enforcement.

(3)　after forgetting the conservation laws.

(4)　with conservation enforcement.

(5)　None of the above.

195. Whom does conservation benefit?

(1)　All living things including man

(2)　All living things but not necessarily man

(3)　All animal life only

(4)　All plants only

(5)　No one

EARTH SCIENCE

ANSWER KEY

Drill: Aspects of Earth Science

1. (4)	15. (1)	29. (3)	43. (5)
2. (1)	16. (4)	30. (3)	44. (3)
3. (3)	17. (3)	31. (3)	45. (3)
4. (4)	18. (2)	32. (1)	46. (3)
5. (2)	19. (3)	33. (4)	47. (2)
6. (3)	20. (1)	34. (1)	48. (3)
7. (1)	21. (2)	35. (2)	49. (3)
8. (3)	22. (4)	36. (4)	50. (4)
9. (5)	23. (1)	37. (3)	51. (5)
10. (4)	24. (2)	38. (2)	52. (3)
11. (1)	25. (5)	39. (4)	53. (3)
12. (1)	26. (3)	40. (1)	54. (3)
13. (3)	27. (1)	41. (3)	55. (1)
14. (5)	28. (2)	42 (2)	56. (2)

Drill: Physics and Chemistry of the Earth

57. (3)	64. (4)	71. (3)	78. (1)
58. (3)	65. (1)	72. (1)	79. (2)
59. (5)	66. (5)	73. (2)	80. (3)
60. (3)	67. (4)	74. (4)	81. (5)
61. (3)	68. (1)	75. (1)	82. (3)
62. (3)	69. (2)	76. (2)	
63. (2)	70. (3)	77. (2)	

Drill: Evolution and Crustal Process

83. (1)	86. (1)	89. (3)	92. (4)
84. (2)	87. (3)	90. (4)	
85. (1)	88. (5)	91. (5)	

Drill: Surface Processes

93. (5)	104. (4)	115. (2)	126. (3)
94. (3)	105. (1)	116. (3)	127. (3)
95. (4)	106. (1)	117. (1)	128. (1)
96. (2)	107. (3)	118. (1)	129. (2)
97. (3)	108. (2)	119. (2)	130 (3)
98. (2)	109. (2)	120. (2)	131. (3)
99. (2)	110. (4)	121. (5)	132. (5)
100. (3)	111. (1)	122. (1)	133. (2)
101. (5)	112. (1)	123. (2)	
102. (1)	113. (2)	124. (1)	
103. (2)	114. (4)	125. (3)	

Drill: Earth's Hazards and Resources

134. (3)	150. (2)	166. (1)	182. (3)
135. (1)	151. (2)	167. (5)	183. (3)
136. (1)	152. (1)	168. (4)	184. (5)
137. (5)	153. (3)	169. (1)	185. (1)
138. (3)	154. (4)	170. (2)	186. (3)
139. (3)	155. (2)	171. (4)	187. (5)
140. (1)	156. (4)	172. (3)	188. (1)
141. (3)	157. (4)	173. (2)	189. (2)
142. (2)	158. (3)	174. (3)	190. (3)
143. (3)	159. (1)	175. (3)	191. (4)
144. (1)	160. (4)	176. (2)	192. (2)
145. (4)	161. (2)	177. (2)	193. (4)
146. (4)	162. (4)	178. (4)	194. (1)
147. (3)	163. (4)	179. (4)	195. (1)
148. (4)	164. (4)	180. (1)	
149. (3)	165. (4)	181. (4)	

V. PHYSICS

A. BASIC CONCEPTS OF PHYSICS

Physics is the study of matter, energy, and the relationships between the two phenomenal areas of study. Relationships between matter and energy have existed as long as the universe has existed, though man has not totally understood all relationships. Every time you lift a baby, push a wheelbarrow, or physically work out, you are demonstrating or applying the principles of physics. Basic principles or concepts of physics may be divided into eight general areas: mechanics (motion and force), energy, magnetism, sound, light, heat, waves, and electricity.

A scientific law is usually constructed after a limited number of experiments or observations have been tried. It summarizes the order that is believed to exist within certain prescribed conditions and can only occasionally be modified or extended to fit new situations. A scientific law is a statement that (1) fits new facts, (2) uses inductive and deductive reasoning, and (3) successfully predicts what is found in nature.

LAW OF ACCELERATION

The amount of acceleration is directly proportional to the acting force and inversely proportional to mass:

$$F = ma.$$

Drop a rock and it falls to the ground. The rock starts its fall from a resting position and gains speed as it falls. This gain in speed indicates the acceleration of the rock as it falls. Gravity (acting force) causes the rock to fall downward once it moves from its resting position. Remember, acceleration is equal to the change in speed divided by the time interval.

ARCHIMEDES' LAW OF BUOYANCY OR ARCHIMEDES' PRINCIPLE

The relationship between buoyancy and displaced liquid was discovered in ancient times by the Greek philosopher Archimedes in the third century B.C. It states that "an immersed object is pushed up by a force equal to the weight of the fluid it displaces." When an object is suspended in water, the pressures on opposite sides cancel each other. The pressure increases with depth, and the upward force on the bottom of the object will be greater than the downward forces on the top. Thus, an object is lighter in water than in air. This relationship, called Archimedes' Principle, is found to be true of both liquids and gases.

BERNOULLI'S LAW

"A moving stream of gas or liquid appears to exert less sideways pressure than if it were at rest." Bernoulli studied the relationship of fluid speed and pressure, and wondered how the fluid got the energy for extra speed. He discovered that the pressure in a fluid decreases as the speed of the fluid increases. This principle is a consequence of the conservation of energy and supports the concept of steady flow. If the flow speed is too great, then it becomes turbulent and follows changing, curling paths known as eddies. Also, this same principle accounts for the flight of birds and aircraft.

BOYLE'S LAW

If the temperature of a gas remains constant,

$$V \propto \frac{1}{P}$$

where P and V are the pressure and volume, respectively. When the density of the gas increases in a given space, the pressure is increased. The density of the gas also can be doubled by simply compressing the air to half its volume. This law is applied when one inflates a tire, balloon, or any other such object.

CHARLES' LAW

"The volume of gas increases as its temperature increases if the pressure stays the same." Charles' measurements suggested that the volume of a gas would become zero at a temperature of -273° C. Thus, this temperature is called absolute zero. This law applies only to gases. Scientists have found all gases become liquids or solids before they are cooled to the temperature of -273°C. Charles' Law is used to explain the kinetic theory as four factors are needed to describe a gas—the mass, the volume, the pressure, and the temperature. Charles' Law explains the increase in volume within tires after traveling long distances or traveling on hot days.

HOOKE'S LAW

The restoring force, F, is directly proportional to the amount by which the spring is stretched from its equilibrium position:

$$F \propto x, \quad F = kx$$

This law is used to explain the property of elasticity. Elasticity is the ability of a body to change shapes when a force is applied and then return to its original shape when that force is removed. Steel is an example of an elastic material. It can be stretched and it can be compressed. Because of its strength and elastic properties, it is used to make springs for construction girders. Also, spring construction and functioning is based on Hooke's Law.

NEWTON'S LAWS

Sir Isaac Newton's laws describe how forces change the motion of an object and are stated in the Three Laws of Motion.

The First Law (Law of Inertia) states that every body remains in a state of rest or uniform motion unless acted upon by forces from the outside.

The Second Law (Law of Constant Acceleration) states that the acceleration of an object increases as the amount of net force applied from outside the object increases. The formula of this law is

Force = mass × acceleration

Force = mass × meter divided by seconds squared (m/s²) $= \dfrac{\mathrm{kg} \cdot \mathrm{m}}{\mathrm{s}^2}$.

Therefore, applying the formula to determine one newton is the force needed to give a mass of one kilogram an acceleration of one meter per second squared, or:

Force (1 newton) = mass 1(kg) × acceleration (1m/s²); 1 N = lkg × 1 m/s²

Newton's Third Law (Law of Conservation of Momentum) states that forces always come in pairs: to every action there is an equal and opposite reaction. When one object exerts a force on a second object, the second object exerts a force that would be equal to and opposite the force of the first object. Mass is a measure of the amount of inertia of a body. The product of mass and velocity is the amount of momentum an object possesses. A quantity that is not changed is said to be conserved. In a collision the total momentum of the colliding bodies is not changed. This is the Law of Conservation of Momentum or Newton's Third Law. Momentum is conserved provided there are no outside forces acting on a set of objects.

LAW OF CONSERVATION OF ENERGY

Energy cannot be created or destroyed; it changes forms but does not cease to exist. This law explains how energy can change from one form to another. As energy can never be created or destroyed, the total energy of the universe remains the same.

LAW OF CONSERVATION OF MECHANICAL ENERGY

In the absence of friction, energy stored in a machine remains constant and work done by the machine is equal to the work done on it. The energy of an object enables it to do work. Mechanical energy is due to the position of something (potential energy) or the movement of something (kinetic energy). Mechanical energy is produced by a machine that is a device for multiplying forces or changing the directions of forces.

LAW OF GRAVITATION

Any two bodies in the universe attract each other with a force that is directly proportional to their masses (m_1 and m_2) and inversely proportional to the square of their distance apart:

$$F = Gm_1 m_2/d^2.$$

Forces are always applied at several different places under normal circumstances, not just at one point. This force on objects found on the Earth is what we call gravity.

LENZ'S LAW

The direction of an induced current is always such that its magnetic field opposes the operation that causes it. This law is the basis for the design of a generator and its ability to function by converting mechanical energy into electrical energy. A changing magnetic field induces an electric field. A generator uses the electromagnetic induction to convert mechanical energy into electrical energy.

OHM'S LAW

The current in a wire is proportional to the potential difference between the ends of the wire:

V (voltage) = I (current) × R (resistance)

Ohm's Law determines the strength of the current that flows into the circuit and the basis for the concept of electrical current. Any path along which electrons can flow is a circuit. A complete circuit is needed to maintain a continuous electron flow.

LAW OF REFLECTION

The angle of incidence equals the angle of reflection. This law explains how a wave changes its direction or how it is reflected back. When light is reflected from a flat surface or plane such as a mirror, the incoming light ray (incident ray) and the reflected ray of light (reflected ray) are measured with respect to a line perpendicular to the flat surface. When a light ray strikes a flat surface, the angle of incidence always equals the angle of reflection. Sunlight is an example showing this law.

LAW OF REFRACTION

Light rays passing through a transparent substance are bent, or refracted; the thicker the substance is, the farther apart its actual and apparent locations will be. The law also states that the incident ray and the refracted ray both lie on one plane.

A theory applies to a broad range of phenomena and is applied to a small aspect of nature. A theory attempts to explain the "how's" and "why's" of science. It is in the establishing and testing of theories that discoveries are made. The primary purpose of a theory is to enable us to see a natural phenomenon as a part of a simple, unified whole as it

1. correlates many facts in a single concept or reasonable assumption;

2. suggests or accommodates new ideas;

3. stimulates research;

4. is useful in solving long-range problems; and

5. makes predictions.

Albert Einstein developed the Theory of Relativity, which is often referred to as Einstein's Theory. The relativity theory is based on mathematical formulas and calculations dealing with gravitation, mass, motion, space, and time. Basic principles of this theory are:

1. The laws of physics will be the same in any reference frame which is moving at constant velocity (non-accelerated).

2. The speed of light in empty space will always have the same value regardless of the motion of the source or the motion of the observer.

Before a hypothesis can be scientific, it must conform to the scientific rule of being testable. Then, one must test by following the scientific method:

1. recognize the problem;

2. formulate your hypothesis;

3. complete related research;

4. perform test-to-test prediction;

5. collect data while performing the test;

6. summarize research and test results in an orderly manner; and

7. draw conclusions.

☞ Drill: Basic Concepts of Physics

<u>DIRECTIONS</u>: Carefully read and answer each of the following questions which are based on the information which you have just read.

1. Physics is the most basic science because
   - (1) you can better understand science if you understand physics principles.
   - (2) the physics ideas extend into more complex science ideas.
   - (3) underneath biology and chemistry concepts lie the physics concepts.
   - (4) All of the above.
   - (5) None of the above.

2. Which of the following statements is not true?
   - (1) Science is a method of answering theoretical questions.
   - (2) Technology is a method of solving practical problems.
   - (3) Science excludes the human factor.
   - (4) A good scientist is influenced by his likes and dislikes as well as friends' opinions.
   - (5) A good scientist is not influenced by his likes and dislikes as well as friends' opinions.

3.   A scientific law is
     (1)   an educated guess that has yet to be proven by experiment.
     (2)   a synthesis of a limited number of experiments or observations that summarizes a belief.
     (3)   close agreements among observations made by competent observers about different ideas.
     (4)   a guess that has been tested and proven without any limitations.
     (5)   usually incorrect.

4.   To test a scientific law,
     (1)   set up one experiment and analyze the results.
     (2)   set up many experiments and analyze the results.
     (3)   use inductive and deductive reasoning in analyzing new facts.
     (4)   find the best result and report only that result.
     (5)   make assumptions based on your opinions.

5.   If the force acting on a cart is doubled, what happens to the cart's acceleration?
     (1)   It is quadrupled.   (4)   It is quartered.
     (2)   It is tripled.   (5)   It is doubled.
     (3)   It is halved.

6.   Acceleration is defined as the
     (1)   change in position divided by the time needed to make that change.
     (2)   change in velocity divided by the time needed to make that change.
     (3)   time it takes to move from one speed to another speed.
     (4)   time it takes to move from one place to another place.
     (5)   change in time.

7.   The acceleration due to gravity _____ over the Earth's surface.
     (1)   is constant
     (2)   is faster than the base rate
     (3)   is slower than the base rate
     (4)   varies
     (5)   creates rain

8.   Archimedes' Principle says that an object is buoyed up by a force that is equal to
     (1)   the weight of the fluid displaced.

    (2)   the volume of the fluid displaced.

    (3)   the mass of the fluid displaced.

    (4)   the mass of the object.

    (5)   the speed at which the object is moving.

9. Pressure in a liquid depends on the
   (1) density of the liquid. (4) Both 1 and 3.
   (2) volume of the liquid. (5) Both 1 and 2.
   (3) depth of the measuring point.

10. The main difference between gases and liquids is that in gases,
    (1) molecules are moving faster.
    (2) forces between molecules are greater.
    (3) distances between molecules are greater.
    (4) molecules collide more frequently.
    (5) molecules are moving slower.

11. When a river narrows, the water in the river flows
    (1) faster. (4) at the same rate.
    (2) more slowly. (5) in the reverse direction.
    (3) at varying rates.

12. Bernoulli's Principle states that
    (1) internal fluid pressure decreases as fluid speed increases.
    (2) as the volume of a gas increases at constant temperature, the pressure decreases.
    (3) an object in air is buoyed up by a force equal to the weight of the air displaced.
    (4) internal fluid pressure increases as fluid speed increases.
    (5) force is equal to mass.

13. The total energy of a liquid depends in part on the liquid's
    (1) specific heat. (4) heat of vaporization.
    (2) volume. (5) color.
    (3) heat of fusion.

14. Boyle's Law relates
    (1) pressure and temperature. (4) temperature and volume.
    (2) pressure and volume. (5) volume and mass.
    (3) pressure and mass.

15. The reason a shower curtain will pull to the inside of a bathtub during a shower is that
    (1) there is more air inside the shower curtain.
    (2) there is less air inside the curtain.
    (3) the pressure is higher inside the curtain.
    (4) the pressure is lower inside the curtain.
    (5) there is a draft in the bathtub.

16. The change in volume of a gas with a change in temperature
    (1) is directly proportional to its volume.
    (2) depends on the nature of the gas.
    (3) is directly proportional to the coefficient of volume expansion.
    (4) All of the above.
    (5) None of the above.

17. As a substance is heated steadily, its temperature increases for a while, then the temperature stops increasing. The temperature stops increasing because
    (1) the molecules are losing kinetic energy.
    (2) the substance is changing from a liquid to a gas.
    (3) the substance is changing from a gas to a liquid.
    (4) the molecules are moving closer together.
    (5) None of the above.

18. Charles' Law can be used to explain
    (1) why car tires are slightly larger after a long trip on a hot day.
    (2) how a liquid-filled thermometer works.
    (3) why a bottle of water cracks when it freezes.
    (4) how large amounts of gas are stored in small containers.
    (5) the Theory of Relativity.

19. The law that explains the principle of elasticity is
    (1) Charles' Law.   (4) Marshall's Law.
    (2) Newton's Law.   (5) Einstein's Law.
    (3) Hooke's Law.

20. The ability of a body to change shapes when a force is applied and then return to its original shape when that force is removed is
    (1) elasticity.   (4) girders.
    (2) compression.   (5) chameleon.
    (3) springforce.

21. Which of the following is made of an elastic material?
    (1) A piece of cookie dough (4) A telephone pole
    (2) Biscuit dough   (5) A bridge girder
    (3) Skis

22. The resistance of an object to changes in its state of motion is called
    (1) momentum.   (4) acceleration.
    (2) inertia.   (5) deceleration.
    (3) torque.

23. The Law of Inertia states that an object
    (1) at rest will remain at rest unless acted on by an outside force.
    (2) will move at the same velocity from an inside force.
    (3) will continue to move in a straight line.
    (4) has more mass when moving.
    (5) All of the above.

24. The Law of Inertia applies to
    (1) only moving objects.
    (2) only objects that are not moving.
    (3) both moving and nonmoving objects.
    (4) all objects at rest only.
    (5) all objects.

25. The acceleration produced by a net force on an object is
    (1) directly proportional to the magnitude of the net force.
    (2) in the same direction as the net force.
    (3) inversely proportional to the mass of the object.
    (4) All of the above.
    (5) None of the above.

26. When an automobile is accelerated forward,
    (1) the tires exert a forward action force on the road.
    (2) the road exerts a forward reaction force on the tires.
    (3) the road exerts a rearward reaction on the tires.
    (4) the tires exert a rearward reaction on the road.
    (5) the tires deflate.

27. The acceleration of a body is
    (1) directly proportional to the force exerted.
    (2) inversely proportional to the mass of the body.

    (3)   in the same direction as the applied force.

    (4)   All of the above.

    (5)   None of the above.

28.   In free fall, the force required to accelerate an object of known weight is
   - (1)   related to velocity and gravity.
   - (2)   not related to acceleration due to gravity.
   - (3)   directly proportional to the acceleration due to gravity.
   - (4)   directly proportional to the weight of the object.
   - (5)   the force of gravity itself.

29.   Newton's Third Law of Motion deals with
   - (1)   one object and two forces.
   - (2)   two objects and one force.
   - (3)   two objects and two forces.
   - (4)   three objects and two forces.
   - (5)   three objects and three forces.

30.   According to Newton's Third Law, if you push on something, it will push
   - (1)   back on you with equal force.
   - (2)   gently on something else.
   - (3)   away from you.
   - (4)   on you if you are not moving.
   - (5)   back with a doubled force.

31.   Energy is
   - (1)   the capacity for doing work.
   - (2)   acquired by an object raised to an elevated position.
   - (3)   acquired by an object which is set in motion.
   - (4)   All of the above.
   - (5)   None of the above.

32.   Energy can
   - (1)   not be created.
   - (2)   not be destroyed.
   - (3)   be changed in form.
   - (4)   All of the above.
   - (5)   None of the above.

33.   Mechanical energy is produced by a machine that is a device for
   - (1)   multiplying forces or changing the directions of forces.
   - (2)   dividing forces or changing the direction of forces.
   - (3)   adding forces.

(4)   subtracting the direction of the force.

(5)   changing speed.

34.   Which of the following is NOT an example of a simple machine?
- (1)   Pulley
- (2)   Fulcrum
- (3)   Inclined plane
- (4)   Lever
- (5)   Piston

35.   Friction acts parallel to the surfaces which are sliding over one another and in the
- (1)   same direction as the motion.
- (2)   opposite direction of the motion.
- (3)   contact line and circular motion.
- (4)   direction of the sliding force.
- (5)   None of the above.

36.   It can be reasoned that the gravitational attraction between the Earth and the moon must be
- (1)   directly proportional to the square of the distance between them.
- (2)   inversely proportional to the square of the distance between them.
- (3)   the same at all distances.
- (4)   independent of distance.
- (5)   related to their speeds.

37.   The gravitational force between two masses
- (1)   is always an attraction.
- (2)   depends on how large the masses are.
- (3)   depends inversely on the square of the distances between the masses.
- (4)   All of the above.
- (5)   None of the above.

38.   Gravitational forces are the weakest forces found in nature. Because of this,
- (1)   the gravitational effect between a pencil and the Earth cannot be seen.
- (2)   there is no gravitational force between two 1-kg masses.
- (3)   there is no movement between two 1-kg masses located near each other in space.
- (4)   gravitational effects can only be observed when a large mass is involved.
- (5)   gravity's effect on humans cannot be seen.

39. A generator uses electromagnetic induction to convert
    (1) mechanical energy into electric energy.
    (2) electric energy into mechanical energy.
    (3) magnetic energy into electromagnetic energy.
    (4) electromagnetic energy into electric energy.
    (5) magnetic energy into electromagnetic energy.

40. The induction of voltage by a change in the magnetic field around a conductor is called
    (1) generated voltage.
    (2) Faraday's induction.
    (3) transformer induction.
    (4) electromagnetic induction.
    (5) transformer voltage.

41. According to Ohm's Law,
    (1) $V = I/R$.
    (2) $V = IR$.
    (3) $R = VI$.
    (4) $I = R/V$.
    (5) $R = I/V$

42. When two light bulbs are connected in series,
    (1) the same amount of current flows through each light bulb.
    (2) the current through each light is proportional to the resistance of the bulb.
    (3) the light bulbs will not work unless there is a fuse in the circuit.
    (4) there are at least two branches in the circuit.
    (5) All of the above.

43. Ohm's Law determines the strength of the current that flows
    (1) through the circuit.
    (2) out of the circuit.
    (3) around the circuit.
    (4) into and through the circuit.
    (5) into the circuit.

44. The Law of Reflection states that
    (1) all waves incident on a mirror are reflected.
    (2) waves incident on a mirror are partially reflected.
    (3) the angle at which a ray is reflected from a mirror is unpredictable.
    (4) the angle of reflection from a mirror equals the angle of incidence.
    (5) what you see is what you get.

45. Reflection occurs
    (1) when the image is located in front of the mirror.
    (2) when one part of the wave travels more slowly than another part.
    (3) when the wave incidence is deflected.
    (4) None of the above.
    (5) All of the above.

46. The reason we can read print from any direction is that
    (1) letters emit black light in all directions.
    (2) letters absorb black light from all directions.
    (3) the white part of a page reflects light in all directions.
    (4) the image is decolored.
    (5) our brain can process information quickly.

47. When refraction occurs, part of a wave
    (1) is bent more than another part.
    (2) slows down before another part.
    (3) is pushed to one side.
    (4) is closer together than it appears.
    (5) is crushed.

48. A rainbow occurs because sunlight
    (1) is refracted by water in the raindrops.
    (2) is refracted by the atmosphere.
    (3) is bent by layers of hot air in the atmosphere.
    (4) falls on different size raindrops.
    (5) has conquered the storm.

49. When light is refracted,
    (1) the rays all lie on different planes.
    (2) the rays lie on one plane.
    (3) the rays lie on one thickness.
    (4) the rays lie behind the plane.
    (5) the rays disappear.

50. Testing
    (1) and establishing theories lead to discoveries.
    (2) explains how discoveries are made.
    (3) correlates all discoveries.
    (4) and establishing myths lead to great discoveries.
    (5) is expensive and dangerous.

51. A major purpose of the theory is to
    (1) bring fame to the scientist.
    (2) prove another scientist wrong.
    (3) stimulate research.
    (4) supply reading material.
    (5) give scientists something to study.

52. Einstein reasoned
    (1) all motion is relative.
    (2) a spaceship can measure its speed only relative to other objects.
    (3) there is no unique spot relative to which all motion can be measured.
    (4) All of the above.
    (5) None of the above.

53. According to the Theory of Relativity, all laws of nature are the same in reference frames that
    (1) accelerate.   (4) oscillate.
    (2) vibrate.   (5) decelerate.
    (3) move at constant speeds.

54. To insure that a hypothesis is scientific, it must conform to the
    (1) ideas of the scientist.
    (2) rule of having been tested before.
    (3) scientific rule of being testable.
    (4) scientific rule of categorizing.
    (5) scientist's opinion.

55. A testing of a hypothesis is accomplished by following the scientific method which includes:
    (1) recognizing the problem.
    (2) formulating a hypothesis.
    (3) completing related research.
    (4) All of the above.
    (5) None of the above.

B. MATTER, MASS, AND DENSITY

Matter is found in everything. Everything is made of atoms. All matter, living or nonliving, is a combination of elements (atoms). Matter is anything that has mass and occupies space. Matter can exist in four states dependent upon its Brownian Motion:(l) solid, (2) liquid, (3) gas, or (4) plasma, which makes up the greatest quantity of matter.

Mass is the quantity of matter in a body that exhibits a response to any effort (energy or movement) made to start it, stop it, or change in any way its state of motion. Mass is measured by the amount of inertia an object has. The greater the mass, the greater the force necessary to change its state of motion. Mass is often confused with weight. Weight is a specific numerical measurement or unit, while mass is anything that takes up space and has weight.

Density is the measure of compactness of a material. It being as light as a feather or heavy as a rock is dependent upon its density. Density is not mass nor is it volume. Density cannot be equated to size in all cases; rather, it is the compactness of the mass per unit of volume. Both the mass of the atoms making up the substance or material and the spacing between the atoms determine the density of materials or state of materials.

☞ Drill: Matter, Mass, and Density

DIRECTIONS: Carefully read and answer each of the following questions which are based on the information which you have just read.

56. Most of the matter of the universe is in which state?
     (1) Liquid   (4) Plasma
     (2) Solid   (5) Air
     (3) Gas

57. Atoms combine to form
     (1) nucleon.   (4) isotopes.
     (2) elements.   (5) molecules.
     (3) more atoms.

58. Mass is measured by the amount of
     (1) inertia an object has.
     (2) motion an object has.
     (3) weight an object has.

(4)   specific numbers of an object.

(5)   force an object exerts.

59.   The greater the mass of an object, the greater the force necessary

(1)   to change its position.

(2)   to change its force.

(3)   to change its weight.

(4)   to change its state of motion.

(5)   to change its shape.

60.   If an object has the density of water and is placed into water, it will

(1)   float.

(2)   sink.

(3)   bounce up and down.

(4)   neither float nor sink, but stay anywhere it is put.

(5)   fill up with water.

61.   The reason an iron ship does not sink is that

(1)   iron is less dense than water.

(2)   iron in the shape of a ship's hull displaces more water than if the same amount of iron were in a solid block.

(3)   the ship is so big.

(4)   the buoyant force equals the volume of the boat.

(5)   iron is waterproof.

C. MOTION

Motion is all around us. Our bodies, no matter how still we think we are, are in a constant state of motion. Motion is easy to see but almost impossible to describe or define. Therefore, when speaking of motion, one must address it as relative to an object rate.

1. VELOCITY

Velocity is the speed in a given direction. Speed and velocity can be used interchangeably if the description is asking for how fast a movement occurs in a certain direction. Velocity can be described as constant or changing. A constant velocity requires that both the speed stay the same and direction not be changed or altered. Motion at constant velocity is motion in a straight line at a constant speed. A body may be moving at a constant speed along a curved path or the speed may vary along a constant path. The latter is referred to as changing velocity.

2. ACCELERATION

Acceleration is a rate that applies to a decreasing speed (deceleration) as well as an increasing speed (acceleration). Acceleration applies to a change in direction as well as the change in speed. Pressing the gas pedal of a car will accelerate the speed of the car; pressing the brakes will retard the speed, or decelerate the car. Like velocity, acceleration is directional.

3. MOMENTUM

Momentum is the mass of an object multiplied by its velocity

$$\text{momentum} = \text{mass} \times \text{velocity} = m \times v.$$

If the momentum of an object changes, either the mass or the velocity or both change. Thus, acceleration occurs.

Gravity causes a rock to fall downward once it has been dropped. This action on movement is referred to as gravitational motion. If there were no air resistance, the motion would be called free fall. The time that it takes an object to fall from the beginning of the fall to the point of rest is called elapsed time. The concept of gravity effects was first credited to Isaac Newton after he was hit on the head with an apple that fell from a tree he was sitting beneath.

4. SPEED

Speed is a measure of how fast something is moving or the rate at which a distance is being covered. Speed is calculated as the distance covered divided by the unit of time. Speed is the rate of change of the position of an object. The average speed describes the motion of objects even if they are not moving at a constant speed. This average speed can be calculated by the total distance traveled divided by the total time taken for travel.

5. INERTIA

Inertia is the resistance an object has to a change in its state of motion. Inertia can be measured by its mass depending upon the amount and type of matter in it. The idea of inertia while in motion is called momentum in reference to moving objects.

☞ Drill: Motion

DIRECTIONS: Carefully read and answer each of the following questions which are based on the information which you have just read.

62. Motion is
    - (1) a constant state.
    - (2) relative to an object.
    - (3) all around us.
    - (4) All of the above.
    - (5) None of the above.

63. Uniform motion in a straight line is the only motion possible for
    - (1) a space ship.
    - (2) an automobile accelerating.
    - (3) an isolated object.
    - (4) a relative force.
    - (5) a boat.

64. If a moving van changes direction, which of the following also changes?
    - (1) mass.
    - (2) speed.
    - (3) weight.
    - (4) inertia.
    - (5) velocity.

65. Velocity can be described as
    - (1) constant.
    - (2) changing.
    - (3) the force exerted.
    - (4) speed.
    - (5) Both 1 and 2.

66. The value of the acceleration due to gravity
    - (1) does not depend on the mass of an object.
    - (2) depends on the shape of the earth.
    - (3) depends on smaller surfaces.
    - (4) depends on the deceleration factor.
    - (5) depends on the weight of an object.

67. Deceleration is
    - (1) an increase in speed.
    - (2) a motion at a constant speed.
    - (3) a decrease in speed.
    - (4) a gain of mass.
    - (5) a loss of mass.

68. Momentum is conserved in all collisions in which no external forces are acting except
    (1)   those in which heat is regenerated.
    (2)   those that are nonelastic.
    (3)   when all changes are equal.
    (4)   when no change occurs.
    (5)   None of the above.

69. An object falling under the influence of gravity with no air resistance is said to be in
    (1)   free fall.   (4)   free motion.
    (2)   elapsed time.   (5)   fall motion.
    (3)   gravitational motion.

70. The time that it takes an object to fall from the beginning of the fall to the point of rest is called
    (1)   free fall time.   (4)   velocity.
    (2)   concept gravity time.   (5)   deceleration.
    (3)   elapsed time.

71. The motion of objects, even if they are not moving at a constant speed, is called the
    (1)   potential speed.   (4)   average speed.
    (2)   calculated speed.   (5)   kinetic speed.
    (3)   rate of change.

72. Speed is calculated by the following formula:
    (1)   speed divided by distance.
    (2)   distance multiplied by the time.
    (3)   adding time, distance, and weight.
    (4)   distance divided by time.
    (5)   force multiplied by mass.

73. The resistance an object has against change in its state of motion is called
    (1)   force.   (4)   friction.
    (2)   velocity.   (5)   acceleration.
    (3)   inertia.

74. Mass can be defined as:
    (1)   the amount of matter in an object.
    (2)   the type of matter in an object.

      (3)   the amount and type of matter in an object.

      (4)   the amount and density of matter in an object.

      (5)   None of the above.

75.   The idea of inertia while in motion is called

      (1)   momentum in reference to moving objects.

      (2)   inertia frame of reference.

      (3)   measurement of momentum.

      (4)   momentum in reference to nonmoving objects.

      (5)   All of the above.

D. FORCE

Force is the push or pull one body exerts on another body. "For every action, there is an equal and opposite reaction" is another way of describing force. Force is the product of acceleration. The combination of all the forces that act on an object is called the net force. When a body is at rest, a force is at work. The fact that the body is at rest rather than accelerating shows another force at work. Force is necessary to maintain balance and reach net force zero. For a book to be at rest on a table, the sum of the forces acting upon the book must equal zero.

The process of determining the components of a vector is called resolution. A person pushes a lawn mower. This in turn applies force against the ground causing the lawn mower to roll forward. In this example, the vector is a combination of two components. Any vector can be represented by a pair of components that are at right angles to each other.

Friction is the name given to the force that acts between materials that are moving past each other. Friction is a result that arises from irregularities in the surfaces of sliding objects. If no friction was present, a moving object would need no force whatever for its motion to continue. Even for a surface that appears to be smooth, there are microscopic irregularities causing friction to occur.

PARALLEL

When the forces on two opposite sides are equal, this is said to be a parallel force. Thus, this produces, considering all forces are equal, an action-reaction situation.

☞ Drill: Force

<u>DIRECTIONS</u>: Carefully read and answer each of the following questions which are based on the information which you have just read.

76. A net force
    (1) changes the state of motion of an object.
    (2) must be a contact force.
    (3) may act over long distances.
    (4) produces a constant velocity.
    (5) grosses change.

77. For a book resting on the horizontal surface of a desk,
    (1) the weight of the book on the desk is a force.
    (2) the force of gravity is only on the book.
    (3) the desk pushes up on the book.
    (4) Both 1 and 3.
    (5) Both 1 and 2.

78. When pushing a lawn mower, with force at an angle of 30° to the ground,
    (1) the desired motion is in the direction of the vertical component.
    (2) the effective force in the direction of the motion is less than the applied force.
    (3) the applied force varies if the handle is raised, but the vertical component becomes less.
    (4) None of the above.
    (5) All of the above.

79. A vector is a quantity that has
    (1) magnitude and time.
    (2) magnitude and direction.
    (3) time and direction.
    (4) magnitude, direction, and time.
    (5) only direction.

80. The weight of a person can be represented by a vector that acts
    (1) perpendicular to the ground underneath the person.
    (2) parallel to the ground.
    (3) straight down, even if the person is standing on a hill.

(4)   in a direction that depends on where the person is standing.
(5)   All of the above.

81. Friction
(1)   acts in a direction opposite to the direction of motion of an object.
(2)   comes from microscopic bumps that act as obstructions to an object's motion.
(3)   is the name given to the force acting between surfaces sliding past one another.
(4)   All of the above.
(5)   None of the above.

82. Which of the following two forces oppose each other when a block of wood slides down a ramp?
(1)   Gravitational force and electrical force
(2)   Electrical force and magnetic force
(3)   Magnetic force and frictional force
(4)   Frictional force and gravitational force
(5)   Electrical force and frictional force

83. The idea of parallel force can be applied to circuits. A parallel circuit would
(1)   have equal currents.
(2)   have action-reaction forces producing static electricity.
(3)   have a constant supply of electricity.
(4)   would have an on-off supply of electricity depending on all forces being constant.
(5)   have unequal currents.

84. When forces on two opposing sides are equal, you have
(1)   an AC circuit.   (4)   Both 1 and 3.
(2)   a DC circuit.   (5)   an AC/DC circuit.
(3)   a parallel force.

E. ENERGY

Energy is the ability of an object to cause change; energy is the ability to do work. Energy is produced when forces are at work. Objects in motion cause change. The greater the speed, the greater the change that occurs. If you experience an energy surge, then you can work more or move faster. Objects as well as people can have energy. Energy can exist in various forms and can change from one form to another form. This energy and its changes can be measured. The unit of measurement of energy is called a joule.

Energy exists in three states: potential, kinetic, and activation energies. An object possessing energy because of its motion has kinetic energy. The energy that an object has as the result of its position or condition is called potential energy. The energy necessary to transfer or convert potential energy into kinetic energy is called activation energy.

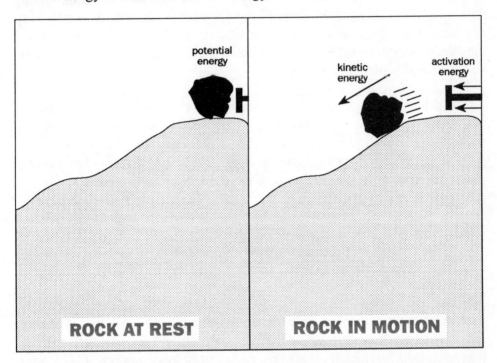

Study the diagram to see that a rock at rest is considered to be potential energy. If a force is used to set that rock in motion, that force would be the activation energy. The rock rolling down the hill until it reaches a point of rest (potential energy) is considered kinetic energy.

Other forms of energy are a result of conditions or combinations of the states of energy. When kinetic and potential energy of lifting, bending, and stretching are grouped together, they are called mechanical energy. If one considers the total energy of the particles that make up an object or body, this is thermal energy. A raised weight possesses potential energy called gravitational potential energy. When it is released, it will return to its former level. This is the principle applied to the functioning of a spring or stretching an object.

Work is the transfer of energy as the result of motion. Most people think of work as an amount of effort exerted. However, if you attempted to move a boulder without any success, you expended energy but no work was accomplished. Work is a derived unit; it may be expressed as any force unit times any distance unit. The only thing that matters in calculating work is the distance moved in the direction of the force.

A machine is any device by which energy can be transferred from one place to another or one form to another. Think back to the diagram of the rock rolling down the hill. This is an example of a machine. Often, when we think of a machine or using a machine, some outside agent — a motor, a battery, your muscles — does the work on the machine. The machine then delivers work to something on which it acts.

The principle of conservation of mechanical energy deals with the functioning of a machine. This principle dictates how two kinds of work are related. "In the absence of other forces that dissipate energy, the total mechanical energy of a system remains constant." So long as any energy that is stored within a machine remains constant, and in the absence of friction, the work done by the machine is exactly equal to the work done on it.

Power is the rate of doing work per unit of time. This is calculated by:

P (power) = W (work) divided by t (time).

Suppose two workers are pushing identical boxes up an inclined plane. One pushes his box up the plane in 20 seconds while the other pushes his box up the plane in 40 seconds. Both do the same amount of work. The difference is the rate of time in which the work is done. The unit for power is watt. One watt is one joule of work per second.

☞ Drill: Energy

DIRECTIONS: Carefully read and answer each of the following questions which are based on the information which you have just read.

85. Objects in motion cause change. The faster the motion,
    (1) the lesser the change that occurs.
    (2) the greater the change that occurs.
    (3) the less the speed increases.
    (4) the more the ability to work has decreased.
    (5) All of the above.

86. Energy is
    (1) the ability to do work.
    (2) objects in motion.
    (3) produced when forces are at work.
    (4) Both 1 and 3.
    (5) Both 2 and 3.

87. As a pendulum swings back and forth,
    (1) potential energy is transformed into kinetic energy.
    (2) its energy is all kinetic at the lowest part of its swing.
    (3) its energy is all potential at the end points of its swing.
    (4) All of the above.
    (5) None of the above.

88. Kinetic energy is
    (1) energy due to the possible position of the mass.
    (2) energy due to the motion of the mass.
    (3) energy due to the orientation of the particles in a mass.
    (4) proportional to the weight of the object.
    (5) energy due to the mass of the motion.

89. Kinetic energy is the energy an object has because of its
    (1) mass.   (4) density.
    (2) location.   (5) speed.
    (3) size.

90. Potential energy
    (1) is due to the potential of the mass.
    (2) is energy due to the motion of a mass.
    (3) is energy due to the orientation of the particles in a mass.
    (4) of position is proportional to the weight of the object concerned.
    (5) is energy due to the mass of the motion.

91. Energy can be transferred
    (1) by the movement of materials in one direction.
    (2) by the movement of cooled gas.
    (3) through matter by mechanical machines.
    (4) through space by electromagnetic waves.
    (5) through gas.

92. A pulse moving along a spiral spring
    (1) carries particles of matter along with it.
    (2) is a method of energy transfer.
    (3) can be a crest or trough of a wave.
    (4) can be compression or a rarefaction in transverse wave motion.
    (5) will die.

93. In physics, work is done
    (1) in lifting an object from the floor to the table.
    (2) in supporting an object on our shoulder.
    (3) in preparing school lessons.
    (4) in earning wages.
    (5) in the laboratory.

94. The two factors which determine the amount of work done are
    (1) magnitude of the force exerted and the weight of the object moved.
    (2) the distance of the object moved in the time required.
    (3) the displacement of the object and the magnitude of the force in the direction of the displacement.
    (4) the magnitude of the force in the direction of the displacement and the time required.
    (5) All of the above.

95. A teacher pushes a stack of papers across the desk. The teacher is showing
    (1) the body used as a machine.
    (2) resistance of papers.
    (3) lever and wheel action.
    (4) the desk's resistance to holding papers.
    (5) None of the above.

96. Machines may be used
    (1) to divide the force.
    (2) to multiply speed.
    (3) to divide force and speed simultaneously.
    (4) to keep the direction of the force constant.
    (5) to change mass.

97. The principle of conservation of mechanical energy dictates how two kinds of work are related. They are

    (1)   friction and mechanical energy.
    (2)   absence of friction and work by a machine.
    (3)   speed and type of machine.
    (4)   time and speed of machine.
    (5)   mass and speed of machine.

98.   The law of conservation of mechanical energy
    (1)   is illustrated in suspending a pendulum.
    (2)   states that the sum of the potential and kinetic energies of an ideal energy system remains constant.
    (3)   involves frictional forces.
    (4)   involves systems where the work done is dependent on the path length.
    (5)   Both 1 and 4.

99.   In science, power is
    (1)   the capacity for doing work.
    (2)   the time rate of doing work.
    (3)   the product of a displacement and the force in the direction of the displacement.
    (4)   the force acquired as an object is being moved.
    (5)   money.

100.   Power is the rate of doing work per unit of time. This can be calculated by applying the formula
    (1)   power equals work divided by time.
    (2)   work equals power.
    (3)   power equals work added to time.
    (4)   power equals time divided by number participating in the work.
    (5)   force equals mass multiplied by time.

F. HEAT

Heat is a necessity of life. It is also a very valuable tool that cooks our food, frees metals from ores, and creates usable products (to mention a few of its uses). Heat is a form of energy and that energy is created by the motion of the molecules making up an object. Heat is the transfer of energy from an object of high temperature to one of lower temperature.

Heat has several properties: it can be conducted, it can be measured, heat can be transferred or radiated, and heat can travel by convection. Nearly all materials will either expand or contract when heat is added or taken away.

When the amount of heat within an object or around an object varies, that object will vary. There is an exact point at which the variation will occur. We call this the specific heat. The specific heat of any substance is defined as the quantity of heat required to raise the temperature of a unit of mass of that substance by one degree. For instance, a gram of water requires one calorie of energy to raise the temperature 1°C.

Heat is commonly measured in calories or kilocalories, although scientifically the SI or joule is preferred. SI is the abbreviation of Le Système International d'Unites (French), which is the international system of measurement. The term applied here would be the degree. The degree is a measure of temperature. Temperature is a measure of the average kinetic energy of the particles in a body. The degree might be stated in terms of Fahrenheit (F), Kelvin (K), or Celsius (C).

Celsius is based on the freezing temperature of a body or substance being 0 degrees. To totally remove all possible internal heat within a body or substance, one must reduce the temperature to -273 degrees. This point is considered to be 0 on the Kelvin scale and is called absolute zero. The Fahrenheit scale measures the freezing point at 32°F. To convert from the Fahrenheit scale to the Celsius scale use the formula:

$$(°F - 32)\,\tfrac{5}{9} = °C$$

unless the temperature is below zero on either scale. In that case, you must place a minus sign in front of its number in the equation.

Heat and work are similar when discussing the transfer of energy. Heat is transferred by convection, conduction, or radiation. As work is accomplished, heat is transferred. One way that heat passes from one object to another is by conduction. Not all objects will conduct heat at the same rate; therefore, they are considered poor heat conductors. A very poor conductor of heat is called an insulator.

Most gases and liquids are poor conductors. They can transfer heat by convection, the mass movement of the heated gas or liquid. This is accomplished by spurring, or sporadic movement of molecules in the mass that pass heat when they bump together. Another method of heat transfer is called radiation. Unlike conduction and convection, radiation does not require direct contact between bodies or masses. Almost all of the energy that comes to Earth is by radiation from the sun. The amount of heat that a body can radiate depends not only on its temperature but on the nature of its surface. Dark, rough surfaces tend to send out more heat than smooth, light-colored surfaces.

☞ Drill: Heat

DIRECTIONS: Carefully read and answer each of the following questions which are based on the information which you have just read.

101. Heat transfer occurs
    (1) from an object of a lower temperature to one of higher temperature.
    (2) from an object of a higher temperature to one of lower temperature.
    (3) when expansion takes place.
    (4) when electrons bump into each other.
    (5) the temperature rises.

102. Heat travels from the sun to the Earth by a process called
    (1) conduction.   (4) insulation.
    (2) convection.   (5) radiation.
    (3) connection.

103. Specific heat is related to the amount of heat
    (1) a specific object has.
    (2) one molecule contains.
    (3) transferred by one molecule.
    (4) needed to change the temperature of one gram of a substance by one degree Celsius.
    (5) two molecules contain.

104. Heat transfer by convection occurs when
    (1) electrons bump into other electrons.
    (2) large numbers of atoms move from place to place.
    (3) atoms give off heat in the form of electromagnetic waves.
    (4) electromagnetic waves travel from one place to another through a vacuum.
    (5) an electron bumps into a neutron.

105. Compared to any other substances, water has
    (1) a high specific heat.
    (2) a low specific heat.
    (3) an average specific heat.
    (4) a high average specific heat.
    (5) no temperature.

106. Heat is measured by
    (1) joule.
    (2) calories.
    (3) kilocalories.
    (4) All of the above.
    (5) None of the above.

107. Temperature is a measure of
    (1) the total energy in a substance.
    (2) the total kinetic energy in a substance.
    (3) the average kinetic energy in a substance.
    (4) the average molecular kinetic energy in a substance.
    (5) air.

108. Internal energy is the
    (1) total amount of energy contained in an object.
    (2) average amount of energy contained in an object.
    (3) amount of energy that is transferred from one object to another object.
    (4) amount of kinetic energy each molecule has.
    (5) amount of potential energy minus the amount of kinetic energy a moledule possesses.

109. Which temperature scale designates the freezing point of water as 0 degrees?
    (1) Celsius.
    (2) Fahrenheit.
    (3) Kelvin.
    (4) joule.
    (5) All of the above.

110. Which temperature scale reads a measurement of 0 at absolute zero?
    (1) Celsius.
    (2) joule.
    (3) Kelvin.
    (4) Fahrenheit.
    (5) None of the above.

111. If the weather reporter stated that it was -10 degrees Fahrenheit outside, what would the temperature be on the Celsius scale?
    (1) 10 degrees
    (2) –5 degrees
    (3) 9 degrees
    (4) None of the above.
    (5) All of the above.

112. Heat transfer by conduction occurs when
    (1) electrons bump into atoms and other electrons.
    (2) large numbers of atoms move from place to place.

(3)   atoms give off heat in the form of electromagnetic waves.

(4)   the atoms are placed in a vacuum.

(5)   atoms are sucked into a vacuum.

113. Styrofoam is a good heat

(1)   emitter.   (4)   insulator.

(2)   absorber.   (5)   None of the above.

(3)   conductor.

114. A piece of metal will feel colder to the touch than a piece of wood at the same temperature. Why is this so?

(1)   Metal is colder than wood.

(2)   Metal, in general, has a higher heat capacity than wood.

(3)   Metal, in general, is a better heat conductor than wood.

(4)   Wood, in general, is a poor insulator.

(5)   Metal cools quicker than wood.

115. The radiant energy emitted from a body can be

(1)   X-rays.   (4)   All of the above.

(2)   infrared rays.   (5)   None of the above.

(3)   radio waves.

116. Two pots are filled with boiling water. The pots are exactly the same size, but one pot is white and the other pot is black. Which pot will cool faster?

(1)   The white pot

(2)   The black pot

(3)   They will cool at the same rate

(4)   A comparison cannot be made as shape is not stated

(5)   None of the above.

G. WAVES

A British physicist, Edward Victor Appleton, received a Nobel Prize in 1947 for his work dealing with waves. His discoveries led to defining an important region of the atmosphere called the "ionosphere." It was established that there were definite layers that would reflect and absorb various radio waves, and thus, the Appleton layers were established. These layers reflect and absorb only the long radio waves used in ordinary radio broadcasts. The shorter waves, used for television broadcasting, pass through, and that is why televisions have a limited range and must use satellite relay stations. The ionosphere is the strongest at the end of the day, after the daylong effect of the sun's radiation, and weakens by dawn because many ions and electrons have recombined. Storms on the sun, intensifying the streams of particles and high-energy radiation sent to the Earth, cause the ionized layers to strengthen and thicken. The regions above the ionosphere also flare up into aurora displays.

A wave is a wiggle in space and time that can extend from one place to another. Light and sound are both forms of energy that move through space as waves. If this wiggle only occurs in time, it is called a vibration. A wave is measured in wavelengths. The high points are called the crests, the low points the troughs, and the distance from the midpoint to the crest is the amplitude. How frequently a vibration occurs is described by its frequency. The time necessary for the wave to complete one cycle is called a period.

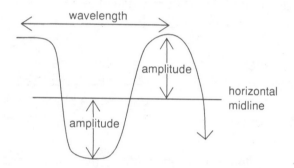

MICROWAVES

Microwaves, having wavelengths shorter than radio waves, are used in communications and to cook food.

☞ Drill: Waves

DIRECTIONS: Carefully read and answer each of the following questions which are based on the information which you have just read.

117. The wave theory assumes that
    (1) light is a train of waves having wave fronts in the same direction as the paths of light rays.
    (2) each point of a wave on a wave front may be regarded as a new source of disturbance.
    (3) the speed of sound in audio-dense media is less than that in air.

(4)   a wave of sound is the line of direction of waves sent out from the base source.

(5)   All of the above.

118. A wave
   (1)   is a disturbance that moves only through solids, liquids, and gases.
   (2)   produces a transfer of energy and matter.
   (3)   involves a quantity which changes location.
   (4)   involves a disturbance which changes in magnitude from place to place at a given time.
   (5)   is made of water.

119. A wave
   (1)   carries energy from one place to another.
   (2)   has a period.
   (3)   has a wavelength.
   (4)   All of the above.
   (5)   None of the above.

120. The time needed for a wave to make one complete cycle is called the wave's
   (1)   frequency.   (4)   velocity.
   (2)   rotation.   (5)   period.
   (3)   wavelength.

121. The distance between successive identical parts of a wave is called the wave's
   (1)   frequency.   (4)   amplitude.
   (2)   period.   (5)   trough.
   (3)   wavelength.

122. The wiggle formed by a wave in time is called the
   (1)   amplitude.   (4)   period.
   (2)   frequency.   (5)   interference.
   (3)   vibration.

123. Microwaves are waves that
   (1)   are shorter.
   (2)   are closer together.
   (3)   are longer.
   (4)   occur less frequently than usual.
   (5)   are flat.

H. LIGHT

The only thing that we can really see is light. Most objects are made visible by the light they reflect from such light sources. Scientists agree that light has a dual nature — part particle and the other part wave. The particles may be measured as photons. The waves are measured by the distance the light travels in one year. This is called a light year. Light is defined as the only visible portion of the electromagnetic spectrum. Light is produced by vibrating electrically charged atoms that have the ability to absorb energy and emit it as light. The transfer of energy by electromagnetic waves is called radiation.

PROPERTIES

The properties of light are reflection, refraction, diffraction, and interference. The amount of the property being demonstrated depends on the amount of light, angle of the light ray, object composition and density. Material that allows all the light to pass through is called transparent. Material that blocks the light is called opaque.

Quantum is an elemental unit that describes the smallest amount of anything. One quantum of light energy is called a photon. In the micro-world, one quantum of anything is an atom. The Quantum Theory is the study of the behavior of the basic elemental form of anything. This can be adapted to all branches of science to explain behavior of matter.

Reflection occurs when a wave bounces off an object. Waves that strike the object are called incident waves, while waves that bounce off are called reflected waves. The angle between the reflected wave and the normal is called the angle of reflection. When the waves are reflected from a surface, the angle of incidence always equals the angle of reflection.

Refraction is the bending of waves toward the direction of slower wave velocity. When wavelengths become shorter, the frequency does not change. Thus, the material will determine the amount of light that is refracted.

DIFFRACTION

The bending of light around the edge of the object blocking its path is called diffraction . The effects of diffraction occur when waves pass either through an opening or around an object that blocks their path.

Light travels in waves that are transverse. This is called polarization. Other waves are longitudinal as they travel. Polarized light waves are waves that travel on one plane. Light vibrating parallel to a molecule is absorbed. The light vibrating at right angles to the rows pass through. This concept is used in the sunglass industry — sunglass lenses are designed to reduce glare.

Illumination is the process of making an object bright by increasing the amount of light per unit of area of a surface.

X-rays are electromagnetic waves with the shortest wavelength and the highest amount of energy. Electrically charged particles are filled with kinetic energy that is changed to radiation when these rays crash into other matter.

Lasers are a source of light that produces a bright and narrow beam of light of one color length and is coherent. Coherent light has the troughs and crests of the light lined up together. Lasers convert one form of energy into light energy. The laser is very bright but extremely inefficient as a light source. They are used extensively by surveyors, welders, surgeons, and by code interpreters for barcoding, as a method of ringing up sales at the supermarket.

☞ Drill: Light

DIRECTIONS: Carefully read and answer each of the following questions which are based on the information which you have just read.

124. Light is measured as
    (1) a light year.
    (2) amps.
    (3) photons.
    (4) a light spectrum.
    (5) amperes.

125. When you approach a light source, the wavelength of emitted light appears
    (1) longer.
    (2) shorter.
    (3) the same.
    (4) to be short and long.
    (5) bright.

126. The energy of a photon is directly proportional to its
    (1) period.
    (2) photos.
    (3) wavelength.
    (4) amplitude.
    (5) frequency.

127. The composition and density of an object will
    (1) directly affect the amount of light passed.

(2)   indirectly affect the amount of light passed.
(3)   not affect light passing.
(4)   cause the object to become opaque.
(5)   enhance light.

128. Glass is transparent to light because
(1)   light beams do not interact with glass molecules.
(2)   glass molecules are relatively far apart.
(3)   glass molecules have a natural frequency in the visible region.
(4)   glass molecules reradiate absorbed light in a relatively short time.
(5)   None of the above.

129. Electron energy states are quantized because
(1)   electrons behave as particles.
(2)   electrons behave as waves.
(3)   the nucleus is quantized.
(4)   only so many electrons will fit in one region of space.
(5)   they are in large quantities.

130. The quantum theory assumes that a transfer of energy between light and matter occurs only in discrete quantities proportionate to
(1)   the intensity of the light.
(2)   the frequency of the radiation.
(3)   the quantity of matter.
(4)   the temperature of matter.
(5)   the mass of matter.

131. The energy states available to an electron are
(1)   continuous.   (4)   nonquantized.
(2)   perpendicular.   (5)   unlimited.
(3)   quantized.

132. When an image is created by reflection from a plane mirror,
(1)   reflected rays diverge.
(2)   the image is located behind the mirror.
(3)   the image is upright.
(4)   All of the above.
(5)   None of the above.

133. The angle between the reflected wave and the normal is called the
(1)   angle of reflection.   (2)   angle of refraction.

(3)   angle of diffraction.   (4)   angle of inference.
(5)   angle of deflection.

134. The bending of waves toward the direction of slower wave velocity is called
(1)   reflection.   (4)   refraction.
(2)   diffraction.   (5)   deflection.
(3)   optifraction.

135. A ray of light passing from one medium into another along the normal is not
(1)   deflected.   (4)   rerefracted.
(2)   reflected.   (5)   inflicted.
(3)   refracted.

136. Diffraction occurs only for
(1)   radio waves.   (4)   Can occur for any wave.
(2)   light.   (5)   Will not occur for any wave.
(3)   X-rays.

137. The effects of diffraction occur either when waves pass through an opening or around an object that
(1)   blocks their path.   (4)   leads to their path.
(2)   opens their path.   (5)   signals their path.
(3)   clears their path.

138. Light traveling in waves that are transverse and travel on one plane is called
(1)   diffracted light.   (4)   distracting light.
(2)   refracted light.   (5)   reflected light.
(3)   polarized light.

139. Light reflected from a lake surface is polarized
(1)   vertically.   (4)   by refraction.
(2)   horizontally.   (5)   equally.
(3)   randomly.

140. Illumination is the process of making an object bright by
(1)   decreasing the area of surface.
(2)   increasing the area of surface.
(3)   decreasing the amount of light per unit of area of a surface.

    (4)   increasing the amount of light per unit of area of a surface.

    (5)   None of the above.

141. X-rays are electromagnetic waves with the shortest wavelength and
    (1)   the lowest amount of energy.
    (2)   the highest amount of energy.
    (3)   no energy.
    (4)   All of the above.
    (5)   None of the above.

142. Electrically charged particles are filled with kinetic energy that is changed to radiation when these rays
    (1)   crash into other matter.
    (2)   avoid other matter.
    (3)   change angles of travel.
    (4)   change to potential energy.
    (5)   Both 2 and 4.

143. Coherent light consists of light rays that all have the same
    (1)   frequency.   (2)   phase.
    (3)   wavelength.   (4)   All of the above.
    (5)   None of the above.

144. Light emitted by a laser is
    (1)   more coherent.   (4)   coherent.
    (2)   less coherent.   (5)   not coherent.
    (3)   incoherent.

I. SOUND

Sound travels about 4 1/2 times faster in seawater than in air. Its speed is affected by temperature, salinity, and pressure; an increase in any of these results in an increase in the speed of sound.

Sound energy does not travel in straight lines in the ocean because of density differences in water. It is refracted, or bent, by variations in sound speed of the water, scattered by suspended material or marine organisms, reflected and scattered by the surface and bottom, and attenuated by the water through which it travels.

Ambient noise refers to any noise or sound produced by the environment or living creatures or organisms.

There are many varieties of sounds that are produced to be captured by the ear and interpreted by the brain. The brain easily distinguishes one sound from another, yet sound is only a longitudinal wave, a rhythmic disturbance of the air that carries energy. Sound waves are compression waves produced by vibrating matter. Ultrasound is used extensively in medical treatment. One way is through picturing a fetus in the womb without any danger to the fetus or the mother.

When any frequency of forced vibrations on an object matches the natural frequency of the object, the measure of the sound increases. The use of tuning forks adjusted to the same frequency and spaced a meter apart is the most common way to demonstrate resonance.

☞ Drill: Sound

DIRECTIONS: Carefully read and answer each of the following questions which are based on the information which you have just read.

145. Sounds are produced by
    (1) matter at rest.
    (2) liquids in motion.
    (3) solids only.
    (4) solids, liquids, or gases.
    (5) your eardrum.

146. An increase in temperature results in
    (1) an increase in the speed of sound.
    (2) a decrease in the speed of sound.
    (3) an increase in the pressure of sound waves.
    (4) a decrease in the pressure of sound waves.
    (5) None of the above.

147. Compared to the speed of light, the speed of sound is
    (1) faster.
    (2) slower.
    (3) the same.
    (4) Cannot be compared.
    (5) Has not been determined.

148. Ambient noise refers to
    (1) wavelengths of sound vibration.
    (2) any sound produced one does not want to hear.
    (3) any noise or sound produced by the environment or living creatures or organisms.

(4)　noise that cannot be heard.

(5)　loud sounds.

149. The most common transmitting medium for sound vibrations is

(1)　metal wires.
(4)　clay.

(2)　earth.
(5)　air.

(3)　water.

150. Ultrasound is a(n)

(1)　type of radio wave.

(2)　sound wave.

(3)　X-ray wave.

(4)　combination of sound and light waves.

(5)　vibration.

151. Resonance occurs when you

(1)　push an object.

(2)　hit an object with a hammer.

(3)　vibrate an object.

(4)　force an object to vibrate at its natural frequency.

(5)　hit your vocal cords.

152. The use of the tuning forks demonstrates

(1)　sound.
(4)　resonance.

(2)　amplitude.
(5)　pitch.

(3)　frequency.

J. ELECTRICITY

An electrical charge resting on an object is called static electricity. If this static electricity is placed in motion, it becomes an electrical current. It is the electrical current that we use in most electrical appliances. This same static electricity can be produced by rubbing a hard rubber rod or sealing wax with a piece of fur or flannel. Also, the same result can be accomplished by rubbing a glass rod with a piece of silk.

Electricity can be carried by matter that is a conductor. Sometimes this is accomplished by a spark, which is a static discharge, or a transfer of static electricity. Materials that are poor conductors, such as wood, plastic, rubber, or glass, are used as insulators or grounds which allow an object to lose its charge in a given direction.

A flow of electrons or charged particles through a conductor is called an electric current. This is demonstrated by use of an electroscope.

Electrical circuits function very efficiently within homes. Most circuits are either alternating current (AC) or direct current (DC). Electricity can be supplied to a water heater to heat water, or through wiring and a bulb to produce artificial light. The energy is carried by means of electrical current from a power plant. One common electrical circuit is the series circuit. A path is formed by electric conductors in the form of wire to carry the current. The series circuit has only one path for the current so the current will be the same through every part.

Another circuit is the parallel circuit, in which there are two or more separate branches for the current to flow. This is the type of circuit used in string lights for a Christmas tree such that when one light goes out, the rest of the lights will stay on. Also, this type of wiring pattern is used for the outlets in our homes. It is not necessary for all the outlets to be in use at all times for electricity to be available at the flip of a switch.

One electronic device that is commonly used is the battery. A battery acts like a pump forcing electrons through a conductor. There are two types of batteries: wet cell battery and dry cell battery. A wet cell battery contains two different metals in a solution containing an electrode. The car battery is an example of the wet cell battery. The dry cell battery contains a carbon rod set in the middle of a zinc holder. A moist paste sets up a chemical reaction that causes electrons to be released.

☞ Drill: Electricity

DIRECTIONS: Carefully read and answer each of the following questions which are based on the information which you have just read.

153. Static electricity compressed will become
    (1) a kilowatt.
    (2) static energy.
    (3) electrical current.
    (4) sound current.
    (5) a shock.

154. Electric energy is measured in
    (1) a kilowatt hour.
    (2) Celsius.
    (3) currents.
    (4) number of wavelengths.
    (5) volts.

155. A property of electricity is that it can
    (1) be carried by a conductor.
    (2) not be carried by a conductor.
    (3) act like static.
    (4) be carried by an insulator.
    (5) change form.

156. An electric current is produced when electrons or charged particles flow through
    (1) an insulator.   (4) an oscilloscope.
    (2) a conductor.   (5) a microscope.
    (3) an electroscope.

157. Alternating current is made by
    (1) alternating the voltage at the energy source.
    (2) alternating current and voltage.
    (3) using huge batteries.
    (4) emptying chemical batteries.
    (5) turning the light switch on and off.

158. Current may be carried in only one path. This is called a(n)
    (1) direct current.   (4) parallel circuit.
    (2) alternating current.   (5) one-way charge.
    (3) series circuit.

159. Electrical elements in our homes are connected in
    (1) series circuits.   (4) switches.
    (2) parallel circuits.   (5) wires.
    (3) outlets.

160. Where there are two or more separate branches for the current to flow, this is called
    (1) current circuits.   (4) parallel circuits.
    (2) outlet circuits.   (5) forked circuits.
    (3) series circuits.

161. A battery acts like a pump forcing electrons through
    (1) a series circuit.   (4) series insulator.
    (2) a parallel circuit.   (5) a conductor.
    (3) an insulator.

162. There are two types of batteries:
    (1)   wet cell battery and dry cell battery.
    (2)   alternating current battery and direct current battery.
    (3)   well cell battery and alternating current battery.
    (4)   direct and dry cell batteries.
    (5)   size AA and D batteries.

K. MAGNETISM

Magnetism is the ability to attract iron and certain other metals that have a molecular structure similar to iron. Magnetism is related to electricity in that it travels in currents. Magnets exert a force on another magnet just like an electrical charge. They can attract or repel each other without touching because of their electrical charges. The strength of their interaction depends on the distance of separation of the two magnets.

Magnetism was explained by Albert Einstein in 1905 in his theory of special relativity when he showed that a magnetic field is a by-product of the electric field. Charges in motion have associated with them both an electric and a magnetic field. A magnetic field is produced by the motion of the electric charge.

A voltmeter is a calibrated device used to measure the electric potential. This electrical current produces a magnetic field. The same principal construction is used in the making of an electric motor. The principal difference is that the current is made to change direction every time the coil makes a half revolution.

Speakers used in car radios, home stereos, and loudspeaker systems belong in the grouping of electromagnets. A speaker consists of a coil of thin wire that goes between the poles of a magnet. The coil is attached to a cone-shaped piece of stiff paper that converts the electrical current into sound.

☞ Drill: Magnetism

DIRECTIONS: Carefully read and answer each of the following questions which are based on the information which you have just read.

163. Magnetic fields are produced by
    (1)   charges at rest.   (4)   magnets.
    (2)   moving particles.   (5)   moving charged particles.
    (3)   moving particles of Earth.

164. Magnetic domains are
     (1) clusters of atoms randomly aligned.
     (2) blocks of material.
     (3) regions that may or may not be magnetized.
     (4) regions of atoms magnetically aligned.
     (5) clusters of magnets.

165. According to Einstein,
     (1) all motion is relative.
     (2) a planet moves around the sun because of the gravitational force exerted by the sun.
     (3) there is a unique spot relative to which all motion can be measured.
     (4) All of the above.
     (5) None of the above.

166. The electromagnetic theory
     (1) was developed by James Clark.
     (2) describes the manner in which radiated energy spreads in dense space.
     (3) predicts that heat radiation travels in space with the speed of light.
     (4) states that the energy of electromagnetic radiations will not split.
     (5) was developed by accident.

167. A speaker converts an electrical current into sound by
     (1) a coil of thin wire that goes between the poles of a magnet.
     (2) a coil of thin wire going around the poles of an electromagnet.
     (3) changing energy forms.
     (4) All of the above.
     (5) None of the above.

PHYSICS

ANSWER KEY

Drill: Basic Concepts of Physics

1.	(4)	15.	(4)	29.	(3)	43.	(5)
2.	(4)	16.	(4)	30.	(1)	44.	(4)
3.	(2)	17	(2)	31.	(4)	45.	(1)
4.	(3)	18.	(1)	32.	(4)	46.	(3)
5.	(5)	19.	(3)	33.	(1)	47.	(2)
6.	(2)	20.	(1)	34.	(2)	48.	(1)
7.	(4)	21.	(5)	35.	(2)	49.	(2)
8.	(1)	22.	(2)	36.	(2)	50.	(1)
9.	(4)	23.	(1)	37.	(4)	51.	(3)
10.	(3)	24.	(3)	38.	(4)	52.	(4)
11.	(1)	25.	(4)	39.	(1)	53.	(3)
12.	(1)	26.	(2)	40.	(4)	54.	(3)
13.	(2)	27.	(4)	41.	(2)	55.	(4)
14.	(2)	28.	(4)	42.	(1)		

Drill: Matter, Mass, and Density

56.	(4)	58.	(1)	60.	(4)	61.	(2)
57.	(5)	59.	(4)				

Drill: Motion

62.	(4)	66.	(1)	70.	(3)	74.	(3)
63.	(3)	67.	(3)	71.	(4)	75.	(1)
64.	(5)	68.	(3)	72.	(4)		
65.	(5)	69.	(1)	73	(3)		

Drill: Force

76.	(1)	79.	(2)	82.	(4)	84.	(4)
77.	(4)	80.	(3)	83.	(3)		
78.	(2)	81.	(4)				

Drill: Energy

85. (2)	89. (5)	93. (1)	97. (2)
86. (4)	90. (3)	94. (3)	98. (2)
87. (4)	91. (4)	95. (1)	99. (2)
88. (2)	92. (2)	96. (2)	100. (1)

Drill: Heat

101. (2)	105. (1)	109. (1)	113. (4)
102. (5)	106. (4)	110. (3)	114. (3)
103. (4)	107. (4)	111. (4)	115. (4)
104. (2)	108. (1)	112. (1)	116. (1)

Drill: Waves

117. (2)	119. (4)	121. (3)	123. (1)
118. (4)	120. (5)	122. (3)	

Drill: Light

124. (3)	130. (2)	136. (4)	142. (1)
125. (2)	131. (3)	137. (1)	143. (4)
126. (5)	132. (4)	138. (3)	144. (4)
127. (1)	133. (1)	139. (2)	
128. (4)	134. (4)	140. (4)	
129. (1)	135. (3)	141. (2)	

Drill: Sound

145. (4)	147. (2)	149. (5)	151. (4)
146. (1)	148. (3)	150. (2)	152. (4)

Drill: Electricity

153. (3)	156. (2)	159. (2)	161. (4)
154. (1)	157. (1)	160. (4)	162. (1)
155. (1)	158. (3)		

Drill: Magnetism

163. (5)	165. (1)	167. (1)
164. (4)	166. (3)	

INTERPRETING LITERATURE AND THE ARTS REVIEW

Chapter 5

INTERPRETING LITERATURE AND THE ARTS REVIEW

I.   INTERPRETING LITERATURE AND THE ARTS TOPICS

II.   READING PROSE

III.   READING POETRY

IV.   READING DRAMA

V.   READING COMMENTARY

This review is meant to help you become familiar with the types of reading passages you will find on the *Interpreting Literature and the Arts* section of the GED. Each of these types of writing communicate ideas in a very distinct way. This review will help you understand how each type differs from the others. It will also help you learn how to handle types of writing that may be unfamiliar to you.

When you begin reading each section, do not become frustrated if some of the vocabulary is new to you. Before too long you will understand the new words. You do not have to try to memorize any of the literary terms that may come up, just so long as you understand them while you are reading the review. Relax and consider all of the points that the review sections make about the individual types of writing. This will train you to handle these same types of writing when you take the actual GED. Here is a breakdown of the questions on the GED *Interpreting Literature and the Arts* section.

I. INTERPRETING LITERATURE AND THE ARTS TOPICS

The topics listed below should be reviewed in order to accurately answer the questions appearing on the Literature and the Arts test of the GED. See the review on the pages which follow.

POPULAR LITERATURE (50% of Test)

1. Fiction
2. Prose
3. Drama

4. Poetry
5. Drama

CLASSICAL LITERATURE (25% of Test)

1. Fiction
2. Prose
3. Drama

4. Poetry
5. Drama

COMMENTARY ABOUT LITERATURE AND THE ARTS (25% of Test)

1. Comments
2. Criticism

3. Reviews

"Popular" literature usually refers to writers of the post-World War II era. This includes everyone from Toni Morrison to William Golding, and Betty Friedan to Ken Kesey.

"Classical" literature usually means writers of the World War II era and preceding. This includes everyone from Edith Wharton to D.H. Lawrence, and Stephen Crane to William Faulkner.

The authors named here are only a very small sample of the authors that could possibly appear on the GED. There is no clear dividing line between the two types of literature. The terms "popular" and "classical" are just rough guides to give you an idea of the content breakdown of the GED.

"Commentary about Literature and the Arts" refers to reviews of the arts by critics. Here you will be asked to interpret reviews and pick out key points in the commentary.

The literature on the GED will range from primarily American authors to a representation of English and Canadian authors, as well as some translations from world literature. These works will include contemporary literature, works from the popular press, fiction, non-fiction, poetry, prose, and criticism, reviews, comments on literature, the fine arts, television, film, and dance.

A casual survey of recent years' exams reveals that the following authors' works are frequently offered for discussion: Edith Wharton, Robert Frost, D.H. Lawrence, Twain, Steinbeck, Emerson, Thoreau, Hemingway, Thomas Wolfe, Tennessee Williams, Stephen Crane, Carl Sandburg, Fitzgerald, Faulkner, Eugene O'Neill, Katherine Ann Porter, G.K. Chesterton, Ralph Ellison, William Golding, Joyce Carol Oates, Mary Gordon, Studs Terkel, James Baldwin, Ken Kesey, Betty Friedan, Gail Godwin, Robert Stone, John Irving, John LeCarré, Toni Morrison, Mary McCarthy, and Maya Aneglou. What these authors' works have in common is their significance and relevance to the human condition, as well as their merit as literary works. They have something to say, and they say it well.

As you read this review, think about how each of the writing types differs from the rest. Keep in mind the objectives of each of the types (prose, poetry, drama, commentary). Finally, be sure you understand one section before you go on to the next. This understanding will do wonders for you when you take the actual GED.

II. READING PROSE

What is prose? Basically, prose is **not** poetry. Prose is what we write and speak most of the time in our everyday lives: unmetered, unrhymed language. Which is not to say that prose does not have its own rhythms — language, whether written or spoken, has cadence and balance. And certainly prose can have instances of rhyme and alliteration. After all, language is **phonic**, or meant to be heard.

Furthermore, **prose** may be either **fiction** or **nonfiction**. A novel (like a short story) is fiction; an autobiography is nonfiction. While a novel (or short story) may have autobiographical elements, an autobiography is presumed to be entirely factual. Essays are usually described in other terms: expository, argumentative, persuasive, critical, narrative. Essays may have elements of either fiction or nonfiction, but are generally classed as a separate type of prose.

READING NOVELS

What is a novel? A good description might be that a novel is a rather long story, filled with many characters and subplots, interlaced with motifs, symbols, and themes, with time and space to develop interrelationships and to present descriptive passages. Much "popular" literature today is formulaic — the endless series of romance novels by various publishers, the sequel upon sequel of sword-and-sorcery novels, and Western novels by genuine cowboys. But popularity alone is not the measure for significance nor for merit. Telling a story whose plot is probable yet refreshingly unpredictable is an art. Characters who seem real and familiar, yet unique and individual, are the creations of skilled writers.

Analyzing novels is a bit like asking the journalist's questions "the five W's and an H": who?, what?, when?, where?, why?, and how? The "**what**" is the story, the narrative, the plot, and subplots. Some students may be familiar with Freytag's Pyramid, originally designed to describe the structure of a five-act drama but now widely used to analyze fiction as well. The stages generally specified are **introduction** or **exposition, complication, rising action, climax, falling action,** and **denouement** or **conclusion**. As the novel's events are charted, the "change which structures the story" should emerge. There are many events in a long narrative, but generally only one set of events comprises the "real" or "significant" story; this is the plot.

Also important, subplots often parallel or serve as counterpoints to the main plot line, serving to enhance the central story. Minor characters sometimes have essentially the same conflicts and goals as the major characters, but the consequences of the outcome seem less important.

Sometimes an author divides the novel into chapters — named or unnamed, perhaps just numbered. Or he might divide the novel into "books" or "parts," with chapters as subsections. Readers should take their cue from these divisions; the author must have had some reason for them. Take note of what happens in each larger section, as well as within the smaller chapters. Whose progress is being followed? What event or occurrence is being foreshadowed or prepared for? What causal or other relationships are there between sections and events? Some writers, such as Steinbeck in *The Grapes of Wrath*, use *intercalary* chapters, alternating between the "real" story (the Joads) and peripheral or parallel stories (the Okies and migrants in general). Look for the pattern of such organization; try to see the interrelationships of these alternating chapters.

Of course, plots cannot happen in isolation from characters, the "who." Not only are there major and minor characters to consider; we need to note whether the various characters are **static** or **dynamic**. Static characters do not change in significant ways — that is, in ways which relate to the story which is structuring the novel. A character may die and still be static, unless his death is central to the narrative. For instance, in Golding's *Lord of the Flies*, the boy with the mulberry birthmark apparently dies in a fire early in the novel. Momentous as any person's death is, this boy's death is not what the novel is about. He is a static character. However, when Simon is killed, and later Piggy, the narrative is directly impacted because the reason for their deaths is central to the novel's theme regarding man's innate evil. Piggy and Simon are dynamic characters. A dynamic character may change only slightly in his attitudes, but those changes may be the very ones upon which the narrative rests.

We describe major characters or "actors" in novels as **protagonists** or **antagonists**. The *pro*tagonist struggles **toward** or for someone or something; the *an*tagonist struggles **against** someone or something. The possible conflicts are usually cited as man against himself, man against man, man against society, man against nature. Sometimes more than one of these conflicts appears in a story, but usually one is dominant and is the structuring device.

A character can be referred to as **stock**, meaning that he exists because the plot demands it. For instance, a Western with a gunman who robs the bank will require a number of **stock** characters: the banker's lovely daughter, the tough but kindhearted barmaid, the cowardly white-shirted citizen who sells out the hero to save his own skin, and the young freckle-faced lad who shoots the bad guy from a second-story hotel window.

Or a character can be a **stereotype**, without unique characteristics. For instance, a sheriff in a small Southern town; a football player who is all brawn; a librarian clucking over her prized books; the cruel commandant of a POW camp.

Characters often serve as **foils** for other characters, enabling us to see one or both of them better. A classic example is Tom Sawyer, the Romantic foil for Huck Finn's Realism. Or, in Harper Lee's *To Kill a Mockingbird*, Scout is the naive observer of events which her brother Jem, four years older, comes to understand from the perspective of the adult world.

Sometimes characters are **allegorical**, or **symbolic**, standing for qualities or concepts rather than for actual people. For instance, Jim Casey (initials "J. C.") in *The Grapes of Wrath* is often regarded as a Christ figure, pure and self-sacrificing in his aims for the migrant workers.

Other characters are fully three-dimensional, "rounded," examples of humans in all their virtue, vice, hope, despair, strength, and weakness. This rich variety aids the author in creating characters who are credible and plausible, without being dully predictable and mundane.

The interplay of plot and characters determines in large part the **theme** of a work, the "why." First of all, we must distinguish between a mere topic and a genuine theme or thesis; and then between a theme and contributing *motifs*. A **topic** is a phrase, such as "man's inhumanity toward man"; or "the fickle nature of fate." A **theme**, however, turns a phrase into a statement: "Man's inhumanity toward man is barely concealed by 'civilization'." Or "Man is a helpless pawn, at the mercy of fickle fate." Many writers may deal with the same **topic**, such as the complex nature of true love; but their **themes** may vary widely, from "True love will always win out in the end" to "Not even true love can survive the cruel ironies of fate."

To illustrate the relationship between plot, character, and theme, let's examine two familiar fairy tales. In "The Ugly Duckling," the structuring story line is "Once upon a time there was an ugly duckling, who in turn became a beautiful swan." In this case, the duckling did nothing to deserve his ugliness or his eventual transformation; but he did not curse fate. He only wept and waited, lonely and outcast. And when he became beautiful, he did not gloat; he eagerly joined the other members of his flock, who greatly admired him. Theme: "Good things come to him who waits," or "Life is unfair — you don't get what you deserve, nor deserve what you get"? What happens to the theme if the ugly duckling remains an ugly duckling: "Some guys just never get a break"?

Especially rewarding to examine for the connection between plot and theme is "Cinderella": "Once upon a time, a lovely, sweet-natured young girl was forced to labor and serve her ugly and ungrateful stepmother and two stepsisters. But thanks to her Fairy Godmother, Cinderella and the Prince marry, and live happily ever after."

We could change events (plot elements) at any point, but let's take the penultimate scene where the Prince's men come to the door with the single glass slipper. Cinderella has been shut away so that she is not present when the other women in the house try on the slipper. Suppose that the stepmother or either of the two stepsisters tries on the slipper — and it fits! Cinderella is in the back room doing the laundry, and her family waltzes out the door to the palace and she doesn't even get an invitation to the wedding. And imagine the Prince's dismay when the ugly, one-slippered lady lifts her wedding veil for the consummating kiss! Theme: "There is no justice in the world, for those of low or high station"; or "Virtue is not its own reward"?

Or let's say that during the slipper-test scene, the stepsisters, stepmother, and finally Cinderella all try on the shoe, but to no avail. And then in sashays the Fairy Godmother, who gives them all a knowing smirk, puts out her slipper-sized foot and cackles hysterically, like the Joker from "Batman." Theme: "You can't trust anybody these days"; or, a favorite statement of theme, "Appearances can be deceiving." The link between plot and theme is very strong, indeed.

Skilled writers often employ **motifs** to help unify their works. A motif is a detail or element of the story which is repeated throughout, and which may even become symbolic. Television shows are ready examples of the use of motifs. A medical show, with many scenes alternately set in the hospital waiting room and operating room, uses elements such as the pacing, anxious parent or loved one, the gradually filling ashtray, the large wall clock whose hands melt from one hour to another. And in the operating room, the half-masked surgeon whose brow is frequently mopped by the nurse; the gloved hand open-palmed to receive scalpel, sponge, and so on; the various oscilloscopes giving readouts of the patient's very fragile condition; the expanding and collapsing bladder manifesting that the patient is indeed breathing; and, again, the wall clock, assuring us that this procedure is taking forever. These are all **motifs**, details which in concert help convince the reader that this story occurs in a hospital, and that the mood is pretty tense, that the medical team is doing all it can, and that Mom and Dad will be there when the patient wakes up.

But motifs can become symbolic. The oscilloscope line quits blipping, levels out, and gives off the ominous hum. And the doctor's gloved hand sets down the scalpel and shuts off the oscilloscope. In the waiting room, Dad crushes the empty cigarette pack; Mom quits pacing and sinks into the sofa. The door to the waiting room swings shut silently behind the retreating doctor. All these elements signal "It's over, finished."

This example is very crude and mechanical, but motifs in the hands of a skillful writer are valuable devices. And in isolation, and often magnified, a single motif can become a controlling image with great significance. For instance, Emma Bovary's shoes signify her obsession with material things; and when her delicate slippers become soiled as she crosses the dewy grass to meet her lover, we sense the impurity of her act as well as its hopelessness. Or when wise Piggy, in *Lord of the Flies*, is reduced to one lens in his glasses, and finally to no glasses at all, we see the loss of insight and wisdom on the island, and chaos follows.

Setting is the "where" of the story: interior — what structure; exterior — in what locality; and even the world or realm — this world or another. But setting is also the "when": time of day, time of year, time period or year; it is the dramatic moment, the precise intersection of time and space when this story is being told. Setting is also the atmosphere: positive or negative, calm, chaotic, Gothic, Romantic. The question for the reader to answer is whether the setting is ultimately essential to the plot/theme, or whether it is incidental; i.e., could this story/theme have been told successfully in another time and/or place? For instance, could the theme in *Lord of the Flies* be made manifest if the boys were not on an island? Could they have been isolated in some other place? Does it matter whether the "war" which they are fleeing is WWII or WWIII or some other conflict, in terms of the theme?

Hopefully, the student will see that the four elements of plot, character, theme, and setting are intertwined and largely interdependent. A work must really be read as a whole, rather than dissected and analyzed in discrete segments.

The final question, "how," relates to an author's style. Style involves language (word choice), syntax (word order, sentence type and length), the balance between narration and dialogue, the choice of narrative voice (first person participant, third person with limited omniscience), use of descriptive passages, and other aspects of the actual words on the page which are basically irrelevant to the first four elements (plot, character, theme, and setting). Stylistic differences are fairly easy to spot among such diverse writers as Jane Austen, whose style is — to today's reader — very formal and mannered; Mark Twain, whose style is very casual and colloquial; William Faulkner, whose prose often spins on without punctuation or paragraphs far longer than the reader can hold either the thought or his breath; and Hemingway, whose dense but spare, pared-down style has earned the epithet, "Less is more."

READING SHORT STORIES

The modern short story differs from earlier short fiction, such as the parable, fable, and tale, in its emphasis on character development through scenes rather than summary: through *showing* rather than *telling*. Gaining popularity in the 19th century, the short story generally was realistic, presenting detailed accounts of the lives of middle-class people. This tendency toward realism dictates that the plot be grounded in *probability*. There was a good chance that these events could really happen. Furthermore, the characters are human with recognizable human motivations, both social and psychological. Setting — time and place — is realistic rather than fantastic. And, as Poe stipulated, the elements of plot, character, setting, style, point of view, and theme all work toward a single *unified* effect.

However, some modern writers have stretched these boundaries and have mixed in elements of nonrealism — such as the supernatural and the fantastic — sometimes switching back and forth between realism and nonrealism, confusing the reader who is expecting conventional fiction. Barth's "Lost in the Funhouse" and Allen's "The Kugelmass Episode" are two stories which are not, strictly speaking, *realistic*. However, if the reader will approach and accept this type of story on its own terms, he will be better able to understand and appreciate them fully.

Unlike the novel, which has time and space to develop characters and relationships, the short story must rely on flashes of insight and revelation to develop plot and characters. The "slice of life" in a short story is much narrower than that in a novel; the time span is much shorter, the focus much tighter. To attempt anything like the grandness available to the novelist would be to view fireworks through a soda straw: occasionally pretty, but ultimately not very satisfying or enlightening.

The elements of the short story are those of the novel, discussed earlier. However, because of the compression of time and concentration of effect, probably the short story writer's most important decision is **point of view**. A narrator may be *objective*, presenting information without bias or comment. Hemingway frequently uses the objective *third-person* narrator, presenting scenes almost dramatically, i.e., with a great deal of dialogue and very little narrative, none of which directly reveals the thoughts or feelings of the characters. We say that such a narrator is fully or partially *omniscient*, depending on how complete his knowledge is of the characters' psychological and emotional makeup. The least objective narrator is the *first-person* narrator, who presents information from the perspective of a single character who is a participant in the action. Such a narrative choice allows the author to present the discrepancies between the writer's/reader's perceptions and those of the narrator.

One reason the choice of narrator, the point of view from which to tell the story, is immensely important in a short story is that the narrator reveals character and event in ways which affect our understanding of theme. For instance, in Faulkner's "A Rose for Emily," the unnamed narrator who seems to be a townsperson tells the story out of order. The narrator withholds information which would explain the events being presented, letting the reader puzzle over Emily Grierson's motivations, a device common in detective fiction. In fact, the narrator presents contradictory information, making the reader alternately pity and resent the spinster. When we examine the imagery and conclude that Miss Emily and her house represent the decay and decadence of the Old South which resisted the invasion of "progress" from the North, we see the importance of setting and symbol in relation to theme.

Similarly, in Mansfield's "Bliss," the abundant description of setting creates the controlling image of the lovely pear tree. But this symbol of fertile life becomes ironic when Bertha Young belatedly feels sincere and overwhelming desire for her husband. The third-person narrator's omniscience is limited to Bertha's thoughts and feelings; otherwise, we would have seen her husband's infidelity with Miss Fulton.

In O'Connor's "Good Country People," the narrator is broadly omniscient, but the reader is still taken by surprise at the cruelty of the Bible salesman who seduces Joy-Hulga. That he steals her artificial leg is perhaps poetic justice, since she (with her numerous degrees) had fully intended to seduce him ("just good country people"). The story's title, the characters' names—Hopewell, Freeman, Joy; the salesman's professed Christianity, the Bibles hollowed out to hold whiskey and condoms, add to the irony of Mrs. Freeman's final comment on the young man: "Some can't be that simple... I know I never could."

The importance of tense is demonstrated in a short story by John Updike. The youthful narrator in "A & P" also uses present tense, but not consistently, which gives his narrative a very casual, even unschooled flavor. Sammy identifies himself in the opening paragraph: "In walks these three girls in nothing but bathing suits. I'm in the third checkout slot, with my back to the door, so I don't see them until they're over by the bread." And later, "Stokesie's married, with two babies chalked up on his fuselage already, but as far as I can tell that's the only difference. He's twenty-two, and I was nineteen this April." The girls incur the wrath of the store manager, who scolds them for their inappropriate dress. And Sammy, in his adolescent idealism, quits on the spot; although he realizes that he does not want to "do this" to his parents, he tells us "… it seems to me that once you begin a gesture it's fatal not to go through with it." But, his gesture is ill-spent: "I look around for my girls, but they're gone, of course… I could see Lengel in my place in the slot, checking the sheep through. His face was dark gray and his back stiff, as if he'd just had an injection of iron, and my stomach kind of fell as I felt how hard the world was going to be to me hereafter."

Answering GED exam questions on short stories is much the same as addressing questions on novels. The student must answer multiple choice questions which require close reading for such elements as tone, style, atmosphere, and inference. Knowing the story beforehand may help the student, but the ability to analyze is the major component of this type of exam.

READING ESSAYS

Essays fall into four rough categories: **speculative, argumentative, narrative**, and **expository**. Depending on the writer's purpose, his essay will fit more or less into one or these groupings.

The **speculative** essay is so named because, as its Latin root suggests, it *looks* at ideas; explores them rather than explains them. While the speculative essay may be said to be *meditative*, it often makes one or more points. But the thesis may not be as obvious or clear-cut as that in an expository or argumentative essay. The writer deals with ideas in an associative manner, playing with ideas in a looser structure than he would in an expository or argumentative essay. This "flow" may even produce *intercalary* paragraphs, which present alternately a narrative of sorts and thoughtful responses to the events being recounted, as in E.B. White's "The Ring of Time."

The purposes of the **argumentative** essay, on the other hand, are always clear: to present a point and provide evidence, which may be factual or anecdotal, and to support it. The structure is usually very formal, as in a debate, with counterpositions and counterarguments. Whatever the organizational pattern, the writer's intent in an argumentative essay is to persuade his reader of the validity of some claim, as Francis Bacon does in "Of Love."

Narrative and **expository** essays have elements of both the speculative and argumentative modes. The narrative essay may recount an incident or a series of incidents and is almost always autobiographical, in order to make a point, as in George Orwell's "Shooting an Elephant." The informality of the story-telling makes the narrative essay less insistent than the argumentative essay, but more directed than the speculative essay.

Students are probably most familiar with the **expository** essay, the primary purpose of which is to explain and clarify ideas. While the expository essay may have narrative elements, that aspect is minor and subservient to that of explanation. Furthermore, while nearly all essays have some element of persuasion, argumentation is incidental in the expository essay. In any event, the four categories — speculative, argumentative, narrative, and expository — are neither exhaustive nor mutually exclusive.

As nonfiction, essays have a different set of elements from novels and short stories: **voice, style, structure,** and **thought**.

Voice in nonfiction is similar to the narrator's tone in fiction; but the major difference is in who is "speaking." In fiction, the author is not the speaker — the **narrator** is the speaker. Students sometimes have difficulty with this distinction, but it is necessary if we are to preserve the integrity of the fictive "story." In an essay, however, the author speaks directly to the reader, even if he is presenting ideas which he may not actually espouse personally. This directness creates the writer's **tone**, his attitude toward his subject.

Style in nonfiction derives from the same elements as style in fiction word choice, syntax, balance between dialogue and narration, voice, use of description — those things specifically related to words on the page. Generally speaking, an argumentative essay will be written in a more formal style than will a narrative essay, and a meditative essay will be less formal than an expository essay. But such generalizations are only descriptive, not prescriptive (rules for writing the essay).

Structure and **thought**, the final elements of essays, are so intertwined as to be inseparable. Just as in our discussion of the interdependence of plot and theme, we must be aware that to change the structure of an essay will alter its meaning. For instance, in White's "The Ring of Time," to abandon the *intercalary* paragraph organization, separating the paragraphs which narrate the scenes with the young circus rider from those which reflect on the nature of time, would alter our understanding of the essay's thesis. Writers signal structural shifts with alterations in focus, as well as with visual clues (spacing), verbal clues (*but, therefore, however*), or shifts in the kind of information being presented (personal, scientific, etc.).

Thought is perhaps the single element which most distinguishes nonfiction from fiction. The essayist chooses his form not to tell a story but to present an idea. Whether he chooses the speculative, narrative, argumentative, or expository format, the essayist has something on his mind that he wants to convey to his readers. And it is this idea which we are after when we analyze his essay.

Often studied is Orwell's "Shooting an Elephant," a narrative essay recounting (presumably) the writer's experience in Burma as an officer of the British law that ruled the poverty-ridden people of a small town. Orwell begins with two paragraphs which explain that, as a white European authority figure, he was subjected to taunts and abuse by the natives. Ironically, he sympathized with the Burmese and harbored fairly strong anti-British feelings, regarding the imperialists as oppressors rather than saviors. He tells us that he felt caught, trapped between his position of authority, which he himself resented, and the hatred of those he was required to oversee.

The body of the essay — some eleven paragraphs — relates the incident with an otherwise tame elephant gone mad which had brought chaos and destruction to the village. Only occasionally does Orwell interrupt the narrative to reveal his reactions directly, but his descriptions of the Burmese are sympathetically drawn. The language is heavily connotative, revealing the helplessness of the villagers against both the elephant and the miserable circumstances of their lives.

Orwell recounts how, having sent for an elephant gun, he found that he was compelled to shoot the animal, even though its destruction was by now unwarranted and even ill-advised, given the value of the elephant to the village. But the people expected it, demanded it; the white man realized that he did not have dominion over these people of color after all. They were in charge, not he.

To make matters worse, Orwell bungles the "murder" of the beast, which takes half an hour to die in great agony. And in the aftermath of discussions of the rightness or wrongness of his action, Orwell wonders if anyone realizes he killed the elephant only to save face. It is the final sentence of the final paragraph which directly reveals the author's feelings, although he has made numerous indirect references to them throughout the essay. Coupled with the opening paragraphs, this conclusion presents British imperialism of the period in a very negative light: "the unable doing the unnecessary to the ungrateful."

Having discovered Orwell's main idea, we must look at the other elements (voice, style, structure) to see *how* he communicates it to the reader. The voice of the first-person narrative is fairly formal, yet remarkably candid, using connotation to color our perception of the events. Orwell's narrative has many complex sentences, with vivid descriptive phrases in series, drawing our eye along the landscape and through the crowds as he ponders his next move. Structurally, the essay first presents a premise about British imperialism. Next the essay moves to a gripping account of the officer's reluctant shooting of the elephant, and finally ends with an admission of his own guilt as an agent of the institution he detests. Orwell frequently signals shifts between his role as officer and his responses as a humane person by using the word *but* or by using dashes to set off his responses to the events he is recounting.

The GED essay exam could conceivably take any work and ask the student to discuss how the writer's attitude toward *time* is revealed; to compare/contrast the attitudes toward time in any pair of essays; to look at the writer's use of language in any essay and discuss the resulting *voice*. The most important thing, as always, is to read and reread the question carefully; the next most important thing is to read and reread the work(s) to be discussed. Try to find the *thought* which the writer means to communicate; then analyze for *voice, style*, and *structure*.

☞ Drill: Reading Prose

<u>DIRECTIONS</u>: Read the following passage and answer the questions which follow.

1   And it was at this moment, as I stood there with the rifle in my hands, that I first grasped the hollowness, the futility of the white man's dominion in the East. Here was I, the white man with his gun, standing in front of the unarmed native crowd—seemingly the

5   leading actor of the piece; but in reality I was only an absurd puppet pushed to and fro by the will of those yellow faces behind. I perceived in this moment that when the white man turns tyrant it is his own freedom that he destroys.

George Orwell, "Shooting an Elephant"

1.   How is the narrator feeling at this moment?
     (1)   Uncomfortable   (4)   Arrogant
     (2)   Joyous   (5)   Resentful
     (3)   Contented

2.   What is the setting of the passage?
     (1)   England   (4)   Australia
     (2)   Alaska   (5)   Texas
     (3)   Asia

3.   "Absurd puppet" in line 5 refers to
     (1)   the elephant.   (4)   the government.
     (2)   the native king.   (5)   the gun.
     (3)   the white man.

III. READING POETRY

Opening a book to study for an examination is perhaps the worst time to read poetry, or read about poetry, because above all, poetry should be enjoyed; it is definitely "reading for pleasure." This last phrase seems to have developed recently to describe the reading we do other than for information or for study. Perhaps you personally would not choose poetry as pleasure reading because of the bad name poetry has received over the years. Some students regard the "old" poetry, such as Donne's or Shelley's, as difficult or dull, or modern poetry as too weird. It is hard to imagine that poetry was the "current language" for students growing up in the Elizabethan or Romantic eras. Whereas in our world information can be retrieved in a nanosecond, in those worlds time was plentiful to sit down, clear the mind, and let poetry take over. Very often the meaning of a poem does not come across immediately and for the modern student this proves very frustrating. Sometimes it takes years for a poem to take on meaning — the reader simply knows that the poem sounds good and it provokes an emotional response that cannot be explained. With time, more emotional experience, more reading of similar experiences, more life, the reader comes to a meaning of that poem that satisfies. In a few more years that poem may take on a whole new meaning. Think of the way lyrics to certain songs affect you — poetry is no different.

This is all very well for reading for pleasure but you are now called upon, in your present experience, to learn poetry for an important examination. Perhaps the first step in the learning process is to answer the question, "Why do people write poetry?" An easy answer is that they wish to convey an experience, an emotion, an insight, or an observation in a startling or satisfying way, one that remains in the memory for years. But why not use a straightforward sentence or paragraph? Why wrap up that valuable insight in fancy words, rhyme, paradox, meter, allusion, symbolism, and all the other seeming mumbo-jumbo that poets use? Why not just come right out and say it like "normal people" do? An easy answer to these questions is that poetry is not a vehicle for conveying meaning alone. Gerard Manley Hopkins, one of the great innovators of rhythm in poetry, claimed that poetry should be "heard for its own sake and interest even over and above its interest or meaning." Poetry provides intellectual stimulus. Of course, one of the best ways of studying a poem is to consider it a jigsaw puzzle presented to you whole. It can then be taken apart piece by piece (word by word), analyzed scientifically, labelled, and put back together again into a whole. Then, the meaning is complete. But people write poetry to convey more than meaning.

T.S. Eliot maintained that the meaning of the poem existed purely to distract us "while the poem did its work." One interpretation of a poem's "work" is that it changes us in some way. We see the world in a new way because of the way the poet has seen it and told us about it. Maybe one of the reasons people write poetry is to encourage us to see things in the first place. Simple things like daffodils take on a whole new aspect when we read the way Wordsworth saw them in his poem "Daffodils." Why did Wordsworth write that poem? His sister had written an excellent account of the scene in her journal. Wordsworth not only evokes nature as we have never seen it before, alive, joyous, exuberant, he shows nature's healing powers, its restorative quality as the scene flashes "upon that inward eye/Which is the bliss of solitude." Bent over your books studying, how many times has a similar quality of nature's power in the memory come to you? Maybe for you a summer beach scene rather than daffodils by the lake is more meaningful, but the poet captures a moment that we have all experienced. The poet's magic is to make that moment new again.

If poets enhance our power of sight, they also awaken the other senses as powerfully. We can hear Emily Dickinson's snake in the repeated "s" sound of the lines:

His notice sudden is —
The Grass divides as with a Comb —
A spotted shaft is seen —

and because of the very present sense of sound, we experience the indrawn gasp of breath of fear when the snake appears. We can touch the little chimney sweep's hair "that curled like a lamb's back" in William Blake's poetry and because of that sense we are even more shocked to read that the child's hair is all shaved off so that the soot will not spoil its color. We can smell the poison gas as Wilfred Owen's soldiers fumble with their gas masks; we can taste the blood gurgling in the poisoned lungs. For that moment, you join those soldiers of WWI.

Poets write to awaken the senses. They have crucial ideas, but the words they use are often more important than the meaning. More important still than ideas and sense awakening is the poet's appeal to the emotions. And it is precisely this area that disturbs a number of students. Our modern society tends to block out emotions — we need reviews to tell us if we enjoyed a film, a critic's praise to see if a play or novel is worth our time. We hesitate to laugh at something in case it is not the "in" thing to do. We certainly do not cry — at least in front of others. Poets write to overcome that blocking (very often it is their own blocking of emotion they seek to alleviate), but that is not to say that poetry immediately sets us laughing, crying, loving, hating. The important fact about the emotional release in poetry is that poets help us explore our own emotions, sometimes by shocking us, sometimes by drawing attention to balance and pattern, sometimes by cautioning us to move carefully in this inner world.

Poets tell us nothing really new. They tell us old truths about human emotions that we begin to restructure anew, to reread our experiences in light of theirs, to reevaluate our world view. Whereas a car manual helps us understand the workings of a particular vehicle, a poem helps us understand the inner workings of human beings. Poets frequently write to help their emotional life — the writing then becomes cathartic, purging or cleansing the inner life, feeding that part of us that makes us human. Many poets might paraphrase Byron who claimed that he had to write or go mad. Writer and reader of poetry enter into a partnership, each helping the other to find significance in the human world, to find safety in a seemingly alien world.

This last point brings any reader of poetry to ask the next question: Why read poetry? One might contend that a good drama, novel, or short story might provide the same emotional experience. But a poem is much more accessible. Apart from the fact that poems are shorter than other genres, there is a unique directness to them which hinges purely on language. Poets can say in one or two lines what may take novelists and playwrights entire works to express. For example, Keats' lines —

Beauty is truth, truth beauty — that is all

Ye know on earth, and all ye need to know —

In your reading of poems remember that poetry is perhaps the oldest art and yet surrounds us without our even realizing it. Listeners thrilled to Homer's poetry; tribes chanted invocations to their gods; today we listen to song lyrics and find ourselves, sometimes despite ourselves, repeating certain rhythmic lines. Advertisements we say we hate have a way of repeating themselves as we use the catchy phrase or repetition. Both lyricists and advertisers cleverly use language, playing on the reader's/listener's/watcher's ability to pick up on a repeated sound or engaging rhythm or inner rhyme. Think of a time as a child when you thoroughly enjoyed poetry: nursery rhymes, ballgame rhythms, jump-rope patterns. Probably you had no idea of the meaning of the words ("Little Miss Muffet sat on a tuffet..." a tuffet?!), but you responded to the sound, the pattern. As adults we read poetry for that sense of sound and pattern. With more experience at reading poetry there is an added sense of pleasure as techniques are recognized: alliteration, onomatopoeia; forms of poetry become obvious — the sonnet, the rondelle. Even greater enjoyment comes from watching a poet's development, tracing themes and ideas, analyzing maturity in growth of imagery, use of rhythm.

To the novice reader of poetry, a poem can speak to the reader at a particular time and become an experience in itself. A freshman's experience after her mother's death exemplifies this. Shortly after the death, the student found Elizabeth Jenning's poem "Happy Families." Using the familiar names of the cards, Mrs. Beef and Master Bun, the poet describes how strangers try to help the family carry on their lives normally although one of the "happy family" is "missing." The card game continues although no one wants it to. At the end the players go back to their individual rooms and give way to their individual grief. The student described the relief at knowing that someone else had obviously experienced her situation where everyone in the family was putting up a front, strangers were being very kind, and a general emptiness prevailed because of that one missing family member. The poem satisfied. The student saw death through another's eyes; the experience was almost the same, yet helped the reader to reevaluate, to view a universal human response to grief as well as encourage her to deal with her own.

On reading a poem the brain works on several different levels: it responds to the sounds; it responds to the words themselves and their connotations; it responds to the emotions; it responds to the insights or learning of the world being revealed. For such a process, poetry is a very good training ground — a boot camp — for learning how to read literature in general. All the other genres have elements of poetry within them. Learn to read poetry well and you will be a more accomplished reader, even of car manuals! Perhaps the best response to reading poetry comes from a poet herself, Emily Dickinson, who claimed that reading a book of poetry made her feel "as if the top of [her] head were taken off!"

Before such a process happens to you, here are some tips for reading poetry before and during the examination.

BEFORE THE EXAM

1. Make a list of poets and poems you remember; analyze poems you liked, disliked, loved, hated, and were indifferent to. Find the poems. Reread them and for each one analyze your *feelings*, first of all, about the poetry itself. Have your feelings changed? Now what do you like or hate? Then paraphrase the meaning of each poem. Notice how the "magic" goes from the poem, i.e., "Daffodils:" the poet sees many daffodils by the side of a lake and then thinks how the sight of them later comforts him.

2. Choose a poem at random from an anthology or one mentioned in this introduction. Read it a couple of times, preferably aloud, because the speaking voice will automatically grasp the rhythm and that will help

the meaning. Do not become bogged down in individual word connotation or the meaning of the poem — let the poetry do its "work" on you; absorb the poem as a whole jigsaw puzzle.

3. Now take the puzzle apart. Look carefully at the title. Sometimes a straightforward title helps you focus. Sometimes a playful title helps you get an angle on the meaning. "Happy Families," of course, is an ironic title because the family playing the card game of that name is not happy.

4. Look carefully at the punctuation. Does the sense of a line carry from one to another? Does a particular mark of punctuation strike you as odd? Ask why that mark was used.

5. Look carefully at the words. Try to find the meaning of words with which you are not familiar within the context. Familiar words may be used differently: ask why that particular use. If you have tapped into your memory bank of vocabulary and find you are still at a loss, go to a dictionary. Once you have the *denotation* of the word, start wondering about the *connotation*. Put yourself in the poet's position and think why that word was used.

6. Look carefully at all the techniques being used. You will gain these as you progress through the test preparation. As soon as you come across a new idea learn the word, see how it applies to poetry, where it is used. Be on the lookout for it in other poetry. Ask yourself questions such as why the poet used alliteration here; why the rhythm changes there; why the poet uses a sonnet form and which sonnet form is in use. Forcing yourself to ask the WHY questions, and answering them, will train the brain to read more perceptively. Poetry is not accidental; poets are deliberate people; they do things for specific reasons. Your task under a learning situation is to discover WHY.

7. Look carefully at the speaker. Is the poet using another persona? Who is that persona? What is revealed about the speaker? Why use that particular voice?

8. Start putting all the pieces of the puzzle together. The rhythm helps the meaning. The word choice helps the imagery. The imagery adds to the meaning. Paraphrase the meaning. Ask yourself simple questions: What is the poet saying? How can I relate to what is being said? What does this poet mean to me? What does this poem contribute to human experience?

9. Write a poem of your own. Choose a particular style; use the sonnet form; parody a famous poem; express yourself in free verse on a crucial,

personal aspect of your life. Then analyze your own poetry with the above ideas.

DURING THE EXAM

You will have established a routine for reading poetry, but now you are under pressure, you must work quickly, and will have no access to a dictionary. You cannot read aloud but you can:

1. Internalize the reading—hear the reading in your head. Read through the poem two or three times following the absorbing procedure.

2. If the title and poet are supplied, analyze the title as before and determine the era of the poetry. Often this pushes you toward the meaning.

3. Look carefully at the questions which should enable you to be able to "tap into" your learning process. Answer the ones that are immediately clear to you: form, technique, language perhaps.

4. Go back for another reading for those questions that challenge you— theme or meaning perhaps — analyze the speaker or the voice at work — paraphrase the meaning—ask the simple question, "What is the poet saying?"

5. If a question asks you about a specific line, metaphor, opening or closing lines, highlight or underline them to force your awareness of each crucial word. Internalize another reading emphasizing the highlighted area—analyze again the options you have for your answers.

6. Do not waste time on a super-tough question. Move onto another section and let the poetry do its "work." Very often the brain will continue working on the problem on another level of consciousness. When you go back to the difficult question, it may well become clear.

7. If you still are not sure of the answer, choose the option that you feel is the closest to correct.

Go home, relax, and forget about the examination!

☞ Drill: Reading Poetry

<u>DIRECTIONS</u>: Read the following poem, then answer the questions which follow.

Why could she not stop for death?

1   Because I could not stop for Death–
He kindly stopped for me–
The Carriage held but just Ourselves–
And Immortality.

5   We slowly drove–He knew not haste
And I had put away
My labor and my leisure too,
For His Civility–

We passed the School, where Children strove
10   At Recess–in the Ring–
We passed the Fields of Gazing Grain–
We passed the Setting Sun–

Or rather–He passed Us–
The Dews drew quivering and chill–
15   For only Gossamer, my Gown–
My Tippet–only Tulle–

We paused before a House that seemed
A Swelling of the Ground–
The Roof was scarcely visible–
20   The Cornice-in the Ground–

Since then–'tis Centuries–and yet
Feels shorter than the Day
I first surmised the Horses' Heads
Were toward Eternity–

Emily Dickinson, 1863.

1.   What is the author's attitude toward dying in the poem?
     (1) She is terrified   (4) She is contented
     (2) She is overjoyed   (5) She is frustrated
     (3) She is angry

2. Death is personified as
    (1) a horse.   (4) the devil.
    (2) a king.   (5) a carriage driver.
    (3) a child.

3. Lines 21–24 signify that
    (1) death is timeless.
    (2) the narrator died yesterday.
    (3) the narrator's horses have died.
    (4) Eternity is a nearby city.
    (5) the horses are lost.

IV. READING DRAMA

The Glass Menagerie by Tennessee Williams begins when one of its four characters, Tom, steps into the downstage light and addresses the audience directly as though he were the chorus from a much earlier play. "I have tricks in my pocket, I have things up my sleeve," says Tom. "But I am the opposite of a stage magician. He gives you illusion that has the appearance of truth. I give you truth in the pleasant disguise of illusion."

To sit among the audience and watch a skillful production of *The Glass Menagerie* is to visit Tom's paradoxical world of theater, a magic place in which known imposters and stagecraft trickery create a spectacle which we know is illusion but somehow recognize as truth. Theater, as a performed event, combines the talents and skills of numerous artists and craftspersons, but before the spectacle must come the playwright's work, the pages of words designating what the audience sees and hears. These words, the written script separate from the theatrical performance of them, is what we call *drama*, and the words give the spectacle its significance because without them the illusion has neither frame nor content. Truth requires boundaries and substance.

Although drama is literature written to be performed, it closely resembles the other genres. In fact, both poetry and prose also can be performed; but as captivating as these public readings sometimes are, only performed drama best creates the immediate living "illusion as truth" Tom promises. Like fiction and narrative poetry, drama tells a tale — that is, it has plot, characters, and setting — but the author's voice is distant, heard only through the stage directions and perhaps some supplementary notes. With rare exceptions, dialogue dominates the script. Some drama is poetry, such as the works of Shakespeare and Molière, and all plays resemble poems as abstractions because both forms are highly condensed, figurative expressions.

A scene set inside a house, for instance, requires a room with only three walls. No audience complains, just as no movie audience feels betrayed by film characters' appearing ridiculously large. Without a thought, audiences employ what Samuel Taylor Coleridge called "a willing suspension of disbelief"; in other words, they know that the images before them are not real but rather representations, reflections in the mirror of which Hamlet speaks, not the real world ("Nature").

A play contains conflict which can be **enacted** immediately on the stage without any alterations in the written word. **Enacted** means performed by an actor or actors free to use the entire stage and such theatrical devices as sets, costumes, makeup, special lighting, and props for support. This differs from the oral interpretation of prose or poetry. No matter how animated, the public reader is not acting. This is the primary distinction between drama and other literary forms. Their most obvious similarity is that any form of literature is a linguistic expression. There is, however, one other feature shared by all kinds of narratives: the pulsating energy which pushes the action along is generated by human imperfection. We speak of tragic characters as having "flaws," but the same is true about comic characters as well. Indeed, nothing is more boring either on a stage or in a written text than a consistently flawless personality, because such characters can never be the real people of our everyday experiences. The most fundamental human truth is human frailty.

Although it can be argued that a play, like a musical composition, must be performed to be understood, the script's linguistic foundation always gives the work potential as a literary experience. Moreover, there is never a "definitive" interpretation. The script, in a sense, remains unfinished because it never stops inviting new variations, and among those invited to participate are individual readers whose imaginations should not be discounted. For example, when *Death of a Salesman* was originally produced, Lee J. Cobb played Willy Loman. Aside from the character's age, Dustin Hoffman's Willy in the revival forty years later bore hardly any physical resemblance to Cobb's. Yet both portrayals "worked." The same could be said about the Willys created by the minds of the play's countless readers. Quite capable of composing its own visions and sounds, the human imagination is the original mirror, the place where all human truths evolve.

PLOT STRUCTURE

As with other narrative types, a play's **plot** is its sequence of events, its organized collection of incidents. At one time it was thought that all the actions within a play should be contained within a single twenty-four hour period. Few lengthy plays have plots which cover only the period of time enacted on the stage. Most plays condense and edit time much as novels do. Decades can be reduced to two hours. Included in the plot is the **exposition**, the revealing of whatever information we need in order to understand the conflict of the play. This exposed material should provide us with a sense of place and time (**setting**), the central participants, important prior incidents, and the play's overall mood. In some plays, such as Shakespeare's, the exposition comes quickly. Notice, for instance, the opening scenes in *Macbeth, Hamlet,* and *Romeo and Juliet*: not one presents us with a central character, yet each — with its witches or king's ghost or street brawl — clearly establishes an essential tension foreshadowing the main conflict to come.

These initial expositions attack the audience immediately and are followed by events in chronological order. The exposition must establish what has come previously, even for an audience familiar with the story, before the plot can advance. Arthur Miller, in his *Death of a Salesman*, continuously interrupts the central action with dislocated expositions from earlier times as though the past were always in the present. He carefully establishes character, place, mood, and conflict throughout the earliest scenes; however, whatever present he places on stage is always caught in a tension between the audience's anticipation of the future and its suspicions of the past. The plots in plays like *Death of a Salesman* tend not to attack us head-on but rather to surround us and gradually close in, the circle made tighter by each deliberately released clue to a mysterious past.

Fairly soon in a play we must experience some incident that incites the fundamental conflict when placed against some previously presented incident or situation. In most plays the conflict's abrasive conditions continuously chafe and even lacerate each other. The play's tempo might provide some interruptions or variations in the pace; nevertheless, conflicts generate the actions which make the characters' worlds worse before they can get better. Any plot featuring only repetitious altercations, however, would soon become tiresome. Potentially, anything can happen in a conflict. The **complication** is whatever presents an element capable of altering the action's direction. Perhaps some new information is discovered or a previously conceived scheme fails, creating a reversal of what had been expected. The plot is not a series of similar events but rather a compilation of related events leading to a culmination, a **crisis**.

In retrospect, we should be able to accept a drama's progression of actions leading to the crisis as inevitable. After the crisis comes the **resolution** (or **denouement**),which gives the play its concluding boundary. This does not mean that the play should offer us solutions for whatever human issues it raises. Rather, the playwright's obligation is to make the experience he presents to us seem filled within its own boundaries. George Bernard Shaw felt he had met this obligation when he ended *Pygmalion* with his two principal characters, Higgins and Eliza, utterly incapable of voicing any romantic affection for each other; and the resolution in Ibsen's *A Doll's House* outraged audiences a hundred years ago and still disturbs some people today, even though it concludes the play with believable consequences.

Terms such as **exposition, complication, crisis,** and **resolution,** though helpful in identifying the conflict's currents and directions, at best only artificially define how a plot is molded. If the play provides unity in its revelations, these seams are barely noticeable. Moreover, any successful play clearly shows that the artist accomplished much more than merely plugging components together to create a finished work. There are no rules which all playwrights must follow, except the central precept that the play's unified assortment of actions be complete and contained within itself.

CHARACTER

Essential to the plot's success are the characters who participate in it. Midpoint in *Hamlet* when Elsinore Castle is visited by the traveling theater company, the prince joyously welcomes the players, but his mood quickly returns to bitter depression shortly after he asks one actor to recite a dramatic passage in which the speaker recalls the fall of Troy and particularly Queen Hecuba's response to her husband's brutal murder. The player, caught by the speech's emotional power, becomes distraught and cannot finish. Left alone on stage, Hamlet compares the theatrical world created by the player with Hamlet's "real" world and asks: "What's Hecuba to him, or he to Hecuba,/ That he should weep for her!" Under ordinary circumstances Hamlet's anxiety would not overshadow his Renaissance sensibilities, because he knows well that fictional characters always possess the potential to move us. As though by instinct, we know the same. We read narratives and go to the theater precisely because we want to be shocked, delighted, thrilled, saddened, titillated, or invigorated by "a dream of passion." Even though some characters are more complex and interesting than others, they come in countless types as the playwright's delegates to our imaginations and as the imitations of reality seeking our response.

TYPES OF PLAYS

When Polonius presents the traveling players to Hamlet, he reads from the theater company's license, which identifies them as

> The best actors in the world, either for tragedy, comedy, history, pastoral, pastoral-comical, historical-pastoral, tragical-historical, tragical-comical-historical-pastoral, scene individable or poem unlimited...

The joke is on those who think all plays somehow can be categorized according to preconceived definitions, as though playwrights follow literary recipes. The notion is not entirely ridiculous, to be sure, since audiences and readers can easily tell a serious play from a humorous one, and a play labeled "tragedy" or "comedy" will generate certain valid expectations from us all, regardless of whether we have read a word by Aristotle or any other literary critic. Still, if beginning playwrights had to choose between writing according to some rigid structures designating the likes of a "tragical-comical-historical-pastoral" or writing a play unrestricted by such rules (a "poem unlimited"), they would probably choose the latter.

We tend to categorize dramatic thought into three clusters: the serious, the comic, and the seriocomic. Thus, in our attempts to interpret life's complexities, it is tempting to place the art forms representing it in precise, fixed designations. After a few centuries, though, it would become clear that there is a better way of explaining what a play's form should be — not so much fixed as organic. In other words, we should think of a play as similar to a plant's growing and taking shape according to its own design. This analogy works well because the plant is not a mechanical device constructed from a predetermined plan, yet every plant is a species and as such contains qualities which identify it with others. So just as Shakespeare could ridicule overly precise definitions for dramatic art, he could still write dramas which he clearly identified as tragedies, comedies, or histories, even though he would freely mix two or more of these together in the same play.

COMEDY

The primary aim of comedy is to amuse us with a happy ending, although comedies can vary according to the attitudes they project, which can be broadly identified as either **high** or **low**, terms having nothing to do with an evaluation of the play's merit. Generally, the amusement found in comedy comes from an eventual victory over threats or ill fortune. Much of the dialogue and plot development might be laughable, yet a play need not be funny to be comic. **Farce** is low comedy intended to make us laugh by means of a series of exaggerated, unlikely situations that depend less on plot and character than on gross absurdities, sight gags, and coarse dialogue. The "higher" a comedy goes, the more natural the characters seem and the less boisterous their behavior. The plots become more sustained, and the dialogue shows more weighty thought. As with all dramas, comedies are about things that go wrong. Accordingly, comedies create deviations from accepted normalcy, presenting problems which we might or might not see as harmless. If these problems make us judgmental about the involved characters and events, the play takes on the features of **satire**, a rather high comic form implying that humanity and human institutions are in need of reform. If the action triggers our sympathy for the characters, we feel even less protected from the incongruities as the play tilts more in the direction of **tragi-comedy**. In other words, the action determines a figurative distance between the audience and the play. Such factors as characters' personalities and the plot's predictability influence this distance. The farther away we sit, the more protected we feel and usually the funnier the play becomes. Closer proximity to believability in the script draws us nearer to the conflict, making us feel more involved in the action and less safe in its presence.

A more consistent play is Oscar Wilde's *The Importance of Being Earnest*, which opened in 1895. In the following scene, Lady Bracknell questions Jack Worthing, who has just announced that Lady Bracknell's daughter, Gwendolyn, has agreed to marry him. Being satisfied with Jack's answers concerning his income and finding his upper-class idleness and careless ignorance about world affairs an asset, she queries him about his family background. In grave tones, the embarrassed Jack reveals his mysterious lineage. His late guardian, Thomas Cardew — "an old gentleman of a very charitable and kindly disposition" — had found the baby Jack in an abandoned handbag.

LADY BRACKNELL: A hand-bag?

JACK: (very seriously): Yes, Lady Bracknell. I was in a hand-bag — a somewhat large, black leather hand-bag, with handles to it — an ordinary hand-bag in fact.

LADY BRACKNELL: In what locality did this Mr. James, or Thomas, Cardew come across this ordinary hand-bag?

JACK: In the cloak-room at Victoria Station. It was given him in mistake for his own.

LADY BRACKNELL: The cloak-room at Victoria Station?

JACK: Yes. The Brighton line.

LADY BRACKNELL: The line is immaterial, Mr. Worthing. I confess I feel somewhat bewildered by what you have just told me. To be born, or at any rate bred, in a hand-bag, whether it had handles or not, seems to me to display a contempt for the ordinary decencies of family life that reminds one of the worst excesses of the French Revolution. And I presume you know what that unfortunate movement led to? As for the particular locality in which the hand-bag was found, a cloak-room at a railway station might serve to conceal a social indiscretion — has probably, indeed, been used for that purpose before now — but it could hardly be regarded as an assured basis for recognized position in good society.

JACK: May I ask you then what would you advise me to do? I need hardly say I would do anything in the world to ensure Gwendolyn's happiness.

LADY BRACKNELL: I would strongly advise you, Mr. Worthing, to try and acquire some relations as soon as possible, and to make a definite effort to produce at any rate one parent, of either sex, before the season is over.

JACK: Well, I don't see how I could possibly manage to do that. I can produce the hand-bag at any moment. It is in my dressing-room at home. I really think that should satisfy you, Lady Bracknell.

LADY BRACKNELL: Me, sir! What has it to do with me? You can hardly imagine that I and Lord Bracknell would dream of allowing our only daughter — a girl brought up with the utmost care — to marry into a cloakroom, and form an alliance with a parcel. Good morning, Mr. Worthing!

(LADY BRACKNELL sweeps out in majestic indignation.)

This dialogue between Lady Bracknell and Jack is typical of what runs throughout the entire play. It is full of exaggerations, in both the situation being discussed and the manner in which the characters, particularly Lady Bracknell, express their reactions to the situation. Under other circumstances an abandoned baby would not be the focus of a comedy, but we are relieved from any concern for the child since the adult Jack is obviously secure, healthy, and, with one exception, carefree. Moreover, we laugh when Lady Bracknell exaggerates Jack's heritage by comparing it with the excesses of the French Revolution. On the other hand, at the core of their discussion is the deeply ingrained and oppressive notion of English class consciousness, a mentality so flawed it almost begs to be satirized. Could there be more there than light, witty entertainment?

TRAGEDY

The term "tragedy" when used to define a play has historically meant something very precise, not simply a drama which ends with unfortunate consequences. This definition originated with Aristotle, who insisted that the play be an imitation of complex actions which should arouse an emotional response combining fear and pity. Aristotle believed that only a certain kind of plot could generate such a powerful reaction. Comedy, as we have seen, shows us a progression from adversity to prosperity. Tragedy must show the reverse; moreover, this progression must be experienced by a certain kind of character, says Aristotle, someone whom we can designate as the **tragic hero**. This central figure must be basically good and noble: "good" because we will not be aroused to fear and pity over the misfortunes of a villain, and "noble" both by social position and moral stature because the fall to misfortune would not otherwise be great enough for tragic impact. These virtues do not make the tragic hero perfect, however, for he must also possess **hamartia** — a tragic flaw—the weakness which leads him to make an error in judgment which initiates the reversal in his fortunes, causing his death or the death of others or both. These dire consequences become the hero's catastrophe. The most common tragic flaw is **hubris**, an excessive pride that adversely influences the protagonist's judgment.

Often the catastrophic consequences involve an entire nation because the tragic hero's social rank carries great responsibilities. Witnessing these events produces the emotional reaction Aristotle believed the audience should experience, the **catharsis**. Although tragedy must arouse our pity for the tragic hero as he endures his catastrophe and must frighten us as we witness the consequences of a flawed behavior which anyone could exhibit, there must also be a purgation, "a cleansing," of these emotions which should leave the audience feeling not depressed but relieved and almost elated. The assumption is that while the tragic hero endures a crushing reversal, somehow he is not thoroughly defeated as he gains new stature through suffering and the knowledge that comes with suffering. Classical tragedy insists that the universe is ordered. If truth or universal law is ignored, the results are devastating, causing the audience to react emotionally; simultaneously, the tragic results prove the existence of truth, thereby reassuring our faith that existence is sensible.

Sophocles' plays give us some of the clearest examples of Aristotle's definition of tragedy. Shakespeare's tragedies are more varied and more modern in their complexities. *Othello* is one of Shakespeare's most innovative and troublesome extensions of tragedy's boundaries. The title character commands the Venetian army and soon becomes acting governor of Cypress. He is also a Moor, a dark-skinned African whose secret marriage to the beautiful Desdemona has infuriated her father, a wealthy and influential Venetian, whose anger reveals a racist element in Venice which Othello tries to ignore. Iago hates Othello for granting a promotion to Cassio which Iago believes should rightfully be his. With unrelenting determination and malicious deception, Iago attempts to persuade Othello that Desdemona has committed adultery with Cassio. The following excerpt catches Iago in the early stages of his successful manipulation:

IAGO: In Venice they [wives] do let heaven see pranks
They dare not show their husbands; their best conscience
Is not to leave 't undone, but keep 't unknown.

OTHELLO: Dost thou say so?

IAGO: She did deceive her father, marrying you;

And when she seem'd to shake and fear your looks,
She lov'd them most.

OTHELLO: And so she did.

IAGO: Why, go to, then;
She that so young could give out such a seeming,
To see her father's eyes up close as oak,
He thought 'twas witchcraft; but I am much to blame;
I humbly do beseech you of your pardon
For too much loving you.

OTHELLO: I am bound to thee for ever.

IAGO: I see, this hath a little dash'd your spirits.

OTHELLO: Not a jot, not a jot.

IAGO: I' faith, I fear it has.
I hope you will consider what is spoke
Comes from my love. But I do see you're mov'd;
I am to pray you not to strain my speech
To grosser issues nor to larger reach
Than to suspicion.

OTHELLO: I will not.

IAGO: Should you do so, my lord,
My speech should fall into such vile success
As my thoughts aim not at. Cassio's my worthy friend —
My lord, I see you're mov'd.

OTHELLO: No, not much mov'd:
I do not think but Desdemona's honest.

IAGO: Long live she so! and long live you to think so!

OTHELLO: And yet, how nature erring from itself, —

IAGO: Ay, there's the point: as, to be bold with you,
Not to affect many proposed matches
Of her own clime, complexion, and degree,
Whereto, we see, in all things nature tends;
Foh! one may smell in such, a will most rank,

Foul disproportion, thoughts unnatural.
But pardon me; I do not in position
Distinctly speak of her, though I may fear
Her will, recoiling to her better judgment,
May fall to match you with her country forms
And happily repent.

OTHELLO: Farewell, farewell:
If more thou dost perceive, let me know more;
Set on thy wife to observe. Leave me, Iago.

IAGO: My lord, I take my leave. (Going)

OTHELLO: Why did I marry? This honest creature, doubtless,
Sees and knows more, much more, than he unfolds.

Notice that Iago speaks much more than Othello. This is typical of their conversations, as though Iago were the superior of the two. Dramatically, for Iago's scheme to compel our interests we must perceive in Othello tragic proportions, both in his strengths and weaknesses; otherwise, *Othello* would slip into a mean tale about a rogue and his dupe. Much of the tension in this scene stems from Othello's reluctance either to accept Iago's innuendos immediately or to dismiss them. This confusion places him on the rack of doubt, a torture made more severe because he questions his own desirability as a husband. Consequently, since Iago is not the "honest creature" he appears to be and Othello is unwilling to confront openly his own self-doubts, Iago becomes the dominant personality — a situation which a flawless Othello would never tolerate.

HISTORY

The playwright's raw material can spring from any source. A passion play, for instance, is a dramatic adaptation of the Crucifixion as told in the gospels. A history play is a dramatic perspective of some event or series of events identified with recognized historical figures. Television docudramas are the most recent examples.

Ever since the 16th century history, plays have seldom risen above the level of patriotic whitewash and political propaganda. Of course there are notable exceptions to this trend: Robert Bolt's *A Man for All Seasons* is one. The title character, Sir Thomas More, is beheaded at the play's conclusion, following his refusal to condone Henry VIII's break from the Roman Catholic Church and the king's establishment of the Church of England with the monarch as its head. Henry wants More to condone these actions because the Pope will not grant Henry a divorce from Queen Catherine so that he can marry Anne Boleyn, who the king believes will bear him the male heir he desperately wants. The central issue for us is not whether More's beliefs are valid but whether any person of conscience can act freely in a world dominated by others far less principled. In Henry's only scene he arrives at Sir Thomas' house hoping his Lord Chancellor will not disappoint him:

[music in background]

HENRY: Son after son she's borne me, Thomas, all dead at birth, or dead within a month; I never saw the hand of God so clear in anything.... I have a daughter, she's a good child, a well-set child — But I have no son. (He flares up.) It is my bounden duty to put away the Queen, and all the Popes back to St. Peter shall not come between me and my duty! How is it that you cannot see? Everybody else does.

MORE: (Eagerly) Then why does Your Grace need my poor support?

HENRY: Because you are honest. What's more to the purpose, you're known to be honest.... There are those like Norfolk who follow me because I wear the crown, and there are those like Master Cromwell who follow me because they are jackals with sharp teeth and I am their lion, and there is a mass that follow me because it follows anything that moves — and there is you.

MORE: I am sick to think how much I must displease Your Grace.

HENRY: No, Thomas, I respect your sincerity. Respect? Oh, man, it's water in the desert.... How did you like our music? That air they played, it had a certain — well, tell me what you thought of it.

MORE: (Relieved at this turn; smiling) Could it have been Your Grace's own?

HENRY: (Smiles back) Discovered! Now I'll never know your true opinion. And that's irksome, Thomas, for we artists, though we love praise, yet we love truth better.

MORE: (Mildly) Then I will tell Your Grace truly what I thought of it.

HENRY: (A little disconcerted) Speak then.

MORE: To me it seemed — delightful.

HENRY: Thomas — I chose the right man for Chancellor.

MORE: I must in fairness add that my taste in music is reputably deplorable.

To what extent Henry and More discussed the king's divorce and its subsequent events nobody knows, let alone what was actually said, although we can be certain they spoke an English distinctively different from the language in the play. Bolt's imagination, funnelled through the dramatist's obligation to tell an interesting story, presides over the historical data and dictates the play's projections of More, Henry, and the other participants. Thus, we do not have "history"; instead, we have a dramatic perception of history shaped, altered, and adorned by Robert Bolt, writing about 16th century figures from a 1960 vantage point. But as the scene above shows, the characters' personalities are not simple reductions of what historical giants should be. Henry struts a royal self-assurance noticeably colored by vanity and frustration; yet although he lacks More's wit and intelligence, the king clearly is no fool. Likewise, as troubled as More is by the controversy before him, he projects a formidable power of his own. *A Man for All Seasons* succeeds dramatically because Bolt provides only enough history to present a context for the characters' development while he allows the resultant implications to touch all times, all seasons. When we read any history play, we should search for similar implications; otherwise, the work can never become more than a theatrical précis with a narrow focus.

MODERN DRAMA

From the 1870's to the present, the theater has participated in the artistic movements reflecting accumulated theories of science, social science, and philosophy which attempt to define reality and the means we use to discern it. First caught in a pendulum of opposing views, modern drama eventually synthesized these perspectives into new forms, familiar in some ways and boldly original in others. Henrik Ibsen's plays began the modern era with their emphasis on **realism**, a seeking of truth through direct observation using the five senses. As objectively depicted, contemporary life received a closer scrutiny than ever before, showing everyday people in everyday situations. Before Ibsen, theatrical sets were limited, with rare exceptions, to castles and country estates. After Ibsen, the farmhouse and city tenement were suitable for the stage. Ibsen's work influenced many others, and from realism came two main variations. The first, **naturalism,** strove to push realism toward a direct transformation of life on stage, a "slice of life" showing how the scientific principles of heredity and environment have shaped society, especially in depicting the plights of the lower classes. The second variation, **expressionism**, moved in a different direction and actually denied realism's premise that the real world could be objectively perceived; instead — influenced by Sigmund Freud's theories about human behavior's hidden, subconscious motivations and by other modernist trends in the arts, such as James Joyce's fiction and Picasso's paintings — expressionism imitated a disconnected dream-like world filled with psychological images at odds with the tangible world surrounding it. While naturalism attempts to imitate life directly, expressionism is abstract and often relies on symbols.

A modern play can employ any number of elements found in the spectrum between these extremes as well as suggest divergent philosophical views about whether humanity has the power to change its condition or whether any of its ideas about the universe are verifiable. Moreover, no work of art is necessarily confined within a particular school of thought. It is quite possible that seemingly unrelated forms can appear in the same play and work well. *The Glass Menagerie, A Man for All Seasons*, and *Death of a Salesman* feature characters and dialogue indicative of realistic drama, but the sets described in the stage directions are expressionistic, offering either framed outlines of places or distorted representations. Conventions from classical drama are also available to the playwright. As previously noted, Tom acts as a Greek chorus as well as an important character in his play; the same is true of the Common Man, whose identity changes from scene to scene. In short, anything is possible in modern drama, a quality which is wholly compatible with the diversity and unpredictability of 20th century human experiences.

In a sense all good drama is modern. No label about a play's origin or form can adequately describe its content. Establishing the people, places, and thought within the play is crucial to our understanding. For the characters to interest us we must perceive the issues that affect their lives, and eventually we will discover why the characters' personalities and backgrounds, together with their social situations, inevitably converge with these issues and create conflicts. *Death of a Salesman* challenges the classical definitions of tragedy by giving us a modern American, Willy Loman, who is indeed a "low man," a person of little social importance and limited moral fiber. His delusionary values have brought him at age sixty-four to failure and despair, yet more than ever he clings to his dreams and painted memories for solace and hope. Late one night, after Willy has returned from an aborted sales trip, his rambling conversation with his wife Linda returns to the topic which haunts him the most, his son Biff.

WILLY: Biff is a lazy bum!

LINDA: They're sleeping. Get something to eat. Go on down.

WILLY: Why did he come home? I would like to know what brought him home.

LINDA: I don't know. I think he's still lost, Willy. I think he's very lost.

WILLY: Biff Loman is lost. In the greatest country in the world a young man with such — personal attractiveness, gets lost. And such a hard worker. There's one thing about Biff — he's not lazy.

LINDA: Never.

WILLY (with pity and resolve): I'll see him in the morning; I'll have a nice talk with him. I'll get him a job selling. He could be big in no time. My God! Remember how they used to follow him around in high school? When he smiled at one of them their faces lit up. When he walked down the street.... (He loses himself in reminiscences.)

LINDA (trying to bring him out of it): Willy, dear, I got a new kind of American-type cheese today. It's whipped.

WILLY: Why do you get American cheese when you know I like Swiss?

LINDA: I just thought you'd like a change —

WILLY: I don't want change! I want Swiss cheese. Why am I always being contradicted?

LINDA (with a covering laugh): I just thought it would be a surprise.

WILLY: Why don't you open a window in here, for God's sake?

LINDA (with infinite patience): They're all open dear.

WILLY: The way they boxed us in here. Bricks and windows, windows and bricks.

LINDA: We should have bought the land next door.

WILLY: The street is lined with cars. There's not a breath of fresh air in the neighborhood. The grass don't grow any more, you can't raise a carrot in the backyard. They should've had a law against apartment houses. Remember those two beautiful elms out there? When I and Biff hung the swing between them?

LINDA: Yeah, like a million miles from the city.

WILLY: They should've arrested the builder for cutting those down. They massacred the neighborhood. (Lost) More and more I think of those days, Linda. This time of year it was lilac and wisteria. And then the peonies would come out, and the daffodils. What fragrance in this room!

LINDA: Well, after all, people had to move somewhere.

WILLY: No, there's more people now.

LINDA: I don't think there's more people. I think —

WILLY: There's more people! That's what's ruining this country! Population is getting out of control. The competition is maddening! Smell the stink from that apartment house! And another on the other side.... How can they whip cheese?

In Arthur Miller's stage directions for *Death of a Salesman*, the Loman house is outlined by simple framing with various floors represented by short elevated platforms. Outside the house the towering shapes of the city angle inward presenting the crowded oppressiveness Willy complains about. First performed in 1949, the play continues to make a powerful commentary on modern American life. We see Willy as more desperate than angry about his condition, which he defines in ways as contradictory as his assessments of Biff. In his suffocating world, Willy gropes for peace while hiding from truth; and although his woes are uniquely American in some ways, they touch broader, more universal human problems as well.

☞ Drill: Reading Drama

<u>DIRECTIONS</u>: The following three questions are based on the previous passage. After reading the passage, answer the following questions.

1. Where does the dialogue in the passage take place?
    (1) At a country cottage   (4) At a seaside resort
    (2) At a city residence   (5) At a western ranch
    (3) At a European villa

2. Why is Willy upset that Linda bought American cheese?
   (1) Because Biff likes American cheese
   (2) Because Willy does not like cheese
   (3) Because the whole city stinks like cheese
   (4) Because Willy fears change
   (5) Because American cheese makes Linda sick

3. What would be a good description of Linda?
   (1) She is cruel   (4) She is selfish
   (2) She is dishonest   (5) She is patient
   (3) She is lazy

V. READING COMMENTARY

When you go to see a movie, and it turns out to be a movie that strikes you in many ways, you just cannot wait to talk about it. Right? That discussion after the movie is a commentary. It is a way of expressing your thoughts and impressions about the film you have just seen. If you were to write down your thoughts and impressions, rather than discuss them, you essentially would have an example of the type of commentary that turns up on the GED.

Commentary is not just about movies. It also takes as its subject dance, art, sculpture, theater, literature, and music. Commentary is a means of conveying feelings about the arts to an audience. The audience may be a teacher for whom you write a report. It may be a friend who receives a letter in which you talk about a play you have just seen. Most likely, the audience is the reader of a newspaper or magazine since this is where the majority of commentary makes its way to the general public. This type of commentary is the kind you will find in the entertainment section of your newspaper. It is also the kind you will encounter on the GED.

What are we looking for when we are presented with a review of something? There are a couple of standard items that we should use as guides when we attempt to understand a review. Here are some important questions to keep in mind as you read such a review:

- What is the author's attitude toward the work? Is the basic opinion favorable to the work or is it disapproving?

- Does the author back up his/her opinion with concrete examples? Are the examples descriptive enough that you understand the critic's point?

You should become able to see how a review works in terms of these points. A critic will *always* have an opinion, and they will *always* cite examples to demonstrate why they feel the way they do. Once you learn to recognize this system, you will be able to follow a reviewer's line of reasoning and understand his interpretations and opinions about a play, poem, or painting. The GED will not expect you to know the background of any of the artists, literature, or works of art discussed. Instead, it will present to you passages which are descriptive enough to answer all questions without any prior knowledge of the work being discussed.

Here is an example of a typical passage that might appear on the GED, with questions that would follow:

Superman, starring Christopher Reeves and Margot Kidder, has the look and feel of a comic book placed on screen. Throughout the movie we are presented with the clear, sharp colors of the original Superman as he was, and is, drawn in Marvel Comics. Not only are the colors clear-cut and bold, but so are the personalities of the characters. There is a simplicity to every character in the movie that lets us clearly know the good guys from the bad guys. In a comic book there just is not the room, nor the inclination, to develop a character in great depth, and so we get characters who are more like cardboard cut-outs than real people. This is what makes comic books so fun. Comic books allow us to escape from the world of real people and give us satisfying conclusions to superheroes' dilemmas. *Superman,* the movie, manages to do the same thing. This is what makes it great entertainment!

In *Superman,* nothing is beyond the hero's control. There is nothing terrible that can happen that Superman cannot fix. His character can bring back a loved one from the dead by turning back time. He is also able to avert nuclear destruction by being faster and more powerful that a ballistic missile. When we, the audience, see the character faced with these situations, we feel as if we are involved in them also. When we see Superman get through these situations and conquer these problems, we feel as if we are also a part of the solution. This gives us the kind power over problems that we do not have in real life. It is that feeling of power that we get by identifying with Superman that allows us a fantasy for just a while. *Superman,* like the comic book that came before it, is guaranteed to entertain with humor, drama, and most importantly, the kind of action that puts you in the sky right alongside the hero himself.

Drill: Reading Commentary

DIRECTIONS: The following questions are based on the passage above. Read each question and choose the correct answer.

1. Which of the following terms would the reviewer most likely use to describe the movie *Superman*?
   - (1) Ridiculous
   - (2) Confusing
   - (3) Satisfying
   - (4) Old-fashioned
   - (5) Boring

2. According to the reviewer, the movie *Superman* is most like
    (1) a circus.   (4) a poem.
    (2) an auto race.   (5) a comic book.
    (3) a war.

3. The author believes that *Superman*
    (1) is an accurate portrayal of real life.
    (2) is an entertaining fantasy.
    (3) is a depressing drama.
    (4) is too wordy.
    (5) lacks humor.

You will notice that the commentator expresses a clear opinion about the movie and uses examples to explain why he felt the way he did. Every commentary will work in this way. Remember that the objective of any commentary is to express an opinion or explain an interpretation; learn to recognize this first in any commentary you pick up. After that, learn to pick out the concrete examples that the reviewer uses to back up his opinions. Knowing how to pick up these things will help you greatly on the GED. Buy a newspaper and read a review of a local play or current movie. Try to pick it apart. This will be good practice so that by the time you take the actual exam you will understand commentary on all of the arts.

INTERPRETING LITERATURE AND THE ARTS

ANSWER KEY

Drill: Reading Prose

1. (1)   2. (3)   3. (3)

Drill: Reading Poetry

1. (4)   2. (5)   3. (1)

Drill: Reading Drama

1. (2)   2. (4)   3. (5)

Drill: Reading Commentary

1. (3)   2. (5)   3. (2)

MATH
REVIEW

Chapter 6

MATH REVIEW

I. STRATEGIES FOR MATH SECTIONS

II. ARITHMETIC

III. ALGEBRA

IV. GEOMETRY

In order to be successful on the mathematics section of the GED, you must first prepare yourself by studying the fundamental concepts in our math review. Our math hints can help increase your chances of answering the problems correctly. The methods that we provide consist of specific steps that illustrate for you the best way to approach particular math problems. These hints will pick up where your math knowledge leaves off. The more familiar you are with our math hints, the better your chances of achieving a top score on the GED Mathematics Exam.

GED math problems test your basic knowledge of arithmetic, algebra, and geometry. Our math review represents the various mathematical topics that will appear on the GED. You will not find any calculus, trigonometry, or imaginary numbers in our math review. Nor will you find any word problems. The mathematical concepts presented on the GED are ones with which you are already familiar and simply need to review in order to score well.

Along with a knowledge to these topics, your speed and accuracy in answering the math questions will have an effect upon your success. Therefore, memorize the directions in order to save time and decrease your chances of making careless mistakes. Then, complete the practice drills that are provided for you in our review. Even if you are sure you know your fundamental math concepts, the drills will help to warm you up so that you can go into the math GED with quick, sharp math skills. Also, make sure to review the Reference Table of mathematical symbols and formulas which appears in the appendix of this book.

I. STRATEGIES FOR MATH SECTIONS

If you know how to solve the problem, this is your plan of attack:

Solve for x:

$3x + 4(x + 1) = 11$

(A) -1 (B) 0 (C) 3/4

(D) 1 (E) 11/7

➤ Step 1   Calculate the answer as quickly as possible.

$$
\begin{aligned}
3x + 4x + 4 &= 11 \\
7x + 4 + (-4) &= 11 + (-4) \\
7x &= 7 \\
x &= 1
\end{aligned}
$$

➤ Step 2   Find your answer among the answer choices.

The answer is (D).

If you do not know how to solve the problem, this is your plan of attack:

A computer generates three consecutive even integers each time it is turned on. If the sum of the three numbers is 54, what is the value of the largest number?

(A) 10   (B) 14   (C) 20

(D) 24   (E) 28

➤ Step 1 | Determine what the question is asking.

This question is asking you to find the largest of three even, consecutive integers.

➤ Step 2 | Try to formulate an equation that solves for the unknown value using all the necessary information given in the question. Look at the answer choices and eliminate any that are obviously wrong.

Let x = the first even integer
Let $x + 2$ = the second even integer
Let $x + 4$ = the third even integer (the largest)
Therefore,
$$x + (x + 2) + (x + 4) = 54$$

By immediately looking at the answer choices, we see that (A) is obviously wrong since if 10 were correct, the other two numbers would be 6 and 8 which, when added together equal only 24. In the same way, (E) is obviously wrong since if 28 was correct, the other two numbers would be 24 and 26 which, when added together, would be much greater than 54.

➤ Step 3 | Plug in the remaining answer choices to find the correct answer.

Plugging in the other choices, we find:

If $x + 4 = 14$, then $x = 10$. Therefore, 10 + 12 + 14 would have to equal 54. However, it only equals 36.

If $x + 4 = 20$, then $x = 16$. Therefore, 16 + 18 + 20 would have to equal 54. It does and therefore, (C) is the correct answer.

➤ Step 4 | If you cannot formulate an equation, try to make an educated guess among the remaining answer choices.

➤ ADDITIONAL HINTS

- **Know all important formulas and concepts in the Mathematics Review.**

- **Draw sketches. This allows you to visualize exactly what the question is asking and what information you need to find.**

- Always look at the answer choices before trying to work out the problem. If all the choices are in a specific format, you would want to do your work in the same format. For example, if the measurements in a problem are given in feet, but the answer choices are given in inches, you must change the feet to inches when working out the problem.

- Remember to work in only one unit and convert if more than one is presented in the problem. For example, if a problem gives numbers in decimals and fractions, convert one in terms of the other and then work out the problem.

- Avoid lengthy computations. If a problem is taking a long time to figure out, go on to another question and come back to it if time remains.

- Do not panic if something looks unusual; it may be easy.

- Use the scratch paper which will be provided.

- When given specific information for a problem, immediately plug these values into your equation.

- Be suspicious of choices that seem too obvious unless it is an easy level question. Many times choices will appear that are simply repetitions of numbers used in the problem. If the question is medium or hard, the chances are that these answers are incorrect.

- After working out an equation, make sure your result is actually answering the question. Otherwise, you may have to perform some extra steps. For example, although you may solve an equation for a specific variable, this may not be the final answer. You may have to use this answer to find another quantity.

Find the greatest of three consecutive integers whose sum is 36.

(A) 11   (B) 13   (C) 15

(D) 17   (E) 19

Let x = the first integer

Let $x + 1$ = the second integer

Let $x + 2$ = the third integer

$x + (x + 1) + (x + 2) = 36$

$3x + 3 = 36$

$3x = 33$

$x = 11$

Although $x = 11$ and answer choice (A) is 11, this is not the correct answer. The questions asks for the *greatest* of three consecutive integers. 11 is the smallest. Therefore, 11 must be plugged into $(x + 2)$ in order to find the greatest integer which is 13.

MATH TOPICS

The topics listed below should be reviewed in order to accurately answer the mathematical GED sections. See the math review on the following pages.

ARITHMETIC (50% of Test)

1. Integers and Real Numbers
2. Fractions
3. Decimals
4. Percentages
5. Radicals
6. Exponents
7. Averages

ALGEBRA (30% of Test)

1. Operations With Polynominals
2. Simplifying Algebraic Expressions
3. Equations
4. Two Linear Equations
5. Absolute Value Equations
6. Inequalities
7. Ratios and Proportions

GEOMETRY (20% of Test)

1. Points, Lines, and Angles
2. Regular Polygons
3. Triangles
4. Quadrilaterals
5. Circles
6. Solids
7. Coordinate Geometry

II. ARITHMETIC

1. INTEGERS AND REAL NUMBERS

Most of the numbers used in algebra belong to a set called the **real numbers** or **reals**. This set can be represented graphically by the real number line.

Given the number line below, we arbitrarily fix a point and label it with the number 0. In a similar manner, we can label any point on the line with one of the real numbers, depending on its position relative to 0. Numbers to the right of zero are positive, while those to the left are negative. Value increases from left to right, so that if a is to the right of b, it is said to be greater than b.

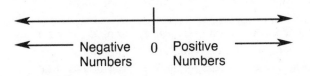

If we now divide the number line into equal segments, we can label the points on this line with real numbers. For example, the point 2 lengths to the left of zero is -2, while the point 3 lengths to the right of zero is $+3$ (the $+$ sign is usually assumed, so $+3$ is written simply as 3). The number line now looks like this:

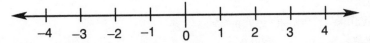

These boundary points represent the subset of the reals known as the **integers**. The set of integers is made up of both the positive and negative whole numbers: $\{\dots -4, -3, -2, -1, 0, 1, 2, 3, 4, \dots\}$. Some subsets of integers are:

Natural Numbers or Positive Numbers — the set of integers starting with 1 and increasing: $\mathcal{N} = \{1, 2, 3, 4, \dots\}$.

Whole Numbers — the set of integers starting with 0 and increasing : $\mathcal{W} = \{0, 1, 2, 3, \dots\}$.

Negative Numbers — the set of integers starting with -1 and decreasing: $\mathcal{Z} = \{-1, -2, -3 \dots\}$.

Prime Numbers — the set of positive integers greater than 1 that are divisible only by 1 and themselves: $\{2, 3, 5, 7, 11, \dots\}$.

Even Integers — the set of integers divisible by 2: $\{\dots, -4, -2, 0, 2, 4, 6, \dots\}$.

Odd Integers — the set of integers not divisible by 2: $\{\dots, -3, -1, 1, 3, 5, 7, \dots\}$.

PROBLEM

Classify each of the following numbers into as many different sets as possible. Example: real, integer ...

(1) 0   (2) 9   (3) $\sqrt{6}$

(4) $\frac{1}{2}$ (5) $\frac{2}{3}$ (6) 1.5

SOLUTION

(1) Zero is a real number, and an integer, and a whole number.

(2) 9 is a real number, an odd number, and a natural number.

(3) $\sqrt{6}$ is a real number.

(4) $\frac{1}{2}$ is a real number.

(5) $\frac{2}{3}$ is a real number.

(6) 1.5 is a real number, and a decimal.

ABSOLUTE VALUE

The **absolute value** of a number is represented by two vertical lines around the number, and is equal to the given number, regardless of sign.

The absolute value of a real number A is defined as follows:

$$|A| = \begin{cases} A \text{ if } A \geq 0 \\ -A \text{ if } A < 0 \end{cases}$$

EXAMPLE

$$|5| = 5, |-8| = -(-8) = 8.$$

Absolute values follow the given rules:

(A) $|-A| = |A|$

(B) $|A| \geq 0$, equality holding only if $A = 0$

(C) $\left|\dfrac{A}{B}\right| = \dfrac{|A|}{|B|}, B \neq 0$

(D) $|AB| = |A| \times |B|$

(E) $|A|^2 = A^2$

Absolute value can also be expressed on the real number line as the distance of the point represented by the real number from the point labeled 0.

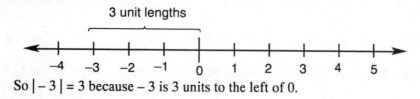

3 unit lengths

So $|-3| = 3$ because -3 is 3 units to the left of 0.

PROBLEM

Classify each of the following statements as true or false. If it is false, explain why.

(1) $|-120| > 1$

(4) $|12 - 3| = 12 - 3$

(2) $|4 - 12| = |4| - |12|$

(5) $|-12a| = 12|a|$

(3) $|4 - 9| = 9 - 4$

SOLUTION

(1)   True

(2)   False, $|4 - 12| = |4| - |12|$

$$|-8| = 4 - 12$$

$$8 \neq -8$$

In general, $|a + b| \neq |a| + |b|$

(3)   True

(4)   True

(5)   True

PROBLEM

Calculate the value of each of the following expressions:

(1) $||2 - 5| + 6 - 14|$

(2) $|-5| \cdot |4| + \dfrac{|-12|}{4}$

SOLUTION

Before solving this problem, one must remember the order of operations: parenthesis, multiplication and division, addition and subtraction.

(1) $||-3| + 6 - 14| = |3 + 6 - 14| = |9 - 14| = |-5| = 5$

(2) $(5 \times 4) + {}^{12}/_4 = 20 + 3 = 23$

PROBLEM

Find the absolute value for each of the following:

(1)   zero

(2) $-\pi$

(2)   4

(4) a, where a is a real number

SOLUTION

(1) $|0| = 0$

(2) $|4| = 4$

(3) $|-\pi| = \pi$

(4)   for $a > 0, |a| = a$

for $a = 0, |a| = 0$

for $a < 0, |a| = -a$

$$\text{i.e., } |a| = \begin{cases} a \text{ if } a > 0 \\ 0 \text{ if } a = 0 \\ a \text{ if } a < 0 \end{cases}$$

POSITIVE AND NEGATIVE NUMBERS

A) **To add two numbers with like signs,** add their absolute values and write the sum with the common sign, So,

$$6 + 2 = 8, (-6) + (-2) = -8$$

B) **To add two numbers with unlike signs,** find the difference between their absolute values, and write the result with the sign of the number with the greater absolute value. So,

$$(-4) + 6 = 2, 15 + (-19) = -4$$

C) **To subtract a number b from another number a,** change the sign of b and add to a. Examples:

$$10 - (3) = 10 + (-3) = 7 \tag{1}$$

$$2 - (-6) = 2 + 6 = 8 \tag{2}$$

$$(-5) - (-2) = -5 + (+2) = -3 \tag{3}$$

D) **To multiply (or divide) two numbers having like signs,** multiply (or divide) their absolute values and write the result with a positive sign. Examples:

$$(5)(3) = 15 \tag{1}$$

$$(-6) / (-3) = 2 \tag{2}$$

E) **To multiply (or divide) two numbers having unlike signs,** multiply (or divide) their absolute values and write the result with a negative sign. Examples:

$$(-2)(8) = -16 \tag{1}$$

$$9 / (-3) = -3 \tag{2}$$

According to the law of signs for real numbers, the square of a positive or negative number is always positive. This means that it is impossible to take the square root of a negative number in the real number system.

☞ DRILL: Integers and Real Numbers

Addition

1. Simplify $4 + (-7) + 2 + (-5)$.

(A) -6 (B) -4 (C) 0 (D) 6 (E) 18

2. Simplify 144 + (– 317) + 213.

(A) – 357   (B) – 40   (C) 40   (D) 357   (E) 674

3. Simplify | 4 + (– 3) | + | – 2 |.

(A) – 2   (B) – 1   (C) 1   (D) 3   (E) 9

4. What integer makes the equation – 13 + 12 + 7 + ? = 10 a true statement?

(A) – 22   (B) – 10   (C) 4   (D) 6   (E) 10

5. Simplify 4 + 17 + (– 29) + 13 + (– 22) + (– 3).

(A) – 44   (B) – 20   (C) 23   (D) 34   (E) 78

Subtraction

6. Simplify 319 – 428.

(A) – 111   (B) – 109   (C) – 99   (D) 109   (E) 747

7. Simplify 91,203 – 37,904 + 1,073.

(A) 54,372   (B) 64,701   (C) 128,034   (D) 129,107   (E) 130,180

8. Simplify | 43 – 62 | – | – 17 – 3|.

(A) – 39   (B) – 19   (C) – 1   (D) 1   (E) 39

9. Simplify – (– 4 – 7) + (– 2).

(A) – 22   (B) – 13   (C) – 9   (D) 7   (E) 9

10. In the Great Smoky Mountains National Park, Mt. Le Conte rises from 1292 feet above sea level to 6593 feet above sea level. How tall is Mt. Le Conte?

(A) 4009 ft   (B) 5301 ft   (C) 5699 ft   (D) 6464 ft   (E) 7885 ft

Multiplication

11. Simplify – 3 * – 18 * – 1.

(A) – 108   (B) – 54   (C) – 48   (D) 48   (E) 54

12. Simplify | – 42 | * | 7 |.

(A) – 294   (B) – 49   (C) – 35   (D) 284   (E) 294

13. Simplify $-6*5*-10*-4*0*2$.

(A) -2400 (B) -240 (C) 0   (D) 280   (E) 2700

14. Simplify $-|-6*8|$.

(A) -48 (B) -42 (C) 2   (D) 42   (E) 48

15. A city in Georgia had a record low temparature of –3°F one winter. During the same year, a city in Michigan experienced a record low that was nine times the record low set in Georgia. What was the record low in Michigan that year?

(A) -31°F   (B) -27°F   (C) -21°F   (D) -12°F   (E) -6°F

Division

16. Simplify $-24 \div 8$.

(A) -4 (B) -3 (C) -2 (D) 3   (E) 4

17. Simplify $(-180) \div (-12)$.

(A) -30 (B) -15 (C) 1.5   (D) 15   (E) 216

18. Simplify $|-76| \div |-4|$.

(A) -21 (B) -19 (C) 13   (D) 19   (E) 21.5

19. Simplify $|216 \div (-6)|$.

(A) -36 (B) -12 (C) 36   (D) 38   (E) 43

20. At the end of the year, a small firm has \$2,996 in its account for bonuses. If the entire amount is equally divided among the 14 employees, how much does each one receive?

(A) \$107   (B) \$114   (C) \$170   (D) \$210   (E) \$214

Order of Operations

21. Simplify $\dfrac{4 + 8 * 2}{5 - 1}$

(A) 4   (B) 5   (C) 6   (D) 8   (E) 12

22. $96 \div 3 \div 4 \div 2 =$

(A) 65   (B) 64   (C) 16   (D) 8   (E) 4

23. $3 + 4 * 2 - 6 \div 3 =$

(A) -1 (B) $5/3$ (C) $8/3$ (D) 9 (E) 12

24. $[(4 + 8) * 3] \div 9 =$

(A) 4 (B) 8 (C) 12 (D) 24 (E) 36

25. $18 + 3 * 4 \div 3 =$

(A) 3 (B) 5 (C) 10 (D) 22 (E) 28

26. $(29 - 17 + 4) \div 4 + |-2| =$

(A) $2^2/_3$ (B) 4 (C) $4^2/_3$ (D) 6 (E) 15

27. $(-3) * 5 - 20 \div 4 =$

(A) -75 (B) -20 (C) -10 (D) $-8^3/_4$ (E) 20

28. $\dfrac{11 * 2 + 2}{16 - 2 * 2} =$

(A) $11/16$ (B) 1 (C) 2 (D) $3\ 2/3$ (E) 4

29. $|-8 - 4| \div 3 * 6 + (-4) =$

(A) 20 (B) 26 (C) 32 (D) 62 (E) 212

30. $32 \div 2 + 4 - 15 \div 3 =$

(A) 0 (B) 7 (C) 15 (D) 23 (E) 63

2. FRACTIONS

The fraction, a/b, where the **numerator** is a and the **denominator** is b, implies that a is being divided by b. The denominator of a fraction can never be zero since a number divided by zero is not defined. If the numerator is greater than the denominator, the fraction is called an **improper fraction**. A **mixed number** is the sum of a whole number and a fraction, i.e., $4^3/_8 = 4 + {}^3/_8$.

OPERATIONS WITH FRACTIONS

A) **To change a mixed number to an improper fraction,** simply multiply the whole number by the denominator of the fraction and add the numerator. This product becomes the numerator of the result and the denominator remains the same. e.g.,

$$5\frac{2}{3} = \frac{(5 \cdot 3) + 2}{3} = \frac{15 + 2}{3} = \frac{17}{3}$$

To change an improper fraction to a mixed number, simply divide the numerator by the denominator. The remainder becomes the numerator of the fractional part of the mixed number, and the denominator remains the same, e.g.,

$$\frac{35}{4} = 35 \div 4 = 8\,\frac{3}{4}$$

To check your work, change your result back to an improper fraction to see if it matches the original fraction.

B) **To find the sum of two fractions having a common denominator,** simply add together the numerators of the given fractions and put this sum over the common denominator.

$$\frac{11}{3} + \frac{5}{3} = \frac{11+5}{3} = \frac{16}{3}$$

Similarly for subtraction,

$$\frac{11}{3} - \frac{5}{3} = \frac{11-5}{3} = \frac{6}{3} = 2$$

C) **To find the sum of the two fractions having different denominators,** it is necessary to find the **lowest common denominator (LCD)** of the different denominators using a process called **factoring**.

To **factor** a number means to find two numbers that when multiplied together have a product equal to the original number. These two numbers are then said to be **factors** of the original number; e.g., the factors of 6 are

(1) 1 and 6 since $1 \times 6 = 6$.

(2) 2 and 3 since $2 \times 3 = 6$.

Every number is the product of itself and 1. A **prime factor** is a number that does not have any factors besides itself and 1. This is important when finding the LCD of two fractions having different denominators.

To find the LCD of $^{11}/_6$ and $^5/_{16}$, we must first find the prime factors of each of the two denominators.

$$6 = 2 \times 3$$

$$16 = 2 \times 2 \times 2 \times 2$$

$$LCD = 2 \times 2 \times 2 \times 2 \times 3 = 48$$

Note that we do not need to repeat the 2 that appears in both the factors of 6 and 16.

Once we have determined the LCD of the denominators, each of the fractions must be converted into equivalent fractions having the LCD as a denominator.

Rewrite 11/6 and 5/16 to have 48 as their denominators.

$6 \times ? = 48$	$16 \times ? = 48$
$6 \times 8 = 48$	$16 \times 3 = 48$

If the numerator and denominator of each fraction is multiplied (or divided) by the same number, the value of the fraction will not change. This is because a fraction b/b, b being any number, is equal to the multiplicative identity, 1.

Therefore,

$$\frac{11}{6} \cdot \frac{8}{8} = \frac{88}{48} \qquad\qquad \frac{5}{16} \cdot \frac{3}{3} = \frac{15}{48}$$

We may now find

$$\frac{11}{6} + \frac{5}{16} = \frac{88}{48} + \frac{15}{48} = \frac{103}{48}$$

Similarly for subtraction,

$$\frac{11}{6} - \frac{5}{16} = \frac{88}{48} - \frac{15}{48} = \frac{73}{48}$$

D)   **To find the product of two or more fractions,** simply multiply the numerators of the given fractions to find the numerator of the product and multiply the denominators of the given fractions to find the denominator of the product. e.g.,

$$\frac{2}{3} \cdot \frac{1}{5} \cdot \frac{4}{7} = \frac{2 \times 1 \times 4}{3 \times 5 \times 7} = \frac{8}{105}$$

E)   To find the quotient of two fractions, simply invert the divisor and multiply; e.g.,

$$\frac{8}{9} \div \frac{1}{3} = \frac{8}{9} \times \frac{3}{1} = \frac{24}{9} = \frac{8}{3}$$

F)   **To simplify a fraction** is to convert it into a form in which the numerator and denominator have no common factor other than 1; e.g.,

$$\frac{12}{18} = \frac{12 \div 6}{18 \div 6} = \frac{2}{3}$$

G)   A **complex fraction** is a fraction whose numerator and/or denominator is made up of fractions. To simplify the fraction, find the LCD of all the fractions. Multiply both the numerator and denominator by this number and simplify.

PROBLEM

If $a = 4$ and $b = 7$, find the value of $\dfrac{a + \frac{a}{b}}{a - \frac{a}{b}}$

SOLUTION

By substitution,

$$\frac{a + \frac{a}{b}}{a - \frac{a}{b}} = \frac{4 + \frac{4}{7}}{4 - \frac{4}{7}}$$

In order to combine the terms, we must find the LCD of 1 and 7. Since both are prime factors, the LCD = $1 \times 7 = 7$.

Multiplying both numerator and denominator by 7, we get:

$$\frac{7(4 + \frac{4}{7})}{7(4 - \frac{4}{7})} = \frac{28 + 4}{28 - 4} = \frac{32}{24}$$

By dividing both numerator and denominator by 8, 32/24 can be reduced to 4/3.

☞ Drill: Fractions

Fractions

<u>DIRECTIONS</u>: Add and write the answer in simplest form.

1.   5/12 + 3/12 =

(A) 5/24   (B)   1/3   (C)   8/12   (D)   2/3   (E)   1 1/3

2.   5/8 + 7/8 + 3/8 =

(A)   15/24   (B)   3/4   (C)   5/6   (D)   7/8   (E)   1 7/8

3.   131 2/15 + 28 3/15 =

(A)   159 1/6   (B)   159 1/5   (C)   159 1/3   (D)   159 1/2   (E)   159 3/5

4.   3 5/18 + 2 1/18 + 8 7/18 =

(A)   13 13/18 (B)   13 3/4   (C)   13 7/9   (D)   14 1/6   (E)   14 2/9

5.   17 9/20 + 4 3/20 + 8 11/20 =

(A)   29 23/60   (B)   29 23/20   (C)   30 3/20

(D)   30 1/5   (E)   30 3/5

Subtract Fractions with the Same Denominator

<u>DIRECTIONS</u>: Subtract and write the answer in simplest form.

6.   4 7/8 – 3 1/8 =

(A)   1 1/4   (B)   1 3/4   (C)   1 12/16 (D)   1 7/8   (E)   2

7.   132 5/12 – 37 3/12 =

(A)   94 1/6   (B)   95 1/12   (C)   95 1/6   (D)   105 1/6   (E)   169 2/3

8.   19 1/3 – 2 2/3 =

(A)   16 2/3   (B)   16 5/6   (C)   17 1/3   (D)   17 2/3   (E)   17 5/6

9.   8/21 – 5/21 =

(A) 1/21   (B)   1/7   (C)   3/21   (D)   2/7   (E)   3/7

10. 82 7/10 – 38 9/10 =

(A) 43 4/5   (B)   44 1/5   (C)   44 2/5   (D)   45 1/5   (E)   45 2/10

Finding the LCD

DIRECTIONS: Find the lowest common denominator of each group of fractions.

11.   2/3, 5/9, and 1/6.

(A) 9   (B)   18   (C)   27   (D)   54   (E)   162

12. 1/2, 5/6, and 3/4.

(A) 2   (B)   4   (C)   6   (D)   12   (E)   48

13. 7/16, 5/6, and 2/3.

(A) 3   (B)   6   (C)   12   (D)   24   (E)   48

14. 8/15, 2/5, and 12/25.

(A) 5   (B)   15   (C)   25   (D)   75   (E)   375

15. 2/3, 1/5, and 5/6.

(A) 15   (B)   30   (C)   48   (D)   90   (E)   120

16. 1/3, 9/42, and 4/21.

(A) 21   (B)   42   (C)   126   (D)   378   (E)   4000

17. 4/9, 2/5, and 1/3.

(A) 15   (B)   17   (C)   27   (D)   45   (E)   135

18. 7/12, 11/36, and 1/9.

(A) 12   (B)   36   (C)   108   (D)   324   (E)   432

19. 3/7, 5/21, and 2/3.

(A) 21   (B)   42   (C)   31   (D)   63   (E)   441

20. 13/16, 5/8, and 1/4.

(A) 4   (B)   8   (C)   16   (D)   32   (E)   64

Adding Fractions With Different Denominators

DIRECTIONS: Add and write the answer in simplest form.

21. $1/3 + 5/12 =$
(A) 2/5   (B) 1/2   (C) 9/12   (D) 3/4   (E) 1 1/3

22. $3\ 5/9 + 2\ 1/3 =$
(A) 5 1/2   (B) 5 2/3   (C) 5 8/9   (D) 6 1/9   (E) 6 2/3

23. $12\ 9/16 + 17\ 3/4 + 8\ 1/8 =$
(A) 37 7/16   (B) 38 7/16   (C) 38 1/2   (D) 38 2/3   (E) 39 3/16

24. $28\ 4/5 + 11\ 16/25 =$
(A) 39 2/3   (B) 39 4/5   (C) 40 9/25   (D) 40 2/5   (E) 40 11/25

25. $2\ 1/8 + 1\ 3/16 + 5/12 =$
(A) 3 35/48   (B) 3 3/4   (C) 3 19/24   (D) 3 13/16   (E) 4 1/12

Subtraction with Different Denominators

DIRECTIONS: Subtract and write the answer in simplest form.

26. $8\ 9/12 - 2\ 2/3 =$
(A) 6 1/12   (B) 6 1/6   (C) 6 1/3   (D) 6 7/12   (E) 6 2/3

27. $185\ 11/15 - 107\ 2/5 =$
(A) 77 2/15   (B) 78 1/5   (C) 78 3/10   (D) 78 1/3   (E) 78 9/15

28. $34\ 2/3 - 16\ 5/6 =$
(A) 16   (B) 16 1/3   (C) 17 1/2   (D) 17   (E) 17 5/6

29. $3\ 11/48 - 2\ 3/16 =$
(A) 47/48   (B) 1 1/48   (C) 1 1/24   (D) 1 8/48   (E) 1 7/24

30. $81\ 4/21 - 31\ 1/3 =$
(A) 47 3/7   (B) 49 6/7   (C) 49 1/6   (D) 49 5/7   (E) 49 13/21

Multiplication of Fractions

DIRECTIONS: Multiply and reduce the answer.

31. 2/3 * 4/5 =

(A) 6/8   (B) 3/4   (C) 8/15   (D) 10/12   (E) 6/5

32. 7/10 * 4/21 =

(A) 2/15   (B) 11/31   (C) 28/210   (D) 1/6   (E) 4/15

33. 5 1/3 * 3/8 =

(A) 4/11   (B) 2   (C) 8/5   (D) 5 1/8   (E) 5 17/24

34. 6 1/2 * 3 =

(A) 9 1/2   (B) 18 1/2   (C) 19 1/2   (D) 20   (E) 12 1/2

35. 3 1/4 * 2 1/3 =

(A) 5 7/12   (B) 6 2/7   (C) 6 5/7   (D) 7 7/12   (E) 7 11/12

Division of Fractions

DIRECTIONS: Divide and reduce the answer.

36. 3/16 ÷ 3/4 =

(A) 9/64   (B) 1/4   (C) 6/16   (D) 9/16   (E) 3/4

37. 4/9 ÷ 2/3 =

(A) 1/3   (B) 1/2   (C) 2/3   (D) 7/11   (E) 8/9

38. 5 1/4 ÷ 7/10 =

(A) 2 4/7   (B) 3 27/40   (C) 5 19/20   (D) 7 1/2   (E) 8 1/4

39. 4 2/3 ÷ 7/9 =

(A) 2 24/27   (B) 3 2/9   (C) 4 14/27   (D) 5 12/27   (E) 6

40. 3 2/5 ÷ 1 7/10 =

(A) 2   (B) 3 4/7   (C) 4 7/25   (D) 5 1/10   (E) 5 2/7

Changing an Improper Fraction to a Mixed Number

DIRECTIONS: Write each improper fraction as a mixed number in simplest form.

41. 50/4

(A) 10 1/4   (B) 11 1/2   (C) 12 1/4   (D) 12 1/2   (E) 25

42. 17/5

(A) 3 2/5   (B) 3 3/5   (C) 3 4/5   (D) 4 1/5   (E) 4 2/5

43. 42/3

(A) 10 2/3   (B) 12   (C) 13 1/3   (D) 14   (E) 21 1/3

44. 85/6

(A) 9 1/6   (B) 10 5/6   (C) 11 1/2   (D) 12   (E) 14 1/6

45. 151/7

(A) 19 6/7   (B) 20 1/7   (C) 21 4/7   (D) 31 2/7   (E) 31 4/7

Changing a Mixed Number to an Improper Fraction

DIRECTIONS: Change each mixed number to an improper fraction in simplest form.

46. 2 3/5

(A) 4/5   (B) 6/5   (C) 11/5   (D) 13/5   (E) 17/5

47. 4 3/4

(A) 7/4   (B) 13/4   (C) 16/3   (D) 19/4   (E) 21/4

48. 6 7/6

(A) 13/6   (B) 43/6   (C) 19/36   (D) 42/36   (E) 48/6

49. 12 3/7

(A) 87/7   (B) 164/14   (C) 34/3   (D) 187/21   (E) 252/7

50. 21 1/2

(A) 11/2   (B) 22/2   (C) 24/2   (D) 42/2   (E) 43/2

3. DECIMALS

When we divide the denominator of a fraction into its numerator, the result is a **decimal**. The decimal is based upon a fraction with a denominator of 10, 100, 1000, ... and is written with a **decimal point**. Whole numbers are placed to the left of the decimal point where the first place to the left is the units place; the second to the left is the tens; the third to the left is the hundreds, etc. The fractions are placed on the right where the first place to the right is the tenths; the second to the right is the hundredths, etc.

EXAMPLE

$$12 \frac{3}{10} = 12.3 \qquad 4 \frac{17}{100} = 4.17 \qquad \frac{3}{100} = .03$$

Since a **rational number** is of the form a/b, $b \neq 0$, then all rational numbers can be expressed as decimals by dividing b into a. The result is either a **terminating decimal**, meaning that b divides a with a remainder of 0 after a certain point; or **repeating decimal**, meaning that b continues to divide a so that the decimal has a repeating pattern of integers.

EXAMPLE

(A) $\frac{1}{2} = .5$

(B) $\frac{1}{3} = .333...$

(C) $\frac{11}{16} = .6875$

(D) $\frac{2}{7} = .285714285714...$

(A) and (C) are terminating decimals; (B) and (D) are repeating decimals. This explanation allows us to define **irrational numbers** as numbers whose decimal form is non-terminating and non-repeating, e.g.,

$$\sqrt{2} = 1.414...$$
$$\sqrt{3} = 1.732...$$

PROBLEM

Express $-\frac{10}{20}$ as a decimal.

SOLUTION

$$-\frac{10}{20} = -\frac{50}{100} = -.5$$

PROBLEM

Write $\frac{2}{7}$ as a repeating decimal.

SOLUTION

To write a fraction as a repeating decimal divide the numerator by the denominator until a pattern of repeated digits appears.

$$2 \div 7 = .285714285714...$$

Identify the entire portion of the decimal which is repeated. The repeating decimal can then be written in the shortened form:

$2/7 = .\overline{285714}$

OPERATIONS WITH DECIMALS

A)   **To add numbers containing decimals,** write the numbers in a column making sure the decimal points are lined up, one beneath the other. Add the numbers as usual, placing the decimal point in the sum so that it is still in line with the others. It is important not to mix the digits in the tenths place with the digits in the hundredths place, and so on.

EXAMPLES

2.558 + 6.391	57.51 + 6.2

$$
\begin{array}{r}
2.558 \\
+\ 6.391 \\
\hline
8.949
\end{array}
\qquad
\begin{array}{r}
57.51 \\
+\ \ 6.20 \\
\hline
63.71
\end{array}
$$

Similarly with subtraction,

78.54 − 21.33	7.11 − 4.2

$$
\begin{array}{r}
78.54 \\
-\ 21.33 \\
\hline
57.21
\end{array}
\qquad
\begin{array}{r}
7.11 \\
-\ 4.20 \\
\hline
2.91
\end{array}
$$

Note that if two numbers differ according to the number of digits to the right of the decimal point, zeros must be added.

.63 − .214	15.224 − 3.6891

$$
\begin{array}{r}
.630 \\
-\ .214 \\
\hline
.416
\end{array}
\qquad
\begin{array}{r}
15.2240 \\
-\ 3.6891 \\
\hline
11.5349
\end{array}
$$

B)   **To multiply numbers with decimals,** simply multiply as usual. Then, to figure out the number of decimal places that belong in the product, find the total number of decimal places in the numbers being multiplied.

EXAMPLES

$$
\begin{array}{r}
6.555 \\
\times\ \ \ 4.5 \\
\hline
32775 \\
26220 \\
\hline
294975 \\
29.4975
\end{array}
\quad
\begin{array}{l}
\text{(3 decimal places)} \\
\text{(1 decimal place)} \\
\\
\\
\\
\text{(4 decimal places)}
\end{array}
\qquad
\begin{array}{r}
5.32 \\
\times\ \ .04 \\
\hline
2128 \\
000 \\
\hline
2128 \\
.2128
\end{array}
\quad
\begin{array}{l}
\text{(2 decimal places)} \\
\text{(2 decimal places)} \\
\\
\\
\\
\text{(4 decimal places)}
\end{array}
$$

C)   **To divide numbers with decimals,** you must first make the divisor a whole number by moving the decimal point the appropriate number of places to the right. The decimal point of the dividend should also be moved the same number of places. Place a decimal point in the quotient, directly in line with the decimal point in the dividend.

EXAMPLES

$$
\begin{array}{r}
12.92 \quad 3.4 \\
3.8 \\
\hline
3{,}4{,}\overline{)12{,}9{,}2} \\
-102 \\
\hline
272 \\
-272 \\
\hline
0
\end{array}
\qquad
\begin{array}{r}
40.376 \quad 7.21 \\
5.6 \\
\hline
7{,}21{,}\overline{)40{,}37{,}6} \\
-3605 \\
\hline
4326 \\
-4326 \\
\hline
0
\end{array}
$$

If the question asks to find the correct answer to two decimal places, simply divide until you have three decimal places and then round off. If the third decimal place is a 5 or larger, the number in the second decimal place is increased by 1. If the third decimal place is less than 5, that number is simply dropped.

PROBLEM

Find the answer to the following to 2 decimal places:

(1)   44.3 ÷ 3

(2)   56.99 ÷ 6

SOLUTION

(1)
$$
\begin{array}{r}
14.766 \\
\hline
3)44.300 \\
-3 \\
\hline
14 \\
-12 \\
\hline
23 \\
-21 \\
\hline
20 \\
-18 \\
\hline
20 \\
-18 \\
\hline
2
\end{array}
$$

(2)
$$
\begin{array}{r}
9.498 \\
\hline
6)56.990 \\
-54 \\
\hline
29 \\
-24 \\
\hline
59 \\
-54 \\
\hline
50 \\
-48 \\
\hline
2
\end{array}
$$

14.766 can be rounded off to 14.77

9.498 can be rounded off to 9.50

D)   When comparing two numbers with decimals to see which is the larger, first look at the tenths place. The larger digit in this place represents the larger number. If the two digits are the same, however, take a look at the digits in the hundredths place, and so on.

EXAMPLES

.518 and .216   .723 and .726

5 is larger than 2, therefore   6 is larger than 3, therefore

.518 is larger than .216   .726 is larger than .723

☞ Drill: Decimals

Addition

1. $1.032 + 0.987 + 3.07 =$

(A) 4.089   (B) 5.089   (C) 5.189   (D) 6.189   (D) 13.972

2. $132.03 + 97.1483 =$

(A) 98.4686   (B) 110.3513   (C) 209.1783

(D) 229.1486   (E) 229.1783

3. $7.1 + 0.62 + 4.03827 + 5.183 =$

(A) 0.2315127   (B) 16.45433   (C) 16.94127

(D) 18.561   (E) 40.4543

4. $8 + 17.43 + 9.2 =$

(A) 34.63   (B) 34.86   (C) 35.63   (D) 176.63   (E) 189.43

5. $1036.173 + 289.04 =$

(A) 382.6573   (B) 392.6573   (C) 1065.077

(D) 1325.213   (E) 3926.573

Subtraction

6. $3.972 - 2.04 =$

(A) 1.932   (B) 1.942   (C) 1.976   (D) 2.013   (E) 2.113

7. $16.047 - 13.06 =$

(A) 2.887   (B) 2.987   (C) 3.041   (D) 3.141   (E) 4.741

8. $87.4 - 56.27 =$

(A) 30.27   (B) 30.67   (C) 31.1   (D) 31.13   (E) 31.27

9.   1046.8 – 639.14 =

(A) 303.84   (B) 313.74   (C) 407.66   (D) 489.74   (E) 535.54

10.   10,000 – 842.91 =

(A) 157.09   (B) 942.91   (C) 5236.09   (D) 9057.91   (E) 9157.09

Multiplication

11.   1.03 * 2.6 =

(A) 2.18   (B) 2.678   (C) 2.78   (D) 3.38   (E) 3.63

12.   93 * 4.2 =

(A) 39.06   (B) 97.2   (C) 223.2   (D) 390.6   (E) 3906

13.   0.04 * 0.23 =

(A) 0.0092   (B) 0.092   (C) 0.27   (D) 0.87   (E) 0.920

14.   0.0186 * 0.03 =

(A) 0.000348   (B) 0.000558   (C) 0.0548   (D) 0.0848   (E) 0.558

15.   51.2 * 0.17 =

(A) 5.29   (B) 8.534   (C) 8.704   (D) 36.352   (E) 36.991

Division

16.   123.39 ÷ 3 =

(A) 31.12   (B) 41.13   (C) 401.13   (D) 411.3   (E) 4,113

17.   1428.6 ÷ 6 =

(A) 0.2381   (B) 2.381   (C) 23.81   (D) 238.1   (E) 2,381

18.   25.2 ÷ 0.3 =

(A) 0.84   (B) 8.04   (C) 8.4   (D) 84   (E) 840

19.   14.95 ÷ 6.5 =

(A) 2.3   (B) 20.3   (C) 23   (D) 230   (E) 2,300

20.   46.33 ÷ 1.13 =

(A) 0.41   (B) 4.1   (C) 41   (D) 410   (E) 4,100

Comparing

21. Which is the **largest** number in this set — {0.8, 0.823, 0.089, 0.807, 0.852}?
(A) 0.8   (B) 0.823   (C) 0.089   (D) 0.807   (E) 0.852

22. Which is the **smallest** number in this set — {32.98, 32.099, 32.047, 32.5, 32.304}?
(A) 32.98   (B) 32.099   (C) 32.047   (D) 32.5   (E) 32.304

23. In which set below are the numbers arranged correctly from smallest to largest?
(A) {0.98, 0.9, 0.993}   (D) {0.006, 0.061, 0.06}
(B) {0.113, 0.3, 0.31}   (E) {12.84, 12.801, 12.6}
(C) {7.04, 7.26, 7.2}

24. In which set below are the numbers arranged correctly from largest to smallest?
(A) {1.018, 1.63, 1.368}   (D) {16.34, 16.304, 16.3}
(B) {4.219, 4.29, 4.9}   (E) {12.98, 12.601, 12.86}
(C) {0.62, 0.6043, 0.643}

25. Which is the **largest** number in this set — {0.87, 0.89, 0.889, 0.8, 0.987}?
(A) 0.87   (B) 0.89   (C) 0.889   (D) 0.8   (E) 0.987

Changing a Fraction to a Decimal

26. What is 1/4 written as a decimal?
(A) 1.4   (B) 0.14   (C) 0.2   (D) 0.25   (E) 0.3

27. What is 3/5 written as a decimal?
(A) 0.3   (B) 0.35   (D) 0.6   (D) 0.65   (E) 0.8

28. What is 7/20 written as a decimal?
(A) 0.35   (B) 0.4   (C) 0.72   (D) 0.75   (E) 0.9

29. What is 2/3 written as a decimal?
(A) 0.23   (B) 0.33   (C) 0.5   (D) 0.6   (E) $0.\overline{6}$

30. What is 11/25 written as a decimal?
(A) 0.1125   (B) 0.25   (C) 0.4   (D) 0.44   (E) 0.5

4. PERCENTAGES

A **percent** is a way of expressing the relationship between part and whole, where whole is defined as 100%. A percent can be defined by a fraction with a denominator of 100. Decimals can also represent a percent. For instance,

$$56\% = 0.56 = 56/100$$

PROBLEM

Compute the value of

(1)   90% of 400

(3)   50% of 500

(2)   180% of 400

(4)   200% of 4

SOLUTION

The symbol % means per hundred, therefore $5\% = 5/100$

(1)   90% of 400 = 90/100 × 400 = 90 × 4 = 360

(2)   180% of 400 = 180/100 × 400 = 180 × 4 = 720

(3)   50% of 500 = 50/100 × 500 = 50 × 5 = 250

(4)   200% of 4 = 200/100 × 4 = 2 × 4 = 8

PROBLEM

What percent of

(1)   100 is 99.5

(2)   200 is 4

SOLUTION

(1) $99.5 = x \times 100$

$99.5 = 100x$

$.995 = x$; but this is the value of x per hundred. Therefore,

$x = 99.5\%$

(2) $4 = x \times 200$

$4 = 200x$

$.02 = x$. Again this must be changed to percent, so

$x = 2\%$

EQUIVALENT FORMS OF A NUMBER

Some problems may call for converting numbers into an equivalent or simplified form in order to make the solution more convenient.

1.   Converting a fraction to a decimal:

$$1/2 = 0.50$$

Divide the numerator by the denominator:

$$\begin{array}{r} .50 \\ 2)\overline{1.00} \\ \underline{-10} \\ 00 \end{array}$$

2. Converting a number to a percent:

    $0.50 = 50\%$

    Multiply by 100:

    $0.50 = (0.50 \times 100)\% = 50\%$

3. Converting a percent to a decimal:

    $30\% = 0.30$

    Divide by 100:

    $30\% = 30/100 = 0.30$

4. Converting a decimal to a fraction:

    $0.500 = {}^1/_2$

    Convert .500 to 500/1000 and then simplify the fraction by dividing the numerator and denominator by common factors:

    $$\frac{2 \times 2 \times 5 \times 5 \times 5}{2 \times 2 \times 2 \times 5 \times 5 \times 5}$$

    and then cancel out the common numbers to get ${}^1/_2$.

PROBLEM

Express

(1) 1.65 as a percent

(2) .07 as a fraction

(3) $- {}^{10}/_{20}$ as a decimal

(4) ${}^4/_2$ as an integer

SOLUTION

(1) $1.65 \times 100 = 165\%$

(2) $0.7 = {}^7/_{10}$

(3) $-{}^{10}/_{20} = -0.5$

(4) ${}^4/_2 = 2$

☞ Drill: Percentages

Finding Percents

1. Find 3% of 80.

(A) 0.24   (B) 2.4   (C) 24   (D) 240   (E) 2,400

2. Find 50% of 182.

(A) 9   (B) 90   (C) 91   (D) 910   (E) 9,100

3. Find 83% of 166.

(A) 0.137   (B) 1.377   (C) 13.778   (D) 137   (E) 137.78

4. Find 125% of 400.

(A) 425   (B) 500   (C) 525   (D) 600   (E) 825

5. Find 300% of 4.

(A) 12   (B) 120   (C) 1200   (D) 12,000   (E) 120,000

6. Forty-eight percent of the 1200 students at Central High are males. How many male students are there at Central High?

(A) 57   (B) 576   (C) 580   (D) 600   (E) 648

7. For 35% of the last 40 days, there has been measurable rainfall. How many days out of the last 40 days have had measurable rainfall?

(A) 14   (B) 20   (C) 25   (D) 35   (E) 40

8. Of every 1000 people who take a certain medicine, 0.2% develop severe side effects. How many people out of every 1000 who take the medicine develop the side effects?

(A) 0.2   (B) 2   (C) 20   (D) 22   (E) 200

9. Of 220 applicants for a job, 75% were offered an initial interview. How many people were offered an initial interview?

(A) 75   (B) 110   (C) 120   (D) 155   (E) 165

10. Find 0.05% of 4,000.

(A) 0.05   (B) 0.5   (C) 2   (D) 20   (E) 400

Changing Percents to Fractions

11. What is 25% written as a fraction?

(A) 1/25   (B) 1/5   (C) 1/4   (D) 1/3   (E) 1/2

12. What is 33 1/3% written as a fraction?

(A) 1/4   (B) 1/3   (C) 1/2   (D) 2/3   (E) 5/9

13. What is 200% written as a fraction?

(A) 1/2   (B) 2/1   (C) 20/1   (D) 200/1   (E) 2000/1

14. What is 84% written as a fraction?

(A) 1/84   (B) 4/8   (C) 17/25   (D) 21/25   (E) 44/50

15. What is 2% written as a fraction?

(A) 1/50   (B) 1/25   (C) 1/10   (D) 1/4   (E) 1/2

Changing Fractions to Percents

16. What is 2/3 written as a percent?

(A) 23%   (B) 32%   (C) 33 1/3% (D) 57 1/3% (E) 66 2/3%

17. What is 3/5 written as a percent?

(A) 30%   (B) 35%   (C) 53%   (D) 60%   (E) 65%

18. What is 17/20 written as a percent?

(A) 17%   (B) 70%   (C) 75%   (D) 80%   (E) 85%

19. What is 45/50 written as a percent?

(A) 45%   (B) 50%   (C) 90%   (D) 95%   (E) 97%

20. What is 1 1/4 written as a percent?

(A) 114%   (B) 120%   (C) 125%   (D) 127%   (E) 133%

Changing Percents to Decimals

21. What is 42% written as a decimal?

(A) 0.42   (B) 4.2   (C) 42   (D) 420   (E) 422

22. What is 0.3% written as a decimal?

(A) 0.0003   (B) 0.003   (C) 0.03   (D) 0.3   (E) 3

23. What is 8% written as a decimal?

(A) 0.0008   (B) 0.008   (C) 0.08   (D) 0.80   (E) 8

24. What is 175% written as a decimal?

(A) 0.175   (B) 1.75   (C) 17.5   (D) 175   (E) 17,500

25. What is 34% written as a decimal?

(A) 0.00034   (B) 0.0034   (C) 0.034   (D) 0.34   (E) 3.4

Changing Decimals to Percents

26. What is 0.43 written as a percent?

(A) 0.0043%   (B) 0.043%   (C) 4.3%   (D) 43%   (E) 430%

27. What is 1 written as a percent?

(A) 1%   (B) 10%   (C) 100%   (D) 111%   (E) 150%

28. What is 0.08 written as a percent?

(A) 0.08%   (B) 8%   (C) 8.8%   (D) 80%   (E) 800%

29. What is 3.4 written as a percent?

(A) 0.0034%   (B) 3.4%   (C) 34%   (D) 304%   (E) 340%

30. What is 0.645 written as a percent?

(A) 64.5%   (B) 65%   (C) 69%   (D) 70%   (E) 645%

5. RADICALS

The **square root** of a number is a number that when multiplied by itself results in the original number. Thus, the square root of 81 is 9 since $9 \times 9 = 81$. However, -9 is also a root of 81 since $(-9)(-9) = 81$. Every positive number will have two roots. The principal root is the positive one. Zero has only one square root, while negative numbers do not have real numbers as their roots.

A **radical sign** indicates that the root of a number or expression will be taken. The **radicand** is the number of which the root will be taken. The **index** tells how many times the root needs to be multiplied by itself to equal the radicand, e.g.,

$$\text{index} \searrow$$
$$\text{radical sign} \longrightarrow \sqrt{} \quad \text{radicand}$$

(1) $\sqrt[3]{64}$;

3 is the index and 64 is the radicand. Since $4 \cdot 4 \cdot 4 = 64$, $\sqrt[3]{64} = 4$

(2) $\sqrt[5]{32}$;

5 is the index and 32 is the radicand. Since $2 \cdot 2 \cdot 2 \cdot 2 \cdot 2 = 32$, $\sqrt[5]{32} = 2$

OPERATIONS WITH RADICALS

A) **To multiply two or more radicals**, we utilize the law that states,

$$\sqrt{a} \cdot \sqrt{b} = \sqrt{ab}.$$

Simply multiply the whole numbers as usual. Then, multiply the radicands and put the product under the radical sign and simplify, e.g.,

(1) $\sqrt{12} \cdot \sqrt{5} = \sqrt{60} = 2\sqrt{15}$

(2) $3\sqrt{2} \cdot 4\sqrt{8} = 12\sqrt{16} = 48$

(3) $2\sqrt{10} \cdot 6\sqrt{5} = 12\sqrt{50} = 60\sqrt{2}$

B) **To divide radicals**, simplify both the numerator and the denominator. By multiplying the radical in the denominator by itself, you can make the denominator a rational number. The numerator, however, must also be multiplied by this radical so that the value of the expression does not change. You must choose as many factors as necessary to rationalize the denominator, e.g.,

(1) $\dfrac{\sqrt{128}}{\sqrt{2}} = \dfrac{\sqrt{64} \cdot \sqrt{2}}{\sqrt{2}} = \dfrac{8\sqrt{2}}{\sqrt{2}} = 8$

(2) $\dfrac{\sqrt{10}}{\sqrt{3}} = \dfrac{\sqrt{10} \cdot \sqrt{3}}{\sqrt{3} \cdot \sqrt{3}} = \dfrac{\sqrt{30}}{3}$

(3) $\dfrac{\sqrt{8}}{2\sqrt{3}} = \dfrac{\sqrt{8} \cdot \sqrt{3}}{2\sqrt{3} \cdot \sqrt{3}} = \dfrac{\sqrt{24}}{2 \cdot 3} = \dfrac{2\sqrt{6}}{6} = \dfrac{\sqrt{6}}{3}$

C)   **To add two or more radicals**, the radicals must have the same index and the same radicand. Only where the radicals are simplified can these simi-larities be determined.

EXAMPLE

(1) $6\sqrt{2} + 2\sqrt{2} = (6+2)\sqrt{2} = 8\sqrt{2}$

(2) $\sqrt{27} + 5\sqrt{3} = \sqrt{9}\sqrt{3} + 5\sqrt{3} = 3\sqrt{3} + 5\sqrt{3} = 8\sqrt{3}$

(3) $7\sqrt{3} + 8\sqrt{2} + 5\sqrt{3} = 12\sqrt{3} + 8\sqrt{2}$

Similarly, to subtract,

(1) $12\sqrt{3} - 7\sqrt{3} = (12-7)\sqrt{3} = 5\sqrt{3}$

(2) $\sqrt{90} - \sqrt{20} = \sqrt{16}\sqrt{5} - \sqrt{4}\sqrt{5} = 4\sqrt{5} - 2\sqrt{5} = 2\sqrt{5}$

(3) $\sqrt{50} - \sqrt{3} = 5\sqrt{2} - \sqrt{3}$

PROBLEM

Simplify $5\sqrt{2} + 3\sqrt{8}$

SOLUTION

To add two radicals we need a common radicand. Here the two radicands are 2 and 8. But 8 factors as 2 * 4, so $5\sqrt{2} + 3\sqrt{8} = 5\sqrt{2} + 3\sqrt{4*2}$, and this can be rewritten as $5\sqrt{2} + 3\sqrt{4} * \sqrt{2}$. Finally we note that $\sqrt{4}$ is 2, so we obtain $5\sqrt{2} + 3*2*\sqrt{2}$, or $5\sqrt{2} + 6\sqrt{2} = 11\sqrt{2}$.

PROBLEM

Simplify the expression $\left(2\sqrt{8}\right)*\left(3\sqrt{2}\right) + \left(\sqrt{12}\right)*\left(7\sqrt{3}\right)$

SOLUTION

The order of operations indicates that we should multiply the radicals first, and then add. Toward that end, $\left(2\sqrt{8}\right)*\left(3\sqrt{2}\right) + \left(\sqrt{12}\right)*\left(7\sqrt{3}\right)$ is the same as $(2)*(3)*\left(\sqrt{8}\right)*\left(\sqrt{2}\right) + (7)*\left(\sqrt{12}\right)*\left(\sqrt{3}\right)$.

This equals $6*\sqrt{8*2} + 7*\sqrt{12*3}$ or $6*\sqrt{16} + 7*\sqrt{36}$. Finally, this can be simplified to $6*4 + 7*6 = 24 + 42 = 66$.

☞ DRILL: Radicals

Multiplication

<u>DIRECTIONS</u>: Multiply and simplify each answer.

1. $\sqrt{6}*\sqrt{5} =$

(A) $\sqrt{11}$ (B) $\sqrt{30}$ (C) $2\sqrt{5}$ (D) $3\sqrt{10}$ (E) $2\sqrt{3}$

2. $\sqrt{3} * \sqrt{12} =$

(A) 3   (B) $\sqrt{15}$ (C) $\sqrt{36}$ (D) 6   (E) 8

3. $\sqrt{7} * \sqrt{7} =$

(A) 7   (B) 49   (C) $\sqrt{14}$ (D) $2\sqrt{7}$ (E) $2\sqrt{14}$

4. $3\sqrt{5} * 2\sqrt{5} =$

(A) $5\sqrt{5}$ (B) 25   (C) 30   (D) $5\sqrt{25}$ (E) $6\sqrt{5}$

5. $4\sqrt{6} * \sqrt{2} =$

A) $4\sqrt{8}$ (B) $8\sqrt{2}$ (C) $5\sqrt{8}$ (D) $4\sqrt{12}$ (E) $8\sqrt{3}$

Division

DIRECTIONS: Divide and simplify the answer.

6. $\sqrt{10} \div \sqrt{2} =$

(A) $\sqrt{8}$ (B) $2\sqrt{2}$ (C) $\sqrt{5}$ (D) $2\sqrt{5}$ (E) $2\sqrt{3}$

7. $\sqrt{30} \div \sqrt{15} =$

(A) $\sqrt{2}$ (B) $\sqrt{45}$ (C) $3\sqrt{5}$ (D) $\sqrt{15}$ (E) $5\sqrt{3}$

8. $\sqrt{100} \div \sqrt{25} =$

(A) $\sqrt{4}$ (B) $5\sqrt{5}$ (C) $5\sqrt{3}$ (D) 2   (E) 4

9. $\sqrt{48} \div \sqrt{8} =$

(A) $4\sqrt{3}$ (B) $3\sqrt{2}$ (C) $\sqrt{6}$ (D) 6   (E) 12

10. $3\sqrt{12} \div \sqrt{3} =$

(A) $3\sqrt{15}$ (B) 6   (C) 9   (D) 12   (E) $3\sqrt{36}$

Addition

DIRECTIONS: Simplify each radical and add.

11. $\sqrt{7} + 3\sqrt{7} =$

(A) $3\sqrt{7}$ (B) $4\sqrt{7}$ (C) $3\sqrt{14}$ (D) $4\sqrt{14}$ (E) $3\sqrt{21}$

12. $\sqrt{5} + 6\sqrt{5} + 3\sqrt{5} =$

(A) $9\sqrt{5}$ (B) $9\sqrt{15}$ (C) $5\sqrt{10}$ (D) $10\sqrt{5}$ (E) $18\sqrt{15}$

13. $3\sqrt{32} + 2\sqrt{2} =$

(A) $5\sqrt{2}$ (B) $\sqrt{34}$ (C) $14\sqrt{2}$ (D) $5\sqrt{34}$ (E) $6\sqrt{64}$

14. $6\sqrt{15} + 8\sqrt{15} + 16\sqrt{15} =$

(A) $15\sqrt{30}$ (B) $30\sqrt{45}$ (C) $30\sqrt{30}$ (D) $15\sqrt{45}$ (E) $30\sqrt{15}$

15. $6\sqrt{5} + 2\sqrt{45} =$

(A) $12\sqrt{5}$ (B) $8\sqrt{50}$ (C) $40\sqrt{2}$ (D) $12\sqrt{50}$ (E) $8\sqrt{5}$

Subtraction

<u>DIRECTIONS</u>: Simplify each radical and subtract.

16. $8\sqrt{5} - 6\sqrt{5} =$

(A) $2\sqrt{5}$ (B) $3\sqrt{5}$ (C) $4\sqrt{5}$ (D) $14\sqrt{5}$ (E) $48\sqrt{5}$

17. $16\sqrt{33} - 5\sqrt{33} =$

(A) $3\sqrt{33}$ (B) $33\sqrt{11}$ (C) $11\sqrt{33}$ (D) $11\sqrt{0}$ (E) $\sqrt{33}$

18. $14\sqrt{2} - 19\sqrt{2} =$

(A) $5\sqrt{2}$ (B) $-5\sqrt{2}$ (C) $-33\sqrt{2}$ (D) $33\sqrt{2}$ (E) $-4\sqrt{2}$

19. $10\sqrt{2} - 3\sqrt{8} =$

(A) $6\sqrt{6}$ (B) $-2\sqrt{2}$ (C) $7\sqrt{6}$ (D) $4\sqrt{2}$ (E) $-6\sqrt{6}$

20. $4\sqrt{3} - 2\sqrt{12} =$

(A) $-2\sqrt{9}$ (B) $-6\sqrt{15}$ (C) 0 (D) $6\sqrt{15}$ (E) $2\sqrt{12}$

6. EXPONENTS

When a number is multiplied by itself a specific number of times, it is said to be **raised to a power**. The way this is written is $a^n = b$ where a is the number or **base**, n is the **exponent** or **power** that indicates the number of times the base is to be multiplied by itself, and b is the product of this multiplication.

In the expression 3^2, 3 is the base and 2 is the exponent. This means that 3 is multiplied by itself 2 times and the product is 9.

An exponent can be either positive or negative. A negative exponent implies a fraction such that if n is a negative integer

$$a^{-n} = \frac{1}{a^n}, \ a \neq 0. \ \text{ So, } 2^{-4} = \frac{1}{2^4} = \frac{1}{16}.$$

An exponent that is zero gives a result of 1, assuming that the base is not equal to zero.

$$a^0 = 1, a \neq 0.$$

An exponent can also be a fraction. If m and n are positive integers,

$$a^{\frac{m}{n}} = \sqrt[n]{a^m}.$$

The numerator remains the exponent of a, but the denominator tells what root to take. For example,

(1) $4^{\frac{3}{2}} = \sqrt[2]{4^3} = \sqrt{64} = 8$ 　　　　　(2) $3^{\frac{4}{2}} = \sqrt[2]{3^4} = \sqrt{81} = 9$

If a fractional exponent were negative, the same operation would take place, but the result would be a fraction. For example,

(1) $27^{-\frac{2}{3}} = \dfrac{1}{27^{2/3}} = \dfrac{1}{\sqrt[3]{27^2}} = \dfrac{1}{\sqrt[3]{729}} = \dfrac{1}{9}$

PROBLEM

Simplify the following expressions:

(1) -3^{-2} 　　　　　(3) $\dfrac{-3}{4^{-1}}$

(2) $(-3)^{-2}$

SOLUTION

(1) Here the exponent applies only to 3. Since

$$x^{-y} = \frac{1}{x^y}, \quad -3^{-2} = -(3)^{-2} = -\frac{1}{3^2} = -\frac{1}{9}$$

(2) In this case the exponent applies to the negative base. Thus,

$$(-3)^{-2} = \frac{1}{(-3)^2} = \frac{1}{(-3)(-3)} = \frac{1}{9}$$

(3) $\dfrac{-3}{4^{-1}} = \dfrac{-3}{\left(\frac{1}{4}\right)^1} = \dfrac{-3}{\frac{1}{4^1}} = \dfrac{-3}{\frac{1}{4}}$

Division by a fraction is equivalent to multiplication by that fraction's reciprocal, thus

$$\frac{-3}{\frac{1}{4}} = -3 \cdot \frac{4}{1} = -12 \quad \text{and} \quad \frac{-3}{4^{-1}} = -12$$

General Laws of Exponents

A) $a^p a^q = a^{p+q}$

$4^2 4^3 = 4^{2+3} = 1024$

B) $(a^p)^q = a^{pq}$

$(2^3)^2 = 2^6 = 64$

C) $\dfrac{a^p}{a^q} = a^{p-q}$

$\dfrac{3^6}{3^2} = 3^4 = 81$

D) $(ab)^p = a^p b^p$

$(3 \cdot 2)^2 = 3^2 \cdot 2^2 = (9)(4) = 36$

E) $\left(\dfrac{a}{b}\right)^p = \dfrac{a^p}{b^p}, \; b \neq 0$

$\left(\dfrac{4}{5}\right)^2 = \dfrac{4^2}{5^2} = \dfrac{16}{25}$

☞ Drill: Exponents

Multiplication

Simplify

1. $4^6 * 4^2 =$

(A) 4^4 (B) 4^8 (C) 4^{12} (D) 16^8 (E) 16^{12}

2. $2^2 * 2^5 * 2^3 =$

(A) 2^{10} (B) 4^{10} (C) 8^{10} (D) 2^{30} (E) 8^{30}

3. $6^6 * 6^2 * 6^4 =$

(A) 18^8 (B) 18^{12} (C) 6^{12} (D) 6^{48} (E) 18^{48}

4. $a^4 b^2 * a^3 b =$

(A) ab (B) $2a^7 b^2$ (C) $2a^{12}b$ (D) $a^7 b^3$ (E) $a^7 b^2$

5. $m^8 n^3 * m^2 n * m^4 n^2 =$

(A) $3m^{16}n^6$ (B) $m^{14}n^6$ (D) $3m^{14}n^5$ (D) $3m^{14}n^5$ (E) m^2

Division

Simplify

6. $6^5 \div 6^3 =$

(A) 0 (B) 1 (C) 6 (D) 12 (E) 36

7. $11^8 \div 11^5 =$

(A) 1^3 (B) 11^3 (C) 11^{13} (D) 11^{40} (E) 88^5

8. $x^{10}y^8 \div x^7y^3 =$

(A) x^2y^5 (B) x^3y^4 (C) x^3y^5 (D) x^2y^4 (E) x^5y^3

9. $a^{14} \div a^9 =$

(A) 1^5 (B) a^5 (C) $2a^5$ (D) a^{23} (E) $2a^{23}$

10. $c^{17}d^{12}e^4 \div c^{12}d^8e =$

(A) $c^4d^5e^3$ (B) $c^4d^4e^3$ (C) $c^5d^8e^4$ (D) $c^5d^4e^3$ (E) $c^5d^4e^4$

Power to a Power

Simplify

11. $(3^6)^2 =$

(A) 3^4 (B) 3^8 (C) 3^{12} (D) 9^6 (E) 9^8

12. $(4^3)^5 =$

(A) 4^2 (B) 2^{15} (C) 4^8 (D) 20^3 (E) 4^{15}

13. $(a^4b^3)^2 =$

(A) $(ab)^9$ (B) a^8b^6 (C) $(ab)^{24}$ (D) a^6b^5 (E) $2a^4b^3$

14. $(r^3p^6)^3 =$

(A) r^9p^{18} (B) $(rp)^{12}$ (C) r^6p^9 (D) $3r^3p^6$ (E) $3r^9p^{18}$

15. $(m^6n^5q^3)^2 =$

(A) $2m^6n^5q^3$ (B) m^4n^3q (C) $m^8n^7q^5$

(D) $m^{12}n^{10}q^6$ (E) $2m^{12}n^{10}q^6$

7.   MEAN, MEDIAN

MEAN

The mean is the arithmetic average. It is the sum of the variables divided by the total number of variables. For example:

$$\frac{4+3+8}{3} = \frac{15}{3} = 5$$

PROBLEM

Find the mean salary for four company employees who make $5/hr., $8/hr., $12/hr., and $15/hr.

SOLUTION

The mean salary is the average.

$$\frac{\$5 + \$8 + \$12 + \$15}{4} = \frac{\$40}{4} = \$10/hr$$

PROBLEM

Find the mean length of five fish with lengths of 7.5 in., 7.75 in., 8.5 in., 8.5 in., 8.25 in.

SOLUTION

The mean length is the average length.

$$\frac{7.5 + 7.75 + 8.5 + 8.5 + 8.25}{5} = \frac{40.5}{5} = 8.1 \, in$$

MEDIAN

The median is the middle value in a set when there is an odd number of values. There is an equal number of values larger and smaller than the median. When the set is an even number of values, the average of the two middle values is the median. For example:

The median of (2, 3, 5, 8, 9) is 5.

The median of (2, 3, 5, 9, 10, 11) is $\frac{5+9}{2} = 7$.

PROBLEM

For this series of observations find the mean and median.

500, 600, 800, 800, 900, 900, 900, 900, 900, 1000, 1100

SOLUTION

The mean is the value obtained by adding all the measurements and dividing by the numbers of measurements.

$$\frac{500 + 600 + 800 + 800 + 900 + 900 + 900 + 900 + 900 + 1000 + 1100}{11}$$

$$= \frac{9300}{11} = 845.45.$$

The median is the observation in the middle. We have 11 observations, so here the sixth, 900, is the median.

Both of these numbers are measures of central tendency. They describe the "middle" or "center" of the data.

PROBLEM

Nine rats run through a maze. The time each rat took to traverse the maze is recorded and these times (in minutes) are listed below.

1, 2.5, 3, 1.5, 2, 1.25, 1, .9, 30

Find the mean and the median.

SOLUTION

The mean is the sum of observations divided by the number of observations. In this case

$$\frac{1 + 2.5 + 3 + 1.5 + 2 + 1.25 + 1 + .9 + 30}{9} = \frac{43.15}{9} = 4.79.$$

The median is the "middle number" in an ordered array of the observations from the lowest to the highest.

0.9, 1.0, 1.0, 1.25, 1.5, 2.0, 2.5, 3.0, 30.0

The median is the fifth observation in this ordered array or 1.5. There are four observations larger than 1.5 and four observations smaller than 1.5.

☞ Drill: Averages

Mean

<u>DIRECTIONS</u>: Find the mean of each set of numbers:

1.   18, 25, and 32.

(A) 3   (B)   25   (C)   50   (D)   75   (E)   150

2.   4/9, 2/3, and 5/6.

(A) 11/18   (B)   35/54   (B)   41/54   (D)   35/18   (E)   54/18

3.   97, 102, 116, and 137.

(A) 40   (B)   102   (C)   109   (D)   113   (E)   116

4.   12, 15, 18, 24, and 31.

(A) 18   (B)   19.3   (C)   20   (D)   25   (E)   100

5.   7, 4, 6, 3, 11, and 14.

(A) 5   (B)   6.5   (C)   7   (D)   7.5   (E)   8

Median

DIRECTIONS: Find the median value of each set of numbers.

6.   3, 8, and 6.

(A)   3   (B)   6   (C)   8   (D)   17   (E)   20

7.   19, 15, 21, 27, and 12.

(A)   19   (B)   15   (C)   21   (D)   27   (E)   94

8.   1 2/3, 1 7/8, 1 3/4, and 1 5/6.

(A)   1 30/48   (B)   1 2/3   (C)   1 3/4   (D)   1 19/24   (E)   1 21/24

9.   29, 18, 21, and 35.

(A)   29   (B)   18   (C)   21   (D)   35   (E)   25

10.   8, 15, 7, 12, 31, 3, and 28.

(A)   7   (B)   11.6   (C)   12   (C)   14.9   (E)   104

ARITHMETIC DRILLS

ANSWER KEY

Drill: Integers and Real Numbers

1.	(A)	9.	(E)	17.	(D)	25.	(D)
2.	(C)	10.	(B)	18.	(D)	26.	(D)
3.	(D)	11.	(B)	19.	(C)	27.	(B)
4.	(C)	12.	(E)	20.	(E)	28.	(C)
5.	(B)	13.	(C)	21.	(B)	29.	(A)
6.	(B)	14.	(A)	22.	(E)	30.	(C)
7.	(A)	15.	(B)	23.	(D)		
8.	(C)	16.	(B)	24.	(A)		

Drill: Fractions

1.	(D)	14.	(D)	27.	(D)	40.	(A)
2.	(E)	15.	(B)	28.	(E)	41.	(D)
3.	(C)	16.	(B)	29.	(C)	42.	(A)
4.	(A)	17.	(D)	30.	(B)	43.	(D)
5.	(C)	18.	(B)	31.	(C)	44.	(E)
6.	(B)	19.	(A)	32.	(A)	45.	(C)
7.	(C)	20.	(C)	33.	(B)	46.	(D)
8.	(A)	21.	(D)	34.	(C)	47.	(D)
9.	(B)	22.	(C)	35.	(D)	48.	(B)
10.	(A)	23.	(B)	36.	(B)	49.	(A)
11.	(B)	24.	(E)	37.	(C)	50.	(E)
12.	(D)	25.	(A)	38.	(D)		
13.	(E)	26.	(A)	39.	(E)		

Drill: Decimals

1.	(B)	9.	(C)	17.	(D)	25.	(E)
2.	(E)	10.	(E)	18.	(D)	26.	(D)
3.	(C)	11.	(B)	19.	(A)	27.	(C)
4.	(A)	12.	(D)	20.	(C)	28.	(A)
5.	(D)	13.	(A)	21.	(E)	29.	(E)
6.	(A)	14.	(B)	22.	(C)	30.	(D)
7.	(B)	15.	(C)	23.	(B)		
8.	(D)	16.	(B)	24.	(D)		

Drill: Percentages

1.	(B)	9.	(E)	17.	(D)	25.	(D)
2.	(C)	10.	(C)	18.	(E)	26.	(D)
3.	(E)	11.	(C)	19.	(C)	27.	(C)
4.	(B)	12.	(B)	20.	(C)	28.	(B)
5.	(A)	13.	(B)	21.	(A)	29.	(E)
6.	(B)	14.	(D)	22.	(B)	30.	(A)
7.	(A)	15.	(A)	23.	(C)		
8.	(B)	16.	(E)	24.	(B)		

Drill: Radicals

1.	(B)	6.	(C)	11.	(B)	16.	(A)
2.	(D)	7.	(A)	12.	(D)	17.	(C)
3.	(A)	8.	(D)	13.	(C)	18.	(B)
4.	(C)	9.	(C)	14.	(E)	19.	(D)
5.	(E)	10.	(B)	15.	(A)	20.	(C)

Drill: Exponents

1.	(B)	9.	(B)
2.	(A)	10.	(D)
3.	(C)	11.	(C)
4.	(D)	12.	(E)
5.	(B)	13.	(B)
6.	(E)	14.	(A)
7.	(B)	15.	(D)
8.	(C)		

Drill: Averages

1.	(B)	6.	(B)
2.	(B)	7.	(A)
3.	(D)	8.	(D)
4.	(C)	9.	(E)
5.	(D)	10.	(C)

III. ALGEBRA

In algebra, letters or variables are used to represent numbers. A **variable** is defined as a placeholder, which can take on any of several values at a given time. A **constant**, on the other hand, is a symbol which takes on only one value at a given time. A **term** is a constant, a variable, or a combination of constants and variables. For example: 7.76, $3x$, xyz, $5z/x$, $(0.99)x^2$ are terms. If a term is a combination of constants and variables, the constant part of the term is referred to as the **coefficient** of the variable. If a variable is written without a coefficient, the coefficient is assumed to be 1.

EXAMPLE

$3x^2$

coefficient : 3

variable: x

y^3

coefficient: 1

variable: y

An **expression** is a collection of one or more terms. If the number of terms is greater than 1, the expression is said to be the sum of the terms.

EXAMPLE

9, $9xy$, $6x + x/3$, $8yz - 2x$

An algebraic expression consisting of only one term is called a **monomial**; of two terms is called a **binomial**; of three terms is called a **trinomial**. In general, an algebraic expression consisting of two or more terms is called a **polynomial**.

1. OPERATIONS WITH POLYNOMIALS

A) **Addition of polynomials** is achieved by combining like terms, terms which differ only in their numerical coefficients, e.g.,

$$P(x) = (x^2 - 3x + 5) + (4x^2 + 6x - 3)$$

Note that the parentheses are used to distinguish the polynomials.

By using the commutative and associative laws, we can rewrite $P(x)$ as:

$$P(x) = (x^2 + 4x^2) + (6x - 3x) + (5 - 3)$$

Using the distributive law, $ab + ac = a(b + c)$, yields:

$$(1 + 4)x^2 + (6 - 3)x + (5 - 3)$$

$$= 5x^2 + 3x + 2$$

B) **Subtraction of two polynomials** is achieved by first changing the sign of all terms in the expression which is being subtracted and then adding this result to the other expression, e.g.,

$$(5x^2 + 4y^2 + 3z^2) - (4xy + 7y^2 - 3z^2 + 1)$$
$$= 5x^2 + 4y^2 + 3z^2 - 4xy - 7y^2 + 3z^2 - 1$$
$$= (5x^2) + (4y^2 - 7y^2) + (3z^2 + 3z^2) - 4xy - 1$$
$$= (5x^2) + (-3y^2) + (6z^2) - 4xy - 1$$

C) **Multiplication of two or more polynomials** is achieved by using the laws of exponents, the rules of signs, and the commutative and associative laws of multiplication. Begin by multiplying the coefficients and then multiply the variables according to the laws of exponents, e.g.,

$$(y^2) (5) (6y^2) (yz) (2z^2)$$
$$= (1) (5) (6) (1) (2) (y^2) (y^2) (yz) (z^2)$$
$$= 60[(y^2) (y^2) (y)] [(z) (z^2)]$$
$$= 60(y^5) (z^3)$$
$$= 60 \, y^5 z^3$$

D) **Multiplication of a polynomial by a monomial** is achieved by multiplying each term of the polynomial by the monomial and combining the results, e.g.,

$$(4x^2 + 3y) (6xz^2)$$
$$= (4x^2) (6xz^2) + (3y) (6xz^2)$$
$$= 24x^3z^2 + 18xyz^2$$

E) **Multiplication of a polynomial by a polynomial** is achieved by multiplying each of the terms of one polynomial by each of the terms of the other polynomial and combining the result, e.g.,

$$(5y + z + 1) (y^2 + 2y)$$
$$[(5y) (y^2) + (5y) (2y)] + [(z) (y^2) + (z) (2y)] + [(1) (y^2) + (1) (2y)]$$
$$= (5y^3 + 10y^2) + (y^2z + 2yz) + (y^2 + 2y)$$
$$= (5y^3) + (10y^2 + y^2) + (y^2z) + (2yz) + (2y)$$
$$= 5y^3 + 11y^2 + y^2z + 2yz + 2y$$

F) **Division of a monomial by a monomial** is achieved by first dividing the constant coefficients and the variable factors separately, and then multiplying these quotients, e.g.,

$$6xyz^2 \div 2y^2z$$
$$= (6/2) (x/1) (y/y^2) (z^2/z)$$
$$= 3xy^{-1}z$$
$$= 3xz/y$$

G) **Division of a polynomial by a polynomial** is achieved by following the given procedure, called long division.

Step 1:   The terms of both the polynomials are arranged in order of ascending or descending powers of one variable.

Step 2:   The first term of the dividend is divided by the first term of the divisor which gives the first term of the quotient.

Step 3:   This first term of the quotient is multiplied by the entire divisor and the result is subtracted from the dividend.

Step 4:   Using the remainder obtained from Step 3 as the new dividend, Steps 2 and 3 are repeated until the remainder is zero or the degree of the remainder is less than the degree of the divisor.

Step 5:   The result is written as follows:

$$\frac{\text{dividend}}{\text{divisor}} = \text{quotient} + \frac{\text{remainder}}{\text{divisor}}$$

$\text{divisor} \neq 0$

e.g. $(2x^2 + x + 6) \div (x + 1)$

$$
\begin{array}{r}
2x - 1 \\
(x+1)\overline{\smash{\big)}\,2x^2 + x + 6} \\
\underline{-(2x^2 + 2x)} \\
-x + 6 \\
\underline{-(-x - 1)} \\
7
\end{array}
$$

The result is $(2x^2 + x + 6) \div (x + 1) = 2x - 1 + \dfrac{7}{x + 1}$

PROBLEM

Simplify $p^2 + 2pq + q^2$ if $p + q = 1$.

SOLUTION

Since $p + q = 1, q = 1 - p$. Thus $p^2 + 2pq + q^2 = p^2 + 2p(1 - p) + (1 - p)^2$. Opening parentheses we obtain $p^2 + (2p - p^2) + 1 + p^2 - 2p)$. Finally we combine like terms and obtain $(p^2 + p^2 - 2p^2) + (2P - 2p) + 1$, and this reduces to 1.

PROBLEM

Simplify $p^2 + 2pq + q^2$.

SOLUTION

Here we are not told that $p + q = 1$. So we rewrite $p^2 + 2pq + q^2$ as $p^2 + pq + pq + q^2 = p(p + q) + q(p + q)$, and this equals $(p + q)(p + q)$ or $(p + q)^2$.

☞ Drill: Operations With Polynomials

Addition

1. $9a^2b + 3c + 2a^2b + 5c =$

(A) $19a^2bc$ 　　　　(B) $11a^2b + 8c$ 　　　　(C) $11a^4b^2 + 8c^2$

(D) $19a^4b^2c^2$ 　　　(E) $12a^2b + 8c^2$

2. $14m^2n^3 + 6m^2n^3 + 3m^2n^3 =$

(A) $20m^2n^3$ 　　　　(B) $23m^6n^9$ 　　　　(C) $23m^2n^3$

(D) $32m^6n^9$ 　　　　(E) $23m^8n^{27}$

3. $3x + 2y + 16x + 3z + 6y =$

(A) $19x + 8y$ 　　　　(B) $19x + 11yz$ 　　　　(C) $19x + 8y + 3z$

(D) $11xy + 19xz$ 　　(E) $30xyz$

4. $(4d^2 + 7e^3 + 12f) + (3d^2 + 6e^3 + 2f) =$

(A) $23d^2e^3f$ 　　　　(B) $33d^2e^2f$ 　　　　(C) $33d^4e^6f^2$

(D) $7d^2 + 13e^3 + 14f$ 　(E) $23d^2 + 11e^3f$

5. $3ac^2 + 2b^2c + 7ac^2 + 2ac^2 + b^2c =$

(A) $12ac^2 + 3b^2c$ 　　(B) $14ab^2c^2$ 　　　　(C) $11ac^2 + 4ab^2c$

(D) $15ab^2c^2$ 　　　　(E) $15a^2b^4c^4$

Subtraction

6. $14m^2n - 6m^2n =$

(A) $20m^2n$ 　(B) $8m^2n$ 　(C) $8m$ 　(D) 8 　(E) $8m^4n^2$

7. $3x^3y^2 - 4xz - 6x^3y^2 =$

(A) $-7x^2y^2z$ 　　　　(B) $3x^3y^2 - 10x^4y^2z$ 　(C) $-3x^3y^2 - 4xz$

(D) $-x^2y^2z - 6x^3y^2$ 　(E) $-7xyz$

8. $9g^2 + 6h - 2g^2 - 5h =$

(A) $15g^2h - 7g^2h$ 　　(B) $7g^4h^2$ 　　　　(C) $11g^2 + 7h$

(D) $11g^2 - 7h^2$ 　　　(E) $7g^2 + h$

9. $7b^3 - 4c^2 - 6b^3 + 3c^2 =$

(A) $b^3 - c^2$ (B) $-11b^2 - 3c^2$ (C) $13b^3 - c$

(D) $7b - c$ (E) 0

10. $11q^2r - 4q^2r - 8q^2r =$

(A) $22q^2r$ (B) q^2r (C) $-2\,q^2r$

(D) $-q^2r$ (E) $2\,q^2r$

Multiplication

11. $5p^2t * 3p^2t =$

(A) $15p^2t$ (B) $15p^4t$ (C) $15p^4t^2$ (D) $8p^2t$ (E) $8p^4t^2$

12. $(2r + s)\,14r =$

(A) $28rs$ (B) $28r^2 + 14sr$ (C) $16r^2 + 14rs$

(D) $28r + 14sr$ (E) $17r^2s$

13. $(4m + p)\,(3m - 2p) =$

(A) $12m^2 + 5mp + 2p^2$ (B) $12m^2 - 2mp + 2p^2$ (C) $7m - p$

(D) $12m - 2p$ (E) $12m^2 - 5mp - 2p^2$

14. $(2a + b)\,(3a^2 + ab + b^2) =$

(A) $6a^3 + 5a^2b + 3ab^2 + b^3$ (B) $5a^3 + 3ab + b^3$

(C) $6a^3 + 2a^2b + 2ab^2$ (D) $3a^2 + 2a + ab + b + b^2$

(E) $6a^3 + 3a^2b + 5ab^2 + b^3$

15. $(6t^2 + 2t + 1)\,3t =$

(A) $9t^2 + 5t + 3$ (B) $18t^2 + 6t + 3$ (C) $9t^3 + 6t^2 + 3t$

(D) $18t^3 + 6t^2 + 3t$ (E) $12t^3 + 6t^2 + 3t$

Division

16. $(x^2 + x - 6) \div (x - 2) =$

(A) $x - 3$ (B) $x + 2$ (C) $x + 3$ (D) $x - 2$ (E) $2x + 2$

17. $24b^4c^3 \div 6b^2c =$

(A) $3b^2c^2$ (B) $4b^4c^3$ (C) $4b^3c^2$ (D) $4b^2c^2$ (E) $3b^4c^3$

18. $(3p^2 + pq - 2q^2) \div (p + q) =$

(A) $3p + 2q$ (B) $2q - 3p$ (C) $3p - q$

(D) $2q + 3p$ (E) $3p - 2q$

19. $(y^3 - 2y^2 - y + 2) \div (y - 2) =$

(A) $(y - 1)^2$ (B) $y^2 - 1$ (C) $(y + 2)(y - 1)$

(D) $(y + 1)^2$ (E) $(y + 1)(y - 2)$

20. $(m^2 + m - 14) \div (m + 4) =$

(A) $m - 2$ (B) $m - 3 + \dfrac{-2}{m + 4}$ (C) $m - 3 + \dfrac{4}{m + 4}$

(D) $m - 3$ (E) $m - 2 + \dfrac{-3}{m + 4}$

2. SIMPLIFYING ALGEBRAIC EXPRESSIONS

To factor a polynomial completely is to find the prime factors of the polynomial with respect to a specified set of numbers.

The following concepts are important while factoring or simplifying expressions.

1. The factors of an algebraic expression consist of two or more algebraic expressions which, when multiplied together, produce the given algebraic expression.

2. A **prime factor** is a polynomial with no factors other than itself and 1. The **least common multiple (LCM)** for a set of numbers is the smallest quantity divisible by every number of the set. For algebraic expressions the least common numerical coefficients for each of the given expressions will be a factor.

3. The **greatest common factor (GCF)** for a set of numbers is the largest factor that is common to all members of the set.

4. For algebraic expressions, the greatest common factor is the polynomial of highest degree and the largest numerical coefficient which is a factor of all the given expressions.

Some important formulas, useful for the factoring of polynomials are listed below.

$$a(c + d) = ac + ad$$
$$(a + b)(a - b) = a^2 - b^2$$
$$(a + b)(a + b) = (a + b)^2 = a^2 + 2ab + b^2$$
$$(a - b)(a - b) = (a - b)^2 = a^2 - 2ab + b^2$$

$$(x + a)(x + b) = x^2 + (a + b)x + ab$$
$$(ax + b)(cx + d) = acx^2 + (ad + bc)x + bd$$
$$(a + b)(c + d) = ac + bc + ad + bd$$
$$(a + b)(a + b)(a + b) = (a + b)^3 = a^3 + 3a^2b + 3ab^2 + b^3$$
$$(a - b)(a - b)(a - b) = (a - b)^3 = a^3 - 3a^2b + 3ab^2 - b^3$$
$$(a - b)(a^2 + ab + b^2) = a^3 - b^3$$
$$(a + b)(a^2 - ab + b^2) = a^3 + b^3$$
$$(a + b + c)^2 = a^2 + b^2 + c^2 + 2ab + 2ac + 2bc$$
$$(a - b)(a^3 + a^2b + ab^2 + b^3) = a^4 - b^4$$
$$(a - b)(a^4 + a^3b + a^2b^2 + ab^3 + b^4) = a^5 - b^5$$
$$(a - b)(a^5 + a^4b + a^3b^2 + a^2b^3 + ab^4 + b^5) = a^6 - b^6$$
$$(a - b)(a^{n-1} + a^{n-2}b + a^{n-3}b^2 + \ldots + ab^{n-2} + b^{n-1}) = a^n - b^n$$

where n is any positive integer (1, 2, 3, 4, ...).

$$(a + b)(a^{n-1} - a^{n-2}b + a^{n-3}b^2 - \ldots - ab^{n-2} + b^{n-1}) = a^n + b^n$$

where n is any positive odd integer (1, 3, 5, 7, ...).

The procedure for factoring an algebraic expression completely is as follows:

Step 1: First find the greatest common factor if there is any. Then examine each factor remaining for greatest common factors.

Step 2: Continue factoring the factors obtained in Step 1 until all factors other than monomial factors are prime.

EXAMPLE

Factoring $4 - 16x^2$,

$$4 - 16x^2 = 4(1 - 4x^2) = 4(1 + 2x)(1 - 2x)$$

PROBLEM

Express each of the following as a single term.

(A) $3x^2 + 2x^2 - 4x^2$

(B) $5axy^2 - 7axy^2 - 3xy^2$

SOLUTION

(A) Factor x^2 in the expression.

$$3x^2 + 2x^2 - 4x^2 = (3 + 2 - 4)x^2 = 1x^2 = x^2.$$

(B) Factor xy^2 in the expression and then factor a.

$$5axy^2 - 7axy^2 - 3xy^2 = (5a - 7a - 3)xy^2$$
$$= [(5 - 7)a - 3]xy^2$$
$$= (-2a - 3)xy^2.$$

PROBLEM

Simplify $\dfrac{\dfrac{1}{x-1} - \dfrac{1}{x-2}}{\dfrac{1}{x-2} - \dfrac{1}{x-3}}$.

SOLUTION

Simplify the expression in the numerator by using the addition rule:

$$\frac{a}{b} + \frac{c}{d} = \frac{ad + bc}{bd}$$

Notice *bd* is the Least Common Denominator, LCD. We obtain

$$\frac{x - 2 - (x - 1)}{(x - 1)(x - 2)} = \frac{-1}{(x - 1)(x - 2)}$$

in the numerator.

Repeat this procedure for the expression in the denominator:

$$\frac{x - 3 - (x - 2)}{(x - 2)(x - 3)} = \frac{-1}{(x - 2)(x - 3)}$$

We now have

$$\frac{\dfrac{-1}{(x-1)(x-2)}}{\dfrac{-1}{(x-2)(x-3)}},$$

which is simplified by inverting the fraction in the denominator and multiplying it by the numerator and cancelling like terms

$$\frac{-1}{(x - 1)(x - 2)} \cdot \frac{(x - 2)(x - 3)}{-1} = \frac{x - 3}{x - 1}.$$

☞ Drill: Simplifying Algebraic Expressions

1. $16b^2 - 25z^2 =$

(A) $(4b - 5z)^2$ (B) $(4b + 5z)^2$ (C) $(4b - 5z)(4b + 5z)$

(D) $(16b - 25z)^2$ (E) $(5z - 4b)(5z + 4b)$

2. $x^2 - 2x - 8 =$

(A) $(x - 4)^2$ (B) $(x - 6)(x - 2)$ (C) $(x + 4)(x - 2)$

(D) $(x - 4)(x + 2)$ (E) $(x - 4)(x - 2)$

3.　$2c^2 + 5cd - 3d^2 =$

(A)　$(c - 3d)(c + 2d)$ (B)　$(2c - d)(c + 3d)$ (C)　$(c - d)(2c + 3d)$

(D)　$(2c + d)(c + 3d)$ (E)　Not possible

4.　$4t^3 - 20t =$

(A)　$4t(t^2 - 5)$ (B)　$4t^2(t - 20)$ (C)　$4t(t + 4)(t - 5)$

(D)　$2t(2t^2 - 10)$ (E)　Not possible

5.　$x^2 + xy - 2y^2 =$

(A)　$(x - 2y)(x + y)$ (B)　$(x - 2y)(x - y)$ (C)　$(x + 2y)(x + y)$

(D)　$(x + 2y)(x - y)$ (E)　Not possible

6.　$5b^2 + 17bd + 6d^2 =$

(A)　$(5b + d)(b + 6d)$ (B)　$(5b + 2d)(b + 3d)$ (C)　$(5b - 2d)(b - 3d)$

(D)　$(5b - 2d)(b + 3d)$ (E)　Not possible

7.　$x^2 + x + 1 =$

(A)　$(x + 1)^2$ (B)　$(x + 2)(x - 1)$ (C)　$(x - 2)(x + 1)$

(D)　$(x + 1)(x - 1)$ (E)　Not possible

8.　$3z^3 + 6z^2 =$

(A)　$3(z^3 + 2z^2)$ (B)　$3z^2(z + 2)$ (C)　$3z(z^2 + 2z)$

(D)　$z^2(3z + 6)$ (E)　$3z^2(1 + 2z)$

9.　$m^2p^2 + mpg - 6q^2 =$

(A)　$(mp - 2q)(mp + 3q)$ (B)　$mp(mp - 2q)(mp + 3q)$

(C)　$mpq(1 - 6q)$ (D)　$(mp + 2q)(mp + 3q)$

(E)　Not possible

10.　$2h^3 + 2h^2t - 4ht^2 =$

(A)　$2(h^3 - t)(h + t)$ (B)　$2h(h - 2t)^2$ (C)　$4h(ht - t^2)$

(D)　$2h(h + t) - 4ht^2$ (E)　$2h(h + 2t)(h - t)$

3. EQUATIONS

An **equation** is defined as a statement that two separate expressions are equal.

A **solution** to an equation containing a single variable is a number that makes the equation true when it is substituted for the variable. For example, in the equation $3x = 18$, 6 is the solution since $3(6) = 18$. Depending on the equation, there can be more than one solution. Equations with the same solutions are said to be **equivalent equations**. An equation without a solution is said to have a solution set that is the **empty** or **null** set and is represented by ϕ.

Replacing an expression within an equation by an equivalent expression will result in a new equation with solutions equivalent to the original equation. Suppose we are given the equation

$$3x + y + x + 2y = 15.$$

By combining like terms we get

$$3x + y + x + 2y = 4x + 3y.$$

Since these two expressions are equivalent, we can substitute the simpler form into the equation to get

$$4x + 3y = 15$$

Performing the same operation to both sides of an equation by the same expression will result in a new equation that is equivalent to the original equation.

A) **Addition or subtraction**

$$y + 6 = 10$$

we can add (-6) to both sides

$$y + 6 + (-6) = 10 + (-6)$$

to get $y + 0 = 10 - 6 \rightarrow y = 4$

B) **Multiplication or division**

$$3x = 6$$

$$3x/3 = 6/3$$

$$x = 2$$

$3x = 6$ is equivalent to $x = 2$.

C) **Raising to a power**

$$a = x^2y$$
$$a^2 = (x^2y)^2$$
$$a^2 = x^4y^2$$

This can be applied to negative and fractional powers as well, e.g.,

$$x^2 = 3y^4$$

If we raise both members to the -2 power, we get

$$(x^2)^{-2} = (3y^4)^{-2}$$

$$\frac{1}{(x^2)^2} = \frac{1}{(3y^4)^2}$$

$$\frac{1}{x^4} = \frac{1}{9y^8}$$

If we raise both members to the $\frac{1}{2}$ power, which is the same as taking the square root, we get:

$$(x^2)^{1/2} = (3y^4)^{1/2}$$

$$x = \sqrt{3}\, y^2$$

D)   The **reciprocal** of both members of an equation are equivalent to the original equation. Note: The reciprocal of zero is undefined.

$$\frac{2x + y}{z} = \frac{5}{2} \qquad\qquad \frac{z}{2x + y} = \frac{2}{5}$$

PROBLEM

Solve for x, justifying each step. $3x - 8 = 7x + 8$.

SOLUTION

$$3x - 8 = 7x + 8$$

Adding 8 to both members, $\qquad\qquad 3x - 8 + 8 = 7x + 8 + 8$

Additive inverse property, $\qquad\qquad 3x + 0 = 7x + 16$

Additive identity property, $\qquad\qquad 3x = 7x + 16$

Adding $(-7x)$ to both members, $\qquad 3x - 7x = 7x + 16 - 7x$

Commuting, $\qquad\qquad\qquad\qquad -4x = 7x - 7x + 16$

Additive inverse property, $\qquad\qquad -4x = 0 + 16$

Additive identity property, $\qquad\qquad -4x = 16$

Dividing both sides by -4, $\qquad\qquad x = {}^{16}/_{-4}$

$$x = -4$$

Check: Replacing x with -4 in the original equation:

$$3x - 8 = 7x + 8$$
$$3(-4) - 8 = 7(-4) + 8$$
$$-12 - 8 = -28 + 8$$
$$-20 = -20$$

LINEAR EQUATIONS

A linear equation with one unknown is one that can be put into the form $ax + b = 0$, where a and b are constants, $a \neq 0$.

To solve a linear equation means to transform it in the form $x = {}^{-b}/_a$.

A) If the equation has unknowns on both sides of the equality, it is convenient to put similar terms on the same sides, e.g.,

$$
\begin{aligned}
4x + 3 &= 2x + 9 \\
4x + 3 - 2x &= 2x + 9 - 2x \\
(4x - 2x) + 3 &= (2x - 2x) + 9 \\
2x + 3 &= 0 + 9 \\
2x + 3 - 3 &= 0 + 9 - 3 \\
2x &= 6 \\
{}^{2x}/_2 &= {}^{6}/_2 \\
x &= 3.
\end{aligned}
$$

B) If the equation appears in fractional form, it is necessary to transform it, using cross-multiplication, and then repeating the same procedure as in A), we obtain:

$$
\frac{3x + 4}{3} \qquad \frac{7x + 2}{5}
$$

By using cross-multiplication we would obtain:

$3(7x + 2) = 5(3x + 4)$.

This is equivalent to:

$21x + 6 = 15x + 20$,

which can be solved as in A):

$$
\begin{aligned}
21x + 6 &= 15x + 20 \\
21x - 15x + 6 &= 15x - 15x + 20 \\
6x + 6 - 6 &= 20 - 6 \\
6x &= 14 \\
x &= {}^{14}/_6 \\
x &= {}^{7}/_3
\end{aligned}
$$

C) If there are radicals in the equation, it is necessary to square both sides and then apply A)

$$
\begin{aligned}
\sqrt{3x + 1} &= 5 \\
(\sqrt{3x + 1})^2 &= 5^2
\end{aligned}
$$

$$3x + 1 = 25$$
$$3x + 1 - 1 = 25 - 1$$
$$3x = 24$$
$$x = {}^{24}/_3$$
$$x = 8$$

PROBLEM

Solve the equation $2(x + 3) = (3x + 5) - (x - 5)$.

SOLUTION

We transform the given equation to an equivalent equation in which we can easily recognize the solution set.

	$2(x + 3)$	$= 3x + 5 - (x - 5)$
Distribute,	$2x + 6$	$= 3x + 5 - x + 5$
Combine terms,	$2x + 6$	$= 2x + 10$
Subtract $2x$ from both sides,	6	$= 10$

Since $6 = 10$ is not a true statement, there is no real number x which will make the original equation true. The equation is inconsistent and the solution set is ϕ, the empty set.

PROBLEM

Solve the equation $2({}^2/_3 y + 5) + 2(y + 5) = 130$.

SOLUTION

The procedure for solving this equation is as follows:

${}^4/_3 y + 10 + 2y + 10 = 130,$	Distributive property
${}^4/_3 y + 2y + 20 = 130,$	Combining like terms
${}^4/_3 y + 2y = 110,$	Subtracting 20 from both sides
${}^4/_3 y + {}^6/_3 y = 110,$	Converting $2y$ into a fraction with denominator 3
${}^{10}/_3 y = 110,$	Combining like terms
$y = 110 \cdot {}^3/_{10} = 33,$	Dividing by ${}^{10}/_3$

Check: Replace y with 33 in the original equation,

$$2({}^2/_3(33) + 5) + 2(33 + 5) = 130$$
$$2(22 + 5) + 2(38) = 130$$
$$2(27) + 76 = 130$$

$$54 + 76 = 130$$
$$130 = 130$$

Therefore the solution to the given equation is $y = 33$.

☞ Drill: Linear Equations

Solve for x:

1. $4x - 2 = 10$

(A) -1 (B) 2   (C) 3   (D) 4   (E) 6

2. $7z + 1 - z = 2z - 7$

(A) -2 (B) 0   (C) 1   (D) 2   (E) 3

3. $\frac{1}{3}b + 3 = \frac{1}{2}b$

(A) 1/2   (B) 2   (C) 3 3/5   (D) 6   (E) 18

4. $0.4p + 1 = 0.7p - 2$

(A) 0.1   (B) 2   (C) 5   (D) 10   (E) 12

5. $4(3x + 2) - 11 = 3(3x - 2)$

(A) -3 (B) -1 (C) 2   (D) 3   (E) 7

4.   INEQUALITIES

An inequality is a statement where the value of one quantity or expression is greater than (>), less than (<), greater than or equal to ($\geq$), less than or equal to ($\leq$), or not equal to ($\neq$) that of another.

EXAMPLE

$5 > 4$.

The expression above means that the value of 5 is greater than the value of 4.

A **conditional inequality** is an inequality whose validity depends on the values of the variables in the sentence. That is, certain values of the variables will make the sentence true, and others will make it false. $3 - y > 3 + y$ is a conditional inequality for the set of real numbers, since it is true for any replacement less than zero and false for all others.

$x + 5 > x + 2$ is an **absolute inequality** for the set of real numbers, meaning that for any real value x, the expression on the left is greater than the expression on the right.

$5y < 2y + y$ is inconsistent for the set of non-negative real numbers. For any y greater than or equal to 0, the sentence is always false. A sentence is inconsistent if it is always false when its variables assume allowable values.

The solution of a given inequality in one variable x consists of all values of x for which the inequality is true.

The graph of an inequality in one variable is represented by either a ray or a line segment on the real number line.

The endpoint is not a solution if the variable is strictly less than or greater than a particular value.

EXAMPLE

$x > 2$

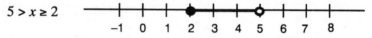

2 is not a solution and should be represented as shown.

The endpoint is a solution if the variable is either (1) less than or equal to, or (2) greater than or equal to, a particular value.

EXAMPLE

$5 > x \geq 2$

In this case 2 is the solution and should be represented as shown.

PROPERTIES OF INEQUALITIES

If x and y are real numbers then one and only one of the following statements is true.

$x > y, x = y,$ or $x < y.$

This is the order property of real numbers.

If a, b, and c are real numbers:

A)   If $a < b$ and $b < c$, then $a < c$.

B)   If $a > b$ and $b > c$, then $a > c$.

This is the transitive property of inequalities.

If a, b, and c are real numbers and $a > b$, then $a + c > b + c$ and $a - c > b - c$. This is the **addition property of inequality**.

Two inequalities are said to have the same **sense** if their signs of inequality point in the same direction.

The sense of an inequality remains the same if both sides are multiplied or divided by the same positive real number.

EXAMPLE

$4 > 3$

If we multiply both sides by 5 we will obtain:

$4 \times 5 > 3 \times 5$

$20 > 15$

The sense of the inequality does not change.

The sense of an inequality becomes opposite if each side is multiplied or divided by the same negative real number.

EXAMPLE

$4 > 3$

If we multiply both sides by $- 5$ we would obtain:

$4 \times - 5 < 3 \times - 5$

$- 20 < -15$

The sense of the inequality becomes opposite.

If $a > b$ and a, b, and n are positive real numbers, then:

$a^n > b^n$ and $a^{-n} < b^{-n}$

If $x > y$ and $q > p$, then $x + q > y + p$.

If $x > y > 0$ and $q > p > 0$, then $xq > yp$.

Inequalities that have the same solution set are called **equivalent inequalities**.

PROBLEM

Solve the inequality $2x + 5 > 9$.

SOLUTION

$2x + 5 + (- 5) > 9 + (- 5)$.   Adding $- 5$ to both sides.

$2x + 0 > 9 + (- 5)$ Additive inverse property

$2x > 9 + (- 5)$ Additive identity property

$2x > 4$ Combining terms

$\frac{1}{2}(2x) > \frac{1}{2} \cdot 4$ Multiplying both sides by $\frac{1}{2}$.

$x > 2$

The solution set is

$X = \{x \,|\, 2x + 5 > 9 \}$

$= \{x \,|\, x > 2\}$

(that is all x, such that x is greater than 2).

PROBLEM

Solve the inequality $4x + 3 < 6x + 8$.

SOLUTION

In order to solve the inequality $4x + 3 < 6x + 8$, we must find all values of x which make it true. Thus, we wish to obtain x alone on one side of the inequality.

Add -3 to both sides:

$$\begin{array}{r} 4x + 3 < 6x\ + 8 \\ -3 \qquad -3 \\ \hline 4x < 6x + 5 \end{array}$$

Add $-6x$ to both sides:

$$\begin{array}{r} 4x < \quad 6x + 5 \\ -6x \qquad -6x \\ \hline -2x < \quad 5 \end{array}$$

In order to obtain x alone we must divide both sides by (-2). Recall that dividing an inequality by a negative number reverses the inequality sign, hence

$$\frac{-2x}{-2} > \frac{5}{-2}$$

Cancelling $-^2/_{-2}$ we obtain, $x > -^5/_2$.

Thus, our solution is $\{x : x > -^5/_2\}$ (the set of all x such that x is greater than $-^5/_2$).

☞ Drill: Inequalities

<u>DIRECTIONS</u>: Find the solution set for each inequality.

1. $3m + 2 < 7$

(A) $m \geq ^5/_3$ (B) $m \leq 2$ (C) $m < 2$

(D) $m > 2$ (E) $m < ^5/_3$

2. $^1/_2 x - 3 \leq 1$

(A) $-4 \leq x \leq 8$ (B) $x \geq -8$ (C) $x \leq \quad 8$

(D) $2 \leq x \leq 8$ (E) $x \geq 8$

3. $-3p + 1 \geq 16$

(A) $p \geq -5$ (B) $p \geq \dfrac{-17}{3}$ (C) $p \leq \dfrac{-17}{3}$

(D) $p \leq -5$ (E) $p \geq 5$

4. $-6 < \frac{2}{3} r + 6 \leq 2$

(A) $-6 < r \leq -3$ (B) $-18 < r \leq -6$ (C) $r \geq -6$

(D) $-2 < r \leq -\frac{4}{3}$ (E) $r \leq -6$

5. $0 < 2 - y < 6$

(A) $-4 < y < 2$ (B) $-4 < y < 0$ (C) $-4 < y < -2$

(D) $-2 < y < 4$ (E) $0 < y < 4$

5.   RATIOS AND PROPORTIONS

The ratio of two numbers x and y written $x : y$ is the fraction x / y where $y \neq 0$. A ratio compares x to y by dividing one by the other. Therefore, in order to compare ratios, simply compare the fractions.

A proportion is an equality of two ratios. The laws of proportion are listed below:

If $a/b = c/d$, then

(A) $ad = bc$

(B) $b/a = d/c$

(C) $a/c = b/d$

(D) $(a + b)/b = (c + d)/d$

(E) $(a - b)/b = (c - d)/d$

Given a proportion $a : b = c : d$, then a and d are called extremes, b and c are called the means and d is called the fourth proportion to a, b, and c.

PROBLEM

Solve the proportion $\dfrac{x + 1}{4} = \dfrac{15}{12}$.

SOLUTION

Cross-multiply to determine x; that is, multiply the numerator of the first fraction by the denominator of the second, and equate this to the product of the numerator of the second and the denominator of the first.

$$(x + 1)\,12 = 4 \cdot 15$$
$$12x + 12 = 60$$
$$x = 4.$$

PROBLEM

Find the ratios of $x : y : z$ from the equations

$$7x = 4y + 8z, \quad 3z = 12x + 11y.$$

SOLUTION

By transposition we have

$$7x - 4y - 8z = 0$$

$$12x + 11y - 3z = 0.$$

To obtain the ratio of $x : y$, we convert the given system into an equation in terms of just x and y. We may eliminate z as follows: Multiply each term of the first equation by 3, and each term of the second equation by 8, and then subtract the second equation from the first. We thus obtain:

$$21x - 12y - 24z = 0$$
$$\underline{-(96x + 88y - 24z = 0)}$$
$$-75x - 100y = 0$$

Dividing each term of the last equation by 25 we obtain:

$$-3x - 4y = 0$$

or, $\quad -3x = 4y.$

Dividing both sides of this equation by 4, and by -3, we have the proportion:

$$\frac{x}{4} = \frac{y}{-3}$$

We are now interested in obtaining the ratio of $y : z$. To do this we convert the given system of equations into an equation in terms of just y and z, by eliminating x as follows: Multiply each term of the first equation by 12, and each term of the second equation by 7, and then subtract the second equation from the first. We thus obtain:

$$84x - 48y - 96z = 0$$
$$\underline{-(84x + 77y - 21z = 0)}$$
$$-125y - 75z = 0.$$

Dividing each term of the last equation by 25 we obtain:

$$-5y - 3z = 0$$

or, $\quad -3z = 5y.$

Dividing both sides of this equation by 5, and by -3, we have the proportion:

$$\frac{z}{5} = \frac{y}{-3}.$$

From this result and our previous result we obtain:

$$\frac{x}{4} = \frac{y}{-3} = \frac{z}{5}$$

as the desired ratios.

☞ Drill: Ratios and Proportions

1. Solve for n : $\dfrac{4}{n} = \dfrac{8}{5}$.

(A) 10   (B) 8   (C) 6   (D) 2.5   (E) 2

2. Solve for n: $\dfrac{2}{3} = \dfrac{n}{72}$.

(A) 12   (B) 48   (C) 64   (D) 56   (E) 24

3. Solve for n: $n : 12 = 3 : 4$.

(A) 8   (B) 1   (C) 9   (D) 4   (E) 10

4. Four out of every five students at West High take a mathematics course. If the enrollment at West is 785, how many students take mathematics?

(A) 628   (B) 157   (C) 705   (D) 655   (E) 247

5. At a factory, three out of every 1,000 parts produced are defective. In a day, the factory can produce 25,000 parts. How many of these parts would be defective?

(A) 7   (B) 75   (C) 750   (D) 7,500   (E) 75,000

6. A summer league softball team won 28 out of the 32 games they played. What is the ratio of games won to games played?

(A) $4 : 5$ (B) $3 : 4$ (C) $7 : 8$ (D) $2 : 3$ (E) $1 : 8$

7. A class of 24 students contains 16 males. What is the ratio of females to males?

(A) $1 : 2$ (B) $2 : 1$ (C) $2 : 3$ (D) $3 : 1$ (E) $3 : 2$

8. A family has a monthly income of $1,250, but they spend $450 a month on rent. What is the ratio of the amount of income to the amount paid for rent?

(A) $16 : 25$ (B) $25 : 9$ (C) $25 : 16$ (D) $9 : 25$ (E) $36 : 100$

9. A student attends classes 7.5 hours a day and works a part-time job for 3.5 hours a day. She knows she must get 7 hours of sleep a night. Write the ratio of the number of free hours in this student's day to the total number of hours in a day.

(A) $1 : 3$ (B) $4 : 3$ (C) $8 : 24$ (D) $1 : 4$ (E) $5 : 12$

10. In a survey by mail, 30 out of 750 questionnaires were returned. Write the ratio of questionnaires returned to questionnaires mailed (write in simplest form).

(A) $30 : 750$ (B) $24 : 25$ (C) $3 : 75$ (D) $1 : 4$ (E) $1 : 25$

ALGEBRA DRILLS

ANSWER KEY

Drill: Operations With Polynomials

1.	(B)	6.	(B)	11.	(C)	16.	(C)
2.	(C)	7.	(C)	12.	(B)	17.	(D)
3.	(C)	8.	(E)	13.	(E)	18.	(E)
4.	(D)	9.	(A)	14.	(A)	19.	(B)
5.	(A)	10.	(D)	15.	(D)	20.	(B)

Drill: Simplifying Algebraic Expressions

1.	(C)	4.	(A)	7.	(E)	10.	(E)
2.	(D)	5.	(D)	8.	(B)		
3.	(B)	6.	(B)	9.	(A)		

Drill: Linear Equations

1.	(C)	4.	(E)
2.	(A)	5.	(B)
3.	(E)		

Drill: Inequalities

1.	(E)	4.	(B)
2.	(D)	5.	(A)
3.	(C)		

Drill: Ratios and Proportions

1.	(D)	4.	(A)	7.	(A)	10.	(E)
2.	(B)	5.	(B)	8.	(B)		
3.	(C)	6.	(C)	9.	(D)		

IV. GEOMETRY

1. POINTS, LINES, AND ANGLES

Geometry is built upon a series of undefined terms. These terms are those which we accept as known in order to define other undefined terms.

A) **Point**: Although we represent points on paper with small dots, a point has no size, thickness, or width.

B) **Line**: A line is a series of adjacent points which extends indefinitely. A line can be either curved or straight; however, unless otherwise stated, the term "line" refers to a straight line.

C) **Plane**: A plane is a collection of points lying on a flat surface, which extends indefinitely in all directions.

If A and B are two points on a line, then the **line segment** AB is the set of points on that line between A and B and including A and B, which are endpoints. The line segment is referred to as AB.

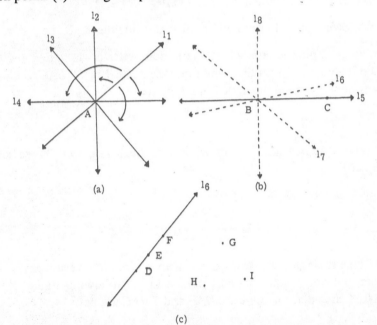

A **ray** is a series of points that lie to one side of a single endpont.

PROBLEM

How many lines can be found that contain (a) one given point (B) two given points (c) three given points?

SOLUTION

(a) *Given one point A,* there are an infinite number of distinct lines that contain the given point. To see this, consider line l_1 passing through point A. By rotating l_1 around A like the hands of a clock, we obtain different lines l_2, l_3, etc. Since we can rotate l_1 in infinitely many ways, there are infinitely many lines containing A.

(b) *Given two distinct points B and C,* there is one and only one straight line passing through both. To see this, consider all the lines containing point B: l_5, l_6, l_7, and l_8. Only l_5 contains both points B and C. Thus, there is only one line containing both points B and C. Since there is always at least one line containing two distinct points and never more than one, the line passing through the two points is said to be determined by the two points.

(c) *Given three distinct points,* there may be one line or none. If a line exists that contains the three points, such as D, E, and F, then the points are said to be **colinear**. If no such line exists (as in the case of points G, H, and I) then the points are said to be **noncolinear**.

INTERSECTION LINES AND ANGLES

An **angle** is a collection of points which is the union of two rays having the same endpoint. An angle such as the one illustrated below can be referred to in any of the following ways:

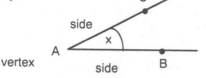

A) by a capital letter which names its vertex, i.e., $\angle A$;

B) by a lower-case letter or number placed inside the angle, i.e., $\angle x$;

C) by three capital letters, where the middle letter is the vertex and the other two letters are not on the same ray, i.e., $\angle CAB$ or $\angle BAC$, both of which represent the angle illustrated in the figure.

TYPES OF ANGLES

A) **Vertical angles** are formed when two lines intersect. These angles are equal.

$$\angle a = \angle b$$

B) **Adjacent angles** are two angles with a common vertex and a common side, but no common interior points. In the following figure, $\angle DAC$ and $\angle BAC$ are adjacent angles. $\angle DAB$ and $\angle BAC$ are not.

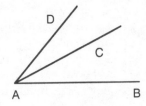

C)   A **right angle** is an angle whose measure is 90°.

D)   An **acute angle** is an angle whose measure is larger than 0°, but less than 90°.

E)   An **obtuse angle** is an angle whose measure is larger than 90° but less than 180°.

F)   A **straight angle** is an angle whose measure is 180°. Such an angle is, in fact, a straight line.

G)   A **reflex angle** is an angle whose measure is greater than 180° but less than 360°.

H)   **Complimentary angles** are two angles whose measures total 90°.

I)   **Supplementary angles** are two angles whose measures total 180°.

J)   **Congruent angles** are angles of equal measure.

PROBLEM

In the figure, we are given $\overleftrightarrow{AB}$ and triangle ABC. We are told that the measure of $\angle$ 1 is five times the measure of $\angle$ 2. Determine the measures of $\angle$ 1 and $\angle$ 2.

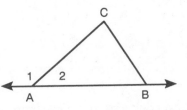

SOLUTION

Since $\angle$ 1 and $\angle$ 2 are adjacent angles whose non-common sides lie on a straight line, they are, by definition, supplementary. As supplements, their measures must total 180°.

If we let x = the measure of $\angle 2$, then, $5x$ = the measure of $\angle$ 1.

To determine the respective angle measures, set $x + 5x = 180$ and solve for x. $6x = 180$. Therefore, $x = 30$ and $5x = 150$.

Therefore, the measure of $\angle$ 1 = 150 and the measure of $\angle$ 2 = 30.

PERPENDICULAR LINES

Two lines are said to be **perpendicular** if they intersect and form right angles. The symbol for perpendicular (or, is therefore perpendicular to) is $\perp$;

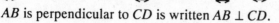

$\overleftrightarrow{AB}$ is perpendicular to $\overleftrightarrow{CD}$ is written $\overleftrightarrow{AB} \perp \overleftrightarrow{CD}$.

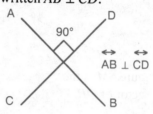

PROBLEM

We are given straight lines $\overleftrightarrow{AB}$ and $\overleftrightarrow{CD}$ intersecting at point P. $\overleftrightarrow{PR} \perp \overleftrightarrow{AB}$ and the measure of $\angle APD$ is 170°. Find the measures of $\angle 1$, $\angle 2$, $\angle 3$, and $\angle 4$. (See figure below.)

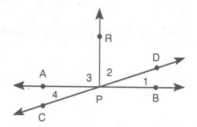

SOLUTION

This problem will involve making use of several of the properties of supplementary and vertical angles, as well as perpendicular lines.

$\angle APD$ and $\angle 1$ are adjacent angles whose non-common sides lie on a straight line, $\overleftrightarrow{AB}$. Therefore, they are supplements and their measures total 180°.

$$m \angle APD + m \angle 1 = 180°.$$

We know $m \angle APD = 170°$. Therefore, by substitution, $170° + m \angle 1 = 180°$. This implies $m \angle 1 = 10°$.

$\angle 1$ and $\angle 4$ are vertical angles because they are formed by the intersection of two straight lines, $\overleftrightarrow{CD}$ and $\overleftrightarrow{AB}$, and their sides form two pairs of opposite rays. As vertical angles, they are, by theorem, of equal measure. Since $m \angle 1 = 10°$, then $m \angle 4 = 10°$.

Since $\overleftrightarrow{PR} \perp \overleftrightarrow{AB}$, at their intersection the angles formed must be right angles. Therefore, $\angle 3$ is a right angle and its measure is 90°. $m \angle 3 = 90°$.

The figure shows us that $\angle APD$ is composed of $\angle 3$ and $\angle 2$. Since the measure of the whole must be equal to the sum of the measures of its parts, $m \angle APD = m \angle 3 + m \angle 2$. We know the $m \angle APD = 170°$ and $m \angle 3 = 90°$, therefore, by substitution, we can solve for $m \angle 2$, our last unknown.

$$170° = 90° + m \angle 2$$

$$80° = m \angle 2$$

Therefore, $m \angle 1 = 10°$, $m \angle 2 = 80°$,

$m \angle 3 = 90°$, $m \angle 4 = 10°$.

PROBLEM

In the accompanying figure $\overline{SM}$ is the perpendicular bisector of $\overline{QR}$, and $\overline{SN}$ is the perpendicular bisector of $\overline{QP}$. Prove that $SR = SP$.

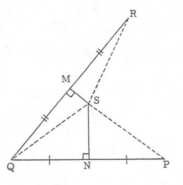

SOLUTION

Every point on the perpendicular bisector of a segment is equidistant from the endpoints of the segment.

Since point S is on the perpendicular bisector of $\overline{QR}$,

$$SR = SQ \tag{I}$$

Also, since point S is on the perpendicular bisector of $\overline{QP}$,

$$SQ = SP \tag{II}$$

By the transitive property (quantities equal to the same quantity are equal), we have:

$$SR = SP. \tag{III}$$

PARALLEL LINES

Two lines are called **parallel lines** if, and only if, they are in the same plane (coplanar) and do not intersect. The symbol for parallel, or is parallel to, is $\|$; $\overleftrightarrow{AB}$ is parallel to $\overleftrightarrow{CD}$ is written $\overleftrightarrow{AB} \| \overleftrightarrow{CD}$.

The distance between two parallel lines is the length of the perpendicular segment from any point on one line to the other line.

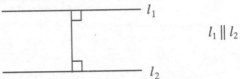

$l_1 \| l_2$

Given a line l and a point P not on line l, there is one and only one line through point P that is parallel to line l.

Two coplanar lines are either intersecting lines or parallel lines.

If two (or more) lines are perpendicular to the same line, then they are parallel to each other.

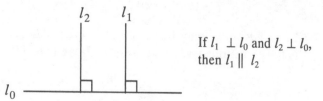

If $l_1 \perp l_0$ and $l_2 \perp l_0$, then $l_1 \parallel l_2$

If two lines are cut by a transversal so that alternate interior angles are equal, the lines are parallel.

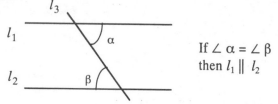

If $\angle \alpha = \angle \beta$ then $l_1 \parallel l_2$

If two lines are parallel to the same line, then they are parallel to each other.

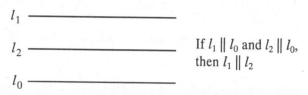

If $l_1 \parallel l_0$ and $l_2 \parallel l_0$, then $l_1 \parallel l_2$

If a line is perpendicular to one of two parallel lines, then it is perpendicular to the other line, too.

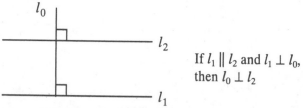

If $l_1 \parallel l_2$ and $l_1 \perp l_0$, then $l_0 \perp l_2$

If two lines being cut by a transversal form congruent corresponding angles, then the two lines are parallel.

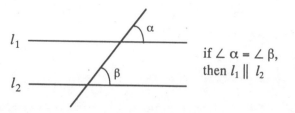

if $\angle \alpha = \angle \beta$, then $l_1 \parallel l_2$

If two lines being cut by a transversal form interior angles on the same side of the transversal that are supplementary, then the two lines are parallel.

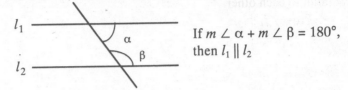

If $m \angle \alpha + m \angle \beta = 180°$, then $l_1 \parallel l_2$

If a line is parallel to one of two parallel lines, it is also parallel to the other line.

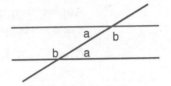

If $l_1 \parallel l_2$ and $l_0 \parallel l_1$ then $l_0 \parallel l_2$

If two parallel lines are cut by a transversal, then:

A)   The alternate interior angles are congruent.

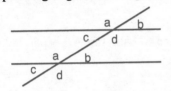

B)   The corresponding angles are congruent.

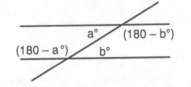

C)   The consecutive interior angles are supplementary.

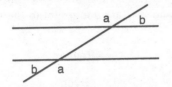

D)   The alternate exterior angles are congruent.

PROBLEM

Given: ∠ 2 is supplementary to ∠ 3.

Prove: $l_1 \parallel l_2$.

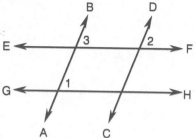

SOLUTION

Given two lines intercepted by a transversal, if a pair of corresponding angles are congruent, then the two lines are parallel. In this problem, we will show that since ∠ 1 and ∠ 2 are supplementary and ∠ 2 and ∠ 3 are supplementary, ∠ 1 and ∠ 3 are congruent. Since corresponding angles ∠ 1 and ∠ 3 are congruent, it follows $l_1 \parallel l_2$.

	Statement		Reason
1.	∠ 2 is supplementary to ∠ 3.	1.	Given.
2.	∠ 1 is supplementary to ∠ 2.	2.	Two angles that form a linear pair are supplementary.
3.	∠ 1 ≅ ∠ 3	3.	Angles supplementary to the same angle are congruent.
4.	$l_1 \parallel l_2$.	4.	Given two lines intercepted by a transversal, if a pair of corresponding angles are congruent, then the two lines are parallel.

PROBLEM

If line $\overleftrightarrow{AB}$ is parallel to line $\overleftrightarrow{CD}$ and line $\overleftrightarrow{EF}$ is parallel to line $\overleftrightarrow{GH}$, prove that $m \angle 1 = m \angle 2$.

SOLUTION

To show ∠ 1 ≅ ∠ 2, we relate both to ∠ 3. Because $\overleftrightarrow{EF} \parallel \overleftrightarrow{GH}$, corresponding angles 1 and 3 are congruent. Since $\overleftrightarrow{AB} \parallel \overleftrightarrow{CD}$, corresponding angles 3 and 2 are congruent. Because both ∠ 1 and ∠ 2 are congruent to the same angle, it follows that ∠ 1 ≅ ∠ 2.

	Statement		Reason
1.	$\overleftrightarrow{EF} \parallel \overleftrightarrow{GH}$	1.	Given.
2.	$m \angle 1 = m \angle 3$	2.	If two parallel lines are cut by a trans-

versal, corresponding angles are of
equal measure.

3. $\overleftrightarrow{AB} \parallel \overleftrightarrow{CD}$

3. Given.

4. $m \angle 2 = m \angle 3$

4. If two parallel lines are cut by a transversal, corresponding angles are equal
in measure.

5. $m \angle 1 = m \angle 2$

5. If two quantities are equal to the same
quantity, they are equal to each other.

☞ Drill: Lines and Angles

Intersection Lines

1. Find *a*.

(A) 38°   (B) 68°   (C) 78°

(D) 90°   (E) 112°

2. Find *c*.

(A) 32°   (B) 48°   (C) 58°

(D) 82°   (E) 148°

3. Determine *x*.

(A) 21°   (B) 23°   (C) 51°

(D) 102°   (E) 153°

4. Find *x*.

(A) 8   (B) 11.75   (C) 21

(D) 23   (E) 32

5. Find *z*.

(A) 29°   (B) 54°   (C) 61°

(D) 88°   (E) 92°

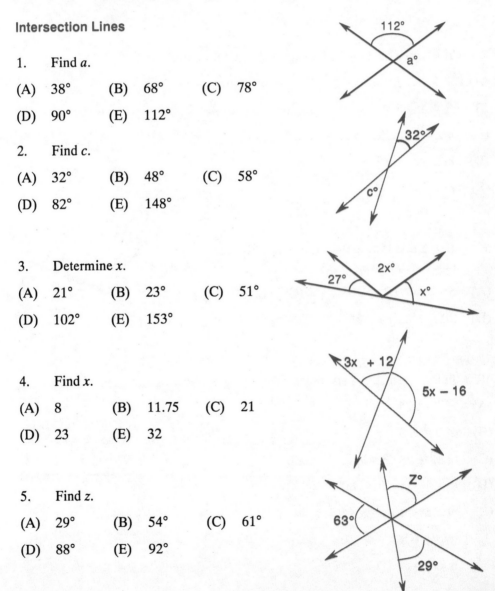

Perpendicular Lines

6. $\overrightarrow{BA} \perp \overrightarrow{BC}$ and $m \angle DBC = 53$. Find $m \angle ABD$.

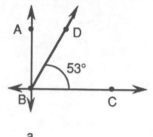

(A) 27°   (B) 33°   (C) 37°

(D) 53°   (E) 90°

7. $m \angle 1 = 90°$. Find $m \angle 2$.

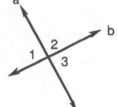

(A) 80°   (B) 90°   (C) 100°

(D) 135°   (E) 180°

8. If $n \perp p$, which of the following statements is true?

(A) $\angle 1 \cong \angle 2$

(B) $\angle 4 \cong \angle 5$

(C) $m\angle 4 + m \angle 5 > m \angle 1 + m \angle 2$

(D) $m \angle 3 > m \angle 2$

(E) $m \angle 4 = 90°$

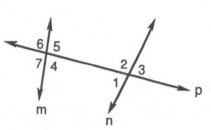

9. $\overleftrightarrow{CD} \perp \overleftrightarrow{EF}$. If $m \angle 1 = 2x$, $m \angle 2 = 30°$, and $m \angle 3 = x$, find x.

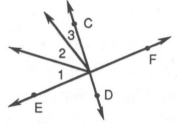

(A) 5°   (B) 10°   (C) 12°

(D) 20°   (E) 25°

10. In the figure, $p \perp t$ and $q \perp t$. Which of the following statements is false?

(A) $\angle 1 \cong \angle 4$

(B) $\angle 2 \cong \angle 3$

(C) $m\angle 2 + m \angle 3 = m \angle 4 + m \angle 6$

(D) $m \angle 5 + m \angle 6 = 180°$

(E) $m \angle 2 > m \angle 5$

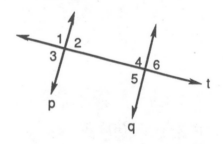

Parallel Lines

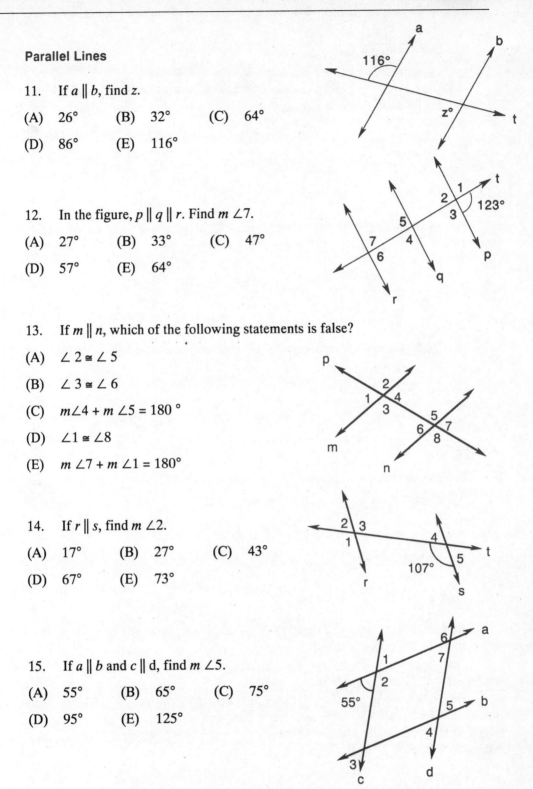

11. If $a \parallel b$, find z.

(A) 26°   (B) 32°   (C) 64°

(D) 86°   (E) 116°

12. In the figure, $p \parallel q \parallel r$. Find $m \angle 7$.

(A) 27°   (B) 33°   (C) 47°

(D) 57°   (E) 64°

13. If $m \parallel n$, which of the following statements is false?

(A) $\angle 2 \cong \angle 5$

(B) $\angle 3 \cong \angle 6$

(C) $m\angle 4 + m \angle 5 = 180°$

(D) $\angle 1 \cong \angle 8$

(E) $m \angle 7 + m \angle 1 = 180°$

14. If $r \parallel s$, find $m \angle 2$.

(A) 17°   (B) 27°   (C) 43°

(D) 67°   (E) 73°

15. If $a \parallel b$ and $c \parallel d$, find $m \angle 5$.

(A) 55°   (B) 65°   (C) 75°

(D) 95°   (E) 125°

2. POLYGONS (CONVEX)

A **polygon** is a figure with the same number of sides as angles.

An **equilateral polygon** is a polygon all of whose sides are of equal measure.

An **equiangular polygon** is a polygon all of whose angles are of equal measure.

A **regular polygon** is a polygon that is both equilateral and equiangular.

PROBLEM

Each interior angle of a regular polygon contains 120°. How many sides does the polygon have?

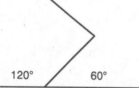

SOLUTION

At each vertex of a polygon, the exterior angle is supplementary to the interior angle, as shown in the diagram.

Since we are told that the interior angles measure 120 degrees, we can deduce that the exterior angle measures 60°.

Each exterior angle of a regular polygon of n sides measure $360°/_n$ degrees. We know that each exterior angle measures 60°, and, therefore, by setting $360°/_n$ equal to 60°, we can determine the number of sides in the polygon. The calculation is as follows:

$$360°/_n = 60°$$

$$60°n = 360°$$

$$n = 6.$$

Therefore, the regular polygon, with interior angles of 120°, has 6 sides and is called a hexagon.

The area of a regular polygon can be determined by using the **apothem** and **radius** of the polygon. The apothem (*a*) of a regular polygon is the segment from the center of the polygon perpendicular to a side of the polygon. The radius (*r*) of a regular polygon is the segment joining any vertex of a regular polygon with the center of that polygon.

(1) All radii of a regular polygon are congruent.

(2) The radius of a regular polygon is congruent to a side.

(3) All apothems of a regular polygon are congruent.

The **area** of a regular polygon equals one-half the product of the length of the apothem and the perimeter.

Area = $^1\!/_2\, a \cdot p$

PROBLEM

Find area of the regular pentagon whose radius is 8 and whose apothem is 6.

SOLUTION

If the radius is 8, the length of a side is also 8. Therefore, the perimeter of the polygon is 40.

$A = ^1\!/_2\, a \cdot p$

$A = ^1\!/_2\, (6)\, (40)$

$A = 120.$

PROBLEM

Find the area of a regular hexagon if one side has length 6.

SOLUTION

Since the length of a side equals 6, the radius also equals 6 and the perimeter equals 36. The base of the right triangle, formed by the radius and apothem, is half the length of a side, or 3. Using the Pythagorean Theorem, you can find the length of the apothem.

$a^2 + b^2 = c^2$

$a^2 + (3)^2 = (6)^2$

$a^2 = 36 - 9$

$a^2 = 27$

$a = 3\sqrt{3}$

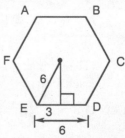

The apothem equals $3\sqrt{3}$. Therefore, the area of the hexagon

$$= \frac{1}{2} a \cdot p$$
$$= \frac{1}{2} (3\sqrt{3})(36)$$
$$= 54\sqrt{3}$$

☞ Drill: Regular Polygons

1. Find the measure of an interior angle of a regular pentagon.

(A) 55   (B) 72   (C) 90   (D) 108   (E) 540

2. Find the measure of an exterior angle of a regular octagon.

(A) 40   (B) 45   (C) 135   (D) 540   (E) 1080

3. Find the sum of the measures of the exterior angles of a regular triangle.

(A) 90   (B) 115   (C) 180   (D) 250   (E) 360

4. Find the area of a square with a perimeter of 12 cm.

(A) 9 cm^2 (B) 12 cm^2 (C) 48 cm^2 (D) 96 cm^2 (E) 144 cm^2

5. A regular triangle has sides of 24 mm. If the apothem is $4\sqrt{3}$ mm, find the area of the triangle.

(A) 72 mm^2 (B) $96\sqrt{3} \text{ mm}^2$ (C) 144 mm^2

(D) $144\sqrt{3} \text{ mm}^2$ (E) 576 mm^2

6. Find the area of a regular hexagon with sides of 4 cm.

(A) $12\sqrt{3} \text{ cm}^2$ (B) 24 cm^2 (C) $24\sqrt{3} \text{ cm}^2$

(D) 48 cm^2 (E) $48\sqrt{3} \text{ cm}^2$

7. Find the area of a regular decagon with sides of length 6 cm and an apothem of length 9.2 cm.

(A) 55.2 cm^2 (B) 60 cm^2 (C) 138 cm^2

(D) 138.3 cm^2 (E) 276 cm^2

8. The perimeter of a regular heptagon (7-gon) is 36.4 cm. Find the length of each side.

(A) 4.8 cm   (B) 5.2 cm   (C) 6.7 cm   (D) 7 cm   (E) 10.4 cm

9.   The apothem of a regular quadrilateral is 4 in. Find the perimeter.

(A)   12 in.   (B)   16 in.   (C)   24 in.   (D)   32 in.   (E)   64 in.

10.   A regular triangle has a perimeter of 18 cm; a regular pentagon has a perimeter of 30 cm; a regular hexagon has a perimeter of 33 cm. Which figure (or figures) have sides with the longest measure?

(A)   regular triangle

(B)   regular triangle and regular pentagon

(C)   regular pentagon

(D)   regular pentagon and regular hexagon

(E)   regular hexagon

---

3. TRIANGLES

A closed three-sided geometric figure is called a **triangle**. The points of the intersection of the sides of a triangle are called the **vertices** of the triangle.

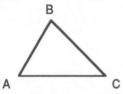

The **perimeter** of a triangle is the sum of the measures of the sides of the triangle.

A triangle with no equal sides is called a **scalene** triangle.

A triangle having at least two equal sides is called an **isosceles** triangle. The third side is called the **base** of the triangle. AB = AC, BC is the base.

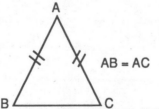

A side of a triangle is a line segment whose endpoints are the vertices of two angles of the triangle.

An interior angle of a triangle is an angle formed by two sides and includes the third side within its collection of points.

An **equilateral triangle** is a triangle having three equal sides. $AB = AC = BC$

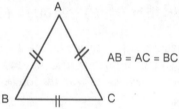

$$AB = AC = BC$$

A triangle with one obtuse angle greater than 90° is called an **obtuse triangle**.

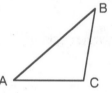

An **acute triangle** is a triangle with three acute angles (less than 90°).

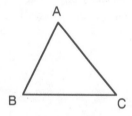

A triangle with a right angle is called a **right triangle**. The side opposite the right angle in a right triangle is called the hypotenuse of the right triangle. The other two sides are called arms or legs of the right triangle.

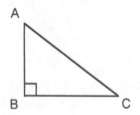

An **altitude** of a triangle is a line segment from a vertex of the triangle perpendicular to the opposite side.

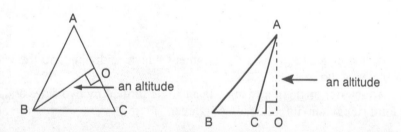

an altitude   an altitude

A line segment connecting a vertex of a triangle and the midpoint of the opposite side is called a **median** of the triangle.

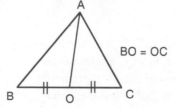

$BO = OC$

A line that bisects and is perpendicular to a side of a triangle is called a **perpendicular bisector** of that side.

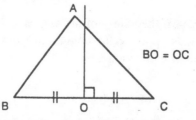

$BO = OC$

An **angle bisector** of a triangle is a line that bisects an angle and extends to the opposite side of the triangle.

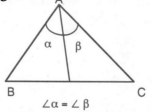

$\angle \alpha = \angle \beta$

The line segment that joins the midpoints of two sides of a triangle is called a **midline** of the triangle.

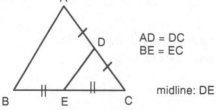

$AD = DC$
$BE = EC$

midline: DE

An **exterior angle** of a triangle is an angle formed outside a triangle by one side of the triangle and the extension of an adjacent side.

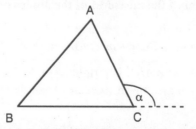

A triangle whose three interior angles have equal measure (60° each) is said to be **equiangular**.

Three or more lines (or rays or segments) are concurrent if there exists one point common to all of them, that is, if they all intersect at the same point.

PROBLEM

The measure of the vertex angle of an isosceles triangle exceeds the measurement of each base angle by 30°. Find the value of each angle of the triangle.

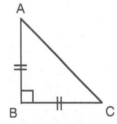

SOLUTION

We know that the sum of the values of the angles of a triangle is 180°. In an isosceles triangle, the angles opposite the congruent sides (the base angles) are, themselves, congruent and of equal value.

Therefore,

(1) Let x = the measure of each base angle.

(2) Then $x + 30$ = the measure of the vertex angle.

We can solve for x algebraically by keeping in mind the sum of all the measures will be 180°.

$$x + x + (x + 30) = 180$$
$$3x + 30 = 180$$
$$3x = 150$$
$$x = 50$$

Therefore, the base angles each measure 50°, and the vertex angle measures 80°.

PROBLEM

Prove that the base angles of an isosceles right triangle have measure 45°.

SOLUTION

As drawn in the figure, $\triangle ABC$ is an isosceles right triangle with base angles BAC and BCA. The sum of the measures of the angles of any triangle is 180°. For $\triangle ABC$, this means

$$m \angle BAC + m \angle BCA + m \angle ABC = 180° \qquad (1)$$

But $m \angle ABC = 90°$ because ABC is a right triangle. Furthermore, $m \angle BCA = m \angle BAC$, since the base angles of an isosceles triangle are congruent. Using these facts in equation (1)

$$m \angle BAC + m \angle BCA + 90° = 180°$$

or $\qquad 2m \angle BAC = 2m \angle BCA = 90°$

or $m \angle BAC = m \angle BCA = 45°$.

Therefore, the base angles of an isosceles right triangle have measure 45°.

The area of a triangle is given by the formula $A = \frac{1}{2} bh$, where b is the length of a base, which can be any side of the triangle and h is the corresponding height of the triangle, which is the perpendicular line segment that is drawn from the vertex opposite the base to the base itself.

$A = \frac{1}{2} bh$

$A = \frac{1}{2} (10) (3)$

$A = 15$

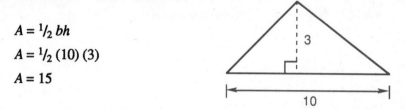

The area of a right triangle is found by taking $\frac{1}{2}$ the product of the lengths of its two arms.

$A = \frac{1}{2} (5) (12)$
$A = 30$

☞ Drill: Triangles

Angle Measures

1. In $\triangle PQR$, $\angle Q$ is a right angle. Find $m \angle R$.

    (A) 27°   (B) 33°   (C) 54°

    (D) 67°   (E) 157°

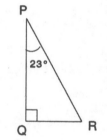

2. $\triangle MNO$ is isosceles. If the vertex angle, $\angle N$, has a measure of 96°, find the measure of $\angle M$.

    (A) 21°   (B) 42°   (C) 64°

    (D) 84°   (E) 96°

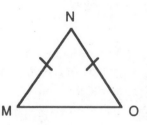

3. Find x.

    (A) 15°   (B) 25°   (C) 30°

    (D) 45°   (E) 90°

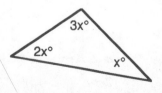

4. Find *m* ∠1.

(A) 40   (B) 66   (C) 74

(D) 114   (E) 140

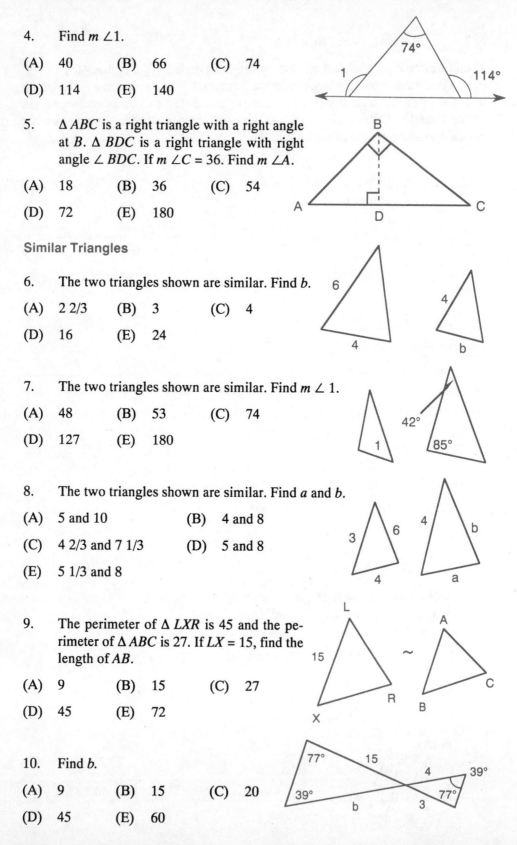

5. Δ *ABC* is a right triangle with a right angle at *B*. Δ *BDC* is a right triangle with right angle ∠ *BDC*. If *m* ∠*C* = 36. Find *m* ∠*A*.

(A) 18   (B) 36   (C) 54

(D) 72   (E) 180

Similar Triangles

6. The two triangles shown are similar. Find *b*.

(A) 2 2/3   (B) 3   (C) 4

(D) 16   (E) 24

7. The two triangles shown are similar. Find *m* ∠ 1.

(A) 48   (B) 53   (C) 74

(D) 127   (E) 180

8. The two triangles shown are similar. Find *a* and *b*.

(A) 5 and 10   (B) 4 and 8

(C) 4 2/3 and 7 1/3   (D) 5 and 8

(E) 5 1/3 and 8

9. The perimeter of Δ *LXR* is 45 and the perimeter of Δ *ABC* is 27. If *LX* = 15, find the length of *AB*.

(A) 9   (B) 15   (C) 27

(D) 45   (E) 72

10. Find *b*.

(A) 9   (B) 15   (C) 20

(D) 45   (E) 60

Area

11. Find the area of △ *MNO*.

(A) 22   (B) 49   (C) 56

(D) 84   (E) 112

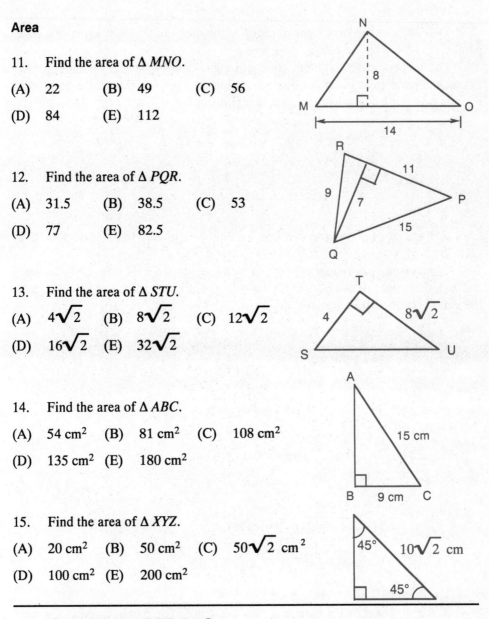

12. Find the area of △ *PQR*.

(A) 31.5   (B) 38.5   (C) 53

(D) 77   (E) 82.5

13. Find the area of △ *STU*.

(A) $4\sqrt{2}$ (B) $8\sqrt{2}$ (C) $12\sqrt{2}$

(D) $16\sqrt{2}$ (E) $32\sqrt{2}$

14. Find the area of △ *ABC*.

(A) 54 cm^2 (B) 81 cm^2 (C) 108 cm^2

(D) 135 cm^2 (E) 180 cm^2

15. Find the area of △ *XYZ*.

(A) 20 cm^2 (B) 50 cm^2 (C) $50\sqrt{2} \text{ cm}^2$

(D) 100 cm^2 (E) 200 cm^2

---

4. QUADRILATERALS

A **quadrilateral** is a polygon with four sides.

PARALLELOGRAMS

A **parallelogram** is a quadrilateral whose opposite sides are parallel.

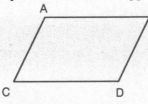

Two angles that have their vertices at the endpoints of the same side of a parallelogram are called **consecutive angles**.

The perpendicular segment connecting any point of a line containing one side of the parallelogram to the line containing the opposite side of the parallelogram is called the **altitude** of the parallelogram.

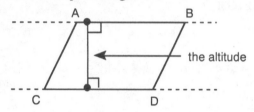

A diagonal of a polygon is a line segment joining any two non-consecutive vertices.

The area of a parallelogram is given by the formula $A = bh$ where b is the base and h is the height drawn perpendicular to that base. Note that the height equals the altitude of the parallelogram.

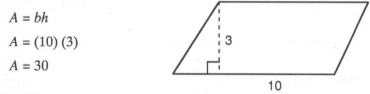

$A = bh$

$A = (10)\,(3)$

$A = 30$

RECTANGLES

A rectangle is a parallelogram with right angles.

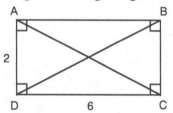

The diagonals of a rectangle are equal.

If the diagonals of a parallelogram are equal, the parallelogram is a rectangle.

If a quadrilateral has four right angles, then it is a rectangle.

The area of a rectangle is given by the formula $A = lw$ where l is the length and w is the width.

$A = lw$

$A = (3)\,(10)$

$A = 30$

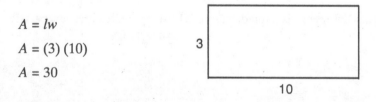

RHOMBI

A rhombus is a parallelogram.

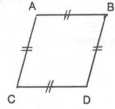

All sides of a rhombus are equal.
The diagonals of a rhombus are perpendicular to each other.

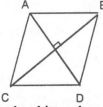

The diagonals of a rhombus bisect the angles of the rhombus.

If the diagonals of a parallelogram are perpendicular, the parallelogram is a rhombus.

If a quadrilateral has four equal sides, then it is a rhombus.

A parallelogram is a rhombus if either diagonal of the parallelogram bisects the angles of the vertices it joins.

SQUARES

A square is a rhombus with a right angle.

A square is an equilateral quadrilateral.

A square has all the properties of parallelograms and rectangles.

A rhombus is a square if one of its interior angles is a right angle.

In a square, the measure of either diagonal can be calculated by multiplying the length of any side by the square root of 2.

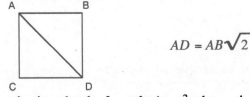

$$AD = AB\sqrt{2}$$

The area of a square is given by the formula $A = s^2$ where s is the side of the square. Since all sides of a square are equal, it does not matter which side is used.

$A = s^2$

$A = 6^2$

$A = 36$

The area of a square can also be found by taking $1/2$ the product of the length of the diagonal squared.

$A = {}^1\!/_2\, d^2$

$A = {}^1\!/_2\, (8)^2$

$A = 32$

TRAPEZOIDS

A **trapezoid** is a quadrilateral with two and only two sides parallel. The parallel sides of a trapezoid are called **bases**.

The **median** of a trapezoid is the line joining the midpoints of the non-parallel sides.

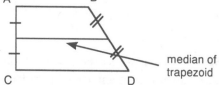

The perpendicular segment connecting any point in the line containing one base of the trapezoid to the line containing the other base is the **altitude** of the trapezoid.

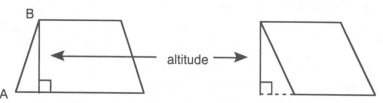

An **isosceles trapezoid** is a trapezoid whose non-parallel sides are equal. A pair of angles including only one of the parallel sides is called **a pair of base angles**.

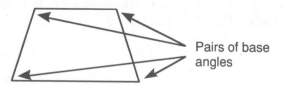

The median of a trapezoid is parallel to the bases and equal to one-half their sum.

The base angles of an isosceles trapezoid are equal.

The diagonals of an isosceles trapezoid are equal.

The opposite angles of an isosceles trapezoid are supplementary.

PROBLEM

Prove that all pairs of consecutive angles of a parallelogram are supplementary. (See figure.)

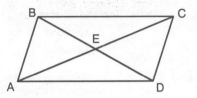

SOLUTION

We must prove that the pairs of angles ∠ BAD and ∠ ADC, ∠ ADC and ∠ DCB, ∠ DCB and ∠ CBA, and ∠ CBA and ∠ BAD are supplementary. (This means that the sum of their measures is 180°.)

Because ABCD is a parallelogram, $\overline{AB} \parallel \overline{CD}$. Angles BAD and ADC are consecutive interior angles, as are ∠ CBA and ∠ DCB. Since the consecutive interior angles formed by 2 parallel lines and a transversal are supplementary, ∠ BAD and ∠ ADC are supplementary, as are ∠ CBA and ∠ DCB.

Similarly, $\overline{AD} \parallel \overline{BC}$. Angles ADC and DCB are consecutive interior angles, as are ∠ CBA and ∠ BAD. Since the consecutive interior angles formed by 2 parallel lines and a transversal are supplementary, ∠ CBA and ∠ BAD are supplementary, as are ∠ ADC and ∠ DCB.

PROBLEM

In the accompanying figure, Δ ABC is given to be an isosceles right triangle with ∠ ABC a right angle and $\overline{AB} \cong \overline{BC}$. Line segment $\overline{BD}$, which bisects $\overline{CA}$, is extended to E, so that $\overline{BD} \cong \overline{DE}$. Prove BAEC is a square.

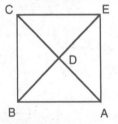

SOLUTION

A square is a rectangle in which two consecutive sides are congruent. This definition will provide the framework for the proof in this problem. We will prove that BAEC is a parallelogram that is specifically a rectangle with consecutive sides congruent, namely a square.

Statement	Reason
1. $\overline{BD} \cong \overline{DE}$ and $\overline{AD} \cong \overline{DC}$	1. Given ($\overline{BD}$ bisects $\overline{CA}$).
2. BAEC is a parallelogram	2. If diagonals of a quadrilateral bisect each other, then the quadrilateral is a parallelogram.
3. ∠ ABC is a right angle	3. Given.
4. BAEC is a rectangle	4. A parallelogram, one of whose angles is a right angle, is a rectangle.
5. $\overline{AB} \cong \overline{BC}$	5. Given.

6. *BAEC* is a square

6. If a rectangle has two congruent con-
    secutive sides, then the rectangle is a
    square.

👉 Drill: Quadrilaterals

Parallelograms, Rectangles, Rhombuses, Squares, Trapezoids

1. In parallelogram *WXYZ*, $\overline{WX}$ = 14, $\overline{WZ}$ = 6,
    ZY = 3*x* + 5, and *XY* = 2*y* – 4. Find *x* and *y*.

    (A)   3 and 5   (B)   4 and 5   (C)   4 and 6

    (D)   6 and 10   (E)   6 and 14

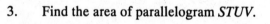

2. Quadrilateral *ABCD* is a parellelogram. If
    m ∠ *B* = 6*x* + 2 and *m* ∠ *D* = 98, find *x*.

    (A)   12   (B)   16   (C)   16 2/3

    (D)   18   (E)   20

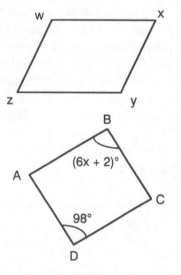

3. Find the area of parallelogram *STUV*.

    (A)   56   (B)   90   (C)   108

    (D)   162   (E)   180

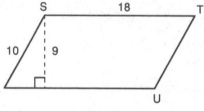

4. Find the area of parallelogram *MNOP*.

    (A)   19   (B)   32   (C) $32\sqrt{3}$

    (D)   44   (E) $44\sqrt{3}$

5. Find the perimeter of rectangle *PQRS*.

    (A)   31 in.   (B)   38 in.

    (C)   40 in.   (D)   44 in.

    (E)   121 in.

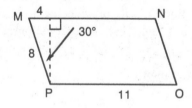

6. In rectangle $ABCD$, $AD = 6$ cm and $\overline{DC} = 8$ cm. Find the length of the diagonal $\overline{AC}$.

(A)   10 cm   (B)   12 cm   (C)   20 cm

(D)   28 cm   (E)   48 cm

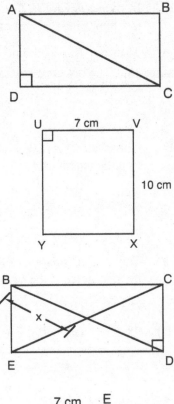

7. Find the area of rectangle $UVXY$.

(A)   17 cm²   (B)   34 cm²   (C)   35 cm²

(D)   70 cm²   (E)   140 cm²

8. Find x in rectangle $BCDE$ if the diagonal $\overline{EC}$ is 17 mm.

(A)   6.55 mm   (B)   8 mm   (C)   8.5 mm

(D)   17 mm   (E)   34 mm

9. In rhombus $DEFG$, $\overline{DE} = 7$ cm. Find the perimeter of the rhombus.

(A)   14 cm   (B)   28 cm   (C)   42 cm

(D)   49 cm   (E)   56 cm

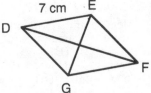

10. In rhombus $RHOM$, the diagonal $\overline{RO}$ is 8 cm and the diagonal $\overline{HM}$ is 12 cm. Find the area of the rhombus.

(A)   20 cm²   (B)   40 cm²   (C)   48 cm²

(D)   68 cm²   (E)   96 cm²

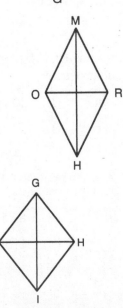

11. In rhombus $GHIJ$, $\overline{GI} = 6$ cm and $\overline{HJ} = 8$ cm. Find the length of $\overline{GH}$.

(A)   3 cm   (B)   4 cm   (C)   5 cm

(D) $4\sqrt{3}$ cm   (E)   14 cm

12. In rhombus *CDEF*, $\overline{CD}$ is 13 mm and $\overline{DX}$ is 5 mm. Find the area of the rhombus.

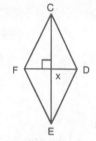

(A) 31 mm²   (B) 60 mm²   (C) 78 mm²

(D) 120 mm²   (E) 260 mm²

13. Quadrilateral *ATUV* is a square. If the perimeter of the square is 44 cm, find the length of $\overline{AT}$.

(A) 4 cm   (B) 11 cm   (C) 22 cm   (D) 30 cm   (E) 40 cm

14. The area of square *XYZW* is 196 cm². Find the perimeter of the square.

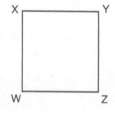

(A) 28 cm   (B) 42 cm   (C) 56 cm

(D) 98 cm   (E) 196 cm

15. In square *MNOP*, $\overline{MN}$ is 6 cm. Find the length of diagonal $\overline{MO}$.

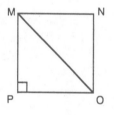

(A) 6 cm   (B) $6\sqrt{2}$ cm   (C) $6\sqrt{3}$ cm

(D) $6\sqrt{6}$ cm   (E) 12 cm

16. In square *ABCD*, *AB* = 3 cm. Find the area of the square.

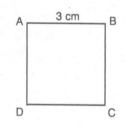

(A) 9 cm²   (B) 12 cm²   (C) 15 cm²

(D) 18 cm²   (D) 21 cm²

17. Find the area of trapezoid *RSTU*.

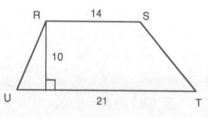

(A) 80   (B) 87.5   (C) 140

(D) 147   (E) 175

18. *ABCD* is an isosceles trapezoid. Find the perimeter.

(A) 21 cm (B) 27 cm (C) 30 cm

(D) 50 cm (E) 54 cm

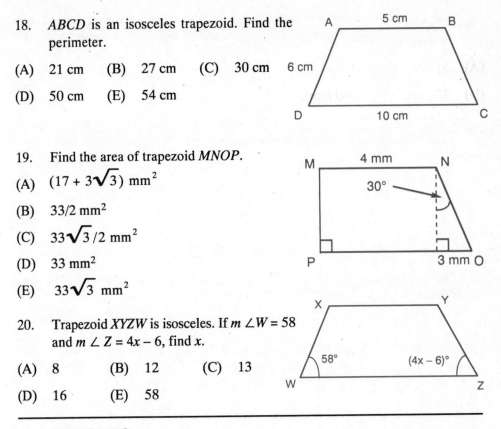

19. Find the area of trapezoid *MNOP*.

(A) $(17 + 3\sqrt{3})$ mm^2

(B) 33/2 mm^2

(C) $33\sqrt{3}/2$ mm^2

(D) 33 mm^2

(E) $33\sqrt{3}$ mm^2

20. Trapezoid *XYZW* is isosceles. If $m \angle W = 58$ and $m \angle Z = 4x - 6$, find *x*.

(A) 8 (B) 12 (C) 13

(D) 16 (E) 58

5. CIRCLES

A **circle** is a set of points in the same plane equidistant from a fixed point, called its center.

A **radius** of a circle is a line segment drawn from the center of the circle to any point on the circle.

A portion of a circle is called an **arc** of the circle.

A line that intersects a circle in two points is called a **secant.**

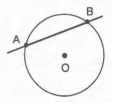

A line segment joining two points on a circle is called a **chord** of the circle.

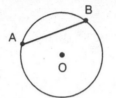

A chord that passes through the center of the circle is called a **diameter** of the circle.

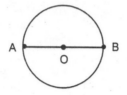

The line passing through the centers of two (or more) circles is called the **line of centers**.

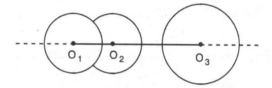

An angle whose vertex is on the circle and whose sides are chords of the circle is called an **inscribed angle**.

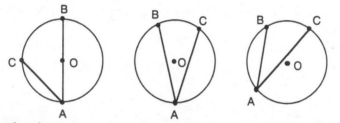

An angle whose vertex is at the center of a circle and whose sides are radii is called a **central angle.**

The measure of a minor arc is the measure of the central angle that intercepts that arc.

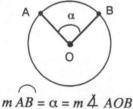

$$m \overarc{AB} = \alpha = m \angle AOB$$

The distance from a point P to a given circle is the distance from that point to the point where the circle intersects with a line segment with endpoints at the center of the circle and point P.

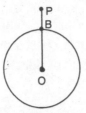

The distance of point P to the diagrammed circle with center O is the line segment $\overline{PB}$ of line segment PO.

A line that has one and only one point of intersection with a circle is called a tangent to that circle, while their common point is called a **point of tangency**.

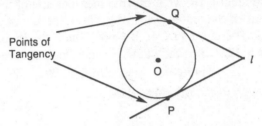

Points of Tangency

Congruent circles are circles whose radii are congruent.

If $O_1A_1 \cong O_2A_2$, then $O_1 \cong O_2$.

The measure of a semicircle is 180°.

A **circumscribed circle** is a circle passing through all the vertices of a polygon.

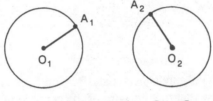

Circles that have the same center and unequal radii are called **concentric circles**.

Concentric Circles

PROBLEM

A and *B* are points on circle *Q* such that △*AQB* is equilateral. If length of side $\overline{AB}$ = 12, find the length of arc $\overset{\frown}{AB}$.

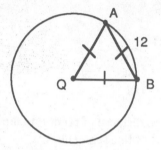

SOLUTION

To find the arc length of $\overset{\frown}{AB}$, we must find the measure of the central angle ∠ *AQB* and the measure of the radius $\overline{QA}$. ∠ *AQB* is an interior angle of the equilateral triangle △ *AQB*. Therefore, $m\angle AQB = 60°$. Similarly, in the equilateral △ *AQB*, $AQ = AB = QB = 12$. Given the radius, *r*, and the central angle, *n*, the arc length is given by $n/360 \cdot 2\pi r$. Therefore, by substitution, $^{60}/_{360} \cdot 2\pi \cdot 12 = ^{1}/_{6} \cdot 2\pi \cdot 12 = 4\pi$. Therefore, length of arc $\overset{\frown}{AB} = 4\pi$.

PROBLEM

In circle *O*, the measure of $\overset{\frown}{AB}$ is 80°. Find the measure of ∠ *A*.

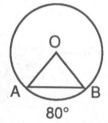

SOLUTION

The accompanying figure shows that $\overset{\frown}{AB}$ is intercepted by central angle *AOB*. By definition, we know that the measure of the central angle is the measure of its intercepted arc. In this case,

$$m\overset{\frown}{AB} = m \angle AOB = 80°.$$

Radius $\overline{OA}$ and radius $\overline{OB}$ are congruent and form two sides of △*OAB*. By a theorem, the angles opposite these two congruent sides must, themselves, be congruent. Therefore, $m \angle A = m \angle B$.

The sum of the measures of the angles of a triangle is 180°. Therefore,

$$m \angle A + m \angle B + m \angle AOB = 180°.$$
Since $m \angle A = m \angle B$, we can write

$$m \angle A + m \angle A + 80° = 180°$$

or $2m\angle A = 100°$

or $m \angle A = 50°$.

Therefore, the measure of ∠ *A* is 50°.

☞ Drill: Circles

Circumference, Area, Concentric Circles

1. Find the circumference of circle A if its radius is 3 mm.

(A) 3π mm (B) 6π mm (C) 9π mm (D) 12π mm (E) 15π mm

2. The circumference of circle H is 20π cm Find the length of the radius.

(A) 10 cm (B) 20 cm (C) 10π cm (D) 15π cm (E) 20π cm

3. The circumference of circle A is how many millimeters larger than the circumference of circle B?

(A) 3 (B) 6 (C) 3π

(D) 6π (E) 7π

4. If the diameter of circle X is 9 cm and if $\pi = 3.14$, find the circumference of the circle to the nearest tenth.

(A) 9 cm (B) 14.1 cm (C) 21.1 cm (D) 24.6 cm (E) 28.3 cm

5. Find the area of circle I.

(A) 22 mm^2 (B) 121 mm

(C) 121π mm^2 (D) 132 mm^2

(E) 132π mm

6. The diameter of circle Z is 27 mm. Find the area of the circle.

(A) 91.125 mm^2 (B) 182.25 mm^2 (C) 191.5π mm^2

(D) 182.25π mm^2 (E) 729 mm^2

7. The area of circle B is 225π cm^2. Find the length of the diameter of the circle.

(A) 15 cm (B) 20 cm (C) 30 cm (D) 20π cm (E) 25π cm

8. The area of circle X is 144π mm^2 while the area of circle Y is 81π mm^2. Write the ratio of the radius of circle X to that of circle Y.

(A) $3:4$ (B) $4:3$ (D) $9:12$ (D) $27:12$ (E) $18:24$

9. The circumference of circle M is 18π cm. Find the area of the circle.

(A) 18π cm^2 (B) 81 cm^2 (C) 36 cm^2 (D) 36π cm^2 (E) 81π cm^2

10. In two concentric circles, the smaller circle has a radius of 3 mm while the larger circle has a radius of 5 mm. Find the area of the shaded region.

(A) 2π mm^2 (B) 8π mm^2

(C) 13π mm^2 (D) 16π mm^2

(E) 26π mm^2

11. The radius of the smaller of two concentric circles is 5 cm while the radius of the larger circle is 7 cm. Determine the area of the shaded region.

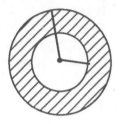

(A) 7π cm^2 (B) 24π cm^2

(C) 25π cm^2 (D) 36π cm^2

(E) 49π cm^2

12. Find the measure of arc MN if $m \angle MON = 62°$.

(A) 16°   (B) 32°   (C) 59°

(D) 62°   (E) 124°

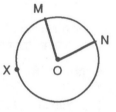

13. Find the measure of arc AXC.

(A) 150°   (B) 160°   (C) 180°

(D) 270°   (E) 360°

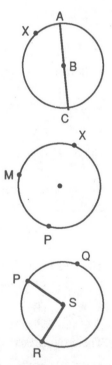

14. If arc $MXP = 236°$, find the measure of arc MP.

(A) 62°   (B) 124°   (C) 236°

(D) 270°   (E) 360°

15. In circle S, major arc PQR has a measure of 298°. Find the measure of the central angle $\angle PSR$.

(A) 62°   (B) 124°   (C) 149°

(D) 298°   (E) 360°

16. Find the measure of arc *XY* in circle *W*.

(A) 40°   (B) 120°   (C) 140°

(D) 180°   (E) 220°

17. Find the area of the sector shown.

(A) 4 cm²   (B) 2π cm²   (C) 16 cm²

(D) 8π cm²   (E) 16π cm²

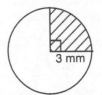

18. Find the area of the shaded region.

(A) 10   (B) 5π   (C) 25

(D) 20π   (E) 25π

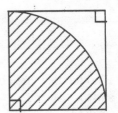

19. Find the area of the shaded sector shown.

(A) $\dfrac{9\pi \text{ mm}^2}{4}$ (B) $\dfrac{9\pi \text{ mm}^2}{2}$ (C) 18 mm²

(D) 6π mm²   (E) 9π mm²

20. If the area of the square is 100 cm², find the area of the shaded sector.

(A) 10π cm²   (B) 25 cm²   (C) 25π cm²

(D) 100 cm²   (E) 100π cm²

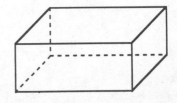

6. SOLIDS

Solid geometry is the study of figures which consist of points not all in the same plane.

RECTANGULAR SOLIDS

A solid with lateral faces and bases that are rectangles is called a **rectangular solid**.

The surface area of a rectangular solid is the sum of the areas of all the faces.

The volume of a rectangular solid is equal to the product of its length, width, and height.

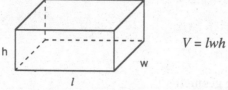

$V = lwh$

PROBLEM

What are the dimensions of a solid cube whose surface area is numerically equal to its volume?

SOLUTION

The surface area of a cube of edge length a is equal to the sum of the areas of its 6 faces. Since a cube is a regular polygon, all 6 faces are congruent. Each face of a cube is a square of edge length a. Hence, the surface area of a cube of edge length a is

$$S = 6a^2.$$

The volume of a cube of edge length a is

$$V = a^3.$$

We require that $A = V$, or that

$$6a^2 = a^3 \quad \text{or} \quad a = 6$$

Hence, if a cube has edge length 6, its surface area will be numerically equal to its volume.

☞ Drill: Solids

1. Find the total area of the rectangular prism shown.

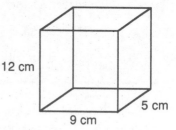

(A) 138 cm² (B) 336 cm² (C) 381 cm²

(D) 426 cm² (D) 540 cm²

2. Find the volume of the rectangular storage tank shown.

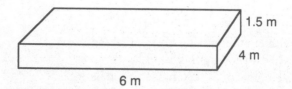

(A) 24 m³ (B) 36 m³ (C) 38 m³ (D) 42 m³ (E) 45 m³

3. The lateral area of a cube is 100 cm². Find the length of an edge of the cube.

(A) 4 cm   (B)   5 cm   (C)   10 cm (D)   12 cm (E)   15 cm

7. COORDINATE GEOMETRY

Coordinate geometry refers to the study of geometric figures using algebraic principles.

The graph shown is called the Cartesian coordinate plane. The graph consists of a pair of perpendicular lines called **coordinate axes**. The **vertical axis** is the *y*-axis and the **horizontal axis** is the *x*-axis. The point of intersection of these two axes is called the **origin**; it is the zero point of both axes.

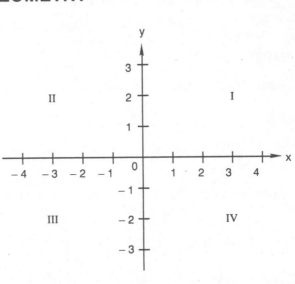

Furthermore, points to the right of the origin on the *x*-axis and above the origin on the *y*-axis represent positive real numbers. Points to the left of the origin on the *x*-axis or below the origin on the *y*-axis represent negative real numbers.

The four regions cut off by the coordinate axes are, in counterclockwise direction from the top right, called the first, second, third, and fourth quadrant, respectively. The first quadrant contains all points with two positive coordinates.

In the graph shown, two points are identified by the ordered pair, (*x*, *y*) of numbers. The *x*-coordinate is the first number and the *y*-coordinate is the second number.

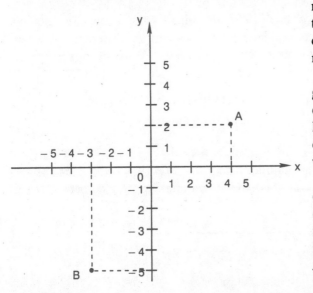

To plot a point on the graph when given the coordinates, draw perpendicular lines from the number-line coordinates to the point where the two lines intersect.

To find the coordinates of a given point on the graph, draw perpendicular lines from the point to the coordinates on the number line. The *x*-coordinate is written before the y-coordinate and a comma is used to separate the two.

In this case, point A has the co-ordinates (4, 2) and the coordinates of point B are (− 3, − 5).

For any two points A and B with coordinates (X_A, Y_A) and (X_B, Y_B), respectively, the distance between A and B is represented by:

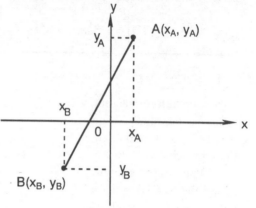

$$AB = \sqrt{(X_A - X_B)^2 + (Y_A - Y_B)^2}$$

This is commonly known as the distance formula.

PROBLEM

Find the distance between the point A(1, 3) and B(5, 3).

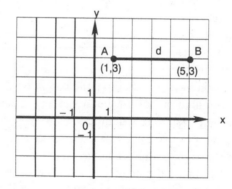

SOLUTION

In this case, where the ordinate of both points is the same, the distance between the two points is given by the absolute value of the difference between the two abscissas. In fact, this case reduces to merely counting boxes as the figure shows.

Let, x_1 = abscissa of A y_1 = ordinate of A

x_2 = abscissa of B y_2 = ordinate of B

d = the distance.

Therefore, $d = |x_1 - x_2|$. By substitution, $d = |1 - 5| = |-4| = 4$. This answer can also be obtained by applying the general formula for distance between any two points

$$d = \sqrt{(x_1 - x_2)^2 + (y_1 - y_2)^2}$$

By substitution,

$$d = \sqrt{(1-5)^2 + (3-3)^2} = \sqrt{(-4)^2 + (0)^2} = \sqrt{16} = 4.$$

The distance is 4.

To find the midpoint of a segment between the two given endpoints, use the formula

$$MP = \left(\frac{x_1 + x_2}{2}, \frac{y_1 + y_2}{2} \right)$$

where x_1 and y_1 are the coordinates of one point; x_2 and y_2 are the coordinates of the other point.

☞ Drill: Coordinate Geometry

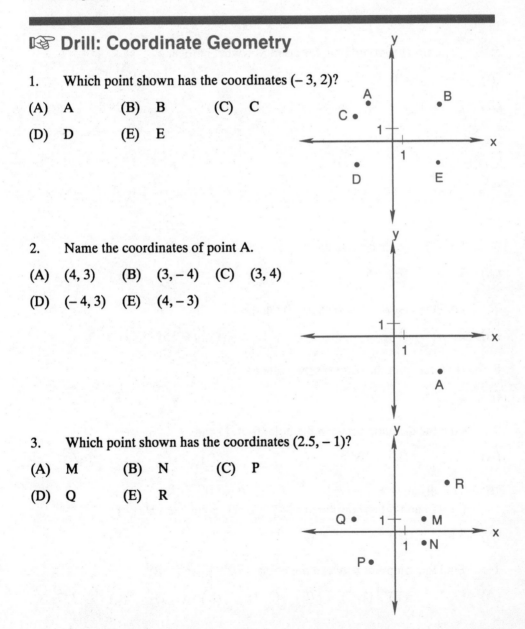

1.   Which point shown has the coordinates $(-3, 2)$?

(A)   A   (B)   B   (C)   C

(D)   D   (E)   E

2.   Name the coordinates of point A.

(A) $(4, 3)$ (B) $(3, -4)$ (C) $(3, 4)$

(D) $(-4, 3)$ (E) $(4, -3)$

3.   Which point shown has the coordinates $(2.5, -1)$?

(A)   M   (B)   N   (C)   P

(D)   Q   (E)   R

4. The correct *x*-coordinate for point *H* is what number?

(A) 3   (B) 4   (C) – 3

(D) – 4   (E) – 5

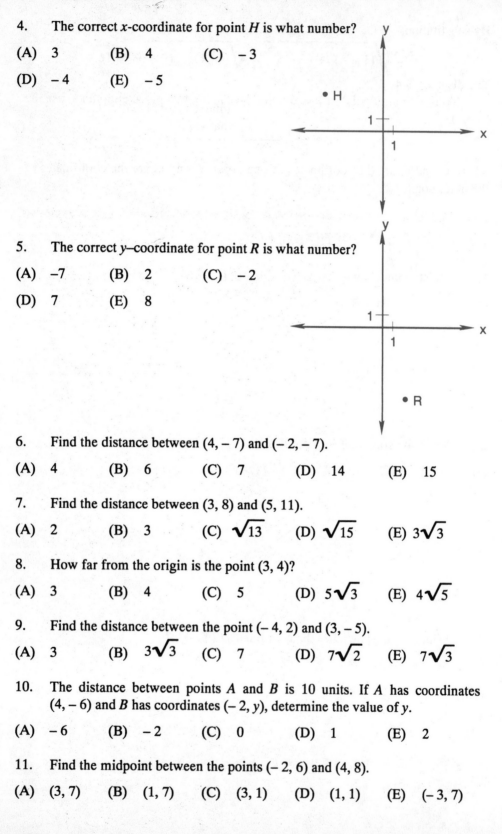

5. The correct *y*–coordinate for point *R* is what number?

(A) –7   (B) 2   (C) – 2

(D) 7   (E) 8

6. Find the distance between (4, – 7) and (– 2, – 7).

(A) 4   (B) 6   (C) 7   (D) 14   (E) 15

7. Find the distance between (3, 8) and (5, 11).

(A) 2   (B) 3   (C) $\sqrt{13}$ (D) $\sqrt{15}$ (E) $3\sqrt{3}$

8. How far from the origin is the point (3, 4)?

(A) 3   (B) 4   (C) 5   (D) $5\sqrt{3}$ (E) $4\sqrt{5}$

9. Find the distance between the point (– 4, 2) and (3, – 5).

(A) 3   (B) $3\sqrt{3}$ (C) 7   (D) $7\sqrt{2}$ (E) $7\sqrt{3}$

10. The distance between points *A* and *B* is 10 units. If *A* has coordinates (4, – 6) and *B* has coordinates (– 2, *y*), determine the value of *y*.

(A) – 6   (B) – 2   (C) 0   (D) 1   (E) 2

11. Find the midpoint between the points (– 2, 6) and (4, 8).

(A) (3, 7)   (B) (1, 7)   (C) (3, 1)   (D) (1, 1)   (E) (– 3, 7)

12. Find the coordinates of the midpoint between the points (– 5, 7) and (3, – 1).

(A) (– 4, 4)   (B) (3, – 1)   (C) (1, – 3)   (D) (– 1, 3)   (E) (4, – 4).

13. The *y*-coordinate of the midpoint of segment $\overline{AB}$ if *A* has coordinates (– 3, 7) and *B* has coordinates (– 3, – 2) is what value?

(A) 5/2   (B) 3   (C) 7/2   (D) 5   (E) 15/2

14. One endpoint of a line segment is (5, – 3). The midpoint is (– 1, 6). What is the other endpoint?

(A) (7, 3)   (B) (2, 1.5)   (C) (– 7, 15)

(D) (– 2, 1.5)   (E) (– 7, 12)

15. The point (– 2, 6) is the midpoint for which of the following pair of points?

(A) (1, 4) and (– 3, 8)   (B) (– 1, – 3) and (5, 9)

(C) (1, 4) and (5, 9)   (D) (– 1, 4) and (3, – 8)

(E) (1, 3) and (– 5, 9)

GEOMETRY DRILLS

ANSWER KEY

Drill: Lines and Angles

1.	(B)	5.	(D)	9.	(D)	13.	(B)
2.	(A)	6.	(C)	10.	(E)	14.	(E)
3.	(C)	7.	(B)	11.	(C)	15.	(A)
4.	(D)	8.	(A)	12.	(D)		

Drill: Regular Polygons

1.	(D)	4.	(A)	7.	(E)	10.	(B)
2.	(B)	5.	(D)	8.	(B)		
3.	(E)	6.	(C)	9.	(D)		

Drill: Triangles

1.	(D)	5.	(C)	9.	(A)	13.	(D)
2.	(B)	6.	(A)	10.	(C)	14.	(A)
3.	(C)	7.	(B)	11.	(C)	15.	(B)
4.	(E)	8.	(E)	12.	(B)		

Drill: Quadrilaterals

1.	(A)	6.	(A)	11.	(C)	16.	(A)
2.	(B)	7.	(D)	12.	(D)	17.	(E)
3.	(D)	8.	(C)	13.	(B)	18.	(B)
4.	(E)	9.	(B)	14.	(C)	19.	(C)
5.	(C)	10.	(C)	15.	(B)	20.	(D)

Drill: Circles

1.	(B)	6.	(D)	11.	(B)	16.	(C)
2.	(A)	7.	(C)	12.	(D)	17.	(B)
3.	(D)	8.	(B)	13.	(C)	18.	(D)
4.	(E)	9.	(E)	14.	(B)	19.	(A)
5.	(C)	10.	(D)	15.	(A)	20.	(C)

Drill: Solids
1. (D)　　　　2. (B)　　　　3. (C)

Drill: Coordinate Geometry
1. (C)	5. (A)	9. (D)	13. (A)
2. (E)	6. (B)	10. (E)	14. (C)
3. (B)	7. (C)	11. (B)	15. (E)
4. (D)	8. (C)	12. (D)	

PRACTICE
EXAM I

GENERAL EDUCATIONAL DEVELOPMENT
PRACTICE EXAM I
ANSWER SHEET

Test 1:

Writing Skills, Part I

1. ① ② ③ ④ ⑤
2. ① ② ③ ④ ⑤
3. ① ② ③ ④ ⑤
4. ① ② ③ ④ ⑤
5. ① ② ③ ④ ⑤
6. ① ② ③ ④ ⑤
7. ① ② ③ ④ ⑤
8. ① ② ③ ④ ⑤
9. ① ② ③ ④ ⑤
10. ① ② ③ ④ ⑤
11. ① ② ③ ④ ⑤
12. ① ② ③ ④ ⑤
13. ① ② ③ ④ ⑤
14. ① ② ③ ④ ⑤
15. ① ② ③ ④ ⑤
16. ① ② ③ ④ ⑤
17. ① ② ③ ④ ⑤
18. ① ② ③ ④ ⑤
19. ① ② ③ ④ ⑤
20. ① ② ③ ④ ⑤
21. ① ② ③ ④ ⑤
22. ① ② ③ ④ ⑤
23. ① ② ③ ④ ⑤
24. ① ② ③ ④ ⑤
25. ① ② ③ ④ ⑤
26. ① ② ③ ④ ⑤
27. ① ② ③ ④ ⑤

28. ① ② ③ ④ ⑤
29. ① ② ③ ④ ⑤
30. ① ② ③ ④ ⑤
31. ① ② ③ ④ ⑤
32. ① ② ③ ④ ⑤
33. ① ② ③ ④ ⑤
34. ① ② ③ ④ ⑤
35. ① ② ③ ④ ⑤
36. ① ② ③ ④ ⑤
37. ① ② ③ ④ ⑤
38. ① ② ③ ④ ⑤
39. ① ② ③ ④ ⑤
40. ① ② ③ ④ ⑤
41. ① ② ③ ④ ⑤
42. ① ② ③ ④ ⑤
43. ① ② ③ ④ ⑤
44. ① ② ③ ④ ⑤
45. ① ② ③ ④ ⑤
46. ① ② ③ ④ ⑤
47. ① ② ③ ④ ⑤
48. ① ② ③ ④ ⑤
49. ① ② ③ ④ ⑤
50. ① ② ③ ④ ⑤
51. ① ② ③ ④ ⑤
52. ① ② ③ ④ ⑤
53. ① ② ③ ④ ⑤
54. ① ② ③ ④ ⑤
55. ① ② ③ ④ ⑤

Test 2:

Social Studies

1. ① ② ③ ④ ⑤
2. ① ② ③ ④ ⑤
3. ① ② ③ ④ ⑤
4. ① ② ③ ④ ⑤
5. ① ② ③ ④ ⑤
6. ① ② ③ ④ ⑤
7. ① ② ③ ④ ⑤
8. ① ② ③ ④ ⑤
9. ① ② ③ ④ ⑤
10. ① ② ③ ④ ⑤
11. ① ② ③ ④ ⑤
12. ① ② ③ ④ ⑤
13. ① ② ③ ④ ⑤
14. ① ② ③ ④ ⑤
15. ① ② ③ ④ ⑤
16. ① ② ③ ④ ⑤
17. ① ② ③ ④ ⑤
18. ① ② ③ ④ ⑤
19. ① ② ③ ④ ⑤
20. ① ② ③ ④ ⑤
21. ① ② ③ ④ ⑤
22. ① ② ③ ④ ⑤
23. ① ② ③ ④ ⑤
24. ① ② ③ ④ ⑤
25. ① ② ③ ④ ⑤
26. ① ② ③ ④ ⑤
27. ① ② ③ ④ ⑤

28. ① ② ③ ④ ⑤
29. ① ② ③ ④ ⑤
30. ① ② ③ ④ ⑤
31. ① ② ③ ④ ⑤
32. ① ② ③ ④ ⑤
33. ① ② ③ ④ ⑤
34. ① ② ③ ④ ⑤
35. ① ② ③ ④ ⑤
36. ① ② ③ ④ ⑤
37. ① ② ③ ④ ⑤
38. ① ② ③ ④ ⑤
39. ① ② ③ ④ ⑤
40. ① ② ③ ④ ⑤
41. ① ② ③ ④ ⑤
42. ① ② ③ ④ ⑤
43. ① ② ③ ④ ⑤
44. ① ② ③ ④ ⑤
45. ① ② ③ ④ ⑤
46. ① ② ③ ④ ⑤
47. ① ② ③ ④ ⑤
48. ① ② ③ ④ ⑤
49. ① ② ③ ④ ⑤
50. ① ② ③ ④ ⑤
51. ① ② ③ ④ ⑤
52. ① ② ③ ④ ⑤
53. ① ② ③ ④ ⑤
54. ① ② ③ ④ ⑤
55. ① ② ③ ④ ⑤
56. ① ② ③ ④ ⑤
57. ① ② ③ ④ ⑤
58. ① ② ③ ④ ⑤
59. ① ② ③ ④ ⑤
60. ① ② ③ ④ ⑤
61. ① ② ③ ④ ⑤
62. ① ② ③ ④ ⑤
63. ① ② ③ ④ ⑤
64. ① ② ③ ④ ⑤

Test 3:

Science

1. ① ② ③ ④ ⑤
2. ① ② ③ ④ ⑤
3. ① ② ③ ④ ⑤
4. ① ② ③ ④ ⑤
5. ① ② ③ ④ ⑤
6. ① ② ③ ④ ⑤
7. ① ② ③ ④ ⑤
8. ① ② ③ ④ ⑤
9. ① ② ③ ④ ⑤
10. ① ② ③ ④ ⑤
11. ① ② ③ ④ ⑤
12. ① ② ③ ④ ⑤
13. ① ② ③ ④ ⑤
14. ① ② ③ ④ ⑤
15. ① ② ③ ④ ⑤
16. ① ② ③ ④ ⑤
17. ① ② ③ ④ ⑤
18. ① ② ③ ④ ⑤
19. ① ② ③ ④ ⑤
20. ① ② ③ ④ ⑤
21. ① ② ③ ④ ⑤
22. ① ② ③ ④ ⑤
23. ① ② ③ ④ ⑤
24. ① ② ③ ④ ⑤
25. ① ② ③ ④ ⑤
26. ① ② ③ ④ ⑤
27. ① ② ③ ④ ⑤
28. ① ② ③ ④ ⑤
29. ① ② ③ ④ ⑤
30. ① ② ③ ④ ⑤
31. ① ② ③ ④ ⑤
32. ① ② ③ ④ ⑤
33. ① ② ③ ④ ⑤
34. ① ② ③ ④ ⑤
35. ① ② ③ ④ ⑤

36. ① ② ③ ④ ⑤
37. ① ② ③ ④ ⑤
38. ① ② ③ ④ ⑤
39. ① ② ③ ④ ⑤
40. ① ② ③ ④ ⑤
41. ① ② ③ ④ ⑤
42. ① ② ③ ④ ⑤
43. ① ② ③ ④ ⑤
44. ① ② ③ ④ ⑤
45. ① ② ③ ④ ⑤
46. ① ② ③ ④ ⑤
47. ① ② ③ ④ ⑤
48. ① ② ③ ④ ⑤
49. ① ② ③ ④ ⑤
50. ① ② ③ ④ ⑤
51. ① ② ③ ④ ⑤
52. ① ② ③ ④ ⑤
53. ① ② ③ ④ ⑤
54. ① ② ③ ④ ⑤
55. ① ② ③ ④ ⑤
56. ① ② ③ ④ ⑤
57. ① ② ③ ④ ⑤
58. ① ② ③ ④ ⑤
59. ① ② ③ ④ ⑤
60. ① ② ③ ④ ⑤
61. ① ② ③ ④ ⑤
62. ① ② ③ ④ ⑤
63. ① ② ③ ④ ⑤
64. ① ② ③ ④ ⑤
65. ① ② ③ ④ ⑤
66. ① ② ③ ④ ⑤

Test 4:

Interpreting

Literature and the Arts

1. ① ② ③ ④ ⑤
2. ① ② ③ ④ ⑤

3. ① ② ③ ④ ⑤
4. ① ② ③ ④ ⑤
5. ① ② ③ ④ ⑤
6. ① ② ③ ④ ⑤
7. ① ② ③ ④ ⑤
8. ① ② ③ ④ ⑤
9. ① ② ③ ④ ⑤
10. ① ② ③ ④ ⑤
11. ① ② ③ ④ ⑤
12. ① ② ③ ④ ⑤
13. ① ② ③ ④ ⑤
14. ① ② ③ ④ ⑤
15. ① ② ③ ④ ⑤
16. ① ② ③ ④ ⑤
17. ① ② ③ ④ ⑤
18. ① ② ③ ④ ⑤
19. ① ② ③ ④ ⑤
20. ① ② ③ ④ ⑤
21. ① ② ③ ④ ⑤
22. ① ② ③ ④ ⑤
23. ① ② ③ ④ ⑤
24. ① ② ③ ④ ⑤
25. ① ② ③ ④ ⑤
26. ① ② ③ ④ ⑤
27. ① ② ③ ④ ⑤
28. ① ② ③ ④ ⑤
29. ① ② ③ ④ ⑤
30. ① ② ③ ④ ⑤
31. ① ② ③ ④ ⑤
32. ① ② ③ ④ ⑤
33. ① ② ③ ④ ⑤
34. ① ② ③ ④ ⑤
35. ① ② ③ ④ ⑤
36. ① ② ③ ④ ⑤

37. ① ② ③ ④ ⑤
38. ① ② ③ ④ ⑤
39. ① ② ③ ④ ⑤
40. ① ② ③ ④ ⑤
41. ① ② ③ ④ ⑤
42. ① ② ③ ④ ⑤
43. ① ② ③ ④ ⑤
44. ① ② ③ ④ ⑤
45. ① ② ③ ④ ⑤

Test 5:

Mathematics

1. ① ② ③ ④ ⑤
2. ① ② ③ ④ ⑤
3. ① ② ③ ④ ⑤
4. ① ② ③ ④ ⑤
5. ① ② ③ ④ ⑤
6. ① ② ③ ④ ⑤
7. ① ② ③ ④ ⑤
8. ① ② ③ ④ ⑤
9. ① ② ③ ④ ⑤
10. ① ② ③ ④ ⑤
11. ① ② ③ ④ ⑤
12. ① ② ③ ④ ⑤
13. ① ② ③ ④ ⑤
14. ① ② ③ ④ ⑤
15. ① ② ③ ④ ⑤
16. ① ② ③ ④ ⑤
17. ① ② ③ ④ ⑤
18. ① ② ③ ④ ⑤
19. ① ② ③ ④ ⑤
20. ① ② ③ ④ ⑤
21. ① ② ③ ④ ⑤
22. ① ② ③ ④ ⑤

23. ① ② ③ ④ ⑤
24. ① ② ③ ④ ⑤
25. ① ② ③ ④ ⑤
26. ① ② ③ ④ ⑤
27. ① ② ③ ④ ⑤
28. ① ② ③ ④ ⑤
29. ① ② ③ ④ ⑤
30. ① ② ③ ④ ⑤
31. ① ② ③ ④ ⑤
32. ① ② ③ ④ ⑤
33. ① ② ③ ④ ⑤
34. ① ② ③ ④ ⑤
35. ① ② ③ ④ ⑤
36. ① ② ③ ④ ⑤
37. ① ② ③ ④ ⑤
38. ① ② ③ ④ ⑤
39. ① ② ③ ④ ⑤
40. ① ② ③ ④ ⑤
41. ① ② ③ ④ ⑤
42. ① ② ③ ④ ⑤
43. ① ② ③ ④ ⑤
44. ① ② ③ ④ ⑤
45. ① ② ③ ④ ⑤
46. ① ② ③ ④ ⑤
47. ① ② ③ ④ ⑤
48. ① ② ③ ④ ⑤
49. ① ② ③ ④ ⑤
50. ① ② ③ ④ ⑤
51. ① ② ③ ④ ⑤
52. ① ② ③ ④ ⑤
53. ① ② ③ ④ ⑤
54. ① ② ③ ④ ⑤
55. ① ② ③ ④ ⑤
56. ① ② ③ ④ ⑤

WRITING SKILLS, Part II

Write your essay for Test 1: Writing Skills, Part II on these lined pages.

EXAM I

TEST 1: WRITING SKILLS, PART I
Tests of General Educational Development

Directions

The Writing Skills Test is intended to measure your ability to use clear and effective English. It is a test of English as it should be written, not as it might be spoken. This test includes both multiple-choice questions and an essay. These directions apply only to the multiple-choice section; a separate set of directions is given for the essay.

The multiple-choice section consists of paragraphs with numbered sentences. Some of the sentences contain errors in sentence structure, usage, or mechanics (spelling, punctuation, and capitalization). After reading the numbered sentences, answer the multiple-choice questions that follow. Some questions refer to sentences that are correct as written. The best answer for these questions is the one which leaves the sentence as originally written. The best answer for some questions is the one which produces a sentence that is consistent with the verb tense and point of view used throughout the paragraph.

You should spend no more than 75 minutes on the multiple-choice questions and 45 minutes on your essay. Work carefully, but do not spend too much time on any one question. You may begin working on the essay part of this test as soon as you complete the multiple-choice section.

Do not mark in this test booklet. Record your answers on the separate answer sheet provided. Be sure that all requested information is properly recorded on the answer sheet.

To record your answers, mark one numbered space on the answer sheet beside the number that corresponds to the question in the test booklet.

FOR EXAMPLE:

Sentence I: **We were all honored to meet governor Phillips.**

What correction should be made to this sentence?

(1)   insert a comma after <u>honored</u>

(2)   change the spelling of <u>honored</u> to <u>honered</u>

(3)   change <u>governor</u> to <u>Governor</u>

(4)   replace <u>were</u> with <u>was</u>

(5)   no correction is necessary.

In this example, the word "governor" should be capitalized; therefore, answer space 3 would be marked on the answer sheet.

Do not rest the point of your pencil on the answer sheet while you are considering your answer. Make no stray or unnecessary marks. If you change an answer, erase your first mark completely. Mark only one answer space for each question; multiple answers will be scored as incorrect. Do not fold or crease your answer sheet. All test materials must be returned to the test administrator.

reprinted with permission of the General Educational Developmental Testing Service of the American Council on Education

Directions: Choose the <u>one best answer</u> to each item.

<u>Items 1 to 5</u> refer to the following paragraph.

(1) Auto Striping Pro's is having a special on pin stripes for all vehicles. (2) Several of our group is going to participate in this special program. (3) Cars brought in today will get special attention from the owner and his son. (4) Cars done by he and his son always get a lot of special touches. (5) In fact, there the best in the business.

1. Sentence 1: **Auto Striping Pro's is having a special on pin stripes for all vehicles.**

    What correction should be made to this sentence?

    (1)   change the spelling of <u>Pro's</u> to <u>Pros</u>

    (2)   change <u>is having</u> to <u>are having</u>

    (3)   place a comma before <u>for</u>

    (4)   change <u>stripes</u> to <u>strips</u>

    (5)   no correction is necessary

2. Sentence 2: **Several of our group is going to participate in this special program.**

    What correction is necessary?

    (2)   change <u>participate</u> to <u>particepate</u>

    (2)   change <u>is going</u> to <u>are going</u>

    (3)   add a comma after <u>participate</u>

    (4)   change <u>in</u> to <u>with</u>

    (5)   no correction is necessary

3. Sentence 3: **Cars brought in today will get special attention from the owner and his son.**

    What correction should be made?

    (1)   change <u>special</u> to <u>speciel</u>

    (2)   change <u>from</u> to <u>with</u>

    (3)   place a comma between <u>attention</u> and <u>from</u>

    (4)   change <u>Cars</u> to <u>cars</u>

    (5)   no correction is necessary

4. Sentence 4: **Cars done by he and his son always get a lot of special touches.**

   What correction should be made?

   (1) change he and to him and
   (2) change a lot to alot
   (3) place a comma after and son
   (4) change always to all ways
   (5) no correction is necessary

5. Sentence 5: **In fact, there the best in the business.**

   What correction is necessary?

   (1) remove the comma after in fact
   (2) change business to buisness
   (3) place a comma after the best
   (4) change there to they're
   (5) no correction is necessary

Items 6 to 10 refer to the following paragraph.

(1) Preparing for a job interview is all ways a hard thing to do. (2) If you now what is going to be asked, it is easier. (3) Its easier to answer questions when you know what to expect. (4) To often, it is not possible to be really prepared. (5) When I go on an interview, me and my friends talk first about what we think we will be asked.

6. Sentence 1: **Preparing for a job interview is all ways a hard thing to do.**

   What correction is necessary?

   (1) change Preparing to Perparing
   (2) change all ways to always
   (3) place a comma between interview and is
   (4) place a comma between thing and to.
   (5) no correction is necessary

7. Sentence 2: **If you now what is going to be asked, it is easier.**

   What correction is necessary?

   (1) remove the comma after asked

(2)   change it to what

(3)   change easier to easyer

(4)   change now to know

(5)   no correction is necessary

8.   Sentence 3: **Its easier to answer questions when you know what to expect.**

What correction is necessary?

(1)   begin a new sentence with the word when

(2)   replace Its with It's

(3)   replace to with too

(4)   replace easier with easyer

(5)   no correction is necessary

9.   Sentence 4: **To often, it is not possible to be really prepared.**

What correction is necessary?

(1)   replace To with Too

(2)   replace To with Two

(3)   remove the comma after often

(4)   replace prepared with perpared

(5)   no correction is necessary

10.   Sentence 5: **When I go on an interview, me and my friends talk first about what we think we will be asked.**

What correction is necessary?

(1)   remove the comma after interview

(2)   change me and my friends to my friends and me

(3)   change me and my friends to my friends and I

(4)   change me and my friends to I and my friends

(5)   no correction is necessary

Items 11 to 18 refer to the following paragraphs.

(1) The Middle Ages in England went from the end of the Roman empire to the 1500's. (2) Barbaric tribes of German's swept into Britain. (3) There they excepted the Christian religion of the retreating Romans. (4) These tribes were governed by chiefs.

(5) The strong system of the Romans were replaced by barbaric laws. (6) The invaders lacked the knowlege to carry on the Roman achievements. (7) Few people could read Latin the language of the well-educated. (8) All of these skills were soon to be forgotten.

11. Sentence 1: **The Middle Ages in England went from the end of the Roman empire to the 1500's.**

    What correction is necessary?

    (1) change 1500's to 1500s
    (2) change end of the to end to the
    (3) change empire to Empire
    (4) change in England to of England
    (5) no correction is necessary

12. Sentence 2: **Barbaric tribes of German's swept into Britain.**

    What correction is necessary?

    (1) change swept to sweeped
    (2) change into to in to
    (3) change Britain to Britin
    (4) change German's to Germans
    (5) no correction is necessary

13. Sentence 3: **There they excepted the Christian religion of the retreating Romans.**

    What correction is necessary?

    (1) change There to Their
    (2) change There to They're
    (3) change excepted to accepted
    (4) place a comma after religion
    (5) no correction is necessary

14. Sentence 4: **These tribes were governed by chiefs.**

    What correction is necessary?

    (1) change were to was
    (2) change governed to govened
    (3) change chiefs to chieves

    (4)   place a comma after <u>governed</u>

    (5)   no correction is necessary

15.   Sentence 5: **The strong system of the Romans were replaced by barbaric laws.**

    What correction is necessary?

    (1)   place a comma after <u>system</u>

    (2)   change <u>Romans</u> to <u>romans</u>

    (3)   change <u>were</u> to <u>was</u>

    (4)   change <u>Romans</u> to <u>Roman</u>

    (5)   no correction is necessary

16.   Sentence 6: **The invaders lacked the knowlege to carry on the Roman achievements.**

    What correction is necessary?

    (1)   change <u>invaders</u> to <u>Invaders</u>

    (2)   change <u>knowlege</u> to <u>knowledge</u>

    (3)   change <u>achievements</u> to <u>achivments</u>

    (4)   place a comma after <u>carry on</u>

    (5)   no correction is necessary

17.   Sentence 7: **Few people could read Latin the language of the well-educated.**

    What correction is necessary?

    (1)   change <u>Latin</u> to <u>latin</u>

    (2)   change <u>language</u> to <u>lanuage</u>

    (3)   change <u>well-educated</u> to <u>well educated</u>

    (4)   place a comma after <u>Latin</u>

    (5)   no correction is necessary

18.   Sentence 8: **All of these skills were soon to be forgotten.**

    What correction is necessary?

    (1)   replace <u>All of these skills</u> with <u>All, of these skills,</u>

    (2)   replace <u>were</u> with <u>was</u>

    (3)   replace <u>forgotten</u> with <u>for gotten</u>

    (4)   replace <u>forgotten</u> with <u>forgot</u>

(5)   no correction is necessary

<u>Items 19 to 30</u> refer to the following paragraph.

(1) Much of what we watch on television is really very boaring. (2) Several times a week, shows are on which are stupid. (3) Why do we even watch shows that make us board? (4) On the other hand there are good and informative serials which can teach and entertain us at the same time. (5) The programmers at television stations must think that were awfully stupid to put on some of the programs that they do. (6) How often do you wish that you could run a television station, or at least all of the programs selection? (7) It can be embarassing to watch television with new friends. (8) When advertisements about private things come on. (9) I know were we could send stupid programmers. (10) We could send them to live with Bart Simpson, then they could have a cow to. (11) What we really need is someone who asks you and I what we want to see.

19. Sentence 1: **Much of what we watch on television is really very boaring.**

What correction should be made?

(1)   change <u>Much</u> to <u>Many</u>

(2)   change <u>television</u> to <u>Television</u>

(3)   place a comma between <u>watch</u> and <u>on</u>

(4)   change <u>boaring</u> to <u>boring</u>

(5)   no correction is necessary

20. Sentence 2: **Several times a week, shows are on which are stupid.**

What correction should be made?

(1)   change <u>week</u> to <u>weak</u>

(2)   change <u>several</u> to <u>alot of</u>

(3)   place a comma after <u>times</u>

(4)   remove the comma after <u>week</u>

(5)   no correction is necessary

21. Sentence 3: **Why do we even watch shows that make us board?**

What correction should be made?

(1)   change <u>that</u> to <u>which</u>

(2)   change <u>board</u> to <u>bored</u>

(3)   replace the question mark with a period

(4) place a comma after shows

(5) no correction is necessary

22. Sentence 4: **On the other hand there are good and informative serials which can teach and entertain us at the same time.**

   What correction should be made?

   (1) place a comma after hand

   (2) place a comma after serials

   (3) place a comma after teach

   (4) place a comma after us

   (5) no correction is necessary

23. Sentence 5: **The programmers at television stations must think that were awfully stupid to put on some of the programs that they do.**

   What correction should be made?

   (1) place a comma after programmers

   (2) place a comma after stupid

   (3) replace were with we're

   (4) replace awfully with awefully

   (5) no correction is necessary

24. Sentence 6: **How often do you wish that you could run a television station, or at least all of the programs selection?**

   What correction should be made?

   (1) remove the comma after station

   (2) replace the question mark with a period

   (3) replace programs with program's

   (4) place a comma after least

   (5) no correction is necessary

25. Sentence 7: **It can be embarassing to watch television with new friends.**

   What correction should be made?

   (1) place a comma after embarassing

   (2) replace new with knew

(3)   replace <u>television</u> with <u>Television</u>

(4)   replace <u>embarassing</u> with <u>embarrassing</u>

(5)   no correction is necessary

26.   Sentence 8: **When advertisements about private things come on.**

What correction should be made?

(1)   change <u>advertisements</u> to <u>advertizements</u>

(2)   place a comma after <u>advertisements</u>

(3)   change <u>When</u> to <u>when</u> and place with previous sentence

(4)   change <u>When</u> to <u>Win</u>

(5)   no correction is necessary

27.   Sentence 9: **I know were we could send stupid programmers.**

What correction should be made?

(1)   change <u>were</u> to <u>we're</u>

(2)   change <u>were</u> to <u>where</u>

(3)   change <u>were</u> to <u>wear</u>

(4)   change <u>programmers</u> to <u>programers</u>

(5)   no correction is necessary

28.   Sentence 10: **We could send them to live with Bart Simpson, then they could have a cow, to.**

What correction should be made?

(1)   remove the comma after <u>Simpson</u>

(2)   place a comma after <u>live</u>

(3)   replace <u>to</u> with <u>two</u>

(4)   replace <u>to</u> with <u>too</u>

(5)   no correction is necessary

29.   Sentence 11: **What we really need is someone who asks you and I what we want to see.**

What correction should be made?

(1)   place a comma after <u>need</u>

(2)   place a comma after <u>I</u>

(3)   replace <u>you and I</u> with <u>me and you</u>

    (4)   replace <u>you and I</u> with <u>you and me</u>

    (5)   no correction is necessary

<u>Items 30 to 43</u> refer to the following paragraph.

    (1) I don't hardly ever get to talk about my favorite summer vacations. (2) The beach is most unique of all the places we visit. (3) I really like going there often. (4) Whose going to want to go any place else in the summer? (5) I guess I should of told you about the best beaches in Texas, Florida, and Alabama. (6) Wether you go or not, you still will know what they look like. (7) Its always fun to talk about the white beaches of Alabama. (8) When we drive threw Alabama, I'm always happy to spend some time on the beach. (9) Me and my family always spend some time on some beach each summer. (10) When we are at the beach, we wear very few cloths and use lots of lotions. (11) If you think i like swimming, you are wrong. (12) My favorite thing to do is to lay on the beach and get a tan. (13) Thats why lotion is so important.

30.   Sentence 1: **I don't hardly ever get to talk about my favorite summer vacations.**

    What correction must be made?

    (1)   change <u>don't</u> to <u>do not</u>

    (2)   change <u>vacations</u> to <u>vacation</u>

    (3)   delete <u>don't</u>

    (4)   delete <u>hardly</u>

    (5)   no correction is necessary

31.   Sentence 2: **The beach is most unique of all the places we visit.**

    What correction needs to be made?

    (1)   place a comma after <u>unique</u>

    (2)   replace <u>is</u> with <u>are</u>

    (3)   replace <u>beach</u> with <u>beaches</u>

    (4)   remove <u>most</u>

    (5)   no correction is necessary

32.   Sentence 3: **I really like going there often.**

    What correction needs to be made?

    (1)   place a comma after <u>there</u>

    (2)   replace <u>there</u> with <u>their</u>

(3) replace <u>really</u> with <u>realy</u>

(4) remove <u>going</u>

(5) no correction is necessary

33. Sentence 4: **Whose going to want to go any place else in the summer?**

What correction needs to be made?

(1) replace <u>whose</u> with <u>who's</u>

(2) place a comma after <u>else</u>

(3) replace <u>else</u> with <u>eles</u>

(4) replace <u>to want to</u> with <u>to want too</u>

(5) no correction is necessary

34. Sentence 5: **I guess I should of told you about the best beaches in Texas, Florida, and Alabama.**

What correction is necessary?

(1) insert <u>that</u> after <u>guess</u>

(2) replac e <u>beaches</u> with <u>beach</u>

(3) replace <u>should of</u> with <u>should have</u>

(4) delete the comma after Florida

(5) no correction is necessary

35. Sentence 6: **Wether you go or not, you still will know what they look like.**

What correction is necessary?

(1) remove the comma after <u>not</u>

(2) add a comma after <u>know</u>

(3) replace <u>wether</u> with <u>weather</u>

(4) replace <u>wether</u> with <u>whether</u>

(5) no correction is necessary

36. Sentence 7: **Its always fun to talk about the white beaches of Alabama.**

What correction needs to be made?

(1) replace <u>Its</u> with <u>It's</u>

(2) replace <u>always</u> with <u>all ways</u>

    (3)   place a comma after <u>beaches</u>

    (4)   replace <u>to</u> with <u>too</u>

    (5)   no correction is necessary

37.   Sentence 8: **When we drive threw Alabama, I'm always happy to spend some time on the beach.**

What correction needs to be made?

    (I1   remove the comma after <u>Alabama</u>

    (2)   replace <u>when</u> with <u>win</u>

    (3)   replace <u>always</u> with <u>all ways</u>

    (4)   replace <u>threw</u> with <u>through</u>

    (5)   no correction is necessary

38.   Sentence 9: **Me and my family always spend some time on some beach each summer.**

What correction needs to be made?

    (1)   change <u>spend</u> to <u>spends</u>

    (2)   change <u>me and my family</u> to <u>I and my family</u>

    (3)   change <u>me and my family</u> to <u>my family and I</u>

    (4)   change <u>me and my family</u> to <u>my family and me</u>

    (5)   no correction is necessary

39.   Sentence 10: **When we are at the beach, we wear very few cloths and use lots of lotions.**

What correction is necessary?

    (1)   change <u>wear</u> to <u>were</u>

    (2)   change <u>cloths</u> to <u>close</u>

    (3)   change <u>lots</u> to <u>alot</u>

    (4)   change <u>cloths</u> to <u>clothes</u>

    (5)   no correction is necessary

40.   Sentence 11: **If you think i like swimming, you are wrong.**

What correction is necessary?

    (1)   place a comma after <u>think</u>

    (2)   remove the comma after <u>swimming</u>

    (3)   replace <u>i</u> with <u>I</u>

(4)   end the sentence with an exclamation mark

(5)   no correction is necessary

41.   Sentence 12: **My favorite thing to do is to lay on the beach and get a tan.**

What correction needs to be made?

(1)   place a comma after <u>beach</u>

(2)   place a comma after <u>is</u>

(3)   replace <u>lay</u> with <u>lay out</u>

(4)   replace <u>lay</u> with <u>lie</u>

(5)   no correction is necessary

42.   Sentence 13: **Thats why lotion is so important.**

What correction needs to be made?

(1)   place a comma after <u>why</u>

(2)   replace <u>lotion</u> with <u>lotions</u>

(3)   replace <u>so</u> with <u>sew</u>

(4)   replace <u>Thats</u> with <u>That's</u>

(5)   no correction is necessary

<u>Items 43 to 55</u> refer to the following paragraphs.

   (1) What sort of entertainment do you prefer to attend when you go out? (2) I like majic shows best of all the types of entertainment that I can think of. (3) Several times a year I get the chance to watch the best majicians do their tricks. (4) I would like to get to meet up with famous entertainers some day. (5) Most majic entertainers are fun to watch, all of the time. (6) Comedy actors are also fun to watch and entertainment. (7) Tradgedy actors might also be fun to be with. (8) But I surely don't like how they have to act. (9) Their always facing some terrible problem, some awful decision, or some huge danger. (10) The best thing about entertainers is that they get to travel. (11) I wonder if that is so grate to them or if it really isn't. (12) Sinse I love to travel, the life of a successful entertainer sounds good. (13) If I got to be famous, I would travel all the time.

43.   Sentence 1: **What sort of entertainment do you prefer to attend when you go out?**

What correction should be made?

(1)   change <u>prefer</u> to <u>perfer</u>

(2)   place a comma after <u>prefer</u>

    (3)   change <u>sort</u> to <u>kind</u>

    (4)   change <u>entertainment</u> to <u>entertainments</u>

    (5)   no correction is necessary

44.   Sentence 2: **I like majic shows best of all the types of entertainment that I can think of.**

What correction should be made?

    (1)   place a comma after <u>shows</u>

    (2)   place a comma after <u>entertainment</u>

    (3)   change <u>entertainment</u> to <u>entertainement</u>

    (4)   change <u>majic</u> to <u>magic</u>

    (5)   no correction is necessary

45.   Sentence 3: **Several times a year I get the chance to watch the best majicians do their tricks.**

What correction should be made?

    (1)   place a comma after <u>year</u>

    (2)   place a comma after <u>chance</u>

    (3)   change <u>several</u> to <u>severel</u>

    (4)   change <u>majicians</u> to <u>magicians</u>

    (5)   no correction is necessary

46.   Sentence 4: **I would like to get to meet up with famous entertainers some day.**

What correction should be made?

    (1)   place a comma after <u>entertainers</u>

    (2)   replace <u>to get to</u> with <u>too get to</u>

    (3)   replace <u>would</u> with <u>wood</u>

    (4)   remove <u>up</u>

    (5)   no correction is necessary

47.   Sentence 5: **Most majic entertainers are fun to watch, all of the time.**

What correction should be made?

    (1)   replace <u>entertainers</u> with <u>entertaners</u>

    (2)   replace <u>majic</u> with <u>magic</u>

(3)   remove the comma after <u>watch</u>

(4)   place a comma after <u>most</u>

(5)   no correction is necessary

48.   Sentence 6: **Comedy actors are also fun to watch and entertainment.**

What correction should be made?

(1)   replace <u>actors</u> with <u>acters</u>

(2)   replace <u>entertainment</u> with <u>entertanement</u>

(3)   place a comma after <u>watch</u>

(4)   replace <u>entertainment</u> with <u>to be entertained by</u>

(5)   no correction is necessary

49.   Sentence 7: **Tradgedy actors might also be fun to be with.**

What correction is necessary?

(1)   change <u>actors</u> to <u>acters</u>

(2)   remove <u>with</u>

(3)   place a comma after <u>fun</u>

(4)   change <u>tradgedy</u> to <u>tragedy</u>

(5)   no correction is necessary

50.   Sentence 8: **But I surely don't like how they have to act.**

What correction is needed?

(1)   place a comma after <u>but</u>

(2)   place a comma after <u>like</u>

(3)   place <u>,but I surely don't like how they have to act</u> after previous
sentence

(4)   remove <u>have to</u>

(5)   no correction is necessary

51.   Sentence 9: **Their always facing some terrible problem, some
awful decision, or some huge danger.**

What correction is needed?

(1)   replace <u>their</u> with <u>there</u>

(2)   replace <u>their</u> with <u>they're</u>

(3)   replace <u>awful</u> with <u>aweful</u>

(4)   replace <u>decision</u> with <u>dicision</u>

(5)   no correction is necessary

52.   Sentence 10: **The best thing about entertainers is that they get to travel.**

What correction is needed?

(1)   place a comma after <u>entertainers</u>

(2)   place a comma after <u>that</u>

(3)   replace <u>entertainers</u> with <u>entertaners</u>

(4)   place a comma after <u>thing</u>

(5)   no correction is necessary

53.   Sentence 11: **I wonder if that is so grate to them or if it really isn't.**

What correction is needed?

(1)   place a comma after <u>wonder</u>

(2)   place a comma after <u>them</u>

(3)   replace <u>grate</u> with <u>great</u>

(4)   place a comma after <u>or</u>

(5)   no correction is necessary

54.   Sentence 12: **Sinse I love to travel, the life of a successful entertainer sounds good.**

What correction is needed?

(1)   change <u>entertainer</u> to <u>entertaner</u>

(2)   change <u>Sinse</u> to <u>Sense</u>

(3)   change <u>successful</u> to <u>succesful</u>

(4)   change <u>Sinse</u> to <u>Since</u>

(5)   no correction is necessary

55.   Sentence 13: **If I became famous, I would travel all the time.**

What correction is necessary?

(1)   remove the comma after <u>famous</u>

(2)   place a comma after <u>travel</u>

(3)   replace <u>famous</u> with <u>famouse</u>

(4)   replace <u>travel</u> with <u>travell</u>

(5)   no correction is necessary

TEST 1: WRITING SKILLS, PART II
Tests of General Educational Development

Directions

This part of the Writing Skills Test is intended to determine how well you write. You are asked to write an essay that explains something or presents an opinion on an issue. In preparing your essay, you should take the following steps.

1. Read carefully the directions and the essay topic given below.

2. Plan your essay carefully before you write.

3. Use scratch paper to make any notes.

4. Write your essay on the lined pages of the separate answer sheet.

5. Read carefully what you have written and make any changes that will improve your essay.

6. Check your paragraphs, sentence structure, spelling, punctuation, capitalization, and usage, and make any necessary corrections.

Be sure you write the <u>letter</u> of the essay topic (given below) on your answer sheet. Write the letter in the box at the upper right-hand corner of the page where you write your essay.

You will have 45 minutes to write on the topic below. Write legibly and use a ballpoint pen so the evaluators will be able to read your writing.

Write your essay on the lined pages of the separate answer sheet. The notes you make on scratch paper will not be scored.

Your essay will be scored by at least two trained evaluators who will judge it according to its <u>overall effectiveness</u>. They will judge how clearly you make the main point of your composition, how thoroughly you support your ideas, and how clearly and correctly you write throughout the essay.

reprinted with permission of the General Educational Development Testing Service of the American Council on Education

Topic A

Some state legislatures are considering making 18 years of age the legal age to get a driver's license. In an essay of approximately two hundred words, tell why you think this is or is not a good idea.

TEST 2: SOCIAL STUDIES

Tests of General Educational Development

Directions

The Social Studies Test consists of multiple-choice questions intended to measure your knowledge of general social studies concepts. The questions are based on short readings which often include a graph, chart, or figure. Study the information given and then answer the question(s) following it. Refer to the information as often as necessary in answering the questions.

You should spend no more than 85 minutes answering the questions in this booklet. Work carefully, but do not spend too much time on any one question. Be sure you answer every question. You will not be penalized for incorrect answers.

Do not mark in this test booklet. Record your answers to the questions on the separate answer sheet provided. Be sure all requested information is properly recorded on the answer sheet.

To record your answers, mark the numbered space on the answer sheet beside the number that corresponds to the question in the test booklet.

FOR EXAMPLE:

Early colonists of North America looked for settlement sites that had adequate water supplies and were accessible by ship. For this reason, many early towns were built near

(1) mountains.   (4) glaciers.
(2) prairies.   (5) plateaus.
(3) rivers.

① ② ● ④ ⑤

The correct answer is "rivers"; therefore, answer space 3 would be marked on the answer sheet.

Do not rest the point of your pencil on the answer sheet while you are considering your answer. Make no stray or unnecessary marks. If you change an answer, erase your first mark completely. Mark only one answer space for each question; multiple answers will be scored as incorrect. Do not fold or crease your answer sheet. Return all test materials to the test administrator.

reprinted with permission of the General Educational Development Testing Service of the American Council on Education

Directions: Choose the <u>one best answer</u> to each item.

<u>Items 1 to 3</u> refer to the following passage.

Along about April 1, 1913, we first tried the experiment of an assembly line. We tried it on assembling the fly-wheel *magneto* ....

I believe that this was the first moving line ever installed. The idea came in a general way from the overhead trolley that the Chicago packers use in dressing beef. We had previously assembled the fly-wheel magneto in the usual method. With one workman doing a complete job he could turn out from thirty-five to forty pieces in a nine-hour day, or about twenty minutes to an assembly. What he did alone was then spread into twenty-nine operations; that cut down the assembly time to thirteen minutes, ten seconds. Then we raised the height of the line eight inches—this was in 1914—and cut the time to seven minutes. Further experimenting with the speed that the work should move at cut the time down to five minutes. In short, the result is this: by the aid of scientific study one man is now able to do somewhat more than four did only a comparatively few years ago. That line established the efficiency of the method and we now use it everywhere. The assembling of the motor, formerly done by one man, is now divided into eighty-four operations—those men do the work that three times their number formerly did. In a short time we tried out the plan on the *chassis* ....

It must not be imagined, however, that all this worked out as quickly as it sounds. The speed of the moving work had to be carefully tried out .... The chassis assembling line, for example, goes at a pace of six feet per minute; the front axle assembly line goes at one hundred eighty-nine inches per minute. In the chassis assembling are forty-five separate operations or stations.... Some men do only one or two small operations, others do more. The man who places a part does not fasten it—the part may not be fully in place until after several operations later. The man who puts in a bolt does not put on the nut; the man who puts on the nut does not tighten it. On operation number thirty-four the budding motor gets its gasoline; it has previously received lubrication; on operation number forty-four the radiator is filled with water, and on operation number forty-five the car drives out....

1. Which famous American, quoted above, pioneered the modern industrial assembly line?

    (1) John D. Rockefeller
    (2) J.P. Morgan
    (3) Andrew Carnegie
    (4) Henry Ford
    (5) Leland Stanford

2. The main reason for creating an assembly line, according to the quote, was

   (1) to make a better product.
   (2) to make better use of skilled labor.
   (3) to make a product more quickly.
   (4) to increase employment.
   (5) to cut down the work day and week.

3. Which was not a factor in making Detroit the "Motor City"?

   (1) Home to early automotive inventors
   (2) Location central to major raw materials
   (3) Access to cheap water transportation
   (4) Availability of a large immigrant labor force
   (5) The crossroads for most of the major east-west railroads

Items 4 to 6 refer to the tables below.

Grain Producers				Grain Importers			
Grain	1st	2nd	3rd	Grain	1st	2nd	3rd
Corn	USA	China	Brazil	Corn	USSR	Japan	Spain
Wheat	USSR	USA	China	Wheat	China	USSR	Japan
Rice	China	India	Indonesia	Rice	Indonesia	Iran	USSR

4. Which nation seems to have the least efficient agricultural system?

   (1) Brazil   (4) India
   (2) Indonesia   (5) China
   (3) USSR

5. Which nation seems to have the most productive agricultural system?

   (1) USA   (4) Indonesia
   (2) China   (5) India
   (3) Brazil

6. Which is not a characteristic of American agriculture?

   (1) The rich ecosystem of North America
   (2) The use of mechanization
   (3) The diversity of climate and soil
   (4) Total free market capitalism
   (5) The trend toward agribusiness

RECORD OF GALLUP POLL ACCURACY

Year	Gallup Final Survey		Election Result		Deviation
1980	47.0%	Reagan	50.8%	Reagan	-3.8
1978	55.0	Democratic	54.6	Democratic	+0.4
1976	48.0	Carter	50.0	Carter	-2.0
1974	60.0	Democratic	58.9	Democratic	+1.1
1972	62.0	Nixon	61.8	Nixon	+0.2
1970	53.0	Democratic	54.3	Democratic	-1.3
1968	43.0	Nixon	43.5	Nixon	-0.5
1966	52.5	Democratic	51.9	Democratic	+0.6
1964	64.0	Johnson	61.3	Johnson	+2.7
1962	55.5	Democratic	52.7	Democratic	+2.8
1960	51.0	Kennedy	50.1	Kennedy	+0.9
1958	57.0	Democratic	56.5	Democratic	+0.5
1956	59.5	Eisenhower	57.8	Eisenhower	+1.7
1954	51.5	Democratic	52.7	Democratic	-1.2
1952	51.0	Eisenhower	55.4	Eisenhower	-4.4
1950	51.0	Democratic	50.3	Democratic	+0.7
1948	44.5	Truman	49.9	Truman	-5.4
1946	58.0	Republican	54.3	Republican	+3.7
1944	51.5	Roosevelt	53.3	Roosevelt	-1.8
1942	52.0	Democratic	48.0	Democratic	+4.0
1940	52.0	Roosevelt	55.0	Roosevelt	-3.0
1938	54.0	Democratic	50.8	Democratic	+3.2
1936	55.7	Roosevelt	62.5	Roosevelt	-6.8

Average deviation for 23 national elections.

2.3 percentage points

Average deviation for 16 national elections since 1950 inclusive.

1.6 percentage points

TREND IN DEVIATION

Elections	Average Error
1936-1950	3.6
1952-1960	1.7
1962-1970	1.6
1972-1980	1.5

Items 7 to 9 refer to the chart above

7. Which is not shown by the chart?

    (1) The average error rate decreased in recent decades.
    (2) Every second poll was a presidential election year.
    (3) There were more negative deviations than positive.
    (4) Non-presidential polls favored the Democrats.
    (5) No president was elected by less than 50%.

8. According to the chart, who won the presidency with the lowest vote?

    (1) Carter   (4) Johnson
    (2) Reagan   (5) Kennedy
    (3) Nixon

9. Why was President Gerald Ford (1974-77) **not** shown in the poll?

    (1) He chose not to run for re-election.
    (2) He died in office.
    (3) He took over while vice-president, and was not elected.

(4) He was impeached.
(5) He resigned.

Items 10 to 12 refer to the following graph.

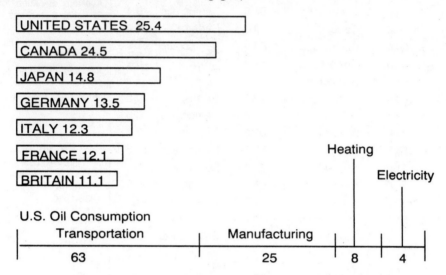

10. Which is not a conclusion that can be drawn from the graphs?

   (1) Transportation takes up too high a portion of U.S. oil usage.
   (2) U.S. per capita consumption is over twice that of most European nations.
   (3) North American oil demands are the highest.
   (4) Manufacturing is a major consumer of oil.
   (5) Heating needs take less than 10% of oil use.

11. Which would be least likely to explain the statistics above?

   (1) The area size of a nation has a relationship to oil usage.
   (2) The European nations consume large quantities of oil.
   (3) The larger the population, the greater the usage.
   (4) Japan is the largest industrial power in Asia.
   (5) Industrial nations' people have lifestyles that use more oil.

12. Which is not true about the petroleum industry?

   (1) It is dealing with a nonrenewable resource.
   (2) It is essential to the plastics industry.
   (3) It reacts quickly to the law of supply and demand.
   (4) It is an example of a monopoly.
   (5) It is truly a multinational industry.

Items 13 to 16 refer to the following speech.

Slavery! How much misery is comprehended in that single word. No one [person] has more right to the full enjoyment of freedom than another. In every man's mind the good seeds of liberty are planted, and he who brings his fellow man down so low, as to make him contented with a condition of slavery, commits the highest crime against God and man. Brethren, your oppressors aim to do this. They endeavor to make you as much like beasts as possible. Then, and not till then, has American slavery done its perfect work.

If you would be free in this generation, here is your only hope. However much you and all of us may desire it, there is not much hope of redemption without the shedding of blood. If you must bleed, let it come all at once—rather die free men than live to be slaves.

In the name of the merciful God, and by all that life is worth, let it no longer be a debatable question, whether it is better to choose liberty or death.

In 1822, Denmark Vesey of South Carolina formed a plan for the liberation of his fellowmen. He was betrayed by the treachery of his own people, and died a martyr to freedom. The patriotic Nathaniel Turner followed Denmark Vesey. He was goaded to desperation by wrong and injustice. Next arose the immortal Joseph Cinque, the hero of the Amistad. He was a native African, and by the help of God he emancipated a whole shipload of his fellowmen on the high seas. Next arose Madison Washington, that bright star of freedom, and took his station in the constellation of true heroism. He was a slave on board the Brig Creole, of Richmond, bound to New Orleans with a hundred and four others. Nineteen struck for liberty or death. Only one life was taken, and the whole party were emancipated.

Brethren, arise, arise! Strike for your lives and liberty. Now is the day and the hour. Let every slave thoughout the land do this, and the days of slavery are numbered. You cannot be more oppressed than you have been—you cannot suffer greater cruelties than you have already. Rather die free men than live to be slaves. Remember that you are FOUR MILLIONS!

13. The speech above must have been given

    (1) during Reconstruction.
    (2) during the American Revolution.
    (3) before the Civil War.
    (4) on the passage of the 13th Amendment.
    (5) when the Brown v. the Topeka Board of Education verdict was announced.

14. Which anti-slavery leader didn't succeed because of his own people?

    (1)   Denmark Vesey   (4)   Madison Washington
    (2)   Nathaniel Turner   (5)   Amistad
    (3)   Joseph Cinque

15. Which statement is most true about the pre-Civil War South?

    (1)   Only whites who owned slaves supported the system.
    (2)   Opposition to slavery was nonexistent.
    (3)   Strict controls prevented any slave revolts from occuring.
    (4)   Blacks had many ways of resisting slavery.
    (5)   The economic system could not exist without slavery.

16. Which would be considered a victory for civil rights over slavery or segregation?

    (1)   Three-fifths Compromise in the Constitution
    (2)   Dred Scott Decision
    (3)   Plessy v. Ferguson
    (4)   15th Amendment
    (5)   Missouri Compromise

Items 17 to 19 refer to the following graph.

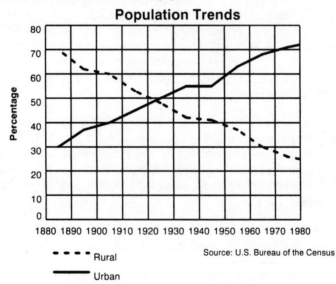

Population Trends

Source: U.S. Bureau of the Census

- - - - Rural

———— Urban

17. Which would be the best title for the graph?

    (1)   Trends in Rural Settlements
    (2)   Trends in Urban Settlements
    (3)   20th century Population Trends
    (4)   Population Growth Trends
    (5)   A Century of Population Trends

18. Which would the graph be most useful in studying?

    (1) The growth of suburbia
    (2) The decline in farm production
    (3) Preferences for urban living
    (4) Urban problems
    (5) Non-farming rural residents

19. A megalopolis is

    (1) a large city.
    (2) several large urban areas joined together.
    (3) smaller than a metropolis.
    (4) the total ring of suburbs around a central city.
    (5) the central city without its suburbs.

Items 20 to 22 refer to the following table.

Educational Statistics, 1870-1910

	Total enrollment public, elementary, and secondary schools	Enrollment, grades 9-12 and postgraduates (public schools)	Percent of population 17 years old graduating from high school	Bachelors, or first professional degrees awarded by institutions of higher education
1870-71	6,871,522	80,277	2.0%	9,371
1880	9,867,505	110,277	2.5%	12,896
1890	12,722,581	202,963	3.5%	15,539
1900	15,503,110	519,251	6.4%	27,410
1910	17,813,852	915,061	8.8%	37,199

20. Which statement is not true?

    (1) Public school enrollment increased over 10 times in a forty-year period.
    (2) There were more people graduating from college in 1910 than had enrolled in high school in 1870.
    (3) High school graduates increased fourfold during the period.
    (4) In 1880, less than ten times as many students enrolled in public schools as graduated from college.
    (5) Public education was becoming more important during this time.

21. Which statement is the most logical conclusion from the statistics?

    (1) School statistics were heavily impacted by the Civil War.
    (2) Many students graduating from high school were younger than 17.
    (3) High school enrollment and graduation rates slumped between 1890 and 1900.

(4)   Most students never made it to high school.
(5)   A high school education was not valued in 1910.

22.   Which is <u>not</u> an influence of the public schools?

(1)   Helping immigrants become citizens.
(2)   Required for all immigrants to become citizens.
(3)   Cooperating with the needs of business employers.
(4)   Helping minorities to improve their status.
(5)   Helping provide greater access to higher education.

<u>Items 23 to 26</u> refer to the following information.

Facts about Central America: Culturally, the region is part of Latin America, which refers to the colonial influence of the Spanish "Latin" rulers from the 1500's until almost the 20th century in some areas. Geographically, it is part of North America. Historically, this was the site of one of the great empires of the Mayas. The variety of experiences have created a people with a rich mixture of ethnic and cultural heritage. Today, Central American nations strive to keep their national independence and to raise their standard of living.

23.   Central America includes all except

(1)   Columbia.   (4)   Costa Rica.
(2)   Nicaragua.   (5)   Guatemala.
(3)   Panama.

24.   Which is not a characteristic of Central America?

(1)   It is part of North America.
(2)   It has access to two oceans.
(3)   Its heritage is modeled solely on the Spanish influence.
(4)   It has strategic importance as a major trade artery.
(5)   It contains nations that need economic assistance.

25. Which physical characteristic compares best to Central America?

   (1) Rocky Mountains   (4) Baja California
   (2) Andes Mountains   (5) Caribbean Sea
   (3) Puerto Rico

26. According to the Theory of Tectonics,

   (1) Central America connects two major shifting plates.
   (2) Central America is very stable and is not part of any faults.
   (3) the Atlantic Ocean is part of a huge plate connecting Africa and the Americas.
   (4) tectonics occurred when the earth was first formed and is now finished.
   (5) the Americas formed the center from which all other land areas were split off.

Items 27 to 29 refer to the following article.

   Miranda's case reached the U.S. Supreme Court in 1966. In a majority opinion, Chief Justice Earl Warren referred to the Court's decision in the case of Danny Escobedo and pointed out its importance in providing protection for individuals against overzealous police practices. Chief Justice Warren wrote: "The constitutional issue we decide... is the admissibility of statements obtained from a defendant questioned while in custody and deprived of his freedom of action."

   The case that Chief Justice Warren was writing about was certainly a difficult one. On the one hand, there was the important question of the rights of a person under the protection of the Constitution. On the other hand, there was the equally important issue of interfering with the work of the police and preventing them from arresting criminals and bringing them to trial. Members of the Supreme Court were deeply divided on how the Court should rule.

   The smallest possible majority of five justices made the historic ruling: "... it is clear that Miranda was not in any way apprised of his right to consult with an attorney and to have one present during the interrogation, nor was his right not to be compelled to incriminate himself effectively protected in any other manner. Without these warnings the statements were inadmissible. The mere fact that he signed a statement which contained a typed-in clause stating that he had 'full knowledge' of his 'legal rights' does not approach the knowing and intelligent waiver required to relinquish constitutional rights."

Source: *Great Trials in American History*, L. Arbetman, R. Roe, West Publishing

27. Which statement is most true about the reading?

   (1) Miranda's case was unique and a first.

(2)   The Supreme Court ruled unanimously on the verdict.
(3)   The Miranda warning bars a suspect from confessing.
(4)   Miranda was one of several cases changing police procedures.
(5)   Miranda involved legal procedure, not Constitutional rights.

28.   Which is not part of the Miranda warning?

(1)   The right to remain silent
(2)   The right to a lawyer
(3)   The right to bail
(4)   The right against self-incrimination
(5)   The right of a lawyer to be with the accused during interrogation

29.   Which instance would violate Miranda?

(1)   A non-English speaking person is told his rights in English.
(2)   A suspect understands his rights but refuses to sign a statement to that effect.
(3)   A person is questioned by police without having been read the Miranda rights, but is not arrested.
(4)   A suspect decides to confess without consulting an attorney after getting his Miranda rights explained.
(5)   An attorney advises his client to accept plea bargaining.

Items 30 to 32 refer to the following article.

"All men have the right to an environment capable of sustaining life and promoting happiness. If the accumulated actions of the past become destructive of this right, men now living have the further right to repudiate the past for the benefit of the future. And it is manifest that centuries of careless neglect of the environment have brought mankind to a final crossroads. The quality of our lives is eroded and our very existence threatened by our abuse of the natural world....

"Recognizing that the ultimate remedy for these fundamental problems is found in man's mind, not his machines, we call on societies and their governments to recognize and implement the following principles:

• We need an ecological consciousness that recognizes man as member, not master, of the community of living things sharing his environment.

• We must extend ethics beyond social relations to govern man's contact with all life forms and with the environment itself.

• We need a renewed idea of community which will shape urban environments that serve the full range of human needs.

• We must find the courage to take upon ourselves as individuals responsibility for the welfare of the whole environment, treating our own back yards as if they were the world and the world as if it were our back yard.

• We must develop the vision to see that in regard to the natural world private and corporate ownership should be so limited as to preserve the interest of society and the integrity of the environment.

• We need greater awareness of our enormous powers, the fragility of the earth, and the consequent responsibility of men and governments for its preservation.

• We must redefine 'progress' toward an emphasis on long-term quality rather than immediate quantity.

"We, therefore, resolve to act. We propose a revolution in conduct toward an environment which is rising in revolt against us. Granted that ideas and institutions long established are not easily changed; yet today is the first day of the rest of our life on this planet. We will begin anew."

Source: U.S. Government statistics

30. Which group is not called upon to act in the statement?

    (1) Private and corporate ownership   (4) Society
    (2) Government   (5) Communities
    (3) Individuals

31. What makes this quote relevant to economics?

    (1) Ethical use of the environment
    (2) Man as a member of the "community of all living things"
    (3) Need for individual responsibility
    (4) References to man's machines and past abuses
    (5) Progress, in terms of quality of life

32. Which is not an example of how environmental concerns can become economic priorities?

    (1) Recycling
    (2) Reforestation
    (3) Strip mining restoration
    (4) Greenhouse effect
    (5) Coal-generated electricity to replace imported oil

Items 33 to 35 refer to the following paragraph.

Suppose a study of the particular situation suggested very strongly that the youth engaged in the gang warfare were having great difficulty in finding what they could do well, in learning useful skills, in finding opportunities for "self-respect producing" employment. Such a finding would pose the question as to what can be done to provide more resources in the school by way of further opportunities for vocational and personal guidance and teaching. It also suggests the question as to what can be done to provide more "real" jobs for the youth in the community. This may require the combined efforts of the employment office, the Chamber of Commerce, the school, the Parent-Teacher Association, and the citizens in the community.

Reprinted from the October, 1964, issue of EDUCATION, Copyright 1964 by the Bobbs-Merrill Co., Inc., Indianapolis, Indiana, "The Causes and Consequences of Behavior," by R. Ojemann.

33. Which would meet the needs of gang members best?

    (1)   More schooling   (4)   Better law enforcement
    (2)   Better schooling   (5)   High paying jobs
    (3)   Vocational programs

34. Which would not be a question posed in the reading?

    (1)   What a gang member could do well
    (2)   What resources can schools provide
    (3)   How the community can create jobs
    (4)   How to learn useful skills
    (5)   Why they belong to a gang

35. Which would be the least likely reason for joining a gang?

    (1)   Security   (4)   Racism
    (2)   Belonging   (5)   Crime
    (3)   Rebellion

Items 36 to 37 refer to the diagram below.

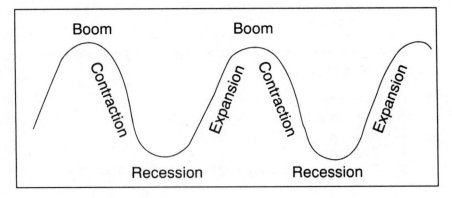

36. Which is the best title for the diagram above?

    (1)   Boom and Bust
    (2)   Causes of Economic Change
    (3)   The Business Cycle
    (4)   Causes of Recession
    (5)   The History of Business Activity

37. In referring to the stages of the cycle above, on the previous page, which would not be a factor considered by economists?

    (1) Unemployment figures   (4) War or peace
    (2) Manufacturing production (5) Retail sales
    (3) Income levels

38. Which is not a method used to encourage expansion during a recession?

    (1) Political crisis, such as war
    (2) Increased government spending
    (3) Increased taxation
    (4) Deregulation of industry
    (5) Restriction of imports

Items 39 to 42 refer to the following passage.

Business functions by public consent, and its basic purpose is to serve constructively the needs of society—to the satisfaction of society.

"Historically, business has discharged this obligation mainly by supplying the needs and wants of people for goods and services, by providing jobs and purchasing power, and by producing most of the wealth of the nation. This has been what American society required of business, and business on the whole has done its job remarkably well....

"In generating... economic growth, American business has provided increasing employment, rising wages and salaries, employee benefit plans, and expanding career opportunities for a labor force....

"Most important, the rising standard of living of the average American family has enabled more and more citizens to develop their lives as they wish with less and less constraint imposed on them by economic need. Thus, most Americans have been able to afford better health, food, clothing, shelter, and education than the citizens of any other nation have ever achieved on such a large scale....

Source: U.S. Government report

39. Which statement best summarizes the attitude of the quote?

    (1) Business has successfully met all the needs of society.
    (2) Business has done a good job supplying the economic needs of society.
    (3) Americans are best off with the least government.
    (4) All Americans have benefited from the rising living standard.
    (5) Government and business, in partnership, have created prosperity.

40. Which organization would be most likely to endorse this quote?

    (1) Chamber of Commerce (4) Socialist Labor Party
    (2) Department of Labor (5) AFL/CIO
    (3) General Accounting Office

41. Which of the following economic goals is not addressed by the quote?

    (1) Economic growth (4) Economic justice
    (2) Economic stability (5) Economic freedom
    (3) Economic security

42. Which is not one of the four basic economic activities of capitalism?

    (1) Production (4) Service
    (2) Distribution (5) Labor
    (3) Manufacturing

Items 43 to 45 refer to the following graph.

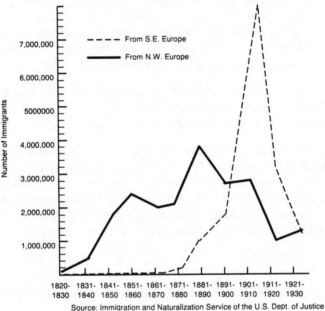

Immigration to the United States, 1820-1930

Source: Immigration and Naturalization Service of the U.S. Dept. of Justice

43. Northern and Western European immigration patterns were

    (1) highest from 1851-60.
    (2) lowest during the Civil War.
    (3) peaking just before the turn of the century.
    (4) declining as Southern and Eastern European immigration increased.
    (5) the highest ever seen in U.S. history in 1841.

44. Which is not true?

    (1) Total immigration from Europe never reached 10 million in a decade.
    (2) Southern and Eastern European immigration didn't equal Northern and Western until after 1900.
    (3) S.E. European immigration remained fairly constant until 1861-70.
    (4) Both waves of immigration had steep increases and decreases.
    (5) By 1930, the 20th century trends had reversed themselves again.

45. Which is most true about U.S. immigration history?

    (1) The Open Door policy has welcomed all groups equally.
    (2) Immigration has come in waves, with non-Europeans being the most recent.
    (3) Political refugees are given the lowest preference.
    (4) Immigration has usually increased during wartime.
    (5) Immigration policy is part of the Constitution.

Items 46 to 48 refer to the following poll.

PRESIDENTIAL PREFERENCES OF DIFFERENT GROUPS

	Reagan	Carter
Total Sample	37	30
Democrats (29%)	18	56
Independents (43%)	32	24
Republicans (24%)	72	9
Detroit (15%)	24	57
Rest of tri-county area (25%)	40	28
Remainder of state (59%)	40	24
Liberal (22%)	26	37
Middle of the road (30%)	33	31
Conservative (42%)	50	25
Labor union households (37%)	30	34
Nonunion households (52%)	42	27
Black (10%)	4	73
White (87%)	41	25
Men (44%)	39	27
Women (56%)	36	32

46. Which conclusion can be made from the chart?

    (1) Reagan was most popular in Detroit.
    (2) There were more liberals than conservatives.
    (3) Republicans felt stronger about Reagan than Democrats about Carter.
    (4) Reagan was more popular with women than with men.
    (5) More people were independents than party members.

47. If you wanted Carter to campaign in his strongest areas, which would you avoid?

    (1) Detroit   (4) Black voters
    (2) Remainder of the state   (5) Liberals
    (3) Union households

48. Who wins the Presidential elections?

    (1) The winner of a majority of the Electoral College in December
    (2) The winner of a majority of the popular vote in November
    (3) The winner of the Electoral College in November
    (4) The candidate with the largest vote total in November
    (5) The party with the greatest popular vote

Items 49 to 52 refer to the following table.

Effects of Common Drugs

Drug	Psychological Dependence	Physical Dependence	Physical Withdrawal Effects	Development of Tolerance
Depressants				
Alcohol Barbituates	Mild to very strong Develops slowly	Very strong Develops slowly	Severe/dangerous Death possible	Minimal
Narcotics				
Opiates (heroin, morphine)	Very strong Develops rapidly	Rapid/increases with dosage	Frightening symptoms but not dangerous	Very high Goes down quickly after withdrawal (Danger if user returns to original dose)
Stimulants				
Amphetamines Cocaine Crack	Strong Very strong	Strong Not in formal sense but body seeks "rush"	Mild None	Extremely high None (Can cause heart spasms and instant death even in healthy)
Psychedelics				
LSD Marijuana	Unpredictable Mild to strong	None Some to high doses	None None	Extremely high None (Some to high doses)

PCP, called "angel dust" This drug is so potent that we have no real information on it. Those who take it become dangerous and lose all contact with reality within a matter of hours. Should never be taken under any circumstances.

49. Which statement is most true about the chart?

    (1) It recommends one drug over others.
    (2) It ranks drugs from mild to severe.
    (3) It gives a user a guide to tolerance.
    (4) It covers all drugs abused.
    (5) It shows how one drug leads to another.

50. Which category of drugs has the fewest physical complications?

 (1) Depressants   (4) Psychedelics
 (2) Narcotics   (5) Amphetamines
 (3) Stimulants

51. Marijuana falls under the category of drugs called

 (1) stimulants.   (4) narcotics.
 (2) depressants.   (5) None of the above.
 (3) psychedelics.

52. Which is <u>not</u> a true statement about heroin?

 (1) Users develop psychological dependence very slowly.
 (2) Users develop very high tolerance to it.
 (3) It is an opiate.
 (4) Users develop rapid physical dependence.
 (5) Its withdrawal effects are freightening, but not dangerous.

<u>Items 53 to 58</u> refer to the following article.

After the Cold War in Asia
Time for U.S. Troops in Japan to Come Home

Defense Monitor in Brief

- Japan maintains one of the world's most powerful military forces and is the third largest military spender.

- The United States forces that occupied Japan at the end of World War II never left, even though a peace treaty was signed in 1951.

- Japan has built up its military despite the intent of the 1947 Japanese Constutition to ban all armed forces.

- The U.S. spends $9 Billion every year on its 50,000 soldiers and 55,000 dependents in Japan.

- Japan pays nothing to the U.S. Treasury for the U.S. forces in Japan.

- The Pentagon plans a modest withdrawal of 5,000 troops from Japan over the next three years.

- The growing potential for Japanese military agencies aggression has rekindled fears among Asian nations.

In 1853 an isolated and reclusive Japan was shocked by the arrival in Tokyo Bay of a U.S. Navy squadron led by Commodore Perry. Threatening to use modern United States military might to shell, blockade, or seize the defenseless country, he forced Japan to its knees and opened it up to the West.

The Japanese found themselves surrounded by hostile military powers, including Britain and Russia as well as the U.S. They responded by building from scratch the most powerful military in Asia over a few decades.

In 1945 after Japan conquered much of East Asia in World War II, the U.S. Navy again sailed into Tokyo Bay and imposed the U.S. will on a defeated Japan. Now, a few short decades later, Japan has again built one of the world's most powerful militaries.

Fortunately there is a difference this time. Japan is no longer surrounded by avaricious, stronger nations waiting to attack. In particular, the Soviet Union has no intention of invading Japan. **Today, unlike in 1853, Japan can safely choose to reduce its military strength.**

The terrible experience of World War II led Japan to develop a series of political understandings constraining its milirary. Although these understandings did not prevent Japan from building a large and powerful military, they did lead Japan to emphasize "defensive" forces designed to fight only in Japan and its home waters.

Today, however, the informal constraints on the Japanese military are in danger. **Japan faces a historic choice. It can either continue the rapid buildup of its armed forces, inevitably threatening its neighbors, and perhaps leading to war, or it can recognize the far-reaching changes in the world, and reduce its military power.**

With the Soviet Union reducing its forces in Asia as well as in Europe, and Japan able to defend itself, the U.S. can now withdraw the forces it bases in Japan. The Cold War is over in Asia just as it is in Europe.

53. The best title for the article would be

    (1)   U.S./Japanese Relations Since World War II.
    (2)   Japan's Relations With Its Asian Neighbors.
    (3)   Military Status of Japan and the U.S.
    (4)   Japanese Treaty Obligations.
    (5)   Japanese Military Aggressions.

54. Which should not be a major concern for the U.S. from a strictly economic viewpoint?

    (1)   The size and strength of the Japanese military.
    (2)   The cost of U.S. dependents in Japan.
    (3)   The contribution of Japan to U.S. forces in Japan.
    (4)   The cost of keeping 50,000 U.S. soldiers in Japan.
    (5)   The non-contribution of the Japanese to the U.S. troop presence.

55. Which is <u>not</u> indicated by the statement?

    (1) Japan does maintain a substantial military.
    (2) The U.S. has no intention to decrease military involvement in Japan.
    (3) The U.S. and Japan have a formal treaty ending World War II.
    (4) Japan is a major military investor in the world.
    (5) The U.S. plans to decrease its military presence in Japan.

56. The Japanese form of government is

    (1) a constitutional monarchy.   (4) a democracy.
    (2) a fascist state.   (5) communist.
    (3) a socialist state.

57. Which of the following is a Constitutional Monarchy?

    (1) Germany   (4) United Kingdom
    (2) U.S.S.R.   (5) France
    (3) China

58. Which of the following is <u>not</u> specified in the U.S. Constitution?

    (1) The role of the court system
    (2) How laws are made
    (3) The rights of individuals
    (4) The rights and responsibilities of local governments
    (5) How the military is controlled

<u>Items 59 to 61</u> refer to the following information:

Maslow's Hierarchy:
Self-Actualization
Self-Esteem
Social Needs
Security
Survival

59. Maslow's famous hierarchy applies to

    (1) psychological needs.   (4) group needs.
    (2) social needs.   (5) All the above.
    (3) individual needs.

60. Which best describes a person's behavior, according to Maslow?

    (1) Once a person achieves a higher level, the lower level may be forgotten.

    (2)   It shows an inevitable progression through life, with the typical person achieving all levels in order.

    (3)   A personal crisis often requires a return to a lower level.

    (4)   The levels may be achieved in random order as long as all are covered.

    (5)   Civilized people start at the top rows, while others start lower.

61.   Which would <u>not</u> be an example of Maslow's Hierarchy?

    (1)   An illiterate person creating great poetry by accidentally banging on a typewriter.

    (2)   A worker who feels his job has no satisfaction.

    (3)   The development of a civilization.

    (4)   A teacher rewarding a student for an original art work.

    (5)   A person protecting his home after a storm.

<u>Items 62 to 64</u> refer to the following paragraph.

I will venture to say [declared Volney] that if a prize were proposed for the scheme of a regimen most calculated to injure the stomach, the teeth, and the health in general, no better could be invented than that of the Americans. In the morning at breakfast they deluge their stomach with a quart of hot water, impregnated with tea, or so slightly with coffee that it is mere colored water; and they swallow, almost without chewing, hot bread, half baked, toast soaked in butter, cheese of the fattest kind, slices of salt or hung beef, ham, etc., all which are nearly insoluble. At dinner they have boiled pastes under the name of puddings, and the fattest are esteemed the most delicious; all their sauces, even for roast beef, are melted butter; their turnips and potatoes swim in hog's lard, butter, or fat; under the name of pie or pumpkin, their pastry is nothing but a greasy paste, never sufficiently baked. To digest these viscous substances they take tea almost instantly after dinner, making it so strong that it is absolutely bitter to the taste, in which state it affects the nerves so powerfully that even the English find it brings on a more obstinate restlessness than coffee. Supper again introduces salt meats or oysters. As Chastellux says, the whole day passes in heaping indigestions on one another; and to give tone to the poor, relaxed, and wearied stomach, they drink Madeira, rum, French brandy, gin, or malt spirits, which complete the ruin of the nervous system.

The excerpt is from *A History of the United States During the Administrations of Jefferson and Madison* by Henry Adams, 1889.

62.   Which was not part of the American diet in the early 1800s, according to this passage?

    (1)   Dairy products   (4)   Strong coffee

    (2)   Pork products   (5)   Alcoholic beverages

    (3)   Vegetables

63. Which statement best expresses the author's opinion of the American diet?

    (1) Very unhealthy
    (2) Designed to keep the digestion calm
    (3) Necessarily based on what was available on farms
    (4) Cuisine that was fatty, but delicious
    (5) A product of the English colonial heritage

64. What does the author describe as being "so strong that it is absolutely bitter to the taste"?

    (1) Tea
    (2) Coffee
    (3) French brandy
    (4) Madeira
    (5) Rum

TEST 3: SCIENCE

Tests of General Educational Development

Directions

The Science Test consists of multiple-choice questions intended to measure your knowledge of the general concepts in science. The questions are based on short readings which often include a graph, chart, or figure. Study the information given and then answer the question(s) following it. Refer to the information as often as necessary in answering the questions.

You should spend no more than 95 minutes answering the questions in this booklet. Work carefully, but do not spend too much time on any one question. Be sure you answer every question. You will not be penalized for incorrect answers.

Do not mark in this test booklet. Record your answers to the questions on the separate answer sheet provided. Be sure all requested information is properly recorded on the answer sheet.

To record your answers, mark the numbered space on the answer sheet beside the number that corresponds to the question in the test booklet.

FOR EXAMPLE:

Which of the following is the smallest unit in a living thing?

(1) Tissue
(2) Organ
(3) Cell

(4) Muscle
(5) Capillary

① ② ● ④ ⑤

The correct answer is "cell"; therefore, answer space 3 would be marked on the answer sheet.

Do not rest the point of your pencil on the answer sheet while you are considering your answer. Make no stray or unnecessary marks. If you change an answer, erase your first mark completely. Mark only one answer space for each question; multiple answers will be scored as incorrect. Do not fold or crease your answer sheet. Return all test materials to the test administrator.

reprinted with permission of the General Educational Development Testing Service of the American Council on Education

Directions: Choose the one best answer to each item.

Items 1 to 4 refer to the following passage.

An easy method of experimentally determining the acceleration due to gravity "g" is by measuring the period of one complete vibration of a simple pendulum of known length. If all the mass of the pendulum can be considered to be concentrated in the bob at the bottom, and if the amplitude of the vibration is kept small (less than a 5° arc), then g will be proportional to the length of the pendulum and inversely proportional to the square of the period. For example, on the Earth's surface where g is about 9.8 meters/sec², a 1-meter long pendulum has a vibrational period of 2.0 seconds and a 2-meter long pendulum has a vibrational period of 2.84 seconds.

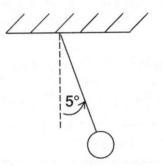

1. If the acceleration due to gravity "g" on the Earth is determined by using a pendulum with a period of 4 seconds, then its length must be about

    (1) 1 meter.   (4) 4 meters.
    (2) 2 meters.   (5) 5 meters.
    (3) 3 meters.

2. On the moon the acceleration due to gravity is about one-sixth what is here on the Earth. If a simple pendulum is to have a two-second period on the moon, its length must be close to

    (1) 1/2 meter.   (4) 1/5 meter.
    (2) 1/3 meter.   (5) 1/6 meter.
    (3) 1/4 meter.

3. Which of the following does not seem to affect the period of a simple pendulum?

    (1) The acceleration due to gravity
    (2) The mass of the bob
    (3) The amplitude of the swing
    (4) The length of the pendulum
    (5) All of the above.

4. The units used to express the acceleration due to gravity express a measure of

    (1) velocity over time.   (4) velocity over distance.
    (2) distance over time.   (5) force over distance.
    (3) weight over time.

Items 5 to 9 refer to the following passage.

Ants are insects with two body parts, a thorax and abdomen, plus a head. Antennae protrude from the head. These antennae serve in communicating with other ants and examining food, and possess several other purposes. Ants have fixed compound eyes which are made of many small lenses. Ants leave a trail when they travel; they never seem to get lost. Ants which have been trapped in resin and preserved for millions of years seem to be very similar to the ants of today.

5. The relationship between human eyelashes and the human eye is similar to the relationship between comblike hooks found on antennae and antennae themselves. What is this relationship?

    (1) The comblike hooks blink periodically to moisten the antennae.
    (2) The comblike hooks keep the antennae free from dust and dirt.
    (3) The comblike hooks are attractive to male ants when female ants move their antennae in a blinking manner.
    (4) The length of the comblike hooks and the antennae determine the age of the ants.
    (5) The comblike hooks help an ant find its way, similar to the function of eyelashes.

6. When an ant finds food, it leaves a trail behind it which has a different odor than the trail left by any other ant colony. This trail is most likely made of

    (1) food.
    (2) broken pieces of antennae.
    (3) drops of liquid from the abdomen.
    (4) lenses of compound eyes.
    (5) tiny pebbles.

7. How is a compound eye advantageous to an ant?

    (1) The ant sees multiple images of everything.
    (2) If one lens breaks, the ant still can see.
    (3) The eye can rotate and gives the ant better vision.
    (4) The ant can see moving objects more easily than objects which stand still.
    (5) Like a compound microscope, a compound eye magnifies objects a thousand times.

8. Ants are considered to be most related to

   (1) bees.   (4) fleas.
   (2) spiders.   (5) crabs.
   (3) fungus.

9. Ants did not change or evolve much from prehistoric ants because

   (1) ants could not adjust themselves to changing conditions.
   (2) ants could not protect themselves against enemies.
   (3) no Earth changes were severe enough to disturb ants.
   (4) ants were unable to find food for their young.
   (5) ants were unable to find shelter.

Items 10 to 12 refer to the following passage.

   All matter can be divided into two categories: pure substances and mixtures. The pure substances can be further subdivided into elements and compounds, while mixtures can either be homogeneous or heterogeneous.

10. According to the paragraph, which one of the following statements is true?

   (1) A homogeneous mixture is a pure substance.
   (2) Pure substances and mixtures are equivalent terms for the same type of matter.
   (3) A compound can be a pure substance.
   (4) A heterogeneous mixture is only composed of one type of element.
   (5) All matter is one lump that cannot be categorized.

11. If a homogeneous mixture is combined with a heterogeneous mixture, what type of matter will result?

   (1) A homogeneous mixture
   (2) A heterogeneous mixture
   (3) A pure substance
   (4) The two mixtures will not combine because they are too different.
   (5) A new type of matter will result that has not yet been classified.

12. A substance that cannot be decomposed is called an element. Which one of the following is not an element?

   (1) Zinc   (2) Sodium
   (3) Iron   (4) Tin
   (5) Zinc sulfide

Items 13 to 17 refer to the following passage.

Scientific investigation involves two areas: pure science and applied science. Pure science is basic research, or the attempt to answer questions simply for the sake of knowledge itself. Applied science uses the knowledge gained from pure science to solve practical problems. Consider the following example: A biologist wants to know how insects attract mates. After much research, observation, and experimentation she discovers a substance called a pheromone is produced by the female insect and released into the air as an invisible gas, much like perfume. Pheromones are chemicals that are given off by organisms and affect or influence the behavior or the development of an individual organism. Pheromones are also known as "sex attractants" and are specific according to the type of organism. She found that pheromones produced by some organisms can be detected miles away by male organisms of the same species. This allows the male to find the female much faster than by looking or listening for the female insect. Pheromones are so powerful that the insect attracted pays no attention to anything other than trying to reach the female so that mating can begin.

13. The biologist that did the research on pheromones was engaged in

   (1) basic research.
   (2) applied research.
   (3) government research.
   (4) library research.
   (5) methods to produce great numbers of insects.

14. Pheromones

   (1) are used only in insects. (4) can be seen.
   (2) are used by all animals. (5) can be felt.
   (3) are found in many organisms.

15. If another biologist placed a cockroach pheromone on a cork and then placed the cork in a dish containing a solution poisonous to cockroaches, what would probably be the result?

   (1) No cockroaches would be affected
   (2) Over a period of time, the dish would gradually be filled with dead cockroaches that crawled through the poison in an attempt to mate with the cork
   (3) Moths would be attracted to the pheromone impregnated cork
   (4) Cockroaches would surround the dish but not cross the poison
   (5) Not enough data has been given

16. If a biologist used pheromones to attract male cockroaches to a cork containing a contact poison in hopes of ridding his home of cockroaches, what would this be an example of?

(1) Pure science
(2) Basic research
(3) Applied science

(4) Government research
(5) The scientific method

17. Pheromones are sexual attractants of insects. This has been a great discovery in itself. If scientists took this information and used it to make a trap where the insects would die, this would be an example of

(1) entomology.
(2) botany.
(3) applied science.

(4) pure science.
(5) scientific method.

Items 18 to 20 refer to the following table.

ERA	PERIOD	EVENTS	BEGAN MILIONS OF YEARS AGO
CENOZOIC	Quaternary	Age of humans. Four major glacial advances.	2
	Tertiary	Increase in mammals. Appearance of primates. Mountain building in Europe and Asia.	65
MESOZOIC	Cretaceous	Extinction of dinosaurs. Increase in flowering plants and reptiles.	140
	Jurassic	Birds. Mammals. Dominance of dinosaurs. Mountain building in western North America.	195
	Triassic	Beginning of dinosaurs and primitive mammals.	230
PALEOZOIC	Permian	Reptiles spread and develop. Evaporate deposits. Glaciation in Southern Hemisphere.	280
	Carboniferous	Abundant amphibians. Reptiles appear.	345
	Devonian	Age of fishes. First amphibians. First abundant forests on land.	395
	Silurian	First land plants. Mountain building in Europe.	435
	Ordovician	First fishes and vertebrates.	500
	Cambrian	Age of marine invertebrates.	600
PRECAMBRIAN TIME		Beginning of life. At least five times longer than all geologic time following.	

Table from *Introduction to Oceanography*, fourth edition, 1988 by David A. Ross, Prentice Hall.

18. Which of the following statements is true?

    (1) Earth's history is divided into time blocks, determined by geologic events only.
    (2) Earth's history is divided into equal divisions of time.
    (3) Earth's history is divided into time blocks of differing amounts of time.
    (4) Each period of Earth's history is divided into time blocks called eras.
    (5) Three major events are grouped under each period.

19. Which sequence of life is correct?

    (1) Invertebrates, Fish, Reptiles, Mammals
    (2) Fish, Invertebrates, Mammals, Birds
    (3) Plants, Invertebrates, Forests, Fish
    (4) Invertebrates, Mammals, Birds, Plants
    (5) Mammals, Plants, Birds, Reptiles

20. According to the table, what period would have marked the appearance of the first relatives of the common alligator?

    (1) Silurian   (4) Carboniferous
    (2) Triassic   (5) Cambrian
    (3) Tertiary

Items 21 to 23 refer to the following passage.

Over three hundred years ago, a British scientist named Robert Hooke was looking through a microscope at thin sections of cork. He noticed that there were many cavities in the cork. He coined the term "cells" to refer to these cavities. In 1835, Felix Dujardin was able to view living cells through a microscope. In 1838, Matthias Schleiden proposed that all plants are composed of cells, and in 1840 Theodor Schwann stated that all animals are made of cells. Approximately twenty years later, Rudolf Virchow published his observations that disease affected only living things. Today, we know that the information gained by these men is summed up in what is known as "The Cell Theory." The Cell Theory states that: 1) all living things are composed of cells; 2) cells carry on the life processes such as using energy, taking in nutrients, organizing protoplasm, having a life span, reproduction, adapting, and having irritability; and 3) all cells are produced from pre-existing cells.

21. Which of the following would not be considered to be a living thing?

    (1) a rose   (4) an amoeba
    (2) a fungus   (5) a sponge
    (3) a virus

22. According to the Cell Theory, an icicle is

    (1)   alive because it grows by the addition of more water.
    (2)   alive because it has a life span which involves a beginning, growth, a period of maturity, a period of decline, and finally, death.
    (3)   alive because it can reproduce.
    (4)   not alive because it is composed of cells.
    (5)   not alive because it is not composed of cells, it cannot reproduce, and it does not carry out any of the life functions.

23. The basic or common unit of life is

    (1)   a cell.   (4)   an organ system.
    (2)   an organ.   (5)   an organism.
    (3)   a chemical compound.

Items 24 to 27 refer to the following information.

Issac Newton was the first to point out that every mass in the universe attracts every other mass. This statement is known as the Law of Universal Gravitation. This attraction between bodies is proportional to the mass of each and is inversely proportional to the square of the distance between their centers. Also, by Newton's Third Law of Motion, this attraction must be the same on each pair of masses but in an opposite direction. For example, it is known that the Earth pulls on the moon with an average force of 2×10^{20} N and the moon pulls on the Earth with an average force of 2×10^{20} N.

**Relative Masses and Average Separations
Moon, Earth, and Sun**

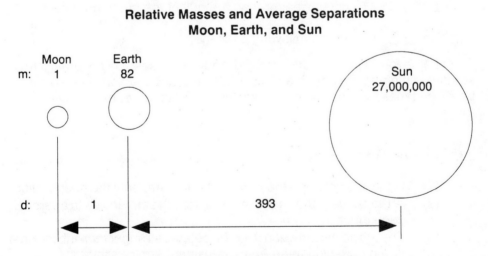

24. Newton's Universal Law of Gravitation implies that

    (1)   the attraction between the moon and the sun is the same as that between the moon and the Earth.
    (2)   the attraction between the Earth and the sun is the same as that between the moon and the Earth.

(3) the pull of the sun on the Earth is the same as the pull of the Earth on the sun.

(4) the pull of the sun on the moon must be 3×10^{19} N.

(5) the pull of the Earth on the sun must be 8×10^{24} N.

25. The pull of the sun on the Earth is

(1) about 82 times stronger than the pull of the sun on the moon.
(2) about 82 times weaker than the pull of the sun on the moon.
(3) about 393 times stronger than the pull of the sun on the moon.
(4) about 393 times weaker than the pull of the sun on the moon.
(5) about the same as the pull of the sun on the moon.

26. If the distance between the moon and the Earth was doubled, then the gravitational pull of the Earth on the moon would be

(1) 8×10^{20} N.   (4) 5×10^{19} N.
(2) 4×10^{20} N.   (5) 1×10^{19} N.
(3) 2×10^{20} N.

27. If the Earth and the sun had the same mass, then the pull of the moon on the Earth would be about

(1) the same as the pull of the moon on the sun.
(2) 393 times greater than the pull of the moon on the sun.
(3) 393 times weaker than the pull of the moon on the sun.
(4) 154,450 times greater than the pull of the moon on the sun.
(5) 154,450 times weaker than the pull of the moon on the sun.

Items 28 to 29 refer to the following passage.

Matter is found in three states: solid, liquid, and gas. Gases are both compressible and expandable. The liquid state and the solid state are both condensed phases since molecules "stick" together by attractive forces.

28. Why do two Br_2 molecules "stick" together at low temperatures?

(1) Ice forms between the molecules and prevents their separation.
(2) An increase in thermal energy causes the molecules to approach each other.
(3) The attraction between the molecules is stronger than the thermal energy pushing them apart, causing them to "stick."
(4) The Br_2 molecules expand quickly and bump into one another.
(5) Br_2 molecules cannot "stick" together because Br_2 is a gas at all temperatures.

29. If the states of matter were organized in terms of randomness of the molecular arrangements, from most random to least random, the order would be

    (1)   solid, liquid, gas.   (4)   gas, liquid, solid.
    (2)   liquid, solid, gas.   (5)   liquid, gas, solid.
    (3)   gas, solid, liquid.

Items 30 to 33 refer to the following passage.

When an Earthquake occurs, some of the energy released travels through the ground as waves. Two general types of waves are generated. One type, called the P wave, is a compression wave that alternately compresses and stretches the rock layers as it travels. A second type is a Shear wave, called the S wave, which moves the rocks in an up and down manner.

A graph can be made of the travel times of these waves.

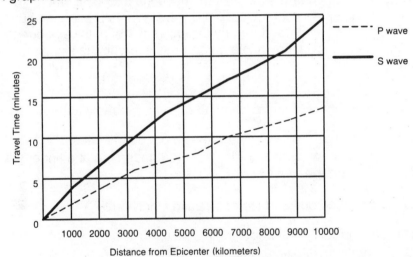

30. The main reason that a Time-Travel graph can be used to determine distance to an Earthquake's point of occurrence is that

    (1)   S waves move up and down.
    (2)   P waves are compressional.
    (3)   P waves travel faster than S waves.
    (4)   S waves travel faster than P waves.
    (5)   P and S waves travel together.

31. Approximately how many minutes does it take a P wave to travel 8000 km?

    (1)   6 minutes   (4)   15 minutes
    (2)   12 minutes   (5)   18 minutes
    (3)   3 minutes

32. An Earthquake occurs at noon, and the recording station receives the S wave at 12:05 pm. How far away is the Earthquake?

(1) 1000 km   (4) 4000 km
(2) 2000 km   (5) 5000 km
(3) 3000 km

33. How far away is an Earthquake if the difference in arrival time between the P and S waves is 7 minutes?

(1) 1000 km   (4) 7000 km
(2) 3000 km   (5) 9000 km
(3) 4000 km

Items 34 to 37 refer to the following passage.

Germs are small living structures that get into plant or animal tissue and get nourishment. Germs can cause infectious diseases, and some infectious diseases are contagious. Germs are always present on human bodies and germs can enter the body through several pathways during breathing, during eating, or while a person has injury to the skin, for example.

34. If a person has a lung infection, the germs probably entered via

(1) the nose.   (4) a cut on the chest.
(2) a cut on the finger.   (5) the underside of a fingernail.
(3) a cut on the foot.

35. Germs on the body surface of a healthy individual

(1) are infecting the body.
(2) are causing disturbance to the body.
(3) are never contagious.
(4) are not infecting the body.
(5) cannot enter the body in any manner.

36. Which one of the following microbes are considered harmful?

(1) Yeast used in making bread
(2) Mold that gives blue cheese its flavor
(3) Bacterial cultures in yogurt
(4) Malaria germs carried by mosquitoes
(5) Microorganisms used in fermentation for beer preparation

37. If a person swallows a great number of microbes with food,

(1) acidic stomach juice will destroy most microbes.
(2) basic stomach juice will destroy most microbes.

    (3)   the destruction of all of the microbes will cause food poisoning.

    (4)   powerful microbes that were not destroyed cannot cause food poisoning.

    (5)   a great proportion of the microbes swallowed are most likely very harmful.

Items 38 to 40 refer to the following information.

Scaling is used by scientists and engineers to make predictions about what will happen if the size of a structure is increased or decreased dramatically. For example, model airplanes are built and studied under different conditions, and then predictions based on scaling arguments are used for understanding how a full-sized airplane will behave under similar circumstances.

For simple objects, the surface area is proportional to the square of its linear dimension. The volume is proportional to the cube of its linear dimension, and the strength is proportional to the cross-sectional area. For like materials, weight is proportional to volume.

38.   Tripling the linear size of a bowling ball will increase its weight by

    (1)   twenty-seven and its surface area by nine.

    (2)   nine and its surface area by three.

    (3)   three and its surface area by nine.

    (4)   nine and its surface area by twenty-seven.

    (5)   twenty-seven and its surface area by three.

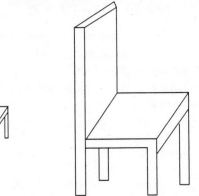

39.   A small wood chair can support 25 lbs. Another wood chair is built with the same design but scaled up four times. Its strength will increase by

    (1)   four and its weight by sixteen.

    (2)   eight and its weight by thirty-two.

    (3)   four and its weight by thirty-two.

    (4)   sixteen and its weight by eight.

    (5)   sixteen and its weight by sixty-four.

40. Suppose apples came in four sizes: A (6 cm), B (7cm), C (8 cm), and D (9 cm). Assuming each has the same density, a kilogram of what sized apples will produce the most skin when peeled?

    (1) A   (4) D
    (2) B   (5) They all produce the same amount of skin.
    (3) C

Items 41 to 44 are based on the following passage.

Every living thing contains proteins. A protein molecule is composed of molecules called amino acids. These amino acids are chemically bonded together to form a chain (the protein molecule). Amino acids are generally composed of carbon, hydrogen, oxygen, and nitrogen. Every amino acid is basically alike except for one molecular component. That component, called the "R" factor, makes the amino acid unique. There are 20 different amino acids that make up hundreds of thousands of different kinds of proteins. Proteins are what make up our skin, our hair, our muscles, our cartilage, and many other components of our body. There is very little that is found in a living organism that is not composed, in part, of protein molecules. Protein molecules are specific to the organism of which they are a part. Therefore cow muscle protein cannot be found in the muscles of humans, and neither can chicken muscle protein be found in the muscles of hawks.

41. If a chain of amino acids makes up a protein molecule, then one protein can be different from another protein by

    (1) only the length of the protein molecule.
    (2) the length of protein molecule, and the order and type of amino acids in the protein molecule.
    (3) only the type of amino acids found in the protein molecule.
    (4) only the number of chemical bonds found in the protein molecule.
    (5) only the order of amino acids in the protein.

42. How many different kinds of "R" factors are there?

    (1) 20   (4) 1000
    (2) 50   (5) 100,000
    (3) 100

43. Proteins are

    (1) chains of sugar molecules.   (4) loops of cellulose molecules.
    (2) chains of fat molecules.   (5) chains of amino acids.
    (3) rings of carbon.

44. Which of the following is not made of protein?

    (1) Hair   (4) Skin
    (2) Fingernails   (5) Muscle tissue
    (3) Rock

Items 45 to 47 refer to the following passage.

   The boiling point of a liquid in an open system is the temperature where atmospheric pressure is equivalent to the vapor pressure of the liquid. Additionally, the boiling point of a liquid is the highest temperature at which there can be liquid as a component of a system.

45. Bubbles form in a boiling liquid because

    (1) air from the atmosphere is entering the liquid.
    (2) the liquid is condensing to form a gas.
    (3) helium gas, which is lighter than any liquid, is rising.
    (4) the liquid is vaporizing.
    (5) microorganisms in the liquid are carrying out respiration.

46. A kettle containing water is heated to a boil. If the water is allowed to boil for fifteen minutes, what effect will this have on the volume of the water?

    (1) The volume will increase as water molecules are created in the hot air over the kettle.
    (2) The volume will remain constant.
    (3) The volume will occasionally increase and decrease due to the effects of atmospheric pressure.
    (4) The volume will decrease.
    (5) The volume will remain constant only if the kettle is uncovered.

47. Which of the following statements about boiling liquids is false?

    (1) Boiling liquids contain both gas and liquid.
    (2) All boiling liquids feel extremely hot to the human touch.
    (3) It will take longer to boil two liters of water compared to one liter of water over the same flame.
    (4) Below the boiling point for a liquid, the external pressure prevents the formation of gas bubbles.
    (5) Vapor pressure equals atmospheric pressure at the boiling point.

Items 48 to 51 refer to the following diagram.

Diagram of the major constellations

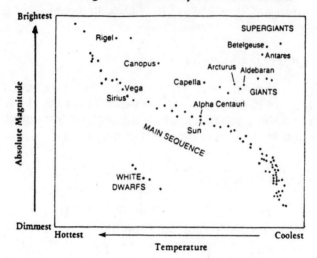

48. Most stars represented belong to which group?

    (1) Giants
    (2) Main Sequence
    (3) Supergiants
    (4) White Dwarfs
    (5) Alpha Centauri

49. Compared to our sun, Sirius is

    (1) cooler and dimmer.
    (2) cooler and brighter.
    (3) warmer and dimmer.
    (4) warmer and brighter.
    (5) similar in all respects.

50. Which star is matched with an incorrect group?

    (1) Vega—main sequence
    (2) Aldebaran—giant
    (3) Betelgeuse—Supergiant
    (4) Canopus—white dwarf
    (5) Antares—supergiant

51. Which statement is correct?

    (1) Our sun is similar to most other stars in the universe.
    (2) Our sun is very unique among stars.
    (3) Distances between stars can accurately be determined from this diagram.
    (4) Our night sky looks like this diagram.
    (5) Stars belonging to the supergiant grouping are by far the largest stars on the diagram.

Items 52 to 57 refer to the following paragraph.

Cells contain chromosomes. The number of chromosomes that are in a cell varies. In sexually reproducing organisms, the cells usually have two sets of chromosomes. Cells like these are said to be "diploid." In organisms that reproduce asexually, the cells are usually "haploid," or having one set of chromosomes. Cells reproduce themselves by means of a process called mitosis. Some organisms can reproduce themselves by budding, or breaking, when there is no sexual reproduction. Sexually reproducing organisms undergo a process whereby they produce haploid cells from diploid cells. These haploid cells are called sperms or eggs. When a sperm and an egg are united, they fuse to form a single cell called a zygote. The zygote of a human has 46 chromosomes. A zygote is a diploid cell and will undergo mitosis to produce a mature organism.

52. There are 46 chromosomes found in the cheek cell of a human male. If this cell were to undergo mitosis, how many chromosomes would be found in each resulting daughter cell?

(1) 2
(2) 10
(3) 24
(4) 46
(5) 92

53. Humans have 46 chromosomes in their body cells. How many chromosomes are found in the zygote?

(1) 2
(2) 10
(3) 23
(4) 46
(5) 92

54. If mitosis were not to occur in both a male and a female human and their sperm and egg were to unite to form a zygote, how many chromosomes would the zygote have?

(1) 2
(2) 23
(3) 46
(4) 92
(5) 184

55. Which of the following relates to a zygote?

(1) A single organism composed of two cells
(2) Haploid
(3) Undergoes meiosis to produce four sperm
(4) Diploid
(5) Undergoes meiosis to produce four eggs

56. Which of the following relates to a sperm?

(1) A single organism composed of two cells

(2) Haploid
(3) Undergoes meiosis to produce four zygotes
(4) Diploid
(5) Undergoes meiosis to produce four eggs

57. Which of the following relates to an egg?

(1) A single organism composed of two cells
(2) Haploid
(3) Undergoes meiosis to produce four sperm
(4) Diploid
(5) Undergoes meiosis to produce four zygotes

Items 58 to 59 refer to the following information.

Substance	Length of Molecules
gasoline	short
tar	long
lubricating oil	medium

A liquid that flows with ease has molecules that do not tend to tangle. Tangles occur easily when long chains of atoms flow by one another. Viscosity is the resistance of liquids to flow.

58. According to the above information, which substance is most viscous?

(1) Tar
(2) Gasoline
(3) Lubricating oil
(4) Tar and lubricating oil are equally viscous
(5) Gasoline and tar have equal viscosity

59. Why does the viscosity of most substances decrease as the temperature rises?

(1) Chains join to form much longer chains.
(2) Thermal energy rises and chains vibrate more, which causes more tangling.
(3) The chains vaporize and less are present to tangle.
(4) Most chains circularize.
(5) Long chains break to form shorter chains.

Items 60 to 66 refer to the following paragraph.

A flower is composed of several different modified leaves. The sepals are modified leaves that encircle the flower when it is in "bud." Sepals are green and protect the bud while it is developing into a flower. Just inside the sepals are the petals. The petals are usually large, showy, and brightly colored. They serve as a means of advertisement for animal pollinators that are attracted to bright patterns. Inside the petals are the stamens. The stamens are a two-part structure made up of the anther and the filament. The filament supports the anther. The anther is a structure which houses the developing pollen grains. In the very center of the flower is the pistil. The pistil is a series of modified leaves (the carpels) that contain the ovules. A pistil is composed of three basic parts: the stigma, the style, and the ovary/ovaries. The stigma is a sticky knob that receives the pollen. The pollen germinate and grow downward into the filamentous style and into the ovary and ultimately fertilize the egg that is contained within the ovary.

60. The modified leaves that produce the ovules are the

   (1) sepals.   (4) stigmas.
   (2) petals.   (5) styles.
   (3) carpels.

61. The flower part that supports the stigma is the

   (1) sepal.   (4) stigma.
   (2) petal.   (5) style.
   (3) anther.

62. These structures fertilize the egg.

   (1) Stigmas   (4) Radicals
   (2) Styles   (5) Anthers
   (3) Pollen

63. Some children pass by a bunch of flowers. After this interaction, bees are no longer attracted to the flowers. What did the children do?

   (1) They separated the sepals from the rest of the bud.
   (2) They crushed the pollen.
   (3) They crushed the stigma, which receives the pollen.
   (4) They plucked off all of the petals.
   (5) They separated the anther from the filament.

64. If a bug invades a flower which has not yet budded and causes damage to the petals, the bug must also have the ability to damage the

   (1) sepals.   (4) style.
   (2) stamens.   (5) ovary.
   (3) pistil.

65. In what way does the stigma most likely receive the pollen?

   (1) Gale winds are necessary to blow the pollen to the stigma.
   (2) Pollen sticks to pollinators and then is transferred to the stigma as the pollinator moves.

(3) Picking flowers causes the flowers to pollinate.

(4) The pollen is negatively charged and the stigma is positively charged.

(5) The pollen slides from the anther to the stigma by way of the style.

66. Flowers are similar to female animals in that

(1) both are composed of modified leaves.
(2) both have ovaries and eggs.
(3) both have ovaries and stigmas.
(4) both have male and female reproductive organs.
(5) both have eggs and sperm.

TEST 4: INTERPRETING LITERATURE AND THE ARTS

Tests of General Educational Development

Directions

The Interpreting Literature and the Arts Test consists of excerpts from classical and popular literature and articles about literature or the arts. Each excerpt is followed by multiple-choice questions about the reading material.

Read each excerpt first and then answer the questions following it. Refer back to the reading material as often as necessary in answering the questions.

Each excerpt is preceded by a "purpose question." The purpose question gives a reason for reading the material. Use these purpose questions to help focus your reading. You are not required to answer these purpose questions. They are given only to help you concentrate on the ideas presented in the reading materials.

You should spend no more than 65 minutes answering the questions in this booklet. Work carefully, but do not spend too much time on any one question. Be sure you answer every question. You will not be penalized for incorrect answers.

Do not mark in this test booklet. Record your answers on the separate answer sheet provided. Be sure all requested information is properly recorded on the answer sheet. To record your answers, mark the numbered space on the answer sheet beside the number that corresponds to the question in the test booklet.

FOR EXAMPLE:

It was Susan's dream machine. The metallic blue paint gleamed, and the sporty wheels were highly polished. Under the hood, the engine was no less carefully cleaned. Inside, flashy lights illuminated the instruments on the dashboard, and the seats were covered by rich leather upholstery.

The subject ("It") of this excerpt is most likely

   (1)   an airplane.   (4)   a boat.
   (2)   a stereo system.   (5)   a motorcycle.
   (3)   an automobile.

                                        (1) (2) ● (4) (5)

The correct answer is "an automobile"; therefore, answer space 3 would be marked on the answer sheet.

Do not rest the point of your pencil on the answer sheet while you are considering your answer. Make no stray or unnecessary marks. If you change an answer, erase your first mark completely. Mark only one answer space for each question; multiple answers will be scored as incorrect. Do not fold or crease your answer sheet. Return all test materials to the test administrator.

reprinted with permission of the General Educational Development Testing Service of the American Council on Education

Directions: Choose the <u>one best answer</u> to each item.

<u>Items 1 to 3</u> refer to the following excerpt from a story.

HOW DO YOU LET GO OF SOMETHING YOU LOVE?

I had decided to let my raccoon make his own decision. But I took off his collar and his leash and put them in a pocket of my corduroy jacket as something to remember him by if he should choose to leave me. We sat together in the canoe, listening to the night sounds all around us, but for one sound in particular.

It came at last, the sound I had been waiting for, almost exactly like the crooning tremolo we had heard when the romantic female raccoon had tried to reach him through the chicken wire. Rascal became increasingly excited. Soon he answered with a slightly deeper crooning of his own. The female was now approaching along the edge of the stream, trilling a plaintive call, infinitely tender and questing. Rascal raced to the prow of the canoe, straining to see through the moonlight and shadow, sniffing the air, and asking questions.

"Do as you please, my little raccoon. It's your life," I told him.

He hesitated for a full minute, turned once to look back at me, then took the plunge and swam to the near shore. He had chosen to join that entrancing female somewhere in the shadows. I caught only one glimpse of them in a moonlit glade before they disappeared to begin their new life together.

Sterling North, from *Rascal*, New York, New York: E.P. Dutton and Company, 1963.

1. What is the overall tone of this passage?

    (1) Uplifting   (4) Cynical
    (2) Melancholy   (5) Sarcastic
    (3) Forlorn

2. Which of the following best describes the narrator's attitude toward his pet's departure?

    (1) Sentimental   (4) Angry
    (2) Bitter yet resigned   (5) Tolerant but disappointed
    (3) Relieved

3. The reader can infer that the narrator and his pet

    (1) would soon forget about one another.
    (2) would never meet again.
    (3) were companions who understood each other.
    (4) would soon be united.
    (5) were never suited for one another.

Items 4 to 6 refer to the following excerpt from a story.

WHAT DISILLUSIONMENTS DOES DEXTER EXPERIENCE?

1   "About Judy Jones."
        Devlin looked at him helplessly.
        "Well, that's—I told you all there is to it. He treats her like the
        devil. Oh, they're not going to get divorced or anything. When he's
5   particularly outrageous she forgives him. In fact, I'm inclined to
        think she loves him. She was a pretty girl when she first came to
        Detroit."
        A pretty girl! The phrase struck Dexter as ludicrous. "Isn't she a
        pretty girl, any more?"
10   "Oh, she's all right."
        "Look here," said Dexter, sitting down suddenly. "I don't under-
        stand. You say she was a 'pretty girl' and now she's 'all right.' I
        don't understand what you mean—Judy Jones wasn't a pretty girl,
        at all. She was a great beauty. Why, I knew her. I knew her. She
15   was—"
        Devlin laughed pleasantly.
        "I'm not trying to start a row," he said. "I think Judy's a nice girl
        and I like her. I can't understand how a man like Lud Simms could
        fall madly in love with her, but he did." Then he added: "Most of
20   the women like her."
        Dexter looked closely at Devlin, thinking wildly that there must
        be a reason for this, some insensitivity in the man or some private
        malice.
        "Lots of women fade just like that," Devlin snapped his fingers.
25   "You must have seen it happen. Perhaps I've forgotten how pretty
        she was at her wedding. I've seen her so much since then, you
        see. She has nice eyes."
        A sort of dullness settled down upon Dexter. For the first time in
        his life he felt like getting very drunk. He knew that he was laugh-
30   ing loudly at something Devlin had said, but he did not know what
        it was or why it was funny. When, in a few minutes, Devlin went he
        lay down on his lounge and looked out the window at the New
        York skyline into which the sun was sinking in dull lovely shades of
        pink and gold.
35   He had thought that having nothing else to lose he was invul-
        nerable at last—but he knew that he had just lost something more,
        as surely as if he had married Judy Jones and seen her fade
        before his eyes.

F. Scott Fitzgerald, *All the Sad Young Men*, New York; New York, Charles Scribner's Sons, copyright
1922, 1950.

4.   The underlying meaning of lines 35-38 is

        (1)   Dexter is saddened but relieved that he never married Judy.
        (2)   Judy was never meant for Dexter.

    (3)   even though they never married, Dexter is still touched by Judy's life.

    (4)   nothing can hurt Dexter any more than Judy did.

    (5)   he still wishes that he and Judy could be united.

5.   Which of the following quotations does not apply to Dexter's situation concerning Judy?

    (1)   It is impossible to love and be wise. —Francis Bacon, *Of Love*

    (2)   Love is blind. —Geoffrey Chaucer, "The Merchant," from *The Canterbury Tales*

    (3)   Love comforteth like sunshine after rain. —Shakespeare, *Venus and Adonis*

    (4)   Speak of me as I am, one that loved not wisely but too well. — Shakespeare, *Othello*

    (5)   Love blinds all men alike, both the reasonable, and the foolish. — Meander, *Andria*

6.   From this dialogue, we can conclude that Devlin is being

    (1)   argumentative and harsh.   (4)   optimistic and charitable.

    (2)   realistic but kind.   (5)   rude but accurate.

    (3)   pessimistic and unforgiving.

<u>Items 7 to 13</u> refer to the following essay.

WHAT IS THE FISHERMAN'S BALM?

1   In a sense I never fish alone, in that a good share of the time, even before dawn and after dark, I'm apt to be fishing "with somebody." It may be somebody I've never known nor ever will, or it may be somebody I have known but will never see again. Be-

5   cause it's with somebody who is in any case absent from the actual scene of my fishing, my own more-than-middle age and the law of averages team up to furnish the likelihood that it is somebody who is no longer living. But that's only natural in any event; you can learn more from the dead than from the living, if only

10   because there are so many more of them. But I still don't mean that all my fishing is "down among the dead men." I'm as ready as the next to take a tip from any passing stranger, when I'm somewhere out on a stream. And a great deal of my fishing is done with people, dead or alive, with whom I have fished in the past, and, in

15   the latter instance, will undoubtedly fish with again but are in any case not around right now....

        Of course, the more you fish, the sooner you reach that stage where you'd rather put the fish back for somebody else to catch, or simply to catch them again yourself rather than take them home

20   to eat, or even to have mounted, for the subsequent amazement of all and sundry. Most wives, for one thing, are less than ecstatic over mounted fish as elements of home decoration, and, for

another, people who mount fish are nowadays even harder to come by than fish that merit being mounted.

25   You'd think, then, that as long as we're not going to keep the fish anyway, going fishless wouldn't be such a dire fate as to warrant our being classified as hardship cases. What's so bad about being skunked, if you set out resolved to return as empty-handed as if you had been anyway? And why moan about the one

30   that got away, when you were going to put him back again even if he hadn't? Well, this is where the element of thinking about it enters in. It only matters, of course, if you think it does. And boy, you find it very hard to think of anything, at least at that moment, that matters more. In fact, the great thing about fishing is that

35   there are very few activities that are open to all men on a virtually equal basis and that can provide you with occasions to feel quite so deeply, to care quite that much.

It's all very well for Izzak Walton to have settled the question centuries ago, on a purely philosophical basis, by reminding us

40   that no man can be said to have lost that which he never had. On that basis, of course, there is no such thing as a lost fish. But if it doesn't exist, why does it hurt so much?

I've never felt such intense compassion for anyone in my life as I felt for Ernest Hemingway in Bimini in 1936, when a marlin that

45   looked the size of a tank car in the sun got away after some thirty jumps, and the hand-forged hook, looking the size of an anchor, came back, pulled out and straightened like a bent bobby-pin. And if I felt that bad, then how bad did he feel?

Arnold Gingrich,"A Balm for Fishlessness," from *Fishing Moments of Truth*, edited by Eric Peper and Jim Rikhoff, copyright 1973, New York, New York: Winchester Press.

7.   Concerning fish which get away, the speaker in lines 38-42

    (1)   totally agrees with Izzak Walton.
    (2)   does not understand Walton's philosophy.
    (3)   applies Walton's wisdom to his own experience.
    (4)   totally disagrees with Walton's premise.
    (5)   needs to learn more about the matter.

8.   The speaker believes that if a person cannot lose that which he/she never had, then

    (1)   you can never gain something you never had.
    (2)   something which you nearly had is never really lost.
    (3)   material objects are never really lost.
    (4)   anything immaterial can never be lost.
    (5)   you also can never really win anything.

9.   In lines 43-48, the fisherman suggests that Ernest Hemingway's feelings about his lost marlin in Bimini were probably

    (1)   stronger than his own emotions.
    (2)   hidden.
    (3)   the same as Izzak Walton's philosophy.
    (4)   known to the public.
    (5)   not as strong as his own feelings.

10.   You can conclude from lines 25-35 that if the act of fishing is a balm to the fisherman, then

    (1)   no one actually needs to catch fish.
    (2)   more fishermen would have healthier personalities.
    (3)   going fishless could still be rewarding.
    (4)   other sports can be just as therapeutic.
    (5)   doctors would not be needed.

11.   Referring to lines 27-28, if you "got skunked," you would

    (1)   not have made a big catch.
    (2)   have made your fishing limit.
    (3)   come home empty-handed.
    (4)   be disappointed.
    (5)   encounter a foul-smelling animal.

12.   In lines 1-10, the fisherman says that he is never alone because

    (1)   thoughts and memories of people, both known and unknown, are always with him.
    (2)   visions of his dead friends come back to him.
    (3)   interesting strangers always stop by.
    (4)   he does not actually need company.
    (5)   fishing is a solitary venture.

13.   Lines 9-15 imply that the fisherman will probably fish once again with friends, dead or still alive, because

    (1)   he believes in reincarnation.
    (2)   this sport is probably not confined to people only on this earth.
    (3)   he happens to be joking.
    (4)   he is only fantasizing.
    (5)   None of the above.

Items 14 to 17 refer to the following excerpt from a story.

CAN DEATH UNITE LOVED ONES?

1   "It is coming, Maggie!" Tom said, in a deep hoarse voice, loosing the oars, and clasping her. The next instant the boat was no longer seen upon the water—and the huge mass was hurrying on in hideous triumph.

5   But soon the keel of the boat reappeared, a black speck on the golden water.

        The boat reappeared—but brother and sister had gone down in an embrace never to be parted: living through again in one supreme moment the days when they had clasped their little hands

10   in love and roamed the daisied fields together.

        Nature repairs her ravages—repairs them with her sunshine, and with human labor. The desolation wrought by that flood had left little visible trace on the face of the earth, five years after. The fifth autumn was rich in golden corn-stacks, rising in thick clusters

15   among the distant hedgerows: with echoes of eager voices, with hopeful lading and unlading.

        And every man and woman mentioned in this history was still living—except those whose end we know.

        Nature repairs her ravages—but not all. The uptorn trees are

20   not rooted again; the parted hills are left scarred: if there is new growth, the trees are not the same as the old, and the hills underneath their green vesture bear the marks of the past rending. To the eyes that have dwelt on the past, there is no thorough repair....

25   Near the brick grave there was a tomb erected, very soon after the flood, for two bodies that were found in close embrace: and it was visited at different moments by two men who both felt that their keenest joy and keenest sorrow were forever buried there....

        The tomb bore the names of Tom and Maggie Tulliver, and

30   below the names it was written:

        "In their death, they were not divided."

George Eliot, *The Mill on the Floss* (abridged excerpt), N.Y., Doubleday Page and Co., 1901.

14. The tone of lines 11-16 is

    (1)   optimistic.   (4)   forboding.
    (2)   pessimistic.   (5)   None of the above.
    (3)   realistic.

15. The tone of lines 19-24 is

    (1)   optimistic.   (4)   sarcastic.
    (2)   encouraging.   (5)   compassionate.
    (3)   realistic.

16. Lines 19-24 reveal the meaning of the passage:

    (1)   nature, like a good doctor, can heal.
    (2)   not everything, once damaged, can be repaired.
    (3)   nothing can be permanently damaged.
    (4)   birth and death are a part of nature's plan.
    (5)   in time, all things can be replaced.

17. The sentence in lines 22-24, "To the eyes that have dwelt on the past, there is no thorough repair..." can be restated as

    (1) once you have known and loved something, you can never completely replace it.
    (2) some things are taken away from us prematurely.
    (3) people who dwell on the past can never be totally happy.
    (4) never "look back."
    (5) None of the above.

Items 18 to 23 refer to the following excerpt from a story.

1   Dear Fred—I try to find heart and life to tell you that it is all over with dear old Nolan. I have been with him on this voyage more than I ever was, and I can understand wholly now the way in which you used to speak of the dear old fellow. I could see that he

5   was not strong, but I had no idea the end was so near....
      "O Danforth," he said, "I know I am dying. I cannot get home. Surely, you will tell me something now?—stop! stop! Do not speak till I say what I am sure you know, that there is not in this ship, that there is not in America—God bless her!—a more loyal man than I

10 am. There cannot be a man who loves the flag as I do, prays for it as I do, or hopes for it as I do...."
      "Mr. Nolan," said I, "I will tell you everything you ask about. Only, where shall I begin?"...
      And he drank it in, and enjoyed it as I cannot tell you. He grew

15 more and more silent, yet I never thought he was tired or faint....
      But in an hour, when the doctor went in gently, he found Nolan had breathed his life away with a smile....
      We looked in his Bible, and there was a slip of paper, at the place where he had marked the text:

20   "They desire a country, even a heaven: wherefore God is not ashamed to be called their God: for he hath prepared for them a city."
      On this slip of paper he had written:
      "Bury me in the sea; it has been my home, and I love it... But

25 will not someone set up a stone for my memory at Fort Adams or at Orleans, that my disgrace may not be more than I ought to say on it

      'In memory of
      Phillip Nolan,
30   Lieutenant in the Army of the United States.

      He loved his country as no other man has loved her; but no man deserved less at her hands.' "

Edward Everett Hale, *The Man Without A Country*, (The first Book Edition,) New York, Franklin Watts, Inc., copyright 1960.

18. From lines 1-5, you can tell that Danforth now regards Nolan

    (1)   with compassion.   (4)   as a traitor.
    (2)   with mixed feelings.   (5)   indifferently.
    (3)   with suspicion.

19. Nolan protests in lines 6-11 that

    (1)   he wishes to go home.
    (2)   he wants to live.
    (3)   he has been treated unfairly.
    (4)   nobody loves his country more than he.
    (5)   no one understands him.

20. From lines 12-17, we can infer that Danforth related to Nolans information

    (1)   which was classified.   (4)   which was incorrect.
    (2)   which gave his spirit peace.   (5)   reluctantly.
    (3)   which caused him further unrest.

21. From a close reading of lines 6-17, we can form this analogy: Danforth's news to Nolan was as

    (1)   exercise is to an athlete.
    (2)   money is to a wealthy man's wallet.
    (3)   peace is to a tormented spirit.
    (4)   a toy is to a small child.
    (5)   food is to a hungry man.

22. From the text Nolan had marked in his Bible, we can conclude that his burning desire was to have

    (1)   a burial at sea.   (4)   a country of his own.
    (2)   an elaborate funeral.   (5)   fame and fortune.
    (3)   a medal of honor.

23. Lines 31 and 32 most nearly mean

    (1)   he loved his country more, and deserved no more than he received.
    (2)   he actually did not love his country.
    (3)   patriotism has its rewards.
    (4)   it is worth suffering for your country.
    (5)   Nolan was a "summer patriot."

Items 24 ro 29 refer to the following excerpt from an article.

VAN GOGH WAS A GENIUS, BUT WAS HE REALLY MAD?

1   It has been almost exactly 100 years since Vincent van Gogh propped his easel against a haystack near the Château d'Auvers in France and fired a bullet into his chest. He managed to crawl back to the house of a family named Ravoux, with whom he was
5 living. Doctors were summoned and the artist's younger brother, Theo, rushed by train from Paris as soon as he heard the news.

    "I wish I could pass away like this," Vincent said as he lay beside his brother, shortly before dying in the early morning of July 29, 1890, leaving behind hundreds of paintings and drawings no
10 one wanted. Theo had tried for years to sell them, not least in the hope of recouping a fraction of the money he had shelled out to support his hapless brother over the course of more than a decade. He had no luck, and neither did the Paris dealer, Julien François (Pére) Tanguy, who had agreed to keep some of
15 Vincent's paintings in the attic of his shop.

    Was Vincent addicted to absinthe? Did he really chase Paul Gauguin with a razor, or was that a story embroidered by Gauguin to justify abandoning van Gogh in Arles? Did Theo die—six months after his brother, at the age of 33, in an asylum near
20 Utrecht—from grief over Vincent's suicide? Was the artist epileptic or manic depressive or did he suffer, as a recent article in the Journal of the American Medical Association suggests, from an inner-ear disorder that finally drove him in the winter of 1888 to lop off part of his left ear in a desperate attempt to alleviate the pain?
25   An earlier generation of van Gogh biographers wove such fanciful tales of the pathetic starving painter driven to drink and lunacy that the latest crop of historians and writers has found it necessary to undo, at least in part, the myth that has obscured the man. As David Sweetman, author of the engaging new "Van
30 Gogh: His Life and His Art," says of the old biographies: "The one significant conclusion that can be reached from them is that whatever he was suffering from cannot be directly 'read' into his art... the image of Vincent as an isolated Holy Fool, artist-sage or whatever, has finally been exposed as the nonsense it always
35 was...."

Michael Kimmelman, "Vincent Obsessed," from *The New York Times, Book Review*, August 12, 1990, New York: copyright 1990, Pp. 1, 22, 23.

24. According to this review, the notion of Vincent van Gogh being a "mad genius" is best explained as

    (1) substantiated by incidents in his life.
    (2) just a myth.
    (3) created by his brother.
    (4) proven by his suicide.
    (5) challenged by recent historians and writers.

25. The series of questions posed in lines 16-24 is used by the reviewer as a literary device to

    (1) prove his point that van Gogh was mad.
    (2) give the reader insight into the controversial stories about van Gogh's life.
    (3) baffle the reader.
    (4) amuse the reader.
    (5) prove that van Gogh was not mad, but physically ill.

26. In lines 25-35 one new biographer

    (1) questions old theories about van Gogh.
    (2) accepts the "old" biographers' and writers' statements.
    (3) rejects past and present theories.
    (4) is uncertain about "old" and "new" reviews.
    (5) None of the above.

27. The tone of this review is generally

    (1) serious and informative. (4) derogatory and inflammatory.
    (2) humorous and entertaining. (5) None of the above.
    (3) slanted and one-sided.

28. You can readily determine in lines 29-35 that van Gogh as the genius and madman

    (1) has no basis in truth.
    (2) has finally been exposed as the truth.
    (3) is still debatable.
    (4) has yet to be resolved.
    (5) is best left for future biographers.

29. In lines 32 and 33, the word "read" as used in the sentence means

    (1) summarized.   (4) interpreted.
    (2) questioned.   (5) removed from.
    (3) painted.

Items 30 to 32 refer to the following excerpt of an article.

WAS THIS MUSICIAN REALLY THE GREATEST BLUES SINGER-GUITARIST-SONGWRITER?

1   What we have in *Robert Johnson: The Complete Recordings* are solid facts in Stephen C. LaVere's meticulously researched liner notes, brief appreciations of Johnson by Keith Richards ("He was like a comet or meteor that came along and, BOOM, suddenly
5   he raised the ante, suddenly you just had to aim that much higher") and Eric Clapton ("I have never found anything more

10

15

20

25

deeply soulful than Robert Johnson. His music remains the most powerful cry that I think you can find in the human voice, really"), lyrics and photos. And, of course, we have the songs—digitally clarified and, as expected, at least as powerful and affecting as ever.

The Robert Johnson recordings are musical art of the highest order, as rich and transcendent as anything produced by an American musician in this century—surely only a racist or classist would argue otherwise. Was he really the greatest blues singer-guitarist-songwriter of all? Listening to Johnson in Frank Abbey's lovingly restored and remastered new versions, the question seems almost irrelevant. Johnson was a great one, all right, and bluesman to the bottom of his soul. But at his most original, when he is almost chilling, Johnson blows genre considerations and invidious comparisons right out of the window.

Technically, Johnson the guitarist was an anomaly. He could sing and play crossrhythms on the guitar, relating the parts in such complex syncopations that, as Richards notes, "You think, 'This guy must have three brains!' "... The music has a power that age cannot dim. Familiarity with his work, even over many years, breeds only a finer appreciation and a more acute sense of awe....

Robert Palmer, *King of the Delta Blues*, in *ROLLING STONE*, October 18, 1990, pp. 97-98, copyright 1990 by Straight Arrow Publishers, 745 Fifth Avenue, New York, New York, 10151.

30. In lines 4 and 5, "... suddenly he raised the ante..." most closely means:

    (1)   The musician raised the salary of musicians.
    (2)   Johnson raised the standards of excellence for musicians.
    (3)   The guitarist created a problem between musicians and the general public.
    (4)   He raised the risk of becoming obscure.
    (5)   Johnson aimed too high to actually achieve his goals.

31. The reviewer answers the question in lines 15 and 16 ("Was he really the greatest...?")

    (1)   affirmatively by saying *yes*.
    (2)   negatively with a firm *no*.
    (3)   evasively by *avoiding* the question.
    (4)   *neither* affirmatively nor negatively by saying the question is of little importance.
    (5)   by *first affirming* then *denying* the question of Johnson's greatness.

32. In a close reading of lines 22 through 27, we can conclude that Robert Johnson's music

    (1)   will soon become outdated.
    (2)   has no popular appeal.
    (3)   will survive the test of time.
    (4)   cannot endure the test of time.
    (5)   is the greatest of all time.

Items 33 to 37 refer to the following excerpt from a story.

WHAT DID THE NARRATOR LEARN DURING HER VISIT?

1   "Have a seat, Marguerite. Over there by the table."

She carried a platter covered with a tea towel. Although she warned that she hadn't tried her hand at baking sweets for some time, I was certain that like everything else about her the cookies

5   would be perfect.

As I ate she began the first of what we later called my "lessons in living." She said that I must always be intolerant of ignorance but understanding of illiteracy. That some people, unable to go to school, were more educated and even more intelligent than

10   college professors. She encouraged me to listen carefully to what country people called mother wit. That in those homely sayings was couched the collective wisdom of generations.

When I finished the cookies she brushed off the table and brought a thick, small book from the bookcase. I had read *A Tale*

15   *of Two Cities* and found it up to my standards as a romantic novel. She opened the first page and I heard poetry for the first time in my life.

"It was the best of times and the worst of times..."

Her voice slid in and curved down through and over the words.

20   She was nearly singing. I wanted to look at the pages. Were they the same that I had read? Or were there notes, music, lines on the pages, as in a hymn book? Her sounds began cascading gently. I knew from listening to a thousand preachers that she was nearing the end of her reading, and I hadn't really heard, heard to under-

25   stand, a single word.

"How do you like that?"

It occurred to me that she expected a response. The sweet vanilla flavor was still on my tongue and her reading was a wonder in my ears. I had to speak.

30   I said, "Yes ma'am." It was the least I could do, but it was the most also.

"There's one more thing. Take this book of poems and memo-rize one for me. Next time you pay me a visit, I want you to recite."

Maya Angelou, from *I Know Why the Caged Bird Sings*, copyright 1969 by Maya Angelou, New York, New York: Bantam Books, Feb., 1980.

33. From the beginning, we can judge that Marguerite's regard for her hostess is one of

    (1) cool reserve.   (4) awe and respect.
    (2) fear.   (5) no consequence.
    (3) distrust.

34. You can equate the writer's "lesson in living," lines 6-12, with

    (1) wisdom.   (4) native intelligence.
    (2) unintelligence.   (5) "book" learning.
    (3) charm.

35. To be "intolerant of ignorance but understanding of illiteracy" implies

    (1) uneducated people are always intelligent.
    (2) illiterate people are always ignorant.
    (3) intolerance always means ignorance.
    (4) ignorant people are always educated.
    (5) educated people can sometimes be ignorant.

36. The author intended lines 16 and 17, "I heard poetry for the first time" to be interpreted

    (1) literally.   (2) figuratively.
    (3) socially.   (4) with "tongue in cheek."
    (5) None of the above.

37. After the poetic reading, lines 29 and 30, the writer reveals that she was

    (1) uneasy.
    (2) offended.
    (3) unable to express her feelings.
    (4) unimpressed.
    (5) eloquent in her praises.

Items 38 to 41 refer to the following poem.

WHY DOES THE SPEAKER STOP, THEN GO ON?

1   Whose woods these are I think I know
His house is in the village though;
He will not see me stopping here
To watch his woods fill up with snow.

5   My little horse thinks it queer
To stop without a farmhouse near
Between the woods and frozen lake
The darkest evening of the year.

He gives his harness bells a shake
10   To ask if there is some mistake.
The only other sound's the sweep
Of easy wind and downy flake.

The woods are lovely, dark and deep,
But I have promises to keep,
15   And miles to go before I sleep,
And miles to go before I sleep.

Robert Frost, "Stopping by Woods on a Snowy Evening," in *An Anthology of the New England Poets*,
Ed. by Louis Untermeyer, N.Y., New York: Random House, 1948.

38. In the first stanza, the speaker stops by the woods because

    (1) his horse is weary.
    (2) he decides to visit a neighbor.
    (3) he enjoys the silent beauty of the woodland.
    (4) it's getting too dark to travel.
    (5) some neighbor beckons him to stop.

39. Stanzas two and three tell us that the horse

    (1) knows this is the wrong path home.
    (2) stops since he is weary.
    (3) has lost the way.
    (4) signals there is no farmhouse here.
    (5) moves along stubbornly.

40. The final stanza reveals that the woods are inviting, but the **speaker**

    (1) decides not to stay since he has obligations.
    (2) is confused.
    (3) must go home to sleep.
    (4) will return soon.
    (5) None of the above.

41. Symbolically, the poem presents a struggle between

    (1) good and evil.   (4) sickness and health.
    (2) wealth and poverty.   (5) past and present.
    (3) life and death.

Items 42 to 43 refer to the following excerpt from an article.

HOW CAN TIME BE IMPRISONED IN A RECTANGLE?

1   Balzac had a "vague dread" of being photographed. Like some
primitive peoples, he thought the camera stole something of the
soul—that, as he told a friend, "every body in its natural state is

made up of a series of ghostly images superimposed in layers to
5   infinity, wrapped in infinitesimal films." Each time a photograph
was made, he believed, another thin layer of the subject's being
would be stripped off to become not life as before but a membrane
of memory in a sort of translucent anti-world.

If that is what photography is up to, then the onion of the world
10   is being peeled away, layer by layer—lenses like black holes
gobbling up life's emanations. Mere images proliferate, while
history pares down to a phosphorescence of itself.

The pictures made by photojournalists have the legitimacy of
being news, fresh information. They slice along the hard edge of
15   the present. Photojournalism is not self-conscious, since it first
enters the room (the brain) as a battle report from the far-flung
Now. It is only later that the artifacts of photojournalism sink into
the textures of the civilization and tincture its memory.

If journalism—the kind done with words—is the first draft of
20   history, what is photojournalism? Is it the first impression of history, the first graphic flash? Yes, but it is also (and this is the
disturbing thing) history's lasting visual impression. The service
that the pictures perform is splendid, and so powerful as to seem
preternatural. But sometimes the power they possess is more than
25   they deserve.

All great photographs have lives of their own, but they can be
as false as dreams. Somehow the mind knows that and sorts out
the matter, and permits itself to enjoy the pictures without getting
sunk in the really mysterious business that they involve.

Lance Morrow, "Imprisoning Time in a Rectangle," Special Collector's Edition of *Time: 150 Years of Photo Journalism*, Fall, 1989, New York: New York, Time Inc. Magazine Company, Rockefeller Center.

42.   The author believes that, at times, photojournalism

    (1)   is not powerful enough.
    (2)   is not "good" journalism.
    (3)   can be more powerful than it is thought to be.
    (4)   is simply entertainment.
    (5)   is underestimated as a news media.

43.   A literary device used effectively in this essay is

    (1)   repetition.   (4)   rhyme.
    (2)   alliteration.   (5)   cacophony.
    (3)   personification.

44.   The writer implies that we should regard photojournalism

    (1)   casually.   (4)   tolerantly.
    (2)   cautiously.   (5)   disrespectfully.
    (3)   suspiciously.

45. According to the essayist, time can be "imprisoned in a rectangle" by

    (1) revealing criminal misuse of photojournalism.
    (2) capturing historic moments in photographs.
    (3) accepting Balzac's dread of photographs.
    (4) discontinuing the use of photojournalism.
    (5) None of the above.

TEST 5: MATHEMATICS

Tests of General Educational Development

Directions

The Mathematics Test consists of multiple-choice questions intended to measure general mathematics skills and problem-solving ability. The questions are based on short readings which often include a graph, chart, or figure.

You should spend no more than 90 minutes answering the questions in this booklet. Work carefully, but do not spend too much time on any one question. Be sure you answer every question. You will not be penalized for incorrect answers.

Formulas you may need are given on the following page. Only some of the questions will require you to use a formula. Not all the formulas given will be needed.

Some questions contain more information than you will need to solve the problem. Other questions do not give enough information to solve the problem. If the question does not give enough information to solve the problem, the correct answer choice is "Not enough information is given."

The use of calculators is not allowed.

Do not mark in this test booklet. The test administrator will give you blank paper for your calculations. Record your answers on the separate answer sheet provided. Be sure all requested information is properly recorded on the answer sheet.

To record your answers, mark the numbered space on the answer sheet beside the number that corresponds to the question in the test booklet.

FOR EXAMPLE:

If a grocery bill totaling $15.75 is paid with a $20.00 bill, how much change should be returned?

(1)	$5.26	(4)	$3.75
(2)	$4.75	(5)	$3.25
(3)	$4.25		

① ② ● ④ ⑤

The correct answer is "$4.25"; therefore, answer space 3 would be marked on the answer sheet.

Do not rest the point of your pencil on the answer sheet while you are considering your answer. Make no stray or unnecessary marks. If you change an answer, erase your first mark completely. Mark only one answer space for each question; multiple answers will be scored as incorrect. Do not fold or crease your answer sheet. Return all test materials to the test administrator.

reprinted with permission of the General Educational Development Testing Service of the American Council on Education

REFERENCE TABLE

SYMBOLS AND THEIR MEANINGS

=	is equal to	≤	is less than or equal to
≠	is unequal to	≥	is greater than or equal to
<	is less than	‖	is parallel to
>	is greater than	⊥	is perpendicular to

FORMULAS

DESCRIPTION	FORUMLA

AREA (A) of a:

square — $A = s^2$; where s = side
rectangle — $A = lw$; where l = length, w = width
parallelogram — $A = bh$; where b = base, h = height
triangle — $A = \frac{1}{2} bh$; where b = base, h = height
circle — $A = \pi r^2$; where π = 3.14, r = radius

PERIMETER (P) of a:

square — $P = 4s$; where s = side
rectangle — $P = 2l + 2w$; where l = length, w = width
triangle — $P = a + b + c$; where a, b, and c are the sides
circumference (C) of a circle — $C = \pi d$, where π = 3.14, d = diameter

VOLUME (V) of a:

cube — $V = s^2$; where s = side
rectangular container — $V = lwh$; where l = length, w = width, h = height

Pythagorean relationship — $c^2 = a^2 + b^2$; where c = hypotenuse, a and b are legs of a right triangle

distance (d) between two points in a plane — $d = \sqrt{(x_2 - x_1)^2 + (y_2 - y_1)^2}$
where (x_1, y_1) and (x_2, y_2) are two points in a plane

mean — $\text{mean} = \dfrac{x_1 + x_2 + \ldots + x_n}{n}$;
where the x's are the values for which a mean is desired, and n = number of values in the series

median — **median** = the point in an ordered set of numbers at which half of the numbers are above and half of the numbers are below this value

simple interest (i) — $i = prt$; where p = principal, r = rate, t = time

distance (d) as function of rate and time — $d = rt$; where r = rate, t = time

total cost (c) — $c = nr$; where n = number of units, r = *cost per unit*

Directions: Choose the one best answer to each item.

1. Solve for x: 2x - 7 = 3x + 2

    (1)   -14   (4)   9/5
    (2)   -9   (5)   14/5
    (3)   1

2. There are 25 students in a chemistry class and 23 students taking physics. Seven students are in both classes. How many individuals are enrolled in either of the classes or both?

    (1)   24   (4)   41
    (2)   34   (5)   48
    (3)   38

3. What percent of 3.6 is 0.9?

    (1)   1/4   (4)   40
    (2)   4   (5)   60
    (3)   25

4. A swimming pool measures 160 feet long and 80 feet wide. What is the perimeter of the pool in yards?

    (1)   40   (4)   280
    (2)   160   (5)   320
    (3)   240

5. Scott can pot 100 plants in 30 minutes. Henri can do the same job in 60 minutes. If they worked together, how many minutes would it take them to pot 200 plants?

    (1)   20   (4)   60
    (2)   30   (5)   90
    (3)   40

6. Twenty-five students rented a bus to attend a play. At the last moment, five students decided not to go. The others were each assessed an additional $1.00 to their share of the fare to cover the total cost of the bus rental. How much was the bus rental?

    (1) $80   (4) $110
    (2) $100   (5) $125
    (3) $120

7. What is 1/2 of 4/5 divided into 2/3 of 60%?

    (1)   4/5   (2)   4/25

(3) 2/5   (4) 1
(5) 1 1/2

8.   a is an even number, b is an odd number, and c is an even number.
     Which one of the following must be false?

     (1) a + b = odd   (4) a + 3b = odd
     (2) a + c = even   (5) a(b + c) = odd
     (3) 2bc = even

9.   The angles of a triangle are in a ratio of 3 : 5 : 10. How many degrees
     is the largest angle?

     (1) 10   (4) 150
     (2) 18   (5) 180
     (3) 100

10. A family earned $40,000 last year. 25% of it paid the mortgage. 25% of
     the remainder paid for their food and clothing. After the food and
     clothing, 20% of the remaining balance was saved for a vacation. What
     percent of the total earnings was saved for the vacation?

     (1) 11 1/ 4   (4) 40
     (2) 20   (5) 45
     (3) 23 1/3

11. What is the least common multiple of 8x and 24xy?

     (1) 2   (4) 48
     (2) 2xy   (5) 72xy
     (3) 6x

12. How many twelfths are there in 33 1/3%?

     (1) 1   (4) 100
     (2) 4   (5) 400
     (3) 33

13. A floor that measures 10 feet by 20 feet is to be tiled with square tiles
     that are 36 square inches in area. How many tiles are needed to cover
     the entire floor?

     (1) 200   (4) 800
     (2) 360   (5) 1200
     (3) 600

14. Pearl's bowling average after 15 games was 162. Her next three games were 187, 175, and 160. Her new average was increased by how much?

(1) 2   (4) 8
(2) 5   (5) 12
(3) 6

15. Neal spent 3/4 of his money for a shirt. If he was left with $20.00, how much did he have originally?

(1) $15   (4) $80
(2) $25   (5) $100
(3) $60

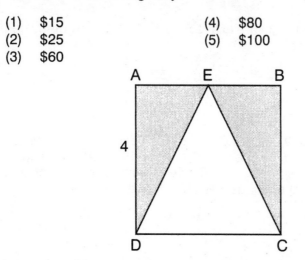

16. ABCD is a square and E is the midpoint of segment AB. Find the area of the shaded region.

(1) 4   (4) 12
(2) 6   (5) 16
(3) 8

17. Solve for all possible values of b: $b^2 - 121 > 0$.

(1) b = 11   (4) b < -11 or b > 11
(2) b = -11 or b = 11   (5) b > -11 or b > 11
(3) b > -11 or b < 11

18. Tracey has 13 more dimes than nickels. In terms of n (for nickels), find an expression for the value of Tracey's coins.

(1) 2n + 13   (4) 5n + 130
(2) 2n + 130   (5) 15n + 130
(3) 15n + 13

19. A recipe for Chicken Divan will serve 8 people. Jann has invited 17 friends over for dinner. By how much does she need to increase the recipe in order to have enough servings?

    (1)   1 3/4 times
    (2)   2 times
    (3)   2 1/4 times
    (4)   3 1/2 times
    (5)   9 times

20. A board 3 feet long is to be cut into 3 pieces such that the first piece is one-third the length of the second and the third piece is five times the length of the first. Find the length of the longest piece.

    (1)   1/3 foot
    (2)   1 foot
    (3)   1 1/2 foot
    (4)   1 2/3 foot
    (5)   1 3/4 foot

21. Lance traveled 90 miles in 2 hours. How much faster does he need to go in order to return in 1.5 hours?

    (1)   15 mph
    (2)   25 mph
    (3)   35 mph
    (4)   45 mph
    (5)   60 mph

22. What is the minimum amount that 534 may be increased by to be a multiple of 7?

    (1)   2
    (2)   5
    (3)   44
    (4)   76 2/7
    (5)   3738

23. Find the area of the polygon.

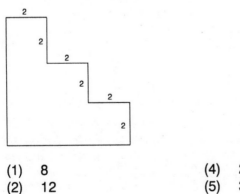

    (1)   8
    (2)   12
    (3)   20
    (4)   24
    (5)   30

24. If $4x - 3 = 2y + 7$, find the value of $2x - y$.

    (1) -21   (4) 5
    (2) 21   (5) 10
    (3) 1

Graph for Problems 25, 26, and 27.

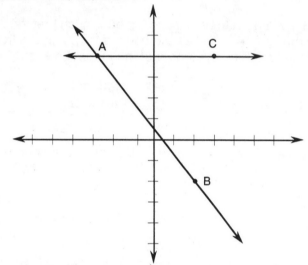

25. Find the equation for the line AC.

    (1) x = 4   (4) x − y = 4
    (2) y = 4   (5) not enough information
    (3) x + y = 4

26. What is the midpoint of segment AB?

    (1) (-1, 2)   (4) (-1, 1/2)
    (2) (0, 0)   (5) (-1, -1/2)
    (3) (-1/2, 1)

27. What is the slope of line AB?

    (1) -2/5   (4) -6/5
    (2) -5/2   (5) -8/5
    (3) 5/6

28. Two cars 660 miles apart start traveling toward each other, agreeing to meet midway. One car averages 40 mph, the other at 55 mph. How long will the faster car have to wait in order to meet the slower car at the halfway point?

    (1) 2 hours   (4) 6 hours
    (2) 2 1/4 hours   (5) 8 1/4 hours
    (3) 4 hours

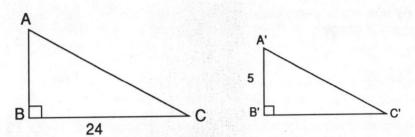

29. Triangles ABC and A'B'C' are similar right triangles. Find the length of side AC.

    (1) 10   (4) 16
    (2) 12   (5) 26
    (3) 13

30. Simplify the following:

$$\frac{\dfrac{1}{3}}{1+\dfrac{2}{4+5}}$$

    (1) 7/24   (4) 1
    (2) 3/11→ 3/11   (5) 1/3
    (3) 8/21

31. The formula to convert Fahrenheit temperature to Celsius is

$$C = \frac{5}{9}\ (F\text{-}32)$$

    Convert 98.6 F to Celsius.

    (1) 19.5 C   (4) 60 C
    (2) 37 C   (5) 66.6 C
    (3) 54.5 C

Chart for Problems 32 and 33.

Kristen's Growth Chart

Age in months:	Birth	6	12	18
Length in inches:	20	27 1/2	30 3/4	33
Weight in lbs./oz.:	7/4	19/15	22/6	24/8

32. How much more did Kristen's weight increase during the first 6 months as compared to her second 6 months?

    (1) 10 lbs. 4 oz.   (4) 7 lbs. 8 oz.
    (2) 2 lbs. 5 oz.   (5) 4 lbs. 4 oz.
    (3) 12 lbs. 11 oz.

33. By how many percent did Kristen's height increase from birth to 18 months of age?

    (1) 13
    (2) 22
    (3) 42

    (4) 65
    (5) 75

34. A restaurant buys cans of corn in bulk. If 3 cans of corn sell for $8.00, how much will one gross cost the restaurant?

    (1) $24
    (2) $80
    (3) $246

    (4) $384
    (5) $1152

35. A cylindrical can measures 4.2 inches in height. Its circular bases of 1 1/2 inch radii are removed, and the cylinder is cut open from top to bottom. What is the surface area of the cylinder? (Use 3.14 for π.)

    (1) 9 3/7 sq. in.
    (2) 6.3 sq. in.
    (3) 39.6 sq. in.

    (4) 1 4/7 sq. in.
    (5) 66 sq. in.

36. A group of children share a package of cookies, each having six. If 2 more children join the group, they can each have four cookies. How many cookies were in the package, assuming none are left over?

    (1) 8
    (2) 10
    (3) 16

    (4) 24
    (5) 36

37. A bike wheel has a radius of 12 inches. How many revolutions will it take to cover 1 mile? (Use 1 mile = 5280 feet, and π = 22/7.)

    (1) 70
    (2) 84
    (3) 120

    (4) 840
    (5) 1020

38. Mike is 8 1/2 times older than his son, Derek. The sum of their ages is 38. How old is Mike?

    (1) 32
    (2) 34
    (3) 36

    (4) 38
    (5) 40

Table for Problems 39 and 40.

The following table shows the rainfall, in inches, over a 5-day period in August for Hilo, Hawaii. It also includes the total rainfall for the year and the average rainfall for a typical year.

	Rainfall	Year	Normal
Monday	0.08	90.88	79.15
Tuesday	0.09	90.97	79.16
Wednesday	0.70	91.67	79.17
Thursday	0.19	91.86	79.17
Friday	0.32	92.18	79.50

39. Find the average rainfall for the week in August.

    (1)   1.38   (4)   0.237
    (2)   0.276   (5)   0.138
    (3)   0.32

40. Using Monday's reading and rounding off to the nearest one percent, the year-to-date record is what percent of the normal reading?

    (1)   13   (4)   105
    (2)   15   (5)   115
    (3)   87

41. Estimate to the nearest hundred:

$$\frac{(7592)\,(4892)}{(3810)\,(70)}$$

    (1)   98   (4)   1000
    (2)   100   (5)   4900
    (3)   980

42. Sam has $1000 to invest. He would like to invest 3/5 of it at 6% simple interest. The remainder would be invested at 8% simple interest. How much interest would he have earned after one year?

    (1) $32   (4) $70
    (2) $36   (5) $140
    (3) $68

43. What is the largest prime number factor of 156?

    (1)   2   (4)   13
    (2)   3   (5)   39
    (3)   12

44. Four less than 3 times x is greater than 6. Find all values of x.

    (1) $x < 10/3$ (4) $x > 2/3$
    (2) $x > 10/3$ (5) $x > 8$
    (3) $x < 5$

45. In the diagram, the triangle is isosceles, how many degrees is x?

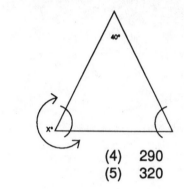

(1)   70
(2)   110
(3)   140

(4)   290
(5)   320

46. Rewrite the repeating decimal 0.252525... in fraction form.

(1)   1/4
(2)   1/25
(3)   4/17

(4)   4/25
(5)   25/99

47. The denominator of a fraction is four more than the numerator. If the numerator is doubled and the denominator is increased by five, the resulting fraction is equal to 1/2. What is the original fraction?

(1)   3/7
(2)   5/9
(3)   1/5

(4)   7/3
(5)   9/5

48. A case of cereal boxes measures 1 foot high, 2 feet wide, and 2 1/2 feet long. Each box of cereal has a volume of 288 cubic inches. How many boxes of cereal are in each case?

(1)   5
(2)   15
(3)   25

(4)   30
(5)   40

49. Sandy was x years old four years ago. What expression represents how old she will be 4 years from now?

(1)   x
(2)   x + 4
(3)   4x + 4

(4)   x + 8
(5)   16x

50. Evaluate the following: $48 - 24 \div 3 + 5 \times 2$

(1)   6
(2)   12
(3)   18

(4)   26
(5)   50

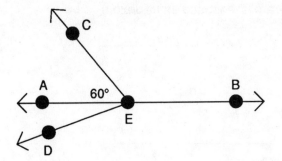

51. Line AB is a straight line. The measure of angle CEB is 8 times the measure of angle AED. Find the degree measure of angle DEB.

    (1) 15   (4) 165
    (2) 60   (5) 175
    (3) 120

52. Simplify: $7.5 \times 1\frac{7}{9} - 1.333...$

    (1) 1/18   (4) 12
    (2) 5 5/8   (5) 17 7/9
    (3) 6 2/3

53. Let $a^*b = a^2 + 2b$

    Find 3 * 1/2.
    (1) -8   (4) 8
    (2) -5   (5) 10
    (3) 7

54. Simplify and express in factored form: $6(x-2) - 4(x+4)$

    (1) 2 (x + 1)   (4) 2 (x – 14)
    (2) 2 (x + 2)   (5) 2 (x – 8)
    (3) 2 (x + 7)

55. Find the area of the isosceles trapezoid.

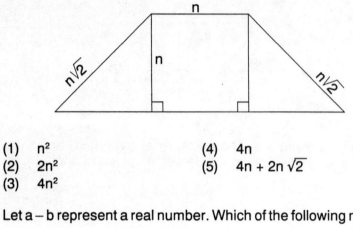

(1) n^2
(2) $2n^2$
(3) $4n^2$

(4) $4n$
(5) $4n + 2n\sqrt{2}$

56. Let $a - b$ represent a real number. Which of the following must be true?

I. $a > b$
II. $a - b < a + b$
III. $a - b < a$

(1) I only
(2) II only
(3) III only

(4) I and III
(5) none

EXAM I

ANSWER KEY

Test 1—Writing Skills

1.	(1)	15.	(3)	29.	(4)	43.	(5)
2.	(2)	16.	(2)	30.	(3)	44.	(4)
3.	(5)	17.	(4)	31.	(4)	45.	(4)
4.	(1)	18.	(5)	32.	(5)	46.	(4)
5.	(4)	19.	(4)	33.	(1)	47.	(2)
6.	(2)	20.	(5)	34.	(3)	48.	(4)
7.	(4)	21.	(2)	35.	(4)	49.	(4)
8.	(2)	22.	(1)	36.	(1)	50.	(3)
9.	(1)	23.	(3)	37.	(4)	51.	(2)
10.	(3)	24.	(5)	38.	(3)	52.	(5)
11.	(3)	25.	(4)	39.	(4)	53.	(3)
12.	(4)	26.	(3)	40.	(3)	54.	(4)
13.	(3)	27.	(2)	41.	(4)	55.	(5)
14.	(5)	28.	(4)	42.	(4)		

Test 2—Social Studies

1.	(4)	17.	(5)	33.	(3)	49.	(3)
2.	(3)	18.	(3)	34.	(5)	50.	(4)
3.	(5)	19.	(2)	35.	(4)	51.	(3)
4.	(3)	20.	(2)	36.	(3)	52.	(1)
5.	(1)	21.	(4)	37.	(4)	53.	(3)
6.	(4)	22.	(2)	38.	(3)	54.	(1)
7.	(3)	23.	(1)	39.	(2)	55.	(2)
8.	(3)	24.	(3)	40.	(1)	56.	(1)
9.	(3)	25.	(5)	41.	(4)	57.	(4)
10.	(1)	26.	(1)	42.	(5)	58.	(4)
11.	(3)	27.	(4)	43.	(4)	59.	(5)
12.	(4)	28.	(3)	44.	(2)	60.	(3)
13.	(3)	29.	(1)	45.	(2)	61.	(1)
14.	(1)	30.	(1)	46.	(3)	62.	(4)
15.	(4)	31.	(4)	47.	(2)	63.	(1)
16.	(4)	32.	(5)	48.	(1)	64.	(1)

Test 3—Science

1.	(4)	18.	(3)	35.	(4)	52.	(4)
2.	(5)	19.	(1)	36.	(4)	53.	(4)
3.	(2)	20.	(4)	37.	(1)	54.	(4)
4.	(1)	21.	(3)	38.	(1)	55.	(4)
5.	(2)	22.	(5)	39.	(5)	56.	(2)
6.	(3)	23.	(1)	40.	(1)	57.	(2)
7.	(4)	24.	(3)	41.	(2)	58.	(1)
8.	(1)	25.	(1)	42.	(1)	59.	(5)
9.	(3)	26.	(4)	43.	(5)	60.	(3)
10.	(3)	27.	(4)	44.	(3)	61.	(5)
11.	(2)	28.	(3)	45.	(4)	62.	(3)
12.	(5)	29.	(4)	46.	(4)	63.	(4)
13.	(1)	30.	(3)	47.	(2)	64.	(1)
14.	(3)	31.	(2)	48.	(2)	65.	(2)
15.	(2)	32.	(1)	49.	(4)	66.	(2)
16.	(3)	33.	(3)	50.	(4)		
17.	(3)	34.	(1)	51.	(1)		

Test 4—Literature and the Arts

1.	(2)	13.	(2)	25.	(2)	37.	(3)
2.	(1)	14.	(1)	26.	(1)	38.	(3)
3.	(3)	15.	(3)	27.	(1)	39.	(4)
4.	(3)	16.	(2)	28.	(1)	40.	(1)
5.	(3)	17.	(1)	29.	(4)	41.	(3)
6.	(2)	18.	(1)	30.	(2)	42.	(3)
7.	(3)	19.	(4)	31.	(4)	43.	(3)
8.	(2)	20.	(2)	32.	(3)	44.	(2)
9.	(1)	21.	(3)	33.	(4)	45.	(2)
10.	(3)	22.	(4)	34.	(1)		
11.	(3)	23.	(1)	35.	(5)		
12.	(1)	24.	(5)	36.	(2)		

Test 5—Math

1.	(2)	15.	(4)	29.	(5)	43.	(4)
2.	(4)	16.	(3)	30.	(2)	44.	(2)
3.	(3)	17.	(4)	31.	(2)	45.	(4)
4.	(2)	18.	(5)	32.	(1)	46.	(5)
5.	(3)	19.	(3)	33.	(4)	47.	(1)
6.	(2)	20.	(4)	34.	(4)	48.	(4)
7.	(4)	21.	(1)	35.	(3)	49.	(4)
8.	(5)	22.	(5)	36.	(4)	50.	(5)
9.	(3)	23.	(4)	37.	(4)	51.	(4)
10.	(1)	24.	(4)	38.	(2)	52.	(4)
11.	(5)	25.	(2)	39.	(2)	53.	(5)
12.	(2)	26.	(3)	40.	(5)	54.	(4)
13.	(4)	27.	(4)	41.	(2)	55.	(2)
14.	(1)	28.	(2)	42.	(3)	56.	(5)

DETAILED EXPLANATIONS
OF ANSWERS

TEST 1: WRITING SKILLS, PART I

1.   **(1) Sentence 1   Pros** is the correct answer, the plural of the word **Pro**. **Pro's** is possessive, showing that **Pro** owns **is**! **Auto Striping Pros is having** is correct. There is one business, so the singular "is" is the correct form. No commas should be added to the sentence. **Stripes** is the correct spelling. The "e" at the end of the word makes the "i" a long "i".

2.   **(2) Sentence 2   Several** is the subject. It is plural and so must have the plural verb phrase **are going**. **Participate** is spelled correctly. There is no need to add commas to the sentence. **In** is correct; **with** would be a poor word choice.

3.   **(5) Sentence 3   The sentence is correct. **Special** is the correct spelling. **From** is the correct word choice, the car owners will receive attention **from** the owner of the shop. No commas should be added; they would make the sentence become two fragments. **Cars** must be capitalized because this word begins the sentence.

4.   **(1) Sentence 4   Cars are done by **him**, not by **he**. **Him** is the correct word choice because **him** is the direct object. **A lot** is always **two words**. A comma placed after son would make two fragments and no complete sentence. **Always** is an adverb and is always one word.

5.   **(4) Sentence 5   They're** is the contraction of they are, and is the correct answer to this sentence. **There** means place. **In fact** needs the comma following it to make the sentence clear. **Business** is the correct spelling. A comma after **the best** would break up the sentence and make it confusing to the reader.

6.   **(2) Sentence 1   Always**, the adverb modifying the verb **is**, is the correct answer. **All ways** is the word "ways" modified by all, meaning every kind of way. **Preparing** is spelled correctly. No commas are necessary.

7.   **(4) Sentence 2   Now** means at this time. **Know** means knowledge. Spelling and punctuation are correct.

8.   **(2) Sentence 3   Its** is possessive. **It's** means it is, the contraction, and is the correct answer. Spellings are all correct.

9. **(1) Sentence 4** **Too** means more than enough, and is the correct answer. **To** means direction, or is used as a preposition, when followed by a noun (to the top).

10. **(3) Sentence 5** When confused, drop everything but the pronoun referring to yourself; you would not say me talk. Also, always list others before yourself.

11. **(3) Sentence 1** **Roman Empire** is a term and both words must be capitalized. Numbers are always followed by an apostrophe, when referred to in the plural form. The other two choices are weaker sentence forms.

12. **(4) Sentence 2** **German's** infers that one German owned barbaric tribes which swept into Britain. The plural form of German, Germans, should be used here, making (4) correct. The other choices are misspellings of the words in the sentence.

13. **(3) Sentence 3** **Except** means to exclude, to not include. **Accept** means to approve of, to receive. The other choices are incorrect spellings for this sentence.

14. **(5) Sentence 4** The sentence is correct. The spelling choices are incorrect spellings, and the punctuation is correct as it is.

15. **(3) Sentence 5** The subject of this sentence is **system**, thus the verb must be the singular form, was. The spelling and punctuation are correct.

16. **(2) Sentence 6** **Knowledge** is the correct spelling. The other spellings are correct and no additional punctuation is necessary.

17. **(4) Sentence 7** A comma is necessary after **Latin** to make the sentence read clearly. The words following **Latin** modify **Latin**. **Well-educated** is correct, as is the spelling of **language**.

18. **(5) Sentence 8** The sentence is correct. No commas are necessary and all spelling is correct.

19. **(4) Sentence 1** **Boring** is the correct answer. **To bore** is to be dull and uninteresting. When adding **ing**, you must drop the "e" first.

20. **(5) Sentence 2** The sentence is correct. **Alot** is not a word. **Many** must be followed by a noun. The word **television** is not capitalized unless it is the beginning of a sentence or is part of a title. No comma is needed in this sentence.

21. **(2) Sentence 3** **Board** is a piece of wood. **Bored** is to be uninterested, finding something dull. No punctuation additions are necessary.

22. **(1) Sentence 4** **On the other hand** is an introductory phrase and must be set off from the main sentence by a comma.

23. **(3) Sentence 5** **Were** is the plural of was. The correct choice, **we're**, means we are. No additional punctuation is needed. **Awfully** is right.

24. **(5) Sentence 6** The sentence is correct.

25. **(4) Sentence 7** **Embarrassing** is the correct spelling choice.

26. **(3) Sentence 8** This item is a fragment and not a sentence. It must be attached to the previous sentence in order to be correct.

27. **(2) Sentence 9** **Were** is the plural of **was**. The word **where** refers to place and is the correct answer for this sentence. **Programmers** is the correct spelling. **Wear** means to put on clothing or to over-use something.

28. **(4) Sentence 10** **Too** means also, here. **To** means direction or is a preposition. **Two** is the number.

29. **(4) Sentence 11** Remember to drop all but reference to yourself, when in doubt about correct pronoun choice. You would not say "Someone who asks I." Also remember to place yourself at the end of listing of people.

30. **(3) Sentence 1** You cannot have two negative words together. "Don't" and "hardly" are both negative words. If you delete "hardly," you are saying that you "don't ever get to talk." If you delete "don't" you mean that you rarely get the chance to talk. "Don't" is the correction of "do not," and is acceptable. **Vacations** or **vacation** is acceptable in this sentence, and so is not the best answer here.

31. **(4) Sentence 2** "Unique" means that it is the absolute most that can be. Adding "most" to "unique" is like saying unique is the best best. Therefore, "most" must be dropped. The other choices are incorrect spelling, punctuation, or verb choice.

32. **(5) Sentence 3** The sentence is correct.

33. **(1) Sentence 4** **Whose** is the possessive form, showing ownership of **who**. **Who's** means who is, and is the correct answer. The other choices are incorrect spelling and punctuation.

34. **(3) Sentence 5** **Should** is part of the verb phrase here and must be attached to another verb. **Of** is a preposition, not a verb. You cannot "of." **Should have** is the correct answer.

35. **(4) Sentence 6** **Whether** means choice. **Weather** refers to tem-

perature and climate conditions. **Wether** is not a word. No punctuation corrections or additions are necessary.

36. **(1) Sentence 7**   **Its** is the possessive form of "it." **It's** means "it is," and is the correct answer. The other choices are all incorrect.

37. **(4) Sentence 8**   **Threw** is the past tense of **throw**, to pitch or hurl something. **Through** means between things. **Win** is to come in first. **Always** is the correct adverb form in this sentence.

38. **(3) Sentence 9**   Dropping "my family," the correct choice is clearly **my family and I**, because these words are in the subject position in this sentence.

39. **(4) Sentence 10**   **Cloths** are pieces of fabric. We wear **clothes** on our bodies.

40. **(3) Sentence 11**   When the letter "i" is used as a pronoun referring to yourself, "I" is always capitalized. No correction is necessary in punctuation.

41. **(4) Sentence 12**   People **lie** when they recline. You **lay** things down, such as books. Hens **lay** eggs. No commas are necessary in this sentence.

42. **(4) Sentence 13**   **That's** means "that is," and is what is meant in this sentence. "**Thats**" would never be correct, because it is only the plural of "that." Everything else is spelled correctly.

43. **(5) Sentence 1**   No comma is necessary. A comma after when would only chop up the sentence. All words are spelled correctly.

44. **(4) Sentence 2**   The word **magic** sounds with a "j" for the "g." The word is correctly spelled **magic**. All words are spelled correctly and no commas are necessary in this sentence.

45. **(4) Sentence 3**   Like the previous sentence, **magic** and **magicians** must be spelled with a "g." **Several** is spelled correctly, and the sentence is punctuated correctly.

46. **(4) Sentence 4**   "Meet up" cannot be done. We "meet" with people, or even simply "meet people." **To** is used correctly in "to get" and "to meet," both infinitives. Spelling and punctuation are correct.

47. **(2) Sentence 5**   **Magic** is the correct spelling. The words **entertainers** and **wood** are spelled correctly. No commas are needed.

48. **(4) Sentence 6**   Sentence structure must remain parallel (using the same word endings when joined by "and" is one example of parallel

structure). Because "fun to watch" is before "and," then **to be entertained by** must follow after the word "and." Spelling and punctuation are correct.

49. **(4) Sentence 7** **Tragedy** is the correct spelling. **With** is a necessary part of the sentence. Punctuation is correct.

50. **(3) Sentence 8** This phrase is clearer when it is attached to the previous sentence. Beginning a sentence with "but" is usually weak writing. **Have to** is acceptable. It could be removed, but is not the best answer choice.

51. **(2) Sentence 9** **They're** is the contraction for "they are." This is what is meant and needed in this sentence. "Their" means "owned by them." "There" means "in that place." **Decision** and **awful** are spelled correctly.

52. **(5) Sentence 10** No correction is necessary. The spelling and punctuation are correct as they are.

53. **(3) Sentence 11** **Great** means outstanding, wonderful. "Grate" is a metal fireplace holder for wood, or a metal cover over an opening on the ground. Any comma would break up the sentence and is not needed.

54. **(4) Sentence 12** **Since** means "because." "Sense" is "an awareness." "Successful" and "entertainer" are spelled correctly.

55. **(5) Sentence 13** No correction is necessary. The words are spelled correctly. Any commas would just chop up the sentence and confuse the reader.

TEST 1: WRITING SKILLS, PART II

Sample Essay — Possible Score of 6 or 5

Making eighteen years of age the minimum age for people to receive their drivers' licenses would be an unfair hardship on young people. Many people below the age of eighteen have regular jobs away from their homes. Many of these people would be unable to reach their job sites, and could not continue to hold down those jobs.

Some families depend upon their under-eighteen family members to help with family finances. The loss of a young person's pay could put an entire family in a serious financial position.

Lots of high school students work toward their college education costs. Not being able to legally drive could put them in a position of not being able to work and not being able to attend college later.

The state lawmakers believe that accident rates would be reduced if young people were taken off of the roads. They also seem to believe that all young people do is to ride around, causing problems. In fact, many accidents are caused by the elderly and those under the influence of drugs or alcohol.

The use of controlled substances is not strictly in the hands of the high school students. What percentage of drug abuse and drinking is done by teenagers? Do they control the statistics on these abuses? What percentage of accidents is caused by and involves teenagers? Statistics need to be fairly collected and fairly presented. Then the public should vote on whether or not people under the age of eighteen should be allowed to drive.

Why this essay scores a 6 or 5

A superior essay goes below the surface. This essay is thoughfully organized and presents adequate support for the main idea which states that it is not a good idea to make 18 years of age the legal age to obtain a driver's license. It is also very well structured, with no obvious problems with the use of standard written English.

This essay addresses both sides of the argument and proposes that the reader is intelligent and can make decisions from the information offered. The essayist begins by presenting his argument. He/she then proceeds to explain the rationale behind each side of the argument, so as to give the reader the complete picture. His conclusion is nicely developed by suggesting possible solutions to the argument.

Sample Essay — Possible Score of 4 or 3

Eighteen year olds are not responsible drivers. Any state legislature that makes eighteen the legal age for a driver's license is not doing enough. The legal driving age should be twenty-one.

Insurance statistics show that most accidents are caused by and involve drivers who are under the age of twenty-one. Most of those are also caused by male drivers. Maybe male drivers should not be able to be licensed to drive until they are twenty-five.

Fatalities are reaching world war proportions. Only major, twentieth century wars have higher fatality statistics.

Somehow, if legislatures could tie alcohol and driving, perhaps our highways could and would be safer.

In Canada, if a driver causes an accident while intoxicated, his or her driver's license is taken away permanently. This rule seems to have affected the behavior of Canadians. Their driving statistics are certainly better then those of this country. We only seem to slap drunk or irrational drivers on the wrist when they take the lives of others.

Maybe legislators should make driving a privilege, only earned by a special few who prove themselves worthy.

Why this essay scores a 4 or 3

This essay is not extensively organized. Errors in sentence structure appear and detract somewhat from the essay. Many of the points presented are repetitive and most of the paragraphs are underdeveloped.

Some of the supporting details are effective, but many contain weaknesses. The essayist presents support for the argument in the form of statistics which show that male drivers under the age of 21 cause a great many automobile accidents. However, he/she then strays from the topic to suggest that since male drivers under the age of 21 cause most accidents, they should therefore not be licensed to drive until they are 25 years of age. The essayist writes about driving while intoxicated, but does not tie this point into the argument. Standing alone, this point has absolutely nothing to do with the essay topic.

Sample Essay — Possible Score of 2 or 1

State legislatures get into the darndest things. Why should they worry themselves over the driving age when there are so many greater problems to be faced?

I am reminded of the old saying: "If it ain't broke, don t fix it!" As a general rule, driving statistics seem to reflect a pretty good record, considering the population of this country.

Today, our states are faced with high crime rates and overcrowded jails. The drug problem is big and getting bigger. In large cities, gangs seem to be a threat to the safety of everyone. State legislators should be trying to figure out ways to improve these situations, and to correct these problems.

Drivers buy gasoline. Drivers pay auto taxes. Drivers pay license taxes. These taxes help to pave our highways and to raise revenues. The boys at the state capitol need to remember this when they are trying to figure out ways to raise the driving age. What they are doing is reducing the number of drivers on the highways. In the long run, this hurts us all in our pocketbooks, perhaps the greatest hurt of all.

Why this essay scores a 2 or 1

This essay has very little structure and does not address the topic. The topic of raising the driving age is mentioned in passing in the first paragraph and then is not mentioned again until the fifth sentence of the last paragraph. Ideas are basically unorganized and do not sufficiently support the essay.

The paragraphs in this essay are not well developed and the essayist does not go into enough detail to support his statements. The essayist begins one sentence with, "As a general rule"; however, he does not cite whose rule it is, therefore giving it no credence. He/she cites that, "our states are faced with high crime rates and overcrowded jails," but he/she does not attribute this information to anyone to support his claim. He/she says the drug problem in this country is getting bigger, but provides no evidence that this is the case. Another unsupported claim is that, "in large cities, gangs seem to be a threat to the safety of everyone." He/she does not tell us how he/she knows this to be true.

Yet, there are still other problems. He/she uses poor word choice. The cliché, "If it ain't broke, don't fix it!" is employed, but does not work well here. Also, the conclusion is poor, in that it touches upon ideas not discussed in the writing and does not really sum up the essay.

TEST 2: SOCIAL STUDIES

1.   **(4)**   Henry Ford is considered the father of assembly line techniques for the manufacture of complex products. (1) Rockefeller created Standard Oil, one of the most efficient monopolies. (2) Morgan was the premier financier of his day, controlling banking and Wall Street. (3) Carnegie created the first billion dollar corporation, which became U.S. Steel. (5) Stanford was one of several railroad millionaires.

2.   **(3)**   is correct. The stress was on saving time, building a product faster and thus more of them. (1) The improving of quality was never mentioned. (2) The job descriptions make it clear that less, not more, skill is needed in this type of operation. (4) The article states that four workers can be replaced by one. (5) The work day is mentioned, but not in terms of shortening it.

3.   **(5)**   Chicago was the recognized rail center of the nation. (1) Ford, Dodge, Durant and many others lived in or near Detroit. (2) The Great Lakes put Detroit centered in access to iron ore and coal. (3) The Detroit River is the connecting link between the upper and lower Great Lakes. (4) Michigan, like the rest of the Midwest, had access to a large immigrant influx whenever jobs were available.

4.   **(3)**   is correct. Despite being a leading wheat producer, the Soviet Union is the only nation that is in the top three in having to import extra grain in all three categories, including extra wheat.

5.   **(1)**   The USA is the only nation listed that is not only an importer, but also listed in two categories as a top producer.

6.   **(4)**   is least correct. The American farmer has traditionally had government assistance available in the form of loan programs, subsidies, price supports, and tariff protection. (1) and (3) are natural assets that American farmers have enjoyed. (2) and (5) have made American farms more efficient and costeffective.

7.   **(3)**   is correct, there were 13 positive deviations and only 10 negative. (1) is shown by the Trend in Deviation table to be decreasing. (2) Non-presidential elections are indicated by listing only party names. These so-called "off-year" elections are for Congress only. (4) The non-presidential years, beginning with 1938, show the Democrats winning every year except 1946. (5) In both 1948 (Truman) and 1968 (Nixon), presidents were elected with less than 50% of the popular vote, largely because of strong third-party candidates.

8.   **(3)**   is correct. In 1968, Nixon won with only 43.5% of the popular vote. (1) Carter won with 50% of the vote in 1976. (2) Reagan won with 50.8% in

1980. (4) Johnson won with 61.3% in 1964. (5) Kennedy won with 50.1% in 1960.

9.   **(3)**   is correct. When Nixon's vice-president, Spiro Agnew, resigned, Ford was chosen by Congress to replace him. When Nixon resigned over the Watergate scandal, Ford became president, but failed in his only election bid in 1976, losing to Carter. (1) He could not run for re-election since he was never elected. (2) He did not die in office. (4) Only Andrew Johnson (1865-69) was impeached, which means to bring to trial, and he was not removed from office. (5) He did not resign. Only Richard Nixon has ever resigned while in office.

10.   **(1)**   is not a proper conclusion because it is an opinion. The facts from the graph may be used to try to prove the need to cut transportation oil consumption, but the graph itself makes no conclusions. (2) This is true if the average of Germany, Italy, France, and Great Britain is used. (3) Since the U.S. and Canada top the chart, this is true. (4) This is true, with 25%. (5) True, about 8%.

11.   **(3)**   This cannot be a conclusion from the graphs, which are per person. Also, Canada, ranking second, has the smallest population on the list. (1) This could be a conclusion because the two largest nations are also the top two consumers. (2) Since four of the top seven consumers are European, this is true. (4) Japan is the only Asian nation listed. (5) This is a probable conclusion, especially when the quantity used for manufacturing in the U.S. is used as an indicator.

12.   **(4)**   This is no longer true. Today's industry is divided between many private and nationalized companies. (1) The supply of petroleum is limited and exhaustible. (2) Oil is the key ingredient in plastics. (3) Prices and supply are very sensitive to many conditions. (5) Oil supplies and prices are affected by conditions all over the world with many producers.

13.   **(3)**   is the logical answer, because the speaker (Henry H. Garnet) is a black who is urging his brothers to rise up against slavery still in existence. (1) is wrong because Reconstruction is the post-Civil War period, when slavery had already been outlawed by the 13th Amendment (4). (2) There is no reference to the Revolution or its time period. (5) This Supreme Court decision desegregating the schools took place in 1954, well after slavery was outlawed.

14.   **(1)**   The speech states that Vesey was "betrayed by the treachery of his fellowmen." None of the others (2), (3) or (4) were cited for failure because of their own people. (5) The *Amistad* was the ship that Joseph Cinque was on.

15.   **(4)**   Blacks could and did resist slavery, using revolts, escape, passive resistance, and social customs. (1) This is not correct. Many poor whites

supported the slave system as a means of keeping a class beneath them. (2) This is a direct contradiction of both (4) and the quoted revolts above. (3) Again, slave revolts did occur despite terrible penalties. Nat Turner's revolt, referred to in the speech, was one of the most famous. (5) This was a myth perpetuated by the supporters of slavery. Obviously, the same agricultural products are grown today without slavery.

16. **(4)** This is one of the 3 Civil War Amendments (13–15) that moved the black population from slavery to citizenship. The 15th Amendment specifically gave the ex-slaves and all other black males the right to vote. (1) This counted the slaves of a state as only three-fifths of a person for the purposes of gaining votes in the House of Representatives. (2) This Supreme Court decision ruled that slaves remained property even when their masters took them into free territory. (3) This 1886 Supreme Court decision declared that segregation was legal as long as it was "separate but equal." (5) This 1820 deal in Congress drew a line across the U.S., allowing slavery in any new states south of the line.

17. **(5)** is most accurate. The graph covers over 100 years and shows total population trends. (1) and (2) are not complete enough. Each is only a partial description. (3) is not accurate because the graph also includes the 1880's and 1890's. (4) is wrong because the graph shows percentages, not growth.

18. **(3)** is most correct because the graph definitely shows a constant increase in urban population. (1) may be assumed as one part of urban increases, but is not specifically shown on the chart. (2) is incorrect. Farm production has not declined, rather fewer farmers are needed to grow more food. (4) is not referred to by the graph. (5) Occupations are not singled out, so there is no way to know anything about this category from the graph.

19. **(2)** is the correct definition. The rising urban population has created several of these, from Boston to Washington and from San Diego to Los Angeles, for example. (1) is called a metropolis. (3) Since a megalopolis is several metropolises joined together, it is obviously larger, not smaller. (4) and (5) do not fit the definition. A megalopolis includes central cities and suburbs over a wide area.

20. **(2)** is the untrue statement; 80,277 were enrolled in grades 9–12, while only 37,199 got higher degrees. (1) Enrollment went to 915,061 by 1910, well over ten times the 80,277 of 1870. (3) High school graduate percentages went from 2% to 8.8%. (4) 12,896 graduated from college, over one-tenth of the 110,277 in grades 9–12. (5) This conclusion can be drawn by the rapid increases in enrollments and graduations.

21. **(4)** is the most logical, because comparing any year's total enrollment to the high school total shows how few were enrolled in grades 9–12. (1) All the years are post-war and there is no reference to the war. (2) There are no statistics that deal with this. (3) Just the opposite, the rate of increase was

highest that decade. (5) The increase in graduation rates over 40 years shows an increasing value placed on getting a degree.

22. **(2)** is not a requirement for citizenship although many immigrants do use the schools to study for their test. (1) As stated above, the citizenship test requirements are often learned in either day or night school. (3) Vocational education and cooperation with business are common programs. (4) Many groups have used education to improve their competitiveness in society. (5) With the increasing numbers of high school graduates came higher enrollments in colleges.

23. **(1)** is not in Central America. It is part of Latin America, but its location south of the isthmus of Panama puts it in South, not North, America. (2), (3), (4), and (5) are all part of the region south of Mexico and north of the isthmus.

24. **(3)** is incorrect because both the Spanish and Mayan influence are discussed. (1) This is stated in the text. (2) This is clear from the map. (4) The Panama Canal is a major shipping artery and any land trade between northern North America and South America must go through Central America. (5) The need to raise the standard of living is stated above.

25. **(5)** is most correct because almost every nation in the region touches the Caribbean. (1) is in northern North America. (2) is in South America. (3) is an island in the Caribbean. (4) is a peninsula in Mexico.

26. **(1)** is most correct. Both South and North America experience tectonic activity and Central America geologically connects them. (2) is not correct. The area has a number of active volcanoes, earthquake activity, and is on fault lines. (3) The opposite is true. The Mid-Atlantic Ridge is an active fault area that pushes the two regions apart more each year. (4) Earthquakes and volcanoes continue to prove the ongoing nature of tectonics. (5) According to the theory, Africa formed the center of the splitting land masses that migrated to their present positions. Theories may vary, but none name the Americas as the center.

27. **(4)** is correct. The reading refers to the Escobedo case as an earlier and related decision. (1) is not right because it is the opposite of (4). Miranda continued and extended rights against "overzealous police practices" established in earlier cases. (2) It states that only 5 of the 9 justices ruled in favor. (3) is wrong. It does not prevent a confession, but rather requires that a suspect knows they do not have to volunteer a statement and can have legal counsel present. (5) Miranda involves legal procedures, but they are directly related to enforcing Constitutional Bill of Rights standards.

28. **(3)** is correct. There is no reference to bail rights in the ruling. The right to bail is in the Bill of Rights (8th Amendment). (1) is part of Miranda as a protection against self-incrimination. (2) is an essential part of Miranda in that the right to a lawyer is key to understanding and having advice on all arrest

rights. (4) Like (1), (2), and (5), the Court ruled that a person must know their rights before they can decide if they wish to waive them in a confession or exercise them by remaining silent. (5) is part of the more general right (2) to have a lawyer present during all stages of the arrest procedure.

29. **(1)** is correct. The Court ruling stated that a person must be told his rights so he understands them. (2) Miranda does not insist that a suspect sign anything, but merely that he has been informed of his rights and given a chance to exercise them. (3) The Court referred to questioning "while in custody," so Miranda rights apply at the time of arrest, but police are free to ask questions to try to determine if a person is a suspect. (4) The Court did not mandate legal counsel, only the suspect's right to have it if he so chooses. (5) Miranda is being obeyed because the suspect is getting legal counsel and it is the suspect's choice whether or not to follow it.

30. **(1)** is taken to task and it is stated that they should be limited. All other groups are called upon to band together to help the environment.

31. **(4)** These are obvious references to the past use of the environment for economic purposes rather than environmental concerns. (1) and (2) are moral statements, not economic ones. (3) This is a call to action. (5) This tries to redefine society's values.

32. **(5)** This is a political, cost concern. Coal is more polluting than oil. (1) This is now used to sell products, changing packaging, and is becoming profitable. (2) This is an attempt to replace trees as a renewable resource. (3) Repair and replacement of topsoil, erosion control, and replanting are attempts to reuse mined areas for agriculture. (4) Concern over this has changed products' chemical contents and created new laws to reduce airborn pollution.

33. **(3)** is the most complete answer in the reading. Referred to are creating useful skills, counseling, and training that leads to jobs. (1) and (2) are referred to in a general sense, but with no specifics. (4) is not mentioned in the article. (5) High pay is not emphasized, rather "real jobs, self-respect producing employment." Money is one criteria for such jobs, but not the only one.

34. **(5)** is correct because the focus of the article is how to get a member out of a gang, not how he or she got there. (1) Learning skills, finding opportunities, getting meaningful jobs are all mentioned as things a gang member could possibly do well. (2) Education, counseling, and career services are mentioned as school functions. (3) Such community resources as the employment office, Chamber of Commerce, and citizens are discussed. (4) The need for skills, not how to learn them, is discussed.

35. **(4)** Racial, ethnic, or cultural differences may be reasons for joining one specific gang over another, but the other reasons are stronger for

desiring gang membership in general. (1) The need to feel safe and/or have allies in your own neighborhood sometimes forces youngsters into gangs for self-protection. (2) Adolescence brings with it a strong need to belong and feel accepted in a group. (3) Sometimes being young or feeling underprivileged leads to a desire to strike out against the establishment. (5) Crime as part of a gang activity provides several rewards, including acceptance, money, excitement, and rebellion.

36. **(3)** Although the chart can be used for several of the choices, it is a simplified version of the Business Cycle. (1) The chart does not refer to "bust" or depression. (2) and (4) Changes are shown, but not causes. (5) If you added data, such as dates, it could be used to track historical fluctuations, but doesn't in this form.

37. **(4)** This may influence the other factors, but can have a variety of effects and is not part of the purely economic picture. (1) The number of people employed is used to define whether we are in a recession or not. (2) Obviously directly related to (1), it also shows prosperity, if products are in demand. (3) Personal earnings rise with an economic boom and help sustain it with spending. (5) This is an important indicator of income, production, and consumer confidence in the economy.

38. **(3)** is the most counterproductive to economic growth because it takes money out of spending circulation and reduces sales. (1) is usually not planned, but has been credited with helping the economy as a side effect because of the increased need for services and products. (2) Keynesian economics calls for "pump-priming" of the economy through government spending to employ people and increase production. (4) Supply-side economics contends that reducing government regulation frees up capital to create products and jobs. (5) This is often used as a short term solution to help specific industries, such as the auto industry in the early 1980's. Long term use may trigger international retaliation and create worse problems.

39. **(2)** is the most specific statement because, although the first paragraph refers to the "needs of society," those needs are specified as economic in the rest of the quote. (1) Many of society's needs—legal rights, social needs, poverty—are not addressed. (3) This is not discussed. (4) The terms "average," "more and more," and "most" are used, not all. (5) The government role is not discussed.

40. **(1)** The Chamber of Commerce represents U.S. business people and this is definitely a pro-business statement. (2) The federal Department of Labor is not anti-business, but it is not its major concern to advocate pro-business stands. (3) The GAO is the auditing branch of the government and doesn't take a stand on pro- or anti-business statements. (4) The Socialist belief would probably be the opposite of the quote. (5) The union position would probably credit workers more and business less.

41. **(4)** Justice means fair treatment for all, sometimes enforced by government regulation. (1) This is specifically referred to in relation to employment, wages, etc. (2) This is indirectly referred to through rising living standards and growth which also provides security (3). (5) This is implied throughout and referred to as "less constraint."

42. **(5)** Labor is a factor in creating all of the others, which are the basic activities.

43. **(4)** is most correct, the N.W. line declined as the S.E. increased. (1) was the second-highest period, after 1881–90. (2) Immigration slowed during 1861-70, but it was lower in 1911–20. (3) It peaked 10 years before 1900, then increased slightly from 1891–1900. (5) The 1901–1910 peak of the S.E. line was much higher.

44. **(2)** is not true because the two lines cross before or right at 1900. (1) Adding the two lines together never equals ten million. (3) This is true as the line indicates. (4) This is evident from the peaks and valleys of both lines. (5) At 1930 the two lines cross, with the N.W. line rising.

45. **(2)** is most correct. Three great waves have occurred, with non-Europeans being the latest. (1) The Open Door Policy was a foreign policy relating to China and did not relate to immigration. Also, many groups, such as the Japanese, have been discriminated against at various times. (3) Victims of political oppression are given priority consideration. (4) War, usually, temporarily cuts off most immigration as people are barred from leaving war zones and travel is dangerous. (5) Immigration laws are passed by Congress and are not required by the Constitution.

46. **(3)** is correct. The chart shows a 72% to 56% margin. (1) is the opposite, with Carter holding a 40% to 24% edge. (2) Conservatives outnumbered liberals, 42% to 22%. (4) Women preferred Reagan by 36% while 39% of men preferred him. (5) Adding together the Democrats (29%) and the Republicans (24%) creates 53% with party membership and only 43% independents.

47. **(2)** is correct, at 24% support, it is his weakest area. (1) Carter (57%) had over twice the support that Reagan had. (3) Carter was favored in union households by a 34% to 30% margin. (4) Black voters gave Carter his strongest margin, 73% to 4%. (5) Liberals gave Carter a 37% to 26% edge over Reagan.

48. **(1)** is correct. The popular vote determines who gets a state's entire Electoral College vote. Those delegates convene in Washington in December of the election year and officially elect the next president. (2) is not correct. It is even possible for the popular vote winner to lose the presidency if the other candidate wins in enough key states to get a majority of Electoral

College votes. (3) The Electoral College meets in December, not November. (4) is not correct because either the situation described in (2) could happen or, with more than two candidates, no one may receive a majority of either the popular or Electoral votes. In that case, the House of Representatives would elect a president. (5) Americans vote for candidates, not parties, and the same rules about the popular vote referred to in (2) and (4) apply.

49. **(3)** is most true, there is a tolerance column that would inform a user. (1) It makes no recommendations. (2) categorizes drugs by chemical/effects, not severity. (4) Many other substances have been abused, alone and in combination. (5) Although this is a popular theory, it is not covered here.

50. **(4)** According to the chart, the 2 drugs in this category have no physical withdrawal effects and only one has any possible physical dependence. (1), (2), and (3) all had some physical withdrawal effects and physical dependence. (5) This is not a category, but a drug within the Stimulants.

51. **(3)** is the correct answer. Reading the chart, it is clearly listed that marijuana is a psychedelic drug.

52. **(1)** is not true. According to the chart, heroin users rapidly develop very strong psychological dependence to it. All of the remaining answer choices are true.

53. **(3)** is the best answer. Each item deals with either the Japanese or U.S. military, including their relationship with each other. (1) is not correct. Only the military aspect is covered; many other areas, such as political and economic, are not. (2) This is mentioned in the last point, but is not the main focus. (4) Only one point mentions an actual treaty. (5) Again, like (2), this is mentioned, but not a main focus.

54. **(1)** This is the least related to economics under present circumstances. Obviously, if the Japanese became aggressive again, this could become an economic factor if U.S. military intervention were required. (2) This is a direct economic issue. (3) This is an economic issue where the U.S. taxpayers are footing the bill to protect Japan. (4) This is a major ($9 billion) economic issue. (5) This is the same point as (3) stated a different way.

55. **(2)** is correct. The U.S. does plan to begin withdrawing troops. So, the phrase, "no intention" is not indicated. (3) This is specified, with 1951 being listed as the treaty date. (4) The statement asserts that Japan is the third largest spender. (5) This is also discussed, with a specific figure of 5000 over three years.

56. **(1)** is most correct. The Japanese modeled their constitution after the U.S., but retained the emperor as a figurehead with strictly ceremonial powers. (2) This was the Japanese ruling military clique before and during

World War II. (3) The Japanese are very capitalistic and have designed their government to encourage private enterprise. (4) This term is used loosely to describe any free society that elects its government, but from a political science view, it only refers to local and small population areas that can meet on all issues without electing representatives. (5) The Japanese are firmly in the Western, non-Communist camp.

57. **(4)** The United Kingdom, which includes England, has maintained an official role for the British monarchy. (1) Germany lost its monarchy when the Kaiser abdicated at the end of World War I. (2) The Russian Revolution overthrew the Tsar and royal family and established the Soviet Union. (3) China's emperor was replaced by a democratic government, which later became a dictatorship and then, finally, communism. (5) France, after several revivals for royalty, finally established a republic.

58. **(4)** is most correct. Federal roles and individual rights are specified, with state and local government responsibilities left to those agencies. (1) The judicial system is specifically described. (2) The legislative branch is spelled out in detail. (3) The Bill of Rights amended the Constitution with these rights. (5) The President's role as Commander-in-Chief, establishing firm civilian control over the military, is part of the executive branch.

59. **(5)** is correct, as it was found that Maslow's original (1) psychological hierarchy for (3) individual behavior was easily adapted to (2) social behavior or (4) group needs.

60. **(3)** Maslow depicts basic needs for everyone in sequence and any threat to a lower level means a return to it until the threat is taken care of. (1) The hierarchy is a building block where lower steps must be continually satisfied in order to function on a higher level. (2) Most people never reach the top level and many only reach the social level. (4) The levels are in sequence, so basic needs are taken care of first. (5) Everyone has to go through all the steps in order and each type of culture may meet its own definition of self-actualization or creativity.

61. **(1)** This does not fit the pattern because it fits no need and there is no evidence of true creativity (self-actualization). (2) This shows someone who is at a social level but unable to reach self-esteem and why he reacts with frustration. (3) The theory applied to history has helped explain the evolution of cultures to higher levels. (4) The student has moved up to the self-esteem level. (5) This is an example of a crisis creating a need for a person to return to a lower level to satisfy that need, i.e., security and survival.

62. **(4)** is correct because of the reference to coffee as "mere colored water." (1) Several dairy products are mentioned, such as butter and cheese. (2) is wrong because lard and ham are referred to. (3) is not correct because turnips and potatoes are among the mentioned vegetables. (4) At least 5 different alcoholic beverages are referred to at the end.

63. **(1)** is correct. It is described as winning the "prize" for most injurious. (2) is wrong. The result of the day's meals was "heaping indigestions on one another." (3) is not correct because this topic is never mentioned. (4) is wrong because the author is very critical of the food's taste. (5) is not complete because only the tea is referred to as an English habit.

64. **(1)** is the correct answer. The author cites, "To digest these viscous substances they take *tea* almost instantly after dinner, making it so strong that it is absolutely bitter to the taste..." Therefore, the remaining answer choices are incorrect.

TEST 3: SCIENCE

1. **(4)** The longer the pendulum, the greater the time for one complete vibrational period. Since the acceleration due to gravity is constant, the length of the pendulum must be directly proportional to the square of the period. Here on the Earth a 2-second pendulum is one meter long. Doubling the period to 4 seconds implies a quadrupling of the length to 4 meters. Tripling the period to 6 seconds implies increasing the pendulum's length 9 times.

2. **(5)** If the period of a pendulum is to remain constant while it is moved to a different position in space, then the length is directly proportional to the acceleration due to gravity "g". On the moon the acceleration due to gravity is one-sixth what it is here on the Earth, so that to have the same-period pendulum on the moon means its length must also be one-sixth what it is here on Earth. Similarly, on Jupiter the acceleration due to gravity at its cloud tops is over 2.3 times what it is here on Earth, so that there the same pendulum would have to be over 2.3 times longer.

3. **(2)** From the information given, it is apparent that the period depends on "g" (1), on the fact that the amplitude must be less than 5 degrees (3), and on the length (4). No mention of the mass (2) was made. Hence, we can assume it makes no difference for what we need here. The only difference a greater mass could make is increasing the effective length of the pendulum by taking up more space. The length of the pendulum is defined to be from the pivot point at the top to the bob's center of mass.

4. **(1)** The units of "g" were given as meters/sec^2. This is distance divided by (time times time). This can be rearranged to read distance (divided by time) divided by time. This is speed divided by time. And that is exactly what acceleration means: how fast is the speed changing in time. Weight (3) and force (5) are concepts which require mass. Distance over time (2) is speed. Velocity over distance (4) is the inverse of time.

5. **(2)** Human eyelashes help keep dust and dirt out of the eye. Similarly, the hooks have tiny comblike ridges on them and they keep the antennae free from dust and dirt. Thus, (2) is correct. (1) is wrong because hooks are structures on the antennae that do not blink. (3) is wrong because the hooks are not involved in attraction between male and female ants. (4) is incorrect because the length of these structures is not indicative of the age of the ant. (5) is wrong because eyelashes do not help people find their way.

6. **(3)** For the trail to be different from any other trail of another ant colony, the trail must have a unique composition. The trail is drops of liquid from the abdomen. Each ant colony has its own odor. Thus, (3) is correct. Ants do not

use food (1), broken pieces of antennae (2), lenses of compound eyes (4), or tiny pebbles (5) to mark their trail.

7.   **(4)**   The compound eye permits the ant to see moving objects more easily than objects which stand still. Thus, (4) is correct. If an ant saw multiple images (1), its perception would be distorted. The same is true if images were highly magnified (5). (3) is wrong because a compound eye is fixed and cannot rotate. (2) is wrong because the whole compound eye works together in vision; all parts of it are needed for good vision.

8.   **(1)**   Ants are most related to bees. Ants, bees, and wasps are all classified in the order called **Hymenoptera**. These insects are social and live in communities rather than living alone. The body is similar to that of a bee. (2), spiders, are different from ants in body structure and number of legs. Fungus (3) is very different from ants since fungus is a simple plantlike organism. Fleas (4) have a different body structure and do not live in communities. Crabs (5) are ten-legged crustaceans and are very different from ants.

9.   **(3)**   Ants did not change much because ants were always able to fight enemies, find food, find shelter, protect their young, and stand up to any environmental changes. Thus, (3) is correct because no changes were severe enough to cause much change in ants through the years. Answer choices (1), (2), (4), and (5) would all have resulted in extinction of the ant population. Since ants are not extinct, these answer choices are all incorrect.

10. **(3)**   The answer to question 1 is (3)—a compound can be a pure substance. The passage states that pure substances are either elements or compounds. It is easier to see the relationships posed in the answer choices by this simple chart:

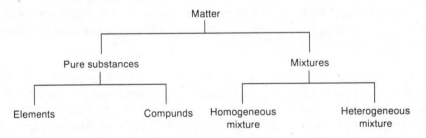

By studying this chart, which shows the relationships described in the passage, it becomes possible to eliminate the incorrect answer choices. (1) is wrong because a homogeneous mixture is a mixture, not a pure substance. (2) is incorrect since pure substances and mixtures are two distinctly different types of matter. (4) is wrong because the term "heterogeneous" implies being composed of parts with visibly different properties. Since one type of element, such as a lump of lead, has consistency with respect to its physical properties, then this one element cannot simultaneously possess visibly different properties. (5) is wrong because matter can be categorized, as shown in the above diagram.

11. **(2)** The right answer is (2). This can be proven by visualizing a homogeneous mixture to be water (which has the same properties throughout) and a heterogeneous mixture to be water with rocks in it (since this combination would be composed of parts with visibly different properties). If the water is combined with water plus rocks, the resulting mixture will be water plus rocks, which is a heterogeneous mixture. (1) is wrong because the mixture will not be homogeneous; rocks have very different properties in comparison to water. (3) is wrong since a pure substance is entirely a different branch of matter from mixtures. (4) is wrong because these two mixtures will indeed be miscible, and (5) is incorrect because the resulting solution can be classified as a heterogeneous mixture.

12. **(5)** Only (5), zinc sulfide, is not an element, because it can undergo a chemical change when it is heated to form two substances, zinc and sulfur. Zinc (1), sodium (2), iron (3) and tin (5) are all elements. They can each be found in a periodic table of the elements. None can be broken down further to any other type of matter.

13. **(1)** Answer choice (1), "basic research," is the correct answer since the biologist was wanting to gain the knowledge simply for the sake of curiosity or knowledge itself. "Applied research" (2) cannot be the correct answer since it involves using knowledge that has been gained from basic research or pure research and used to solve a problem. "Government research" (3) cannot be the correct answer since it may be either basic research or applied research, and in the paragraph there is no mention of who is funding the research. "Library research" (4) cannot be the correct answer even though in scientific research there is work done in the library; the paragraph deals with the major theme of a biologist doing "basic research." "Methods to produce great amounts of insects" (5) cannot be the correct answer since nothing is mentioned in the paragraph concerning a reason for producing large numbers of insects.

14. **(3)** Answer choice (3), "are found in many organisms" is the correct answer since there are organisms other than insects that produce chemical sexual attractants. "Are used only in insects" (1) cannot be the correct answer since there are other animals that produce chemical sexual attractants. "Are used by all animals" (2) cannot be the correct answer since there are some animals, especially the "lower" such as sponges and coelenterates, that have not been found to produce sexual attractants. "Can be seen" (4) cannot be the correct answer since the pheromones are invisible. "Can be felt" (5) cannot be the correct answer since no mention of feeling is mentioned in the paragraph, and it would be like standing next to someone wearing a perfume, and "feeling it."

15. **(2)** Answer choice (2), "over a period of time, the dish would gradually

be filled with dead cockroaches that crawled through the poison in an attempt to mate with the cork," is the correct answer since they would attempt to crawl to the cork thinking that it is a female. "No cockroaches would be affected" (1) cannot be the correct answer since the pheromone would definitely affect the insect. "Moths would be attracted to the pheromone impregnated cork" (3) cannot be the correct answer since the biologist in the question was not using a moth pheromone and pheromones are specific. "Cockroaches would surround the dish but not cross the poison" (4) cannot be the correct answer since the cockroach would not notice what it is crawling through. "Not enough data has been given" (5) cannot be the correct answer since it is mentioned that the pheromone is so powerful that the insect does not pay attention to its own safety.

16. **(3)**   Answer choice (3), "Applied science" would be the correct answer since the biologist is solving a problem by applying the information gained from the basic research or pure science. "Pure science" (1) cannot be the correct answer since the biologist is not experimenting out of curiosity or for only the sake of knowledge. "Basic research" (2) cannot be the correct answer since it is the same thing as "pure science." "Government research" (4) cannot be the correct answer since "government" would imply who is sponsoring the research, and not whether it is pure science/basic research or applied science/research. "The scientific method" (5) cannot be the correct answer since there is no mention of the methodology of a controlled experiment.

17. **(3)**   Answer choice (3), "applied science" would be the correct answer since the scientists are using information gained from basic research/pure science to solve a problem. "Entomology" (1) cannot be the correct answer since it is the study of insects. "Botany" (2) cannot be the correct answer since it is the study of plants. "Pure science" (4) cannot be the correct answer since the scientists are not trying to gain knowledge simply for the sake of knowledge itself. "Scientific method" (5) cannot be the correct answer since it does not address the question of why the information is being sought or how the information is being used.

18. **(3)**   Examination of the fourth column reveals that there is no pattern to the divisions of time, therefore (3) is the correct answer. (1) is incorrect because the events listed are biological in nature rather than geological. (2) is incorrect, as the time blocks are of differing amounts. (4) is wrong because the eras are divided into periods and not the reverse.

19. **(1)**   The sequence of life listed is correct, so answer choice (1) should be chosen. (2) is incorrect because invertebrates evolved before fish. (3) is incorrect because the first fish appeared much earlier than the first forests. Plants were present before birds, so (4) is wrong, and (5) is incorrect because reptiles had evolved before mammals.

20. **(4)** The common alligator is a reptile. Answer choice (4) is correct because the Carboniferous Period saw the emergence of the first reptiles. Answer choices (1), (2), (3) and (5) are incorrect, because they represent they emergence periods of organisms other than reptiles.

21. **(3)** Answer choice (3), "a virus" would be the correct answer since a virus is not composed of cells, nor does it organize protoplasm into cells, and it does not come from pre-existing cells. "A rose" (1) cannot be the correct answer since it is a living thing composed of cells; it came from a cell; it carries on all of the life processes. "A fungus" (2) cannot be the correct answer since it is a living thing composed of cells; it came from a cell; it carries on all of the life processes. "An amoeba" (4) cannot be the correct answer since it is a living thing composed of cells; it came from a cell; it carries on all of the life processes. "A sponge" (5) cannot be the correct answer since it is a living thing composed of cells; it came from a cell; it carries on all of the life processes.

22. **(5)** Answer choice (5), "not alive because it is not composed of cells, it cannot reproduce, and it does not carry out any of the life functions" is correct since icicles are made of only water and not cells. "Alive because it grows by the addition of more water" (1) cannot be the correct answer since icicle growth is by accumulation of water freezing to the outside, and not by assimilation where food is chemically broken down, absorbed, and incorporated into the body of the organism. "Alive because it has a life span which involves a beginning, growth, a period of maturity, a period of decline and finally, death" (2) is wrong because there is no proper beginning (from a pre-existing cell); growth is not of the right kind; no "maturity" is exhibited; no decline (breaking down of cells due to age) is exhibited; no death is exhibited. "Alive because it can reproduce" (3) cannot be the correct answer since icicles cannot reproduce. "Alive because it is composed of cells" (4) cannot be the correct answer since icicles are composed of water, not cells.

23. **(1)** Answer choice (1), "a cell" is the correct answer since all living things are composed of cells. "An organ" (2) cannot be the correct answer since organs are composed of tissues, which are composed of cells. "A chemical compound" (3) cannot be the correct answer since living things must be composed of cells, and chemical compounds are not cells. "An organ system" (4), or "an organism" (5) cannot be the correct answer since an organism is composed of organ systems, which are composed of organs, which are composed of tissues, which are composed of cells.

24. **(3)** By Newton's Third Law of Motion, the gravitational pull of a first body on a second must be equal and opposite to the pull of the second back on the first, no matter what the mass of each body is or what the motion of each body is. Therefore, I pull back on the (1) with the same force the Earth pulls on me, but in the opposite direction. But, because my mass is so small, I accelerate downward a great deal (9.8 m/s^2) while the mass of the Earth is so large that it accelerates minutely.

25. **(1)**   The gravitational pull between two masses is proportional to the product of their masses. Hence, doubling the two masses would increase the pull by 4 times. Since the Earth is 82 times more massive than the moon, the pull between the sun and Earth must be 82 times greater than the pull between the Earth and moon if their separations were the same. Actually, the smaller distance between the Earth and moon makes the pull between the sun and Earth only 175 times the pull between the Earth and moon.

26. **(4)**   The gravitational pull between any two masses is inversely proportional to the square of the distance between them. The pull between the moon and Earth was given as 2×10^{20} N. If their separation was increased by two, then the force between them would have to decrease by four. A force of 2×10^{20} N divided by four is 5×10^{19} N.

27. **(4)**   Since each answer given involves the pull between the moon and sun, the key factor is the relative distances between the bodies. The distance between the sun and moon is on the average 393 times greater than the distance between the moon and Earth. Remembering that the pull is inversely proportional to the square of the distance, the pull between the moon and Earth must be 393^2 or 154,449 times the pull between the sun and moon.

28. **(3)**   The Br_2 molecules "stick" together at low temperatures because attractive forces between the molecules become stronger than the thermal energy, which tends to cause separation of molecules. Thus, choice (3) is correct. Choice (1) does not apply because the electrostatic forces of attraction are what cause the molecules to "stick." Ice is not involved. (2) is incorrect because molecules at low temperatures have decreased thermal energy, not increased thermal energy. (4) is wrong because gases tend to condense at low temperatures, not expand. (5) is wrong because Br_2 molecules, and most elements in general, will compress at low temperatures and go into a liquid phase.

29. **(4)**   The correct answer is (4). Gases contain molecules that move freely in space. Gases are thus the most random. Liquids still move but attractive forces between molecules prevent totally random motion. The solid state contains molecules that are ordered and close together. Thus, the rigid state of a solid renders it least random. The correct order is gas, liquid, solid.

30. **(3)**   is correct, because of the difference between the P and S waves, the P wave travels faster. It can be seen on the graph that the P wave covers a greater distance in less time. (1) and (2) are incorrect as they are descriptions of the waves rather than an explanation. (4) is incorrect as an examination of the graph reveals the S wave to be slower. (5) is incorrect; if the P and S wave traveled together they would both occupy the same line.

31. **(2)**   is correct, locate the position labeled 8000 km and look up until you reach the P wave line and read across to the time. (1) is incorrect, it would

be 3000 km. (3) is incorrect, it would be 1000 km. (4) is incorrect, it would be > 10,000 km. (5) is incorrect, it would be > 10,000.

32. **(1)** is correct, you must locate the place on the graph where the S wave has traveled 5 minutes and read down to find the distance. (2) is incorrect; it would be 7 minutes. (3) is incorrect; it would be 10 minutes. (4) is incorrect; it would be 13 minutes. (5) is incorrect; it would be 15 minutes.

33. **(3)** is correct. You must locate on the graph the place where the space between the P and S wave lines is 7 minutes; then look down and read the distance scale. (1) is incorrect; it would be 2 minutes. (2) is incorrect; it would be 4 minutes. (4) is incorrect; it would be 9 minutes. (5) is incorrect; it would be 10 minutes.

34. **(1)** The nose provides a direct route to the lungs via the bronchi. Thus, choice (1) is correct. A cut on the finger (2), the foot (3), or the chest (4) may cause infectious organisms to enter the body but these are not direct routes to the lungs like the nose is. (5), the underside of the fingernail, is not an entrance because skin blocks organisms from entering this way in a healthy organism.

35. **(4)** Germs on the body surface of a healthy individual are not infecting the body. They are simply living on the body surface without causing disturbance to the body. Thus, choices (1) and (2) are wrong. Only if germs grow and affect the body does infection take place. These germs on the surface can be contagious, so (3) is wrong. Also, these germs can indeed enter the body if the opportunity arises, so choice (5) is incorrect.

36. **(4)** Of all of the types of microbes mentioned in choices (1)–(5), only the malaria microbe is harmful. Malaria is an infectious disease. Yeast (1), cheese mold (2), yogurt cultures (3), and fermenting microorganisms (5) are used in the preparation of food and drink. They are approved methods because these microbes are not harmful.

37. **(1)** Acidic stomach juice can destroy many microbes which otherwise could cause food poisoning. Thus, choice (1) is correct. (2) is wrong because stomach juice is acidic, not basic. (3) is wrong because destroying the microbes will eliminate the cause of food poisoning. (4) is wrong because any microbes that do survive have the possibility of causing food poisoning. (5) is wrong because most microbes swallowed are not harmful; food poisoning is a relatively rare occurrence.

38. **(1)** Weight is proportional to size cubed. Surface area is proportional to size squared. Tripling the size of the ball means the weight goes up by 3^3 and the surface area up by 3^2. The weight then is 27 times larger and the surface area is 9 times larger.

39. (5) Strength is proportional to size squared while weight is proportional to size cubed. Having the size increase by a factor of four means the strength increases by 4^2 and the weight increases by 4^3. The strength is 16 times greater and the weight is 64 times greater.

40. (1) The amount of apple skin is proportional to the surface area of the apples. If we take a cube and slice it into eighths as shown below, it is apparent that the total surface area of the eight little cubes is greater than that of the large cube since the inside dotted surfaces of the small cubes are not available to the larger cube as surface area.

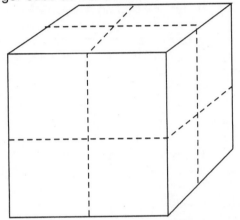

For the same mass, the smaller apples will provide the greater skin area. Since the A apples are the smallest, they will generate the most skin.

41. (2) Answer choice (2), "the length of the protein molecule, and the order and type of amino acids in the protein molecule" is the correct answer since proteins can be of different lengths; they can contain different types of amino acids; the amino acids can be in different orders in the protein. "Only the length of the protein molecule" (1) cannot be the correct answer since proteins can also differ by the order of their amino acids and/or by the types of amino acids they contain. "Only the type of amino acids in the protein molecule" (3) cannot be the correct answer since proteins can also differ in length and/or by the order of their amino acids. "Only the number of chemical bonds found in the protein molecule" (4) cannot be the correct answer since it is not mentioned as being one of the factors by which proteins can be different. "Only the order of amino acids found in the protein" (5) cannot be the correct answer since proteins can differ by the length of the protein and/or the type of amino acids found in the protein.

42. (1) Answer choice (1), 20, is the correct choice since there are 20 different types of "R" factor which produce 20 different types of amino acids. "50" (2) cannot be the correct answer since there are only 20 different types of "R" factor which produce 20 different types of amino acids. "100" (3) cannot be the correct answer since there are only 20 different types of "R" factor which produce 20 different types of amino acids. "1000" (4) cannot be the correct answer since there are only 20 different types of "R" factor which produce 20 different types of amino acids. "100,000" (5) cannot be the correct answer since there are only 20 different types of "R" factor which produce 20 different types of amino acids.

43. **(5)** Answer choice (5), "chains of amino acids" is the correct choice since amino acids are bonded together to form a chain. "Chains of sugar molecules" (1) cannot be the correct answer since only amino acid chains make protein. "Chains of fat molecules" (2) cannot be the correct answer since fat molecules are not part of a protein chain, and they are not mentioned in the paragraph. "Rings of carbon" (3) cannot be the correct answer since carbon rings form structures other than protein, and proteins which are composed of amino acids have no carbon rings. "Loops of cellulose molecules" (4) cannot be the correct answer since proteins are composed of amino acid chains.

44. **(3)** Answer choice (3), "rock" is the correct choice since rock is not composed of amino acids. "Hair" (1) cannot be the correct answer since hair is composed of protein. "Fingernails" (2) cannot be the correct answer since they are composed of protein. "Skin" (4) cannot be the correct answer since its major components are protein. "Muscle tissue" (5) cannot be the correct answer since its bulk is derived from protein.

45. **(4)** The correct answer is (4). The liquid is vaporizing to form a gas at the boiling point. Air does not enter from the atmosphere (1) because the atmospheric pressure is equivalent to the vapor pressure; there is not a higher external pressure forcing air into the liquid. (2) is wrong because although liquid does form a gas at the boiling point, it does so by expanding, not by condensing. (3) is incorrect because the passage does not mention helium gas in the liquid as the cause of the bubbles. Helium gas is rare on Earth. (5) is wrong because microorganisms do not cause bubbles in boiling liquid. In fact, most microorganisms would not thrive at the boiling points of most naturally occurring liquids, such as water.

46. **(4)** Choice (4) is correct. As water boils, the liquid water evaporates. Water loss occurs in the form of steam, and the volume of water decreases. Choice (1) is incorrect because water molecules are not created over the hot steam. Choice (2) is wrong because the volume decreases rather than remains constant. Atmospheric pressure will not cause the volume to increase and decrease as statement (3) describes, and statement (5) is also incorrect.

47. **(2)** Choice (2) is the false statement. Many liquids boil below 100°C (when water boils) and thus would not be considered extremely hot. Liquid nitrogen boils at room temperature, for instance. (1) and (5) are true statements that are discussed briefly in the passage. (3) is true because more heat will be needed to heat more water. (4) is also true in that the external

pressure is relatively higher in comparison to the lower vapor pressure below the boiling point and thus prevents gas bubble formation.

48. **(2)** The dots representing the most number of stars are clustered in the area called Main Sequence, therefore (2) is the correct answer. (1), (3), and (4) are incorrect because the number of stars in these areas is less than those of the Main Sequence area, and (5) is incorrect because Alpha Centauri is the name of a star, not of a group.

49. **(4)** (4) is correct. Sirius is located to the upper left of the sun in this diagram, which shows it a warmer and brighter position than the sun. (1), (2), (3), and (5) are all locations that Sirius is not in.

50. **(4)** is false. Canopus is a Main Sequence star.

51. **(1)** Answer choice (1) is correct because our sun is located in the middle of the diagram, making it average in many respects. (2) is incorrect. The sun is a Main Sequence star, making it similar to many other stars. (3) is incorrect because distances are not included on this diagram. (4) is incorrect because many of these stars are invisible to the unaided eye. (5) is incorrect because no data regarding star size is provided.

52. **(4)** Answer choice (4), "46" is the correct answer since a cell undergoing mitosis will first double its chromosome number and then divide and during that division the chromosomes will be evenly and correctly divided between the two daughter cells. "2" (1) cannot be the correct answer since the information in the questions states that a cell starts out with 46 chromosomes. "10" (2) cannot be the correct answer since this number is still too small to make up even one set of chromosomes, much less two. "24" (3) cannot be the correct answer since humans are sexually reproducing organisms and in a body cell there are two sets of chromosomes; therefore, 24 would be more than a single set but less than two sets. "92" (5) cannot be the correct answer since this number would indicate a doubling of the chromosome number without a cell division taking place.

53. **(4)** Answer choice (4), "46", is the correct answer since the zygote of a human is a cell derived from a sperm containing 23 chromosomes and an egg containing 23 chromosomes. "2" (1) cannot be the correct answer since it represents too few chromosomes for either a haploid sex cell or a diploid body cell. "10" (2) cannot be the correct answer since it also represents too few chromosomes for either a haploid sex cell or a diploid body cell. "23" (3) cannot be the correct answer since it represents the number of chromosomes in a sperm or an egg. "92" (5) cannot be the correct answer since it represents the number of chromosomes in a diploid cell that has doubled its chromosome number without dividing.

54. **(4)** Answer choice (4), "92" is the correct answer since the egg and the sperm, in this case, would have the diploid number of chromosomes (46), and

if they were to unite, then the number of chromosomes would be doubled. "2" (1) cannot be the correct answer since this number represents too few chromosomes for even a human sex cell. "23" (2) cannot be the correct answer since this is the haploid chromosome number of a normal human sex cell. "46" (3) cannot be the correct answer since this is the diploid chromosome number of a normal zygote. "184" (5) cannot be the correct answer since this number is greater than a zygote with twice the normal number of chromosomes.

55. **(4)**   Answer choice (4), "diploid" is the correct answer since a zygote is a diploid cell formed from the union of two haploid sex cells. "A single organism composed of two cells" (1) cannot be the correct answer since a zygote is not composed of two cells, it is composed of one cell. "Haploid" (2) cannot be the correct answer since a zygote is formed from the union of two haploid sex cells and is a diploid cell. "Undergoes meiosis to produce four sperm" (3) cannot be the correct answer since zygotes do not undergo meiosis. "Undergoes meiosis to produce four eggs" (5) cannot be the correct answer since zygotes do not undergo meiosis.

56. **(2)**   Answer choice (2), "haploid" is the correct answer since a sperm is a product of meiosis and has only one set of chromosomes. "A single organism composed of two cells" (1) cannot be the correct answer since a sperm is a single cell that has only one set of chromosomes. "Undergoes meiosis to produce four zygotes" (3) cannot be the correct answer since sperm do not undergo meiosis, and zygotes are not produced by meiosis. "Diploid" (4) cannot be the correct answer since sperm contain only one set of chromosomes and are haploid. "Undergoes meiosis to produce eggs" (5) cannot be the correct answer since sperm do not undergo meiosis and they do not produce eggs.

57. **(2)**   Answer choice (2), "haploid" is the correct answer since an egg is a product of meiosis and has only one set of chromosomes. "A single organism composed of two cells" (1) cannot be the correct answer since an egg is a single cell that has only one set of chromosomes. "Undergoes meiosis to produce four sperm" (3) cannot be the correct answer since eggs do not undergo meiosis, and they do not produce sperm. "Diploid" (4) cannot be the correct answer since sperm contain only one set of chromosomes and are haploid. "Undergoes meiosis to produce eggs" (5) cannot be the correct answer since eggs do not undergo meiosis and they do not produce zygotes.

58. **(1)**   The correct response is (1). Tar is the most viscous because the molecules composing tar are long and thus tangle easily. Lubricating oil (3) and gasoline (2) are composed of shorter molecules and thus flow easier, or are less viscous. (4) is wrong because tar and lubricating oil, or gasoline and tar (5) have molecules of different lengths and thus different viscosities.

59. **(5)**   is correct. Long chains breaking to form shorter chains will help the substance to flow better, and viscosity will be reduced. (1) is wrong because

the formation of long chains will result in increased viscosity. (2) is wrong because although thermal energy does increase, it will cause chain break-age, not increased tangling. (3) is wrong because chain vaporization has never been observed. (4) is wrong for the same reason.

60. **(3)** Answer choice (3), "carpels," is the correct answer since these are the modified leaves that produced the ovules. "Sepals" (1) cannot be the correct answer since the sepals are the modified leaves that surround the flower while it is in bud. "Petals" (2) cannot be the correct answer since these are the modified showy leaves used to attract insects to aid in pollination. "Stigmas" (4) cannot be the correct answer since they are the portions of the pistil that are sticky and receive the pollen. "Styles" (5) cannot be the correct answer since they are the portions of the pistil that are beneath the stigmas.

61. **(5)** Answer choice (5), "style" is the correct answer since it is the portion of the pistil that is beneath the stigmas. "Sepals" (1) cannot be the correct answer since the sepals are the modified leaves that surround the flower while it is in bud. "Petals" (2) cannot be the correct answer since these are the modified showy leaves used to attract insects to aid in pollination. "Carpels" (3) cannot be the correct answer since these are the modified leaves that produced the ovules. "Stigmas" (4) cannot be the correct answer since they are the portions of the pistil that are sticky and receive the pollen.

62. **(3)** Answer choice (3), "pollen," is the correct answer since the pollen contain the nucleus that combines with the nucleus in the ovule to produce the embryonic plant. "Stigmas" (1) cannot be the correct answer since stigmas receive the pollen. "Styles" (2) cannot be the correct answer since styles are found beneath stigmas. "Radicals" (4) cannot be the correct answer since these are growing regions that produce the root system. "Anthers" (5) cannot be the correct answer since an anther is a container that produces the pollen.

63. **(4)** The reason why bees are attracted to flowers is because of the bright and showy petals. If these are removed, the bees will not notice the flowers. Thus, (4) is correct. In (1), separating the sepals from the bud will still put the petals in a prominent position to be viewed by the bees. (2) is wrong because the pollen does not affect the bees' attraction for the flowers. (3) is incorrect because crushing the stigma will affect pollination but not bee attraction. (5), separating the anther from the filament, will break structures within the flower but will not affect the ability of the petals to attract bees.

64. **(1)** Since the sepal is the protective covering over the petals, the sepal must have been invaded if the petals are to be reached. Stamens (2), the pistil (3), the style (4), and the ovary (5) are all reproductive portions of the flower and are not involved in protecting the petals from damage.

65. **(2)** The main way in which the pollen travels to the stigma is by way of pollinators that transfer the pollen to the stigma through their movements.

Thus, choice (2) is correct. (1) is false because although wind may help in pollination, gale winds (very strong winds) are not necessary. (3) is incorrect because picking flowers simply does not stimulate pollination. (4) is an incorrect statement because the pollen and stigma do not possess opposite charges. (5) is wrong because the style is the structure through which an already germinated pollen structure is passed to the ovary.

66. **(2)** It is true that female animals, like female humans, possess both ovaries and eggs. Flowers also possess ovaries and eggs. (1) is wrong because animals are not composed of modified leaves. (3) is wrong because animals do not have stigmas. (4) is wrong because animals in general possess either male or female organs, but not both. (5) is wrong because only animals have sperm; flowers do not.

TEST 4: LITERATURE AND THE ARTS

1.   **(2)**   Melancholy is the pervasive tone, not uplifting (1), since the narrator treasured his last moments with his pet while it "hesitated for a full minute." Forlorn (3) is incorrect since there is mention of a "new life." (4) and (5) are wrong since there is no hint of cynicism or sarcasm in the narration.

2.   **(1)**   The tone is sentimental but hopeful since the narrator has prepared himself for the separation, lovingly pocketing the raccoon's chain and collar in case it chooses to go off with the "entrancing female." This passage ends with promise of "new life" for pet and mate; therefore, disappointed (5) as well as bitter yet resigned (2) and angry (4) do not apply. Since the boy allows his pet freedom, relieved (3) is also not a wise choice.

3.   **(3)**   The narrator and his pet are companions who understand each other since the narrator lets his pet leave. (1) is incorrect since the narrator pockets the collar to remember his pet; this act of love proves they were once suited for each other, so (5) is incorrect. There is no immediate hope of reunion (4), but there is no evidence that (2) they would never meet again.

4.   **(3)**   Still affected by her life, Dexter loses Judy twice, proving he is still emotionally vulnerable, overreacting to Devlin's account of her fading beauty and unhappy marriage. (1) and (2) are not correct since Dexter wanted to marry Judy, never hinting that it was not meant to be. (4) is not the best choice since he is still being hurt by Judy, long after her rejection. Nothing suggests that Dexter still wished they could be united (5).

5.   **(3)**   Attention should be brought to the question which asks which of the following does <u>not</u> apply to Dexter's dilemma. Answers (1) and (4) <u>do</u> apply since they concern the lack of wisdom concerning love. Also, (2) and (5) do apply, since they state that love is blind.

6.   **(2)**   Here the emphasis is on Devlin and his account of Judy Jones. He "tells it like it is," but tempers his description with kindness, speaking of her "nice eyes," mentioning "most of the women like her." No other answers apply.

7.   **(3)**   The fisherman does not wholly agree (1) or totally disagree (4) with Walton. Lines 38–42 ask, if it doesn't exist, why does a "lost fish" hurt so much? He obviously understands (2) and knows enough (5) about Walton's theory.

8.   **(2)**   The speaker still feels the pain felt over "the one that got away," or the one he nearly had. (2) is correct because he'll always remember that feeling and never truly lose it.

9. **(1)** The depth of Hemingway's feelings are implied as stronger than the narrator's in the question in line 48. Therefore, hidden (2), same as (3), and known (4) are not correct. Since not as strong (5) is the direct opposite of what is implied, it is also incorrect.

10. **(3)** "Balm" is used figuratively and transcends personality (2) and physical aspects (5). (4) is incorrect since no other sport is mentioned. (1) is incorrect since it is contradictory to the entire message of the essay.

11. **(3)** "Skunked" is explicitly defined in lines 27–29 as a fishing term for coming home "empty-handed."

12. **(1)** The speaker explains that the "somebody" he fishes with may be known, never known, nor ever will. This goes beyond visions (2) and interesting strangers (3) completely, and (4) and (5) which describe fishing as a "solitary" encounter.

13. **(2)** Nothing in the dialogue touches on reincarnation (1) or suggests that he is joking (3) or only fantasizing (4). However, he does say that he "will probably fish with friends, dead or alive." (5) is also incorrect.

14. **(1)** Adjectives such as rich, golden, thick, eager, and hopeful abound through this passage, giving hope and promise and negating pessimistic (2) and foreboding (4) as possible answers. Realistic (3) is not the best choice because of the poetic promise within the passage.

15. **(3)** Realistic is the best choice even though the passage begins with the same phrase as the optimistic paragraph before it. This time, "but not all" is added with adjectives such as "scarred" and such phrases as "no thorough repair." Therefore, positive possible answers such as (1) optimistic, (2) encouraging, and (5) compassionate are not good choices. There is no hint of (4) sarcasm in the paragraph.

16. **(2)** By the use of contrast and the words "no" and "not," the author shows that not all devastation can be repaired. Answers (1), (3), and (5) are incorrect since they speak of healing, restoration, and replacement. (4) is also not a correct choice since the passage does not give the reader any reason to draw that conclusion.

17. **(1)** is the best answer since the writer's intended meaning transcends the notion of just looking back on the past. Although (2) and (3) are astute observations of life in general, they have very little to do with the passage. (4) does not apply.

18. **(1)** "Now" is the key word for choosing the answer, since we discover that Nolan had initially been received with (2) mixed feelings and accepted with reluctance. (4) and (5) are not answers which are supported by the passage.

19. **(4)** Nolan's message is explicit that "not in America" is there one more loyal, nor is there one who loves and prays for its flag more. No other answer approaches Nolan's heartfelt protests.

20. **(2)** The feeling that Nolan died in peace is substantiated and is apparent by the smile he had with his last breath. This eliminates further unrest (3) as a possible choice. There is no hint that this information is classified, thus (1) is also incorrect as well as (5), given reluctantly, since Danforth declares he will tell Nolan "everything you asked about it."

21. **(3)** Danforth's news transcends the material and physical since we witnessed that Nolan's death is made easier by it. Therefore all the following are incorrect since they appeal to material or physical gratification: (1) exercise-athlete, (2) money-wallet, (4) toy-child, (5) food-man.

22. **(4)** Although burial at sea (1) is mentioned, the biblical text alludes to desiring a country and excludes the more materialistic desires such as (2) an elaborate funeral, (3) a medal of honor, (5) fame and fortune.

23. **(1)** Philip Nolan's epitaph leaves no doubt about how much he loved his country since he felt he deserved no better treatment than what he received. This totally excludes (2) and (5).

24. **(5)** Challenged by recent historians and writers is the best answer. Even though "myth" is used in line 28, it is qualified by the phrase "to undo, at least in part." Only alleged incidents about the artist's life appear and cannot be presumed to be substantiated, therefore (1) is incorrect. Van Gogh's brother, Theo, was close to him and van Gogh's suicide is still not understood.

25. **(2)** The literary technique of stringing critical questions is most effective here, capsulizing the controversy. (1) and (5) are poor choices since the writer takes no specific stand; likewise, (3) and (4) are poor choices, since it is the writer's intent to inform and not to amuse or baffle the reader.

26. **(1)** Descriptives such as "fanciful tales" and "Holy Fool" are quoted from a new biographer who questions old van Gogh stories. Sweetman does not (2) accept these nor does he (3) reject past and present theories. He is quite clear in his endorsement, negating any uncertainty (4).

27. **(1)** The informative nature of this review is immediately apparent from the onset. It chronicles important information in reverse order, beginning with van Gogh's self-inflicted wound. (2) Humor is nowhere introduced. (3) is a poor choice since the review presents both "old" and "new" schools of thought. Derogatory and inflammatory (4) is inaccurate because the writer presents his information with little bias.

28. **(1)** Sweetman leaves no doubt as to his conviction that van Gogh (as "Holy Fool") is nonsense. Therefore, his madness is neither (2) true nor (3) debatable. Since he so emphatically believes it is true, it cannot be resolved (4) or left for future biographers (5).

29. **(4)** "Read" in this context means interpreted. The writer feels that whatever maladies may have been present in van Gogh's life, they cannot be found in his art. Since (5) removed from would mean the opposite, it is incorrect. Contextually, (1) summarized, (2) questioned, and (3) painted are not precise.

30. **(2)** Line 5 clarifies this informally used poker term to mean that musicians' standards of excellence were raised. Neither salary (1) nor public problems (3) were mentioned nor implied. Obscurity (4) is incorrect since lines 24–25 reveal that his music will not be outdated with time. Line 11 negates that (5) Johnson "aimed too high" since his music is called "art of the highest order."

31. **(4)** The reviewer answers his question neither affirmatively (1) nor negatively (2) in lines 15–17—"comparisons seem almost irrelevant." Evasively (3) is incorrect in lines 20–21—"blows... comparisons right out of the window."

32. **(3)** Implicit in lines 25–26 is the message of surviving time—"has a power that age cannot dim." Therefore (4) is wrong as is (1), see lines 26 and 27—"over many years... finer appreciation." This entire review is a tribute to the artist excluding (2) no popular appeal. (5) is neither affirmed nor negated (see explanation to preceding question).

33. **(4)** From the first paragraph of this excerpt, the writer tells us that she knows everything about her hostess' cookies would be as "perfect" as her hostess is; "perfect," therefore, suggests awe and respect, which logically excludes (1) cool reserve, as well as fear (2) and distrust (3). (5) is a poor choice of answers since it suggests there is no regard for her hostess at all.

34. **(1)** Wisdom is suggested here since the author mentions such things as "mother wit" emanating from "country people"; people more educated than college professors. Unintelligence (2) as well as book learning (5) are polar opposites and incorrect. Neither charm (3) nor native intelligence (4) are implied.

35. **(5)** Buried beneath this statement is the lesson, "some people, unable to go to school, were more educated and even more intelligent than college professors." Therefore, numbers (1), (2), (3), and (4) are incorrect because they contain the absolute "always," but miss the entire point—"sometimes."

36. **(2)** Since Marguerite had read the novel and "found it up to my standards," we can disregard (1) a literal meaning. Socially (3) is incorrect

since the visit was not social, but scholarly, in its intent. Marguerite was too much in awe of her hostess for "tongue in cheek" (4) comments.

37. **(3)** Lines 29–30 reveal that all Marguerite could manage was, "Yes ma'am." Uneasy (1) might have been an appropriate answer, if she had not earlier compared her hostess' recitation to music, to which she had listened mesmerized. Therefore offended (2), unimpressed (4) as well as eloquent (5) in her praises are entirely incorrect.

38. **(3)** The best answer, "enjoy the silent beauty," is suggested in line 4. Since he admits the neighbor "will not see me", (2) is incorrect. There is no neighbor about to beckon him, so (5) is incorrect. No mention is made here of his horse (1) or of darkness (4).

39. **(4)** Lines 5, 9, and 10 tell us that his "little horse" stops and signals to the poet that there is no farmhouse so there must be a mistake in stopping. Wrong path (1) and lost the way (3) are immediate poor choices since we know there is a rapport and friendship between the man and his horse. No mention is made of weariness (2) or of stubbornness (5).

40. **(1)** The key word in the last stanza is "promises," and the idea that the poet goes on, which suggests that he has made his choice by resuming to meet his obligations. Although we might infer that (4) he will return soon, there is no hint of that possibility in the last stanza. Confused (2) is a poor choice because we sense determination. The effect of repeating lines 15 and 16 rule out (3) as a possible answer.

41. **(3)** If this poem is read on the symbolic level, "sleep" in the final two lines of the last stanza can be equated with death. Therefore the serenity and peace of the winter scene can be interpreted as the lure of death, while the "miles to go" can be read as the obligations of life. There is nothing literal or figurative that would suggest any of the other answers as appropriate choices.

42. **(3)** The power of photojournalism is prevalent throughout this essay, but lines 24 and 25 are the most explicit. Line 24 speaks of its "power" which makes not powerful (1) a very poor choice. (2) is incorrect since photojournalism is called "splendid" in line 23. Simply entertainment (4) is negated throughout the entire piece; likewise (5), underestimated, is incorrect since its power is called "preternatural" in line 24.

43. **(3)** Personification is effectively used throughout, especially in lines 26–27 wherein photographs are personified as having "lives of their own." Alliteration (2), rhyme (4) and cacophony (5) have to do with sound, and they are not present. Any sense of repetition (1) is underlying within the message of the essay and not technically used as a literary device.

44. **(2)** Implicit within the message of the essay with its emphasis on the power of photojournalism, is a precautionary note that the power of pictures may be "more than they deserve." Casually (1) implies the opposite, so it is incorrect. Suspiciously (3) presents an averse connotation, not found within the essay's context. Both tolerantly (4) and disrespectfully (5) are poor choices for answers since neither is suggested by the author.

45. **(2)** The author has cleverly entitled his essay, "Imprisoning Time in a Rectangle," and equated it with photojournalism's method of capturing history in a rectangular-shaped mode. Although permeating the piece is a caution concerning the media's power, there is no mention of (1) criminal misuse or (4) discontinuing its use. Balzac's dread of photography is presented in the opening paragraph only to emphasize the power of photography itself; therefore, (3) is incorrect.

TEST 5: MATHEMATICS

1. **(2)** To solve any equation, use some simple rules of algebra. First, get the like terms on one side of the equation, then simplify to solve for the variable.

$$2x - 7 = 3x + 2 \text{ becomes}$$
$$2x - 3x = 2 + 7$$
$$-x = 9 \text{ or}$$
$$x = -9$$

2. **(4)** Of the 25 chemistry students, 7 are also in physics. There are 23 − 7 = 16 remaining students taking only Physics. Therefore, 25 + 16 = 41 individual students are enrolled in the two science classes.

3. **(3)** Percents that are set up as proportions such as

$$\frac{\text{Percent}}{100} = \frac{\text{is}}{\text{of}}$$

or

$$\frac{\text{Percent}}{100} = \frac{\text{part}}{\text{whole}}$$

are the easiest to remember and solve. Identify the various parts of the proportion in the problem such as:

Percent = ?
"is" or "part" = 0.9
"of" or "whole" = 3.6
Now set up the proportion:

$$\frac{?}{100} = \frac{0.9}{3.6}$$

Simplify:

$$\frac{0.9}{3.6} = \frac{9}{36} = \frac{1}{4}$$

Therefore,

$$\frac{?}{100} = \frac{1}{4}$$

$$? = 25$$

4. **(2)** The perimeter or measure around the pool will use the formula:

2 (lengths) + 2 (widths) = perimeter
2 (160) + 2 (80) = 320 + 160 = 480 feet

Because the question asks for the answer in terms of yards,

$$\frac{480 \text{ ft.}}{3 \text{ ft.}} = 160 \text{ yards}$$

5. **(3)** Because this is a rate of work problem, consider what fraction of the job would get done in one minute. Scott would get 1/30th of the job done while Henri would get 1/60th of the job done in one minute. Together, they would get:

$$\frac{1}{30} + \frac{1}{60} = \frac{2}{60} + \frac{1}{60} = \frac{3}{60} = \frac{1}{20}$$

of the job done in one minute. Therefore, 20 minutes would be needed to pot 100 plants, and 40 minutes to pot all 200 pants.

6. **(2)** The twenty students that actually went to the play were assessed an additional $20.00 total to cover the remaining cost of the bus when the other 5 students decided not to go. Therefore, each of the 5 students were paying $4.00 for their share of the bus rental along with the other 20 students.

$$(\$4.00)\ (25\ students) = \$100.00$$

was he cost of the bus rental.

7. **(4)** 1/2 of 4/5 is interpreted as:

$$\frac{1}{2}\ \frac{4}{5} = \frac{2}{5}$$

2/3 of 60% is translated into:

$$\frac{2}{3} \times \frac{60}{100} = \frac{2}{3} \times \frac{3}{5} = \frac{2}{5}$$

Following the problem then:

$$\frac{2}{5} + \frac{2}{5} = 1$$

8. **(5)** Using actual numbers as examples will help to find the false choice. Let a = 4, b = 5, and c = 6, then substitute these values into the multiple choice answers of the problem. The choices are:

    1. a + b = 4 + 5 = 9 True
    2. a + c = 4 + 6 = 10 True
    3. 2bc = 2(5)(6) = 10(6) = 60 True
    4. a + 3b = 4 + 3(5) = 4 + 15 = 19 True
    5. a(b + c) = 4(5 + 6) = 4(11) = 44 False

Following rules may be recalled. (1) odd + even = odd (2) odd + odd = even (3) even + even = even (4) odd • even = even (5) odd • odd = odd (6) even • even = even

9. **(3)** The ratio 3 : 5 : 10 indicates that the 180 degrees of the triangle must be divided into 3 + 5 + 10 = 18 equal parts or 10 degrees for each part. The largest angle is made up of ten 10 degree parts or 100 degrees.

10. **(1)**   25% or 1/4 of $40,000 = $10,000 was for the mortgage, leaving $30,000. 25% or 1/4 of $30,000 = $7500 was used for food and clothing, leaving a $22,500 balance. 20% or 1/5 of $22,500 = $4500 was saved for a vacation. The problem, then, can be restated as: $4500 is what percent of $40,000? Using proportions:

$$\frac{?}{100} = \frac{4500}{40,000}$$

or

$$\frac{?}{100} = \frac{9}{80}$$

$$? = \frac{900}{80} = \frac{90}{8} = 11\frac{1}{4}\%$$

Method 2:   Although $40,000 was used as a base figure, in a problem like this one, any number would have worked. If $100 was used instead, the figures would have yielded the same results; in fact, it would have eliminated one step.

25% or 1/4 of $100 = $25, leaving $75
25% or 1/4 of $75 = $18.75, leaving $56.25
20% or 1/5 of $56.25 = $11.25
$11.25 of $100 is 11 1/4% of $100

11. **(5)**   The least common multiple or LCM of 18x and 24xy is the smallest number that both of these numbers can divide into evenly without a remainder. To find the LCM, prime factorize 18x and 24xy into:

$$18x = (2)(3)(3)(x)$$
$$24xy = (2)(2)(2)(3)(x)(y)$$

Now, take the largest group of each number and variable represented. Of the 2's, the larger group is the (2)(2)(2) from the 24xy. Of the 3's, the larger group is the (3)(3) from the 18x. There is also one x and one y to be represented. Therefore, the LCM of 18x and 24xy is (2)(2)(2)(3)(3(xy) = 72xy.

Method 2: The LCM may also be calculated by a modified form of long division, as follows:

$$6x \lfloor 18x \quad 24xy$$

$$3 \lfloor 3 \quad 4y$$

$$4y \lfloor 1 \quad 4y$$
$$1$$

Then (6x)(3)(4y) = 72 xy.

12. **(2)**   Convert 33 1/3% into a fraction, remembering that the percent sign is equivalent to 1/100.

$$33\frac{1}{3}\% = \frac{100}{3} \times \frac{1}{100} = \frac{1}{3}$$

Now,
$$\frac{1}{3} = \frac{4}{12}$$

Therefore, there are 4 twelfths in 33 1/3%.

13. **(4)** The floor that measures 10 ft. by 20 ft. has an area of 10 x 20 = 200 sq. ft. The tiles with 36 sq. in. of area must measure 6 in. by 6 in. or 1/2 ft. by 1/2 ft. for 1/4 sq. ft. of area. Because it would take 4 tiles to cover 1 sq. ft., 4(200 sq. ft.) = 800 tiles would be needed to cover the entire floor.

14. **(1)** Any average score is calculated by adding all the scores and dividing the sum by the number of games. An average of 162 out of 15 games came from a total pin count of (162)(15 games) = 2430 pins. Adding the last three scores to the total will yield 187 + 175 + 160 + 2430 = 2952 pins for 18 games. Pearl's new average is:

$$2952 \div 18 = 164$$

and so her average increased by 2 pins.

Method 2: The number of pins that an average is increased (or decreased) by can also be calculated by finding the differences between the scores and the 162 average, adding the differences together, then dividing by the total number of games.

$$187 - 162 = 25$$
$$175 - 162 = 13$$
$$160 - 162 = -2$$
Now, 25 + 13 − 2 = 36
Therefore: 36 ÷ 18 = 2

15. **(4)** Since Neal was left with only $20.00 or 1/4 of what he had originally, he must have spent 3($20.00) = $60.00 for his shirt. The cost of the shirt added to the $20.00 is $80.00 that he originally had.

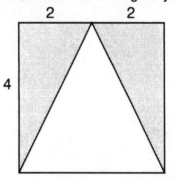

16. **(3)** The shaded regions of the square are two right triangles with heights of 4 and bases of 2. Each region has an area of (1/2)(base)(height) = (1/2)(4)(2) = 4. Two of the areas will equal 8 sq. units.

17. **(4)** The interpretation of the sign "> 0." means that all the answers derived from the inequality $b^2 - 121 > 0$ must be of positive value. Therefore, the values of b when it is squared must be greater than 121 in order for the difference to be positive. Because the product of two negative numbers is positive, negative values less than -11 must be considered, as well as all the positive values greater than +11.

18. **(5)** Let n = the number of nickels and n + 13 = the number of dimes. Then let 5n = the value of the n nickels and 10(n + 13) = the value of the dimes. The total value of Tracey's coins may now be represented by the expression:

$$5n + 10(n + 13) =$$
$$5n + 10n + 130 =$$
$$15n + 130$$

19. **(3)** There will be a total of 18 people for dinner, Jann and her 17 guests. Doubling her recipe will serve only 16 people, so another 1/4 of the recipe must be included to feed the remaining 2 people. Jann needs to increase her recipe to 2 1/4 times the original.

20. **(4)** To make the problem easier to understand, first translate the phrase "the first piece is one-third the length of the second" into "the second piece is three times the first." Because the third piece is five times the first, the pieces are in a ratio of 1 : 3 : 5. The board must be divided into 9 equal parts of 1/3 ft. which equals 4 inches. The longest piece takes 5 parts or 20 inches, which is:

$$\frac{20 \text{ inches}}{12 \text{ inches}} = 1\frac{2}{3} \text{ ft.}$$

21. **(1)** Ninety miles in 2 hours is equivalent to 45 miles in 1 hour (60 minutes) or 45 mph. If Lance has only 1.5 hours or 90 minutes to cover the same 90 miles when he returns, he needs to travel 1 mile a minute, which translates into 60 mph, 15 mph faster than his original speed.

22. **(5)** In order for 534 to be a multiple of 7, it must be divisible by 7 with no remainder. Doing some long division gives:

$$\begin{array}{r} 76 \\ 7\overline{)534} \\ \underline{49} \\ 44 \\ \underline{42} \\ 2 \end{array}$$

If the remainder 2 is increased by 5, then 534 + 5 = 539 will be a multiple of 7.

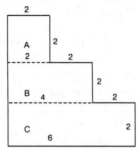

23. **(4)** The polygon can be divided into 3 rectangles whose areas are easy to calculate by using the formula: area = (length)(width).

Rectangle A = 2(2) = 4
Rectangle B = 2(4) = 8
Rectangle C = 2(6) = 12

The sum 4 + 8 + 12 = 24 is the area of the polygon.

24. **(4)** Using some rules of algebra,

$4x - 3 = 2y + 7$ becomes
$4x - 2y = 7 + 3$ or
$4x - 2y = 10$

Dividing by 2: $2x - y = 5$

25. **(2)** Identify several ordered pairs that are on Line A such as (0,4), (1,4), (2,4), and (3,4) . Notice that the y-term or second term of the ordered pairs is always 4. Therefore, the equation is $y = 4$.

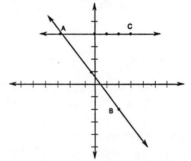

26. **(3)** The ordered pairs for points A and B, respectively, are (-3,4) and (2,-2). The midpoint is calculated by finding the averages of the x and y coordinates. In other words, the midpoint is:

$$\left(\frac{-3 + 2}{2}, \frac{4 + (-2)}{2} \right) = \left(\frac{-1}{2}, 1 \right)$$

27. **(4)** The slope of a line uses the formula:

$$m = \frac{y^2 - y^1}{x_2 - x_1}$$

Assigning point A(-3, 4) as (x , y) and point B(2, -2) as (x , y), the formula yields:

$$m = \frac{4 - (-2)}{-3 - 2} = \frac{6}{-5} = -\frac{6}{5}$$

28. **(2)** The car traveling 55 mph can get to the halfway point 330 miles away in 330/55 = 6 hours. The 40 mph car covers the same distance in 330/40 = 8 1/4 hours. The faster car will have to wait:

$$8\frac{1}{4} - 6 = 2\frac{1}{4} \text{ hours}$$

29. **(5)** The sides of similar triangles are in proportion. Using the Pythagorean Theorem the length of B'C' is:

$$5^2 + (B'C')^2 = 13^2$$
$$25 + (B'C')^2 = 169$$
$$(B'C')^2 = 144$$
$$B'C' = 12$$

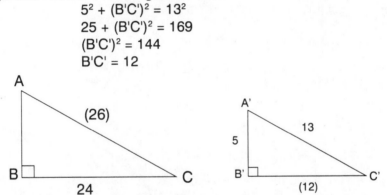

BC and B'C' are corresponding sides of similar triangles in a ratio of 24 : 12 or 2 : 1. Similarly side AC and A'C' have the same ratio; AC must be twice as long as A'C'. In other words, AC = 2(13) = 26.

30. **(2)** Complex fractions such as this one can be solved one of two ways. The first method would be to work on the numerator and denominator separately so they are each simplified to simple fractions, then treat them as a quotient of two fractions. Therefore,

$$\frac{\dfrac{1}{3}}{1 + \dfrac{2}{4 + 5}} =$$

$$\frac{\dfrac{1}{3}}{1 + \dfrac{2}{9}} = \frac{\dfrac{1}{3}}{\dfrac{11}{9}} =$$

$$\frac{1}{3} \times \frac{9}{11} = \frac{3}{11}$$

In the second method, multiply every term by the common denominator (g) to cancel all of the denominators of the complex fraction, then work to simplify what is left:

$$\frac{\dfrac{1}{3}}{1 + \dfrac{2}{4+5}} = \frac{\dfrac{1}{3}}{1 + \dfrac{2}{9}}$$

$$\frac{9 \times \dfrac{1}{3}}{(9 \times 1) + \left(9 \times \dfrac{2}{9}\right)} =$$

$$\frac{3}{9+2} = \frac{3}{11}$$

31. **(2)** Substitute 98.6 F into the formula for F:

$$C = \frac{5}{9}(F - 32)$$

$$C = \frac{5}{9}(98.6 - 32)$$

$$C = \frac{5}{9}(66.6)$$

$$C = 5(7.4)$$

$$C = 37°$$

32. **(1)** In the first 6 months, Kristen's weight gain is:

19 lbs. 15 oz. − 7 lbs. 4 oz. = 12 lbs. 11 oz.

During the following 6 months, her weight gain is:

22 lbs. 6 oz. − 19 lbs. 15 oz. = 21 lbs. 22 oz. − 19 lbs. 15 oz. = 2 lbs. 7 oz.

Therefore, Kristen gained:

12 lbs. 11 oz. − 2 lbs. 7 oz. = 10 lbs. 4 oz. more.

33. **(4)** Kristen grew 13 inches in 18 months. Setting up a proportion yields the following:

$$\frac{\text{percent}}{100} = \frac{13}{20}$$

$$\text{percent} = \frac{13}{20}(100)$$

$$\text{percent} = 65$$

34. **(4)** One gross amounts to 144 cans. Since each set of 3 cans will cost $8.00, and there are 144/3 = 48 sets, (48 sets)($8) = $384.

35. **(3)** When the can is cut open and flattened out, its shape will be a rectangle.

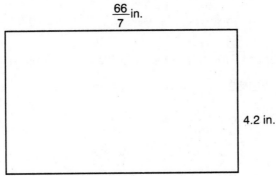

$\frac{66}{7}$ in.

4.2 in.

The length, which is the circumference of the circular base, is:

$$C = 2\pi \text{ (radius)}$$
$$C + 2\pi \left(\frac{3}{2} \text{ inches }\right)$$
$$C = 3\pi$$
$$C = 3\left(\frac{22}{7}\right) = \frac{66}{7} \text{ in.}$$

The area of the rectangle is (length)(width):

$$A = \left(\frac{66}{7}\right)(4.2)$$
$$A = (66.6)(.6) = 39.6 \text{ sq. in.}$$

36. **(4)** Using some algebraic expressions to represent the unknown should help here. Let:

x = the number of children in the original group
$6x$ = the number of cookies in the package.

When 2 more children join the group, the expressions are:

$x + 2$ = the number of children
$4(x + 2)$ = the number of cookies in the package.

Notice that there are 2 expressions for "the number of cookies in the package." These are equivalent expressions so set up an equation and solve for x.

$$6x = 4(x + 2)$$
$$6x = 4x + 8$$
$$2x = 8$$
$$x = 4$$

There were 4 children in the original group, and therefore, 6x = 6(4) = 24 cookies in the package.

37. **(4)** The circumference of the wheel is:

$$C = 2\pi \ (1 \text{ ft.})$$

$$C = 2\left(\frac{22}{7}\right) = \frac{44}{7} \text{ ft.}$$

To find the number of revolutions the wheel takes, calculate:

$$5280 \div \left(\frac{44}{7}\right) =$$

$$5280 \times \frac{7}{44} =$$

$$120 \times 7 = 840 \text{ revolutions}$$

38. **(2)** Because the indicated operation in this problem is addition, find the 2 expressions that are to be added together. Let:

$$x = \text{Derek's age}$$
$$(17/2)x = \text{Mike's age}$$

Now add the expressions for a sum of 38.

$$\frac{17}{2}x + x = 38$$

$$17x + 2x = 76$$

$$19x = 78$$

$$x = 4$$

Derek is 4 years old, and Mike is 38 − 4 = 34 years old.

39. **(2)** To find the average rainfall for the week, add the five amounts in the "rainfall" column, then divide by five.

$$\frac{0.08 + 0.09 + 0.70 + 0.19 + 0.32}{5} =$$

$$\frac{1.38}{5} = 0.276 \text{ in.}$$

40. **(5)** The problem may be restated, "90.88 is what percent of 79.15?" Rounding off the numbers will simplify the calculations and not change the answer significantly. Therefore, set up the proportion and solve:

$$\frac{\text{percent}}{100} = \frac{91}{79}$$

$$\text{percent} = \frac{9100}{79} = 115$$

41. **(2)**   In estimating an answer to the nearest hundred, round off to the nearest hundred all the numbers of the expression. This will create a much easier problem to simplify with less chance of a mistake.

$$\frac{(7592)\ (4892)}{(3810)\ \ (70)}$$

is rounded off to:

$$\frac{(7600)\ (4900)}{(3800)\ \ (100)} =$$

$$(2)\ (49) = 98$$

98 rounded off to the nearest hundred is 100.

42. **(3)**   Because Sam is making 2 investments, first find 3/5 of $1000. Divide $1000 into 5 equal parts ($1000/5 = $200) and take 3 parts ($600). $600 is invested at 6% simple interest, which yields:

$$\$600\ (6\%) = \$600\ (.06) = \$36$$

The remaining $400 is invested at 8% simple interest, which yields:

$$\$400\ (8\%) = \$400\ (.08) = \$32$$

The total interest earned is $36 + $32 = $68

43. **(4)**   Prime factorize 156:

$$156 = 2 \times 78$$
$$= 2 \times 2 \times 39$$
$$= 2 \times 2 \times 3 \times 13$$

The largest prime factor of 156 is 13.

44. **(2)**   Set up the inequality in mathematical symbols and solve.

$$3x - 4 > 6$$
$$3x > 6 + 4$$
$$3x > 10$$
$$x > 10/3$$

45. **(4)**   The diagram is of an isosceles triangle, as indicated by the 2 equal base angles.

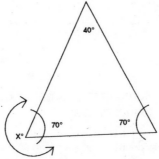

Because the total degree measure of any triangle is 180 degrees, the 2 base angles must be:

$$\frac{180° - 40°}{2} = \frac{140°}{2} = 70°$$

The angle represented outside of the triangle can be imagined as a partial circle. A circle contains 360 degrees, therefore:

$$360° - 70° = 290°$$

is the value of x.

46. **(5)**   The most difficult part to deal with in a repeating decimal is the fact that it seemingly continues indefinitely. Eliminate this difficulty by eliminating the repeating portion of the decimal number using this algebraic method. Let:

$$x = 0.252525... \text{ and}$$
$$100x = 25.252525...$$

By subtracting the first equation from the second, obtain:

$$100x = 25.252525...$$
$$- \ (x = 0.252525...)$$
$$99x = 25$$
$$x = 25/99$$

47. **(1)**   Let x = the numerator and x + 4 = the denominator. Therefore, the fraction is expressed as:

$$\frac{x}{x+4}$$

When the numerator is doubled and the denominator is increased by five, the expression for the new fraction is:

$$\frac{2x}{(x+4) + 5}$$

Now set up the equation and solve for x:

$$\frac{2x}{x + 9} = \frac{1}{2}$$
$$4x = x + 9$$
$$3x = 9$$
$$x = 3$$
$$x + 4 = 7$$

The original fraction is 3/7.

48. **(4)**   Because the volume of the cereal boxes is cubic inches, convert the measure of the case to inches also.

$$1 \text{ ft.} = 12 \text{ in.}$$
$$2 \text{ ft.} = 24 \text{ in.}$$

2 1/2 ft. = 30 in.

The volume of the case is calculated by using the volume formula:

$$V = (\text{length})(\text{width})(\text{height})$$
$$= (30)(24)(12)$$
$$= 8649 \text{ cubic in.}$$

Now find how many boxes of cereal are needed:

$$\frac{8640}{288} = 30 \text{ boxes}$$

49. **(4)**   x represents Sandy's age 4 years ago. Therefore, she is now x + 4 years old. Adding another 4 years to x + 4, in other words, (x + 4) + 4, will yield x + 8 as Sandy's age 4 years from now.

50. **(5)**   When evaluating an expression without grouping symbols to indicate what operation should be done first, always do all multiplication and division first as they appear from left to right, then do any addition or subtraction, again as they appear from left to right. Therefore,

$$48 - 24 \div 3 + 5 \times 2 =$$
$$48 - 8 + 10 =$$
$$40 + 10 = 50$$

51. **(4)**   Line AB is a straight line and also a straight angle measuring 180 degrees. Angle CEA = 40, therefore Angle CEB = 120. Because Angle CEB is 8 times Angle AED, Angle AED must be 120/5 = 15 degrees. Angle AED and Angle DEB form another straight angle: Angle AED + Angle DEB = 180 or 15 degrees + Angle DEB = 180. Therefore, Angle DEB = 165 degrees.

52. **(4)**   First, change all the numbers to the same form. All are easily converted to fractions and simplify:

$$7.5 \times 1\frac{7}{9} - 1.333... =$$
$$7\frac{1}{2} \times \frac{16}{9} - 1\frac{1}{3} =$$
$$\frac{15}{2} \times \frac{16}{9} - \frac{4}{3} =$$

$$\frac{15}{2} \times \frac{16}{9} - \frac{4}{3} = 12$$

53. **(5)** What is needed here is some substitution: a = 3 and b = 1/2. Now simplify:

$$a * b = a^2 + 2b$$
$$3 * \frac{1}{2} = 3^2 + 2\left(\frac{1}{2}\right)$$
$$= 9 + 1 = 10$$

54. **(4)** Use the distributive property and collect like terms:
$$6(x - 2) - 4(x + 4) =$$
$$6x - 12 - 4x - 16 =$$
$$2x - 28 =$$
$$2x - 28 = 2(x - 14) \text{ In factored form.}$$

55. **(2)** The formula for the area of a trapezoid is:
$$A = (1/2)(\text{height})(\text{first base} + \text{second base}).$$

To find the length of the second base, use the Pythagorean Theorem to find the bases of the 2 congruent triangles on either side of the square.
$$(\text{base})^2 + n^2 = (n\sqrt{2})^2$$
$$(\text{base})^2 + n^2 = 2n^2$$
$$\text{base}^2 = n^2$$
$$\text{base} = n$$

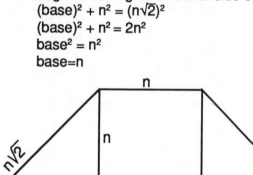

The base of the trapezoid is 3n. Using the area formula:

$$A = \left(\frac{1}{2}\right)(n)(n + 3n)$$

$$A = \left(\frac{1}{2}\right)(n)(4n)$$

$$A = 2n^2$$

56. **(5)** Although it may seem time consuming, if numbers are substituted in for the variables, the problem may not be so difficult. In this case, try to find contradictions to the statements to find the true statements, if any.

Case I.   For a – b, a > b is not always true.

2 – 3 = –1, which is a real number.

Case II.   a – b > a + b will be false when a and b are both negative numbers.

(–2) – (–3) < (–2) + (-3) yields 1 < -5 which is not true.

Case III.   a – b < a is also nullified by this example:

(–2) – (–3) < –2 which yields

1 < –2

All 3 statements in this problem are false.

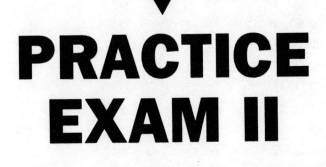

PRACTICE
EXAM II

GENERAL EDUCATIONAL DEVELOPMENT
PRACTICE EXAM II
ANSWER SHEET

Test 1:

Writing Skills, Part I

1. ① ② ③ ④ ⑤
2. ① ② ③ ④ ⑤
3. ① ② ③ ④ ⑤
4. ① ② ③ ④ ⑤
5. ① ② ③ ④ ⑤
6. ① ② ③ ④ ⑤
7. ① ② ③ ④ ⑤
8. ① ② ③ ④ ⑤
9. ① ② ③ ④ ⑤
10. ① ② ③ ④ ⑤
11. ① ② ③ ④ ⑤
12. ① ② ③ ④ ⑤
13. ① ② ③ ④ ⑤
14. ① ② ③ ④ ⑤
15. ① ② ③ ④ ⑤
16. ① ② ③ ④ ⑤
17. ① ② ③ ④ ⑤
18. ① ② ③ ④ ⑤
19. ① ② ③ ④ ⑤
20. ① ② ③ ④ ⑤
21. ① ② ③ ④ ⑤
22. ① ② ③ ④ ⑤
23. ① ② ③ ④ ⑤
24. ① ② ③ ④ ⑤
25. ① ② ③ ④ ⑤
26. ① ② ③ ④ ⑤
27. ① ② ③ ④ ⑤

28. ① ② ③ ④ ⑤
29. ① ② ③ ④ ⑤
30. ① ② ③ ④ ⑤
31. ① ② ③ ④ ⑤
32. ① ② ③ ④ ⑤
33. ① ② ③ ④ ⑤
34. ① ② ③ ④ ⑤
35. ① ② ③ ④ ⑤
36. ① ② ③ ④ ⑤
37. ① ② ③ ④ ⑤
38. ① ② ③ ④ ⑤
39. ① ② ③ ④ ⑤
40. ① ② ③ ④ ⑤
41. ① ② ③ ④ ⑤
42. ① ② ③ ④ ⑤
43. ① ② ③ ④ ⑤
44. ① ② ③ ④ ⑤
45. ① ② ③ ④ ⑤
46. ① ② ③ ④ ⑤
47. ① ② ③ ④ ⑤
48. ① ② ③ ④ ⑤
49. ① ② ③ ④ ⑤
50. ① ② ③ ④ ⑤
51. ① ② ③ ④ ⑤
52. ① ② ③ ④ ⑤
53. ① ② ③ ④ ⑤
54. ① ② ③ ④ ⑤
55. ① ② ③ ④ ⑤

Test 2:

Social Studies

1. ① ② ③ ④ ⑤
2. ① ② ③ ④ ⑤
3. ① ② ③ ④ ⑤
4. ① ② ③ ④ ⑤
5. ① ② ③ ④ ⑤
6. ① ② ③ ④ ⑤
7. ① ② ③ ④ ⑤
8. ① ② ③ ④ ⑤
9. ① ② ③ ④ ⑤
10. ① ② ③ ④ ⑤
11. ① ② ③ ④ ⑤
12. ① ② ③ ④ ⑤
13. ① ② ③ ④ ⑤
14. ① ② ③ ④ ⑤
15. ① ② ③ ④ ⑤
16. ① ② ③ ④ ⑤
17. ① ② ③ ④ ⑤
18. ① ② ③ ④ ⑤
19. ① ② ③ ④ ⑤
20. ① ② ③ ④ ⑤
21. ① ② ③ ④ ⑤
22. ① ② ③ ④ ⑤
23. ① ② ③ ④ ⑤
24. ① ② ③ ④ ⑤
25. ① ② ③ ④ ⑤
26. ① ② ③ ④ ⑤
27. ① ② ③ ④ ⑤

28. ① ② ③ ④ ⑤
29. ① ② ③ ④ ⑤
30. ① ② ③ ④ ⑤
31. ① ② ③ ④ ⑤
32. ① ② ③ ④ ⑤
33. ① ② ③ ④ ⑤
34. ① ② ③ ④ ⑤
35. ① ② ③ ④ ⑤
36. ① ② ③ ④ ⑤
37. ① ② ③ ④ ⑤
38. ① ② ③ ④ ⑤
39. ① ② ③ ④ ⑤
40. ① ② ③ ④ ⑤
41. ① ② ③ ④ ⑤
42. ① ② ③ ④ ⑤
43. ① ② ③ ④ ⑤
44. ① ② ③ ④ ⑤
45. ① ② ③ ④ ⑤
46. ① ② ③ ④ ⑤
47. ① ② ③ ④ ⑤
48. ① ② ③ ④ ⑤
49. ① ② ③ ④ ⑤
50. ① ② ③ ④ ⑤
51. ① ② ③ ④ ⑤
52. ① ② ③ ④ ⑤
53. ① ② ③ ④ ⑤
54. ① ② ③ ④ ⑤
55. ① ② ③ ④ ⑤
56. ① ② ③ ④ ⑤
57. ① ② ③ ④ ⑤
58. ① ② ③ ④ ⑤
59. ① ② ③ ④ ⑤
60. ① ② ③ ④ ⑤
61. ① ② ③ ④ ⑤
62. ① ② ③ ④ ⑤
63. ① ② ③ ④ ⑤
64. ① ② ③ ④ ⑤

Test 3:
Science

1. ① ② ③ ④ ⑤
2. ① ② ③ ④ ⑤
3. ① ② ③ ④ ⑤
4. ① ② ③ ④ ⑤
5. ① ② ③ ④ ⑤
6. ① ② ③ ④ ⑤
7. ① ② ③ ④ ⑤
8. ① ② ③ ④ ⑤
9. ① ② ③ ④ ⑤
10. ① ② ③ ④ ⑤
11. ① ② ③ ④ ⑤
12. ① ② ③ ④ ⑤
13. ① ② ③ ④ ⑤
14. ① ② ③ ④ ⑤
15. ① ② ③ ④ ⑤
16. ① ② ③ ④ ⑤
17. ① ② ③ ④ ⑤
18. ① ② ③ ④ ⑤
19. ① ② ③ ④ ⑤
20. ① ② ③ ④ ⑤
21. ① ② ③ ④ ⑤
22. ① ② ③ ④ ⑤
23. ① ② ③ ④ ⑤
24. ① ② ③ ④ ⑤
25. ① ② ③ ④ ⑤
26. ① ② ③ ④ ⑤
27. ① ② ③ ④ ⑤
28. ① ② ③ ④ ⑤
29. ① ② ③ ④ ⑤
30. ① ② ③ ④ ⑤
31. ① ② ③ ④ ⑤
32. ① ② ③ ④ ⑤
33. ① ② ③ ④ ⑤
34. ① ② ③ ④ ⑤
35. ① ② ③ ④ ⑤

36. ① ② ③ ④ ⑤
37. ① ② ③ ④ ⑤
38. ① ② ③ ④ ⑤
39. ① ② ③ ④ ⑤
40. ① ② ③ ④ ⑤
41. ① ② ③ ④ ⑤
42. ① ② ③ ④ ⑤
43. ① ② ③ ④ ⑤
44. ① ② ③ ④ ⑤
45. ① ② ③ ④ ⑤
46. ① ② ③ ④ ⑤
47. ① ② ③ ④ ⑤
48. ① ② ③ ④ ⑤
49. ① ② ③ ④ ⑤
50. ① ② ③ ④ ⑤
51. ① ② ③ ④ ⑤
52. ① ② ③ ④ ⑤
53. ① ② ③ ④ ⑤
54. ① ② ③ ④ ⑤
55. ① ② ③ ④ ⑤
56. ① ② ③ ④ ⑤
57. ① ② ③ ④ ⑤
58. ① ② ③ ④ ⑤
59. ① ② ③ ④ ⑤
60. ① ② ③ ④ ⑤
61. ① ② ③ ④ ⑤
62. ① ② ③ ④ ⑤
63. ① ② ③ ④ ⑤
64. ① ② ③ ④ ⑤
65. ① ② ③ ④ ⑤
66. ① ② ③ ④ ⑤

Test 4:
Interpreting
Literature and the Arts

1. ① ② ③ ④ ⑤
2. ① ② ③ ④ ⑤

3. ① ② ③ ④ ⑤
4. ① ② ③ ④ ⑤
5. ① ② ③ ④ ⑤
6. ① ② ③ ④ ⑤
7. ① ② ③ ④ ⑤
8. ① ② ③ ④ ⑤
9. ① ② ③ ④ ⑤
10. ① ② ③ ④ ⑤
11. ① ② ③ ④ ⑤
12. ① ② ③ ④ ⑤
13. ① ② ③ ④ ⑤
14. ① ② ③ ④ ⑤
15. ① ② ③ ④ ⑤
16. ① ② ③ ④ ⑤
17. ① ② ③ ④ ⑤
18. ① ② ③ ④ ⑤
19. ① ② ③ ④ ⑤
20. ① ② ③ ④ ⑤
21. ① ② ③ ④ ⑤
22. ① ② ③ ④ ⑤
23. ① ② ③ ④ ⑤
24. ① ② ③ ④ ⑤
25. ① ② ③ ④ ⑤
26. ① ② ③ ④ ⑤
27. ① ② ③ ④ ⑤
28. ① ② ③ ④ ⑤
29. ① ② ③ ④ ⑤
30. ① ② ③ ④ ⑤
31. ① ② ③ ④ ⑤
32. ① ② ③ ④ ⑤
33. ① ② ③ ④ ⑤
34. ① ② ③ ④ ⑤
35. ① ② ③ ④ ⑤
36. ① ② ③ ④ ⑤

37. ① ② ③ ④ ⑤
38. ① ② ③ ④ ⑤
39. ① ② ③ ④ ⑤
40. ① ② ③ ④ ⑤
41. ① ② ③ ④ ⑤
42. ① ② ③ ④ ⑤
43. ① ② ③ ④ ⑤
44. ① ② ③ ④ ⑤
45. ① ② ③ ④ ⑤

Test 5:
Mathematics

1. ① ② ③ ④ ⑤
2. ① ② ③ ④ ⑤
3. ① ② ③ ④ ⑤
4. ① ② ③ ④ ⑤
5. ① ② ③ ④ ⑤
6. ① ② ③ ④ ⑤
7. ① ② ③ ④ ⑤
8. ① ② ③ ④ ⑤
9. ① ② ③ ④ ⑤
10. ① ② ③ ④ ⑤
11. ① ② ③ ④ ⑤
12. ① ② ③ ④ ⑤
13. ① ② ③ ④ ⑤
14. ① ② ③ ④ ⑤
15. ① ② ③ ④ ⑤
16. ① ② ③ ④ ⑤
17. ① ② ③ ④ ⑤
18. ① ② ③ ④ ⑤
19. ① ② ③ ④ ⑤
20. ① ② ③ ④ ⑤
21. ① ② ③ ④ ⑤
22. ① ② ③ ④ ⑤

23. ① ② ③ ④ ⑤
24. ① ② ③ ④ ⑤
25. ① ② ③ ④ ⑤
26. ① ② ③ ④ ⑤
27. ① ② ③ ④ ⑤
28. ① ② ③ ④ ⑤
29. ① ② ③ ④ ⑤
30. ① ② ③ ④ ⑤
31. ① ② ③ ④ ⑤
32. ① ② ③ ④ ⑤
33. ① ② ③ ④ ⑤
34. ① ② ③ ④ ⑤
35. ① ② ③ ④ ⑤
36. ① ② ③ ④ ⑤
37. ① ② ③ ④ ⑤
38. ① ② ③ ④ ⑤
39. ① ② ③ ④ ⑤
40. ① ② ③ ④ ⑤
41. ① ② ③ ④ ⑤
42. ① ② ③ ④ ⑤
43. ① ② ③ ④ ⑤
44. ① ② ③ ④ ⑤
45. ① ② ③ ④ ⑤
46. ① ② ③ ④ ⑤
47. ① ② ③ ④ ⑤
48. ① ② ③ ④ ⑤
49. ① ② ③ ④ ⑤
50. ① ② ③ ④ ⑤
51. ① ② ③ ④ ⑤
52. ① ② ③ ④ ⑤
53. ① ② ③ ④ ⑤
54. ① ② ③ ④ ⑤
55. ① ② ③ ④ ⑤
56. ① ② ③ ④ ⑤

WRITING SKILLS, Part II

Write your essay for Test 1: Writing Skills, Part II on these lined pages.

EXAM II

TEST 1: WRITING SKILLS, PART I

Tests of General Educational Development

Directions

The Writing Skills Test is intended to measure your ability to use clear and effective English. It is a test of English as it should be written, not as it might be spoken. This test includes both multiple-choice questions and an essay. These directions apply only to the multiple-choice section; a separate set of directions is given for the essay.

The multiple-choice section consists of paragraphs with numbered sentences. Some of the sentences contain errors in sentence structure, usage, or mechanics (spelling, punctuation, and capitalization). After reading the numbered sentences, answer the multiple-choice questions that follow. Some questions refer to sentences that are correct as written. The best answer for these questions is the one which leaves the sentence as originally written. The best answer for some questions is the one which produces a sentence that is consistent with the verb tense and point of view used throughout the paragraph.

You should spend no more than 75 minutes on the multiple-choice questions and 45 minutes on your essay. Work carefully, but do not spend too much time on any one question. You may begin working on the essay part of this test as soon as you complete the multiple-choice section.

Do not mark in this test booklet. Record your answers on the separate answer sheet provided. Be sure that all requested information is properly recorded on the answer sheet.

To record your answers, mark one numbered space on the answer sheet beside the number that corresponds to the question in the test booklet.

FOR EXAMPLE:

Sentence 1: **We were all honored to meet governor Phillips.**

What correction should be made to this sentence?

    (1)   insert a comma after <u>honored</u>

    (2)   change the spelling of <u>honored</u> to <u>honered</u>

    (3)   change <u>governor</u> to <u>Governor</u>

    (4)   replace <u>were</u> with <u>was</u>

    (5)   no correction is necessary.   ①②●④⑤

In this example, the word "governor" should be capitalized; therefore, answer space 3 would be marked on the answer sheet.

Do not rest the point of your pencil on the answer sheet while you are considering your answer. Make no stray or unnecessary marks. If you change an answer, erase your first mark completely. Mark only one answer space for each question; multiple answers will be scored as incorrect. Do not fold or crease your answer sheet. All test materials must be returned to the test administrator.

reprinted with permission of the General Educational Development Testing Service of the American Council on Education

Directions: Choose the one best answer to each item.

Items 1 to 5 refer to the following paragraph.

(1) The word "home" may be considered in many ways but, each will always be a positive one. (2) For instance home is where a child goes after a neighborhood quarrel. (3) Mother would bandage any wounds and serve milk and cookies. (4) But whatever she might do, you would feel safe and secure. (5) Home is where one should recieve a great deal of comfort and support.

1. Sentence 1: **The word "home" may be considered in many ways but, each will always be a positive one.**

   Which correction should be made to this sentence?

   (1)   place the word way after each
   (2)   put the comma before but
   (3)   place a comma after home
   (4)   replace each with home
   (5)   no correction is necessary

2. Sentence 2: **For instance home is where a child goes after a neighborhood quarrel.**

   Which correction should be made to this sentence?

   (1)   place a comma after goes
   (2)   change quarrel to quarrell
   (3)   place a comma after instance
   (4)   change where to were
   (5)   no correction is necessary

3. Sentence 3: **Mother would bandage any wounds and serve milk and cookies.**

   Which correction should be made to this sentence?

   (1)   change bandage to bandaid
   (2)   change cookies to cookys
   (3)   place a comma after milk
   (4)   place a comma after bandage
   (5)   no correction is necessary

4. Sentence 4: **But whatever she might do you would feel safe and secure.**

    Which correction should be made to this sentence?

    (1) change whatever to what ever
    (2) change secure to sicure
    (3) place a comma after whatever
    (4) place a comma after But
    (5) no correction is necessary

5. Sentence 5: **Home is where one should receive a great deal of comfort and support.**

    Which correction should be made to this sentence?

    (1) change recieve to receive
    (2) change support to suport
    (3) place a comma after where
    (4) place a comma after recieve
    (5) no correction is necessary

Items 6 to 18 refer to the following paragraph.

(1) Do you have a favorite sport that you like to play? (2) Soccer is one of the latest fades to come to this country. (3) This is a dangerous sport however and people can suffer real injuries. (4) I know of a young man who had to have surgury because of a serious injury to his knee. (5) He lost his balance during a game and twisted his knee severly. (6) The tendons suffered some damage but the cartilage was damaged the most. (7) Because of this injury, the player had to sit out the entire season. (8) This injury has kept him from his best outlet, soccer. (9) He has suffered both mentally and physically from this inactivity. (10) He finally had surgury on his knee. (11) He hopes to be able to play this next season. (12) The injury dosen't seem to have made him afraid of soccer. (13) In fact his doctor says his knee is stronger than before.

6. Sentence 2: **Soccer is one of the latest fades to come to this country.**

    Which correction should be made to this sentence?

    (1) change Soccer to Soccar
    (2) change fades to fads
    (3) place a comma after fades

(4)   place a comma after is

(5)   no correction is necessary

7.   Sentence 3: **This is a dangerous sport however and people can suffer real injuries.**

Which correction should be made to this sentence?

(1)   change dangerous to dangrous

(2)   change injuries to ingeries

(3)   place a comma after sport

(4)   place a comma before and after however

(5)   no correction is necessary

8.   Sentence 4: **I know of a young man who had to have surgury because of a severe injury to his knee.**

Which correction should be made to this sentence?

(1)   place a comma after surgury

(2)   place a comma after injury

(3)   change surgury to surgery

(4)   change injury to ingury

(5)   no correction is necessary

9.   Sentence 5: **He lost his balance during a game and twisted his knee severly.**

Which correction should be made to this sentence?

(1)   place a comma after balance

(2)   place a comma after knee

(3)   change during to durning

(4)   change severly to severely

(5)   no correction is necessary

10.   Sentence 6: **The tendons suffered some damage but the cartilage was damaged the most.**

Which correction should be made to this sentence?

(1)   place a comma after damage

(2)   place a comma after but

       (3)   change <u>tendons</u> to <u>tendens</u>

       (4)   change <u>cartilage</u> to <u>cartiledge</u>

       (5)   no correction is necessary

11.   Sentence 9: **He has suffered both mentally and physically from this inactivity.**

      Which correction should be made to this sentence?

       (1)   place commas after <u>suffered</u> and <u>physically</u>

       (2)   place commas after <u>mentally</u> and <u>physically</u>

       (3)   change <u>physically</u> to <u>physicaly</u>

       (4)   change <u>inactivity</u> to <u>unactivity</u>

       (5)   no correction is necessary

12.   Sentence 11: **He hopes to be able to play this next season.**

      Which correction should be made to this sentence?

       (1)   place a comma after <u>hopes</u>

       (2)   place a comma after <u>be</u>

       (3)   place a comma after <u>play</u>

       (4)   place a comma after <u>this</u>

       (5)   no correction is necessary

13.   Sentence 13: **In fact his doctor says his knee is stronger than before.**

      Which correction should be made to this sentence?

       (1)   place a comma after <u>fact</u>

       (2)   place a comma after <u>doctor</u>

       (3)   place a comma after <u>knee</u>

       (4)   place a comma after <u>stronger</u>

       (5)   no correction is necessary

<u>Items 14 to 20</u> refer to the following paragraph.

    (1) Do you have pecular friends that you hang around with? (2) I know a strange person who never lets a dull moment slip by him. (3) Making strange noises, and saying off-the-wall comments. (4) His plesure in these distasteful talents never seems to alter. (5) His unending enjoyment in these shenanigans will probably never change. (6) Everyday, his warped brain begins to click. (7) Looking around to see if he is in the clear

he finds a trick to pull. (8) He becomes overwhelmed with happiness when he pulls off some crazy trick of his. (9) Each day he ponders and lets his warped brain begin to click. (10) He always appears to be an angel instead of a demon.

14. Sentence 1: **Do you have pecular friends that you hang around with?**

    Which correction should be made to this sentence?

    (1) change pecular to peculiar
    (2) change pecular to peculiur
    (3) place a comma after friends
    (4) place a comma after around
    (5) no correction is necessary

15. Sentence 2: **I know a strange person who never lets a dull moment slip by him.**

    Which correction should be made to this sentence?

    (1) place a comma after person
    (2) replace lets with let's
    (3) place a comma after lets
    (4) place a comma after moment
    (5) no correction necessary

16. Sentence 2 and Sentence 3: **I know a strange person who never lets a dull moment slip by him. Making strange noises, and saying off-the-wall comments.**

    Which correction should be made to this sentence?

    (1) slip by him and making
    (2) slip by him, making strange
    (3) slip by him, thus making
    (4) slip by him; making strange
    (5) no correction is necessary

17. Sentence 4: **His plesure in these distasteful talents never seems to alter.**

    Which correction should be made to this sentence?

    (1) change plesure to pleasure

(2)   change <u>distasteful</u> to <u>untasteful</u>

(3)   place a comma after <u>plesure</u>

(4)   place a comma after <u>talents</u>

(5)   no correction is necessary

18.   Sentence 6: **Everyday, his warped brain begins to click.**

Which correction should be made to this sentence?

(1)   change <u>Everyday</u> to <u>Every day</u>

(2)   change <u>warped</u> to <u>wharped</u>

(3)   remove the comma after <u>Everyday</u>

(4)   place a comma after <u>begins</u>

(5)   no correction is necessary

19.   Sentence 7: **Looking around to see if he is in the clear he finds a trick to pull.**

Which correction should be made to this sentence?

(1)   place a comma after <u>around</u>

(2)   place a comma after <u>to see</u>

(3)   place a comma after <u>clear</u>

(4)   place a comma after <u>trick</u>

(5)   no correction is necessary

20.   Sentence 9: **Each day he ponders and lets his warped brain begin to click.**

Which correction should be made to this sentence?

(1)   place a comma after <u>day</u>

(2)   place a comma after <u>ponders</u>

(3)   place a comma after <u>and</u>

(4)   place a comma after <u>brain</u>

(5)   no correction is necessary

<u>Items 21 to 27</u> refer to the following paragraph.

(1) In todays society, people are always asking about where you went to school. (2) Education is getting more and more important, especially concerning employment. (3) Often, potential employers ask more about education than they do about skills abilities. (4) Major companies find that they have to teach basic educational skills to new employees before they

can train these employees to work. (5) What is happening in the public school system that is not preparing young people to enter the work world? (6) Are we passing students, letting them move on from one grade to the next without really making sure that they have learned? (7) How do people get out of school without learning how to read or do simple arithmatic? (8) Do these same young people fool teachers, or do teachers except poor papers and bad work, just letting these students graduate without proving themselves academically? (9) What can we all do to improve the national educational system? (10) We certainly do not want our children to go through twelve years of school and not be able to read. (11) Companies certainly should not have to step in after people have graduated high school. (12) We should of learned academic skills in high school and elementary classes. (13) I know that I would like to be hired for any job I wanted, and be able to do it when I was hired. (14) Me and my family want to live comfortably and have enough money. (15) With good reading and math skills I should be able to get a good job. (16) Its not being prepared for the work market that makes getting a good job hard to do.

21. Sentence 1: **In todays society, people are always asking about where you went to school.**

Which correction should be made to this sentence?

(1) remove the comma after <u>society</u>

(2) place a comma after <u>where</u>

(3) change <u>todays</u> to <u>today's</u>

(4) change <u>society</u> to <u>sosiety</u>

(5) no change is necessary

22. Sentence 7: **How do people get out of school without learning how to read and do simple arithmatic?**

Which correction should be made to this sentence?

(1) place a comma after <u>school</u>

(2) change <u>arithmatic</u> to <u>arithmetic</u>

(3) place a period after <u>school</u>

(4) change <u>simple</u> to <u>simply</u>

(5) no correction is necessary

23. Sentence 8: **Do these same young people fool teachers, or do teachers except poor papers and bad work?**

Which correction should be made to this sentence?

(1)   remove the comma after <u>teachers</u>

(2)   place a comma after <u>papers</u>

(3)   change <u>people</u> to <u>peopel</u>

(4)   change <u>except</u> to <u>accept</u>

(5)   no correction is necessary

24.   Sentence 12: **We should of learned academic skills in high school and elementary classes.**

Which correction should be made to this sentence?

(1)   change <u>high school</u> to <u>High School</u>

(2)   change <u>of</u> to <u>have</u>

(3)   place a comma after <u>skills</u>

(4)   place a comma after <u>high school</u>

(5)   no correction is necessary

25.   Sentence 14: **Me and my family want to live comfortably and have enough money.**

Which correction should be made to this sentence?

(1)   change <u>comfortably</u> to <u>comfortbly</u>

(2)   change <u>enough</u> to <u>enuff</u>

(3)   change <u>Me and my family</u> to <u>I and my family</u>

(4)   change <u>Me and my family</u> to <u>My family and I</u>

(5)   no correction is necessary

26.   Sentence 15: **With good reading and math skills I should be able to get a good job.**

Which correction should be made to this sentence?

(1)   place a comma after <u>reading</u>

(2)   place a comma after <u>skills</u>

(3)   place a comma after <u>able</u>

(4)   place a comma after <u>get</u>

(5)   no correction is necessary

27.   Sentence 16: **Its not being prepared for the work market that makes getting a good job hard to do.**

Which correction should be made to this sentence?

(1) change <u>work market</u> to <u>work-market</u>

(2) change <u>Its</u> to <u>It's</u>

(3) place a comma after <u>prepared</u>

(4) place a comma after <u>market</u>

(5) no correction is necessary

<u>Items 28 to 34</u> refer to the following paragraphs.

(1) This country is football-crazy to a extreme. (2) Every weekend people all over the United States root for teams. (3) Their is no way that every team can win every game. (4) High school ball players are the town heros when they win. (5) Whole families plan the weekend around the local game. (6) My favorite team has had a winning season this year and it has been lots of fun. (7) It is gonna be lots of fun having a winning season. (8) Our special team always runs the ball back on kick-offs. (9) They seem to break tackels right and left. (10) Last week, we were the receiving team first and ran the first play for a touchdown. (11) Boy! Was that a fun night—creaming the other team.

28. Sentence 1: **This country is football crazy to a extreme.**

    Which correction should be made to this sentence?

    (1) change <u>football</u> to <u>foot ball</u>

    (2) change <u>crazy</u> to <u>crasy</u>

    (3) change <u>a extreme</u> to <u>an extreme</u>

    (4) place a comma after <u>crazy</u>

    (5) no correction is necessary

29. Sentence 2: **Every weekend people all over the United States root for teams.**

    Which correction should be made to this sentence?

    (1) change <u>weekend</u> to <u>week end</u>

    (2) change <u>root</u> to <u>rote</u>

    (3) place a comma after <u>weekend</u>

    (4) place a comma after <u>United States</u>

    (5) no correction is necessary

30. Sentence 3: **Their is no way that every team can win every game.**

    Which correction should be made to this sentence?

(1)   place a comma after <u>way</u>

(2)   place a comma after <u>win</u>

(3)   change <u>Their</u> to <u>There</u>

(4)   change <u>Their</u> to <u>They're</u>

(5)   no correction is necessary

31.   Sentence 4: **High school ball players are the town heros when they win.**

Which correction should be made to this sentence?

(1)   change <u>High school</u> to <u>High School</u>

(2)   change <u>ball players</u> to <u>ball-players</u>

(3)   change <u>heros</u> to <u>heroes</u>

(4)   place a comma after <u>heros</u>

(5)   no correction is necessary

32.   Sentence 6: **My favorite team has had a winning season this year and it has been lots of fun.**

Which correction should be made to this sentence?

(1)   place a comma after <u>team</u>

(2)   place a comma after <u>season</u>

(3)   place a comma after <u>year</u>

(4)   place a comma after <u>been</u>

(5)   no correction is necessary

33.   Sentence 7: **It is gonna be lots of fun having a winning season.**

Which correction should be made to this sentence?

(1)   change <u>It is</u> to <u>Its</u>

(2)   change <u>gonna</u> to <u>going to</u>

(3)   place a comma after <u>lots</u>

(4)   place a comma after <u>fun</u>

(5)   no correction is necessary

34.   Sentence 9: **They seem to break tackels right and left.**

Which correction should be made to this sentence?

(1)   change <u>break</u> to <u>brake</u>

    (2)   change tackels to tackles

    (3)   place a comma after right

    (4)   place a comma after tackels

    (5)   no correction is necessary

Items 35 to 41 refer to the following passage.

(1) During America's recent encounter with Iraq in the Persian Gulf, anti-war protests sprang up throughout the country. (2) From this many people were reminded of the violent protests associated with the Vietnam War. (3) Many people attributed these similar incidents to a sign of progressive change in the country's attitude toward piece. (4) The fact is however that anti-war protest has been a feature of this country through every major war, excluding World War II. (5) The reason being the attack on Pearl Harbor. (6) Moreover, many have tried to argue that Roosevelt engineered the attack on Pearl Harbor to stem America's anti-war sentiments. (7) While this is a rather extreme proof of America's anti-war history, the fact remains that the last two wars have indicated nothing new about this country's attitude, yet they have shown that the roots of America's war philosophy have remained unchanged.

35.   Sentence 1: **During America's recent encounter with Iraq in the Persian Gulf, anti-war protests had sprang up throughout the country.**

    Which correction should be made to this sentence?

    (1)   change America's to Americas

    (2)   change encounter to encountre

    (3)   change Gulf to gulf

    (4)   change sprang to sprung

    (5)   no correction is necessary

36.   Sentence 2: **From this many people were reminded of the violent protests associated with the Vietnam War.**

    Which correction should be made to this sentence?

    (1)   insert a comma after this

    (2)   insert a comma after people

    (3)   change were to was

    (4)   change associated to associates

    (5)   no correction is necessary

37. Sentence 3: **Many people attributed these similar incidents to a sign of progressive change in the country's attitude toward piece.**

    Which correction should be made to this sentence?

    (1) insert a comma after people
    (2) change similar to similiar
    (3) change country's to countries
    (4) change piece to peace
    (5) no correction is necessary

38. Sentence 4: **The fact is however that anti-war protest has been a feature of this country through every major war, excluding World War II.**

    Which correction should be made to this sentence?

    (1) change is to being
    (2) insert commas before and after however
    (3) change has to have
    (4) omit excluding World War II
    (5) no correction is necessary

39. Sentence 5: **The reason being the attack on Pearl Harbor.**

    Which rewrite of Sentence 5 is correct?

    (1) The reason not being the attack on Pearl Harbor.
    (2) The reason for this was the attack on Pearl Harbor.
    (3) The reason for this being the attack on Pearl Harbor.
    (4) The reason for this were the attack on Pearl Harbor.
    (5) The sentence is correct as it stands.

40. Sentence 6: **Moreover, many have tried to argue that Roosevelt engineered the attack on Pearl Harbor to stem America's anti-war sentiments.**

    Which correction should be made to this sentence?

    (1) change Moreover to More over
    (2) change many to much
    (3) change attack to attak
    (4) change Pearl to Perl
    (5) no correction is necessary

41. Sentence 7: **While this is a rather extreme proof of America's anti-war history, the fact remains that the last two wars have indicated nothing new about this country's <u>attitude, yet</u> they have shown that the roots of America's war philosophy have remained unchanged.**

Which of the following is the best way to write the underlined portion of this sentence? If you think the original is the best way, choose option (1).

(1) attitude, yet
(2) attitude, as
(3) attitude. Yet
(4) attitude, as yet
(5) attitude. As

<u>Items 42 to 48</u> refer to the following passage.

(1) The past decad saw a rising interest, mostly negative, in the role-playing game, Dungeons & Dragons. (2) Complaints ranged from calling it a devil worshipers' game, hold it responsible for witchcraft use, and, worst of all, blaming it for teenage suicide. (3) Talk shows have even invited practically evangelical speakers denounce players of the game as being in league with Satan. (4) Creater Gary Gygax disagrees. (5) He says that the purpose of the game is merely to broaden the imaginations of those who play, without influencing their every day lives; at least not in a negative sense. (6) However, one might see why others could misconstrue his game's purposes. (7) The game allows characters to encounter demons such as Mephiṣtopheles and Baalzebul, traditional names in Biblical texts. (8) In fact, despite Gygax's denial of demonic worship as part of the game, there has been a flurry of activity by its makers. (9) A whole new edition of the game has been produced, excluding the demons and disallowing players to be of an evil code of ethics.

42. Sentence 1: **The past decad saw a rising interest, mostly negative, in the role-playing game, Dungeons & Dragons.**

Which correction should be made to this sentence?

(1) change <u>decad</u> to <u>decade</u>
(2) change <u>saw</u> to <u>sees</u>
(3) omit the commas around <u>mostly negative</u>
(4) change <u>Dragons</u> to <u>Dragens</u>
(5) no change is necessary

43. Sentence 2: **Complaints ranged from calling it a devil worshipers' game, hold it responsible for witchcraft use, and, worst of all, blaming it for teenage suicide.**

Which correction should be made to this sentence?

(1)   change <u>ranged</u> to <u>ranges</u>

(2)   change <u>worshipers'</u> to <u>worshipper's</u>

(3)   change <u>hold</u> to <u>holding</u>

(4)   insert <u>by</u> before <u>worst</u>

(5)   no corrections are necessary

44.   Sentence 3: **Talk shows have even invited practically evangelical speakers denounce players of the game as being in league with Satan.**

Which of the following is the best way to write the underlined portions of this sentence? If you think the original is the best way, choose option (1).

(1)   invited... denounce

(2)   invited... to denounce

(3)   inviting... to denounce

(4)   inviting... denounce

(5)   been invited... denounce

45.   Sentence 4: **Creater Gary Gygax disagrees.**

Which correction should be made to this sentence?

(1)   change <u>Creater</u> to <u>Creator</u>

(2)   insert <u>With</u> before <u>creater</u>

(3)   change <u>disagrees</u> to <u>disagreeing</u>

(4)   change <u>disagrees</u> to <u>agreeing</u>

(5)   change <u>disagrees</u> to <u>disagreed</u>

46.   Sentence 5: **He says that the purpose of the game is merely to broaden the imaginations of those who play, without influencing their every day lives; at least not in a negative sense.**

Which correction should be made to this sentence?

(1)   insert quotation marks before <u>that</u> and after <u>sense</u>

(2)   change <u>merely</u> to <u>meerly</u>

(3)   change <u>influencing</u> to <u>influenceing</u>

(4)   change <u>every day</u> to <u>everyday</u>

(5)   no correction is necessary

47. Sentence 8: **In fact, despite Gygax's denial of demonic worship as part of the game, there has been a flurry of activity by its makers.**

Which correction should be made to this sentence?

(1) change Gygax's to Gygax'

(2) change denial to denied

(3) insert a comma after worship

(4) change its to his

(5) no correction is necessary

48. Sentence 9: **A whole new edition of the game has been produced, excluding the demons and disallowing players to be of an evil code of ethics.**

Which correction should be made to this sentence?

(1) change has to have

(2) change produced to prodused

(3) change disallowing to unallowing

(4) change ethics to ethicks

(5) no correction is necessary

Items 49 to 55 refer to the following passage.

(1) Many movie criticks complain that there has been a literary glut in the films produced within the past decade. (2) They attribute this to the rise of the "Hollywood genre." (3) That is, the recurrence of certain movie plots. (4) Examples of this so-called "Hollywood genre" include movies about intergalactic wars, visits by cute aliens from space, and an intelligent pet. (5) The cause of these genres, say critics, stem from an original movie which has been a box office success. (6) For example, the movie *Gremlins* motivated a whole slew of movies involving miniature creatures who were cute but deadly; such as, *Critters* and *Ghoulies*. (7) Hollywood producers, however, counter these critiques, saying that audiences are pleased with recurring plots that appear more than once. (8) They argue that movies are too expensive to produce to be constantlly risking new ideas.

49. Sentence 1: **Many movie criticks complain that there has been a literary glut in the films produced within the past decade.**

Which correction should be made to this sentence?

(1) change Many to Much

(2) change criticks to critics

    (3)   insert a comma after <u>glut</u>

    (4)   change <u>glut</u> to <u>glutt</u>

    (5)   no correction is necessary

50.   Sentences 2-3: **They attribute this to the rise of the "Hollywood genre". That is, the recurrence of certain movie plots.**

Which of the following is the best way to write the underlined portion of this sentence? If you think the original is the best way, choose option (1).

    (1)   genre." That is, the recurrence

    (2)   genre. That is," the recurrence

    (3)   genre." In other words, the recurrence

    (4)   genre," or rather, the recurrence

    (5)   genre." Rather, the recurrence

51.   Sentence 4: **Examples of this so-called "Hollywood genre" include movies about intergalactic wars, visits by cute aliens from space, and an intelligent pet.**

Which of the following is the best way to write the underlined portion of this sentence? If you think the original is the best way, choose option (1).

    (1)   and an intelligent pet.

    (2)   and also an intelligent pet.

    (3)   and intelligent pets.

    (4)   or an intelligent pet.

    (5)   but an intelligent pet.

52.   Sentence 5: **The cause of these genres, say critics, stem from an original movie which has been a box office success.**

Which correction should be made to this sentence?

    (1)   change <u>say</u> to <u>says</u>

    (2)   change <u>critics</u> to <u>criticks</u>

    (3)   change <u>stem</u> to <u>stems</u>

    (4)   change <u>has</u> to <u>have</u>

    (5)   no correction is necessary

53. Sentence 6: **For example, the movie *Gremlins* motivated a whole slew of movies involving miniature creatures who were cute but deadly; such as, *Critters* and *Ghoulies*.**

   Which correction should be made to this sentence?

   (1) remove the comma after <u>example</u>

   (2) change <u>motivated</u> to <u>motivating</u>

   (3) insert a comma after <u>slew of movies</u>

   (4) remove the comma after <u>such as</u>

   (5) no correction is necessary

54. Sentence 7: **Hollywood producers, however, counter these critiques, saying that audiences are pleased with recurring plots that appear more than once.**

   Which correction should be made to this sentence?

   (1) remove the commas around <u>however</u>

   (2) remove the comma after <u>critiques</u>

   (3) remove <u>recurring</u>

   (4) insert a comma after <u>plots</u>

   (5) no correction is necessary

55. Sentence 8: **They argue that movies are too expensive to produce to be constantlly risking new ideas.**

   Which correction should be made to this sentence?

   (1) change <u>to produce</u> to <u>productive</u>

   (2) change <u>constantlly</u> to <u>constantly</u>

   (3) add a semicolon after <u>risking</u>

   (4) change <u>risking</u> to <u>riskly</u>

   (5) no correction is necessary

TEST 1: WRITING SKILLS, PART II

Tests of General Educational Development

Directions

This part of the Writing Skills Test is intended to determine how well you write. You are asked to write an essay that explains something or presents an opinion on an issue. In preparing your essay, you should take the following steps.

1. Read carefully the directions and the essay topic given below.

2. Plan your essay carefully before you write.

3. Use scratch paper to make any notes.

4. Write your essay on the lined pages of the separate answer sheet.

5. Read carefully what you have written and make any changes that will improve your essay.

6. Check your paragraphs, sentence structure, spelling, punctuation, capitalization, and usage, and make any necessary corrections.

Be sure you write the <u>letter</u> of the essay topic (given below) on your answer sheet. Write the letter in the box at the upper right-hand corner of the page where you write your essay.

You will have 45 minutes to write on the topic below. Write legibly and use a ballpoint pen so that the evaluators will be able to read your writing.

Write your essay on the lined pages of the separate answer sheet. The notes you make on scratch paper will not be scored.

Your essay will be scored by at least two trained evaluators who will judge it according to its <u>overall effectiveness</u>. They will judge how clearly you make the main point of your composition, how thoroughly you support your ideas, and how clearly and correctly you write throughout the essay.

reprinted with permission of the General Educaional Development Testing Service of the American Council on Education

Topic A

This country is faced with crime, health problems, a possibility of war, financial problems, and a lessening of world respect.

Is this true? If so, what can we do about it? If not, why do people say it is true? What can we do to improve our image internationally? Respond to this statement in an essay of approximately two hundred words.

TEST 2: SOCIAL STUDIES

Tests of General Educational Development

Directions

The Social Studies Test consists of multiple-choice questions intended to measure your knowledge of general social studies concepts. The questions are based on short readings which often include a graph, chart, or figure. Study the information given and then answer the question(s) following it. Refer to the information as often as necessary in answering the questions.

You should spend no more than 85 minutes answering the questions in this booklet. Work carefully, but do not spend too much time on any one question. Be sure you answer every question. You will not be penalized for incorrect answers.

Do not mark in this test booklet. Record your answers to the questions on the separate answer sheet provided. Be sure all requested information is properly recorded on the answer sheet.

To record your answers, mark the numbered space on the answer sheet beside the number that corresponds to the question in the test booklet.

FOR EXAMPLE:

Early colonists of North America looked for settlement sites that had adequate water supplies and were accessible by ship. For this reason, many early towns were built near

    (1)   mountains.   (4)   glaciers.
    (2)   prairies.   (5)   plateaus.
    (3)   rivers.

                                              ① ② ● ④ ⑤

The correct answer is "rivers"; therefore, answer space 3 would be marked on the answer sheet.

Do not rest the point of your pencil on the answer sheet while you are considering your answer. Make no stray or unnecessary marks. If you change an answer, erase your first mark completely. Mark only one answer space for each question; multiple answers will be scored as incorrect. Do not fold or crease your answer sheet. Return all test materials to the test administrator.

---

reprinted with permission of the General Educational Development Testing Service of the American Council on Education

<u>Directions</u>: Choose the <u>one best answer</u> to each item.

<u>Items 1 to 5</u> refer to the following letter.

Department of State,
Washington, May 13, 1915

To Ambassador Gerard:

Please call on the Minister of Foreign Affairs and after reading to him this communication leave with him a copy.

In view of recent acts of the German authorities in violation of American rights on the high seas which culminated in the torpedoing and sinking of the British steamship *Lusitania* on May 7, 1915, by which over 100 American citizens lost their lives, it is clearly wise and desirable that the Government of the United States and the Imperial German Government should come to a clear and full understanding as to the grave situation which has resulted.

The sinking of the British passenger steamer *Falaba* by a German submarine on March 28, through which Leon C. Thrasher, an American citizen, was drowned; the attack on April 28 on the American vessel *Cushing* by a German aeroplane; the torpedoing on May 1 of the American vessel *Gulflight* by a German submarine, as a result of which two or more Americans citizens met their death; and finally, the torpedoing and sinking of the steamship *Lusitania*, constitute a series of events which the Government of the United States has observed with growing concern, distress, and amazement....

The Government of the United States has been apprised that the Imperial German Government considered themselves to be obliged by the extraordinary circumstances of the present war and the measures adopted by their adversaries in seeking to cut Germany off from all commerce, to adopt methods of retaliation which go much beyond the ordinary methods of warfare at sea, in the proclamation of a war zone from which they have warned neutral ships to keep away. This Government has already taken occasion to inform the Imperial German Government that it cannot admit the adoption of such measures or such a warning of danger to operate as in any degree an abbreviation of the rights of American shipmasters or of American citizens bound on lawful errands as passengers on merchant ships of belligerent nationality; and that it must hold the Imperial German Government to a strict accountability for any infringement of those rights, intentional or incidental.

1.   The stated purpose of the letter was to

   (1)   declare war.
   (2)   demand payment for all damages.
   (3)   create an alliance.

    (4)   make sure no American ships were attacked.

    (5)   issue a warning.

2.   From the quote, the war going on was

    (1)   the American Civil War.   (4)   World War II.

    (2)   the Spanish-American War.   (5)   the Vietnam War.

    (3)   World War I.

3.   The letter acknowledges that the Germans have done all except what?

    (1)   Used submarines to attack ships

    (2)   Bombed ships from planes

    (3)   Used poison gas

    (4)   Created a war zone to stop shipping

    (5)   Warned neutral nations away from war zones

4.   Which is not stated in the letter?

    (1)   Germany is being cut off from trade by her enemies.

    (2)   Americans claim the right to safely sail on merchant ships of warring nations.

    (3)   American ships will observe war zones.

    (4)   Neutral nations have rights.

    (5)   The war circumstances are extraordinary.

5.   The President who sent this letter and eventually lead the U.S. to declare war was

    (1)   T. Roosevelt.   (4)   H. Hoover.

    (2)   W. Wilson.   (5)   F. Roosevelt.

    (3)   W. Harding.

<u>Items 6 to 10</u> refer to the following table.

Parliamentary	Restricted Parliamentary	One Party
Canada	Brazil	Syria
United States	Colombia	Algeria
Venezuela	Turkey	Sudan
India	Eygpt	Kenya
Spain	Indonesia	Ivory Coast

6.   What would be the best title tor the table?

    (1)   World government forms

    (2)   Sample government organization

(3)   Capitalism v. communism
(4)   First World v. Third World government
(5)   Poor v. rich governments

7.   The term parliamentary refers to

   (1)   a representative form of government.
   (2)   the name of the governing body.
   (3)   an ex-British colony.
   (4)   the lack of an elected leader.
   (5)   a written constitution.

8.   One pattern of the one-party system is that

   (1)   all are ex-British colonies.
   (2)   all have kings.
   (3)   all are Arabic.
   (4)   all are on the Mediterranean Sea.
   (5)   all are from the same continent.

9.   Which is the most likely definition of restricted parliamentary rule?

   (1)   Elected for short terms
   (2)   Only allowed to veto laws
   (3)   Countered by a strong executive
   (4)   Only meets for limited sessions
   (5)   Limited to one term

10.   Which would not be a government that would fit under a one-party system?

   (1)   Fascist   (4)   Dictatorship
   (2)   Militarist   (5)   Republic
   (3)   Monarchy

Items 11 to 15 refer to the graphs below.

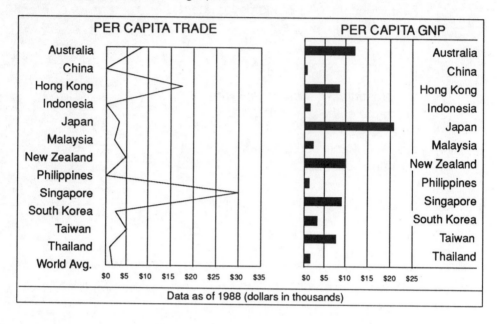

11. Comparing the two charts, the best conclusion is that

    (1) there is a direct relationship between GNP and trade.
    (2) the nations all have increased their GNP.
    (3) they all exceeded the world average in trade.
    (4) Japan is the leader in both GNP and trade.
    (5) China ranks lowest in both categories.

12. Which is not true about both charts?

    (1) Both are figured per person.
    (2) Both are in thousands of dollars.
    (3) Both compare the same nations.
    (4) Both are the same type of graph.
    (5) Both use the same year's data.

13. Which economic region of the world is reflected in the graphs?

    (1) East Asia   (4) All Pacific
    (2) All Asia   (5) All ex-British colonies
    (3) North West Asia

14. The nation that is increasing its prosperity the most is probably

    (1) Australia.   (4) Singapore.
    (2) Hong Kong.   (5) Taiwan.
    (3) Japan.

15. Which is the best way to describe the GNP?

    (1) Total goods and services
    (2) Total national production
    (3) Greater national production
    (4) Government natural production
    (5) Gross national resources

Items 16 to 20 refer to the following information.

Total Area:	1,040 km².
Population:	5,709,330 (1989)
Government:	Colony of U.K. Due to revert back to People's Republic of China in 1997. Local administrative powers are limited.
Natural Resources:	Deepwater harbor.
Agriculture:	Must import food products. Natural resources and agricultural land are in very limited supply. (Population density is high—Colony is 1/7th the size of Ireland with twice the population.)
GNP:	$45 billion.
Per Capita GNP:	$9220.
Major Industries:	Textiles, electronics, manufacturing, finance, and distribution services.
Industrial Output:	+16.4% (1988).
Merchandise Trade:	(1988) Exports = $48.5 billion; Imports = $48.5 billion.
Per Capita Trade:	$17,017.
Foreign Debt:	$9.6 billion (1988).
Inflation (CPI): 1980-88	6.7%.

16. The area being described is

    (1) Australia.   (4) Gibraltar.
    (2) Northern Ireland.   (5) Singapore.
    (3) Hong Kong.

17. Which occupation is particularly suited to this area?

    (1) Farmer   (4) Teacher
    (2) Merchant   (5) Tourist guide
    (3) Autoworker

18. Statistics would indicate this about population patterns?

    (1) High density   (4) Uneven distribution
    (2) Low density   (5) Heavily rural
    (3) Even distribution

19. The statistics contained in the list above would lead to what conclusion?

    (1) This is a poor nation.
    (2) This is a rich nation.
    (3) The nation is industrially efficient.
    (4) The nation is weak industrially.
    (5) The nation has a one-product economy.

20. The statistics indicate what kind of trade balance?

    (1) Favorable   (4) Reasonable debt
    (2) Unfavorable   (5) Balanced
    (3) Excessive debt

Items 21 to 25 refer to the following graph.

Category	Male	Female	National Average
Were spanked as a child: often	33%	31%	32%
occasionally	62	61	61
Have spanked a child	78	90	84
OK for a teacher to hit a child	53	46	49
Approve of strong discipline by parents	84	89	86
Approve of hitting a spouse	25	17	21
Have been hit by another adult	16	8	12
Have hit another adult	21	8	15

21. The most appropriate title for the graph would be

    (1) Trends in violence.   (4) Adult vs. child violence.
    (2) Experiences in violence.   (5) Limits in violent behavior.
    (3) Reasons for violence.

22. In which area did women practice violence more than men?

    (1) Spanking children   (4) As teachers
    (2) Hitting adults   (5) As strong disciplinarians
    (3) Hitting spouses

23. In which area did the least sex difference occur?

    (1) Approval of strong discipline
    (2) Having received a spanking often
    (3) Having spanked a child
    (4) Having received occasional spankings
    (5) Having hit another adult

24. Which conclusion cannot be made from the statistics?

    (1) Men are more violent than women.
    (2) Most people have experienced some form of violence.
    (3) Parents today are not as strong in discipline as their parents.
    (4) More adults have hit others than have been hit.
    (5) Most people agree that spanking is acceptable.

25. Which generalization applies best to the study of violence?

    (1) Violence is a product of psychology, not sociology.
    (2) Violence is a product of sociology, not psychology.
    (3) Violence is a product of both sociology and psychology.
    (4) Violence is a product of environment, not genetics.
    (5) Violence is a product of genetics, not environment.

Items 26 to 30 refer to the following information.

Caucus Standing Rules

1. This caucus shall be governed by Robert's Rules of Order (newly revised), unless the caucus rules provide otherwise.

2. Membership in this caucus is based on both of the following criteria:

    a. ...being either a member in good standing of the Party or a precinct delegate of the Party (in accordance with the rules of the state convention).

    b. ...being an active member, a retired member, or a professional staff member.

3. Voting privileges shall be extended to all qualified caucus members as defined in Section 2.

4. Officers of the caucus shall be the chairperson, vice-chairperson, and secretary.

    a. The officers shall be elected by the majority of those persons present and voting.

    b. The officers shall be elected for a two-year term in accordance with the election of the State Party officers at the spring convention held in February of the odd-numbered years.

c. The chairperson shall fill vacancies by appointment, subject to the approval of the Executive Committee.

d. In the event the chairperson can no longer serve, the secretary shall call an Executive Committee meeting within 30 days. At the meeting, the Executive Committee shall appoint a chairperson to serve until the next regularly scheduled election, at which point, the caucus will elect a chairperson to fill the unexpired term.

5. Each congressional district will elect one coordinator and one alternate at the spring convention.

---

26. The presiding officer of the organization is the

    (1) president.
    (2) caucus leader.
    (3) chairperson.
    (4) chief executive.
    (5) chief executive officer.

27. A caucus is part of a

    (1) political party.
    (2) local government.
    (3) state government.
    (4) national government.
    (5) corporation.

28. Who could not vote in the caucus?

    (1) A party member
    (2) A precinct delegate
    (3) A staff member
    (4) A retired member
    (5) All can vote.

29. The caucus is organized by

    (1) cities.
    (2) states.
    (3) counties.
    (4) congressional districts.
    (5) age.

30. The caucus meets

    (1) every spring.
    (2) annually.
    (3) every two years.
    (4) quarterly.
    (5) monthly.

Items 31 to 35 refer to the following graphs.

TOP IMPORTERS FROM U.S. in billions of dollars, 1989		TOP EXPORTERS TO U.S. in billions of dollars, 1989		U.S. TRADE BALANCE with MEXICO in billions of dollars, 1989
$78.6	Canada	$93.6	Japan	
$44.6	Japan	$88.2	Canada	27.2
$25.0	Mexico	$27.2	Mexico	25.0
$20.9	Britain	$24.8	Germany	-2.2
$16.9	Germany	$24.3	Taiwan	Exports Imports Deficit

SOURCE: Commerce Dept.

31. Which nation is a top importer, but not a top exporter?

    (1) Britain
    (2) Canada
    (3) Germany
    (4) Japan
    (5) Mexico

32. Taken together, which area imports the most from the U.S.?

    (1) Northern North America
    (2) Latin America
    (3) Asia
    (4) Africa
    (5) Europe

33. Taken together, which area exports the most to the U.S.?

    (1) Northern North America
    (2) Latin America
    (3) Asia
    (4) Africa
    (5) Europe

34. Who has the most favorable trade balance with the U.S.?

    (1) Britain
    (2) Canada
    (3) Germany
    (4) Japan
    (5) Mexico

35. If exports exceed imports, it is called

    (1)   favorable balance of payments.
    (2)   unfavorable balance of payments.
    (3)   favorable balance of trade.
    (4)   unfavorable balance of trade.
    (5)   deficit spending.

Items 36 to 39 refer to the following paragraph.

The account of the physical condition of the manufacturing population in the large towns in the northeastern District of England is less favourable. It is of this district that the Commissioners state, "We have found undoubted instances of children five years old sent to work thirteen hours a day; and frequently of children nine, ten, and eleven consigned to labour for fourteen and fifteen hours." The effects ascertained by the Commissioners in many cases are, "deformity," and in still more "stunted growth, relaxed muscles, and slender conformation": "twisting of the ends of the long bones, relaxation of the ligaments of the knees, ankles, and the like." "The representation that these effects are so common and universal as to enable some persons invariably to distinguish factory children from other children is, I have no hesitation in saying, an exaggerated and unfaithful picture of their general condition; at the same time it must be said, that the individual instances in which some one or other of those effects of severe labour are discernible are rather frequent than rare....

"Upon the whole, there remains no doubt upon my mind, that under the system pursued in many of the factories, the children of the labouring classes stand in need of, and ought to have, legislative protection against the conspiracy insensibly formed between their masters and parents, to tax them to a degree of toil beyond their strength.

In conclusion, I think it has been clearly proved that children have been worked a most unreasonable and cruel length of time daily, and that even adults have been expected to do a certain quantity of labour which scarcely any human being is able to endure. I am of opinion no child under fourteen years of age should work in a factory of any description for more than eight hours a day. From fourteen upwards I would recommend that no individual should, under any circumstances, work more than twelve hours a day; although if practicable, as a physician, I would prefer the limitation of ten hours, for all persons who earn their bread by their industry."

Source: Commission for Inquiry into the Employment of Children in Factories, *Second Report, with Minutes of Evidence and Reports by the Medical Commissioners*, Vol. V, Session 29 January-20 August, 1833 (London: His Majesty's Printing Office, 1833), pp. 5, 26-28.

36. Which is the best title for the quote above?

    (1)   Child labor health problems

    (2)   Unsafe working conditions in English factories
    (3)   Parental abuse of minor children
    (4)   Health problems of minor children
    (5)   Arguments for the eight-hour day

37.   Which is not cited as a cause of the work problems?

    (1)   Excessive work hours
    (2)   The age of the employee
    (3)   Poor nutrition
    (4)   Work beyond the worker's strength
    (5)   Unreasonable quantity of labor

38.   The type of conditions described in the article were created as a result of what historical event?

    (1)   The Age of Revolution
    (2)   The creation of capitalism
    (3)   The rise of communism
    (4)   The rise of fascism
    (5)   The Industrial Revolution

39.   Which was not used to try to solve working condition problems?

    (1)   Organized unions   (4)   Blacklists
    (2)   Legislation   (5)   Boycotts
    (3)   Political protests

Items 40 to 44 refer to the following passage.

It is an ugly, elusive war, fought with all the clever stunts in the guerrilla's handbook, not all of them deadly. Gangs disguised as official mosquito-spray teams walk into villages to confiscate farm equipment in the name of the government; sometimes they tear up peasants' identity cards to disrupt local administration; the Communists even managed to sabotage the national census by substituting falsified lists in some areas. The Viet Cong, which is what the Communist Vietnamese are called, are everywhere: tossing grenades into isolated villages in the rice fields in the south, sowing unrest among the border tribesmen in the thickly wooded Annamese highlands to the north. By day Saigon, a city of 2,000,000, is safe enough. But no one willingly sets his foot outside town after dark.

Fueled by Communist North Viet Nam with supplies and men smuggled through Laos over the clandestine Ho Chi Minh Trail, this wasting war has been going on for seven years. Its object is the destruction of South Viet Nam's stubby, stubborn President Ngo Dinh Diem, 60, who runs the war, the government, and everything else in South Viet Nam from a massive desk in his yellow stucco Freedom Palace in Saigon. President Diem had fought the Communists in his country long before World War II. At war's end, he was arrested by them; his brother was shot by them. He has stood in their way ever since.

Faced with this Communist challenge, the U.S. has made a major decision: South Viet Nam must be defended at all costs. While all Asia watched, the U.S., by fumbling unpreparedness and the lack of a dependable local fighting force to attach itself to, last spring abandoned Laos to its fate. South Viet Nam has been U.S.-sponsored from the start; its government is militantly anti-Communist, and its soldiers are willing to fight. If the U.S. cannot or will not save South Viet Nam from the Communist assault, no Asian nation can ever again feel safe in putting its faith in the U.S.—and the fall of all of Southeast Asia would only be a matter of time.

40. At the time of the quote, the Viet Nam War

    (1) was winding down.
    (2) was just beginning the U.S. involvement.
    (3) was at its height.
    (4) had become a UN police action.
    (5) had just been lost by the French.

41. Which of the following was a U.S. ally in the conflict?

    (1) Laos   (4) Ngo Dinh Diem
    (2) Viet Cong   (5) Southeast Asia
    (3) Ho Chi Minh

42. The fear of all Southeast Asia falling to communism was known as

    (1) the Truman Doctrine.   (4) the Red Scare.
    (2) SEATO.   (5) the Domino Theory.
    (3) the Marshall Plan.

43. Which of the following did not fall to Communism?

    (1) Thailand   (4) Cambodia
    (2) South Viet Nam   (5) Laos
    (3) North Viet Nam

44. The events in the passage occurred during the same time as the construction of the Berlin Wall, which places them in the administration of

    (1) Truman.   (4) L. Johnson.
    (2) Eisenhower.   (5) Nixon.
    (3) Kennedy.

Items 45 to 49 refer to the following table.

Nation	Chemical Fertilizers	Oil Spills	Acid Rain
United States	moderate	moderate	severe
France	severe	severe	moderate
Japan	severe	small	moderate
Australia	small	small	small
USSR	small	small	moderate

45. The best title for this graph is

   (1) Pollution problems.
   (2) Modern industry.
   (3) National problems.
   (4) Leading polluters.
   (5) Western pollution problems.

46. The chart reflects

   (1) all major polluters.
   (2) the major world polluters.
   (3) land, sea, and air problems.
   (4) similar national problems.
   (5) problems of heavy industrialization.

47. What do the nations have in common?

   (1) They are the richest nations.
   (2) Capitalism ignores pollution in these nations.
   (3) They have a world-wide distribution.
   (4) They have a western hemisphere problem.
   (5) They are all major oil-producing nations.

48. According to the chart, the nation with the least problems is

   (1) United States.
   (2) France.
   (3) Japan.
   (4) Australia.
   (5) USSR.

49. According to many scientists, the end result of continuing pollutions will be all except

   (1) greenhouse effect.
   (2) health problems.
   (3) depleted resources.
   (4) more rain forests.
   (5) water shortages.

Items 50 to 54 refer to the following passage.

Hoover had been in office less than a year, stocks had been falling for over a month; they had lost, on the average, about 1/6 of their quoted value, and looked "cheap" according to the opinion of important bankers, economists, and government officials. Business was still good—the economic position of the country was "sound" and technically the stock market itself had been improved by a "healthy reaction." Almost everyone thought a rally must be close at hand.

The market opened steady with prices little changed from the previous day, though some rather large blocks, of 20,000 to 25,000 shares, came out at the start. It sagged easily for the first half hour, and then around eleven o'clock the deluge broke.

It came with a speed and ferocity that left men dazed. The bottom simply fell out of the market. From all over the country a torrent of selling orders poured onto the floor of the Stock Exchange and there were no buying orders to meet it. Quotations of representative active issues, like Steel, Telephone, and Anaconda, began to fall two, three, five, and even ten points between sales. Less active stocks became unmarketable. Within a few moments the ticker service was hopelessly swamped and from then on no one knew what was really happening. By 1:30 the ticker tape was nearly two hours late; by 2:30 it was 147 minutes late. The last quotation was not printed on the tape until 7:08:05 P.M., four hours, eight and one-half minutes after the close. In the meantime, Wall Street had lived through an incredible nightmare.

50. What is the event the quote describes?

    (1) The Panic of 1837
    (2) The Great Depression
    (3) The Crash of 1929
    (4) Pearl Harbor Day
    (5) The assassination of John Kennedy

51. What compounded the problems of the day?

    (1) The ticker tape was running slow.
    (2) Business leaders were pessimistic.
    (3) Government leaders were pessimistic.
    (4) Major issues were not affected.
    (5) There was a lack of selling orders.

52. The stock prices were driven down by

    (1) lack of activity.
    (2) massive activity at the open of the market.

    (3)   the market's rising trend over several months.
    (4)   the general collapsing of businesses nationwide.
    (5)   sell orders overwhelming buy orders.

53.   The results of the Crash were partially blamed on the administration of

    (1)   Woodrow Wilson.   (4)   Herbert Hoover.
    (2)   Warren Harding.   (5)   Franklin Roosevelt.
    (3)   Calvin Coolidge.

54.   Which was not a reform created to try to prevent a repetition of 1929?

    (1)   SEC
    (2)   Margin restrictions
    (3)   FDIC
    (4)   Restrictions on corporation issuing stocks
    (5)   Restrictions on insider trading

Items 55 to 59 refer to the following information.

Social Influence =	Influencing Agent +	Social Power
(changed behavior)	(change agent)	(techniques: information, reward, coercion, expert, authority, modeling)

55.   The formula above refers to what?

    (1)   Socializing behavior   (4)   Being more influential
    (2)   Altering behavior   (5)   Creating power
    (3)   Preventing change

56.   Enrolling someone in a drug-education program would fit the formula in what way?

    (1)   The influencing agent would be the drugs.
    (2)   The course would be coercive.
    (3)   The instructor would model behavior.
    (4)   The course would create social pressure.
    (5)   The course information would influence change.

57.   A parent telling a child to obey is an example of

    (1)   modeling.   (4)   information.
    (2)   expert.   (5)   influencing.
    (3)   authority.

58. Telling a child that his or her allowance will go either up or down based on behavior is a combination of

    (1) modeling/coercion.   (4) reward/coercion.
    (2) authority/modeling.   (5) influencing/modeling.
    (3) information/reward.

59. When an advertising campaign uses a celebrity to advertise a product that has nothing to do with the celebrity's fame, the product hopes to alter behavior through

    (1) modeling.   (4) informing.
    (2) coercion.   (5) authority.
    (3) reward.

Items 60-64 refer to the following chart.

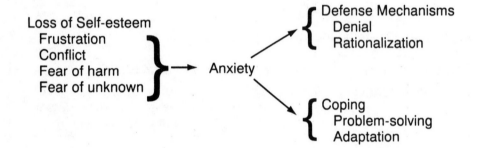

60. The term closest in meaning to anxiety is

    (1) crisis.   (4) stress.
    (2) apprehension.   (5) action.
    (3) reaction.

61. A cause of anxiety could be all except

    (1) a death in the family.   (4) a divorce.
    (2) being fired from a job.   (5) All could.
    (3) a crime wave.

62. A teenager's feeling of being invincible is an example of

    (1) problem-solving.   (4) adaptation.
    (2) rationalization.   (5) anxiety.
    (3) denial.

63. Buying a burglar alarm is an example of

    (1) adaptation.
    (2) loss of self-esteem.
    (3) denial.

    (4) rationalization.
    (5) All of the above.

64. From the examples above, the problem with a defense mechanism is what?

    (1) It does not solve the problem.
    (2) It creates more anxiety.
    (3) It does not make excuses for behavior.
    (4) It causes a person to change to match the anxiety.
    (5) It is always based on fear.

TEST 3: SCIENCE

Tests of General Educational Development

Directions

The Science Test consists of multiple-choice questions intended to measure your knowledge of the general concepts in science. The questions are based on short readings which often include a graph, chart, or figure. Study the information given and then answer the question(s) following it. Refer to the information as often as necessary in answering the questions.

You should spend no more than 95 minutes answering the questions in this booklet. Work carefully, but do not spend too much time on any one question. Be sure you answer every question. You will not be penalized for incorrect answers.

Do not mark in this test booklet. Record your answers to the questions on the separate answer sheet provided. Be sure all requested information is properly recorded on the answer sheet.

To record your answers, mark the numbered space on the answer sheet beside the number that corresponds to the question in the test booklet.

FOR EXAMPLE:

Which of the following is the smallest unit in a living thing?

   (1)   Tissue   (4)   Muscle
   (2)   Organ   (5)   Capillary
   (3)   Cell

                                                     ① ② ● ④ ⑤

The correct answer is "cell"; therefore, answer space 3 would be marked on the answer sheet.

Do not rest the point of your pencil on the answer sheet while you are considering your answer. Make no stray or unnecessary marks. If you change an answer, erase your first mark completely. Mark only one answer space for each question; multiple answers will be scored as incorrect. Do not fold or crease your answer sheet. Return all test materials to the test administrator.

Directions: Choose the <u>one best answer</u> to each item.

Items 1 to 4 refer to the following paragraph.

Skin is the flexible outer covering on the bodies of vertebrate animals. The thickness varies on different body areas. Human skin is composed of an outer layer called the epidermis and an inner layer called the dermis. The epidermis has several layers. Near the outside is the stratum corneum. Under it is the layer of Malpighi which quickly grows to replace the cells of the stratum corneum which wear away. Human skin protects the body from injury, helps get rid of waste products, regulates water, and regulates temperature.

1. What area of the skin is most likely the thinnest?

    (1) The soles of the feet   (4) The back
    (2) The palms of the hand   (5) The heel
    (3) Skin covering the eyeballs

2. What is the order of the layers of skin from the outside of the body proceeding inward?

    (1) layer of Malpighi, stratum corneum, epidermis
    (2) stratum corneum, layer of Malpighi, epidermis
    (3) dermis, layer of Malpighi, stratum corneum
    (4) dermis, stratum corneum, layer of Malpighi
    (5) stratum corneum, layer of Malpighi, dermis

3. How does the body regulate temperature or water through the skin?

    (1) Respiration   (4) Sensation
    (2) Transpiration   (5) Coagulation
    (3) Perspiration

4. Since the stratum corneum is constantly wearing away, structures such as blood vessels, nerve endings, and sweat glands must be found in

    (1) the layer of Malpighi.   (4) the dermis.
    (2) the stratum corneum.   (5) the muscle tissue.
    (3) the epidermis.

Items 5 to 7 refer to the following information.

The discoveries of Galileo Galilei (1564–1642) and Isaac Newton (1642–1727) precipitated the scientific revolution of the 17th century. Stressing the use of detailed measurements during experimentation enabled them to frame several universal laws of nature and to overthrow many of Aristotle's (384–322 B.C.) erroneous ideas about motion which were based on sheer reasoning alone. One of these universal laws is now known as the "Law of Inertia" or Newton's First Law of Motion. According to this law, objects in motion tend to stay in motion and objects at rest tend to stay at rest unless acted upon by external force. The more mass (inertia) an object has, the more resistance it offers to changes in its state of motion.

5. According to the Law of Inertia, which of the following would offer the greatest resistance to a change in its motion?

   (1) A pellet of lead shot   (4) A feather
   (2) A golf ball   (5) A sheet of notepaper
   (3) A large watermelon

6. When astronauts sleep aboard the Space Shuttle, they strap themselves to a wall or bunk. If one of the thruster rockets was fired, resulting in a change of Shuttle velocity, any unstrapped, sleeping astronauts would be injured by slamming into a Shuttle wall. The sleeping astronauts need to be strapped down because

   (1) their bodies have inertia.
   (2) gravity is not strong enough to keep them touching their beds.
   (3) their body functions need to be constantly monitored.
   (4) astronauts cannot sleep while floating free in space.
   (5) their bodies need a reaction force.

7. In Einstein's famous equation, $E = mc^2$, which of the following is most closely associated with a body's inertia?

   (1) The energy $= E$
   (2) The mass $= m$
   (3) The speed of light $= c$
   (4) The speed of light squared $= c^2$
   (5) The momentum $= mc$

Items 8 to 10 refer to the following map.

   It has been known that ocean conditions influence the weather on land. Look at the following map showing circulation patterns in the oceans and answer the following questions.

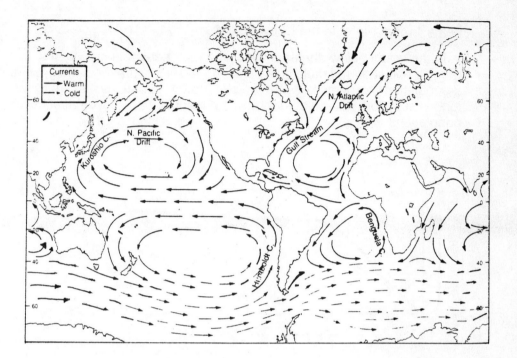

8. Which statement is true?

   (1) The east coasts of the continents are usually washed by warm currents.
   (2) The west coasts of the continents are usually washed by warm currents.
   (3) The east coasts of continents are washed by cold currents.
   (4) No pattern exists.
   (5) The pattern is hard to distinguish.

9. Both London, England, and Hudson Bay, Canada, are on the same North Latitude, yet London's winters average 35°F. warmer. What could account for this difference?

   (1) England is an island.
   (2) The waters of the Gulf Stream wash the English coast.
   (3) Latitude is not a factor in determining temperature.
   (4) Warm winds from France moderate the weather in England.
   (5) The waters of the Gulf Stream wash the Canadian coast.

10. A bottle with a message is tossed into the ocean on the east side of Japan. Where can it be expected to wash ashore?

   (1) Australia   (4) Eastern Mexico
   (2) Western North America   (5) Western South America
   (3) Siberian Peninsula, U.S.S.R.

Items 11 to 14 refer to the following graph.

In the graph below, the dark black line represents the growth in a ranch's population of mule deer. The shaded line represents the growth of a population of whitetail deer in the same area. In both cases, sufficient food is supplied, and no other outside influences or diseases affect either populations.

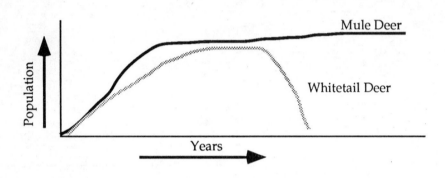

11.   According to the graph, two species with the same living requirements cannot live long together in the same environment. Competition will eliminate one of the two.

   (1)   This conclusion is supported by the data.
   (2)   This conclusion is not supported by the data.
   (3)   This conclusion includes the effect of hunting and is supported by the data.
   (4)   This conclusion includes the effect caused by a drought and is supported by the data.
   (5)   This conclusion takes into consideration that a fire ruined half of the ranch and is supported by the data.

12.   If one comes to the conclusion that the idea of survival of the fittest is supported by this graph, then

   (1)   the conclusion is supported by the data.
   (2)   the conclusion is refuted by the data.
   (3)   the conclusion is refuted because only one kind of deer survived.
   (4)   the conclusion is refuted because the two kinds of deer do not compete with each other, and the data supports this.
   (5)   the conclusion is right, but the data is wrong.

13. If one comes to the conclusion that the mule deer are better adapted to the environment than are the whitetail deer, then

   (1) the conclusion is supported by the data.
   (2) the conclusion is refuted by the data.
   (3) the conclusion is neither supported nor refuted by the data.
   (4) the data gives plenty of information concerning the mule deer's adaptability, which supports the conclusion.
   (5) the data gives plenty of information concerning the type of terrain, which supports the conclusion.

14. One could come to the conclusion that for a period of time the mule deer and the whitetail deer did not compete so one could see a significant growth in the whitetail population. In this case,

   (1) the conclusion is supported by the data.
   (2) the conclusion is refuted by the data.
   (3) the conclusion is neither supported nor refuted by the data.
   (4) the data gives plenty of information concerning the mule deer's adaptability, which supports the conclusion.
   (5) the data gives plenty of information concerning the type of terrain, which supports the conclusion.

Items 15 to 16 refer to the following diagram.

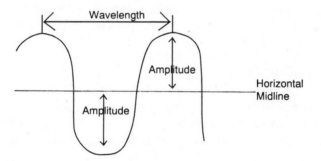

15. The wavelength is

   (1) the distance between any two peaks.
   (2) the distance between two adjacent peaks.
   (3) the distance between the height of a wave and the low point of a wave.
   (4) the rate of motion of the peak.
   (5) the length of the horizontal midline.

16. A wave does not carry along the medium through which it travels. Thus, it follows that

   (1) molecules of water in the ocean are pushed to shore by waves.

(2) the ocean's water molecules are thoroughly mixed each day by waves.

(3) debris in the ocean is washed ashore by waves.

(4) individual water molecules do not travel toward shore, but wave peaks do.

(5) waves move water, not swimmers.

Items 17 to 20 refer to the following paragraph.

Protein synthesis is very important in living things. All cells contain protein and the making of protein is controlled by DNA (deoxyribonucleic acid), which is a major constituent of the chromosomes. DNA molecules contain information in the form of 64 chemical "code words." This informa- tion is also known as the "genetic code." Since DNA is only found in the nucleus of cells, the information that is needed for protein synthesis must be carried to the portion of the cell involved with protein synthesis, the endoplasmic reticulum (ER) and the ribosomes. This is done by a mol- ecule called messenger ribonucleic acid (mRNA), which is made by DNA. Once the mRNA is in the ER, the ribosomes begin to "read" the instruc- tions on the mRNA. As the instructions are read, transfer ribonucleic acid (tRNA) brings to the ribosomes, from the cytoplasm, the proper amino acids. The ribosomes then bond these amino acids together in the proper order until a long chain of amino acids (the protein) is formed.

17. Imagine that a cosmic ray obliterates a "code word" in a single DNA molecule. What happens when the DNA molecule is read so that mRNA can be built?

(1) Nothing happens.
(2) The message of the mRNA is different from the DNA was before the event.
(3) mRNA cannot be made.
(4) Triplets can no longer be produced, so doublets are used.
(5) DNA repairs itself perfectly.

18. DNA nucleotides are found in what part of the cell?

(1) The lysosomes
(2) The endoplasmic reticulum
(3) The cytoplasmic matrix
(4) The nucleus
(5) The golgi bodies

19. DNA strands that are coiled around and interwoven with protein molecules form

(1) RNA.   (2) chromosomes.

(3) nucleotides.   (4)   genes.

(5) ribosomes.

20. If the "code words" for a DNA molecule were changed around, or reversed, what would happen to the resulting protein?

(1) The resulting protein would remain the same.

(2) The resulting protein would definitely be smaller.

(3) The resulting protein would definitely be larger.

(4) The resulting protein would be wrapped around the DNA.

(5) The resulting protein would be changed in some way, either in length, number, or type or arrangement of amino acids.

Items 21 to 22 refer to the following information.

It has been suggested (R. McNeill Alexander, *Dynamics of Dinosaurs and Other Extinct Giants*, New York: Columbia University Press, 1989) that one can figure out what a dinosaur sounded like by measuring the length of its nasal cavity. One dinosaur has a cavity about 150 cm long that runs from the nose to the back of its throat. It was a plant eater that ground its food much like cows and horses do. The cavity is assumed to function much like an open-tube instrument such as the flute. The frequency in cycles per second played by the tube is approximately 170 divided by the length of the tube in meters. The frequencies of some standard musical notes are given below:

Note	Frequency*	Note	Frequency*
F_2	87	D_3	147
G_2	98	E_3	165
A_2	110	F_3	175
B_2	123	G_3	196
C_3	131	A_3	220

*Notice that the same note one octave higher is doubled in frequency.

21. The note sounded by this dinosaur when grinding its food is closest to

(1) F_2.   (4) G_3.

(2) A_2.   (5) A_3.

(3) C_3.

22. A baby dinosaur which has a skull one-third the size of an adult would sound

(1) a note six times higher in frequency than the adult.

(2) a note six times lower in frequency than the adult.

(3) the same note as the adult.

(4)   a note three times higher in frequency than the adult.
(5)   a note three times lower in frequency than the adult.

Items 23 to 25 refer to the following diagram.

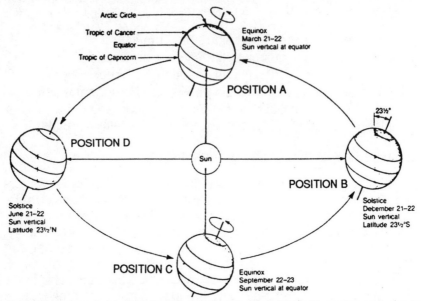

Picture: *The Atmosphere: An introduction to Meteorology*, 1989, Fourth Edition, Fredrick K. Lutgens, Edward J. Tarbuck. Prentice Hall.

23.   Which position(s) in the above diagram result(s) in the North Polar regions being referred to as the Land of the Midnight Sun?

(1)   Position A   (4)   Position D
(2)   Position B   (5)   Positions B and D
(3)   Position C

24.   Which position results in equal day and night?

(1)   Position A   (4)   Position D
(2)   Position B   (5)   Positions A and C
(3)   Position C

25.   The Earth's seasons are caused by the

(1)   tilt of the Earth's axis.
(2)   distance from the sun to the planet.
(3)   rotation of the sun.
(4)   rotation of the Earth.
(5)   effects of the moon's position.

Items 26 to 28 refer to the following paragraph.

   Chameleons are lizards found mainly in Africa. The popular belief that chameleons change color to match their environment is largely false. Temperature, sunlight, and emotion affect the chameleon more than the color of its surroundings. A chameleon can swiftly shoot out its sticky tongue to a distance longer than the length of its body. In this way, it can catch its food.

26. If chameleons are mainly found in Africa, it follows that

   (1)   no chameleons can be found on any other continent.
   (2)   the greater proportion of chameleons are found on the other continents.
   (3)   a lizard found on another continent cannot be a chameleon.
   (4)   chameleons tend to migrate to all parts of the world in great numbers.
   (5)   some species may possibly live in India, but in small number.

27. A chameleon sitting on a black rock turns black in color. This color change is most likely because

   (1)   the chameleon is hiding from a predator.
   (2)   the chameleon is attempting to blend into its surroundings.
   (3)   the chameleon is most likely dying.
   (4)   the chameleon is cold, causing the animal to darken.
   (5)   the animal is preparing to extend its long tongue.

28. The chameleon's tongue catches prey because

   (1)   prey will stick to the sticky substance covering the tongue.
   (2)   the fork on the end of the tongue spears the prey.
   (3)   the tongue wraps around the prey in the same way that a snake will squeeze its prey to death.
   (4)   the tongue contains poisonous glands that kill their prey.
   (5)   the prey is stunned to see the chameleon change color.

Items 29 to 31 refer to the following information.

   The solubility of a substance is the maximum amount of that substance that can dissolve in a given quantity of solvent. A like substance can dissolve a like substance. A solution containing the maximum amount of solute is saturated.

29. If a solid substance is added to a solution but will not dissolve, one can hypothesize that

   (1)   the solution is unsaturated.

(2)   the substance is insoluble in that solvent.
(3)   the solution is saturated.
(4)   one solution may never contain more than one type of solute.
(5)   (2) or (3)

30.   A solute dissolves in a solvent because

(1)   like substances dissolve in like substances, such as oil dissolving in water.
(2)   like substances do not dissolve in like substances.
(3)   like substances dissolve in unlike substances.
(4)   like substances do not dissolve in unlike substances, such as NaCl not dissolving in water.
(5)   like substances dissolve like substances.

31.   If a liquid-liquid solution is made, then

(1)   the liquid in greater quantity is the solute.
(2)   the appearance of two separate layers means that the liquids are miscible.
(3)   no solutes can be dissolved in this solution.
(4)   the liquid in greater quantity is always the solvent.
(5)   (1) or (3)

Items 32 to 34 refer to the following informa. on.

Surface water waves are fundamentally different from sound waves in that the vibration of the former is perpendicular to the direction of motion, while that of sound is always parallel to the direction of motion. If a large disturbance in a material is created by a strong external blow, then it is possible for shear or transverse waves (like water waves) to propagate through the material. However, it is impossible for these shear waves to travel through the inside of a liquid or gas; the attractive forces between the molecules are so weak that there is little restoring force to cause displaced sections of the liquid or gas to return to their original positions which is required for a continuous wave. These shear or S-waves are known to travel through the earth at about 4.25 kilometers/sec.

32.   Shear (transverse) waves, set up by a strong blow to the material, are able to travel through which of the following at room temperature?

(1)   Water   (4)   Air
(2)   Carbon dioxide   (5)   Granite
(3)   Mercury

33. Shear (or S-waves) created by an Earthquake are known to stop at a depth of about 2900 kilometers below the Earth's surface. This is evidence that the Earth has

    (1) a diameter of 2900 kilometers.
    (2) a liquid portion that starts 2900 kilometers below the Earth's surface.
    (3) a solid core that starts 2900 kilometers below the Earth's surface.
    (4) a radius of 2900 kilometers.
    (5) mostly a liquid surface to reflect the waves down to 2900 kilometers.

34. Earthquakes cause pressure-type waves (P-waves), which travel about twice as fast as the associated S-waves. If a seismographic station records an Earthquake's P-waves arriving 4 minutes after the earthquake occurs, its distance away from the station must be about

    (1) 500 kilometers.   (4) 3000 kilometers.
    (2) 1000 kilometers.   (5) 4000 kilometers.
    (3) 2000 kilometers.

Items 35-38 refer to the following map.

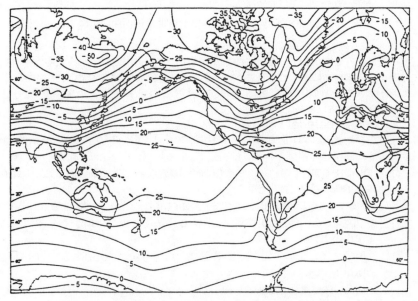

WORLD MEAN SEA-LEVEL TEMPERATURES IN JANUARY IN °C

Picture: *The Atmosphere: An introduction to Meteorology*, 1989, Fourth Edition, Fredrick K. Lutgens, Edward J. Tarbuck. Prentice Hall.

35. Latitude is the distance in degrees north or south of the equator. The latitude of the equator is zero degrees, and the poles are at 90 degrees. Longitude is the distance in degrees east or west of the prime meridian.

The meridians are semicircles drawn around the globe from pole to pole. Which statement is true?

(1)   The distance between latitude lines increases as you move toward the poles.
(2)   The distance between longitude lines increases as you move toward the poles.
(3)   The distance between latitude lines decreases as you move toward the poles.
(4)   The distance between longitude lines decreases as you move toward the poles.
(5)   The distance between latitude and longitude is never changing.

36.   Contour lines are used in map making. Contour lines give exact elevation above sea level and show the shape of the land at the same time. Which statement is false?

(1)   When contour lines are close together, the land is steep.
(2)   When contour lines cross, this indicates the top of a hill or mountain.
(3)   Closed circles or ovals indicate the top of a hill or mountain.
(4)   A contour line will bend in the direction that the slope of the land changes.
(5)   The distance between contour lines varies with the slope.

37.   In setting forth his Theory on Continental Drift, Alfred Wegner gave a series of proofs which supported his theory that the continents at one time were all connected. Which of the below statements would not support his idea?

(1)   The coasts of South America and Africa fit together like a jigsaw puzzle.
(2)   When continents are placed together, their mountain ranges connect.
(3)   The weather conditions on matching continents are similar.
(4)   Fossils of the same age and type are found on connecting continents.
(5)   Rocks of the same age and type are found on connecting continents.

38.   Two main factors of climate are temperature and rainfall, and these factors depend on a whole set of conditions called climatic controls. Which of the following would not be a climatic control?

(1)   Latitude   (4)   Topography
(2)   Prevailing winds   (5)   Distance from large bodies of water
(3)   Population density

Items 39 to 41 refer to the following passage.

For five years Charles Darwin traveled around the world aboard the H.M.S. Beagle. During that time he observed many things, especially the plants and animals of South America and the Galapagos Islands. Later, he published his famous book, *On The Origin of Species*, which made sense of what he saw. His theory may be summarized by the following four observations: (1) individuals vary genetically; (2) generally, organisms will produce more offspring than the environment can support; (3) even though there are large numbers of offspring, the population remains fairly constant; and (4) the environment all over the planet is in a constant state of change. From these four observations Darwin concluded that: (1) in every population there is competition for available resources, (2) those organisms that have favorable genetic variation will be able to live and reproduce, and (3) those genetic variations that allowed the parents to survive will be handed down to offspring through generations and will accumulate in the population until the whole population will have these favorable genes. In this way, Darwin could see how things change or evolve.

39. It is a well-known fact that clams release millions of eggs and sperm. If 50% of all eggs were fertilized, would this be consistent with Darwin's conclusions?

   (1)   Yes, because favorable variations occur.
   (2)   Yes, because there are more offspring produced than the environment could support, and only some of the clams would survive.
   (3)   Yes, because the environment is constantly changing.
   (4)   No, because individual sperm and egg are different genetically.
   (5)   No, because genetic variation does not allow for natural selection.

40. It is estimated that a single fern can produce upwards of 50 million spores in a single year. It is easy to realize that all of the spores do not grow into a mature adult fern, because if they did, whole continents would be covered with ferns. What did Darwin observe that would explain this?

   (1)   Organisms produce more offspring than the environment can support, so a population will remain constant because there are not enough resources for all offspring.
   (2)   The environment is slowly changing all over the world, which prevents all of the offspring from maturing.
   (3)   Genetic variation is allowing the ferns to keep the same level of population.
   (4)   Genetic variation, which allows for survival, will increase.
   (5)   Individuals vary genetically.

41. Which person would be helped by having a better understanding of Darwin's observations and conclusions in order to have a more productive business?

    (1) Cattle rancher
    (2) Oilman
    (3) Engineer
    (4) Refinery chemist
    (5) Hair stylist

Items 42 to 44 refer to the passage below.

Most substances are denser during the solid phase than during the liquid phase. Water is an exception to this rule. Additionally, water has a very high boiling point compared to other hydrides of nonmetals. Water has several other unusual properties that are related to the structure and composition of the water molecules.

42. Which of the following statements is not a true statement about water?

    (1) Ice cubes float because solid water is less dense than liquid water.
    (2) Water exists as both a liquid and a solid at normal Earth temperatures.
    (3) Hydrogen bonding is especially weak in water.
    (4) The bonds between the oxygen and the hydrogens of water are covalent.
    (5) A water molecule can be both an electron donor and an electron acceptor.

43. The unusually high boiling and melting points of water result from

    (1) a great amount of intermolecular attraction in water.
    (2) low surface tension.
    (3) low amount of hydrogen bonding between water molecules.
    (4) the low heat capacity of water.
    (5) strong covalent bonds between water molecules.

44. On the centigrade temperature scale, water freezes at _____ °C and boils at _____ °C.

    (1) 32; 100
    (2) 0; 212
    (3) 32; 98.6
    (4) 32; 212
    (5) 0; 100

Items 45 to 49 refer to the following graphs.

Assume you have grown some bacterial cultures in a test tube. You carefully keep track of how they grow. The graphs below represent some possible growth curves. Use the following graphs to answer the next five questions.

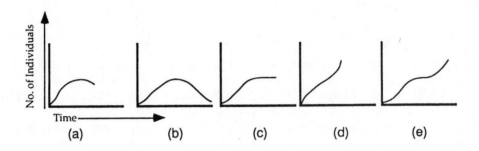

45. Which of the statements would be best represented by graph (a)?

    (1) The number of bacteria being produced by mitosis is equal to the number of bacteria dying.
    (2) Nothing was done to the culture of bacteria at first, but after a while some of the waste products were removed.
    (3) Bacteria "love" this growth curve because it represents ideal conditions.
    (4) The growth of the bacteria is represented by a normal growth curve.
    (5) While growing the bacteria, the test tube was inoculated with poison.

46. Which of the statements would be best represented by graph (b)?

    (1) The number of bacteria being produced by mitosis is equal to the number of bacteria dying.
    (2) Nothing was done to the culture of bacteria at first, but after a while some of the waste products were removed.
    (3) Bacteria "love" this growth curve because it represents ideal conditions.
    (4) The growth of the bacteria is represented by a normal growth curve.
    (5) While growing the bacteria, the test tube was inoculated with poison.

47. Which of the statements would be best represented by graph (c)?

    (1) The number of bacteria being produced by mitosis is equal to the number of bacteria dying.
    (2) Nothing was done to the culture of bacteria at first, but after a while some of the waste products were removed.

(3) Bacteria "love" this growth curve because it represents ideal conditions.

(4) The growth of the bacteria is represented by a normal growth curve.

(5) While growing the bacteria, the test tube was inoculated with poison.

48. Which of the statements would be best represented by graph (d)?

(1) The number of bacteria being produced by mitosis is equal to the number of bacteria dying.

(2) Nothing was done to the culture of bacteria at first, but after a while some of the waste products were removed.

(3) Bacteria "love" this growth curve because it represents ideal conditions.

(4) The growth of the bacteria is represented by a normal growth curve.

(5) While growing the bacteria, the test tube was inoculated with poison.

49. Which of the statements would be best represented by graph (e)?

(1) The number of bacteria being produced by mitosis is equal to the number of bacteria dying.

(2) Nothing was done to the culture of bacteria at first, but after a while some of the waste products were removed.

(3) Bacteria "love" this growth curve because it represents ideal conditions.

(4) The growth of the bacteria is represented by a normal growth curve.

(5) While growing the bacteria, the test tube was inoculated with poison.

Items 50 to 51 refer to the following information.

The average home use of electricity in the United States as compared to a developing country like Brazil is shown in the table below. The amount of electrical energy used is given in kilowatt-hours (KWH) per household per year. (October 1990, *Scientific American*, p. 113)

Use	United States	Brazil
Lighting	1000	350
Cooking	635	15
Water Heating	1540	380
Air-Conditioning	1180	45
Refrigeration	1810	470
Other	1180	200

50. Which of the statements below is the best conclusion based on the data provided?

(1) The total electrical consumption by the average U.S. household is about twice that of the typical Brazilian home wired for electricity.

(2) Because it is warmer in Brazil, the percentage of electricity used in air-conditioning is greater than that used in the United States.

(3) The greatest amount of electricity use in both countries is for lighting.

(4) United States households use more electricity for water heating than lighting, while Brazilian households use more electricity for lighting than water heating.

(5) Both countries have a somewhat similar pattern of electricity consumption.

51. How much more electrical energy per household does the United States consume than developing Brazil?

(1) 3 times
(2) 4 times
(3) 5 times
(4) 6 times
(5) 7 times

Items 52 to 57 refer to the following information.

One way of describing animals is to describe how their body parts are arranged. The arrangement of body parts is called symmetry. If an organism has no definite shape, then it is said to be asymmetrical. No matter which way the organism is sliced, no two halves will look similar. If an organism is shaped like a ball, then it is said to have spherical symmetry. No matter how you slice it, both halves will look similar. If an organism is bilaterally symmetrical, then it will have a right and a left side. If an organism has radial symmetry, then it will have the general shape of a cylinder, with its body parts extending outward from the middle of the cylinder (radiating). However, one must be careful when considering radial symmetry. Sometimes the cylindrical shape will be flattened.

52. What type of symmetry is exhibited by the organism shown to the right?

(1) Asymmetry
(2) Radial symmetry
(3) Spherical symmetry
(4) Bilateral symmetry
(5) Longitudinal symmetry

53. The organism to the right exhibits what type of symmetry?

   (1) Asymmetry
   (2) Radial symmetry
   (3) Bilateral symmetry
   (4) Spherical symmetry
   (5) Triradial symmetry

54. What type of symmetry is exhibited by the figure on the right?

   (1) Asymmetry
   (2) Radial symmetry
   (3) Spherical symmetry
   (4) Bilateral symmetry
   (5) Longitudinal symmetry

55. What type of symmetry is exhibited by the organism shown at the right?

   (1) Asymmetry
   (2) Radial symmetry
   (3) Bilateral symmetry
   (4) Spherical symmetry
   (5) Longitudinal symmetry

56. If an organism has a right side and a left side, it is said to be

   (1) asymmetrical.   (4) cylindrically symmetrical.
   (2) bilaterally symmetrical. (5) radially symmetrical.
   (3) spherically symmetrical.

57. A starfish, since it has rays radiating out from a central point, would be

   (1) asymmetrical.   (4) cylindrically symmetrical.
   (2) bilaterally symmetrical. (5) radially symmetrical.
   (3) spherically symmetrical.

Items 58 to 61 refer to the following information.

   When assigning oxidation numbers, simple rules can be followed: (1) The sum of all oxidation numbers of the atoms in an electrically neutral chemical substance is zero. (2) The sum of the oxidation numbers must equal the charge on the ion for polyatomic ions. (3) The oxidation number of an atom in a monatomic ion is its charge. (4) Hydrogen always has the oxidation number +1 when combined with nonmetals and -1 when combined with metals.

58. Which rule(s) must be applied to find the oxidation number of H_2S?

    (1) 1
    (2) 4
    (3) 1, 2

    (4) 1, 4
    (5) 2, 4

59. What is the oxidation number of the Mn in the neutral compound $KMnO_4$ if the oxidation number of K is +1 and the oxidation number for one oxygen atom (O) is -2?

    (1) +1
    (2) +7
    (3) 0

    (4) +3
    (5) -3

60. Calculate the oxidation number of the P atom in HPO_4^{2-} if the oxidation number of one oxygen atom is -2?

    (1) +1
    (2) +7
    (3) +5

    (4) 0
    (5) +2

61. Which rule(s) is/are used to find the oxidation numbers of HPO_4^{2-} and the oxidation numbers of the atoms comprising this compound?

    (1) 2
    (2) 3, 4
    (3) 4

    (4) 2, 4
    (5) 1, 2, 4

Items 62 to 65 refer to the following paragraphs.

Carolus Linnaeus introduced a scientific system of naming organisms. He developed this because there were so many names for the same organism. For example, a mountain lion could be called a puma, mountain lion, panther, cougar, red lion, etc. In order to avoid this confusion, he set up what is known as the binomial system of nomenclature. This means that for the name of the animal, one would use two names. Carolus used Latin names because Latin is a dead language that is not spoken by anyone; therefore, it is not subject to change. In a two-word name, the first name refers to the animals' genus and the second name to its species.

Carolus Linnaeus also set up a system of grouping organisms. He began by dividing up all living things into two groups. These he named kingdoms. Today there are five kingdoms: Animalia, Plantae, Monera, Protista, and Fungi. The classification (grouping) hierarchy of today is: kingdom, phylum, class, order, family, genus, species. Note that members of a genus group can have a special name like *Felis* (cat), or *Canis* (dog). Every type of animal has a unique species name, which also places them in a single grouping. For example, *Canis lupis* (wolf) and *Canis latrans* (coyote) are two different species of the dog family. *Canis* is the genus name; *latrans* and *lupis* are species names. *Felis domesticus* and *Canis familiaris* are not the same and their genus names tell us so.

62. The panda bear, *Aleropoda melanoleuca*, is not a bear like the black bear, *Ursus americanus*, or the grizzly bear, *Ursus horribilis*. How can this distinction be shown?

    (1) Panda bears live only in China.
    (2) Pandas are not bears, and their genus name, *Aleropoda*, indicates this.
    (3) Pandas are not bears, and their species name, *melanoleuca*, indicates this.
    (4) Pandas are on the endangered list and have black and white fur.
    (5) Pandas are not bears because they are really called "pandas."

63. Given: 2 animals. Animal #1 is called *Linius alba*, and animal #2 is called *Canis alba*. Which of the following is true?

    (1) The species name indicates that there is a close genetic relationship.
    (2) The species name indicates a filial relationship.
    (3) The genus names indicate that there is no relationship.
    (4) The genus name indicates there is a filial relationship.
    (5) Both animals are totally black.

64. Some members of the kingdom Animalia include the

    (1) insects, amphibians, reptiles, fish, birds, and mammals
    (2) insects, fungus, amphibians, reptiles, fish, birds, and mammals
    (3) mushrooms, amphibians, reptiles, fish, birds, and mammals
    (4) slime molds, autotrophic algae, rusts, trees, and blue-green algae
    (5) insects, crabs, sponges, trees, fish, birds, and reptiles

65. The first name of a scientific name, such as *Happlopappus gracilis*, is the

    (1) kingdom name.
    (2) phylum name.
    (3) class name.
    (4) order name.
    (5) genus name.

Item 66 refers to the following information.

The graph below shows how the relative light energy given off by a tungsten lamp (3000 K) and a fluorescent lamp compared with that of average sunlight at the earth's surface. The wavelength of 4000 A is at the blue end of the spectrum, and 7000 A is at the red end.

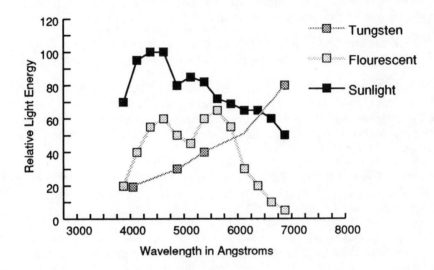

66. Which source tends to be the reddest?

    (1) Tungsten filament lamp
    (2) Fluorescent lamp
    (3) Sunlight
    (4) Sunlight and fluorescent lamp
    (5) Each lamp has the same amount of red

TEST 4: INTERPRETING LITERATURE AND THE ARTS

Tests of General Educational Development

Directions

The Interpreting Literature and the Arts Test consists of excerpts from classical and popular literature and articles about literature or the arts. Each excerpt is followed by multiple-choice questions about the reading material.

Read each excerpt first and then answer the questions following it. Refer back to the reading material as often as necessary in answering the questions.

Each excerpt is preceded by a "purpose question." The purpose question gives a reason for reading the material. Use these purpose questions to help focus your reading. You are not required to answer these purpose questions. They are given only to help you concentrate on the ideas presented in the reading materials.

You should spend no more than 65 minutes answering the questions in this booklet. Work carefully, but do not spend too much time on any one question. Be sure you answer every question. You will not be penalized for incorrect answers.

Do not mark in this test booklet. Record your answers on the separate answer sheet provided. Be sure all requested information is properly recorded on the answer sheet. To record your answers, mark the numbered space on the answer sheet beside the number that corresponds to the question in the test booklet.

FOR EXAMPLE:

It was Susan's dream machine. The metallic blue paint gleamed, and the sporty wheels were highly polished. Under the hood, the engine was no less carefully cleaned. Inside, flashy lights illuminated the instruments on the dashboard, and the seats were covered by rich leather upholstery.

The subject ("It") of this excerpt is most likely

(1) an airplane.   (4) a boat.
(2) a stereo system.   (5) a motorcycle.
(3) an automobile.

(1) (2) ● (4) (5)

The correct answer is "an automobile"; therefore, answer space 3 would be marked on the answer sheet.

Do not rest the point of your pencil on the answer sheet while you are considering your answer. Make no stray or unnecessary marks. If you change an answer, erase your first mark completely. Mark only one answer space for each question; multiple answers will be scored as incorrect. Do not fold or crease your answer sheet. Return all test materials to the test administrator.

Directions: Choose the <u>one best answer</u> to each item.

<u>Items 1 to 8</u> refer to the following conversation.

WHAT IS THE RELATIONSHIP BETWEEN THESE MEN?

1   George still stared morosely at the fire. "When I think of the swell time I could have without you, I go nuts. I never get no peace."

      Lennie still knelt. He looked off into the darkness across the

5   river. "George, you want I should go away and leave you alone?"

      "Where the hell could you go?"

      "Well, I could go off in the hills there. Some place I'd find a cave."

      "Yeah? How'd you eat? You ain't got sense enough to find

10   nothing to eat."

      "I'd find things, George. I don't need no nice food with ketchup. I'd lay out in the sun and nobody'd hurt me. An' if I foun' a mouse, I could keep it. Nobody'd take it away from me."

      George looked quickly and searchingly at him. "I been mean,

15   ain't I?"

      "If you don' want me I can go off in the hills and find a cave. I can go away any time."

      No—look! I was jus' foolin', Lennie. 'Cause I want you to stay with me. Trouble with mice is you always kill 'em." He paused.

20   "Tell you what I'll do, Lennie. First chance I get I'll give you a pup. Maybe you wouldn't kill it. That'd be better than mice. And you could pet it harder."

      Lennie avoided the bait. He had sensed his advantage. "If you don't want me, you only jus' got to say so, and I'll go off in those

25   hills right there—right up in those hills and live by myself. An' I won't get no mice stole from me."

      George said, "I want you to stay with me, Lennie, Jesus Christ, somebody'd shoot you for a coyote if you was by yourself. No, you stay with me. Your Aunt Clara wouldn't like you running off by

30   yourself, even if she is dead."

      Lennie spoke craftily, "Tell me—like you done before."

      "Tell you what?"

      "About the rabbits."

      George snapped, "You ain't gonna put nothing over on me."

35   Lennie pleaded, "Come on, George. Tell me, please George. Like you done before."

      "You get a kick outta that, don't you? Awright, I'll tell you, and then we'll eat our supper...." George's voice became deeper. He repeated his words rhythmically as though he had said them many

40   times before....

      Lennie was delighted. "That's it—that's it. Now tell how it is with us."

      George went on. "With us it ain't like that. We got a future. We

45 got somebody to talk to that gives a damn about us. We don't
have to sit in no barroom blowin' our jack jus because we
got no place to go....
"O.K. Someday—we're gonna get the jack together and we're
gonna have a little house and a couple of acres an' a cow and
some pigs and—"
50 "An' live off the fatta the lan'!," Lennie shouted.

John Steinbeck, *Of Mice and Men*, New York, New York: Bantam Books, copyright 1965 by John Steinbeck, pp. 15, 16, 17.

1. You can tell from the dialogue that

   (1) each man is bonded in friendship with the other.
   (2) neither one really cares what happens to the other.
   (3) George will stay angry with Lennie this time.
   (4) Lennie sincerely intends to leave.
   (5) George intends to abandon Lennie soon.

2. It becomes clear when studying the conversation that

   (1) George has little compassion for Lennie.
   (2) Lennie has learned to manipulate George.
   (3) George has the "upper hand" at all times.
   (4) Lennie intends to hurt George.
   (5) Lennie is a survivor.

3. You can best compare the relationship of George and Lennie with one of

   (1) best friends.   (4) feuding neighbors.
   (2) father and son.   (5) complete strangers.
   (3) casual acquaintances.

4. Lines 18-22 provide insight into

   (1) George's inner conflict.
   (2) George's intelligence.
   (3) Lennie's attitude.
   (4) both men's devotion to each other.
   (5) George's impatience.

5. The fact that Lennie accidentally kills mice while he pets them indicates

   (1) he is careless.   (4) he is kind.
   (2) he is cruel.   (5) he is stubborn.
   (3) he is not aware of his own strength.

6. The conflict within George appears to be one concerning

    (1) his relationship with Lennie.
    (2) his lack of money.
    (3) his lack of education.
    (4) his job.
    (5) his bad luck.

7. The fact that Lennie knows George's story by heart means

    (1) Lennie created it.
    (2) he has heard it many times.
    (3) it is probably untrue.
    (4) there is cause for concern.
    (5) nothing in particular.

8. Essentially the story gives each man

    (1) something to talk about.   (4) cause for concern.
    (2) hope for the future.   (5) nothing in particular.
    (3) reason to leave town.

Items 9 to 14 refer to the following poem.

WHAT DOES THE SCOTTISH POET SAY ABOUT LIFE TO THE MOUSE?

1
    Wee, Sleekit, cowrin, tim'rous beastie
    O what a panic's in thy breastie!
    Thou ned na start awa sae hasty,
        Wi' bickering brattle!
5
    I wad be laith to rin an' chase thee,
        Wi' murdering pattle!
    I'm truly sorry man's dominion
    Has broken Nature's social union,
        An' justifies that ill opinion
10
            Which makes thee startle
    At me, thy poor, earth-born companion,
        An' fellow-mortal!
    I doubt na, whyles, but thou may thieve;
    What then? poor beastie, thou maun live!
15
        A daimen icker in a thrave
            'S a sma' request;
    I'll get a blessin' wi' the lave,
        An' never miss 't!
    Thy wee-bit housie, too, in ruin!
20
        Its silly wa's the win's are strewin!
    An' naething now to big a new ane,
        O' foggage green!

An bleak December's win's ensuin,
Baith snell an' keen!
25 Thou saw the fields laid bare an' waste,
An' weary winter coming fast,
An' cozie here, beneath the blast,
Thou thought to dwell—
Till, crash! the cruel coulter passed
30 Out thro' thy cell.
That wee bit heap o' leaves an' stibble
Has cost thee monie a weary nibble!
Now thou's turned out, for a' thy trouble,
But house or hald
35 To thole the winter's sleety dribble,
An' cranreuch cauld!
But mousie, thou art no thy lane
In proving foresight may be vain:
The best-laid schemes o'mice an' men
40 Gang aft agley,
An' lea'e us naught but grief an' pain
For promised joy!
Still thou art blest compared wi' me!
The present only toucheth thee:
45 But och! I backward cast my e'e,
On prospects drear!
An' forward, tho' I canna see,
I guess an' fear!

Robert Burns, from *Anthology of Romanticism*, Ed., Ernest Bosbaum, New York, New York: The Ronald Press Co., Copyright 1929, 1930, 1933, 1948, p. 87.

9. Using dialect, the poet successfully describes the mouse in line 1 as

    (1) brave, bold, and aggressive. (4) Nature's masterpiece.
    (2) small, sleek, and afraid.   (5) a useless creature.
    (3) innocent but menacing.

10. Lines 7 and 8 concerning "man's dominion" and "Nature's social union" can be translated as meaning

    (1) both man and beast rule the earth.
    (2) man's rule over beast surpasses any kinship nature may have intended.
    (3) although man rules, he still has a social kinship with all creatures.
    (4) his "wee beastie" actually dominates mankind.
    (5) None of the above.

11. Lines 13 through 18 tell the reader that Burns intends to do what with the mouse?

(1)	Keep it as a pet.	(4)	Give it to his son.
(2)	Destroy it.	(5)	Rebuild its house.
(3)	Let it live.		

12. What is the author's attitude toward the tiny creature's demolished home as revealed in lines 19–36?

(1)	Sarcastic	(4)	Uncaring
(2)	Humble	(5)	Business-like
(3)	Compassionate		

13. The best laid plans of mice and men "gang aft agley" (lines 39–40), which means they

(1)	usually work out.	(4)	never work out.
(2)	often go astray.	(5)	are useless.
(3)	take hard work.		

14. Comparing his life to the mouse's, in lines 43—48 we can tell the author's tone is

(1)	self-pitying.	(4)	fearful.
(2)	exaggerating.	(5)	impartial.
(3)	angry.		

Items 15 to 17 refer to the following conversation.

WHAT CODE OF MANHOOD DOES THE OLD MAN PORTRAY?

1   "Santiago," the boy said.
    "Yes," the old man said. He was holding his glass and thinking of many years ago.
    "Can I go out to get sardines for you for tomorrow?"
5   "No. Go and play baseball. I can still row and Rogelio will throw the net."
    "I would like to go. If I cannot fish with you, I would like to serve in some way."
    "You bought me a beer," the old man said. "You are already a
10 man."
    "How old was I when you first took me in a boat?"
    "Five and you nearly were killed when I brought the fish in too green and he nearly tore the boat to pieces. Can you remember?"
    "I can remember the tail slapping and banging and the thwart
15 breaking and the noise of the clubbing. I can remember you throwing me into the bow where the wet coiled lines were and feeling the whole boat shiver and the noise of you clubbing him like chopping a tree down and the sweet blood smell all over me."
    "Can you really remember that or did I just tell it to you?"
20   "I remember everything from when we first went together."

The old man looked at him with his sun-burned confident loving eyes.

"If you were my boy I'd take you out and gamble," he said. "But you are your father's and your mother's and you are in a lucky
25   boat."

"May I get the sardines? I know where I can get four baits, too."

15. From the preceding selection, what can be concluded about the old man and the boy?

(1) They are father and son.
(2) They have a deep, bonding friendship.
(3) They are merely casual acquaintances.
(4) They care very little for one another.
(5) They most likely have just met.

16. In line 13 "fish too green" means

(1) the fish was spoiled.
(2) the fish was brought aboard too soon.
(3) the fisherman was only a novice.
(4) the boy was careless.
(5) the incident happened by chance.

17. This passage is most likely from a story primarily concerned with

(1) mystery and intrigue.   (4) character portrayal.
(2) geographical location.   (5) science fiction.
(3) humor.

Items 18 to 22 refer to the following passage.

1   "How do you feel, fish?" he asked aloud. "I feel good and my left hand is better and I have food for a night and a day. Pull the boat, fish."

He did not truly feel good because the pain from the cord
5   across his back had almost passed pain and gone into a dullness that he mistrusted. But I have had worse things than that, he thought. My hand is only cut a little and the cramp is gone from the other. My legs are all right. Also now I have gained on him in the question of sustenance.
10   It was dark now as it becomes dark quickly after the sun sets in September. He lay against the worn wood of the bow and rested all that he could. The first stars were out. He did not know the name of Rigel but he saw it and knew soon they would all be out and he would have all his distant friends.
15   "The fish is my friend too," he said aloud. "I have never seen or

heard of such a fish. But I must kill him. I am glad we do not have
to try to kill the stars."

Imagine if each day a man must try to kill the moon, he thought.
The moon runs away. But imagine if a man each day should have
20   to try to kill the sun? We were born lucky, he thought.

Then he was sorry for the great fish that had nothing to eat and
his determination to kill him never relaxed in his sorrow for him.
How many people will he feed, he thought. But are they worthy to
eat him? No, of course not. There is no one worthy of eating him
25   from the manner of his behaviour and his great dignity.

I do not understand these things, he thought. But it is good that
we do not have to try to kill the sun or the moon or the stars. It is
enough to live on the sea and kill our true brothers.

Ernest Hemingway, selections from *The Old Man and the Sea*, New York, New York: Charles
Scribner's Sons, (p.b.), copyright 1952 by Ernest Hemingway, pp. 12, 13, 74, 75.

18.   The preceding selection reveals that the story primarily emphasizes
which of the following aspects of the old man's character?

    (1)   Determination and endurance
    (2)   Wit and humor
    (3)   Intelligence and formal schooling
    (4)   Irrational stubbornness
    (5)   Blind hatred

19.   In lines 16–17, Santiago reveals that he must

    (1)   kill the fish with no remorse.
    (2)   kill the fish with deep regret.
    (3)   let the fish go.
    (4)   soon give up.
    (5)   find someone worthy of eating this fish.

20.   Which of Santiago's personality traits are evident in his self-dialogue?

    (1)   Appreciation and compassion for all creation
    (2)   Self-centered interest in achieving this goal
    (3)   Pride in his fishing ability
    (4)   Blind hatred of losing
    (5)   Total disregard for danger

21.   On a literal level, lines 23–25 refer to the "great fish"; on a deeper level,
they convey what universal idea?

    (1)   Honor and dignity once earned should not be carelessly cast
away.

(2) Youth should respect old age.
(3) The fish should be fed to the poor of the village.
(4) The fisherman himself would eat the fish.
(5) None of the above.

22. Lines 26–27 suggest that Santiago considers the fish his "true brothers"

(1) literally. (4) humorously.
(2) figuratively. (5) satirically.
(3) paradoxically.

Items 23 to 30 refer to the poem below.

WHAT IS THE POET'S MESSAGE CONCERNING NATURE'S BEAUTY?

1   In May, when sea winds pierced our solitudes,
     I found the fresh Rhodora in the woods,
     Spreading its leafless blooms in a damp nook,
     To please the desert and the sluggish brook.
5   The purple petals, fallen in the pool,
     Made the black water with their beauty gay;
     Here might the redbird came his plumes to cool,
     And court the flower that cheapens his array.
     Rhodora! If the sages ask thee why
10   This charm is wasted on the earth and sky,
     Tell them, dear, that if eyes were made for seeing,
     Then Beauty is its own excuse for being:
     Why thou wert there, O rival of the rose!
     I never thought to ask, I never knew;
15   But, in my simple ignorance suppose
     The selfsame Power that brought me there brought you.

Ralph Waldo Emerson, "The Rhodora," *American Literature: A College Survey*, New York: McGraw-Hill Company, Clarence A. Brown and John T. Flanagan, Eds. copyright 1961, p. 197.

23. The theme of the entire poem is

(1) nature. (4) religion.
(2) philosophy. (5) love.
(3) patriotism.

24. In general, what is the poet's attitude toward the natural world?

(1) Callousness (4) Fear
(2) Scorn (5) Admiration
(3) Envy

25. Line 1 tells the reader that

    (1) it is time for sailing.
    (2) it is time for solitude.
    (3) spring has penetrated winter's isolation.
    (4) May is a month of solitude.
    (5) spring is a time for rejoicing.

26. Literally, lines 7 and 8 most closely mean that

    (1) the flower is more resplendent than the bird's plumage.
    (2) the bird is more beautiful than the flower.
    (3) neither the bird nor the flower are as glorious as nature.
    (4) both the bird and the flower equal nature's beauty.
    (5) None of the above.

27. Lines 9 through 12 are an apostrophe, a poetic device which

    (1) compares implicitly two unlike objects.
    (2) uses language with some kind of incongruity.
    (3) addresses inanimate things or absent persons as if alive or present.
    (4) expresses less than what the poet actually means.
    (5) mimics a words meanings with its sounds.

28. Lines 9 through 12 translated literally most nearly mean

    (1) If wisemen ask, tell them that nature's beauty needs no other purpose.
    (2) If wisemen ask, tell them that nature's beauty is no excuse for its lack of purpose.
    (3) Beauty in nature is difficult to find.
    (4) Nature's beauty is wasteful.
    (5) There is no purpose for nature's beauty.

29. In line 13, the flower is called

    (1) an enemy of the rose.
    (2) not nearly as beautiful as the rose.
    (3) one which is as beautiful as the rose.
    (4) a wildflower.
    (5) All of the above.

30. Lines 13 through 16 suggest that the poet feels, without question, that

    (1) he is simply ignorant.
    (2) he never thought about nature's beauty.

(3)   the same Power who created the flower created him.
(4)   the selfsame Power who created man did not create the flower.
(5)   nature and humanity are not created by the same Power.

Items 31 to 36 refer to the following story.

WHAT HARDSHIPS DID THIS YOUNG, MODERN WRITER ENDURE IN CHILDHOOD?

1   She was born in 1949 into tropical poverty. Her father was a
carpenter and her mother kept house. They had no electricity, no
bathroom, no running water. Every Wednesday she registered
their outhouse at the Public Works Department so that the "night
5   soil men," as they were called, would take away their full tub and
replace it with a clean one. And every morning she went to a
public pipe and drew four pails of water for her mother—more if it
was a wash day. After school, she went to the pipe for more water.
At night she had to wipe the soot from the lampshade and trim the
10   wick. If the lamp was out of oil she would buy more kerosene.
Those were her duties.
         As a young child, the only child in the family, she was happy
and deeply connected to her mother. But when she was nine the
first of her three brothers was born, and life became complicated.
15   Not only did her mother's focus shift from her to the new baby, but
an enlarged family caused a keener sense of their poverty. Around
this time she entered adolescence, with its attendant emotional
storms. For the first time, her intelligence demanded its own realm,
but on a 10-by-12-mile outpost of British rule, the intellectual
20   needs of a gifted, indeed brilliant, child could find no organized
outlet. That was when she began to steal books, hide them under
the house and read in secret.
         Her formal education was at Government schools, where she
was considered bright but troublesome. "I was sullen," she says. "I
25   was always accused of being rude, because I gave some back
chat. I moved very slowly. I was never where I should be. I wasn't
really angry yet. I was just incredibly unhappy."
         I ask her if any teachers in her school recognized her talent,
and she says, with a tight smile: "Absolutely not. Everyone thought
30   I had a way with words, but it came out as a sharp tongue. No one
expected anything from me at all. Had I just sunk in the cracks it
would not have been noted. I would have been lucky to be a
secretary somewhere."

Leslie Garis, "Through West Indian Eyes," *The New York Times Magazine*, 7 October 1990, Section
6, pp. 44, 70.

31.   The first paragraph suggests that the woman lived

    (1)   in a small town.   (4)   in an apartment complex.
    (2)   a large city.   (5)   on a houseboat.
    (3)   on an island.

32. Her life first became complicated by

    (1) family poverty.   (4) catastrophic events.
    (2) bad luck.   (5) poor schooling.
    (3) her mother's emotional abandonment and poverty.

33. The passage infers that the woman was

    (1) intellectually undemanding, until adolescence.
    (2) a demanding child.
    (3) unintellectual.
    (4) unhappy.
    (5) uneducated.

34. In the phrase "attendant adolescent storms," attendant most closely means

    (1) uncontrolled.   (4) severe.
    (2) accompanying.   (5) mild.
    (3) numerous.

35. The woman admits that she stole books because

    (1) she was bored.
    (2) she was revengeful.
    (3) she needed to use her gifted mind.
    (4) she was intimidated by her friends.
    (5) None of the above.

36. From the woman's viewpoint, memories of her childhood could be described most appropriately as

    (1) happy.   (4) normal.
    (2) unexamined.   (5) abnormal.
    (3) misunderstood.

Items 37 to 45 refer to the following poem.

WHAT OR WHO IS THIS MYSTERIOUS BIRD?

1 Once upon a midnight dreary, while I pondered, weak and weary,
        Over many a quaint and curious volume of forgotten lore—
   While I nodded nearly napping, suddenly there came a tapping
        As of someone gently rapping, rapping at my chamber door.
5   "Tis some visitor," I muttered, "tapping at my chamber door—
            Only this and nothing more."
     Ah, distinctly I remember it was in the bleak December,
   And each separate dying ember wrought its ghost upon the floor.

Eagerly I wished the morrow, vainly I had sought to borrow

10　From my books surcease of sorrow—sorrow for the lost Lenore—

For the rare and radiant maiden whom the angels named Lenore—

Nameless here for evermore.

.....

Open here I flung the shutter, when, with many a flirt and flutter,

In there stepped a stately Raven of the saintly days of yore.

15　Not the least obeisance made he; not a minute stopped or stayed he;

But, with mien of lord or lady, perched above my chamber door,

Perched upon a bust of Pallas just above my chamber door—

Perched and sat, and nothing more.

Then this ebony bird beguiling my sad fancy into smiling,

20　　By the grave and stern decorum of the countenance it wore,

"Though thy crest be shorn and shaven, thou," I said, "art sure no craven;

Ghastly, grim, and ancient raven, wandering from the nightly shore,

Tell me what thy lordly name is on the night's Plutonian shore?"

Quoth the raven, "Nevermore!"

.....

25　　"Prophet!" said I, "thing of evil—prophet still, if bird or devil!

By that heaven that bends above us, by that God we both adore,

Tell this soul with sorrow laden, if within the distant Aidenne,

It shall clasp a sainted maiden, whom the angels name Lenore,

Clasp a fair and radiant maiden, whom the angels name Lenore!"

30　　　　　　　Quoth the raven, "Nevermore!"

.....

And the raven, never flitting, still is sitting, still is sitting

On the pallid bust of Pallas, just above my chamber door;

And his eyes have all the seeming of a demon that is dreaming,

And the lamplight o'er him streaming throws his shadow on the floor;

35　And my soul from out that shadow that lies floating on the floor shall be

lifted—nevermore!

Edgar Allan Poe, "The Raven" *The Best Loved Poems of the American People*, selected by Hazel Felleman, Garden City, New York: Doubleday and Company, copyright, 1936, pp. 209-11.

37.　The setting of the poem as revealed in the first stanza presents

    (1)　the narrator in his study, browsing sleepily over old books.

    (2)　the narrator writing in his diary.

    (3)　the narrator, daydreaming.

    (4)　the narrator, working at his business.

    (5)　the narrator, ill.

38.　In the second stanza, the narrator's thoughts are preoccupied by

    (1)　concern about the stormy weather.

    (2)　involvement in some business venture.

    (3)　mourning over a loved one who has died.

    (4)   he is mulling over ghostly memories.
    (5)   preoccupied with the supernatural.

39.   Imagery of the bird perching above the chamber door suggests

    (1)   pearls and diamonds.
    (2)   feathers arrayed on silk.
    (3)   red emblazoned on gold.
    (4)   ebony on alabaster.
    (5)   marble.

40.   What does the narrator ask the raven in lines 25–29?

    (1)   What do you want?
    (2)   Where do you live?
    (3)   Are you of this world or of a spiritual world?
    (4)   Are you sincere?
    (5)   Is there a maiden by the name Lenore, in Paradise?

41.   The narrator in his setting is presented as

    (1)   a poet deeply involved in his work.
    (2)   an involved reporter.
    (3)   a bereft lover.
    (4)   a businessman at his desk.
    (5)   a student.

42.   In the third paragraph, the raven appears with "mien of lord or lady," which is the same as one who is

    (1)   acting savagely.
    (2)   acting as a person with position or royal birth.
    (3)   acting harshly or "mean."
    (4)   acting haughty or superior.
    (5)   acting in a benevolent manner.

43.   The mood of the poem is

    (1)   happy.   (4)   angry.
    (2)   optimistic.   (5)   morose.
    (3)   indecisive.

44.   Lines 35–36 mean

    (1)   the raven will return no more.
    (2)   the poet's soul will never be free.

(3) there is another life after death.
(4) Lenore will return once more.
(5) the raven will remain forever.

45. What is the poem's theme?

(1) Death is final and hopeless.
(2) Love is fleeting.
(3) There is hope for those who have loved and lost.
(4) Love is fickle.
(5) Loved ones lost are soon replaced.

TEST 5: MATHEMATICS

Tests of General Educational Development

Directions

The Mathematics Test consists of multiple-choice questions intended to measure general mathematics skills and problem-solving ability. The questions are based on short readings which often include a graph, chart, or figure.

You should spend no more than 90 minutes answering the questions in this booklet. Work carefully, but do not spend too much time on any one question. Be sure you answer every question. You will not be penalized for incorrect answers.

Formulas you may need are given on the following page. Only some of the questions will require you to use a formula. Not all the formulas given will be needed.

Some questions contain more information than you will need to solve the problem. Other questions do not give enough information to solve the problem. If the question does not give enough information to solve the problem, the correct answer choice is "Not enough information is given."

The use of calculators is not allowed.

Do not mark in this test booklet. The test administrator will give you blank paper for your calculations. Record your answers on the separate answer sheet provided. Be sure all requested information is properly recorded on the answer sheet.

To record your answers, mark the numbered space on the answer sheet beside the number that corresponds to the question in the test booklet.

FOR EXAMPLE:

If a grocery bill totaling $15.75 is paid with a $20.00 bill, how much change should be returned?

(1)	$5.26	(4)	$3.75
(2)	$4.75	(5)	$3.25
(3)	$4.25		

The correct answer is "$4.25"; therefore, answer space 3 would be marked on the answer sheet.

Do not rest the point of your pencil on the answer sheet while you are considering your answer. Make no stray or unnecessary marks. If you change an answer, erase your first mark completely. Mark only one answer space for each question; multiple answers will be scored as incorrect. Do not fold or crease your answer sheet. Return all test materials to the test administrator.

REFERENCE TABLE

SYMBOLS AND THEIR MEANINGS

=	is equal to	≤	is less than or equal to
≠	is unequal to	≥	is greater than or equal to
<	is less than	‖	is parallel to
>	is greater than	⊥	is perpendicular to

FORMULAS

DESCRIPTION	FORUMLA

AREA (A) of a:

square	$A = s^2$; where s = side
rectangle	$A = lw$; where l = length, w = width
parallelogram	$A = bh$; where b = base, h = height
triangle	$A = \frac{1}{2} bh$; where b = base, h = height
circle	$A = \pi r^2$; where π = 3.14, r = radius

PERIMETER (P) of a:

square	$P = 4s$; where s = side
rectangle	$P = 2l + 2w$; where l = length, w = width
triangle	$P = a + b + c$; where a, b, and c are the sides
circumference (C) of a circle	$C = \pi d$, where π = 3.14, d = diameter

VOLUME (V) of a:

cube	$V = s^2$; where s = side
rectangular container	$V = lwh$; where l = length, w = width, h = height
Pythagorean relationship	$c^2 = a^2 + b^2$; where c = hypotenuse, a and b are legs of a right triangle
distance (d) between two points in a plane	$d = \sqrt{(x_2 - x_1)^2 + (y_2 - y_1)^2}$ where (x_1, y_1) and (x_2, y_2) are two points in a plane
mean	$\text{mean} = \frac{x_1 + x_2 + \ldots + x_n}{n}$; where the x's are the values for which a mean is desired, and n = number of values in the series
median	**median** = the point in an ordered set of numbers at which half of the numbers are above and half of the numbers are below this value
simple interest (i)	$i = prt$; where p = principal, r = rate, t = time
distance (d) as function of rate and time	$d = rt$; where r = rate, t = time
total cost (c)	$c = nr$; where n = number of units, r = *cost per unit*

Directions: Choose the <u>one best answer</u> to each item.

1. What is the name of this figure?

    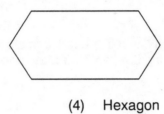

    (1) Rectangle   (4) Hexagon
    (2) Trapezoid   (5) Heptagon
    (3) Pentagon

2. Joan won at tennis 4 out of 6 matches. What percentage did she win?

    (1) 33-1/3%   (4) 60%
    (2) 66-2/3%   (5) 80%
    (3) 40%

3. Solve for the value of x. 4x + 7 = 27

    (1) 27/4   (4) 5
    (2) 17/2   (5) -5
    (3) 4

4. Find the net bank deposit: Deposit $348 in currency, $30.54 in coins, and checks of $553.67 and $30.09. Subtract $150 for cash received.

    (1) $367.54   (4) $812.30
    (2) $932.21   (5) $782.21
    (3) $962.30

5. Classify this triangle.

    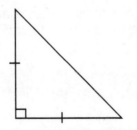

    (1) Scalene   (4) Equilateral
    (2) Ososceles   (5) Acute
    (3) Obtuse

6. 1/4 x + 3 = 15

    (1) 15-1/4   (4) 12
    (2) 12-1/4   (5) 48
    (3) 3

7. Toby runs track. Last week she ran: 8 miles Monday, 3 miles Tuesday,
    9 miles Wednesday, 5 miles Thursday, and 10 miles Friday. Find the
    mean.

    (1) 7 mi.   (4) 5 mi.
    (2) 35 mi.   (5) There is no mean.
    (3) 8 mi.

8. What is the measure of angle Q?

    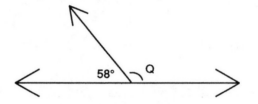

    (1) 58°   (4) 32°
    (2) 100°   (5) 180°
    (3) 122°

9. Evaluate the expression $x^2 + 2x - y + 3$ when x = -2 and y = 3.

    (1) -5   (4) -3
    (2) 3   (5) 5
    (3) 0

10. Joey has seven marbles in his pocket. 2 are red, 4 are blue, and 1 is
    white. What is the probability he will **not** pull out a red marble, if he picks
    one at random?

    (1) 2/7   (4) 3/7
    (2) 1/7   (5) 5/7
    (3) 4/7

11. What is the measure of angle A?

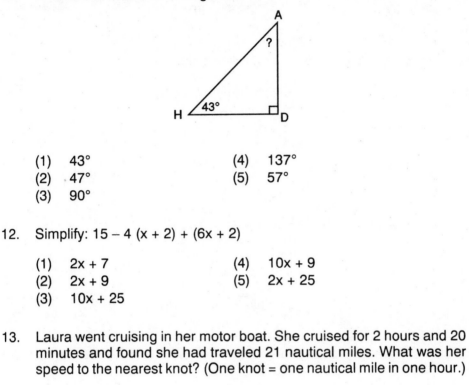

(1) 43°   (4) 137°
(2) 47°   (5) 57°
(3) 90°

12. Simplify: 15 – 4 (x + 2) + (6x + 2)

(1) 2x + 7   (4) 10x + 9
(2) 2x + 9   (5) 2x + 25
(3) 10x + 25

13. Laura went cruising in her motor boat. She cruised for 2 hours and 20 minutes and found she had traveled 21 nautical miles. What was her speed to the nearest knot? (One knot = one nautical mile in one hour.)

(1) 7 knots   (4) 9 knots
(2) 2-1/3 knots   (5) 49 knots
(3) 21 knots

14. Simplify: 38 + (-17) + 91 + (-58)

(1) 204   (4) -58
(2) 58   (5) 54
(3) -54

15. Line a is parallel to line b. Angle BFE measures 80°. What is the measure of angle CGF?

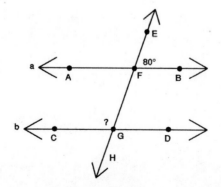

(1) 100°   (4) 120°
(2) 40°   (5) 80°
(3) 180°

<u>Items 16 to 17</u> are based on the following graph.

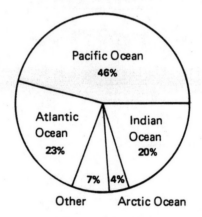

16. The total area of our world's oceans is about 140,000,000 square miles. What is the area of the Pacific Ocean?

(1) 46,000,000 sq. mi.   (4) 86,000,000 sq. mi.
(2) 64,400,000 sq. mi.   (5) 6,440,000 sq. mi.
(3) 94,000,000 sq. mi.

17. The total area of our world is about 200,000,000 square miles. What percent of our world's surface is covered with water?

(1) 7%   (4) 28%
(2) 70%   (5) 60%
(3) 14%

18. Multiply: $(x + 1)(4x + 3)$

(1) $4x^2 + 4$ (4) $4x^2 + 7x + 3$
(2) $4x^2 + 3$ (5) $4x^2 - 7x - 4$
(3) $4x^2 + 4x + 3$

19. How many degrees in angle X?

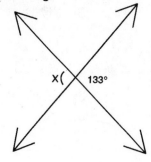

(1) 47°
(2) 360°
(3) 180°

(4) 223°
(5) 133°

20. Pat went shopping with a $100.00 bill. She spent $14.99 for a shirt, $29.95 for a skirt, and $19.90 for shoes. **About** how many dollars did she get in change?

(1) $65
(2) $45
(3) $35

(4) $60
(5) $50

21. Multiply: 10 (-3w + 2)

(1) 30w + 2
(2) -30w + 2
(3) -30w − 2

(4) -30w − 20
(5) -30w + 20

22. **About** how much is 75% of $9.89?

(1) $75.00
(2) $7.50
(3) $5.00

(4) $2.50
(5) $6.00

23. $\overline{AB}$ is perpendicular to $\overline{BC}$. How many degrees is angle ABD?

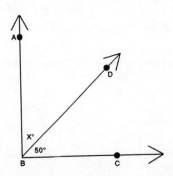

(1) 90°	(4) 40°
(2) 50°	(5) 100°
(3) 45°	

24. Alex's grades in math class were 90, 75, 100, 60, & 75. Find the mean.

(1) 400	(4) 100
(2) 75	(5) 60
(3) 80	

25. What would Sammy's score on the next algebra test have to be to have an average of 95? His grades so far are 93, 100, 92, and 100.

(1) 95	(4) 90
(2) 93	(5) 100
(3) 96	

26. Johnny is 6 feet tall and casts a shadow of 3 feet. At the same time, a tree next to Johnny casts a shadow of 35 feet. How tall is the tree?

(1) 30 ft.	(4) 75 ft.
(2) 60 ft.	(5) 100 ft.
(3) 70 ft.	

27. Laura spent $3.89 for milk, $1.29 for bread, and $4.99 for lunch meat. Lana spent $3.45 for milk, $1.39 for bread, and $5.50 for lunch meat. Who spent more and how much more?

(1) Laura spent 27 cents more.	(4) Lana spent 17 cents more.
(2) Lana spent 27 cents more.	(5) They spent the same amount.
(3) Laura spent 17 cents more.	

28. The sum of an even integer and twice the next consecutive even integer is 40. To find the integers, which equation represents the correct solution?

(1) $x \cdot x = 40$	(4) $x(x + 2) = 40$
(2) $x(x + 1) = 40$	(5) $x + 2(x + 2) = 40$
(3) $x + 2(x + 1) = 40$	

29. Out of a 52-card deck, what is the probability of drawing one of the 4 kings?

(1) 1/12	(4) 52/4
(2) 1/4	(5) 1/13
(3) 4/1	

30. A sports car lease is $621 per month. This is 8% more than the lease for last year's model. How much was the monthly lease last year?

    (1) $670.68
    (2) $571.32
    (3) $613.00
    (4) $575.00
    (5) $579.32

31. In triangle ABC what is the measure of angle B?

    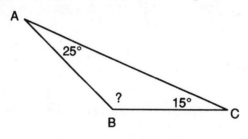

    (1) 140°
    (2) 25°
    (3) 15°
    (4) 40°
    (5) 100°

32. What is the probability of rolling a "two" on a six-sided die?

    (1) 2/6
    (2) 1/3
    (3) 1/6
    (4) 5/6
    (5) 1/2

33. Simplify: $4x^4 \cdot x^6$

    (1) $4x^{10}$
    (2) $4x^{24}$
    (3) $16x^{10}$
    (4) $24x^4$
    (5) x^{22}

34. What is the probability of the spinner stopping on "5"?

    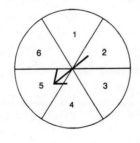

    (1) 1/5
    (2) 1/2
    (3) 1/3
    (4) 1/6
    (5) 5/6

35. Factor completely: $x^4 - 81$

    (1) $(x^2 + 9)(x^2 + 9)$ (4) $(x^2 + 9)(x + 3)(x - 3)$
    (2) $(x^2 + 9)(x^2 - 9)$ (5) $(x^2 - 9)(x^2 - 9)$
    (3) $(x^2 + 9)(x - 3)(x - 3)$

36. The students were having a bake sale at Mountain Elementary School. Maria baked 5-1/2 dozen cookies. Her little brother ate 1/3 of a dozen of them. How many cookies did Maria have left to take to the bake sale?

    (1) 62   (4) 63
    (2) 60   (5) 52
    (3) 66

37. What is the volume, in cubic centimeters, of this cylinder?

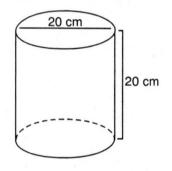

20 cm

20 cm

    (1) 6,280 cu. cm.   (4) 200 cu. cm.
    (2) 25,120 cu. cm.   (5) 628 cu. cm.
    (3) 400 cu. cm.

38. Sam Sanchez got a new compact car. His car can go 100 miles on 3 gallons of gas. He drove 300 miles on a weekend trip. How many gallons of gas did he use?

    (1) 100 gal.   (4) 3 gal.
    (2) 33 gal.   (5) 10 gal.
    (3) 9 gal.

39. Factor: $x^2 - 6x + 9$

    (1) $x(x + 6)$ (4) $(x + 3)^2$
    (2) $(x + 3)(x + 3)$ (5) $(x + 3)(x - 3)$
    (3) $(x - 3)^2$

40. Mary's new car got the following gas mileage during the first five months she had the car: 35.5 mpg, 37 mpg, 34.25 mpg, 40.5 mpg, and 39.25 mpg. What was her average mpg (miles per gallon)?

(1) 46.63 mpg   (4) 37.5 mpg
(2) 37.3 mpg   (5) 40.5 mpg
(3) 37.1 mpg

41. George took his dog for 3 long walks Saturday. First they walked 1 mile, then they walked 720 yards, and for the last walk they walked 3,500 feet. How many feet did they walk?

(1) 4,221 ft.   (4) 11,340 ft.
(2) 9,500 ft.   (5) 10,660 ft.
(3) 3,780 ft.

42. $g(x) = x^2 + 4$, find $g(-3)$.

(1) -3   (4) 3
(2) 4   (5) 13
(3) -5

43. Mary wants to cover a small chest with contact paper. The chest is 24" x 12" x 10". How much contact paper is needed?

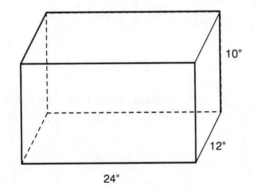

10"

12"

24"

(1) 5 sq. ft.   (4) 1-2/3 sq. ft.
(2) 4 sq. ft.   (5) 720 sq. ft.
(3) 9 sq. ft.

44. Harry bought a sofa priced at $995 and a chair priced at $149. The sales tax is 8%. How much must he pay for the sofa and chair and tax?

(1) $1,144   (4) $1,224.72
(2) $91.52   (5) $1,235.52
(3) $1,134

45. Juan found a portable TV that normally costs $225, but now it is on sale at 30% off. What is the sale price?

    (1) $157.50
    (2) $67.50
    (3) $199.95
    (4) $195.00
    (5) Not enough information is given.

46. Fresh pears are 2 pounds for $0.96. How much would 3 pounds cost?

    (1) $5.76
    (2) $4.80
    (3) $0.48
    (4) $1.44
    (5) $1.50

47. A shirt sold at a 20% discount. The sale price was $36. What was the original price before the sale?

    (1) $43.20
    (2) $45.00
    (3) $56.00
    (4) $39.95
    (5) $49.95

48. Solve: 10^2 times 10^3 =

    (1) 10^6
    (2) 10^{23}
    (3) 10,000
    (4) 100,000
    (5) 10, 000,000

49. Mountain High has 245 sophomores. 60% have brown eyes. What percent of them do **not** have brown eyes?

    (1) 60%
    (2) 40%
    (3) 147%
    (4) 98%
    (5) 50%

50. John was looking for the smallest wrench in his tool box. If he has 5 wrenches, and the sizes are 1/2 inch, 3/8 inch, 7/8 inch, 3/4 inch, and 9/16 inch, then which is smallest?

    (1) 1/2 in.
    (2) 3/8 in.
    (3) 7/8 in.
    (4) 3/4 in.
    (5) 9/16 in.

51. There are 650 seniors at Warm Weather High School. What percentage of the seniors are girls if 351 of the seniors are boys?

    (1) 85.1%
    (2) 2.17%
    (3) 46%
    (4) 54%
    (5) 299%

52. Jerry wanted to buy a new pickup truck. In his home town he found one he liked for $11,558, but the sales tax in his state is 6% on vehicles. He lived near another state with lower sales tax. He found a truck there for $11,599. How much would it cost him to buy it in the next state?

    (1) $12,251.48
    (2) $12,294.94
    (3) $12,178.95
    (4) $12,062.95
    (5) Not enough information is given.

53. The planet Jupiter is said to be about 480 million miles from the sun. How is that distance written in scientific notation?

    (1) 4.8×10^8
    (2) 48×10^8
    (3) 4.8×10^6
    (4) 480×10^2
    (5) 48×10

54. Bowling Balls Unlimited wants to know how much to sell their new shipment of bowling balls for if they bought them for $68.00 each?

    $S = (p \times 1.6) + \$4.00$ Where S = selling price and p = purchase price

    (1) $73.60
    (2) $108.80
    (3) $278.40
    (4) $112.80
    (5) $272.00

55. Shawn bought a 10-foot board. He found it actually measured 9 feet 11 and 5/8 inches. He cut off a piece exactly 5 and 1/2 feet long. How much is left?

    (1) 4-1/2 ft.
    (2) 4 ft. 6 in.
    (3) 4 ft. 5-5/8 in.
    (4) 5 ft. 5-5/8 in.
    (5) 4 ft. 6-5/8 in.

56. Robert is doing a population study and needs to find 36.59% of 11,356. He should multiply 11,356 by

    (1) 36.59
    (2) 3.659
    (3) .3659
    (4) .03659
    (5) 365.9

TEST I

ANSWER KEY

Test 1—Writing Skills

1.	(2)	15.	(5)	29.	(3)	43.	(3)
2.	(3)	16.	(2)	30.	(3)	44.	(2)
3.	(4)	17.	(1)	31.	(3)	45.	(1)
4.	(4)	18.	(1)	32.	(3)	46.	(4)
5.	(1)	19.	(3)	33.	(2)	47.	(1)
6.	(2)	20.	(1)	34.	(2)	48.	(5)
7.	(4)	21.	(3)	35.	(4)	49.	(2)
8.	(3)	22.	(5)	36.	(1)	50.	(4)
9.	(4)	23.	(4)	37.	(4)	51.	(3)
10.	(1)	24.	(2)	38.	(2)	52.	(3)
11.	(1)	25.	(4)	39.	(2)	53.	(4)
12.	(5)	26.	(2)	40.	(5)	54.	(3)
13.	(1)	27.	(2)	41.	(3)	55.	(2)
14.	(1)	28.	(5)	42.	(1)		

Test 2—Social Studies

1.	(5)	17.	(2)	33.	(3)	49.	(4)
2.	(3)	18.	(1)	34.	(4)	50.	(3)
3.	(3)	19.	(3)	35.	(3)	51.	(1)
4.	(3)	20.	(5)	36.	(1)	52.	(5)
5.	(2)	21.	(2)	37.	(3)	53.	(4)
6.	(2)	22.	(1)	38.	(5)	54.	(3)
7.	(1)	23.	(4)	39.	(4)	55.	(2)
8.	(5)	24.	(3)	40.	(2)	56.	(5)
9.	(3)	25.	(3)	41.	(4)	57.	(3)
10.	(5)	26.	(3)	42.	(5)	58.	(4)
11.	(5)	27.	(1)	43.	(1)	59.	(1)
12.	(4)	28.	(5)	44.	(3)	60.	(2)
13.	(1)	29.	(4)	45.	(1)	61.	(5)
14.	(4)	30.	(3)	46.	(3)	62.	(3)
15.	(1)	31.	(1)	47.	(3)	63.	(1)
16.	(3)	32.	(1)	48.	(4)	64.	(1)

Test 3—Science

1.	(3)	18.	(4)	35.	(4)	52.	(4)
2.	(5)	19.	(2)	36.	(2)	53.	(1)
3.	(3)	20.	(5)	37.	(3)	54.	(3)
4.	(4)	21.	(2)	38.	(3)	55.	(2)
5.	(3)	22.	(4)	39.	(2)	56.	(2)
6.	(1)	23.	(4)	40.	(1)	57.	(5)
7.	(2)	24.	(5)	41.	(1)	58.	(4)
8.	(1)	25.	(1)	42.	(3)	59.	(2)
9.	(2)	26.	(5)	43.	(1)	60.	(3)
10.	(2)	27.	(4)	44.	(5)	61.	(4)
11.	(1)	28.	(1)	45.	(5)	62.	(2)
12.	(1)	29.	(5)	46.	(4)	63.	(3)
13.	(3)	30.	(5)	47.	(1)	64.	(1)
14.	(1)	31.	(4)	48.	(3)	65.	(5)
15.	(2)	32.	(5)	49.	(2)	66.	(1)
16.	(4)	33.	(2)	50.	(5)		
17.	(2)	34.	(3)	51.	(3)		

Test 4—Literature and the Arts

1.	(1)	13.	(2)	25.	(3)	37.	(1)
2.	(2)	14.	(1)	26.	(1)	38.	(3)
3.	(2)	15.	(2)	27.	(3)	39.	(4)
4.	(1)	16.	(2)	28.	(1)	40.	(5)
5.	(3)	17.	(4)	29.	(3)	41.	(3)
6.	(1)	18.	(1)	30.	(3)	42.	(2)
7.	(2)	19.	(2)	31.	(3)	43.	(5)
8.	(2)	20.	(1)	32.	(3)	44.	(2)
9.	(2)	21.	(1)	33.	(1)	45.	(1)
10.	(2)	22.	(2)	34.	(2)		
11.	(3)	23.	(1)	35.	(3)		
12.	(3)	24.	(5)	36.	(3)		

Test 5—Math

1.	(4)	15.	(1)	29.	(5)	43.	(3)
2.	(2)	16.	(2)	30.	(4)	44.	(5)
3.	(4)	17.	(2)	31.	(1)	45.	(1)
4.	(4)	18.	(4)	32.	(3)	46.	(4)
5.	(2)	19.	(5)	33.	(1)	47.	(2)
6.	(5)	20.	(3)	34.	(4)	48.	(4)
7.	(1)	21.	(5)	35.	(4)	49.	(2)
8.	(3)	22.	(2)	36.	(1)	50.	(2)
9.	(3)	23.	(4)	37.	(1)	51.	(3)
10.	(5)	24.	(3)	38.	(3)	52.	(5)
11.	(2)	25.	(4)	39.	(3)	53.	(1)
12.	(2)	26.	(3)	40.	(2)	54.	(4)
13.	(4)	27.	(4)	41.	(4)	55.	(3)
14.	(5)	28.	(5)	42.	(5)	56.	(3)

DETAILED EXPLANATIONS OF ANSWERS

TEST 1: WRITING SKILLS, PART I

1. **(2) Sentence 1** With the use of the word "but" in a sentence, the comma always goes before it. The word choices in the sentence are good, and the punctuation is correct as it is.

2. **(3) Sentence 2** A comma is needed after "for instance" for clarity. The reader needs to be clear, and "for instance" is an introductory phrase in this sentence. Spelling is correct, and no other punctuation is needed.

3. **(4) Sentence 3** Because "milk" is combined with "cookies" by "and," a comma after "wounds" makes the sentence clearer and easier to read. "Bandage" is the correct word choice here, and a comma after "bandage" would break the sentence up in a confusing manner.

4. **(4) Sentence 4** While a sentence started with "but" is usually not a strong sentence, **But** is the best answer choice in this sentence. **Whatever** and **secure** are correctly spelled words. A comma after **whatever** would break up the sentence incorrectly.

5. **(1) Sentence 5** The general rule is "I before E, except after C." **Receive** is the correct spelling. **Support** is spelled correctly also. No added commas are necessary or needed.

6. **(2) Sentence 2** **Fads** means favorite new activities. **Soccer** is spelled correctly, and no commas are necessary.

7. **(4) Sentence 3** A comma before and after "however" makes the sentence clearer and easier to understand. The spelling is all correct.

8. **(3) Sentence 4** The correct spelling is **surgery**. **Injury** is spelled correctly. No commas are necessary.

9. **(4) Sentence 5** **Sever** means "to cut." **Severe** means "serious, critical." The "ly" is added to **severe** because it is an adverb modifying the verb "twisted." **During** is spelled correctly, and no commas are needed in this sentence.

10. **(1) Sentence 6** Because this is a compound sentence, a comma is

needed to separate the two parts of the sentence. **Cartilage** and **tendons** are spelled correctly.

11. **(1) Sentence 9**   The main sentence is **He has suffered from this inactivity**. **Both mentally and physically** tell how he has suffered and are set off from the main sentence by commas. All spelling is correct.

12. **(5) Sentence 11**   No commas are needed anywhere.

13. **(1) Sentence 13**   **In fact** is an introductory phrase and must be followed by a comma for clarity. No other commas are needed.

14. **(1) Sentence 1**   **Peculiar** is the correct spelling. No commas are needed.

15. **(5) Sentence 2**   **Let's** means "let us," and would be incorrect. The sentence needs no commas.

16. **(2) Sentences 2 and 3**   **Making strange noises, and saying off-the-wall comments** is a fragment, not a sentence. It must be combined with the preceding sentence for it to be correct.

17. **(1) Sentence 4**   **Pleasure** is the correct spelling. **Untasteful** is not a word. No commas are needed in this sentence.

18. **(1) Sentence 6**   Day is modified by every, every is a separate word and an adjective here. Warped is spelled correctly. No commas are necessary.

19. **(3) Sentence 7**   The main sentence is: **He finds a trick to pull**. The first part is then an introduction and must be set off from the main sentence by a comma.

20. **(1) Sentence 9**   **Each day** is an introductory phrase and must be set off from the main sentence by a comma.

21. **(3) Sentence 1**   **Today's** is the possessive form, meaning "the society of today." This is the correct answer in this sentence. Spelling and punctuation are all correct.

22. **(2) Sentence 7**   **Arithmetic** is the correct spelling. No commas are needed.

23. **(4) Sentence 8**   **Accept** means to take in, allow to happen. "Except" means everything but that. All other spelling and punctuation is correct.

24. **(2) Sentence 12**   "Of" is incorrect; it is not a verb. The choice must be **should have**. Spelling and punctuation are correct.

25. **(4) Sentence 14** Spellings are correct. When confused on what pronoun to use to refer to yourself, drop the other part of that phrase. You would not say, "Me want to live." Also, remember to list others before yourself.

26. **(2) Sentence 15** **With good reading and math skills** is the introductory statement and must be set off by a comma.

27. **(2) Sentence 16** **It's** means "it is," and is the correct choice for this sentence. Work market is correct. No commas are necessary.

28. **(2) Sentence 1** The indefinite article **an** should be used with **extreme**.

29. **(3) Sentence 2** **Every weekend** modifies and introduces the sentence. It must be separated from the main sentence by a comma. Other spelling and punctuation are correct.

30. **(3) Sentence 3** **There**, meaning in that place, is the correct answer in this sentence. **They're** means they are, and would be incorrect here. No commas are necessary in this sentence.

31. **(3) Sentence 4** The correct spelling is **heroes**. **Ball players** is correctly spelled as two words. **High School** is not capitalized unless following a proper noun. No commas are necessary.

32. **(3) Sentence 6** Place a comma after **year**. This is a compound sentence, and the comma gives clarity to the sentence.

33. **(2) Sentence 7** **Going** to is the correct answer choice. **Gonna** is not a word, and not standard English. **It is** would have to be replaced by **It's**. No commas are needed.

34. **(2) Sentence 9** **Tackles** is the correct spelling. **Brake** means to stop. No commas are needed.

35. **(4) Sentence 1** The past of "spring" is "sprung"; **sprang** is an optional use of the past tense. **America's** is obviously possessive, and there are no spelling or capitalization errors.

36. **(1) Sentence 2** Without the comma after **this**, its role would be changed from that of demonstrative pronoun to demonstrative adjective modifying **people**. Because this makes no syntactic sense, there is likewise no comma placed after **people**. People is the subject, which agrees with **were**. Changing to associates makes no syntactic sense.

37. **(4) Sentence 3** **Piece** means a portion of, not an opposite to war. There are no other spelling or structural errors.

38. **(2) Sentence 4**   When used in this way, **however** must be surrounded by commas. There is no reason to omit **excluding World War II**, as this hardly constitutes Sentence 4 as a run-on sentence.

39. **(2) Sentence 5**   All the sentences listed are fragments except (2), because (2) is the only one that contains a main verb (which agrees with the subject **reason**, which (4)'s **were** does not.

40. **(5) Sentence 6**   There are no errors in this sentence. When used in this context, **moreover** is always a single word.

41. **(3) Sentence 7**   This run-on sentence would best be broken up into two sentences. **As** is not suitable, for it introduces a subordinate clause which would accompany no main clause.

42. **(1) Sentence 1**   "Decade" is misspelled, not **Dragons**. **Sees** is not suitable because it does not coincide with the adjective **past**, which implies a past verb.

43. **(3) Sentence 2**   Verbs in a series must be of the same tense and form. There are no spelling or structural errors.

44. **(2) Sentence 3**   **Invited** in this use calls for an infinitive verb. **Inviting** is not suitable with the auxiliary have. **Been invited** would only have been usable if **denounce** was in the infinitive.

45. **(1) Sentence 4**   **Creater** is misspelled; it is one of the misleading "or" ending nouns. **Disagreeing** would only fit with an auxiliary verb (e.g. "was disagreeing").

46. **(4) Sentence 5**   **Everyday** is one word when used as an adjective. **That** introduces an indirect statement that does not require quotation marks. There are no other spelling errors.

47. **(1) Sentence 8**   Two or more syllable words ending in "x" or "s" do not receive an extra "s" after the possessive apostrophe. Only if there is one syllable in the word is this extra "s" tagged to the end of the word. **His** before **makers** would refer to the makers of Gary Gygax, not his game.

48. **(5) Sentence 9**   There are no corrections necessary. **Unallowing** is not a word.

49. **(2) Sentence 1**   **Critic** does not end in a "k."

50. **(4) Sentences 2 and 3**   Sentence 3 is a fragment, and incorporating it to Sentence 2 excuses its verbal deficiency without forming a run-on sentence from the two single-clause sentences.

51. **(3) Sentence 4**   **Wars** and **visits** both agree in number with the word, **movies**, which they elaborate, but **pet** stands out in its singular number. The other selections all retained this flaw in number agreement.

52. **(3) Sentence 5**   **Stem** does not agree with the subject, **cause**, but this is difficult to spot due to the structural intervention of the plural noun **genres** and the plural noun **critics** (which is spelled correctly). **Say** agrees with **critics**; **says** would agree with a singular noun.

53. **(4) Sentence 6**   The comma before *Critters* and *Ghoulies* denotes that the two proper nouns are in apposition, but in apposition to no other noun, which is not possible. Therefore, the comma is structurally wrong. No comma is required after **slew of movies** because this would create an unnatural break which would separate **movies** from **involving**, whose clause modifies **movies**.

54. **(3) Sentence 7**   Using **recurring** and **appear more than once** is redundant; therefore, one of them must be omitted. **However** in this context must retain its commas.

55. **(2) Sentence 8**   **Constantlly** is spelled incorrectly. The other choices are syntactically harmful to the sentence's structure.

TEST 1: WRITING SKILLS, PART II

Sample Essay — Possible Score of 6 or 5

Crime rates are rising alarmingly. Newspapers and television newscasts report frightening situations in all of our major cities. Young people form gangs, doing illegal activities and atrocities that were unheard of only a few years ago.

HIV and AIDS are common terms, when we had never heard of this national health threat twenty years ago. Many diseases were growing out of control, and overtaking the health of our country.

War in the Middle East is not something that we wanted to become involved in, yet our young American troops were in that area, in great numbers. Were we defending oil fields or were we taking a stand against world aggression? Was this all to the greater benefit of the greater number of people, or were we jeopardizing the credibility of the United States in the eyes of the world?

Could we afford to take such a step? Not only was the cost in human lives great, but the cost in money was great. Our nation was already running "in the red." Preparing a defense in the Middle East was certainly going to increase the deficit in America's finances.

Is involvement in the Middle East going to enhance our image in the eyes of the world or is it only going to further tarnish us? Who can answer these questions? Not I.

Why this essay scores a 6 or 5

This essay is thoughtfully organized and is well structured. The topic states that the U.S. is faced with crime, health problems, a possibility of war, financial problems, and a lessening of world respect. The essayist uses this as an outline for his essay by writing on each point in order in which it is presented.

The essayist's thoughts flow together nicely which makes the essay easy to read. There are, also, no obvious errors in use of standard written English. In addition, adequate support for the main idea has been presented, and is drawn upon and tied together in the conclusion.

Sample Essay — Possible Score of 4 or 3

The United States of America is the greatest country in the world, today or at any other time in history. We have more to offer, more freedoms, more goods, more opportunities than any other country in the world has, ever.

When people criticize us, they make me angry. When our own citizens do not stand for "The Pledge of Allegiance" and "The Star Spangled Banner," I am furious. These people should have to spend time as "guests" in Iraq. That might clarify for them what is great in this country.

Few countries allow people the freedom to publically state their beliefs, if these are against State doctrine. Few countries have so many opportunities available to the general populace.

Granted, we have homeless who would argue about opportunities. This is a fact which must be faced. But, the homeless situation is not one which is strictly to be found in America. Homeless are found in all parts of the world. Maybe, the public cry over the plight of the homeless in America is yet another example of how free we are in our rights to criticize, as well as to praise what is America.

For the most part, praise is what America deserves.

Why this essay scores a 4 or 3

This essay is not well organized. It attacks the essay topic in a rather roundabout manner. Support presented in this essay is only partially related to the topic of the problems this country faces, and basically only deals with a lessening of respect for our country, although the essay topic deals with "a lessening of world respect."

Support for the main idea is very weak and is made worse by the use of poor sentence structure and the misspelling of words, such as "publicly" in the third sentence which is spelled "publically." To say that the conclusion of this essay is not well developed would be an understatement—it is not developed at all. One sentence is presented which does not tie together any of the points in the essay.

Sample Essay — Possible Score of 2 or 1

Can you imagine a wall going across this country? In reality, there seems to be an imaginary wall running from east to west, across America's mid-section.

This wall separates north from south, "Yankee" from "Southerner," "yes" from "Yes ma'am." Why is it that people in Boston think a Texan is being "smart" when he uses what he has been raised to know as good manners? Why is it that North Carolinians think a New Yorker is being rude when he says "Sure" instead of "Yes, sir" to a question?

Do Americans speak different languages? Absolutely. In our family clans, our ethnic groups, we speak languages which we do not share with strangers. This does not make us weaker; it makes us stronger. We accept other Americans outside of our own smaller cultures. This, in turn, makes us a more tolerant and kinder nation. This may be the greatest strength we have.

The United States of America is faced with problems only because this country continually tries to improve itself, to grow, and to be a better nation. The rest of this planet should know this and know that we are a caring, intelligent, learning, teaching community of the world.

Why this essay scores a 2 or 1

This essay has one main problem—it does not address the topic. The only mention of the problems faced by the U.S. appears in the last paragraph and this point is not developed. Even if this point was developed, it would appear too late in the essay to mean anything.

In addition, there is no organization of ideas. Apparently, not a great deal of planning was put into this essay. As it stands, the essay is wordy and has no purpose whatsoever.

TEST 2: SOCIAL STUDIES

1. **(5)** is most correct. The German government is being warned that a "grave situation…has resulted…" from the loss of American lives. (1) There is no statement declaring war by the U.S. (2) No mention of payments or compensation is made. (3) The U.S. is claiming to be neutral in the conflict. (4) It is stated that American ships have already been attacked.

2. **(3)** World War I began in Europe in 1915, and incidents like the *Lusitania's* sinking helped bring the U.S. into the war in 1917.

3. **(3)** is most correct. Although the Germans do introduce poison gas in the trench warfare in France, this is not discussed in the letter. All the other tactics are discussed in the letter.

4. **(3)** is the opposite of the letter's intent, which is to insist on the right of the U.S. to trade anywhere. The other points are stated in the letter, (1) and (2) being disagreed with.

5. **(2)** is correct. Woodrow Wilson finally had to ask for a declaration of war because of increasing German attacks on Atlantic shipping.

6. **(2)** is most correct. There is a sampling of both government types and nations with those types. A sampling means it is not an all-inclusive list. (1) is partially correct, but not all government forms are included. Others include despotic, military, and colonial rule. (3) refers to economic, not political, systems, and would not be a good title. (4) and (5) describe living standards, and the first column contains a mix of these.

7. **(1)** is correct, because a representative form of government is where elected officials represent the people in a legislature. (2) The legislative body may take other names, such as the U.S. Congress. (3) Most ex-British colonies have parliaments, but not all. (4) All governments have leaders, most parliamentary forms have elected ones. (5) Most modern governments have a written constitution like the U.S., but the oldest parliamentary government, Britain, has no written constitution.

8. **(5)** is correct, all are African states. (1) all are ex-colonies of various European powers, not just Britain. (2) most have some form of military rule, with or without kings. (3) and (4) Algeria is Arab and on the Mediterranean, the others are in sub-Saharan Africa.

9. **(3)** is the most correct pattern, usually the legislature has become a rubber-stamp for a strong leader. For answers (1), (4), and (5), length of term or limits may exist, but these do not deal with the power of the parliament, which is what "restricted" refers to.

10. **(5)** is correct, a republic is a government of elected representatives that debates issues, which implies several factions or parties. The other choices are all versions of one-person or single-action rule.

11. **(5)** is correct. (1) is not correct, because there are some variances between nations high in GNP while not so high in trade. (2) is incorrect because there is no data comparing previous years. (3) is incorrect. Thailand, the Philippines, and Indonesia did not exceed the world average in trade. (4) is incorrect; Japan was not the leader in trade.

12. **(4)** is not true, the trade graph is a line graph, and the GNP is a bar graph. All the others are true. (1) per capita means per person.

13. **(1)** is most accurate; all are on the eastern edge of Asia. (2) is incorrect because all of Asia is not represented, for example, India or the Persian Gulf. (3) is wrong; North West Asia would be either the Persian Gulf area or Asian USSR. (4) is incorrect; Malaysia and Thailand are as close to the Indian Ocean as to the Pacific. (5) is wrong; only Australia, Hong Kong, Malaysia, New Zealand, and Singapore were ever British colonies. Japan and Thailand were never colonized by foreigners.

14. **(4)** Singapore shows the greatest growth rate because its per capita trade is not only highest, but exceeds its GNP, which means its people are producing exportable products which bring money back into the nation. Hong Kong is second.

15. **(1)** GNP is the gross national product and is defined as the total goods and services produced by the nation in a given year. (2) is only partially correct because services are not specified. The others are not correct.

16. **(3)** is correct, the key fact being the proximity to China.

17. **(2)** is most correct, with the key data being on the importance of trade. (1) is not correct because of the statistic on scarcity of agricultural area. (3), (4), and (5) have no supporting data from which a conclusion may be drawn.

18. **(1)** is correct. Density means the number of people per set area. The high population and small area would indicate high density. (3) and (4) have no data to come to a conclusion about how the population is scattered or distributed. (5) The data indicating little farming area and high manufacturing and trade would indicate an urban population.

19. **(3)** is most correct, again with data to support good manufacturing and trade, which must be efficient to compete on the world market as well as they do. The statistics show a 16% increase, which is very high.

20. **(5)** is most correct, with the export and import figures exactly tied. (3) and (4) have no supporting data.

21. **(2)** is most appropriate because the categories describe experiences. (1) is not right because trends indicate a comparison over different time periods. (3) is not correct because the graph does not offer reasons, although conclusions could be drawn using the data. (4) Several of the categories examine this but others, like teacher and parent discipline, do not necessarily. (5) This issue is not directly addressed by the graph.

22. **(1)** is the only category in which women exceeded men in the use of force. (2), (3), and (4) are areas where men practiced violence more. (5) was an area where women exceeded men, but discipline does not always mean the use of violence.

23. **(4)** is correct with only a one percent difference. All the others had a greater difference.

24. **(3)** There is no data comparing past and present parents. (1) In either using or approving the use of violence men led in every category except one (having spanked a child). (2) As children, over sixty percent of both men and women received at least an occasional spanking. (4) This is true if you compare the last two categories. (5) This can be concluded by the fact that a majority of people have used spanking as a discipline technique.

25. **(3)** is most correct because it covers both group (sociology) and individual (psychology) instances. (1) and (2) are too exclusive, since there are instances of both causing violent behavior. (4) and (5) is partially a rewording of (1) and (2), since environment is influenced by interaction with others, and genetics refers to built-in psychological factors.

26. **(3)** is correct. Section 4 describes the officers, with chairperson listed first and with the most power. None of the other choices are mentioned.

27. **(1)** is correct, as the rules refer to the "Party" several times. (2), (3), and (4) are not correct, although political parties obviously exist to control these governments. (5) is not mentioned anywhere.

28. **(5)** is correct, all are mentioned specifically in section 2 as eligible to vote.

29. **(4)** is correct, as mentioned in section 5.

30. **(3)** is correct, as mentioned in section 4a. Other groups, like the Executive Board, meet more frequently.

31. **(1)** is correct, Britain is the only top importing nation that does not appear among the top five exporters.

32. **(1)** is correct. Canada is the largest importer. Even the two European nations, Britain and Germany, combined to import less.

33. **(3)** is correct. Japan was the largest single exporter, and combining with Taiwan made it even larger. No other region had two exporters listed.

34. **(4)** is correct, with the difference between exports and imports being the greatest in Japan's favor. The others are relatively close, with no comparisons available for Britain.

35. **(3)** is correct. If your nation sells more exports than it buys imports, it creates a surplus of capital coming in or a profit. (1) and (2) refer to the payments made for many things, including trade. So they may reflect on trade balances, but are not the same. (4) is the opposite. In the graph, the U.S.'s imports from Japan reflect a balance of trade unfavorable for the U.S. and favorable for Japan. (5) This can result from unfavorable trade balances, but reflects many other spending and revenue factors.

36. **(1)** Although the other choices are referred to, the focus of the article is on the health problems of children caused by their labor working conditions. (2) is too broad a title because other safety problems, such as machinery design and adult safety, are not addressed. (3) is incorrect because parents are accused of allowing their children to work, but not singled out for blame or abuse. (4) is too general, as only work-related problems are cited. (5) is incorrect because the length of the work day is cited, but it is not the main focus, and different hours for different ages are recommended.

37. **(3)** This is a logical problem with child labor, but is not studied in this report. (1) is incorrect, because the main focus of the report is excessive work hours in combination with (2). (4) and (5) are given as examples of child labor abuses in working too many hours.

38. **(5)** The early years of mass-production and the factory system saw many abuses of laborers until attitudes and laws balanced the needs of owners and workers. (1) is a political era rather than economic. (2) is incorrect because capitalism existed before the Industrial Revolution, although its free market theories were used to justify poor working conditions. (3) is wrong because Karl Marx observed the abuses of capitalism and envisioned communism as a solution with workers in control. (4) is incorrect because fascism was a 20th Century political/economic dictatorship, but did not advocate these conditions.

39. **(4)** is a management tactic which identified and banned workers who advocated factory reforms. (1) is incorrect because unions became the major force to pressure for reform. (2) is wrong because, eventually, governments had to respond to the record of abuses and the political pressures. Political protests, (3), is incorrect. This was one tactic used by unions and other reformers to pressure legislation and elect favorable representatives. (5) is wrong because organized protests often involved trying to ruin the sales of products created by abusive manufacturers.

40. **(2)** is correct. The statement is that the "U.S. has made a decision— defend at all costs." (1) is incorrect; all the statements point to an ongoing war, with no end in sight. (3) is incorrect because there is no statement to support this. (4) is incorrect because all the discussions revolve around U.S., not UN involvement. (5) is incorrect; although this had already happened in the past, there is nothing to indicate when.

41. **(4)** is correct, as the second paragraph discusses his anti-communist feelings. The U.S. support for his government is clear in the last paragraph. (1) is not a correct choice, because Laos is cited as part of the communist supply line. Viet Cong, (2), is wrong because they were the South Vietnamese branch of the Communist party. (3) is incorrect; he was the legendary leader of Vietnamese communists, who opposed the U.S.. (5) is wrong because this would include North Viet Nam and Laos, areas already communist.

42. **(5)** is correct. As expressed in the last paragraph, the failure of the U.S. to stop communism in South Viet Nam was seen as the first domino that would result in the entire region being taken over. (1) is incorrect because this was the post-World War II policy to help nations resist communist aggression anywhere. (2) is not a good choice, because SEATO was the specific alliance formed by the U.S. in the region (South East Asia Treaty Organization) to implement the Truman Doctrine. (3) is incorrect; this was the postwar economic recovery plan for Europe. The Red Scare, (4), is incorrect; several waves of fear of communism created irrational actions in the U.S., such as McCarthyism in the 1950's.

43. **(1)** is correct. The "dominoes" stopped after North and South Viet Nam, Laos, and Cambodia had fallen.

44. **(3)** is correct. Kennedy had to deal with the first escalation of the conflict to the South by increasing military advisors and warning that this must be fought by the Vietnamese, not the Americans. (1) is a poor choice. Truman's administration saw the first communist rebellion against French colonial rule in Viet Nam. (2) is incorrect because Eisenhower saw the French withdraw from the area and sent in the first advisors to South Viet Nam. (4) is incorrect, because Johnson saw the war get beyond local control and began the mass escalation of American military. (5) is wrong, because Nixon inherited a large war, expanded, and then reduced it.

45. **(1)** This is the only one that fits specifically. (2) is a poor choice, because the problems come from industry, and the title is too general. There are other national problems besides pollution, so (3) is wrong. (4) Several of the nations listed have small pollution problems in these areas. (5) is wrong because only the U.S. and France are geographically "western" nations.

46. **(3)** is most accurate, with one pollution problem from each area represented. (1) and (2) have no data to say whether either all or the major ones are all represented. The variety of problems, from small to severe,

suggests they are not similar to all nations, so (4) is incorrect. (5) is wrong because the category of fertilizers is an agricultural problem.

47. **(3)** is most correct, with four continents and all hemispheres represented. (1) is incorrect. The Soviet Union is not among the wealthiest nations economically. (2) is incorrect. The USSR's problems were created under communism. (4) is incorrect. Only the U.S. is in the Western Hemisphere. (5) is incorrect. The U.S. and USSR are the only major oil-producing nations from the list.

48. **(4)** is correct, with small classification in all areas.

49. **(4)** is the opposite of what is predicted, with air pollution destroying the rain forests. All the others are predicted results.

50. **(3)** is correct because the event was obviously a stock market crash, with no outside event cited as a cause. Historical references, such as ticker tape and Anaconda, help pinpoint the era. (1) is incorrect, because modern references, such as telephone, eliminate this era. (2) is incorrect. This will be a partial result of the crash, but no references to it are made. Pearl Harbor Day (4) is also incorrect. No reference to this is made, plus historically the attack occurred on a weekend when the market is closed. (5) is incorrect because there is no reference to point to this event, which occurred in the afternoon while the crash began in the morning.

51. **(1)** The quote says that once the tape lost track no one knew what was happening. This lack of information would increase the panic. (2) and (3) are cited as being the opposite, with a sound economy waiting for a stock market rally. (4) is incorrect, because three major issues, steel, telephone, and anaconda (copper) were listed. (5) is incorrect. This is the opposite of what happened, there were "no buying orders...."

52. **(5)** is most correct as cited, with sell orders coming in from all over the country, with no buy orders to meet them. (1) is wrong. The passage states that there was so much activity that the ticker tape was overwhelmed. (2) is incorrect. The quote says that the market opened "steady." (3) is incorrect. The opening sentence discusses the general falling market recently. (4) is incorrect. There is no evidence of this in the quote.

53. **(4)** is correct, even though he had been in office for less than a year, and the economic conditions were already in place. (1), (2), and (3) were the three presidents before Hoover, and (5) was elected after Hoover to try to solve the depression that followed.

54. **(3)** is most correct. FDIC or federal bank account insurance was part of the New Deal to restore confidence in banks, not stocks. (1) is incorrect; the Securities and Exchange Commission was created to regulate the stock market after the crash. Among its reforms were (2), which reduced the percentage of stock that could be bought on credit (margin), tighter checks on the economic soundness of businesses issuing stocks (4), and checks on

how people inside a company can buy and sell their own stocks (5).

55. **(2)** is correct. If you apply the equation, the goal is to have someone use various power techniques to change someone else's behavior. (1) is incorrect. Socialization, or getting along with others, is not mentioned. (3) is incorrect. This is the opposite of the formula. (4) and (5) are not stated goals, although they may be techniques.

56. **(5)** is most correct, with information being one of the social powers listed that can change behavior. The others may occur but are not the prime example.

57. **(3)** The parent has a legal authority over a minor child. The others are examples of arguments that a parent can use to persuade, but the phrase "had to obey" implies power of authority.

58. **(4)** is most correct. It is the "carrot and stick" approach of either positive or negative consequences for a behavior.

59. **(1)** Modeling behavior influences because people like to copy those they admire, and, even though the connection may not be rational (a famous person liking a soft drink), it is human nature to favor that behavior.

60. **(2)** Apprehension includes the most categories in the diagram above. Not all the conditions lead to crisis (1), or stress (4). Reaction (3) and action (5) are physical behaviors that may or may not be related to anxiety.

61. **(5)** is correct. Almost any condition, good or bad, can create anxiety, depending on how an individual reacts to it.

62. **(3)** is most correct. Young people often feel that death is removed from them by age and that somehow their risk-taking will not be harmful because death is something that happens to others, not them or their friends. Problem-solving (1) is too practical an approach and would not create a feeling of invincibility. Rationalizing, (2), could be part of a denial process because it means to justify an action, so it is incorrect. (4) is incorrect because this means adjusting to a situation, which would not fit. (5) is incorrect because this would not lead to feelings of invincibility, or "it can't happen to me".

63. **(1)** is most correct. If a person's security needs or demands change, doing something to solve the problem is adapting to the changes. (2) Buying an alarm by itself is not a sign of lower self-esteem, but being robbed could lead to lower self-esteem. (3) Not protecting yourself would be denial, so the alarm is the opposite. (4) If there is a real danger, it is not rationalization; an imagined one could be, but there is no evidence of this.

64. **(1)** The two examples, denial and rationalization, either refuse to accept the problem or make an excuse for it. Neither solve it. (2), (4), and (5) do not match the examples. (3) is the opposite of the examples.

TEST 3: SCIENCE

1.   **(3)**   Skin covering the eyeballs is generally the thinnest skin on the body. The soles of the feet (1), the palms of the hand (2), and the heel (5) are often involved in laborious activities, and the skin is thick in these areas. The back (4) also has thick skin. Thus, (3) is the correct answer.

2.   **(5)**   The epidermis is made of two layers: the layer of Malpighi and the stratum corneum. The stratum corneum is the outer layer, and the layer of Malpighi is directly under it. Under these two layers of the epidermis is the dermis. Answer choices (1) through (4) do not have these layers arranged in the correct order. (1) and (2) are wrong because the two layers mentioned are both part of the epidermis. (3) is wrong because this is the order from the inside out. (4) is wrong because the dermis is not on the outside.

3.   **(3)**   The body regulates water and heat through perspiration. Transpiration describes a process not involving humans. Thus, (2) is not correct. Respiration (1) is breathing in humans and will cause some water loss. However, the question asks for how the body regulates substances through the skin. (4), sensation, is the ability to process or perceive. The skin does have nerve endings that can sense, but this does not involve temperature or water regulation. Coagulation (5) is a term referring to a change from a liquid to a thickened mass. This term does not relate to the question.

4.   **(4)**   The nerve endings, blood vessels, and sweat glands are found in the dermis. They are not in the layer of Malpighi, since this layer's main function is to grow to replace the stratum corneum that quickly wears away. Thus, (1) is wrong. It would not be beneficial to have these important structures in a layer that wears away; thus, they are not found in the stratum corneum. (2) must be wrong. Since the layer of Malpighi and the stratum corneum are the two layers of the epidermis, (3) must be wrong. Since it is known that nerve endings and sweat glands are in skin, they could not be contained in the muscle tissue, or (5). (4) must be correct.

5.   **(3)**   The property of an object which determines the object's resistance to motion is its mass. A large watermelon (3) has a far greater mass than the pellet of lead shot, golf ball, feather, or notepaper. The mass of an object never changes. It is equal to an object's weight divided by the acceleration due to gravity "g" at its current position in space.

6.   **(1)**   The sleeping astronauts would continue their motion in a straight line if the Shuttle suddenly changed velocity due to the firing of its thrusters. If the Shuttle slowed down, the astronauts would move forward relative to the walls. This is all due to the fact that the astronauts have mass, or inertia. Gravity is so weak that it is negligible on the astronauts. They can be

monitored by battery driven devices which allow them to move around, and they can certainly sleep without being strapped. Bodies do not need a reaction force to sleep.

7. **(2)** Inertia is measured by mass, m, which is choice (2). Choices (1) and (5) do contain mass but also involve other complicating factors like the speed of light, c, which invalidate the choice. There are two ways to measure mass: gravitationally through an object's weight, and inertially through an object's resistance to motion. Both measures, gravitational mass and inertial mass, have always been found to be the same for a given object.

8. **(1)** is correct, and examination of the ocean currents shows that the eastern seaboards of all the continents are washed by warm currents from the equator, and the western seaboards are washed by cold polar currents. (2) is incorrect as west coasts are washed by cold water from the poles. (3) is incorrect as it is the opposite of statement (1). (4) is incorrect because a pattern clearly exists.

9. **(2)** is correct. The Gulf Stream consists of warm equatorial currents that raise the temperature of the winds that pass over England, thus warming the land. (1) is incorrect. Being an island would not make it warmer. (3) is incorrect. Latitude does affect temperature, the higher the latitude the greater the sun's angle and the cooler the air. (4) is incorrect as the winds that affect England do not come from France.

10. **(2)** is correct. A bottle tossed from Japan will ride the Kuroshio current to the North Pacific Drift and wash ashore on the western side of North America. (1), (3), (4), and (5) are all incorrect as no currents travel from Japan to these locations.

11. **(1)** Answer choice (1), "this conclusion is supported by the data," is the correct answer since the gray line representing the whitetail deer population drops over a period of time, and the mule deer (black line) stays the same or shows an increase in population. "This conclusion is not supported by the data" (2) cannot be the correct answer since one can determine that there are fewer whitetail deer over a period of time. "This conclusion includes the effect of hunting and is supported by the data" (3) cannot be the correct answer since it is stated in the paragraph that hunting was not allowed. "This conclusion includes the effect caused by drought and is supported by the data" (4) cannot be the correct answer since no drought was mentioned in the data. "The conclusion is right but the data is wrong" (5) cannot be the correct answer since a proper conclusion can only be based on the data, and if that data is incorrect, then the conclusion must also be incorrect.

12. **(1)** Answer choice (1), "the conclusion is supported by the data" is the correct answer since the mule deer survived and the whitetail deer did not survive. "The conclusion is refuted by the data" (2) cannot be the correct answer since the fittest, in this case, were the mule deer. "The conclusion is

refuted because only one survived" (3) cannot be the correct answer since there is no data indicating that any of the whitetail deer survived. "The conclusion is refuted because both deer do not compete with each other and the data supports this" (4) cannot be the correct answer since both animals had the same food and opportunities. "The conclusion is right but the data is wrong" (5) cannot be the correct answer since a conclusion is based on data and if the data is wrong, then the conclusion must also be wrong, and there is no evidence of that.

13. **(3)** Answer choice (3), "the conclusion is neither supported nor refuted by the data," is correct since there is no data concerning any special adaptations to the environment. "The conclusion is supported by the data" (1) cannot be the correct answer since there is no data concerning any special adaptations to the environment. "The conclusion is refuted by the data" (2) cannot be the correct answer since environmental adaptations are not addressed by the graph. "The data gives plenty of information concerning the mule deers' adaptability, which supports the conclusion" (4) cannot be the correct answer since there are no data about adaptability. "The data gives plenty of information concerning the type of terrain, which supports the conclusion" (5) cannot be the correct answer since no information is given about the terrain.

14. **(1)** Answer choice (1), "the conclusion is supported by the data," is the correct answer since the graph shows an early increase in both populations of deer. "The conclusion is refuted by the data" (2) cannot be the correct answer since the graph shows an early increase in both populations of deer. "The conclusion is neither supported nor refuted by the data" (3) cannot be the correct answer since the conclusion is supported by the early increase in both populations of deer. "The data gives plenty of information concerning the mule deer's adaptability, which supports the conclusion" (4) cannot be the correct answer since adaptability is not a part of the graph. "The data gives plenty of information concerning the type of terrain, which supports the conclusion" (5) cannot be the correct answer since no data is given concerning the terrain.

15. **(2)** is correct since, as the diagram shows, the distance between the two adjacent peaks is labelled as the wavelength. If the peaks are not adjacent, more than one wavelength will be measured, as in (1). (3) is wrong because the distance described is twice the wave amplitude, not wavelength. (4) is describing velocity, not wavelength. (5) is incorrect because the horizontal midline is only an imaginary line to divide the height of a wave from a trough.

16. **(4)** is correct. The water molecules, which is the medium, is not carried, but the wave peaks do move toward shore. (1) states the opposite of what is mentioned in the question. (2) is wrong because although the ocean is somewhat mixed each day, this mixing is due to currents and turbulence, not by waves. (3) is wrong because debris washes ashore by

currents and turbulence, not by waves. (5) is incorrect because waves move neither water nor swimmers. The waves travel through the water and the swimmer will bob up and down but will not be carried by the wave. Again, currents and turbulence are responsible for moving both water and swimmers.

17. **(2)**   Answer choice (2), "the message of the mRNA is different from the DNA before the event," is the correct answer. Since the DNA contains the information for the mRNA, the mRNA made after the event will be different because the DNA will be changed. Since DNA makes mRNA, the mRNA will be changed whenever the DNA is changed. "Nothing happens" (1) cannot be the correct answer since the removal of a "code word" is at least considered a point mutation, and the resulting mRNA will be changed. "mRNA cannot be made" (3) cannot be the correct answer since many of the DNA "code words" would have to be destroyed before this would happen. "Triplets can no longer be produced, so doublets are used" (4) cannot be the correct answer since "code words" are always "read" by threes (triplets). "DNA repairs itself" (5) cannot be the correct answer since although DNA can repair itself, the mechanism for repair is often flawed.

18. **(4)**   Answer choice (4), the nucleus, is the correct answer since the nucleus contains the chromosomes, which are composed of DNA nucleotides and some protein. The lysosomes (1) cannot be the correct answer since lysosomes contain digestive enzymes. The endoplasmic reticulum (2) cannot be the correct answer since it is a series of membranes found in the cytoplasm and it serves as a site of protein synthesis. "They are found floating in the cytoplasmic matrix" (3) cannot be the correct answer since DNA nucleotides are not found outside of the nucleus. Ribosomes (5) cannot be the correct answer since ribosomes are found in the cytoplasm and are in the endoplasmic reticulum.

19. **(2)**   Answer choice (2), chromosomes, is the correct answer since DNA and its associated proteins form these rodlike or threadlike structures. RNA (1) cannot be the correct answer since RNA does not interweave itself with proteins to form chromosomes. Nucleotides (3) cannot be the correct answer since DNA strands are composed of nucleotides; DNA and protein cannot make nucleotides. Genes (4) cannot be the correct answer since genes are composed of DNA and make up chromosomes. Ribosomes (5) cannot be the correct answer since ribosomes are composed of RNA.

20. **(5)**   Answer choice (5), "the resulting protein would be changed in some way, either in length, number or type of arrangement of amino acids" would be the correct answer since all proteins are made of amino acids, which are bonded together sequentially as dictated by the mRNA which was made by the DNA. "The resulting protein would be exactly as it would be before the change occurred" (1) cannot be the correct answer since any change in the DNA molecule would result in the change of the mRNA which would result in a changed protein. "The resulting protein would definitely be

smaller" (2) cannot be the correct answer since only the order of the amino acids would be changed. "The resulting protein would definitely be larger" (3) cannot be the correct answer since only the order of the amino acids would be changed. "The resulting protein would be wrapped around the DNA" (4) cannot be the correct answer since DNA does not enter into the actual construction of the protein molecule.

21. **(2)**   The formula given to find the note is: 170 divided by the length of the cavity in meters will equal the frequency. Here, 170 is divided by 1.5 m (150 cm) which gives 113 cycles per second. The closest note in the table is at 110 cycles per second, or A_2, more than 1 octave below middle C, which is at 262 cycles per second. All musical scales use A_4 or 440 cycles per second as a standard reference.

22. **(4)**   The size of the skull will give the length of the nasal cavity. If the baby's skull is one-third the adult size, then the nasal cavity is also one-third in length. The frequency sounded by the baby grinding its teeth will be 170 divided by (1.5 meters/3) which is 170 divided by 0.5, which is 340 cycles per second or about 3 times greater than the adult.

23. **(4)**   (4) is correct, because at this location, the North Pole is tilted toward the sun, resulting in continual daylight. (1) and (3) are incorrect, because in this position the pole is neither pointing toward nor from the sun, and equal hours of night and day would occur. (2) is not the right answer because the North Pole is pointing away from the sun and is in continual darkness. (5) is incorrect; these two positions are so very different.

24. **(5)**   (5) is the correct answer because both of these positions are parallel to the sun, and this results in equal day and night. (2) is not the right answer because the North Pole is pointing away from the sun and is in continual darkness. (4) is not the right answer as the North Pole is facing the sun and is in continual daylight. (1) and (3) are only partially correct.

25. **(1)**   It is the varying angle of the sunrays in relationship to the poles that causes the change in seasons, therefore answer (1) is correct. (2) is incorrect, because the changes in distance as the Earth revolves around the sun are not great enough to account for the changes in the seasons. (3), (4), and (5) have no bearing on the seasons.

26. **(5)**   It is true that chameleons are mostly found in Africa, but this does not prohibit the existence of some chameleons on other continents. In fact, some species do live in India. Thus, (5) is correct, and it follows that (1) is incorrect. (2) is incorrect because the majority of the chameleons are found in Africa, and this must be the greater proportion. (3) is wrong because a chameleon may be found on another continent. (4) is wrong because chameleons tend to be located in Africa; they are not evenly spread throughout the world.

27. **(4)** A chameleon changes color mostly due to temperature, sunlight, and emotion. Thus, a black chameleon is probably black because it is cold. Thus, (4) is correct. It is a false belief that chameleons change color to match their environment. Thus, (2) is wrong. (1) is wrong because hiding is a possibility for a color change but not a main reason why a color change occurs. (3) is wrong because color changes are normal occurrences for chameleons and do not signify that the animal is dying. (5) is incorrect because extending the tongue is not necessarily preceded by a color change.

28. **(1)** The sticky substance on the tongue aids in catching prey. Thus, (1) is correct. (2) is incorrect because the fork on the end of a tongue is too soft to spear prey. (3) is wrong because the tongue flicks the prey into the chameleon's mouth; the tongue does not squeeze the prey. In this case, the length of the tongue is helpful for catching prey at a distance. (4) is wrong because the chameleon does not have poisonous glands. (5) is wrong because the color change of a chameleon will not distract the prey.

29. **(5)** is correct because either the added substance may be insoluble in the solvent, or the solution may already be saturated, or both may be true. (1) is wrong because the substance would dissolve in an unsaturated solution. (4) is wrong because a solution often does contain more than one type of solute.

30. **(5)** is correct. The rule is that like substances dissolve in like substances. Here, "like" means that both substances are polar or both are nonpolar. (1) is wrong because oil will dissolve in water. (2) is incorrect because like does dissolve in like. (3) is wrong for the same reason. (4) is incorrect because again, the example states incorrect information. NaCl does, in fact, dissolve in water.

31. **(4)** The correct answer is (4). The major component of a solution is the solvent. (1) is thus wrong. (2) is wrong because two layers indicate the two liquids are immiscible. (3) is wrong because additional solutes can be dissolved in a solution until the saturation point. Since (1) and (3) are wrong, (5) is wrong.

32. **(5)** Liquid substances and gases are unable to transmit transverse shear waves. Each of the choices provided are liquids or gases at standard conditions except the igneous rock, granite (5). Mountains of granite on the earth transmit the three types of waves generated by earthquakes: P-, S-, and L-waves.

33. **(2)** If the S-waves are stopped at 2900 kilometers below the surface, then there must be liquid present there. The radius of the Earth is about 6400 kilometers, or 3960 miles. This implies that this liquid outer core must have a radius of about 3500 kilometers, or about 2170 miles.

34. **(3)** For this problem, S-waves travel at 4.25 km/sec and the P-waves at about 8.5 km/sec. Using the equation that distance equals rate multiplied by time, we see that the distance must be equal to 8.5 km/sec times 4 minutes (240 seconds) to get 2040 kilometers. This is closest to the 2000 km of choice (3). The associated S-waves would arrive about 4 minutes after the P-waves.

35. **(4)** is correct; all longitude lines converge at the poles. (1) and (3), are incorrect; latitude lines never vary in distance. (2) is incorrect as it is opposite to the correct answer. (5) is incorrect, since longitude lines vary, the relationship between latitude and longitude must change.

36. **(2)** is the false statement; if two lines cross then, that place would have two elevations, which is not possible. (1), (3), (4), (5) are all correct statements.

37. **(3)** is the false statement; weather is a modern-day phenomenon and is not a reflection on past conditions. (1), (2), (4), (5) are all true statements.

38. **(3)** is the correct statement; the number of people in an area does not affect the weather at that location. (1) affects the weather by changing the amount of sunlight received; (2) winds bring weather from other locations; (4) the shape of the land influences rainfall. (5) distance from water influences rainfall.

39. **(2)** Answer choice (2), "yes, because there are more offspring produced than the environment could support, and only some of the clams would survive," would be the correct answer since it is consistent with the second of Darwin's observations and the first of his conclusions. "Yes, because favorable variations occur" (1) cannot be the correct answer since the question has nothing to do with the variation. "Yes, because the environment is constantly changing" (3) cannot be the correct answer since even though the environment is constantly changing, the change is not fast enough to affect the single release of clam's sex cells. "No, because individual sperm and egg are different" (4) cannot be the correct answer since this is not consistent with any of Darwin's observations nor with any of his conclusions. "No, because genetic variation does not allow for natural selection" (5) cannot be the correct answer since it is not consistent with any of Darwin's observations or conclusions.

40. **(1)** Answer choice (1), "organisms produce more offspring than the environment can support so a population will remain constant since there are not enough resources for all offspring," is the correct answer since it is consistent with Darwin's observations and conclusions. "The environment is slowly changing all over the world which prevents all of the offspring from maturing." (2) cannot be the correct answer since the environment does not change that quickly. "Genetic variation is allowing the ferns to keep the same level of population" (3) cannot be the correct answer since genetic variation has nothing to do with the leveling of the population of ferns. "Genetic

variation that allows for survival will accumulate" (4) cannot be the correct answer since the survival characteristics, which can accumulate, do not do so quickly enough for this to occur in a single year. "Individuals vary genetically" (5) cannot be the correct answer since this is not a source which would prevent all of the spores from maturing.

41. **(1)**   Answer choice (1), "cattle rancher," is the correct answer since cattle ranchers are always trying to have the best-bred cattle. "Oilman" (2) cannot be the correct answer since this person would be more interested in the finding and refining of oil. "Engineer" (3) cannot be the correct answer since engineers function in constructing things. "Refinery chemist" (4) cannot be the correct answer since a refinery chemist's main function is to develop new products or to maintain the quality control of the products produced at the refinery. "Hair stylist" (5) cannot be the correct answer since a hair stylist is mainly interested in hair fashions.

42. **(3)**   is the answer. Hydrogen bonding is especially strong in water, not weak. (1), (2), (4), and (5) are all true statements about water.

43. **(1)**   is correct. Intermolecular attraction, namely, hydrogen bonding, leads to the high boiling and melting point. (2) is wrong because water has high surface tension. (3) is wrong because there is a great deal of hydrogen bonding between water molecules. (4) is wrong because water has a high heat capacity. (5) is wrong because hydrogen bonds, not covalent bonds, are present between the oxygen and hydrogen of one water molecule.

44. **(5)**   Water, at standard atmospheric pressure, freezes at 0°C and boils at 100°C. Therefore, the correct answer is (5). Choice (4) is the freezing and boiling points of water on the Fahrenheit scale. The other answers are also incorrect.

45. **(5)**   Answer choice (5), "While growing the bacteria, the test tube was inoculated with poison," is the correct answer since the graph indicates that the bacteria increase their population and then as the poison was assimilated the population decreased, and then all of the bacteria died. "The number of bacteria being produced by mitosis is equal to the number of bacteria dying" (1) cannot be the correct answer since this answer is best represented by graph (c). "Nothing was done to the culture of bacteria at first, but after a while some of the waste products were removed" (2) cannot be the correct answer since this answer is best represented by graph (e). "Bacteria 'love' this growth curve because it represents ideal conditions" (3) cannot be the correct answer since this statement is best represented by graph (d). "The growth of the bacteria is represented by a normal growth curve" (4) cannot be the correct answer since this statement is best represented by graph (a).

46. **(4)**   Answer choice (4), "The growth of the bacteria is represented by a normal growth curve," is the correct answer since the graph indicates that the bacteria increase their population and then the population decreases

when waste products accumulate or the population becomes too dense. "The number of bacteria being produced by mitosis is equal to the number of bacteria dying" (1) cannot be the correct answer since this statement is best represented by graph (c). "Nothing was done to the culture of bacteria at first, but after a while some of the waste products were removed." (2) cannot be the correct answer since this statement is best represented by graph (e). "Bacteria 'love' this growth curve because it represents ideal conditions" (3) cannot be the correct answer since this statement is best represented by graph (d). "While growing the bacteria, the test tube was inoculated with poison." (5) cannot be the correct answer since this answer is best represented by graph (b).

47. **(1)**   Answer choice (1), "The number of bacteria being produced by mitosis is equal to the number of bacteria dying," is the correct answer since the population line is horizontal. "Nothing was done to the culture of bacteria at first, but after a while some of the waste products were removed" (2) cannot be the correct answer since this answer is best represented by graph (e). "Bacteria 'love' this growth curve because it represents ideal conditions" (3) cannot be the correct answer since this answer is best represented by graph (d). "The growth of the bacteria is represented by a normal growth curve" (4) cannot be the correct answer since this statement is best represented by graph (a). "While growing the bacteria, the test tube was inoculated with poison" (5) cannot be the correct answer since this answer is best represented by graph (b).

48. **(3)**   Answer choice (3), "Bacteria 'love' this growth curve because it represents ideal conditions," is the correct answer since there is nothing preventing the growth of the bacteria. "The number of bacteria being produced by mitosis is equal to the number of bacteria dying" (1) cannot be the correct answer since this answer is best represented by graph (c). "Nothing was done to the culture of bacteria at first, but after a while some of the waste products were removed" (2) cannot be the correct answer since this statement is best represented by graph (e). "The growth of the bacteria is represented by a normal growth curve" (4) cannot be the correct answer since this answer is best represented by graph (a). "While growing the bacteria, the test tube was inoculated with poison" (5) cannot be the correct answer since this answer is best represented by graph (b).

49. **(2)**   Answer choice (2), "Nothing was done to the culture of bacteria at first, but after a while some of the waste products were removed," is the correct answer since there is an initial increase in population, then a leveling off, then another increase in the population. "The number of bacteria being produced by mitosis is equal to the number of bacteria dying" (1) cannot be the correct answer since this statement is best represented by graph (c). "Bacteria 'love' this growth curve because it represents ideal conditions" (3) cannot be the correct answer since this statement is best represented by graph (d). "The growth of the bacteria is represented by a normal growth curve" (4) cannot be the correct answer since this response is best represented

by graph (a). "While growing the bacteria, the test tube was inoculated with poison" (5) cannot be the correct answer since this answer is best represented by graph (b).

50. **(5)** Choice (1) is unacceptable because in each area of use, the U.S. household utilizes far more than twice the electrical energy of the Brazilian household. Choice (2) is incorrect because the percent used in air-conditioning is greater in the U.S. than in Brazil. Choice (3) is invalid since the greatest use in both countries is for refrigeration. Choice (4) is incorrect since in Brazil more electrical energy is used for water heating than for lighting. By the process of elimination, choice (5) is left and supported by the observations that both countries use the least for cooking and the most for refrigeration.

51. **(3)** Both columns of electrical energy in KWH must be totaled. The U.S. household consumes 7345 KWH while the Brazilian household consumes 1460 KWH per year. This is a ratio of 5 to 1. It is interesting to note that the Third World developing countries mimic the United States in their usage of technology.

52. **(4)** Answer choice (4), "bilateral symmetry," is the correct answer since the bird has a right and a left side. "Asymmetry" (1) cannot be the correct answer since asymmetry refers to something that has no definite shape. "Radial symmetry" (2) cannot be the correct answer since radial symmetry refers to organisms that have their parts radiating outward as in a cylindrical shape or a flattened cylindrical shape. "Spherical symmetry" (3) cannot be the correct answer since the bird is not shaped like a sphere. "Longitudinal symmetry" (5) cannot be the correct answer since there is no such terminology.

53. **(1)** Answer choice (1), "asymmetry," is the correct answer since the amoeba is constantly changing shape. "Radial symmetry" (2) cannot be the correct answer since radial symmetry refers to organisms that have their parts radiating outward as in a cylindrical shape or a flattened cylindrical shape. "Spherical symmetry" (3) cannot be the correct answer since the amoeba is not shaped like a sphere. "Bilateral symmetry" (4) cannot be the correct answer since the figure has no right or left side. "Triradial symmetry" (5) cannot be the correct answer since there is no such terminology.

54. **(3)** Answer choice (3), "spherical symmetry," is the correct choice since the figure is ball-shaped. "Asymmetry" (1) cannot be the correct answer since asymmetry refers to something that has no definite shape. "Radial symmetry" (2) cannot be the correct answer since radial symmetry refers to organisms that have their parts radiating outward as in a cylindrical shape or flattened cylindrical shape. "Bilateral symmetry" (4) cannot be the correct answer since the figure has no right or left side. "Longitudinal symmetry" (5) cannot be the correct answer since there is no such terminology.

55. **(2)** Answer choice (2), "radial symmetry," is the correct answer since the organism resembles a flattened cylinder with body parts radiating

outward. "Asymmetry" (1) cannot be the correct answer since asymmetry refers to something that has no definite shape. "Spherical symmetry" (3) cannot be the correct answer since the organism is not shaped like a sphere. "Bilateral symmetry" (4) cannot be the correct answer since the figure has no right or left side. "Triradial symmetry" (5) cannot be the correct answer since there is no such terminology.

56. **(2)** Answer choice (2), "bilaterally symmetrical," is the correct answer since bilateral organisms have a right and left side. "Asymmetrical" (1) cannot be the correct answer since asymmetrical organisms have no definite shape. "Spherically symmetrical" (3) cannot be the correct answer since balls have no right or left side. "Cylindrically symmetrical" (4) cannot be the correct answer since no definition was given for this term. "Radially symmetrical" (5) cannot be the correct answer since body parts do not necessarily radiate outward in an organism with a right and left side.

57. **(5)** Answer choice (5), "radially symmetrical," is the correct answer since the "rays" of the starfish radiate outward from a central disk. "Asymmetry" (1) cannot be the correct answer since asymmetrical organisms have no definite shape. "Bilateral symmetry" (2) is not the correct answer since bilateral organisms have a right and a left side. "Spherically symmetrical" (3) cannot be the correct answer since a starfish is not shaped like a ball. "Cylindrically symmetrical" (4) cannot be the correct answer since no definition was given for this term.

58. **(4)** is correct. To find the oxidation number of H_2S, rule 1 says that the sum of the oxidation numbers of the atoms must be zero. Rule 1 is important here, so choices (2) and (5) can be disqualified from being correct. Also rule 4 states that hydrogen has a charge of +1 when combined with nonmetals (such as sulfur). Rule 2 concerns polyatomic ions. H_2S, however, is not an ion. It is not monatomic, but polyatomic, so rule 3 does not apply.

59. **(2)** is correct. The sum of all of the oxidation numbers must equal zero. O_4 must be $4 \times 2 = -8$. K is +1. $-8 + 1 = 7$. To equal zero, then, Mn must equal +7.

60. **(3)** is correct. Since H is combined with a nonmetal (P), H must have a charge of +1. The four oxygen atoms have a combined charge of -8 since $4 \times -2 = -8$. The charge on the ion is -2. Thus, P must have a charge of +5 since $5 + 1 - 8 = -2$.

61. **(4)** is correct since rules 2 and 4 are necessary to find the charges of H, P, O_4, and the combined ion. Specifically, rule 2 states that HPO_4^{2-} must have a net charge of -2. Rule 4 helps in determining the charge of the hydrogen. Rule 1 is not applicable since HPO_4^{2-} is not a neutral substance. Rule 3 does not apply because HPO_4^{2-} is polyatomic, not monatomic.

62. **(2)** Answer choice (2), "pandas are not bears and their genus name, *Aleropoda*, indicates this," is the correct answer. Since *Ursus* is the genus name of bears, *Aleropoda* would indicate that the panda is not a bear. "Panda bears live only in China" (1) cannot be the correct answer since where a panda lives does not indicate that it is a bear. "Pandas are not bears and their species name, *melanoleuca*, indicates this" (3) cannot be the correct answer since species names are not used to designate the grouping. "Pandas are on the endangered list and have black and white fur" (4) cannot be the correct answer since being on the endangered list and the color of fur does not make the panda a bear. "Pandas are not bears because they are really called "pandas" (5) cannot be the correct answer since the only way to tell what pandas are is to compare the genus name of the bear *Ursus* and the genus name of the panda, *Aleropoda*, and, if they are the same, then the panda is a bear. Simply calling it a "panda" is using its common name which tells one nothing about its classification.

63. **(3)** Answer choice (3), "the genus names indicate that there is no relationship" is the correct answer since the genus names of the two animals are different. "The species name indicates that there is a close genetic relationship" (1) cannot be the correct answer since the species name does not show genetic relationships. "The species name indicates a filial relationship" (2) cannot be the correct answer since the species name is not used to show a genetic relationship. "The genus name indicates there is a filial relationship" (4) cannot be the correct answer since the two names are different. "Both animals are totally black" (5) cannot be the correct answer since not enough information is given.

64. **(1)** Answer choice (1), "insects, amphibians, reptiles, fish, birds, and mammals," is the correct answer since every organism listed is a member of the kingdom Animalia. "Insects, fungi, amphibians, reptiles, fish, birds, and mammals" (2) cannot be the correct answer since fungus is in the kingdom Fungi. "Mushrooms, amphibians, reptiles, fish, birds, and mammals" (3) cannot be the correct answer since mushrooms are in the kingdom Fungi. "Slime molds, autotrophic algae, rusts, trees, and blue-green algae" (4) cannot be the correct answer since these are members of several kingdoms, none of which are animals. "Insects, crabs, sponges, trees, fish, birds, and reptiles" (5) cannot be the correct answer since trees are members of the kingdom Plantae.

65. **(5)** Answer choice (5), "genus name," is the correct answer since all scientific names begin with the genus name. "Kingdom name" (1) cannot be the correct answer since a kingdom name is never used in an organism's scientific name. "Phylum name" (2) cannot be the correct answer since a phylum name is never used in an organism's scientific name. "Class name" (3) cannot be the correct answer since a class name is never used in an organism's scientific name. "Order name" (4) cannot be the correct answer since an order name is never used in an organism's scientific name.

66. **(1)**   Visible light consists of waves which have wavelengths from blue at 4000 angstroms to red at 7000 angstroms. For the three sources plotted in the displayed graph, the tungsten filament lamp has the greatest relative energy output at the red end, with a reading of slightly greater than 80. This compares with the lower red readings of about 57 for daylight and about 7 for the fluorescent lamp. Note average daylight is far brighter than the other two sources, explaining why camera exposures inside under artificial lights need to be longer than those for outside on a normal day.

TEST 4: LITERATURE AND ARTS

1. **(1)** It is evident that this friendship is deeply rooted since each man threatens to leave the other but will not. Neither one cares (2) is incorrect since George shows his remorse with, "I been mean, ain't I?" in line 14. Lennie intends to leave (4) and George intends to abandon him (5) are not good choices since Lennie "senses his advantage" in line 23 and George says he is "jus' foolin" in line 18. (3) is a poor choice since George is no longer angry at the end of his speech.

2. **(2)** The author states clearly in line 23 that Lennie, despite his limited intellect, has learned to manipulate George: "Lennie avoided the bait. He had sensed his advantage." These lines make (3) George has the upper hand, a poor choice. (1) is incorrect since George demonstrates compassion in lines 27–29 by asking Lennie to stay with him. This paragraph also makes (4) Lennie intends to hurt George and (5) George is a survivor incorrect.

3. **(2)** Because of Lennie's dependence on George and his childlike nature, father and son is the best choice. It is not a reciprocal relationship as in most cases with best friends, so (1) is incorrect. Their bonding is too apparent throughout their dialogue to consider them (3) casual acquaintances, (4) feuding neighbors, or (5) complete strangers.

4. **(1)** First, George entertains himself with thoughts of "the swell time" he could have without Lennie, but lines 18 to 21, however, reverse this idea and reveal his inner conflict. There is no intellect demonstrated by George (2); neither is impatience (5) apparent. This dialogue does not reveal devotion (4), but rather appeasement when George offers Lennie a pup.

5. **(3)** It is evident that the childlike Lennie is totally unaware of his brute strength when George offers him a pup so he can "pet it harder." When he threatens to leave George, Lennie says, "An' if I foun' a mouse, I could keep it. Nobody'd take it away from me." This fondness suggests Lennie is neither careless (1) nor cruel (2). Neither (4) kindness nor (5) stubbornness have anything to do with the reason Lennie kills mice.

6. **(1)** George's ambivalence, his inner conflict, has to do with his relationship with Lennie. The dialogue introducing conflict begins with his expressed desire to leave Lennie; a few paragraphs on, he daydreams of the farm they will buy, living "off the fatta the lan'."

7. **(2)** George's story about buying a farm and prospering have been memorized word for word by Lennie. Lennie is not intelligent enough to create it (1), and he appears to be too childlike to fabricate it (3). Since it is the story which seems to delight both men, it apparently is not cause for concern (4) or nothing in particular (5).

8. **(2)** George's voice deepens and his words are repeated rhythmically and Lennie "is delighted" with the story of their hope and future. Although it does give them something to talk about (1), it is more than casual conversation (5); it's a dream, not cause for concern (4). (3) is incorrect, since they must earn their money in this town.

9. **(2)** With the effective use of dialogue, Burns addresses the "wee," small, "sleekit," sleek, "tim'rous," frightened beast. He makes no judgment concerning the mouse (1) brave, (3) innocent, (4) nature's masterpiece, or (5) useless.

10. **(2)** Lines 7 and 8 clearly state that man's dominion is the reason why man must dictate the mouse's fate. Therefore, man and beast do not rule (1); nor is their social kinship maintained (3); rather it is "broken." (4) is a poor choice, since the mouse is declared—from the onset—to be dominated by man.

11. **(3)** Lines 13 through 18 tell the reader what Burns intends to do, "poor beastie, thou maun live." None of the other possible choices are appropriate.

12. **(3)** The author's attitude is compassionate, rather than humble, since he puts himself in the beast's position "til crash! the cruel coulter passed out throu' thy cell!" and again, compassionately, "Has cost thee many monie a weary nibble!" Sarcastic (1), uncaring (2), business-like (5) therefore are incorrect.

13. **(2)** Even without the aid of interpretation of Scottish dialogue, the poetic cadence of "gang aft agley" and the context of Burns' lament concerning the mouse's plight, make (2) the best choice. (4) is not a good choice, since it states **never** (not "aft"). (1) is a poor choice because its message is opposite of the intended one.

14. **(1)** Reflecting on his own plight, ("Still thou art blest compared wi' me!"), Burns begins to pity himself in a subjective, not impartial (5) manner. Even though there could be a hint of exaggeration (2), the thrust of these lines is not like that; neither is there a hint of anger (3) nor of fear (4).

15. **(2)** The only accurate conclusion is that there is a deep bond between the two. (1) is a poor choice because Santiago says in line 23, "If you were my boy." The boy himself wants to be of service to the old man in every possible way, even if his fishing is "unlucky." This rules out (3) casual acquaintances, (4) little care for one another, or (5) just met as correct answers.

16. **(2)** Santiago remembers the incident when the fish was "too green" and the boy, five years old, was "nearly killed," obviously from the thrashings of the still strong fish. There is no suggestion of the fish being (1) spoiled or of (4) the boy being careless. Neither is there mention of the incident being

a "chance" happening (5). Santiago admits he brought it in too green, too soon.

17. **(4)** The old fisherman's gentleness, wisdom, and endurance are evident throughout the selection; therefore character is the focus. Mystery (1) as well as humor (3) are never evident. Even though the sea is important to the plot, there is no preoccupation by the author with geography (2).

18. **(1)** Determination and endurance is the correct answer since, despite the pain, his injured hand, and his weakened condition, the old man struggles on, determined. There is no hint of wit and humor (2) or of blind hatred (5)— Santiago feels sorry for the fish. Although the old man demonstrates intelligence in philosophic musing (3), there is no hint of formal schooling, except that Santiago apparently reads baseball scores. (4) is incorrect since Santiago is stubborn, but quite rational in his thought process.

19. **(2)** Santiago reveals that he must kill him, but he is glad that he does not have to "kill the stars." This statement negates (1), no remorse, as well as (3) let the fish go, and (4) soon give up.

20. **(1)** Santiago declares that the fish "is my friend, too." He then goes on to say that he is glad that he does not have to try and kill the stars, then, the sun, the moon, thus displaying appreciation and compassion for all of mankind. Never once, through this dialogue, has Santiago demonstrated (2) self-centered interest in achieving his goal, or (3) pride in fishing, or (4) hatred. Although Santiago demonstrates bravery, there is no disregard of danger.

21. **(1)** A more universal idea is honor and dignity, earned, should not be carelessly cast away. Santiago is explicit, "There is no one worthy of eating him from the manner of his behaviour and his great dignity."

22. **(2)** Figuratively is correct since "true brothers" is used out of literal (1) or ordinary use. Paradoxically (3) is incorrect since the passage does not involve two opposite statements. It is evident that humor (4) is missing from Santiago's statement, as well as satire (5), since there is no use of wit or ridicule.

23. **(1)** Nature's beauty, petals, the brook as well as the resplendent redbird, is the theme. (2) Although there is a hint of philosophical look at life, neither (2) philosophy nor (3) patriotism nor (4) religion are correct. Although love of nature is evident, (5) love is not the theme.

24. **(5)** Admiration for all of nature's beauty is the only correct answer and is evident not only in the poet's apostrophe but also throughout the entire poem; therefore all the other choices—(1) callousness, (2) scorn, (3) envy, and (4) fear are entirely inappropriate.

25. **(3)** The "sea winds" of May pierce winter's isolation, signaling that spring has arrived is disclosed in line 1. (1) sea winds is used figuratively, (2) and (4) are entirely incorrect since spring generally produces a rebirth of activity. (5) although spring is a time of rejoicing, this is not the intent of line 1.

26. **(1)** The brillant plumage of the redbird is "cheapened" by the flower in lines 7 and 8, therefore, all the other answers are not suitable.

27. **(3)** In lines 9 through 12 the poet addresses the flower, giving it personage and advising her how to respond to the "sages."

28. **(1)** "Beauty is its own excuse for being" rephrased, literally, most nearly means that nature's beauty is reason enough for its existence; therefore, "nature's beauty needs no other purpose."

29. **(3)** In line 13, the "rhodora" is called the "rival of the rose," therefore (1) and (2) cannot be correct. Although the rhodora does grow "wild," the poet does not call it (4) wildflower.

30. **(3)** The poet is explicit in lines 13 through 15 that he never questioned the flower's creator but presumed the "Selfsame Power" created both man and nature. (1) "Simple ignorance" connotes a trusting faith, not ignorance, in a denotative sense. (2) the theme of the poem is nature's beauty, (4) and (5) are opposite of the intended meaning of the poem.

31. **(3)** No electricity, no bathroom, no running water and "night soil men," in addition to "tropical poverty," suggest that island is the best answer. A small town (1), a large city (2), and apartment complex (4) are all incorrect since they would provide the subject with necessary utilities and facilities. A houseboat (5) might be a possible answer were it not for the "outhouse" mentioned.

32. **(3)** Since the author is explicit that her mother's focus on the new baby came at a period of adolescent "storm" when she needed her the most, (3) is correct. She suggests that family poverty (1) was always there, and more children compounded the problem. There was no mention of (2) bad luck, nor was there mention of (4) catastrophic events. Although schooling was not a pleasant experience, there is no basis for concluding that her education was a poor one (5).

33. **(1)** The article reveals that it is in early adolescence that the gifted intellect of the writer interviewed began expanding. (2) is incorrect since there is no hint of overt demands, just intellectual queries, which also makes answer (3) a very poor choice. Unhappy (4) is a possible answer although it does not specify that she was a happy child up until her turbulent adolescent days. If even in a basic sense, the reader is lead to infer that she was educated; therefore (5) is incorrect.

34. **(2)** Contextual clues within the sentence leads the reader to choose "accompanying" as the best synonym for "attendant". None of the others are as suitable in context.

35. **(3)** Quite candidly the gifted author admits in lines 17–22 that she stole books because the intellectual demands of her gifted mind were not met. Bored (1) might have been a good choice if lines 17–22 were not as explicit, since boredom can be a natural consequence of not fulfilling intellectual demands. Never is there a hint of the subject being revengeful (2), even though she does confess to giving teachers "back chat." (4) is a poor choice for an answer, since in these selected excerpts friends are not mentioned.

36. **(3)** Lines 28–33 strongly suggest that, all in all, her strongest memories of her childhood are of being "misunderstood." Neither (1) happy nor (2) unexamined fit appropriately since she admits, "Had I just sunk in the cracks, it would not have been noticed," and that her facility with words was interpreted as "a sharp tongue." For those reasons, we should not assume that her adolescence was neither (4) normal nor (5) abnormal, however misunderstood it might have been.

37. **(1)** The first three lines lead us to infer that the narrator is in his study since he "pondered" over quaint and curious volumes; he also tells us that he was "nearly napping." There is no mention of a diary (2). Daydreaming (3) might have been a viable alternative, except that it would exclude the presence of books. Since he is apparently at leisure, we cannot presume that he is (4) working or (5) ill.

38. **(3)** The narrator explains that he seeks "surcease of sorrow," of the lost Lenore, named by angels—now nameless. (4) is not correct; although the mourner is musing over memories of Lenore, we must not assume that they are ghostly, or that he is in this stanza (5) preoccupied with the supernatural world. Weather (1) and business (2) are too mundane to select and make no appearance in stanzas one and two.

39. **(4)** The provocative imagery of an ebony bird in lines 19 and 20 who also "Perched upon a bust of Pallas," in line 17 suggests the ebony of the raven upon alabaster marble.

40. **(5)** The narrator addresses the raven as if it were nonhuman in line 25: "'Prophet!' said I, 'thing of evil." Essentially the question is, Is there a maiden by the name of Lenore in paradise (Aidenne)?

41. **(3)** Bereft, lamenting the death of the beautiful lost maiden, the poet/ lover bares his soul in every stanza although stanza one finds him trying to forget his lost Lenore by occupying himself with volumes (1). Reporter (2) is an inappropriate answer since there is no suggestion that the speaker is one; nor is businessman (4) a substantiated answer. If the poet happens to be a

student (5), there is no hint of this, although through his allusions to Greek mythology we can infer he is a scholar.

42. **(2)** The raven's appearance with royal "mien" tells us that he is of stately and regal birth; it further suggests that he might be a harbinger of some distant shore, or world beyond. Haughty or superior (4) might seem to be a viable alternative, but the term "mien" presents an image of demeanor and suggests stateliness.

43. **(5)** Images of the poet, alone, pondering, mourning and lamenting his lost love, abound throughout the poem; therefore, morose or sullen is the best choice. Happy (1) and optimistic (2) are completely inappropriate answers, while indecisive (3) and angry (4) are also weak choices since there is little, if anything, to substantiate them.

44. **(2)** The poet is emphatic in his declaration, "And my soul from out that shadow... shall be lifted—nevermore!" We can infer with finality that there is no hope; therefore, (3) another life and (4) Lenore will return are clearly poor choices. Since his statement transcends the mortal presence of a bird, (1) and (5), both of which have to do with the raven, are not correct.

45. **(1)** The poem leaves us with a hopeless, morose message in which the poet reiterates the finality of death. Therefore (3) and (5), which speak of hope and replacement, are poor choices. Love is fleeting (2) might be a choice to consider, but it really is too weak when one investigates the poem's bleak imagery.

TEST 5: MATHEMATICS

1. **(4)** The figure has 6 sides; this is a hexagon. A rectangle has 4 sides, a pentagon has 5 sides, and a heptagon has 7 sides.

2. **(2)** 4 divided by 6 is 4/6 and reduces to 2/3, or use long division to divide 6 into 4. Either way, this is 66-2/3%. Answer (1) is the percent she **lost**.

3. **(4)** Subtracting 7 from each side of the equation gives $4x = 20$. Divide both sides of the equation by 4 and get $x = 5$. Answer (1) is not correct because 7 was not subtracted before dividing by 4. Answer (2) is not correct because 7 was **added** to 27. Answer (5) is not correct because of the incorrect sign.

4. **(4)** To find the net deposit, add the value of the currency, coins, and checks: $348 + $30.54 + $553.67 + $30.09 = $962.30. Now subtract the amount of cash received: $962.30 − $150 = $812.30, the correct answer. Answer (1) is the total of only the currency and coins. Answer (2) omits one check. Answer (3) is the total deposit before subtracting the cash received. Answer (5) is the error in answer (2) minus the $150 cash received.

5. **(2)** This right triangle is isosceles. A scalene triangle has no sides the same length. An equilateral triangle has all sides the same length. An obtuse triangle has one obtuse angle, and an acute triangle has 3 acute angles.

6. **(5)** First subtract 3 from both sides of the equation, then multiply both sides by 4. This gives $x = 48$. Answer (3) is the result if 12 is mistakenly multiplied by 1/4 rather than by 4.

7. **(1)** The mean is the average obtained by adding each day's miles and dividing by the number of days. For the week, she ran a total of 35 miles. Divide this by 5 days, and the mean is 7 miles. Answer (2) is the total miles she ran. Answer (3) is the median.

8. **(3)** The two angles pictured form a **linear pair**, and together they form a straight angle. The sum of the measures of angle **Q** and 58 is 180°, the number of degrees in a straight angle. To obtain the correct answer, subtract 58 from 180.

9. **(3)** To evaluate an expression, simply replace the **x** or **y** with the equivalent number, $(-2)^2 + 2(-2) − 3 + 3 = 4 − 4 − 3 + 3 = 0$.

10. **(5)** To find the probability, make a fraction with the total number of possibilities on the bottom (as the denominator) and the number of ways to fulfill the given condition on top (as the numerator). There are seven marbles,

so 7 is the denominator. Joey will be successful and will **not** pull out a red one if he pulls out any of the 5 that are not red. So 5/7 is the correct answer.

11. **(2)** The sum of the measures of the angles of a triangle is 180 degrees. Angle **D** is marked as a right angle, which is 90 degrees. This leaves the other two angles to make up the other 90 degrees. So the correct answer is obtained by subtracting 43 from 90. Also you could add 90 and 43 to get 133 and subtract 133 from 180. The answer is the same.

12. **(2)** To simplify, remove parentheses and collect like terms. $15 - 4x - 8 + 6x + 2 = 2x + 9$. The most common error is failure to distribute the minus sign with the 4.

13. **(4)** The formula $D = rt$ is the one to use for this problem. $21 = r \cdot 2\ 1/3$ and $r = 9$ knots. Answer (2) is the time, answer (3) is the distance, and answer (5) is obtained by multiplying 21 by 2 rather than by dividing.

14. **(5)** You may either combine each two terms as you get to them, $38 - 17 = 21$ & $21 + 91 = 112$ & $112 - 58 = 54$, or you may combine all of the positive numbers and then combine all of the negative numbers and then combine the two answers. This gives $38 + 91 = 129$ and $-17 + -58 = -75$, and $129 - 75 = 54$.

15. **(1)** Angle BFG and Angle CGF are **alternate interior angles** and are therefore congruent, or equal in measure. If we can find the measure of either one, we will know the measure of Angle CGF. We know that Angle BFG and Angle BFE form a **linear pair**, and are supplementary, and we know Angle BFE measures 80 degrees. Subtracting 80 from 180 we find that Angle BFG is 100 degrees. Since CGF is an alternate interior angle and congruent to Angle BFG, the measure of Angle CGF is 100 degrees.

16. **(2)** The Pacific is 46% of the 140 million square miles, or $.46 \times 140,000,000$. Answer (5) has a misplaced decimal point, answer (2) is the 46 written as 46 million, and answer (3) subtracts 46 million from 140 million.

17. **(2)** In problem 6 you were told that about 140 million square miles of our Earth's surface are covered with oceans. This problem adds the information that the total surface of our Earth is about 200 million square miles. The percentage is 140 divided by 200, or about 70%. Answer (1) has a misplaced decimal point, and answer (5) is $200 - 140$.

18. **(4)** Multiplying x and 4x gives $4x^2$. Multiplying x and 3 gives 3x. Multiplying 1 and 4x gives 4x. Multiplying 1 and 3 gives 3, collecting like terms gives $4x^2 + 7x + 3$. Answer (1) is incorrect because 1 and 3 were **added**, and the middle term is missing. Answer (2) is incorrect because the middle term is missing. Answer (3) is incorrect because the middle term is incorrect. Answer (5) is incorrect because the sign of the middle term is incorrect and the last term is incorrect.

19. **(5)** Two lines intersect to form vertical angles. The angle marked 133° and the one marked X are vertical angles. Vertical angles are congruent. This means X = 133°.

20. **(3)** For this problem, you should **estimate**. She spent **about** 15 + 30 + 20 = 65, and 100 − 65 = 35. If you did not estimate and calculated her change exactly, $35.16, then you still mark answer (3), because that is the nearest or **best** one.

21. **(5)** Distribute the 10 to both terms inside the parenthesis. Answer (5) is correct because 10 times (-3w) is (-30w) and 10 times 2 is 20. Answer (1) is incorrect because the negative sign was omitted from the first term, and the second term was not multiplied by 10. Answer (2) is incorrect because the second term was not multiplied by 10. In answer (3), the second term was not multiplied by 10, but the sign was changed. Answer (4) is incorrect because the sign of the second term was erroneously changed.

22. **(2)** This is another estimation problem. $9.89 is about $10.00, and 75% of $10.00 is $7.50. Answer (1) has a misplaced decimal point.

23. **(4)** Since the two segments are perpendicular, they form a right angle. A right angle measures 90°, so the two marked angles must add up to 90°. 50 + X = 90, therefore X = 40.

24. **(3)** The mean is the average we usually find for grades. Add the scores and divide by the number of scores. The sum is 400, and 400 divided by 5 is 80. Answer (1) is the total points, answer (2) is both the median and the mode, answer (4) is the high score, answer (5) is the low score.

25. **(4)** All of his grades added together and divided by 5 must equal 95. Multiply both sides of that equation by 5 and 93 + 100 + 92 + 100 + x = 475. Then 385 + x = 475 and x = 90.

26. **(3)** Draw two right triangles, a small one to represent Johnny and his shadow and a larger one to represent the tree and its shadow. These triangles are similar. A proportion can be set up between Johnny's height and the length of his shadow and the tree's height and the length of its shadow.

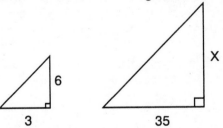

$\dfrac{6}{3} = \dfrac{x}{35}$ 3x = 210 and x = 70.

You may have noticed that Johnny is twice as tall as his shadow and realized that the tree is twice as tall as its shadow.

27. **(4)** Laura spent $10.17 and Lana spent $10.34, so Lana spent 17 cents more than Laura. Answer (2) represents a subtraction error.

28. **(5)** If one integer is represented by x, then the next consecutive **even** integer is (x + 2). The product of one even integer and twice the next even integer is represented by x + 2(x + 2). This is set equal to 40 to form the equation. Answer (1) is simply an integer times itself. Answer (2) represents the product of any two consecutive integers. Answer (3) represents the sum of one integer and twice the next consecutive integer. Finally answer (4) represents the **product** of two even or odd integers.

29. **(5)** There are 4 kings in the 52 card deck, so the probability is 4/52, this fraction reduces to 1/13. Answer (4) uses the two numbers in a fraction but in the wrong positions.

30. **(4)** Let x equal the amount of the lease last year. This year is 8% more. x + .08x = 621 is the equation. Add 1 and .08 and get 1.08x = 621, then x = $575.

31. **(1)** The sum of the measures of the angles of a triangle equals 180°. 25 + 15 = 40 and 180 − 40 = 140.

32. **(3)** The fraction is 1/6. A common error is to put 2 over 6, which reduces to answer (2).

33. **(1)** The form $a^m\ a^n = a^{m+n}$. This is the same form as 4 $(x^4 \bullet x^6)$, which equals $4x^{10}$. Answer (2) represents a common mistake of multiplying the exponents.

34. **(4)** There is the same chance or probability that the spinner will stop on any one of the numbers. This is 1 out of 6 or 1/6.

35. **(4)** We want to find what binomials multiplied together would give $(x^4 - 81)$. $(x^2 + 9)$ and $(x^2 - 9)$ would give the results, but $(x^2 - 9)$ can also be factored into $(x + 3)$ and $(x - 3)$, so $(x^2 + 9)$ $(x + 3)$ $(x - 3)$ are the prime factors. Answer (2) is not the **best** answer because it is not the prime factors.

36. **(1)** There are 12 in a dozen, so Maria baked 66 cookies. Her little brother ate 1/3 of 12 or 4 cookies. This left 62 (66 − 4 = 62).

37. **(1)** The volume of any solid is the area of the base multiplied by the height. The base of a cylinder is a circle. The formula for the area of a circle is $A = \pi r^2$. The diameter is marked 20 cm on the figure, so the radius is 10 cm. 10 x 10 = 100 and 100 x 3.14 = 314. This is the area of the base. Now multiply

by the height, 20, and the answer is 6,280 cubic cm.

38. **(3)** His car can go 100 on 3 gallons, so it can go 300 miles on x gallons. Set up a proportion $\dfrac{100}{3} = \dfrac{300}{x}$. Then X = 9.

39. **(3)** This expression is of the form $A^2 - 2AB + B^2$, which is the square of a binomial $(A - B)^2$. So the answer is $(x - 3)^2$. Answer (1) ignores the third term. When answer (4) is squared, the middle term is positive. Answer (2) is the same as answer (4) only in a different form. When the factors of answer (5) are multiplied together, the last term of the trinomial formed is negative.

40. **(2)** To find the average, add the five figures and divide by 5. 186.5 divided by 5 = 37.3. Answer (1) is 186.5 divided by 4. Answers (3) and (4) are produced by addition errors.

41. **(4)** First convert all measurements to **feet**, since the answers are in feet. One mile is 5,280 ft., 720 yds. is 2,160 ft. The sum is 11,340 ft. Answer (1) is obtained by adding all numbers without converting them to the same measure. Answer (2) is obtained by converting 1 mile to 5,280 ft. and then adding 720 and 3,500. Answer (5) mistakenly converts 1 mile to 5,000 ft.

42. **(5)** To find g (-3) simply substitute (-3) for x. This gives g (-3) = (-3)² + 4. (-3)² is 9 and 9 + 4 equals 13.

43. **(3)** The problem is really to find the surface area of the rectangular solid. This is done by finding the sum of the areas of every side, including the top and bottom. This problem is complicated by the fact that the measurements in the problem are given in inches, and the answers are given in square feet. We must convert to the same unit of measure. If we convert the inches to feet, the dimensions of the chest are 1' x 2' x 5/6'. A formula to find the lateral area (area of all the sides, but not the top and bottom) is L = ph, where p = perimeter of the base and h = the height. The perimeter of the base is 1 + 2 + 1 + 2 or 6. Then 6 x 5/6 = 5 sq. ft. for the sides. Now find the area of the top and bottom and add it to the sides. The bottom is a rectangle and the area = lw, where l = length and w = width. So the area is 2 x 1 or 2 sq. ft. This is the bottom, but the top is the same. Finally add the area of the sides and the top and the bottom: 5 + 2 + 2 = 9 sq. ft.

44. **(5)** 995 + 149 = 1,144 and 1,144 x .08 = 91.52 tax. $1,144 + $91.52 = $1,235.52. Answer (1) is the cost of the sofa and chair without tax. Answer (2) is the tax. Answer (3) results from an addition error, and answer (4) results from adding tax to the incorrect answer (3).

45. **(1)** An easy way to work this is to think that if the TV set is 30% OFF, then it is 70% ON, and 70% of $225 is $157.50. The traditional way to work this is to take 30% of $225, which is $67.50, and subtract this from $225,

giving $157.50. Answer (2) is the 30% discount. Answer (4) is obtained by simply subtracting $30.00 from $225.

46. **(4)** 96 divided by 2 gives the cost of one pound, which is $0.48. Then $0.48 times 3 is $1.44. Answer (1) incorrectly multiplies 2 times 96 times 3. Answer (2) multiplies 96 times 3. Answer (3) is the cost for one pound, and answer (5) is a distractor.

47. **(2)** Let x equal the original price. Then $x - .20x = 36$ and $.80x = 36$ and $x = 45$. Answer (1) adds 36 and 20% of 36 while answer (3) adds 20 and 36. Answers (4) and (5) are distractors for those who might want to guess.

48. **(4)** The exponents of 10 are added, so the answer is 10^5 or a one and five zeros: 100,000.

49. **(2)** If 60% have brown eyes then $100\% - 60\% = 40\%$ **do not** have brown eyes. 40% of 245 is 98 and is written as a percent for answer (4); 60% of 245 is 147 and that is written as a percent for answer (3).

50. **(2)** Answers (3), (4), and (5) are each more than 1/2. Answer (1) is 1/2. Only answer (2) is less than 1/2.

51. **(3)** You may either find the percent of boys (351 divided by 650) and then subtract from 100% to find the percent of girls, or you may subtract 351 from 650 and find that there are 299 girls and divide this by 650 to get 46% girls. Answer (1) is 650 divided by 351, and answer (2) is 650 divided by 299. Answer (4) is the percent of boys, and answer (5) is the number of girls written as a percent.

52. **(5)** There is not enough information given to find the cost in the next state. The tax rate in that state is needed. Answer (1) is the cost in his state, and the other answers are costs with tax rates of 6%, 5%, and 4% respectively.

53. **(1)** Scientific notation writes numbers as a product of numbers from 1 to 10 and a power of 10. Only two answers have numbers less than 10, they are answers (1) and (3). 480 million is 480,000,000, that is 4.8×10^8, moving the decimal point eight places.

54. **(4)** Substitute the values given into the formula: $s = (68 \times 1.6) + 4$, then $108.8 + 4 = \$112.80$.

55. **(3)** subtract   9 ft. 11-5/8 in.
                          5 ft. 6 in.
                          ─────────────
                          4 ft. 5-5/8 in.

Answer (1) is obtained by subtracting 5-1/2 from 10. Answer (2) is the same, only written in feet and inches. Answer (4) represents a subtraction error. Answer (5) mistakenly subtracts 5.5 as 5 ft. 5 in.

56. **(3)** To change 36.59% to a decimal, divide by 100, or move the decimal point two places to the left.

PRACTICE
EXAM III

GENERAL EDUCATIONAL DEVELOPMENT
PRACTICE EXAM III
ANSWER SHEET

Test 1:
Writing Skills, Part I

1. ① ② ③ ④ ⑤
2. ① ② ③ ④ ⑤
3. ① ② ③ ④ ⑤
4. ① ② ③ ④ ⑤
5. ① ② ③ ④ ⑤
6. ① ② ③ ④ ⑤
7. ① ② ③ ④ ⑤
8. ① ② ③ ④ ⑤
9. ① ② ③ ④ ⑤
10. ① ② ③ ④ ⑤
11. ① ② ③ ④ ⑤
12. ① ② ③ ④ ⑤
13. ① ② ③ ④ ⑤
14. ① ② ③ ④ ⑤
15. ① ② ③ ④ ⑤
16. ① ② ③ ④ ⑤
17. ① ② ③ ④ ⑤
18. ① ② ③ ④ ⑤
19. ① ② ③ ④ ⑤
20. ① ② ③ ④ ⑤
21. ① ② ③ ④ ⑤
22. ① ② ③ ④ ⑤
23. ① ② ③ ④ ⑤
24. ① ② ③ ④ ⑤
25. ① ② ③ ④ ⑤
26. ① ② ③ ④ ⑤
27. ① ② ③ ④ ⑤

28. ① ② ③ ④ ⑤
29. ① ② ③ ④ ⑤
30. ① ② ③ ④ ⑤
31. ① ② ③ ④ ⑤
32. ① ② ③ ④ ⑤
33. ① ② ③ ④ ⑤
34. ① ② ③ ④ ⑤
35. ① ② ③ ④ ⑤
36. ① ② ③ ④ ⑤
37. ① ② ③ ④ ⑤
38. ① ② ③ ④ ⑤
39. ① ② ③ ④ ⑤
40. ① ② ③ ④ ⑤
41. ① ② ③ ④ ⑤
42. ① ② ③ ④ ⑤
43. ① ② ③ ④ ⑤
44. ① ② ③ ④ ⑤
45. ① ② ③ ④ ⑤
46. ① ② ③ ④ ⑤
47. ① ② ③ ④ ⑤
48. ① ② ③ ④ ⑤
49. ① ② ③ ④ ⑤
50. ① ② ③ ④ ⑤
51. ① ② ③ ④ ⑤
52. ① ② ③ ④ ⑤
53. ① ② ③ ④ ⑤
54. ① ② ③ ④ ⑤
55. ① ② ③ ④ ⑤

Test 2:
Social Studies

1. ① ② ③ ④ ⑤
2. ① ② ③ ④ ⑤
3. ① ② ③ ④ ⑤
4. ① ② ③ ④ ⑤
5. ① ② ③ ④ ⑤
6. ① ② ③ ④ ⑤
7. ① ② ③ ④ ⑤
8. ① ② ③ ④ ⑤
9. ① ② ③ ④ ⑤
10. ① ② ③ ④ ⑤
11. ① ② ③ ④ ⑤
12. ① ② ③ ④ ⑤
13. ① ② ③ ④ ⑤
14. ① ② ③ ④ ⑤
15. ① ② ③ ④ ⑤
16. ① ② ③ ④ ⑤
17. ① ② ③ ④ ⑤
18. ① ② ③ ④ ⑤
19. ① ② ③ ④ ⑤
20. ① ② ③ ④ ⑤
21. ① ② ③ ④ ⑤
22. ① ② ③ ④ ⑤
23. ① ② ③ ④ ⑤
24. ① ② ③ ④ ⑤
25. ① ② ③ ④ ⑤
26. ① ② ③ ④ ⑤
27. ① ② ③ ④ ⑤

28. ① ② ③ ④ ⑤	**Test 3:**	36. ① ② ③ ④ ⑤
29. ① ② ③ ④ ⑤	**Science**	37. ① ② ③ ④ ⑤
30. ① ② ③ ④ ⑤	1. ① ② ③ ④ ⑤	38. ① ② ③ ④ ⑤
31. ① ② ③ ④ ⑤	2. ① ② ③ ④ ⑤	39. ① ② ③ ④ ⑤
32. ① ② ③ ④ ⑤	3. ① ② ③ ④ ⑤	40. ① ② ③ ④ ⑤
33. ① ② ③ ④ ⑤	4. ① ② ③ ④ ⑤	41. ① ② ③ ④ ⑤
34. ① ② ③ ④ ⑤	5. ① ② ③ ④ ⑤	42. ① ② ③ ④ ⑤
35. ① ② ③ ④ ⑤	6. ① ② ③ ④ ⑤	43. ① ② ③ ④ ⑤
36. ① ② ③ ④ ⑤	7. ① ② ③ ④ ⑤	44. ① ② ③ ④ ⑤
37. ① ② ③ ④ ⑤	8. ① ② ③ ④ ⑤	45. ① ② ③ ④ ⑤
38. ① ② ③ ④ ⑤	9. ① ② ③ ④ ⑤	46. ① ② ③ ④ ⑤
39. ① ② ③ ④ ⑤	10. ① ② ③ ④ ⑤	47. ① ② ③ ④ ⑤
40. ① ② ③ ④ ⑤	11. ① ② ③ ④ ⑤	48. ① ② ③ ④ ⑤
41. ① ② ③ ④ ⑤	12. ① ② ③ ④ ⑤	49. ① ② ③ ④ ⑤
42. ① ② ③ ④ ⑤	13. ① ② ③ ④ ⑤	50. ① ② ③ ④ ⑤
43. ① ② ③ ④ ⑤	14. ① ② ③ ④ ⑤	51. ① ② ③ ④ ⑤
44. ① ② ③ ④ ⑤	15. ① ② ③ ④ ⑤	52. ① ② ③ ④ ⑤
45. ① ② ③ ④ ⑤	16. ① ② ③ ④ ⑤	53. ① ② ③ ④ ⑤
46. ① ② ③ ④ ⑤	17. ① ② ③ ④ ⑤	54. ① ② ③ ④ ⑤
47. ① ② ③ ④ ⑤	18. ① ② ③ ④ ⑤	55. ① ② ③ ④ ⑤
48. ① ② ③ ④ ⑤	19. ① ② ③ ④ ⑤	56. ① ② ③ ④ ⑤
49. ① ② ③ ④ ⑤	20. ① ② ③ ④ ⑤	57. ① ② ③ ④ ⑤
50. ① ② ③ ④ ⑤	21. ① ② ③ ④ ⑤	58. ① ② ③ ④ ⑤
51. ① ② ③ ④ ⑤	22. ① ② ③ ④ ⑤	59. ① ② ③ ④ ⑤
52. ① ② ③ ④ ⑤	23. ① ② ③ ④ ⑤	60. ① ② ③ ④ ⑤
53. ① ② ③ ④ ⑤	24. ① ② ③ ④ ⑤	61. ① ② ③ ④ ⑤
54. ① ② ③ ④ ⑤	25. ① ② ③ ④ ⑤	62. ① ② ③ ④ ⑤
55. ① ② ③ ④ ⑤	26. ① ② ③ ④ ⑤	63. ① ② ③ ④ ⑤
56. ① ② ③ ④ ⑤	27. ① ② ③ ④ ⑤	64. ① ② ③ ④ ⑤
57. ① ② ③ ④ ⑤	28. ① ② ③ ④ ⑤	65. ① ② ③ ④ ⑤
58. ① ② ③ ④ ⑤	29. ① ② ③ ④ ⑤	66. ① ② ③ ④ ⑤
59. ① ② ③ ④ ⑤	30. ① ② ③ ④ ⑤	
60. ① ② ③ ④ ⑤	31. ① ② ③ ④ ⑤	**Test 4:**
61. ① ② ③ ④ ⑤	32. ① ② ③ ④ ⑤	**Interpreting**
62. ① ② ③ ④ ⑤	33. ① ② ③ ④ ⑤	**Literature and the Arts**
63. ① ② ③ ④ ⑤	34. ① ② ③ ④ ⑤	1. ① ② ③ ④ ⑤
64. ① ② ③ ④ ⑤	35. ① ② ③ ④ ⑤	2. ① ② ③ ④ ⑤

3. ① ② ③ ④ ⑤
4. ① ② ③ ④ ⑤
5. ① ② ③ ④ ⑤
6. ① ② ③ ④ ⑤
7. ① ② ③ ④ ⑤
8. ① ② ③ ④ ⑤
9. ① ② ③ ④ ⑤
10. ① ② ③ ④ ⑤
11. ① ② ③ ④ ⑤
12. ① ② ③ ④ ⑤
13. ① ② ③ ④ ⑤
14. ① ② ③ ④ ⑤
15. ① ② ③ ④ ⑤
16. ① ② ③ ④ ⑤
17. ① ② ③ ④ ⑤
18. ① ② ③ ④ ⑤
19. ① ② ③ ④ ⑤
20. ① ② ③ ④ ⑤
21. ① ② ③ ④ ⑤
22. ① ② ③ ④ ⑤
23. ① ② ③ ④ ⑤
24. ① ② ③ ④ ⑤
25. ① ② ③ ④ ⑤
26. ① ② ③ ④ ⑤
27. ① ② ③ ④ ⑤
28. ① ② ③ ④ ⑤
29. ① ② ③ ④ ⑤
30. ① ② ③ ④ ⑤
31. ① ② ③ ④ ⑤
32. ① ② ③ ④ ⑤
33. ① ② ③ ④ ⑤
34. ① ② ③ ④ ⑤
35. ① ② ③ ④ ⑤
36. ① ② ③ ④ ⑤

37. ① ② ③ ④ ⑤
38. ① ② ③ ④ ⑤
39. ① ② ③ ④ ⑤
40. ① ② ③ ④ ⑤
41. ① ② ③ ④ ⑤
42. ① ② ③ ④ ⑤
43. ① ② ③ ④ ⑤
44. ① ② ③ ④ ⑤
45. ① ② ③ ④ ⑤

Test 5:
Mathematics

1. ① ② ③ ④ ⑤
2. ① ② ③ ④ ⑤
3. ① ② ③ ④ ⑤
4. ① ② ③ ④ ⑤
5. ① ② ③ ④ ⑤
6. ① ② ③ ④ ⑤
7. ① ② ③ ④ ⑤
8. ① ② ③ ④ ⑤
9. ① ② ③ ④ ⑤
10. ① ② ③ ④ ⑤
11. ① ② ③ ④ ⑤
12. ① ② ③ ④ ⑤
13. ① ② ③ ④ ⑤
14. ① ② ③ ④ ⑤
15. ① ② ③ ④ ⑤
16. ① ② ③ ④ ⑤
17. ① ② ③ ④ ⑤
18. ① ② ③ ④ ⑤
19. ① ② ③ ④ ⑤
20. ① ② ③ ④ ⑤
21. ① ② ③ ④ ⑤
22. ① ② ③ ④ ⑤

23. ① ② ③ ④ ⑤
24. ① ② ③ ④ ⑤
25. ① ② ③ ④ ⑤
26. ① ② ③ ④ ⑤
27. ① ② ③ ④ ⑤
28. ① ② ③ ④ ⑤
29. ① ② ③ ④ ⑤
30. ① ② ③ ④ ⑤
31. ① ② ③ ④ ⑤
32. ① ② ③ ④ ⑤
33. ① ② ③ ④ ⑤
34. ① ② ③ ④ ⑤
35. ① ② ③ ④ ⑤
36. ① ② ③ ④ ⑤
37. ① ② ③ ④ ⑤
38. ① ② ③ ④ ⑤
39. ① ② ③ ④ ⑤
40. ① ② ③ ④ ⑤
41. ① ② ③ ④ ⑤
42. ① ② ③ ④ ⑤
43. ① ② ③ ④ ⑤
44. ① ② ③ ④ ⑤
45. ① ② ③ ④ ⑤
46. ① ② ③ ④ ⑤
47. ① ② ③ ④ ⑤
48. ① ② ③ ④ ⑤
49. ① ② ③ ④ ⑤
50. ① ② ③ ④ ⑤
51. ① ② ③ ④ ⑤
52. ① ② ③ ④ ⑤
53. ① ② ③ ④ ⑤
54. ① ② ③ ④ ⑤
55. ① ② ③ ④ ⑤
56. ① ② ③ ④ ⑤

WRITING SKILLS, Part II

Write your essay for Test 1: Writing Skills, Part II on these lined pages.

_____

_____

_____

_____

_____

_____

_____

_____

_____

_____

_____

_____

_____

_____

_____

_____

_____

_____

_____

_____

_____

EXAM III

TEST 1: WRITING SKILLS, PART I

Tests of General Educational Development

Directions

The Writing Skills Test is intended to measure your ability to use clear and effective English. It is a test of English as it should be written, not as it might be spoken. This test includes both multiple-choice questions and an essay. These directions apply only to the multiple-choice section; a separate set of directions given for the essay.

The multiple-choice section consists of paragraphs with numbered sentences. Some of the sentences contain errors in sentence structure, usage, or mechanics (spelling, punctuation, and capitalization). After reading the numbered sentences, answer the multiple-choice questions that follow. Some questions refer to sentences that are correct as written. The best answer for these questions is the one which leaves the sentence as originally written. The best answer for some questions is the one which produces a sentence that is consistent with the verb tense and point of view used throughout the paragraph. You should spend no more than 75 minutes on the multiple-choice questions and 45 minutes on your essay. Work carefully, but do not spend too much time on any one question. You may begin working on the essay part of this test as soon as you complete the multiple-choice section.

Do not mark in this test booklet. Record your answers on the separate answer sheet provided. Be sure that all requested information is properly recorded on the answer sheet.

To record your answers, mark one numbered space on the answer sheet beside the number that corresponds to the question in the test booklet.

FOR EXAMPLE:

Sentence 1: **We were all honored to meet governor Phillips.**

What correction should be made to this sentence?

(1)   insert a comma after honored

(2)   change the spelling of honored to honered

(3)   change governor to Governor

(4)   replace were with was

(5)   no correction is necessary   ① ② ● ④ ⑤

In this example, the word "governor" should be capitalized; therefore, answer space 3 would be marked on the answer sheet.

Do not rest the point of your pencil on the answer sheet while you are considering your answer. Make no stray or unnecessary marks. If you change an answer, erase your first mark completely. Mark only one answer space for each question; multiple answers will be scored as incorrect. Do not fold or crease your answer sheet. All test materials must be returned to the test administrator.

reprinted with permission of the General Educational Development Testing Service of the American Council on Education

Directions: Choose the <u>one best answer</u> to each item.

<u>Items 1 to 8</u> refer to the following paragraph.

(1) Nowadays people visit a shoping mall for many different reasons. (2) A number of people goes to exercise, walking the length of the mall several times. (3) Often, especially on weekends, young people stand around and ogle members of the opposite sex. (4) And try to attract the attention of some. (5) Many of the men who have accompanied females sit on the benches outside stores, looking and acting bored, others enjoy watching people or browsing in the specialty shops. (6) In the same manner, some women simply like to browse, trying to escape other responsibilities, or to avoid boredom. (7) Of course, some people, who visit a mall, are serious about shopping; they are looking for a particular item or have a specific purpose. (8) Buying clothes for school or for a special event, for instance. (9) Actually people have varied reasons for visiting a shopping mall.

1. Sentence 1: **Nowadays people visit a shoping mall for many different reasons.**

    What correction should be made to this sentence?

    (1) change <u>Nowadays</u> to <u>Nowdays</u>
    (2) change <u>shoping</u> to <u>shopping</u>
    (3) place a comma after <u>mall</u>
    (4) change <u>different</u> to <u>diversified</u>
    (5) no correction is necessary

2. Sentence 2: **A number of people goes to exercise, walking the length of the mall several times.**

    What correction should be made to this sentence?

    (1) change <u>A number</u> to <u>The number</u>
    (2) change <u>goes</u> to <u>go</u>
    (3) remove the comma after <u>exercise</u>
    (4) change <u>walking the length</u> to <u>walking for the length</u>
    (5) no correction is necessary

3. Sentences 3 and 4: **Often, especially on weekends, young people stand around and ogle members of the opposite sex. And try to attract the attention of some.**

Which of the following is the best way to write the underlined portion of these sentences? If you think that the original is the best way choose option (1).

(1) sex. And try
(2) sex, and try
(3) sex and try
(4) sex; try
(5) sex; and try

4. Sentence 5: **Many of the men who have accompanied females sit on the benches outside stores, looking and acting bored, others enjoy watching people or browsing in the specialty shops.**

    What correction should be made to this sentence?

    (1) place a comma after men and after females

    (2) place a comma after benches

    (3) remove the comma after stores

    (4) use a semicolon instead of a comma after bored

    (5) no correction is necessary

5. Sentence 6: **In the same manner, some women simply like to browse, trying to escape other responsibilities, or to avoid boredom.**

    What correction should be made to this sentence?

    (1) remove the comma after manner

    (2) place a comma before and after simply

    (3) remove the comma after browse

    (4) remove the comma after responsibilities

    (5) no correction is necessary

6. Sentence 7: **Of course, some people, who visit a mall, are serious about shopping; they are looking for a particular item or have a specific purpose.**

    What correction should be made to this sentence?

    (1) remove the comma after course

    (2) remove the commas after people and mall

    (3) use a comma instead of a semicolon after shopping

    (4) change particular to particlar

    (5) no correction is necessary

7. Sentences 7 and 8: **Of course, some people, who visit a mall, are serious about shopping; they are looking for a particular item or have a specific** purpose. Buying clothes **for school or for a special event, for instance.**

   Which of the following is the best way to write the underlined portion of these sentences? If you think that the original is the best way, choose option (1).

   (1) purpose. Buying clothes   (4) purpose—buying clothes
   (2) purpose, buying clothes   (5) purpose buying clothes
   (3) purpose; buying clothes

8. Sentence 9: **Actually people have varied reasons for visiting a shopping mall.**

   What correction should be made to this sentence?

   (1) place a comma after Actually

   (2) change have varied reasons to have varied their reasons

   (3) change people have varied reasons to varied people have reasons

   (4) change shopping to shoping

   (5) no correction is necessary

Items 9 to 16 refer to the following two paragraphs.

   (1) In most organizations, the employees can be divided into two groups, one of which is the doers. (2) Often the doers, an integral part of the organization, is industrious. (3) They take on any task; even if they have to learn the process after making some mistakes. (4) Because they are self-driving, they cannot be detered by criticism or temporary failure.

   (5) Their counterparts, the critics, are always ready to tell the doers how to perform, however, more of this group's advice is offered as the result of hindsight than of foresight. (6) Usually appearing disgruntled, the critics posess the answers to all questions, at least in their own opinions. (7) This group often rationalizes when an error is made; in addition, to claim credit, these people are quick when a job is done well. (8) Most organizations need less critics than doers, since the doers perform most of the tasks.

9. Sentence 1: **In most organizations, the employees can be divided into two groups, one of which is the doers.**

   What correction should be made to this sentence?

(1)   change employees to employes

(2)   change divided to devided

(3)   change into to in

(4)   change is to are

(5)   no correction is necessary

10.   Sentence 2: **Often the doers, an integral part of the organization, is industrious.**

What correction should be made to this sentence?

(1)   place a comma after often

(2)   change integral to intregral

(3)   change is to are

(4)   change industrious to industreous

(5)   no correction is necessary

11.   Sentence 3: **They take on any task; even if they have to learn the process after making some mistakes.**

What correction should be made to this sentence?

(1)   change take to took

(2)   change the semicolon after task to a comma

(3)   change process to proscess

(4)   place a comma after process

(5)   no correction is necessary

12.   Sentence 4: **Because they are self-driving, they cannot be detered by criticism or temporary failure.**

What correction should be made to this sentence?

(1)   change self-driving to self driving

(2)   remove the comma after self-driving

(3)   change cannot to canot

(4)   change detered to deterred

(5)   no correction is necessary

13.   Sentence 5: **Their counterparts, the critics, are always ready to tell the doers how to perform, however, more of this group's advice is offered as a result of hindsight than of foresight.**

What correction should be made to this sentence?

(1) change <u>counterparts</u> to <u>counteparts</u>
(2) change <u>perform</u> to <u>preform</u>
(3) change the comma after <u>perform</u> to a semicolon
(4) change <u>foresight</u> to <u>forsight</u>
(5) no correction is necessary

14. Sentence 6: **Usually appearing disgruntled, the critics posess the answers to all questions, at least in their own opinions.**

What correction should be made to this sentence?

(1) change <u>Usually</u> to <u>Usualy</u>
(2) change <u>disgruntled</u> to <u>disgruntle</u>
(3) change <u>posess</u> to <u>possess</u>
(4) move the comma after <u>questions</u> to after <u>at least</u>
(5) no correction is necessary

15. Sentence 7: **This group often rationalizes when an error is made; in addition, to claim credit, these people are quick when a job is done well.**

What correction should be made to this sentence?

(1) move <u>often</u> from after <u>group</u> to after <u>rationalizes</u>
(2) place a comma after <u>rationalizes</u>
(3) change the semicolon after <u>made</u> to a comma
(4) change <u>in addition, to claim credit, these people are quick when a job is done well.</u> to <u>in addition, these people are quick to claim credit when a job is done well.</u>
(5) no correction is necessary

16. Sentence 8: **Most organizations need less critics than doers, since the doers perform most of the tasks.**

What correction should be made to this sentence?

(1) change <u>less</u> to <u>fewer</u>
(2) place a comma after <u>critics</u>
(3) remove the comma after <u>doers</u>

(4)　change <u>since the doers perform most of the tasks</u> to <u>since most</u>
<u>of the tasks are performed by the doers.</u>

(5)　no correction is necessary

<u>Items 17 t0 23</u> refer to the following paragraph.

(1) Sitting on the bank of the Mississippi River and watching the sun set
is a breathe-taking experience for anyone. (2) The observer has a double
treat, since he sees not only the beauty of the sky but the reflection also
on the river. (3) No artist can realisticly capture first the brilliance and then
the softening hues against the gradually darkening blue canvas. (4) First,
a giant ball spreads its fireyness in different directions. (5) Next, the
striated pinks and purples that follow the oranges, reds, and yellows
inspire a feeling of inner peace. (6) As these pastels finally were absorbed
by the indigo, the onlooker alternately feels a calmness and disappointment that the experience has ended so quickly. (7) He realizes, though,
just how sensational watching the sun set is.

17.　Sentence 1: **Sitting on the bank of the Mississippi River and**
watching the sun set is a breathe-taking experience for anyone.

What correction should be made to this sentence?

(1)　change <u>Mississippi</u> to <u>Missippi</u>
(2)　place a comma after <u>River</u>
(3)　change <u>breathe-taking</u> to <u>breath-taking</u>
(4)　place a comma after <u>experience</u>
(5)　no correction is necessary

18.　Sentence 2: **The observer has a double treat, since he sees not**
only the beauty of the sky but the reflection also on the river.

What correction should be made to this sentence?

(1)　change <u>double treat</u> to <u>doubletreat</u>
(2)　remove the comma after <u>treat</u>
(3)　change <u>he</u> to <u>they</u>
(4)　change <u>but the reflection also on the river</u> to <u>but also the reflection</u>
<u>on the river</u>
(5)　no change is necessary

19.　Sentence 3: **No artist can realisticly capture first the brilliance and**
then the softening hues against the gradually darkening blue
canvas.

What correction should be made to this sentence?

(1) change realisticly to realistically

(2) change brilliance to brillance

(3) change softening to softning

(4) change darkening to darkning

(5) no change is necessary

20. Sentence 4: **First, a giant ball spreads its fireyness in different directions.**

What correction should be made to this sentence?

(1) remove the comma after First

(2) change its to it's

(3) change fireyness to fieriness

(4) change different to diffrent

(5) no correction is necessary

21. Sentence 5: **Next, the striated pinks and purples that follow the oranges, reds, and yellows inspire a feeling of inner peace.**

What correction should be made to this sentence?

(1) remove the comma after Next

(2) change striated to straited

(3) place a comma after purples

(4) place a comma after yellows

(5) no correction is necessary

22. Sentence 6: **As these pastels finally were absorbed by the indigo, the onlooker alternately feels a calmness and disappointment that the experience has ended so quickly.**

What correction should be made to this sentence?

(1) change were to are

(2) change absorbed to absorped

(3) place a comma after calmness

(4) place a comma after disappointment

(5) no correction is necessary

23. Sentence 7: **He realizes, though, just how sensational watching the sun set is.**

    What correction should be made to this sentence?

    (1) change realizes to relizes
    (2) remove the commas after realizes and after though
    (3) change just how sensational watching the sun set is to just how sensational is watching the sun set
    (4) change sensational to sensasional
    (5) no correction is necessary

Items 24 to 30 refer to the following paragraph.

(1) Almost every where one goes nowadays, he encounters a crowd. (2) In a gymnasium, on a ballfield, or in a park, the week end leisure seekers are abundant. (3) To enter a sports event a person has a long wait, which often results in his having to scramble to find a seat. (4) At shopping malls, especially on Friday and Saturday nights, people cannot move about freely because of the number of amblers and shoppers. (5) Sometimes even to pay a bill, an impatient person has to join others waiting impatiently. (6) Particularly on paydays, people frequently stand in a bank in long lines. (7) Wherever one goes, he often becomes a part of a throng or an assembly.

24. Sentence 1: **Almost every where one goes nowadays, he encounters a crowd.**

    What correction should be made to this sentence?

    (1) change Almost to Most
    (2) change every where to everywhere
    (3) remove the comma after nowadays
    (4) change he to they
    (5) no correction is necessary

25. Sentence 2: **In a gymnasium, on a ballfield, or in a park, the week end leisure seekers are abundant.**

    What correction should be made to this sentence?

    (1) change gymnasium to gymnaisum
    (2) change ballfield to ball field
    (3) remove the comma after park

    (4)   change week end to weekend

    (5)   no correction is necessary

26.   Sentence 3: **To enter a sports event a person has a long wait, which often results in his having to scramble to find a seat.**

    What correction should be made to this sentence?

    (1)   place a comma after event

    (2)   remove the comma after wait

    (3)   change his to him

    (4)   place a comma after scramble

    (5)   no correction is necessary

27.   Sentence 4: **At shopping malls, especially on Friday and Saturday nights, people cannot move about freely because of the number of amblers and shoppers.**

    What correction should be made to this sentence?

    (1)   remove the comma after malls

    (2)   place a comma after Friday

    (3)   change nights to night

    (4)   place a comma after freely

    (5)   no correction is necessary

28.   Sentence 5: **Sometimes even to pay a bill, an impatient person has to join others waiting impatiently.**

    What correction should be made to this sentence?

    (1)   place a comma after Sometimes

    (2)   remove the comma after bill

    (3)   remove impatient before person and change an to a

    (4)   change others to others'

    (5)   no correction is necessary

29.   Sentence 6: **Particularly on paydays, people frequently stand in a bank in long lines.**

    What correction should be made to this sentence?

    (1)   change Particularly to Particlarly

    (2)   place a comma after <u>Particularly</u>

    (3)   remove the comma after <u>paydays</u>

    (4)   change <u>stand in a bank in long lines</u> to <u>stand in long lines in a bank</u>

    (5)   no correction is necessary

30.   Sentence 7: **Wherever one goes, he often becomes a part of a throng or assembly.**

    What correction should be made to this sentence?

    (1)   change <u>Wherever</u> to <u>Whereever</u>

    (2)   change <u>goes</u> to <u>go</u>

    (3)   change <u>often becomes</u> to <u>becomes often</u>

    (4)   place a comma after <u>throng</u>

    (5)   no correction is necessary

<u>Items 31 to 36</u> refer to the following paragraph.

    (1) To enjoy many different activities in the summer, a person needs to be knowledgable and to exercise caution. (2) One danger that he may encounter, especially if he is outside for long periods of time, is heat stroke. (3) He certainly needs to avoid prolonged direct exposure to the sun. (4) Seeking shade when he has the opportunity. (5) Drinking water or some liquid can help him to retain necessary fluids. (6) At work or at play, a person needs to pace himself so he don't become too hot. (7) By being aware of potential problems and by dealing with them wisely, you can enjoy summer activities.

31.   Sentence 1: **To enjoy many different activities in the summer, a person needs to be knowledgable and to exercise caution.**

    What correction should be made to this sentence?

    (1)   place a comma after <u>activities</u>

    (2)   remove the comma after <u>summer</u>

    (3)   change <u>knowledgable</u> to <u>knowledgeable</u>

    (4)   place a comma after <u>knowledgable</u>

    (5)   no correction is necessary

32.   Sentence 2: **One danger that he may encounter, especially if he is outside for long periods of time, is heat stroke.**

    What correction should be made to this sentence?

    (1)   place a comma after <u>danger</u>

    (2)   remove the comma after <u>encounter</u>

    (3)   change <u>outside</u> to <u>out side</u>

    (4)   change <u>heat stroke</u> to <u>heatstroke</u>

    (5)   no correction is necessary

33.   Sentences 3 and 4: **He certainly needs to avoid prolonged direct exposure to the sun. <u>Seeking shade</u> when he has the opportunity.**

    Which of the following is the best way to write the underlined portion of these sentences? If you think the original is the best way, choose option (1).

    (1)   sun. Seeking shade   (4)   sun—seeking shade

    (2)   sun. Seek shade   (5)   sun; seeking shade

    (3)   sun by seeking shade

34.   Sentence 5: **Drinking water or some liquid can help him to retain necessary fluids.**

    What correction should be made to this sentence?

    (1)   place a comma after <u>water</u>

    (2)   change <u>some liquid</u> to <u>some other liquid</u>

    (3)   change <u>him</u> to <u>you</u>

    (4)   change <u>necessary</u> to <u>neccessary</u>

    (5)   no correction is necessary

35.   Sentence 6: **At work or at play, a person needs to pace himself so that he don't become too hot.**

    What correction should be made to this sentence?

    (1)   remove the comma after <u>play</u>

    (2)   change <u>himself</u> to <u>hisself</u>

    (3)   change <u>don't</u> to <u>does'nt</u>

    (4)   change <u>don't</u> to <u>does not</u>

    (5)   no correction is necessary

36.   Sentence 7: **By being aware of potential problems and by dealing with them wisely, you can enjoy summer activities.**

    What correction should be made to this sentence?

    (1)   change <u>potential</u> to <u>potentual</u>

(2) place a comma after <u>problems</u>

(3) place a comma after <u>them</u>

(4) change <u>you</u> to <u>a person</u>

(5) no correction is necessary

<u>Items 37 to 43</u> refer to the following paragraph.

(1) A person who likes to be outside during the winter may encounter problems resulting from exposure to the elements, frostbite and hypothermia, for example. (2) A person can become too cold without realizing their condition. (3) Since sometimes the cold numbs not only one's body but also his brain. (4) When one knows that he is going to be outside, he can take certain preventive measures: dressing warmly, avoid getting wet, and generally just use common sense. (5) If, for example, he feels that his extremeties are becoming too cold, he can engage his arms and legs in vigorous exercise to stimulate circulation. (6) In addition, avoiding the intake of much alcohol which affects the circulation of the blood and gives a person the feeling of being warmer than he is. (7) Simply by exercising good judgment, a person can enjoy winter activities safe.

37. Sentence 1: **A person who likes to be outside during the winter may encounter problems resulting from exposure to the elements, frostbite and hypothermia, for example.**

What correction should be made to this sentence?

(1) place a comma after <u>person</u>

(2) place a comma after <u>winter</u>

(3) place a comma after <u>problems</u>

(4) change the comma after <u>elements</u> to a dash

(5) no correction is necessary

38. Sentence 2: **A person can become too cold without realizing their condition.**

What correction should be made to this sentence?

(1) change <u>can become</u> to <u>became</u>

(2) change <u>too</u> to <u>to</u>

(3) place a comma after <u>cold</u>

(4) change <u>their</u> to <u>his</u>

(5) no correction is necessary

39. Sentences 2 and 3: **A person can become too cold without realizing their condition. Since sometimes the cold numbs not** only one's body but also his brain.

   Which of the following, is the best way to write the underlined portion of these sentences? If you think that the original is the best way, choose option (1).

   (1) condition. Since sometimes
   (2) condition; since sometimes
   (3) condition: since sometimes
   (4) condition, since sometimes
   (5) condition—since sometimes

40. Sentence 4: **When one knows that he is going to be outside, he can take certain preventive measures: dressing warmly, avoid getting wet, and generally just use common sense.**

   What correction should be made to this sentence?

   (1) place a comma after knows
   (2) change he to they
   (3) change the colon after measures to a comma
   (4) change dressing warmly, avoid getting wet, and generally just use common sense to dressing warmly, avoiding getting wet, and generally just using common sense
   (5) no correction is necessary

41. Sentence 5: **If, for example, he feels that his extremeties are becoming too cold, he can engage his arms and legs in vigorous exercise to stimulate circulation.**

   What correction should be made to this sentence?

   (1) remove the comma after If
   (2) change extremeties to extremities
   (3) change engage to engauge
   (4) change vigorous to vigerous
   (5) no correction is necessary

42. Sentences 5 and 6: **If, for example, he feels that his extremeties are becoming too cold, he can engage his arms and legs in vigorous exercise to stimulate circulation. In addition, avoiding**

the intake of much alcohol which affects the circulation of the blood and gives a person the feeling of being warmer than he is.

Which of the following is the best way to write the underlined portion of these sentences? If you think that the original is the best way, choose option (1).

(1)   circulation. In addition, avoiding

(2)   circulation; in addition, avoiding

(3)   circulation; in addition, he can avoid

(4)   circulation, in addition, avoiding

(5)   circulation, in addition; avoiding

43.   Sentence 7: **Simply by exercising good judgment, a person can enjoy winter activities safe.**

What correction should be made to this sentence?

(1)   change Simply to Simpley

(2)   place a comma after Simply

(3)   change judgment to judgement

(4)   change a person can enjoy winter activities safe to a person can safely enjoy winter activities

(5)   no correction is necessary

Items 44 to 49 refer to the following paragraph.

(1) Reminding us of an icicle, the young girl came to our school along with the chilling tempratures. (2) Though she created a chill of her own, she possesses a special beauty. (3) Soft tint—the semitransparent blue of her eyes and the pale pink of her lips—highlighted her creamy complexion. (4) Lending to the atmosphere of mystery about her was her eyes—sometimes with a faraway look. (5) And sometimes with an almost mischievous sparkle, as if she knew something that the rest of us did not. (6) When we showed any warmth toward her, she disappeared, no one could touch her in any way.

44.   Sentence 1: **Reminding us of an icicle, the young girl came to our school along with the freezing tempratures.**

What correction should be made to this sentence?

(1)   change icicle to icecicle

(2)   remove the comma after icicle

    (3)   place a comma after <u>school</u>

    (4)   change <u>tempratures</u> to <u>temperatures</u>

    (5)   no correction is necessary

45.   Sentence 2: **Though she created a chill of her own, she possesses a special beauty.**

    What correction should be made to this sentence?

    (1)   change <u>though</u> to <u>tho</u>

    (2)   change <u>created</u> to <u>creates</u>

    (3)   remove the comma after <u>own</u>

    (4)   change <u>possesses</u> to <u>possessed</u>

    (5)   no correction is necessary

46.   Sentence 3: **Soft tints—the semitransparent blue of her eyes and the pale pink of her lips—highlighted her creamy complexion.**

    What correction should be made to this sentence?

    (1)   change the dash after <u>tints</u> to a comma

    (2)   change <u>semitransparent</u> to <u>semi-transparent</u>

    (3)   change <u>highlighted</u> to <u>highlited</u>

    (4)   change <u>complexion</u> to <u>complection</u>

    (5)   no correction is necessary

47.   Sentence 4: **Lending to the atmosphere of mystery about her was her eyes—sometimes with a faraway look.**

    What correction should be made to this sentence?

    (1)   change <u>Lending</u> to <u>Loaning</u>

    (2)   change <u>atmosphere</u> to <u>environment</u>

    (3)   place a comma after <u>about her</u>

    (4)   change <u>faraway</u> to <u>far away</u>

    (5)   no correction is necessary

48.   Sentences 4 and 5: **Lending to the atmosphere of mystery about her was her eyes—sometimes with a faraway look. And sometimes with an almost mischievous sparkle, as if she knew something that the rest of us did not.**

Which of the following is the best way to write the underlined portion of these sentences? If you think that the original is the best way, choose option (1).

(1) look. And sometimes

(2) look, and sometimes

(3) look; and sometimes

(4) look and sometimes

(5) look—sometimes

49. Sentence 6: **When we showed any warmth toward her, she disappeared, no one could touch her in any way.**

What correction should be made to this sentence?

(1) change <u>showed</u> to <u>show</u>

(2) change <u>disappeared</u> to <u>dissappeared</u>

(3) change the comma after <u>disappeared</u> to a semicolon

(4) change <u>no one</u> to <u>noone</u>

(5) no correction is necessary

<u>Items 50 to 55</u> refer to the following paragraph.

(1) After deciding to observe the drivers in my city on three successive Friday afternoons, I precluded that these vehicle operators had to be the worst in the world. (2) Evidently some of these drivers could not read street signs, they thought that yield meant to speed up before another car approached or to play "dodge 'em" if one was already there. (3) Some impatient people passed on the shoulder of the road, while others pulled out of driveways, seemingly daring anyone to hit them, in fact, one driver actually held up his hand for everyone to stop while he pulled out into heavy traffic. (4) One lady traveling in the inside lane of a boulevard suddenly makes a right turn across the path of a car in the right lane. (5) Some drivers crept along, posing as great a problem as some speeders did, still others impeded the flow of traffic in different ways. (6) On one street with two narrow lanes edged by deep ditches; for example, a man picking up goods for a charitable organization stopped the truck right in the middle of the road, causing all traffic to come to a standstill. (7) At one stop sign, two different drivers hardly decreased their speed and ran up into a yard, one driver hitting the porch of a house. (8) The drivers in my city certainly proved, in my opinion, that they are some of the worst in the world.

50. Sentence 1: **After deciding to observe the drivers in my city on three successive Friday afternoons, I precluded that these vehicle operators had to be the worst in the world.**

What correction should be made to this sentence?

    (1)   place a comma after <u>drivers</u>

    (2)   place a comma after <u>city</u>

    (3)   change <u>successive</u> to <u>sucessive</u>

    (4)   change <u>precluded</u> to <u>concluded</u>

    (5)   no correction is necessary

51.   Sentence 2: **Evidently some of these drivers could not read street signs, they thought that yield meant to speed up before another car approached or to play "dodge 'em" if one was already there.**

    What correction should be made to this sentence?

    (1)   change <u>Evidently</u> to <u>Evidentally</u>

    (2)   change the comma after <u>signs</u> to a semicolon

    (3)   change <u>yield</u> to <u>yeild</u>

    (4)   place a comma after <u>approached</u>

    (5)   no correction is necessary

52.   Sentence 3: **Some impatient people passed on the shoulder of the road, while others pulled out of driveways, seemingly daring anyone to hit them, in fact, one driver actually held up his hand for everyone to stop while he pulled out into heavy traffic.**

    What correction should be made to this sentence?

    (1)   change <u>impatient</u> to <u>impacient</u>

    (2)   remove the comma after <u>road</u>

    (3)   change the comma after <u>them</u> to a semicolon

    (4)   place a comma after <u>stop</u>

    (5)   no correction is necessary

53.   Sentence 4: **One lady traveling in the inside lane of a boulevard suddenly makes a right turn across the path of a car in the right lane.**

    What correction should be made to this sentence?

    (1)   place a comma after <u>lady</u>

    (2)   change <u>traveling</u> to <u>travelling</u>

    (3)   place a comma after <u>boulevard</u>

    (4)   change <u>makes</u> to <u>made</u>

    (5)   no correction is necessary

54. Sentence 5: **Some drivers crept along, posing as great a problem as some speeders did, still others impeded the flow of traffic in different ways.**

    What correction should be made to this sentence?

    (1)   change crept to creeped
    (2)   remove the comma after along
    (3)   change posing to poseing
    (4)   change the comma after did to a semicolon
    (5)   no correction is necessary

55. Sentence 6: **On one street with two narrow lanes edged by deep ditches; for example, a man picking up goods for a charitable organization stopped the truck right in the middle of the road, causing all traffic to come to a standstill.**

    What correction should be made to this sentence?

    (1)   place a comma after lanes
    (2)   change On one street with two narrow lanes edged by deep ditches; for example, a man picking up goods for a charitable organization stopped the truck right in the middle of the road, causing all traffic to come to a standstill to In the middle of one narrow street, a man picking up goods for a charitable organization parked his truck, causing all traffic to come to a standstill.
    (3)   place a semicolon after ditches
    (4)   change road, causing all traffic to road, and caused all traffic
    (5)   no correction is necessary

TEST 1: WRITING SKILLS, PART II

Tests of General Educational Development

Directions

This part of the Writing Skills Test is intended to determine how well you write. You are asked to write an essay that explains something or presents an opinion on an issue. In preparing your essay, you should take the following steps.

1. Read carefully the directions and the essay topic given below.

2. Plan your essay carefully before you write.

3. Use scratch paper to make any notes.

4. Write your essay on the lined pages of the separate answer sheet.

5. Read carefully what you have written and make any changes that will improve your essay.

6. Check your paragraphs, sentence structure, spelling, punctuation, capitalization, and usage, and make any necessary corrections.

Be sure you write the _letter_ of the essay topic (given below) on your answer sheet. Write the letter in the box at the upper right-hand corner of the page where you write your essay.

You will have 45 minutes to write on the topic below. Write legibly and use a ballpoint pen so that the evaluators will be able to read your writing.

Write your essay on the lined pages of the separate answer sheet. The notes you make on scratch paper will not be scored.

Your essay will be scored by at least two trained evaluators who will judge it according to its <u>overall effectiveness</u>. They will judge how clearly you make the main point of your composition, how thoroughly you support your ideas, and how clearly and correctly you write throughout the essay.

reprinted with permission of the General Educational Development Testing Service of the American Council on Education

---

TOPIC A

Many experts agree that the influence of high technology in the workplace has created stressful working conditions. Experts also agree that in order to be more productive, such job-related pressures must be relieved. In a composition of about 200 words, explain how you relieve job-related pressures.

TEST 2: SOCIAL STUDIES

Tests of General Educational Development

Directions

The Social Studies Test consists of multiple-choice questions intended to measure your knowledge of general social studies concepts. The questions are based on short readings which often include a graph, chart, or figure. Study the information given and then answer the question(s) following it. Refer to the information as often as necessary in answering the questions.

You should spend no more than 85 minutes answering the questions in this booklet. Work carefully, but do not spend too much time on any one question. Be sure you answer every question. You will not be penalized for incorrect answers.

Do not mark in this test booklet. Record your answers to the questions on the separate answer sheet provided. Be sure all requested information is properly recorded on the answer sheet.

To record your answers, mark the numbered space on the answer sheet beside the number that corresponds to the question in the test booklet.

FOR EXAMPLE:

Early colonists of North America looked for settlement sites that had adequate water supplies and were accessible by ship. For this reason, many early towns were built near

(1) mountains.
(2) prairies.
(3) rivers.
(4) glaciers.
(5) plateaus.

① ② ● ④ ⑤

The correct answer is "rivers"; therefore, answer space 3 would be marked on the answer sheet.

Do not rest the point of your pencil on the answer sheet while you are considering your answer. Make no stray or unnecessary marks. If you change an answer, erase your first mark completely. Mark only one answer space for each question; multiple answers will be scored as incorrect. Do not fold or crease your answer sheet. Return all test materials to the test administrator.

reprinted with permission of the General Educational Development Testing Service of the American Council on Education

Directions: Choose the <u>one best answer</u> to each item.

<u>Items 1 to 5</u> refer to the following poll.

PUBLIC OPINION: RESPONSES TO THE QUESTION "WHY DO PEOPLE BECOME CRIMINALS?"

Cause	Percentage Naming Cause
Upbringing	38
Bad environment	30
Mentally ill	15
Wrong companions	14
No education	14
Broken homes	13
Greed	13
Too much money around	11
Not enough money in home	10
Liquor, drugs	10
Laziness	9
For kicks	8
No religion	8
No job	8
No chance by society	7
Born bad	5
Feeling of hopelessness	4
Moral breakdown of society	3
Degeneracy	2
Failure of police	2

1. Which statement best expresses public opinion?

   (1) Most criminals have only themselves to blame.
   (2) Crime is almost always the fault of environment.
   (3) Poverty creates the most crime.
   (4) Crime is worse than it used to be.
   (5) None of the above.

2. Given the opinions on crime causes, what would be the most logical solution?

   (1) Longer prison sentences   (4) More money for education
   (2) Improved social services   (5) Birth control
   (3) Stricter drug enforcement

3. If you believed in environmental rather than genetic causes for criminal behavior, which would be most likely to cause an increase in criminal activity?

    (1) Ineffectual court procedures   (4) Natural greed
    (2) Availability of weapons   (5) Laziness
    (3) Economic turndown

4. Which would be least likely to apply to sociology?

    (1) How much human behavior is influenced by groups?
    (2) How do people interact with each other?
    (3) How are people influenced by their past?
    (4) How do family members influence each other?
    (5) Why are similar people often different in many ways?

5. When a person acts out their hatred of a group of people it is called

    (1) scapegoating.   (4) fascism.
    (2) prejudice.   (5) hostility.
    (3) racism.

Items 6 to 8 refer to the following paragraph.

In the Confederate states, as in the Union states, the opening of the Civil War on April 12, 1861 was marked by enthusiasm and unity of sentiment of a high degree. The capture of Fort Sumter and Lincoln's subsequent call for troops had the effect of solidifying public opinion in the seven seceded states of the lower South. In addition, these events touched off a second secession movement in the border slaveholding states of Virginia, North Carolina, Tennessee, and Arkansas. The governors of these states indignantly rejected Lincoln's appeal for soldiers, and, within a few weeks, the four states seceded and joined the Confederacy. Thus was effected a political union of upper and lower South, and in this enlarged Confederacy (outside of a few pro-Union areas, primarily in the hill country) there was firm popular approval of the war policy in the early months of the conflict. Charleston, Montgomery, and New Orleans witnessed similar scenes of excited crowds ardently voicing their support of the government. "The South is now united to a man," wrote the sister-in-law of Salmon P. Chase (Lincoln's Secretary of the Treasury) from New Orleans; her phrases were strikingly like those used by George Ticknor to describe the prevailing mood in the Union states.

Pressly, *Americans Interpret their Civil War*, The Free Press, New York, 1962.

6. Which event occurred first?

    (1) Capture of Ft. Sumter
    (2) Lincoln's call for troops

(3)   Secession of 7 lower South states
(4)   Secession of 4 border states
(5)   Political union of upper and lower South

7.   Which best describes the public opinion about the beginning of the Civil War?

(1)   The South was enthusiastic, the North fearful.
(2)   The North was enthusiastic, the South fearful.
(3)   Both sides were enthusiastic.
(4)   Both sides were fearful.
(5)   Neither side was excited.

8.   Which is most true about the causes of the Civil War?

(1)   It was fought in the 1850's over secession and slavery.
(2)   It was fought in the 1860's over secession and slavery.
(3)   It was fought in the 1870's over secession and slavery.
(4)   The main issue was Lincoln's plan to outlaw all slavery.
(5)   The main cause was the federal government's refusal to allow Southern cotton to be sold overseas.

Items 9 to 11 refer to the following passage.

The struggle of socialism against capitalism is part of the historic rhythm in the concentration and dispersion of wealth. The capitalist, of course, has fulfilled a creative function in history: he has gathered the savings of the people into productive capital by the promise of dividends or interest; he has financed the mechanization of industry and agriculture, and the rationalization of distribution; and the result has been such a flow of goods from producer to consumer as history has never seen before. He has put the liberal gospel of liberty to his use by arguing that business-men left relatively free from transportation tolls and legislative regulation can give the public a greater abundance of food, homes, comfort, and leisure than has ever come from industries managed by politicians, manned by governmental employees, and supposedly immune to the laws of supply and demand. In free enterprise the spur of competition and the zeal and zest of ownership arouse the productiveness and inventive-ness of men; nearly every economic ability sooner or later finds its niche and reward in the shuffle of talents and the natural selection of skills; and a basic democracy rules the process insofar as most of the articles to be produced, and the services to be rendered, are determined by public demand rather than by governmental decree. Meanwhile competition compels the capitalist to exhaustive labor, and his products to ever-rising excellence.

Will and Ariel Durant, The Lessons of History, Simon and Schuster, New York, 1968.

9. Capitalism is seen as a positive influence because of all except

    (1) its immunity from the laws of supply and demand.
    (2) creating capital from savings.
    (3) creating more consumer goods.
    (4) rewarding ability and skills.
    (5) meeting consumer demands.

10. The best conclusion on the author's feelings about capitalism is

    (1) it is a useful system with some serious flaws.
    (2) it is best used in partnership with socialism.
    (3) it fits into the basic ideals of democracy.
    (4) it functions best in partnership with government.
    (5) it is a new concept that did not influence history.

11. Which saying best describes capitalism?

    (1) The greatest good for the greatest number
    (2) Ask not what you can do for yourself, ask what you can do for your country
    (3) To each according to his needs
    (4) No work, no eat
    (5) Man does not live by bread alone

Items 12 to 15 refer to the following map.

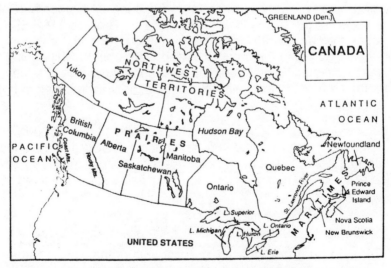

12. Which best describes the chart's arrangement?

    (1) From South to North   (4) From West to East
    (2) From North to South   (5) Random
    (3) From East to West

13. Lakes Erie and Ontario are mostly in which region?

    (1) Maritimes
    (2) Canadian Shield/Northern Territories
    (3) St. Lawrence Lowlands
    (4) Prairies
    (5) Mountain/Coastal

14. Alberta, Manitoba, and Saskatchewan are in

    (1) Maritimes.
    (2) Canadian Shield/Northern Territories.
    (3) St. Lawrence Lowlands.
    (4) Prairies.
    (5) Mountain/Coastal.

15. Which is not true about Canada?

    (1) Part of it is above the Arctic Circle.
    (2) Most of the population is close to the U.S. border.
    (3) All the Great Lakes are partially in Canada.
    (4) Quebec is a French-culture province.
    (5) Canada adapted its government system from Britain.

Items 16 to 19 refer to the following passage.

What became known as the Watergate crisis began during the 1972 presidential campaign. Early on the morning of June 17, James McCord, a security officer for the Committee to Re-elect the President (CREEP), and four other men broke into Democratic headquarters at the Watergate apartment complex in Washington, D.C. and were caught while going through files and installing electronic eavesdropping devices. On June 22, Nixon announced that the administration was in no way involved in the burglary attempt.

The trial of the burglars began in early 1973, with all but McCord, who was convicted, pleading guilty. Before sentencing, McCord wrote a letter to Judge John J. Sirica arguing that high Republican officials had known in advance about the burglary and that perjury had been committed at the trial.

Soon Jeb Stuart Magruder, head of CREEP, and John W. Dean, Nixon's attorney, stated that they had been involved. Dean testified before a Senate Watergate investigating committee that Nixon had been involved in covering up the incident. Over the next several months, extensive involvement of the administration, including payment of "silence" money to the burglars, destruction of FBI records, forgery of documents, and wiretapping, was revealed. Dean was fired and H.R. Haldeman and

John Ehrlichman, who headed the White House Staff, and Attorney General Richard Kleindienst, resigned. Nixon claimed that he had not personally been involved in the cover-up but refused, on the grounds of executive privilege, to allow investigation of White House documents.

Under considerable pressure, Nixon agreed to the appointment of a special prosecutor, Archibald Cox of Harvard Law School. When Cox obtained a subpoena for tape recordings of White House conversations (whose existence had been revealed during the Senate hearings)—and the administration lost an appeal in the appellate court—Nixon ordered Elliot Richardson, now the attorney general, to fire Cox. Both Richardson and his subordinate, William Ruckelshaus, resigned, leaving Robert Bork, the solicitor general, to carry out the order. This "Saturday Night Massacre," which took place on October 20, 1973, aroused a storm of controversy. The House Judiciary Committee, headed by Peter Rodino of New Jersey, began looking into the possibilities of impeachment. Nixon agreed to turn the tapes over to Judge Sirica and named Leon Jaworski as the new special prosecutor. But it soon became known that some of the tapes were missing and that a portion of another had been erased.

16. Who was president of the United States during the Watergate crisis?

   (1) James McCord
   (2) John W. Dean
   (3) Richard M. Nixon
   (4) Archibald Cox
   (5) Richard Kleindienst

17. The date of the Watergate break-in was

   (1) October 20, 1973.
   (2) June 17, 1973.
   (3) June 22, 1972.
   (4) June 17, 1972.
   (5) June 22, 1973

18. The Saturday Night Massacre refers to

   (1) Nixon's firing of Watergate special prosecutor, Archibald Cox, and his staff, in October, 1973.
   (2) the bombing of the Marine Corps barracks in Lebanon by a suicide truck bomber in October, 1983.
   (3) Reagan's bombing of military bases in Libya in April, 1986.
   (4) Oliver North's destruction of files related to the Iran-Contra scandal, the day before his office was searched by the FBI.
   (5) the slaughter of Vietnamese villagers in My Lai by American soldiers under the command of Lt. William Calley.

19. The two *Washington Post* reporters who "broke" the Watergate scandal to the American public were

(1)	Cronkite-Rather.	(4)	Woodward-Bernstein.
(2)	Hearst-Pulitzer.	(5)	Liddy-Dean.
(3)	Ervin-Baker.		

Items 20 to 22 refer to the following paragraph.

At the time of the Crusades, most of Western Europe was a decentralized feudal society, living a self-sufficient hand-to-mouth existence. A few scholars, chiefly in the monasteries, kept alive some learning. In the city states of northern Italy, a surviving merchant class carried on limited commerce, chiefly with the Byzantine Empire, and so had some contact with the slightly higher Byzantine civilization. For the most part, though, the cultural achievements of the Greeks and Romans had been lost. All of the peasants and most of the nobles were entirely illiterate. At that same time, Moslems generally, and especially the Moors in Spain and the Saracens in the Near East, enjoyed a much higher culture. They lived better, had more commerce, and had kept alive the learning of the classical Greeks and of the Hellenistic age. They traded indirectly, through caravans to Persia, with India and China, and so had contact with those civilizations.

Samuel A. Johnson, *An Interpretation of American History*, Barron's Inc., Woodbury, New York, 1968.

20. Western Europe was backward because

(1) the advancements of Greek and Roman civilizations had not been kept up.
(2) Moslems ruled them and lived better.
(3) Europe had no trade with others.
(4) there were no nearby civilizations to imitate.
(5) no one could read or write.

21. Which of the western civilizations in existence during the Crusades was the most advanced?

(1)	Western Europe	(4)	The Roman Empire
(2)	The Byzantine Empire	(5)	Moors and Saracens
(3)	Classical Greece		

22. The Crusades were an attempt to do all except

(1) free the Holy Land from Moslem control.
(2) increase trade with the rest of the world.
(3) destroy all Moslems.
(4) protect Christian pilgrims.
(5) expand wealth and territory.

Items 23 to 26 refer to the following graph.

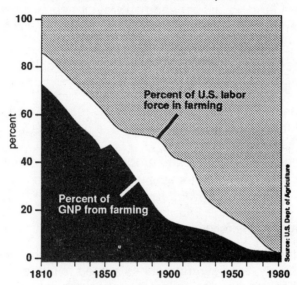

The Growth of Nonfarm Activities, 1810 – 1980

23. The graph most clearly shows

    (1)   the economic impact of farming was always more important than the number of people working in the field.

    (2)   GNP and labor force maintained a constant relationship to each other.

    (3)   farming remained the most important economic activity until about 1900.

    (4)   the decline in farming importance finally reversed itself in the 1970's.

    (5)   recently, the farming GNP and the farm labor force have more accurately matched each other.

24. Which statement is most true about American agriculture and the graph?

    (1)   Farming is no longer an important occupation.

    (2)   It is not possible to make a good living from farming.

    (3)   Farming is becoming more automated.

    (4)   American agriculture's production is now possible with fewer workers.

    (5)   There was never a time when either GNP or labor force actually increased.

25. Which does not apply to American agriculture?

    (1) Farmers usually have to borrow money to operate.
    (2) The U.S. farmer almost always creates a surplus.
    (3) Farming is one of the last areas to resist big corporations.
    (4) Modern farming still depends on weather conditions.
    (5) Modern farmers have depended heavily on government aid.

26. The best description of American agricultural problems in the near future is

    (1) increasing numbers of Americans will return to agriculture.
    (2) world food supplies will increase and need for U.S. exports will diminish.
    (3) efficiency will increase and production will need fewer workers.
    (4) water supplies and chemical fertilizers will both increase.
    (5) Third World food growing needs will diminish.

Items 27 to 29 refer to the following information.

The words of the Fourth Amendment recognize that, while individuals have a right to privacy, the government has a need to gather information. The police, for example, need to collect evidence against criminals in order to protect society against crime. The amendment considers the interests of both the public and the government.

The Fourth Amendment does not give an absolute right to privacy. It does not prohibit all searches and seizures—only those that are unreasonable. In deciding if a search is reasonable, the courts look at the facts and circumstances of each case. As a general rule, courts usually rule that searches and seizures are unreasonable unless authorized by a valid warrant or justified by special situations. In these special situations, police have a lawful or justifiable reason to discover the evidence. For instance, a person may consent to a search. The evidence, such as a gun on a seat of a car, may be in plain view of the officer. When a lawful arrest is being made, police may search a suspect for their own protection. Also, when an emergency situation arises, such as a bomb threat or house fire, police may find evidence of crime in the course of doing their duty.

L. Arbetman, R. Roe, *Great Trials in American History*, West Publishing, p. 100.

27. The best title for this reading would be

    (1) Citizen's Rights under the Fourth Amendment.
    (2) Search and Seizure—What's Legal.
    (3) Limits on the Fourth Amendment.
    (4) How to Search for Evidence.
    (5) Court Rulings on the Fourth Amendment.

28. Which would be an illegal search?

    (1) Any search without a warrant
    (2) Searching for weapons while arresting a person
    (3) A suspect voluntarily allows a search
    (4) Illegal drugs are found while investigating a shooting
    (5) Searching a house without a warrant

29. Which is not part of the Bill of Rights?

    (1) The right to a jury trial
    (2) Freedom of religion
    (3) Freedom from quartering of troops in private quarters
    (4) The freedom from slavery
    (5) The right to bear arms

Items 30 to 33 refer to the following list.

    Department of State
    Department of the Treasury
    Department of Defense
    Department of Justice
    Department of the Interior
    Department of Agriculture
    Department of Commerce
    Department of Labor
    Department of Housing and Urban Development
    Department of Transportation
    Department of Energy
    Department of Health and Human Services
    Department of Education
    Department of Veterans Affairs

30. Which department is responsible for foreign policy?

    (1) State   (4) Commerce
    (2) Defense   (5) Transportation
    (3) Justice

31. Which department supervises the FBI?

    (1) State   (4) Justice
    (2) Treasury   (5) Interior
    (3) Defense

32. Which is not a role of the Department of Health and Human Services?

   (1) Social Security   (4) Food and Drug Administration
   (2) Medicare   (5) Disease research
   (3) National Parks

33. Which is not part of the Executive Branch?

   (1) Secret Service
   (2) Pentagon
   (3) National Security Council
   (4) Securities and Exchange Commission
   (5) Council of Economic Advisors

Items 34 to 36 refer to the following chart.

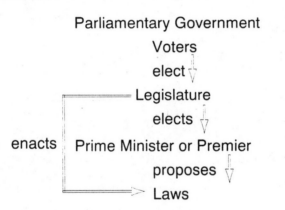

Parliamentary Government

Voters

elect

Legislature

elects

enacts   Prime Minister or Premier

proposes

Laws

34. In a parliamentary system

   (1) there is no popular election of the government leader.
   (2) the voters directly create laws.
   (3) the legislature has less power than our Congress.
   (4) only the prime minister or premier can enact laws.
   (5) only the legislature is responsible for law-making.

35. The term "parliament" comes from the legislature of

   (1) the USA.   (4) Germany.
   (2) the Soviet Union.   (5) China.
   (3) Great Britain.

36. Many legislatures are bicameral, which means

   (1) two political parties.   (4) two Houses.
   (2) elected by the people.   (5) constitutional.
   (3) supreme.

Items 37 to 39 refer to the following map.

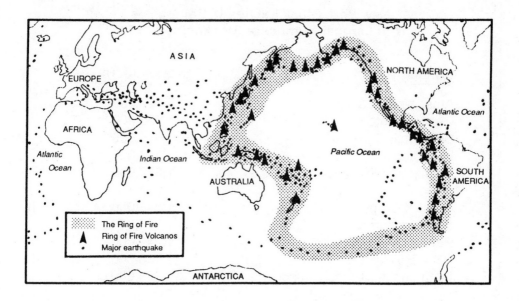

37. What geographic features have created the "Ring of Fire"?

    (1) Geothermics   (4) Tectonics
    (2) Oceanography   (5) Landforms
    (3) Ecosystems

38. Which would not be a characteristic of the area?

    (1) Volcanoes   (4) Island Formations
    (2) Earthquakes   (5) Fault Lines
    (3) Tornadoes

39. Partly as a result of volcanic activity, many Asian nations are on chains of islands known as

    (1) atolls.   (4) lagoons.
    (2) archipelagoes.   (5) continental shelves.
    (3) barrier reefs.

Items 40 to 42 refer to the following table.

New York Stock Exchange Companies With Largest Number of Stockholders, 1985	
Company	**Stockholders**
American Tel & Tel	2,927,000
General Motors	1,990,000
Bell South Corp.	1,685,000
Bell Atlantic	1,413,000
American Information Tech.	1,382,000
NYNEX Corp.	1,348,000
Southwestern Bell	1,320,000
Pacific Telesis Group	1,242,000
US WEST	1,156,000
International Business Machines	798,000
Exxon Corp.	785,000
General Electric	490,000
GTE Corp.	442,000
Bell Canada Enterprises	332,000
Sears Roebuck	326,000

From *1986 Fact Book*, copyright New York Stock Exchange, Inc., 1986.

40. Which is most true about the table?

    (1) Telephone companies have the largest number of stockholders.
    (2) Manufacturing companies have more stockholders than service companies.
    (3) Retail merchandise companies have the largest number of stockholders.
    (4) Only domestic companies are represented.
    (5) Oil companies do not have large numbers of stockholders.

41. Which company would you buy if you wanted the greatest voice in its management ?

    (1) American Tel & Tel   (4) GTE
    (2) Southwestern Bell   (5) Sears Roebuck
    (3) Exxon

42. Stockholders control a company through

    (1)   the chief executive officer.
    (2)   the chairperson of the board.
    (3)   the president of the company.
    (4)   the elected board of directors.
    (5)   stock options.

Items 43 to 45 refer to the following graph.

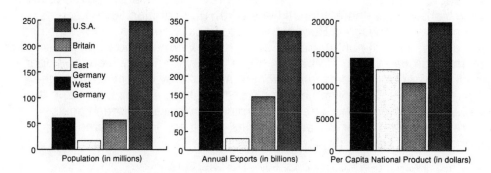

43. Under a unified Germany,

    (1)   the U.S. continues to be the leading exporter.
    (2)   Britain will export about 60% of Germany's total.
    (3)   the East will increase Germany's exports by nearly 10%.
    (4)   the U.S. and Germany will almost be tied in exports.
    (5)   British and German exports together will total nearly $600 billion.

44. The best indicator of people's standard of living is the

    (1)   per capita gross national product.
    (2)   the population divided into the annual exports.
    (3)   the annual exports.
    (4)   the per capita gross national product divided into the exports.
    (5)   the per capita national product multiplied by the population.

45. Which statement would be most true?

    (1)   The U.S. leads in productivity and GNP.
    (2)   Germany will go from 4th to 2nd in GNP by unifying.
    (3)   For its population, the U.S. produced the fewest exports.
    (4)   For its population, Britain produced the most exports.
    (5)   Unified Germany's per capita income will surpass the U.S.

Items 46 to 48 refer to the following paragraph.

LAND

The exploitation of the beasts took hunter and trader to the west, Mormons went west to escape persecution, the exploitation of the grasses took the rancher west, and the exploitation of the virgin soil of the river valleys and prairies attracted the farmer. Good soils have been the most continuous attraction to the farmer's frontier. The land hunger of the Virginians drew them down the rivers into Carolina, in early colonial days; the search for soils took the Massachusetts men to Pennsylvania and to New York. As the eastern lands were taken up migration flowed across them to the west. Daniel Boone, the great backwoodsman, who combined the occupations of hunter, trader, cattle-raiser, farmer, and surveyor— learning probably from the traders of the fertility of the lands on the upper Yadkin, where the traders were wont to rest as they tool their way to the Indians, left his Pennsylvania home with his father, and passed down the Great Valley road to that stream. Learning from a trader whose posts were on the Red River in Kentucky of its game and rich pastures, he pioneered the way for the farmers to that region.

From "The Significance of the Frontier in American History", by Fredrick Jackson Turner

46. Which of the reasons given for moving West is strongest?

    (1) Better hunting   (4) Owning land
    (2) Good soils   (5) Trade
    (3) River valleys

47. Daniel Boone's fame came from

    (1) being the best farmer in Kentucky.
    (2) being the first white man to reach Kentucky.
    (3) being the first to trade with the Indians in Kentucky.
    (4) being the largest cattle raiser in Kentucky.
    (5) being the pioneer for a route to Kentucky.

48. Which statement is most true about American settlement?

    (1) Thomas Jefferson bought the Louisiana Purchase from Spain.
    (2) California did not have permanent settlements until the Gold Rush.
    (3) The Mormons deliberately chose Utah because it was isolated.
    (4) American expansion finally stopped on the West Coast.
    (5) Only the Indians resisted U.S. expansion westward.

Items 49 to 52 refer to the following table.

THE STRESS OF CHANGE

Any change—even a pleasant one—produces stress (Holmes and Rake, 1967). In order to study the extent of stress produced by change, Thomas Holmes and his colleagues constructed a scale of stress values. They assigned an arbitrary baseline value of 50 life change units (LCU) to the act of marrying and then asked people from several countries to rate other actions and events in terms of it. Using this scale, the researchers found evidence that changes totaling more than 300 LCU within one year could result in serious illness within the next two years (Holmes and Holmes, 1970). Here are the life events and their scale values (Holmes and Rake, 1967).

Life Event	*Scale Value*
Death of spouse	100
Divorce	73
Marital separation	65
Jail term	63
Death of close family member	63
Personal injury or illness	53
Marriage	50
Fired from work	47
Marital reconciliation	45
Retirement	45
Change in family member's health	44
Pregnancy	40
Sex Difficulties	39
Gain of new family member	39
Business readjustment	39
Change in financial state	38
Death of close friend	37
Career change	36
Change in number of arguments with spouse	35
Mortgage over $10,000	31
Foreclosure of mortgage or loan	30
Change in responsibilities at work	29
Son or daughter leaving home	29
Trouble with in-laws	29
Outstanding personal achievement	28
Spouse begins or stops work	26
Starting or finishing school	26

Life Event	Scale Value
Change in living conditions	25
Revision of personal habits	24
Trouble with boss	23
Change in work hours or conditions	20
Change in residence	20
Change in schools	20
Change in recreation habits	19
Change in church activities	19
Change in social activities	18
Mortgage or loan less than $10,000	17
Change in sleeping habits	16
Change in number of family gatherings	15
Change in eating habits	15
Vacation	13
Christmas season	12
Minor violations of the law	11

49. Which best describes the items on the chart?

    (1) Normal life events
    (2) Events that create a crisis
    (3) Events that create family problems
    (4) Events that change routine
    (5) Negative events

50. The chart is measuring

    (1) universal experiences.   (4) reasons for joining a religion.
    (2) stressful situations.   (5) life expectancy factors.
    (3) causes of mental illness.

51. Psychologically, which of the following could be of the most help with the situations above?

    (1) Winning the lottery   (4) Repression
    (2) Assertiveness   (5) Transference
    (3) Experience

52. Society's inability to cope with rapid change has been labeled

    (1) transference.   (4) future shock.
    (2) stress.   (5) repression.
    (3) tension.

Items 53 to 55 refer to the following passage.

Although the Thirteen States lacked a great political leader to call forth a spirit of sacrifice, Washington did his best to fill the political as well as the military role. He was more than a general: the embodiment of everything fine in American character. With no illusions about his own grandeur, no thought of the future except an intense longing to return to Mount Vernon, he assumed every responsibility thrust upon him, and fulfilled it. He not only had to lead an army but constantly to write letters to Congress, state leaders, and state governments, begging them for the wherewithal to maintain his army. He had to compose quarrels among his officers and placate cold, hungry, unpaid troops. Intrigues against his authority he ignored, and the intriguers came to grief. In his relations with French officers he proved to be a diplomat second only to Franklin. Refusing to accept a salary, he dipped into his modest fortune to buy comforts for the soldiers and to help destitute families of his companions in battle. Thus Washington brought something more important to the cause than military ability and statesmanship: the priceless gift of character.

Although Washington was scrupulous in his respect for the civil power, there was a certain jealousy of him in Congress and the state governments, largely from fear that he would be too successful and become a dictator. Yet, inconsistently, several members, especially Richard Henry Lee of his own state, and James Lovell of Massachusetts, thought he was not successful enough and played with the idea of relieving him by Charles Lee, or Gates, or the French Duc de Broglie. Just how far the "Conway cabal" of 1777 intended to go; whether it was an officer's plot to supersede Washington, or mere grumbling by ambitious malcontents, is still a mystery. But it is certain that the commander in chief was regarded by the rank and file, and by the people in all parts of the country, with deep respect and affection. He did not have the personality of a Napoleon, a Nelson, or a Stonewall Jackson to arouse men to fanatical loyalty; but the soldiers knew that they could depend on him for valor, for military wisdom, and for justice.

Reprinted from *The Oxford History of the American People*, Samuel Eliot Morison, Oxford University Press, NY, 1965.

53. The article discusses which part of Washington's career?

    (1) Young British colonial army officer
    (2) General of the Continental rebels
    (3) President of the Constitutional Convention
    (4) President of the new United States
    (5) Author of the Declaration of Independence

54. Among the problems Washington faced was

    (1) lack of confidence by his troops.

(2)   accusations of dishonesty.
(3)   opposition by the commander-in-chief.
(4)   lack of popular support.
(5)   fear that he was either too successful or not successful enough.

55.   Which does not describe Washington?

(1)   First President of the United States
(2)   Father of the Constitution
(3)   "Father of his country"
(4)   Commander-in-chief of the Continental army
(5)   Owner of Mount Vernon

Items 56 to 58 refer to the following article.

The idea of a global shortage seems incredible when 70% of the Earth's surface is covered by H_2O. But 98% of that water is salty, making it unusable for drinking or agriculture. Desalinization is technically feasible, but it is far too expensive to use anywhere except in an ultra-rich, sparsely populated country like Saudi Arabia. Other options, like towing icebergs from the poles, are also beyond the means of poor nations.

The scarcity of fresh water for agriculture makes famines more likely every year. The world consumes more food than it produces, and yet there are few places to turn for additional cropland. Only by drawing on international stockpiles of grain have poorer countries averted widespread starvation. But those supplies are being depleted. From 1987 to 1989, the world's stock of grain fell from a 101-day surplus to a 54-day one. A drought in the U.S. bread-basket could rapidly lead to a global food calamity.

Even if rainfall stays at normal levels, current world food production will be difficult to maintain, much less increase. The food supply has kept pace with population growth only because the amount of land under irrigation has doubled in the past three decades. Now, however, agriculture is losing millions of hectares of this land to the effects of improper watering.

Reprinted from *Time Magazine*, August 20, 1990.

56.   The best title for the article would be

(1)   Alternative Water Supplies.   (2)   Problems for Poor Nations.
(3)   Famine Around the World.   (4)   World Grain Supplies.
(5)   Possible Water Problems.

57.   World food supply is in danger because

(1)   individual people are eating more.

    (2)   grain-growing nations have been unwilling to share surpluses.
    (3)   population is growing faster than the surplus of world grain.
    (4)   irrigated farmland is now being lost.
    (5)   poor nations waste money on desalination projects.

58.   Which of the following would least influence fresh water supplies?

    (1)   Annual rainfall   (4)   Soil drainage types
    (2)   Temperature patterns   (5)   Greenhouse effect
    (3)   Hydrologic cycle

Items 59 to 61 refer to the following passage.

If you start by making a list of all the social customs of one particular culture, you will find equivalents to nearly all of them in nearly all other cultures. Only the details will differ, and they will differ so wildly that they will sometimes obscure the fact that you are dealing with the same basic social patterns.

To give an example: in some cultures ceremonies of mourning involve the wearing of black costumes; in others, by complete contrast, the mourning dress is white. Furthermore, if you cast the net wide enough, you can find still other cultures that employ dark blue, or grey, or yellow, or natural brown sackcloth. Having grown up yourself in a culture where, from early childhood, one of these colours, say black, has been heavily associated with death and mourning, it will be startling to think of wearing such colours as yellow or blue in this context. Therefore, your immediate reaction on discovering that these colours are worn as mourning dress in other places is to remark on how different they are from your own familiar custom. Herein lies the trap, so neatly set by the demands of cultural isolation. The superficial observation that the colours vary so dramatically obscures the more basic fact that all these cultures share the performance of a mourning 'display', and that in all of them it involves the wearing of a costume that is strikingly different from the non-mourning costume.

Reprinted from *The Human Zoo*, by Desmond Morris, Dell Publishing Co. Inc., New York 1969.

59.   The main point of the article is

    (1)   cultures have a variety of customs.
    (2)   details differ, but customs are alike.
    (3)   colorful clothes are important in a mourning custom.
    (4)   people wear their best clothes in mourning.
    (5)   it's easy to understand another culture's customs.

60.   Which would be the best title for the article?

    (1)   Observing Customs   (2)   Use of Color in Mourning

(3)   Cultural Differences   (4)   Cultural Isolation
(5)   Cultural Similarities

61.   Which field would the excerpt be from?

(1)   History   (4)   Psychology
(2)   Geography   (5)   Economics
(3)   Anthropology

Items 62 to 64 refer to the following cartoon.

reprinted with permission of Bill Day; Detroit Free Press, Tribune Media Services

62.   Which group would be most in favor of this cartoon?

(1)   NRA   (4)   OPEC
(2)   Commerce Department   (5)   NATO
(3)   Greenpeace

63.   Which problem in the cartoon would be found in an underdeveloped nation?

(1)   Acid rain   (4)   Ozone layer depletion
(2)   Nuclear Waste   (5)   Destroyed rain forests
(3)   Toxic Waste

64.   According to scientists, which would not be a major result of the greenhouse effect?

(1)   Average temperature rising
(2)   Higher sea levels
(3)   Higher disease rates
(4)   Polar ice caps receding
(5)   Lowered sun radiation levels

TEST 3: SCIENCE

Tests of General Educational Development

Directions

The Science Test consists of multiple-choice questions intended to measure your knowledge of the general concepts in science. The questions are based on short readings which often include a graph, chart, or figure. Study the information given and then answer the question(s) following it. Refer to the information as often as necessary in answering the questions.

You should spend no more than 95 minutes answering the questions in this booklet. Work carefully, but do not spend too much time on any one question. Be sure you answer every question. You will not be penalized for incorrect answers.

Do not mark in this test booklet. Record your answers to the questions on the separate answer sheet provided. Be sure all requested information is properly recorded on the answer sheet.

To record your answers, mark the numbered space on the answer sheet beside the number that corresponds to the question in the test booklet.

FOR EXAMPLE:

Which of the following is the smallest unit in a living thing?

(1)	Tissue	(4)	Muscle	
(2)	Organ	(5)	Capillary	
(3)	Cell			① ② ● ④ ⑤

The correct answer is "cell"; therefore, answer space 3 would be marked on the answer sheet.

Do not rest the point of your pencil on the answer sheet while you are considering your answer. Make no stray or unnecessary marks. If you change an answer, erase your first mark completely. Mark only one answer space for each question; multiple answers will be scored as incorrect. Do not fold or crease your answer sheet. Return all test materials to the test administrator.

reprinted with permission of the General Educational Development Testing Service of the American Council on Education

Directions: Choose the one best answer to each item.

Items 1 to 4 refer to the following information.

A graph of a car's instantaneous speed is shown below for a time period of 30 seconds. Assume that when the car's speed is negative, it is backing up, and that it can only move in a straight line.

Instantaneous Speed vs. Time

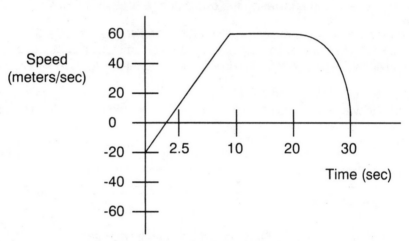

1. How long in seconds is the car moving forward?

    (1) 30 seconds   (4) 10 seconds
    (2) 27.5 seconds   (5) 2.5 seconds
    (3) 15 seconds

2. During what time period is the car moving at constant speed?

    (1) Never   (4) 20–30 seconds
    (2) 0–10 seconds   (5) 2.5–10 seconds
    (3) 10–20 seconds

3. During the first 30 seconds, the maximum speed reached by the car is

    (1) 20 meters/sec.   (4) 50 meters/sec.
    (2) 30 meters/sec.   (5) 60 meters/sec.
    (3) 40 meters/sec.

4. The car changes its speed the greatest (i.e., has the greatest accelera-tion or deceleration) during the period

    (1) 0–2.5 seconds.   (2) 2.5–10 seconds.

(3)   15–20 seconds.   (4)   20–25 seconds.
(5)   25–30 seconds.

Items 5 to 9 refer to the following paragraph.

   Most of the land plants that one observes have vascular tissue. This
tissue transports substances between various regions of the plant. There
are two types of vascular tissue: phloem and xylem. The phloem transports or conducts organic materials, mainly food, from where they are
made to various storage sites or regions of use. Xylem transports water
and minerals from the roots to the stems and leaves and flowers. Another
function of the xylem is that of support. To prevent drying out, the surface
of a plant is covered with a waxy cuticle. The cuticle is impermeable to
gases such as carbon dioxide and oxygen, and to water. Since the plant
needs carbon dioxide and oxygen to carry on photosynthesis, these
gases are exchanged through tiny pores in the leaf called stomata. Each
stomata is surrounded by two guard cells which regulate the size of the
opening of the pore.

5.   The tissue that is able to conduct food to specialized areas in the plant
      is the

      (1)   xylem.   (4)   stomata.
      (2)   phloem.   (5)   cuticle.
      (3)   precambrium.

6.   The tissue that is able to prevent the plant from drying out is the

      (1)   xylem.   (4)   stomata.
      (2)   phloem.   (5)   cuticle.
      (3)   precambrium.

7.   Guard cells make up the

      (1)   xylem.   (4)   stomata.
      (2)   phloem.   (5)   cuticle.
      (3)   precambrium.

8.   The amount of carbon dioxide and oxygen is regulated by the

      (1)   xylem.   (4)   stomata.
      (2)   phloem.   (5)   cuticle.
      (3)   precambrium.

9.   Another term that refers to xylem and phloem is

      (1)   roots.   (2)   stems.

(3)   vascular tissue.   (4)   muscular tissue.
(5)   woody tissue.

Items 10 to 11 refer to the following passage.

In an ionic bond, the entities bonded together are ions of opposite charge. Electrons must be transferred to form an ionic bond. In a covalent bond, which is a strong bond, electrons are shared between two neutral atoms. Hard substances, such as diamonds, consist of covalently bonded atoms.

10.   Sodium chloride is best described as a(n)

(1)   covalent compound consisting of Na^+ cations and Cl^- anions.
(2)   ionic compound consisting of Na^+ cations and Cl^- anions.
(3)   covalent compound consisting of Na^- anions and Cl^+ cations.
(4)   ionic compound consisting of Na^- anions and Cl^+ cations.
(5)   ionic compound consisting of Na^+ anions and Cl^- cations.

11.   An example of a substance joined by one or several covalent bonds would be

(1) H_2.   (4)   a diamond.
(2) Cl_2.   (5)   1, 2, and 4.
(3)   NaCl.

Items 12 to 13 refer to the following map.

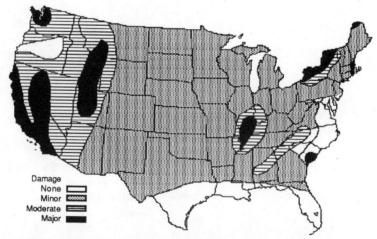

Damage
None
Minor
Moderate
Major

Seismic risk map for the U.S. issued January 1969, showing earthquake damage areas of reasonable expectancy in the next 100 years (Derived from U.S. Coast and Geodetic Survey, ESSA Rel. ES-1, January 14, 1969.

12. People living in which state have little need for Earthquake insurance?

    (1) Rhode Island   (4) California
    (2) Wyoming   (5) Washington
    (3) Illinois

13. Data from the map indicates that

    (1) a major Earthquake will definitely occur within 100 years.
    (2) a major Earthquake will definitely occur in California within 100 years.
    (3) an Earthquake can never occur in Texas.
    (4) nothing can be concluded from this map concerning the location of Earthquakes.
    (5) few states are safe from Earthquakes.

Items 14 to 16 refer to the following passage.

The term "volcanic activity" can mean erupting volcanoes complete with lava and pyroclastic display, or it can mean a simple gaseous emission. It is believed that volcanic activity formed the early Earth's atmosphere. Volcanic gases typically include water vapor, carbon dioxide, hydrogen sulfide, sulfur dioxide, chlorine, and fluorine.

14. Which statement can be drawn in conclusion from the above information?

    (1) Volcanic gases can be more dangerous than lava.
    (2) Erupting volcanoes always emit both lava and gas.
    (3) The term "volcanic activity" is always clear in its meaning.
    (4) Erupting volcanoes emit lava only.
    (5) Erupting volcanoes emit gases only.

15. Which statement is false?

    (1) The early Earth's atmosphere contained no free oxygen.
    (2) The early Earth's atmosphere was poisonous to present day life forms.
    (3) Current Earth's atmosphere must be formed by factors other than volcanic activity.
    (4) Volcanic activity today emits oxygen to the atmosphere.
    (5) None of the above.

16. "Pyroclastic display" is best defined as

    (1) a fallout of ice and snow.   (4) a hot, green vapor.
    (2) trees that fall near the volcano. (5) fire and rock particles.
    (3) a mushroom-type cloud.

Items 17 to 20 refer to the following information.

Pressure is a concept in physics that has a very precise definition. It is the force acting divided by the area upon which it acts. Air pressure at the Earth's surface is 14.7 lbs/in² or 1.013 x 105 N/m². (1.0 lb/in² is known as a PSI.) This pressure is enough to support a 34-foot high, 1-inch square column of water in a vacuum or 2.5-foot high, 1-inch square column of mercury in a vacuum. Water weighs 62.4 lbs per cubic foot or 9797 N per cubic meter.

17. Comparing identical volumes of liquid, mercury weighs

    (1)   157 times more than water.
    (2)   68.1 times more than water.
    (3)   13.6 times more than water.
    (4)   2.3 times more than water.
    (5)   the same as water.

18. A 200 lb man standing on snow with boots each having a bottom area of 35 square inches will exert a downward pressure due to his weight equal to

    (1)   200 PSI   (4)   2.86 PSI
    (2)   100 PSI   (5)   1.93 PSI
    (3)   5.71 PSI

19. A young girl wearing snow skis weighs 110 lbs. If the total area of the skis touching the snow is 330 square inches, then the air pressure on the snow is about

    (1)   11 times that of the girl.   (4)   44 times that of the girl.
    (2)   22 times that of the girl.   (5)   55 times that of the girl.
    (3)   33 times that of the girl.

20. An air pressure of 14.7 PSI can support a one square foot column of water in a vacuum that is

    (1)   34 feet high.   (4)   2.83 inches high.
    (2)   17 feet high.   (5)   less than an inch high.
    (3)   2.83 feet high.

Items 21 to 25 refer to the following paragraph.

A bean seed is a reproductive structure produced by a flower. It contains a plant embryo that is in an arrested stage of development. It also contains the food supply that nourishes the embryo as it begins to grow. The outer covering of the bean is its protective seed coat. Inside of the seed coat is the embryonic plant and two large "seed leaves" or cotyledons. The seed leaves contain nutrients that help the embryo grow until the plant can depend on photosynthesis to make its own food. The embryo has two meristems. Meristems are growth points where the dividing cells promote growth in length or diameter. One of the meristems is located in the plumule which is found between the first foliage leaves. The other meristem is found at the tip of the radical. The meristem located in the plumule promotes the growth of the shoot system (stem, leaves, etc.), and the meristem located at the tip of the radical promotes the growth of the root system. Since the meristems are located at the "tips" of the embryonic plant, they are referred to as apical meristems. Apical meristems promote primary growth or growth in length.

21. A seed leaf is also known as a

    (1) plumule.   (4) seed coat.
    (2) radical.   (5) cotyledon.
    (3) apical meristem.

22. A generalized term referring to a region of actively dividing cells that promotes growth is known as the

    (1) plumule.   (4) seed coat.
    (2) radical.   (5) cotyledon.
    (3) apical meristem.

23. The apical meristem that promotes the growth of the shoot system of a plant is the

    (1) plumule.   (4) seed coat.
    (2) radical.   (5) cotyledon.
    (3) internode.

24. The apical meristem that promotes the growth of the root system of a plant is the

    (1) plumule.   (4) seed coat.
    (2) radical.   (5) cotyledon.
    (3) node.

25. The embryonic plant receives nourishment from the

    (1) plumule.   (4) seed coat.
    (2) radical.   (5) cotyledons.
    (3) apical meristem.

Items 26 to 28 refer to the following information.

Electrons are arranged in orbitals, each possessing various amounts of energy. A hydrogen atom has only one electron and its electron configuration is 1s. When two electrons reside in the same orbital, their spins must be paired as opposed to being parallel.

26. Rank the orbitals from highest energy to lowest energy as found in a multielectron atom.

    (1) 1s, 2s, 2p, 3s, 3p   (4) 3s, 3p, 2s, 2p, 1s
    (2) 3p, 3s, 2p, 2s, 1s   (5) 3d, 2p, 2s, 1p, 1s
    (3) 1s, 2p, 2s, 3p, 3s

27. An example of two electrons in the same orbital with paired spin quantum numbers (m_s) would be

    (1) $m_s = +1/2$, $m_s = -1/2$ (4) $m_s = +1$, $m_s = +1$
    (2) $m_s = +1/2$, $m_s = +1/2$ (5) 2 and 3
    (3) $ms = -1/2$, $m_s = -1/2$

28. Flourine has nine electrons. What is its ground state electronic configuration?

    (1) 1s nine   (4) $1s^2 2p^2 2s^5$
    (2) 1s2s2p   (5) $2p^3$
    (3) $1s^2 2s^2 2p^5$

Items 29 to 31 refer to the following diagram.

An artesian well system is based on the fact that a water-bearing rock layer (aquifer) is trapped between two impermeable rock layers.

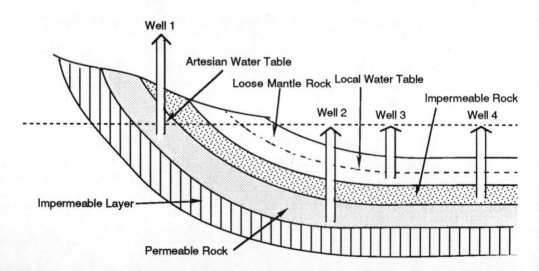

29. Which well is an artesian well that will flow out under its own power?

    (1) Well 1   (4) Well 4
    (2) Well 2   (5) None of the above.
    (3) Well 3

30. Which well is an aquifer well that would require a pumping stem to bring water to the surface?

    (1) Well 1   (4) Well 4
    (2) Well 2   (5) None of the above.
    (3) Well 3

31. Which well is a common well subject to regional weather conditions?

    (1) Well 1   (4) Well 4
    (2) Well 2   (5) None of the above.
    (3) Well 3

Items 32 to 38 refer to the following paragraph.

An animal cell is composed of many parts. The outside of the cell is surrounded by a membrane. The cell membrane is selective, which means that it only allows certain things in or out of the cell. The inside of the cell is composed of various cell organelles (little organs) and the matrix in which they are suspended. The matrix is called the cytoplasm. One of the most conspicuous objects in the cytoplasm is the nucleus. The nucleus is a large spherical structure. It is composed of a nuclear membrane which, like the cell membrane, is selective. Inside the nucleus is a viscous matrix, the nucleoplasm. Suspended in the nucleoplasm are the chromosomes and the nucleoli. The nucleoli are dark staining spherical structures that are thought to function in the production of ribosomes, structures that are involved in protein synthesis. The chromosomes, the number of which may vary from organism to organism, are elongated threadlike structures that cannot be seen with a normal microscope. However, during cell division, the chromosomes coil up and become visible. Some other cell organelles include the mitochondria and the vacuoles. The mitochondria produce energy for the cell. The vacuoles are used as storage centers. They may store food, water, or waste products.

32. Which of the following is the first barrier of defense that a foreign molecule must face upon entering an animal cell?

    (1) Nucleoplasm   (4) Chromosomes
    (2) Cytoplasm   (5) Cell membrane
    (3) Nuclear membrane

33. The number of elongated threadlike chromosomes that can be visualized during cell division

    (1) depends on the random manner in which the chromosomes reassemble during coiling.
    (2) varies among the different types of somatic cells within one organism.
    (3) depends on the strength of the microscope.
    (4) is the same for somatic cells within one individual.
    (5) is influenced by the presence of the nucleoli, which are also suspended in the nucleoplasm.

34. Since nucleoli are involved in the formation of ribosomes, it follows that

    (1) ribosomes must be located in the nucleus so as not to be far from their origin.
    (2) ribosomes must be transferred from the nucleus to the cytoplasm in order to function in protein synthesis.
    (3) ribosomes must be transferred to the area where they can produce energy for the cell.
    (4) the coiling of the chromosomes always hinders the formation of the ribosomes.
    (5) ribosomes must also be dark staining.

35. Since the cell membrane and nuclear membrane are selective in nature, they can be considered

    (1) totally permeable.   (4) opaque.
    (2) nonpermeable.   (5) translucent.
    (3) semipermeable.

36. Dark staining spherical structures in the nucleus are

    (1) nucleoplasm.   (4) chromosomes.
    (2) cytoplasm.   (5) mitochondria.
    (3) nucleoli.

37. Which of the following are used as storage structures in a cell?

    (1) Ribosomes   (4) Nucleoli
    (2) Mitochondria   (5) Chromosomes
    (3) Vacuoles

38. Which structures are thought to be involved in making ribosomes?

    (1) Chromosomes   (4) Mitochondria
    (2) Nucleoli   (5) Cytoplasm
    (3) Vacuoles

Items 39 to 41 refer to the following information.

Ernest Rutherford's (1871-1937) experiment provided the basis for the description of an atom's structure. In his experiment, alpha particles were directed toward a thin gold foil. Most particles went through the foil in a fairly straight line, but a few particles were deflected at sharp angles. A diagram of the experiment is shown below.

RUTHERFORD'S APPARATUS FOR OBSERVING THE SCATTERING OF ALPHA PARTICLES BY A METAL FOIL (within a vacuum chamber)

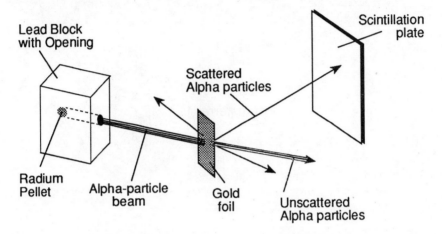

39. Why were some alpha particles deflected at sharp angles?

    (1) The particles did not have enough velocity to penetrate the gold foil, which may have been too thick in some areas.
    (2) The alpha particles were hitting electrons.
    (3) The alpha particles were colliding with atomic nuclei.
    (4) The alpha particles were being repelled from the gold since both alpha particles and gold possess the the same charge.
    (5) The surrounding air pulled the alpha particles from the area where the gold foil was located.

40. Why do most alpha particles pass through the gold foil without being deflected?

    (1) Most of the atom is empty space which alpha particles can pass through unaffected.
    (2) The gold foil was mostly thin enough to allow alpha particles to pass through.
    (3) The electrons did not get in the way.
    (4) The atomic nuclei are semipermeable.
    (5) The alpha particles move so fast that they push the atomic nuclei out of the way.

41. The symbol for gold is

(1) Ga. (4) Na.
(2) Hg. (5) Au.
(3) He.

Items 42 to 44 refer to the following map.

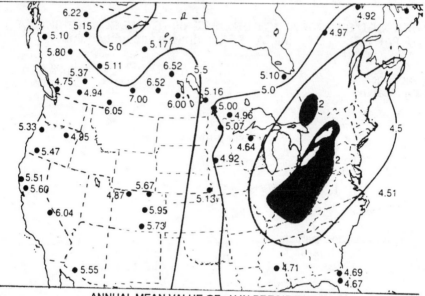

ANNUAL MEAN VALUE OF pH IN PRECIPITATION
IN NORTH AMERICA FOR 1980

42. Which part of the United States and Canada has the most serious acid rain problem?

(1) Northern (4) Southwest
(2) Southern (5) Northwest
(3) Northeast

43. The Great Lake(s) in most serious danger from acid rain are

(a) Superior. (d) Erie.
(b) Huron. (e) Ontario.
(c) Michigan.

(1) All the above. (4) d and e.
(2) a and b. (5) None of the avove.
(3) b and c.

44. Which factor could not account for variation in pH readings?

(1) Forest cover (4) Population densities
(2) Industry (5) Rainfall variations
(3) Prevailing westerly winds

Items 45 to 48 refer to the following paragraph.

Sharks are vertebrate animals and their skeleton is composed of cartilage. Sharks are not in the class Osteichthyes because sharks do not have bony skeletons. The shark is a member of the class Chondrichtheyes. Other members of this class included the rays, skates, and dogfishes. Sharks have a very rough skin which is covered with little toothlike appendages called denticles. Their teeth are enlarged versions of the denticles. Even though most sharks are ferocious predators, the two largest sharks are filter feeders. Sharks have internal fertilization with the female retaining the eggs within her body. Some of these sharks are ovoviparous, which means that the embryo gets all of its nourishment or food from the yolk of the egg. Other sharks are viviparous, which means that the embryo gets its nourishment from close contact of the blood vessels of the mother's oviduct with the blood vessels of the yolk.

45. Sharks have what type of fertilization?

    (1)   Denticle   (4)   External
    (2)   Viviparous   (5)   Internal
    (3)   Ovoviparous

46. Sharks are members of the

    (1)   phylum Reptilia.   (4)   class Osteichthyes.
    (2)   class Aves.   (5)   class Chondrichthyes.
    (3)   class Vertebrata.

47. If a shark is said to be viviparous, then

    (1)   as an embryo it eats its brothers and sisters before they hatch.
    (2)   as an embryo it gets nourishment from the yolk.
    (3)   as an embryo it gets its nourishment directly from the mother's blood.
    (4)   as an embryo it gets its nourishment by eating the mother's oviduct.
    (5)   as an embryo it gets its nourishment from the yolk's blood vessels which are close to the the oviduct's blood vessels.

48. The part of a whale most related to fish scales would be the

    (1)   denticles.   (4)   embryos.
    (2)   yolks.   (5)   internal fertilization.
    (3)   oviducts.

<u>Items 49 to 51</u> refer to the following information.

An electroscope is a device used to detect the presence of electric charge. One such device consists of a pair of gold foil leaves suspended from a metal rod that is electrically connected to the outside of a metal and glass enclosure as shown below. An insulator prevents charge from leaking from the leaves and metal rod to the enclosure.

ELECTROSCOPE

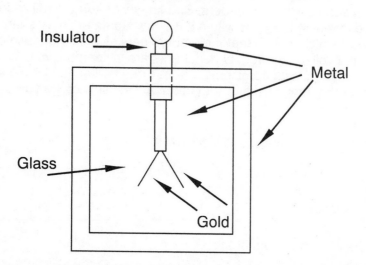

If a piece of vinyl is rubbed with a wool cloth and then brought near the top metal knob, then the gold leaves separate, indicating that the vinyl has acquired a certain amount of charge, either positive or negative. Only electrons (negatively charged particles) are allowed to move on the surface of the metal rod and gold leaves. The amount of spread in the gold leaves indicates the strength of the charge. Touching the top knob with your finger immediately makes the leaves come together, indicating that electrons are either added to or taken away from the electroscope to neutralize it.

49. An electroscope measures

    (1) only the presence of electrons.
    (2) only the absence of electrons.
    (3) the presence of nearby charge.
    (4) the amount of gold electrons.
    (5) the presence of protons in the knob.

50. Suppose a positively charged vinyl rod is brought near the top knob of a neutral electroscope.

    (1) The gold leaves will not spread.

(2) The gold leaves spread because they become positively charged and they repel each other.

(3) The gold leaves become negatively charged.

(4) The top knob becomes positively charged.

(5) The top knob remains neutral.

51. Suppose a negatively charged vinyl rod is brought near the top knob of an electroscope with its gold leaves separated because they both are negatively charged and repel each other.

(1) The top knob will become more negative.

(2) The gold leaves will tend to separate even more.

(3) The gold leaf separation will remain the same.

(4) The gold leaves will tend to come together.

(5) Both (1) and (4) are true.

Items 52 to 56 refer to the following paragraph.

Life in the sea has its advantages and its disadvantages. Most of the food is found near the surface. The fish, which are vertebrates, have the advantage of being able to maintain position while cruising through the sea looking for food. Few invertebrates are powerful enough swimmers to do this. However, invertebrates have become adapted to remain small enough to float. These zooplankton are subject to the whims of the currents. An alternate adaptation that is exhibited by some invertebrates is to remain firmly anchored (sessile) to the sea floor or some solid object in the sea. Some of these animals, such as oysters and clams, are filter feeders, and filter the water for microscopic animals and plants which are their food. Since they are sessile, they must also have a means of protection from the mobile predators of the sea. That is why many of these animals have either a passive protection such as a thick, hard, outer shell, or an active protection such as stinging cells, or an unappetizing, toxic mucus covering their body.

52. Fish are

(1) filter feeders.
(2) invertebrates.
(3) vertebrates.
(4) zooplankton.
(5) phytoplankton.

53. Zooplankton are

(1) invertebrates.
(2) vertebrates.
(3) fish.
(4) toxic mucus.
(5) mobile predators.

54. Those organisms that strain their food from the water could be called

    (1)   fish.
    (2)   vertebrates.
    (3)   phytoplankton.

    (4)   filter feeders.
    (5)   toxic mobile predators.

55. Sessile means to

    (1)   move around.
    (2)   swim freely.
    (3)   crawl along the sea floor.

    (4)   float on the surface.
    (5)   be firmly attached.

56. Invertebrates such as zooplankton are

    (1)   voracious predators.
    (2)   powerful swimmers.
    (3)   fish.
    (4)   voluntarily able to move from one ocean current to another.
    (5)   tiny enough to float near the surface.

<u>Items 57 to 59</u> refer to the following graph.

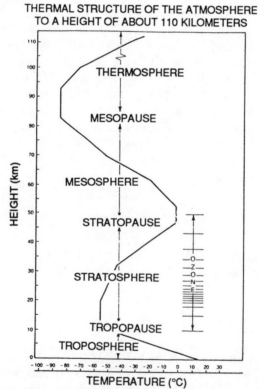

THERMAL STRUCTURE OF THE ATMOSPHERE
TO A HEIGHT OF ABOUT 110 KILOMETERS

The Atmosphere: An Introduction to Meteorology, 1989, Fourth Edition, Frederick K. Lutgens, Edward J. Tarbuck, Prentice Hall.

57. The warmest place in the atmosphere is near the ground because

    (1)   the ground is under the ozone layer.
    (2)   the ground can store heat.
    (3)   the ground is covered by ice in some regions.
    (4)   the Earth is both land and water.
    (5)   All of the above.

58. The coolest layer of the atmosphere is the

    (1)   Mesopause.   (4)   Stratopause.
    (2)   Thermosphere.   (5)   Stratosphere.
    (3)   Mesosphere.

59. Which would be a reason for temperature changes as you travel up through the atmosphere?

    (1)   Distance from the sun decreases.
    (2)   Weather disruptions cause mixing of the temperatures.
    (3)   Presence of ozone.
    (4)   Presence of man.
    (5)   Changes in composition.

Items 60 to 65 refer to the following paragraph.

    A plant contains organs arranged in what is known as the shoot system and the root system. The shoot system is that portion of the plant that is above the ground, and the root system is that portion of the plant that is usually under the ground. The root system functions as an anchor, and absorbs water and minerals from the ground. Roots have no internodes and nodes like the stem does. The stem supports the leaves and the flowers. The points where the leaves grow out of the stem are called nodes, and the space between two nodes is called an internode. The leaves function in photosynthesis while the flowers function as reproductive organs which ultimately produce seeds.

60. That portion of the plant that is involved with the absorption of water and minerals is the
    (1)   flower.   (4)   stomata.
    (2)   stem.   (5)   leaves.
    (3)   root.

61. Seeds are produced from

    (1)   nodes.   (4)   flowers.
    (2)   internodes.   (5)   tubers.
    (3)   stomata.

62. Leaves grow from

    (1) stems.   (4) internodes.
    (2) roots.   (5) stomata.
    (3) nodes.

63. Which term best relates to "guard cells"?

    (1) Stems   (4) Internodes
    (2) Roots   (5) Stomata
    (3) Nodes

64. Which term best relates to "leaves"?

    (1) Stems   (4) Internodes
    (2) Roots   (5) Seeds
    (3) Nodes

65. Which term best relates to plants' "reproductive organs"?

    (1) Stems   (4) Flowers
    (2) Roots   (5) Fruits
    (3) Leaves

Item 66 refers to the following passage.

Salinity is a measure of dissolved solids in water. On the average, 1000 grams of typical sea water contains 35 grams of salts. The level of salinity is below average in areas where large amounts of fresh water enter the ocean, and above average in hot, arid climates.

66. The Mediterranean Sea and the Red Sea are adjacent to deserts. The water in these two seas would be expected to have

    (1) above-average salinity.
    (2) below-average salinity.
    (3) average salinity.
    (4) no salt content whatsoever.
    (5) cold temperatures.

TEST 4: INTERPRETING LITERATURE AND THE ARTS

Tests of General Educational Development

Directions

The Interpreting Literature and the Arts Test consists of excerpts from classical and popular literature and articles about literature or the arts. Each excerpt is followed by multiple-choice questions about the reading material.

Read each excerpt first and then answer the questions following it. Refer back to the reading material as often as necessary in answering the questions.

Each excerpt is preceded by a "purpose question." The purpose question gives a reason for reading the material. Use these purpose questions to help focus your reading. You are not required to answer these purpose questions. They are given only to help you concentrate on the ideas presented in the reading materials.

You should spend no more than 65 minutes answering the questions in this booklet. Work carefully, but do not spend too much time on any one question. Be sure you answer every question. You will not be penalized for incorrect answers.

Do not mark in this test booklet. Record your answers on the separate answer sheet provided. Be sure all requested information is properly recorded on the answer sheet. To record your answers, mark the numbered space on the answer sheet beside the number that corresponds to the question in the test booklet.

FOR EXAMPLE:

It was Susan's dream machine. The metallic blue paint gleamed, and the sporty wheels were highly polished. Under the hood, the engine was no less carefully cleaned. Inside, flashy lights illuminated the instruments on the dashboard, and the seats were covered by rich leather upholstery.

The subject ("It") of this excerpt is most likely

(1)	an airplane.	(4)	a boat.
(2)	a stereo system.	(5)	a motorcycle.
(3)	an automobile.		① ② ● ④ ⑤

The correct answer is "an automobile"; therefore, answer space 3 would be marked on the answer sheet.

Do not rest the point of your pencil on the answer sheet while you are considering your answer. Make no stray or unnecessary marks. If you change an answer, erase your first mark completely. Mark only one answer space for each question; multiple answers will be scored as incorrect. Do not fold or crease your answer sheet. Return all test materials to the test administrator.

reprinted with permission of the General Educational Development Testing Service of the American Council on Education

Directions: Choose the <u>one best answer</u> to each item.

Items 1 to 5 refer to the following passage.

WHAT CHARACTERISTICS OF THE SCHOOLTEACHER'S PERSONALITY CAN THE READER INFER FROM THE PASSAGES BELOW?

1   The schoolmaster is generally a man of some importance in the female circle of a rural neighborhood; being considered a kind of idle gentlemanlike personage, of vastly superior taste and accomplishments to the rough country swains, and, indeed,

5   inferior in learning only to the parson. His appearance, therefore, is apt to occasion some little stir at the tea-table of a farmhouse, and the addition of a supernumerary dish of cakes or sweetmeats, or, peradventure, the parade of a silver tea-pot. Our man of letters, therefore, was peculiarly happy in the smiles of all the country

10   damsels. How he would figure among them in the churchyard, between services on Sundays! Gathering grapes for them from the wild vines that overrun the surrounding trees; reciting for their amusement all the epitaphs on the tombstones; or sauntering, with a whole bevy of them, along the banks of the adjacent mill-pond;

15   while the more bashful country bumpkins hung sheepishly back, envying his superior elegance and address.

      From his half itinerant life, also, he was a kind of travelling gazette, carrying the whole budget of local gossip from house to house; so that his appearance was always greeted with satisfac-

20   tion. He was, moreover, esteemed by the women as a man of great erudition, for he had read several books quite through, and was a perfect master of Cotton Mather's History of New England Witchcraft, in which, by the way, he most firmly and potently believed.

The Legend of Sleepy Hollow, Washington Irving, New York, New York: Franklin Watts, Inc., 575 Lexington Avenue, copyright 1966, pp.10 and 11.

1.   Lines 1–8 suggest that the local schoolmaster

    (1)   is highly esteemed by all.
    (2)   is held in high esteem particularly by the women.
    (3)   is not held in high regard.
    (4)   is considered a "country bumpkin."
    (5)   is held in higher esteem than the parson.

2.   From lines 8–16, the reader can infer that the schoolmaster

    (1)   is clearly shy and retiring.
    (2)   is modest and unassuming.
    (3)   is extremely humble.

(4)   thrives on all this attention.
(5)   strives to keep out of the limelight.

3.   In line 17, "half itinerant" means

    (1)   he wandered through the countryside a great deal.
    (2)   he was only half literate.
    (3)   his life was only half fulfilled.
    (4)   he had two jobs.
    (5)   None of the above.

4.   Lines 17–20 suggest that the schoolmaster

    (1)   sold newspapers.
    (2)   engaged in gossiping with the ladies.
    (3)   was a man of high esteem.
    (4)   never encouraged gossiping.
    (5)   was on a very strict budget.

5.   Lines 19–24 lead the reader to conclude that the schoolmaster

    (1)   was well read.   (4)   loved classical literature.
    (2)   was well educated.   (5)   enjoyed reading fiction.
    (3)   was well read in certain subjects.

Items 6 to 10 refer to the following passage.

WHAT INFERENCES CAN WE DRAW REGARDING THE SCHOOLMASTER'S COMPETITOR?

1   Among these the most formidable was a burly, roaring, roystering blade, of the name of Abraham, or, according to the Dutch abbreviation, Brom Van Brunt, the hero of the country round, which rang with his feats of strength and hardihood. He

5   was broad-shouldered and double-jointed, with short curly black hair, and a bluff, but not unpleasant, countenance, having a mingled air of fun and arrogance. From his Herculean frame and great powers of limb, had received the nickname of BROM BONES, by which he was universally known. He was famed for

10   great knowledge and skill in horsemanship, being as dexterous on horseback as a Tartar. He was foremost at all races and cock-fights; and, with the ascendency which bodily strength acquires in rustic life, was the umpire in all disputes, setting his hat on one side, and giving his decisions with an air and tone admitting of no

15   gainsay or appeal. He was always ready for either a fight or a frolic; but had more mischief than ill-will in his composition; and, with all his overbearing roughness, there was a strong dash of waggish good humor at bottom. He had three or four boon com-

20 panions, who regarded him as their model, and at the hand of
whom he scoured the country, attending every scene of feud or
merriment for miles round. In cold weather he was distinguished
by a fur cap, surmounted with a flaunting fox's tail; and when the
folks at a country gathering descried this well-known crest at a
distance, whisking about among a squad of hard riders, they
25 always stood by for a squall. Sometimes his crew would be heard
dashing along past the farmhouses at midnight, with whoop and
haloo, like a troop of Don Cossacks; and the dames, startled out
of their sleep, would listen for a moment till the hurry-scurry had
clattered by, and then exclaim, "Ay, there goes Brom Bones and
30 his gang!" The neighbors looked upon him with a mixture of awe,
admiration, and good will; and when any madcap prank, or rustic
brawl occurred in the vicinity, always shook their heads, and
warranted Brom Bones was at the bottom of it.

—*Ibid.*, pp. 19, 20.

6. Which of the following best describes the author's attitude toward the schoolmaster's competitor?

    (1) Admiration   (4) Anger
    (2) Hostility   (5) Tongue-in-cheek
    (3) Indifference

7. Lines 1–12 indicate that Brom Bones was renowned most for his

    (1) intellectual knowledge.   (4) physical skills and prowess.
    (2) family background.   (5) love of nature.
    (3) formal education.

8. Lines 15–18 suggest that Brom

    (1) was completely quarrelsome.
    (2) had a sense of humor and a high spirit.
    (3) was frivolous of nature.
    (4) was feared throughout the countryside.
    (5) was regarded lightly.

9. In line 27, "like a troop of Don Cossacks" most closely means

    (1) like a bunch of school boys.
    (2) like a bunch of lovesick young men.
    (3) like a bunch of dignified gentlemen.
    (4) like a bunch of rowdy ruffians.
    (5) like a bunch of horsemen.

10. Lines 30–33 indicate that the neighbors clearly regard Brom

    (1)   with terror.
    (2)   as a young and immature fellow.
    (3)   with honor.
    (4)   with awe, admiration, and good fellowship.
    (5)   as an intellectual.

Items 11 to 14 refer to the following passage.

IS THIS ARTIST "AMERICA'S FIRST MODERNIST PAINTER?"

1   The atmosphere is one of sunlit charm. Children ride merry-go-rounds. Tourists festively promenade up the Spanish steps in Rome. Parasol-toting weekenders buy balloons on the South Boston Pier. This is the turn-of-the century world brought to life in

5   Maurice Prendergast's paintings and watercolors. This world view is also, unfortunately, the main reason that Prendergast has remained a neglected artist. Ostensibly, such vibrant images were the product of an artist who has taken all the work out and left only the joy. Little wonder, then that the modernist movement found

10   Prendergast's work too easy and tranquil and shouldered him to the sidelines. Now, it is startling to learn that some historians consider him America's first modernist painter: the first to journey to Paris, to become familiar with the new trends in art, and to spread the word back in America....

15   Boston was Prendergast's home for all but twelve years of his life, although his five trips to Europe and his many sojourns to New York City—where he became a member of the group known as "The Eight" and exhibited in the famous 1913 Armory Show— were the greatest influences on his work. His art, as with any true

20   pathfinder, resists easy classification. From the Impressionists he took his improvisational brushwork; from the Postimpressionists, his subjective, stylized view of reality; from the Nabis—Pierre Bonnard in particular—his decorative expression of color. This rich stew was then flavored with a gentle simplicity to create a uniquely

25   American mix.
        Above all, his color—or rather, the amount he used—was new. He would have none of the "brown sauce" with which many Bostonian artists of the day served up their paintings. In fact, he used so many colors, one critic called his work "an explosion in a

30   color factory." To this spectrum, he added a sparklingly animated line that blocked out forms as fluidly as an abstractionist—forms he also used in more than two hundred masterful monotypes.
        As this show reveals, Prendergast (1859–1924) was an important link between the masters of the nineteenth century and the

35   new ones of the twentieth....

Thoroughly Modern Maurice, AMERICAN PAINTER, "Exhibits," ed. Robert I. C. Fisher, October, 1990, p. 12, Copyright 1990, by BPI Communications, Inc., a subsidiary of Affiliated Publications,1515 Broadway, New York.

11. Which of the following statements best expresses the **irony**, or turn of events, involving the artist reviewed?

    (1) The modernist movement rejected him.
    (2) His art resists easy classification.
    (3) Although rejected by modernists, some historians consider him America's first modernist painter.
    (4) He is an important link between the 19th and 20th centuries.
    (5) He combines richness and simplicity.

12. Lines 5–11 suggest that modernist critics felt that Prendergast's work was too

    (1) conservative.   (4) ordinary.
    (2) careless.   (5) suggestive.
    (3) carefree.

13. In line 20, the description "pathfinder" most closely means

    (1) his work was unlike any of his predecessors.
    (2) his work was difficult to classify.
    (3) the artist was a hard worker.
    (4) the artist made it easier for his successors.
    (5) the artist was influenced by the Impressionists.

14. Of all Prendergast's techniques, the most revolutionary was

    (1) his improvisational brushwork.
    (2) his stylized view of reality.
    (3) his decorative expression of color.
    (4) the amount of color he used.
    (5) All of the above.

Items 15 to 18 refer to the following passage.

WHAT ARE THE HUSBAND'S AND WIFE'S ATTITUDES TOWARD EACH OTHER?

"Father!"

"What is it?"

"What are them men diggin' over there in the field for?"

There was a sudden dropping and enlarging of the part of the old man's face, as if some heavy weight had settled therein; he shut his mouth tight, and went on harnessing the bay mare. He hustled the collar on to her neck with a jerk.

"Father!"

The old man slapped the saddle upon the mare's back.

"Look here, father, I want to know what them men are diggin' over in the field for, an' I'm goin' to know."

"I wish you'd go into the house, mother, an' 'tend to your own affairs," the old man said then. He ran his words together, and his speech was almost as inarticulate as a growl.

But the woman understood; it was her most native tongue. "I ain't goin' into the house till you tell me what them men are doin' over there in the field," said she.

The old man glanced doggedly at his wife as he tightened the last buckles on the harness. She looked as immovable to him as one of the rocks in his pasture-land, bound to the earth with generations of blackberry vines. He slapped the reins over the horse, and started forth from the barn.

"Father!" said she.

The old man pulled up. "What is it?"

"I want to know what them men are diggin' over there in that field for."

"They're digging a cellar, I s'pose, if you've got to know."

"A cellar for what?"

"A barn."

"A barn? You ain't goin' to build a barn over there where we was goin' to have a house, father?"

The old man said not another word. He hurried the horse into the farm wagon, and clattered out of the yard, jouncing as sturdily on his seat as a boy.

From "The Revolt of Mother" Mary Wilkins Freeman (c. 1892).

15. By saying, "I wish you'd go into the house, mother, an' tend to your own affairs," father implies

(1) her work is not done.
(2) he has no time to talk.
(3) he will meet her inside.
(4) they will talk later.
(5) she has no business in the goings on outside the house.

16. This passage is a good example of

(1) rhyme.
(2) meter.
(3) irony.
(4) dialect.
(5) exaggeration.

17. Mother can be best described as

(1) quiet.
(2) strong-willed.
(3) subservient.
(4) humorous.
(5) pleasant.

18. Mother's question, "...barn? You ain't goin' to build a barn over there where we was goin' to have a house, father?" suggests that

    (1) father is going back on his promise to build her a house.
    (2) father changed the location of the barn.
    (3) mother is pleased with father's intentions.
    (4) mother wants to help with the construction.
    (5) mother doesn't think they can afford to build a barn.

Items 19 to 25 refer to the following poem.

IN EXCERPTS FROM HIS NARRATIVE POEM, WHAT TECHNIQUES DOES THE POET USE TO TELL HIS STORY?

1   The wind was a torrent of darkness among the gusty trees,
The moon was a ghostly galleon tossed upon cloudy seas,
The road was a ribbon of moonlight over the purple moor,
And the highwayman came riding—
5   Riding—riding—
The highwayman came riding, up to the old inn-door.

He'd a French cocked-hat on his forehead, a bunch of lace at his chin,
A coat of the claret velvet, and breaches of brown doe-skin:
10   They fitted with never a wrinkle: his boots were up to the thigh!
And he rode with a jewelled twinkle,
His pistol butts a twinkle,
His rapier hilt a-twinkle, under the jewelled sky.
Over the cobbles he clattered and clashed in the dark inn-yard,
15   And he tapped with his whip on the shutters, but all was locked and barred;
He whistled a tune to the window, and who should be waiting there
But the landlord's black-eyed daughter,
20   Bess, the landlord's daughter,
Plaiting a dark red love-knot into her long black hair.

And dark in the dark old inn-yard a stable-wicket creaked
Where Tim the ostler listened, his face was white and peaked;
His eyes were hallows of madness, his hair like mouldy hay,
25   But he love the landlord's daughter,
The landlord's red-lipped daughter,
Dumb as a dog he listened, and he heard the robber say—
"One kiss, my bonny sweetheart, I'm after a prize to-night,
But I shall be back with the yellow gold before the morning light;
30   Yet, if they press me sharply, and harry me through the day,
Then look for me by moonlight,
Watch for me by moonlight,
I'll come to thee by moonlight, though hell should bar the way."

—passages from *The Highwayman*, by Alfred Noyes, *The Family Book of Verse*, selected and edited by Lewis Gannett, New York: Harper and Row, 1961, pp. 75–76.

19. These stanzas tell a story and are excerpts from

    (1) a sonnet.   (4) a folk ballad.
    (2) a narrative poem.   (5) an epic poem.
    (3) a limerick.

20. Lines 1, 2, and 3 are examples of a poetic technique which

    (1) explicitly compares two essentially unlike objects.
    (2) implicitly compares two objects.
    (3) rhymes.
    (4) grossly exaggerates.
    (5) entertains the reader.

21. In lines 6–14, the highwayman is described as

    (1) a villain.   (4) a soldier in the king's army.
    (2) a nondescript individual.   (5) a coward.
    (3) a dashing and romantic figure.

22. In line 21, the red ribbon is most likely a symbol of Bess'

    (1) vanity.   (4) availability.
    (2) patriotism.   (5) greed.
    (3) love.

23. The one implicit comparison of two unlike objects, a metaphor, used in lines 22–27 is

    (1) "His face was white and peaked."
    (2) "His eyes were hallows of madness."
    (3) "His hair like mouldy hay."
    (4) "The landlord's red-lipped daughter."
    (5) "Dumb as a dog he listened."

24. A close reading of the dialogue in lines 28–33 suggest that the hero

    (1) has reformed.   (4) will join the king's army.
    (2) will marry Bess.   (5) None of the above.
    (3) has planned a robbery tonight.

25. The meter of the poem is somewhat suggestive of

    (1)   a waterfall.   (4)   horses' hoof beats.
    (2)   a bugle call.   (5)   a folk song.
    (3)   a drumroll.

Items 26 to 32 refer to the following passage.

WHAT IS THE AUTHOR REVEALING TO YOU CONCERNING THE NARRATOR'S STATE OF MIND?

1   True!—nervous—very, very dreadfully nervous I had been and am! but why will you say that I am mad? The disease had sharpened my senses—not destroyed—not dulled them. Above all was the sense of hearing acute. I heard all things in the heaven and in

5   the earth. I heard many things in hell. How, then, am I mad? Hearken! and observe how healthily—how calmly I can tell you the whole story.

        It is impossible to say how first the idea entered my brain: but once conceived, it haunted me day and night. Object there was

10   none. Passion there was none. I loved the old man. He had never wronged me. He had never given me insult. For his gold I had no desire. I think it was his eye! yes, it was this! One of his eyes whenever it fell upon me, my blood ran cold; and so by degrees— very gradually—I made up my mind to take the life of the old man,

15   and thus rid myself of the eye forever.

        Now this is the point. You fancy me mad. Madmen know nothing. But you should have seen me. You should have seen how wisely I proceeded— with what caution—with what foresight—with what dissimilation I went to work!

20   I was never kinder to the old man than during the whole week before I killed him. And every night, about midnight, I turned the latch of his door and opened it—oh, so gently! And then, when I had made an opening sufficient for my head, I put in a dark lantern, all closed, closed so that no light shone out, and then I thrust

25   in my head. Oh, you would nave laughed to see how cunningly I thrust it in! I moved it slowly—very, very slowly, so that I might lay upon his bed. Ha!—would a madman have been so wise as this? And then, when my head was well in the room, I undid the lantern cautiously—oh, so cautiously—cautiously (for the hinges

30   creaked)—I undid it just so much that a single ray fell upon the vulture eye. And this I did for seven long nights—every night just at midnight—but I found the eye always closed; and so it was impossible to do the work; for it was not the old man who vexed me, but his Evil Eye. And every morning, when the day broke, I

35   went boldly into the chamber, and spoke courageously to him, calling him by name in a hearty tone, and inquiring how he had passed the night. So you see he would have been a very profound old man, indeed, to suspect that every night, just at twelve I looked in upon him while he slept.

The Tell-Tale Heart, Edgar Allan Poe, *Collected Works of Edgar Allan Poe* (Tales and Sketches, 1843–1849), Edited by Thomas Olive Mabbott, Cambridge, Ma: The Belknap Press of Harvard University Press, 1978, pp. 792–793.

26. In lines 1–7, the reader can sense that the speaker is

   (1) clever.   (4) intelligent.
   (2) angry.   (5) suicidal.
   (3) crazy.

27. The statement, "For his gold I had no desire," (Lines 11–12) suggests that the old man

   (1) is penniless.
   (2) is financially well off.
   (3) is charitable.
   (4) hoards (or accumulates) all of his money.
   (5) collects cans.

28. The only motive mentioned in lines 9–15 is

   (1) to find peace and tranquility without the old man.
   (2) to gain wealth from old man's gold.
   (3) to win power and respect.
   (4) to rid himself of the eye.
   (5) None of the above.

29. The statement —"Ha! would a madman have been so wise as this?" proves that the speaker

   (1) is mad.
   (2) wishes us to believe he is not mad.
   (3) is not mad.
   (4) is very clever.
   (5) is concerned about the old man.

30. On each of his seven attempts to kill the old man, the speaker finds

   (1) the door locked.
   (2) someone thwarting his plans.
   (3) he has a change of heart.
   (4) the old man's eye is closed.
   (5) the old man has not fallen asleep.

31. The narrator's intentions in lines 34–39 are best described as

    (1) proud and self-serving. (4) hesitant.
    (2) sincere and honorable.   (5) frivolous.
    (3) charitable.

32. The general tone of the narration is

    (1) tranquil.   (4) hostile.
    (2) fearful.   (5) anxious.
    (3) reverential.

Items 33–37 refer to the following passage.

WHAT IS DISTURBING THE NARRATOR?

Well, the Fourth of July is over! The people are all gone, and I am tired out. John thought it might do me good to see a little company, so we just had Mother and Nellie and the children down for a week.

Of course I didn't do a thing. Jennie sees to everything now. But it tired me all the same.

I cry at nothing, and cry most of the time.

Of course I don't when John is here, or anybody else, but when I am alone.

And I am alone a good deal just now. John is kept in town very often by serious cases, and Jennie is good and lets me alone when I want her to.

So I walk a little in the garden or down that lovely lane, sit on the porch under the roses, and lie down up here a good deal.

I'm getting really fond of the room in spite of the wallpaper. Perhaps because of the wallpaper.

It dwells in my mind so!

I lie here on this great immovable bed—it is nailed down, I believe—and follow that pattern about by the hour.

I know a little of the principle of design, and I know this thing was not arranged on any laws of radiation, or alternation, or repetition, or symmetry, or anything else that I ever heard of.

I makes me tired to follow it. I will take a nap, I guess.

I don't know why I should write this.

I don't want to.

I don't feel able.

And John would think it absurd. But I must say what I feel and think in some way—it is such a relief!

But the effort is getting to be greater than the relief.

"The Yellow Wallpaper," *The Charlotte Perkins Gilman Reader*, (c. 1892).

33. The narrator seems to be

    (1) in a state of bliss.   (4) ill.
    (2) recovering from an accident. (5) exuberant.
    (3) worried about her family.

34. From the passage it can be inferred that the narrator's thoughts are being

    (1) tape recorded.   (4) sung.
    (2) overheard.   (5) dictated.
    (3) written.

35. It is suggested by the narrator that her husband, John, is

    (1) supportive of her.
    (2) sympathetic.
    (3) there when she writes.
    (4) skeptical of her illness and writing.
    (5) ill.

36. The narrator is obsessed with

    (1) her mother.   (4) Nellie.
    (2) the wallpaper. (5) the Fourth of July activities.
    (3) her children.

37. What emotion does the narrator feel most toward her husband?

    (1) Total love and devotion (4) Friendship
    (2) Pity   (5) Anger
    (3) Fear

Items 38 to 45 refer to the following passage.

WHAT IS THE SPEAKER'S VIEW OF LIFE AND NATURE AS REVEALED IN EXCERPTS FROM HIS ESSAYS BELOW?

Why should we be in such desperate haste to succeed, and in such desperate enterprises? If a man does not keep pace with his companions, perhaps it is because he hears a different drummer. Let him step to the music which he hears, however measured or
5   far away. It is not important that he should mature as soon as an apple-tree or an oak. Shall he turn his spring into summer? If the condition of things which we were made for is not yet, what were any reality which we can substitute? We will not be shipwrecked on a vain reality. Shall we with pains erect a heaven of blue glass
10 over ourselves, though when it is done we shall be sure to gaze

still at the true ethereal heaven far above, as if the former were not?

However mean your life is, meet it and live it; do not shun it and call it hard names. It is not so bad as you are. It looks poorest
15   when you are richest. The fault-finder will find faults even in paradise. Love your life, poor as it is. You may perhaps have some pleasant, thrilling, glorious hours, even in a poorhouse. The setting sun is reflected from the windows of the alms-house as brightly as from the rich man's abode; the snow melts before its
20   door as early in the spring. I do not see but a quiet mind may live as contentedly there, and have as cheering thoughts, as in a palace.

Rather than love, than money, than fame, give me truth. I sat at a table where were rich food and wine in abundance and obsequi-
25   ous attendance, but sincerity and truth were not; and I went away hungry from the inhospitable board. The hospitality was as cold as the ices. I thought that there was no need of ice to freeze them. They talked to me of the age of the wine and the fame of the vintage; but I thought of an older, newer, and purer wine, of a
30   more glorious vintage, which they had not got, and could not buy. The style, the house and the grounds and "entertainment" pass for nothing with me. I called on the king, but he made me wait in his hall, and conducted like a man incapacitated for hospitality. There was a man in my neighborhood who lived in a hollow tree. His
35   manners were truly regal. I should have done better had I called on him.

—Excerpts from *Walden*, (XVIII, Conclusions), by Henry David Thoreau, ed. Walter Harding, New York: Washington Square Press, a division of Simon and Schuster, Copyright dates, 1962, 1967, pp. 247, 248, 250.

38.   The essential message of lines 1–12 have to do mainly with

      (1)   salvation of souls.
      (2)   society's pressure for success.
      (3)   surviving in nature.
      (4)   economy.
      (5)   playing a musical instrument.

39.   Lines 2 and 3, "If a man does not keep pace with his companions, perhaps it is because he hears a different drummer," are used

      (1)   as a figures of speech.   (4)   as a paradox.
      (2)   in their literal sense.   (5)   as a touch of humor.
      (3)   as an overstatement.

40.   The imagery used in the excerpt deals primarily with

      (1)   nature.   (2)   material wealth.

(3)   animals.   (4)   heaven.
(5)   death.

41.   The term "mean," in line 13, most closely is a synonym for

(1)   unkind.   (4)   humble.
(2)   benevolent.   (5)   lonely.
(3)   wealthy.

42.   Lines 13–17 suggest

(1)   material wealth and happiness are compatible.
(2)   wealthy people cannot attain true happiness.
(3)   people who are not wealthy are happy.
(4)   true happiness is not a result of material wealth.
(5)   true happiness is not attainable.

43.   Which of the following best describes the author's attitude toward material wealth in the second paragraph?

(1)   Sympathetic   (4)   Contemptuous
(2)   Accepting   (5)   Nonappreciative
(3)   Envious

44.   What is the general theme of the third paragraph?

(1)   Those who live with truth and sincerity are wealthy.
(2)   Material gain is the only truth.
(3)   Vintage wine and hospitality are solely for the rich.
(4)   Mankind is basically greedy.
(5)   Man has dominion over nature.

45   The "older, newer, and purer wine" referred to in line 29 is most probably

(1)   nature.   (4)   a rare, vintage wine.
(2)   material wealth. (5)   heaven.
(3)   truth and sincerity.

TEST 5: MATHEMATICS

Tests of General Educational Development

Directions

The Mathematics Test consists of multiple-choice questions intended to measure general mathematics skills and problem-solving ability. The questions are based on short readings which often include a graph, chart, or figure.

You should spend no more than 90 minutes answering the questions in this booklet. Work carefully, but do not spend too much time on any one question. Be sure you answer every question. You will not be penalized for incorrect answers.

Formulas you may need are given on the following page. Only some of the questions will require you to use a formula. Not all the formulas given will be needed.

Some questions contain more information than you will need to solve the problem. Other questions do not give enough information to solve the problem. If the question does not give enough information to solve the problem, the correct answer choice is "Not enough information Is glven."

The use of calculators is not allowed.

Do not mark in this test booklet. The test administrator will give you blank paper for your calculations. Record your answers on the separate answer sheet provided. Be sure all requested information is properly recorded on the answer sheet.

FOR EXAMPLE:

If a grocery bill totaling $15.75 is paid with a $20.00 bill, how much change should be returned?

   (1) $5.26   (4) $3.75
   (2) $4.75   (5) $3.25
   (3) $4.25

                                      (1) (2) ● (4) (5)

The correct answer is "$4.25"; therefore, answer space 3 would be marked on the answer sheet.

Do not rest the point of your pencil on the answer sheet while you are considering your answer. Make no stray or unnecessary marks. If you change an answer, erase your first mark completely. Mark only one answer space for each question; multiple answers will be scored as incorrect. Do not fold or crease your answer sheet. Return all test materials to the test administrator.

---

reprinted with permission of the General Educational Development Testing Service of the American Council on Education

REFERENCE TABLE

SYMBOLS AND THEIR MEANINGS

=	is equal to	≤	is less than or equal to
≠	is unequal to	≥	is greater than or equal to
<	is less than	‖	is parallel to
>	is greater than	⊥	is perpendicular to

FORMULAS

DESCRIPTION	FORUMLA

AREA (A) of a:

square	$A = s^2$; where s = side
rectangle	$A = lw$; where l = length, w = width
parallelogram	$A = bh$; where b = base, h = height
triangle	$A = \frac{1}{2} bh$; where b = base, h = height
circle	$A = \pi r^2$; where π = 3.14, r = radius

PERIMETER (P) of a:

square	$P = 4s$; where s = side
rectangle	$P = 2l + 2w$; where l = length, w = width
triangle	$P = a + b + c$; where a, b, and c are the sides
circumference (C) of a circle	$C = \pi d$, where π = 3.14, d = diameter

VOLUME (V) of a:

cube	$V = s^2$; where s = side
rectangular container	$V = lwh$; where l = length, w = width, h = height
Pythagorean relationship	$c^2 = a^2 + b^2$; where c = hypotenuse, a and b are legs of a right triangle
distance (d) between two points in a plane	$d = \sqrt{(x_2 - x_1)^2 + (y_2 - y_1)^2}$ where (x_1, y_1) and (x_2, y_2) are two points in a plane
mean	$\textbf{mean} = \dfrac{x_1 + x_2 + \ldots + x_n}{n}$; where the x's are the values for which a mean is desired, and n = number of values in the series
median	**median** = the point in an ordered set of numbers at which half of the numbers are above and half of the numbers are below this value
simple interest (i)	$i = prt$; where p = principal, r = rate, t = time
distance (d) as function of rate and time	$d = rt$; where r = rate, t = time
total cost (c)	$c = nr$; where n = number of units, r = *cost per unit*

Directions: Choose the one best answer to each item.

1. Solve x + 35 = 70 for x

    (1)   105   (4)   -35
    (2)   35   (5)   2
    (3)   -105

2. What is the measure of angle R?

    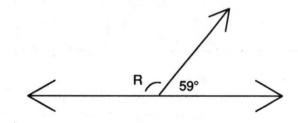

    (1)   59°   (4)   31°
    (2)   100°   (5)   180°
    (3)   121°

3. Johnny has 17 marbles. Mary has twice as many marbles as Johnny
    and half as many as Joe. How many marbles does Mary have?

    (1)   9   (4)   17
    (2)   43   (5)   Not enough information is given.
    (3)   34

4. Solve for x: 12x = 156

    (1)   144   (4)   15
    (2)   -13   (5)   -15
    (3)   13

5. What is the measure of angle S as shown in figure below?

    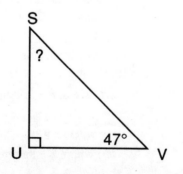

(1)   43°   (4)   54°
(2)   47°   (5)   133°
(3)   90°

6.   Taxi fare from a large hotel to the airport is $15. How much would a taxi driver earn if he made 10 trips to the airport, but had to return to the hotel without a fare?

(1) $1.50   (4) $150.00
(2) $25.00   (5) $300.00
(3) $15.00

7.   Multiply: (x + 1) (3x + 4)

(1) $3x^2 + 5$ (4) $3x^2 - 7x + 5$
(2) $3x^2 + 4$ (5) $3x^2 + 7x + 4$
(3) $3x^2 - 7x - 4$

8.   What is the measure of exterior angle ACD as shown in the figure below?

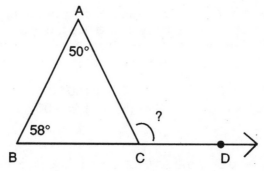

(1)   58°   (4)   108°
(2)   50°   (5)   130°
(3)   72°

9.   Apples are 2 pounds for $0.98. How much would 5 pounds cost?

(1) $9.80   (4) $2.45
(2) $4.90   (5) $0.49
(3) $1.96

10.   Multiply: 7 (-4y + 2)

(1)   28y + 2   (4)   -42y
(2)   28y + 14   (5)   -28y + 14
(3)   -14y

11. The figure below shows two parallel lines l and m. Line H is intersecting both lines l and m. Angle GEB measures 40°. What is the measure of angle CFE?

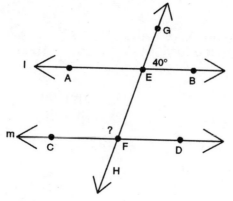

(1) 40°
(2) 180°
(3) 140°
(4) 120°
(5) Not enough information is given.

12. John travels to work Monday through Friday by riding a bus to the train station and then a train into town. The bus fare is $0.50, and the train ride is $2.00. How much does it cost him to commute (to and from work) each week?

(1) $5.00
(2) $12.50
(3) $25.00
(4) $100.00
(5) $1,250.00

13. Which ordered pair is the solution for the following system?

$$x - 3y = 9$$
$$3x + y = 7$$

(1) (-3, -2)
(2) (3, -2)
(3) (3, 2)
(4) No solutions.
(5) Infinitely many solutions.

14. Ira has enough seed to plant a garden of 220 square feet. He has a place 20 feet long to put the garden. How wide must it be to have exactly 220 square feet?

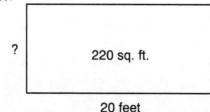

20 feet

(1)	20 ft.	(4)	11 ft.
(2)	10 ft.	(5)	9.5 ft.
(3)	12 ft.		

15. A travel agent earns 10% commission on each ticket sold. If the agent sold one ticket for $210 and two for $400, how much would be his commission?

(1)	$18.60	(4)	$80.00
(2)	$21.00	(5)	$101.00
(3)	$40.00		

16. An airplane made a 6-hour trip with the wind which blew in the same direction as the airplane. The return flight against the wind took 8 hours. What was the speed of the airplane in still air?

(1)	420 km./hr.	(4)	400 km./hr.
(2)	480 km./hr.	(5)	500 km./hr.
(3)	360 km./hr.		

17. What is the height (altitude) of an equilateral triangle with the length of a side 6 centimeters?

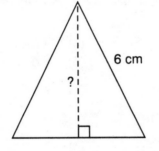

(1)	$3\sqrt{2}$cm.	(4)	9 cm.
(2)	$3\sqrt{3}$cm.	(5)	3 cm.
(3)	6 cm.		

18. A bus leaves Jane's house at 7:09 AM. It arrives in front of her office at 7:32 AM. What is her travel time?

(1)	23 mins.	(4)	82 mins.
(2)	41 mins.	(5)	30 mins.
(3)	46 mins.		

19. Mary has some nickels and some quarters worth $4.65. She has 3 more nickels than quarters. How many coins does she have?

(1)   15   (4)   33
(2)   18   (5)   Not enough information.
(3)   23

20.   What is the length of the hypotenuse of a triangle having angles 45°, 45°, 90° and the length of a leg 4m?

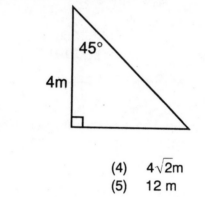

(1)   4 m   (4) $4\sqrt{2}$m
(2)   16 m   (5)   12 m
(3) $4\sqrt{3}$m

21.   Find the total cost of these items if the sales tax rate is 5%. Two bottles of aspirin at $4.19 each, 2 cans of shoe polish at $0.69 each, and 3 cans of hair spray at $1.15 each.

(1) $8.38   (4) $13.87
(2) $13.21   (5) $79.26
(3) $66.05

22. $f(x) = -x + 4$, find $f(-3)$.

(1)   -3   (4)   3
(2)   4   (5)   7
(3)   1

23.   What is the area of the parallelogram as shown in the figure below?

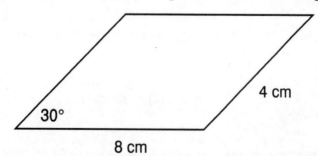

(1) 32 cm²	(4) 28 cm²
(2) 16 cm²	(5) Not enough information is given.
(3) 24 cm²	

24. Juan's house is valued at $55,000. The property tax rate is $2.10 per $100 value. What is his property tax?

(1) $210	(4) $115.50
(2) $550	(5) $115,500
(3) $1,155	

25. What percent of 80 is 32?

(1) 40%	(4) 25%
(2) 0.4%	(5) 400%
(3) 2.5%	

26. Robert's fish tank is 48 centimeters long, 35 centimeters wide and 52 centimeters high. What is the volume of the water in the tank if he leaves 2 centimeters at the top without water?

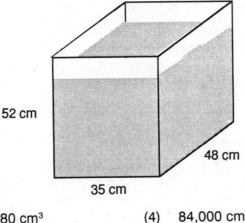

52 cm

48 cm

35 cm

(1) 1,680 cm³	(4) 84,000 cm³
(2) 87,360 cm³	(5) 3,360 cm³
(3) 83,720 cm³	

27. Paul had to rent some tools for 3 days for a repair job. He rented a drill at $5 per day and a cement mixer for $20 per day. What was the total rental charge?

(1) $75.00	(4) $25.00
(2) $60.00	(5) $15.00
(3) $35.00	

28. Solve D = rt for t.

    (1) D = rt
    (2) t = rD
    (3) t = Dr

    (4) t = r/D
    (5) t = D/r

29. Find the area of a regular hexagon with sides 8 inches.

    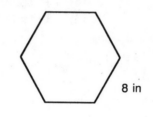

    8 in

    (1) $16\sqrt{3}$in²
    (2) $96\sqrt{2}$in²
    (3) 64 in²

    (4) 128 in²
    (5) $96\sqrt{3}$in²

30. Ruben tuned up his car. He bought

    > spark plugs $ 9.96
    > distributor cap $16.95 and
    > rotor $ 6.45.

    What was his total cost if the tax rate on parts is 6%?

    (1) $33.36
    (2) $32.36
    (3) $2.00

    (4) $34.36
    (5) $35.36

31. Simplify: $3x^3 \cdot x^5$

    (1) $3x^{15}$
    (2) $9x^5$
    (3) $3x^8$

    (4) $8x^3$
    (5) x^{14}

32. Find the area of a circle with a diameter 10 inches. (Use pi = 3.14).

    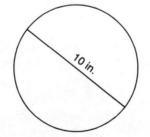

    10 in.

(1)   31.4 sq. in.
(2)   15.7 sq. in.
(3)   31.4 sq. in.

(4)   78.5 sq. in.
(5)   85.25 sq. in.

33.   Medical insurance costs Maria $26.03 per week. What is the annual cost?

(1) $312.36
(2) $1,301.50
(3) $1,353.56

(4) $104.12
(5) $1,367.60

34.   Simplify: $\left(\dfrac{x^2}{y}\right)^5$

(1) $\dfrac{x^2}{y^5}$

(4) x^8

(2) $\dfrac{x^7}{y}$

(5) $\dfrac{x^{10}}{y^5}$

(3) $\dfrac{x^7}{y^5}$

35.   One medical study says golfers consume 300 calories per hour. Jose Gonzalez played golf for 3 1/2 hours. How many calories did he use?

(1)   100 calories
(2)   150 calories
(3)   85.71 calories

(4)   250 calories
(5)   1,050 calories

36.   Simplify: $\dfrac{x^{11}}{x^4}$

(1) x^{44}

(4) $\dfrac{1}{x^4}$

(2) x^7

(5) $\dfrac{1}{x^7}$

(3) x^6

37.   A government fact sheet reveals that the average farmworker produces enough food for 76 people. Approximately how many farm workers are needed to feed a city of 4 million people?

(1) 304
(2) 50,000
(3) 57,000

(4) 304,000,000
(5) 40,000

38. Factor: $x^4 - 1$

(1) $(x^2 + 1)(x^2 + 1)$
(2) $(x^2 + 1)(x^2 - 1)$
(3) $(x^2 + 1)(x - 1)(x - 1)$

(4) $(x^2 + 1)(x + 1)(x - 1)$
(5) $(x^2 - 1)(x^2 - 1)$

39. Which is the best buy for pencils:

$0.10 each or
2 dozen for $2.50 or
10 for $0.99?

(1) $0.10 each
(2) 2 dozen for $2.50
(3) 10 for $0.99

(4) There is no difference.
(5) Not enough information is given.

40. Factor: $x^2 + 6x + 9$

(1) $x(x + 6)$
(2) $(x - 3)(x - 3)$
(3) $(x + 3)^2$

(4) $(x - 3)^2$
(5) $(x - 3)(x - 3)$

41. Sally entered a certain sweepstakes 8 times. There were 1600 entries. What are her chances of winning?

(1) 0.5%
(2) 5%
(3) 50%

(4) 12.8%
(5) 128%

42. There were 350 tickets sold for a concert. Adult tickets were $5.00 each, and student tickets were $3.50 each. The total amount received for tickets sold was $1,306.00. How many of each kind to tickets were sold?

(1) 296 students & 54 adults
(2) 300 students & 50 adults
(3) 175 students & 175 adults

(4) 54 students & 296 adults
(5) 50 students & 300 adults

43. The product of two consecutive integers is 72. Which equation represents this?

(1) $x + x = 72$
(2) $x \cdot x = 72$
(3) $x(x + 1) = 72$

(4) $x(x + 2) = 72$
(5) $x + (x + 1) = 72$

The bar graph shows the amount of real estate sold by the XYZ Company. It is for questions 44 and 45.

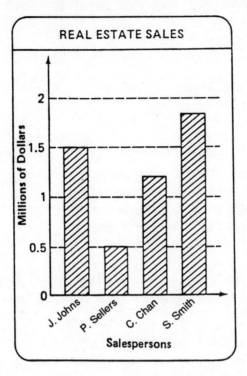

44. Which salesperson sold $1,500,000 worth of real estate?

    (1)   J. Johns   (4)   S. Smith
    (2)   P. Sellers   (5)   None of the above.
    (3)   C. Chan

45. Which person sold about three times the amount of property as P. Sellers?

    (1)   J. Johns   (4)   All of the above.
    (2)   C. Chan   (5)   None of the above.
    (3)   S. Smith

46. Find the simple interest: Jerry borrowed $2,000 for 2 years at 10.5% interest.

    (1) $210   (4) $42,000
    (2) $21,000   (5) $21
    (3) $420

47. Samantha works at a clothing store. Employees are given a 20% discount on clothes they buy there. Last year she spent $592.86 on clothes there. What was her annual benefit (employee discount)?

    (1) $592.86
    (2) $612.86
    (3) $474.29
    (4) $118.57
    (5) $711.43

48. Compare these two jobs:

    Job #1 pays $298 per week
    Job #2 pays $14,900 per year

    (1) Job #1 pays $283.10 more per year
    (2) Job #2 pays $14,602.00 more per year
    (3) Job #1 pays $596.00 more per year
    (4) Job #2 pays $11.46 more per year
    (5) They are the same.

49. Mike's Machine Repair pays repairmen $0.19 per mile for travel to and from repair jobs. Manny traveled an average of 367 miles per week last year for a 50-week work year. What was his annual travel benefit?

    (1) $367.00
    (2) $69.73
    (3) $278.92
    (4) $3,625.96
    (5) $3,486.50

50. George and Mary open a savings account with $550 in it. They earn 8.2% annual interest if they leave the money in the account for one full year. How much will they have at the end of one year?

    (1) $45.10
    (2) $595.10
    (3) $541.20
    (4) $1,091.20
    (5) $451.00

51. Alfred and Joe ordered pizza. It was cut into 12 pieces. As they each were about to get 1/2 of it, Bobby came over. Now they want to divide it into thirds. How many pieces will Bobby get?

    (1) 2
    (2) 6
    (3) 16
    (4) 4
    (5) 36

52. There are 90 students in the junior class at Mountain High School. Of these, 36 are girls. What percent are boys?

    (1) 36%
    (2) 54%
    (3) 40%
    (4) 60%
    (5) Not enough information is given.

53. Add: 3 5/6 + 1/3 + 7/6

    (1)   23/6   (4)   5-5/6
    (2)   4   (5)   5-1/3
    (3)   4-5/6

The graph is for questions 54–56

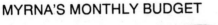

MYRNA'S MONTHLY BUDGET

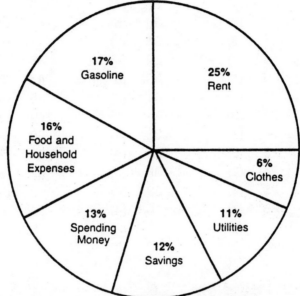

54. If Myrna makes a monthly salary of $2,500.00, how much will she spend on rent in one year?

    (1) $7,500   (4) $156.25
    (2) $625   (5) $2,500
    (3) $32,500

55. What percentage does she spend for utilities?

    (1)   275%   (4)   16%
    (2)   11%   (5)   13%
    (3)   132%

56. What amount does she save each month?

    (1) $12   (4) $1,200
    (2) $300   (5) $325
    (3) $3,600

EXAM III

ANSWER KEY

Test 1—Writing Skills

1.	(2)	15.	(4)	29.	(4)	43.	(4)
2.	(2)	16.	(1)	30.	(5)	44.	(4)
3.	(3)	17.	(3)	31.	(3)	45.	(4)
4.	(4)	18.	(4)	32.	(4)	46.	(5)
5.	(4)	19.	(1)	33.	(3)	47.	(5)
6.	(2)	20.	(3)	34.	(2)	48.	(4)
7.	(4)	21.	(5)	35.	(4)	49.	(3)
8.	(1)	22.	(1)	36.	(4)	50.	(4)
9.	(5)	23.	(5)	37.	(4)	51.	(2)
10.	(3)	24.	(2)	38.	(4)	52.	(3)
11.	(2)	25.	(4)	39.	(4)	53.	(4)
12.	(4)	26.	(1)	40.	(4)	54.	(4)
13.	(3)	27.	(5)	41.	(2)	55.	(2)
14.	(3)	28.	(3)	42.	(3)		

Test 2—Social Studies

1.	(5)	17.	(4)	33.	(4)	49.	(4)
2.	(2)	18.	(1)	34.	(1)	50.	(2)
3.	(3)	19.	(4)	35.	(3)	51.	(3)
4.	(3)	20.	(1)	36.	(4)	52.	(4)
5.	(1)	21.	(5)	37.	(4)	53.	(2)
6.	(3)	22.	(3)	38.	(3)	54.	(5)
7.	(3)	23.	(5)	39.	(2)	55.	(2)
8.	(2)	24.	(4)	40.	(1)	56.	(5)
9.	(1)	25.	(3)	41.	(5)	57.	(4)
10.	(3)	26.	(3)	42.	(4)	58.	(2)
11.	(4)	27.	(2)	43.	(3)	59.	(2)
12.	(1)	28.	(5)	44.	(1)	60.	(5)
13.	(3)	29.	(4)	45.	(3)	61.	(3)
14.	(4)	30.	(3)	46.	(2)	62.	(3)
15.	(3)	31.	(4)	47.	(5)	63.	(5)
16.	(3)	32.	(3)	48.	(3)	64.	(5)

Test 3—Science

1.	(2)	18.	(4)	35.	(3)	52.	(3)
2.	(3)	19.	(4)	36.	(3)	53.	(1)
3.	(5)	20.	(1)	37.	(3)	54.	(4)
4.	(5)	21.	(5)	38.	(2)	55.	(5)
5.	(2)	22.	(3)	39.	(3)	56.	(5)
6.	(5)	23.	(1)	40.	(1)	57.	(2)
7.	(4)	24.	(2)	41.	(5)	58.	(2)
8.	(4)	25.	(5)	42.	(3)	59.	(5)
9.	(3)	26.	(2)	43.	(4)	60.	(3)
10.	(2)	27.	(1)	44.	(5)	61.	(4)
11.	(5)	28.	(3)	45.	(5)	62.	(3)
12.	(2)	29.	(2)	46.	(5)	63.	(5)
13.	(5)	30.	(1)	47.	(5)	64.	(3)
14.	(1)	31.	(3)	48.	(1)	65.	(4)
15.	(4)	32.	(5)	49.	(3)	66.	(1)
16.	(5)	33.	(4)	50.	(2)		
17.	(3)	34.	(2)	51.	(2)		

Test 4—Literature and the Arts

1.	(2)	13.	(1)	25.	(4)	37.	(3)
2.	(4)	14.	(4)	26.	(3)	38.	(2)
3.	(1)	15.	(5)	27.	(2)	39.	(1)
4.	(2)	16.	(4)	28.	(4)	40.	(1)
5.	(3)	17.	(2)	29.	(2)	41.	(4)
6.	(5)	18.	(1)	30.	(4)	42.	(4)
7.	(4)	19.	(2)	31.	(1)	43.	(5)
8.	(2)	20.	(2)	32.	(5)	44.	(1)
9.	(4)	21.	(3)	33.	(4)	45.	(3)
10.	(4)	22.	(3)	34.	(3)		
11.	(3)	23.	(2)	35.	(4)		
12.	(3)	24.	(3)	36.	(2)		

Test 5—Math

1.	(2)	15.	(5)	29.	(5)	43.	(3)
2.	(3)	16.	(1)	30.	(5)	44.	(1)
3.	(3)	17.	(2)	31.	(3)	45.	(1)
4.	(3)	18.	(1)	32.	(4)	46.	(3)
5.	(1)	19.	(4)	33.	(3)	47.	(4)
6.	(4)	20.	(4)	34.	(5)	48.	(3)
7.	(5)	21.	(4)	35.	(5)	49.	(5)
8.	(4)	22.	(5)	36.	(2)	50.	(2)
9.	(4)	23.	(2)	37.	(2)	51.	(4)
10.	(5)	24.	(3)	38.	(4)	52.	(4)
11.	(3)	25.	(1)	39.	(4)	53.	(5)
12.	(3)	26.	(4)	40.	(3)	54.	(1)
13.	(2)	27.	(1)	41.	(1)	55.	(2)
14.	(4)	28.	(5)	42.	(1)	56.	(2)

DETAILED EXPLANATIONS OF ANSWERS

TEST 1: WRITING SKILLS, PART I

1. **(2) Sentence 1** The correct answer is choice (2). **Shopping** is spelled with two p's. In choice (1) **nowadays** is the correct form of the word; **nowdays** is not a word. In choice (3), no comma is needed to set off a prepositional phrase at the end of a sentence, unless that phrase is clearly parenthetical. In choice (4), **different** ("various") is the correct choice; **diversified** suggests some manipulation to achieve variety. Choice (5) is incorrect.

2. **(2) Sentence 2** The correct answer is choice (2). **Go** is the verb that agrees with **A number**. **A number** takes a plural verb. Though **The number** (1) takes a singular verb, the meaning of the sentence changes with this choice. Choice (3) is incorrect because a comma is needed to set off the phrase that comes at the end of the sentence and modifies the subject. Choice (4), **walking the length**, is correct as written and should not be changed. The noun **length** is used as an adverb and modifies **walking** and answers **how much**? Choice (5) is incorrect.

3. **(3) Sentences 3 and 4** The correct answer is choice (3). Sentence 4 is a fragment and should be attached to Sentence 3. After the two are joined, the sentence has compound parts and should not have a period (1), a comma (2), a semicolon (4), or a semicolon and conjunction (5)

4. **(4) Sentence 5** The correct answer is choice (4). Since the sentence has two independent clauses and no coordinating conjunction, a semicolon is needed to separate the clauses. No comma (1) is needed after **men** because the adjective clause that follows is essential. No comma (2) is needed after benches because the succeeding prepositional phrase modifies **benches**. The comma (3) after **stores** is needed to set off the participial phrase that follows. Choice (5) is incorrect.

5. **(4) Sentence 6** The correct answer is choice (4). No comma is needed in compound parts. The comma (1) is needed after **manner** to prevent misreading. Commas (2) are not needed to set off **simply,** which modifies **like**. The comma (3) is needed to set off the participial phrase which follows. Choice (5) is incorrect.

6. **(2) Sentence 7** The correct answer is choice (2). An essential adjective clause should not be enclosed by commas. The comma (1) is needed to set off the parenthetical expression **Of course**. The semicolon (3) is needed

to separate the independent clauses, since there is no coordinating conjunction. **Particular** (4) is the correct spelling. Choice (5) is incorrect.

7. **(4) Sentences 7 and 8** The correct answer is choice (4). Sentence 8 contains an appositive that should be attached to Sentence 7 and set off with a dash since the appositive contains a comma. Choice (1) is incorrect since Sentence 8 is a fragment. Choice (2) is incorrect because the appositive contains a comma and needs something stronger than a comma to set it off. Choice (3) is incorrect since a semicolon can separate only parallel elements. Choice (5) is incorrect because the appositive needs to be set off.

8. **(1) Sentence 9** The correct answer is choice (1). The introductory adverb **Actually** is parenthetical. Choices (2) and (3) are incorrect because each choice changes the meaning of the sentence. Choice (4) is incorrect because **shopping** is spelled with two **p**'s. (5) is incorrect.

9. **(5) Sentence 1** The correct answer is choice (5). The sentence contains no error. Choices (1) and (2) are not correct because **employees** and **divided** are spelled correctly. Choices (3) and (4) are wrong because **into** is the correct preposition and is is the verb that agrees with the subject **one**.

10. **(3) Sentence 2** The correct answer is choice (3). The subject **doers** needs the plural verb **are** instead of the singular verb **is**. Choice (1) is incorrect because **Often** is not parenthetical and should not be set off by a comma. Choices (2) and (4) are not correct because **integral** and **industrious** are spelled correctly. (5) is incorrect.

11. **(2) Sentence 3** The correct answer is choice (2). The sentence contains an independent and a dependent clause; a semicolon can be used to separate only parallel elements. A comma is needed to set off the parenthetical adverb clause. Choice (1) is incorrect, since **took** would constitute a tense shift. Choice (3) is wrong, since **process** is spelled correctly. No comma (4) is needed to set off the prepositional phrase. (5) is incorrect.

12. **(4) Sentence 4** The correct answer is choice (4). **Deterred** contains two **r**'s. Choices (1) and (3) are incorrect because **self-driving** is hyphenated and **cannot** contains two **n**'s. The comma (2) is needed after **self-driving** to set off the introductory adverb clause. (5) is incorrect.

13. **(3) Sentence 5** The correct answer is choice (3). **However** is a conjunctive adverb which is not strong enough to link independent clauses; therefore, a semicolon is necessary to separate the clauses. Choices (1), (2), and (4) are incorrect because **counterparts**, **perform**, and **foresight** are spelled correctly. (5) is incorrect.

14. **(3) Sentence 6** The correct answer is choice (3). **Possess** contains two **s**'s in the middle, also. Choice (1) is incorrect because **Usually** is spelled

correctly. **Disgruntled** (2) is the correct form of the participle. A comma is needed after **questions** (4) to set off the parenthetical element which follows. (5) is incorrect.

15. **(4) Sentence 7** The correct answer is choice (4). The original sentence contains a misplaced modifier. **To claim credit** is an infinitive phrase which modifies **quick**. The adverb clause **when a job is done well** modifies the infinitive **to claim**. The modifier **often** (1) is placed correctly. No comma is needed after **rationalizes** (2) because the adverb clause which follows is needed. The semicolon after **made** is needed to separate the independent clauses; the adverbial expression **in addition** is not strong enough to link independent clauses (3).

16. **(1) Sentence 8** The correct answer is choice (1). **Fewer** is used for things that can be counted and **less** for a fractional part of a whole. No comma is needed after **critics** (2). The comma is needed after **doers** to set off the adverb clause which is parenthetical (3). (According to some grammar texts, an adverb clause introduced by **as** or **since** meaning "because" is set off by a comma when the clause comes at the end of the sentence.) Choice (4) is incorrect because the change would constitute a shift in the voice of the verb—from active to passive. (5) is incorrect.

17. **(3) Sentence 1** The correct answer is choice (3). The correct form of the word is **breath-taking**. Choice (1) is incorrect because **Mississippi** is spelled correctly in the original sentence. Commas are not needed in compound parts (2). No comma is needed after **experience** (4). Choice (5) is incorrect.

18. **(4) Sentence 2** The correct answer is choice (4). The correlative conjunction **not only... but also** is used to link **the beauty** and **the reflection**. **Double treat** (1) is the correct form. The comma after **treat** (2) is correct because it sets off the adverb clause beginning with **since** ("because"). The singular pronoun **he** (3) is needed to agree in number with its antecedent **observer**. (5) is incorrect.

19. **(1) Sentence 3** The correct answer is choice (1). The correct spelling is **realistically**. Choices (2), (3), and (4) are incorrect because **brilliance**, **softening**, and **darkening** are spelled correctly in the original sentence. (5) is incorrect.

20. **(3) Sentence 4** The correct answer is choice (3). The correct spelling is **fieriness**. A comma is needed after **First** (1) because the word is clearly parenthetical. The correct spelling of the possessive pronoun is **its** (2). **Different** (4) is spelled correctly in the original sentence. (5) is incorrect.

21. **(5) Sentence 5** The correct answer is choice (5). The sentence contains no error. The comma after **Next** (1) is needed because the word is clearly parenthetical. **Striated** (2) is the correct spelling. No comma is

needed after **purples** (3) or after **yellows** (4) because the adjective clause is essential.

22. **(1) Sentence 6** The correct answer is choice (1). Since the paragraph is written in the present tense, **are** is the correct auxiliary verb; **were** is past tense. **Absorbed** (2) is the correct spelling. No comma is needed after calmness (3) to separate parallel parts. No comma is needed after disappointment (4) because the adjective clause which follows is essential. (5) is incorrect.

23. **(5) Sentence 7** The correct answer is choice (5). The sentence contains no error. **Realizes** (1) is spelled correctly in the original sentence. The commas are needed after **realizes** and after **though** to set off **though**, a parenthetical expression (2). The change in choice (3) is worded awkwardly. **Sensational** (4) is the correct spelling.

24. **(2) Sentence 1** The correct answer is choice (2). **Everywhere** is one word. The adverb **Almost** ("nearly") is the correct choice to modify the adverb **everywhere**; **most** ("the greater number or part of") is an adjective. A comma is needed to set off the introductory adverb clause (3). **He** (4) is the pronoun that agrees with the antecedent **one**. (5) is incorrect.

25. **(4) Sentence 2** The correct answer is choice (4). **Weekend** is the correct form of the word. **Gymnasium** (1) is spelled correctly in the original sentence. **Ballfield** (2) is written as one word. The comma after **park** is needed to set off a series of introductory prepositional phrases (3). Choice (5) is incorrect.

26. **(1) Sentence 3** The correct answer is choice (1). A comma is needed after **event** to set off an introductory infinitive phrase. A comma is needed after wait because the adjective clause is nonessential (2). The possessive pronoun **his** (3) is needed to show ownership. No comma is needed after **scramble** because the infinitive phrase **to find a seat** answers the question **why?** about **scramble** (4). Choice (5) is incorrect.

27. **(5) Sentence 4** The correct answer is choice (5). The sentence contains no error. A comma is needed after **malls** (1) to set off the parenthetical expression which follows. Choice (2) is wrong because no comma is used in compound parts. **Nights** (3) is the correct choice because of **Friday and Saturday**. No comma is needed after **freely** because the prepositional phrase which follows is not parenthetical (4).

28. **(3) Sentence 5** The correct answer is choice (3). One should avoid using the same root word twice in one sentence: **impatient** and **impatiently** are from the same root. No comma is placed after **Sometimes** (1) because in one reading of the sentence the word is a modifier in the infinitive phrase. The comma is needed after **bill** (2) to set off the introductory infinitive phrase. No apostrophe is needed for **others** because the word is not showing

ownership (4); **waiting impatiently** is a participial phrase, not a gerund phrase. (5) is incorrect.

29. **(4) Sentence 6** The correct answer is choice (4). The prepositional phrases need to be rearranged so that **in a bank** is placed after **lines**, the word that the phrase modifies. **Particularly** (1) is the correct spelling. No comma goes after **Particularly** because the adverb modifies **on paydays** (2). A comma is needed after paydays (3) to prevent misreading. (5) is incorrect.

30. **(5) Sentence 7** The correct answer is choice (5). The sentence contains no error. **Wherever** (1) is spelled correctly in the original sentence. The verb that agrees with **one** is **goes** (2). **Often** modifies **becomes** (3). No comma is needed after **throng** in compound parts (4).

31. **(3) Sentence 1** The correct answer is choice (3). To keep the soft **g** sound, **knowledgeable** has to retain the **e**. No comma is needed after **activities** because the introductory infinitive phrase also contains the following prepositional phrase (1); the comma is placed after summer (2), the word that ends the introductory infinitive phrase. No comma is placed after **knowledgable** (4) in the compound parts. (5) is incorrect.

32. **(4) Sentence 2** The correct answer is choice (4). **Heatstroke** is written as one word. No comma goes after **danger** (1), since the adjective clause that follows is essential. A comma is needed after **encounter** (2) to set off the parenthetical phrase which follows. **Outside** (3) is written as one word. (5) is incorrect.

33. **(3) Sentences 3 and 4** The correct answer is choice (3). Sentence 4, a fragment, needs to be attached to sentence 3; the problem can be corrected by adding the word **by** and making the fragment a prepositional phrase modifying **to avoid** and telling **how**. Since sentence 4 is a fragment, choice (1) is incorrect. In choice (2), sentence 4 becomes imperative and causes both a person shift (with **you** as the understood subject) and a mood shift (from indicative to imperative). The dash (4) is not the correct punctuation mark for setting off a participial phrase that comes at the end of the sentence but modifies the subject; a comma can be used to set off that type of element. A semicolon (5) is used between elements that are parallel; a clause and a phrase do not rank equally.

34. **(2) Sentence 5** The correct answer is choice (2). Since **water** is a **liquid**, **water** has to be excluded from the group by saying **some other liquid**; otherwise, the writer is saying drinking **water** or **water** (part of the **liquid** group). No comma goes after **water** (1) in compound parts. The use of (3) is a shift in persons. **Necessary** (4) is the correct spelling. (5) is incorrect.

35. **(4) Sentence 6** The correct answer is choice (4). The informal con-

traction **don't** does not agree in number with the subject **he**. The comma is needed after **play** (1) to set off the two introductory prepositional phrases, as well as to prevent misreading. In choice (2), **hisself** is not a word. Though **doesn't** (3) agrees in number with the subject **he**, contractions are informal; the remainder of the paragraph is more formal. (5) is incorrect.

36. **(4) Sentence 7**   The correct answer is choice (4). Since the paragraph has been written in third person and **you** is second person, **a person** avoids a shift in voice. **Potential** (1) is the correct spelling. No comma is needed after **problems** (2) in compound parts or after **them** (3), which is not the last word of the introductory prepositional phrases. (5) is incorrect.

37. **(4) Sentence 1**   The correct answer is choice (4). A dash is needed after **elements** to set off the appositive which follows, since the appositive contains a comma. No comma is needed after **person** (1) because the adjective clause that follows is essential; no comma goes after **winter**, the last word in the essential adjective clause (2). No comma is needed after **problems** (3) because the following participial phrase is needed. (5) is incorrect.

38. **(4) Sentence 2**   The correct answer is choice (4). The pronoun **his** is needed to agree in number with its singular antecedent **person**. The use (1) of **became**, a past tense verb, causes a tense shift, since the paragraph is in present tense. The correct spelling of the adverb is **too** (2). No comma goes after **cold** (3) because the prepositional phrase that follows is essential to the sense of the sentence. (5) is incorrect.

39. **(4) Sentences 2 and 3**   The correct answer is choice (4). Sentence 3 is a dependent clause which needs to be attached to sentence 2, an independent clause; a comma goes before an adverb clause beginning with **since** when the subordinate conjunction means "because." Choices (1) and (2) are incorrect, since sentence 3 is a dependent clause and does not rank equally with sentence 2. Choice (3) is incorrect because sentence 3 is not an independent clause explaining the former clause (sentence 2). A dash is not the correct mark of punctuation to attach the dependent clause which is not an abrupt break in thought or does not need particularly to be emphasized.

40. **(4) Sentence 4**   The correct answer is choice (4). The appositives following **measures** need to be parallel in structure: **dressing, avoiding**, and **using** are parallel. No comma goes after **knows** (1), since what follows is a noun clause used as the direct object. **He** (2) is the correct pronoun to agree with its antecedent **one**. In (3), the colon after **measures** is correct before a list of appositives (renaming or explaining **measures**). (5) is incorrect.

41. **(2) Sentence 5**   The correct answer is choice (2). The correct spelling is **extremities**. The comma after **If** (1) is needed to set off the parenthetical expression which follows. **Engage** (3) and **vigorous** (4) are spelled correctly. (5) is incorrect.

42. **(3) Sentences 5 and 6**   The correct answer is choice (3). **In addition** is an adverbial expression serving somewhat as a link between parallel elements. Though the phrase is not strong enough to link two independent clauses and has to be preceded by a semicolon, it is conjunctive in nature. The material following **In addition** needs also to have an independent clause, since the material preceding the the expression does. Choices (1) and (2) are incorrect because sentence 6 is only a fragment. Simply attaching sentence 6 (4) with a comma results in illogical construction. Choice (5) is wrong because the adverbial expression is preceded by a semicolon and usually followed by a comma.

43. **(4) Sentence 7**   The correct answer is choice (4). The adjective **safe** should be changed to the adverb **safely**, which modifies **can enjoy** and tells **how**. **Simply** (1) and **judgment** (3) are spelled correctly in the original sentence. No comma goes after **Simply,** which modifies the introductory prepositional phrase. (5) is incorrect.

44. **(4) Sentence 1**   The correct answer is choice (4). **Temperatures** is the correct spelling. **Icicle** (1) is the correct spelling. The comma after **icicle** is needed to set off the introductory participial phrase (2). No comma is needed after **school**, since the element which follows is not parenthetical (3). Choice (5) is incorrect.

45. **(4) Sentence 2**   The correct answer is choice (4). The past tense verb **possessed** is consistent with the tense in the paragraph. **Though** (1) is the correct spelling for the subordinate conjunction. **Created** (2) is consistent with the other past tense verbs in the paragraph. In (3), the comma after **own** is necessary to set off the introductory adverb clause. (5) is incorrect.

46. **(5) Sentence 3**   The correct answer is choice (5) . The sentence contains no error. The dash after **tints** (1) is needed to set off the appositive which contains material that needs to be emphasized. **Semitransparent** (2) is the correct form of the word, according to one current dictionary. **Highlighted** (3) and **complexion** (4) are correct spellings.

47. **(5) Sentence 4**   The correct answer is choice (5). The sentence contains no error. **Lending** (1) and **atmosphere** (2) are the correct word choices for the context. No comma is needed after **about her** (3) in this inverted sentence. **Faraway** (4) is the correct form of the word.

48. **(4) Sentences 4 and 5**   The correct answer is choice (4). Sentence 5 is a fragment which needs to be attached to sentence 4, an independent clause. Choices (1) and (3) are incorrect, since sentence 5 is a fragment. No comma (2) is needed in compound parts. Dashes (5), instead of a coordinate conjunction, are not used to separate parallel parts within a sentence.

49. **(3) Sentence 6**   The correct answer is choice (3). A sentence containing two independent clauses and no coordinate conjunction needs a semi-

colon to separate the clauses. **Showed** (1) is the correct past tense verb. **Disappeared** (2) is the correct spelling. **No one** (4) is the correct form of the pronoun. (5) is incorrect.

50. **(4) Sentence 1**   The correct answer is choice (4). **Precluded** is a malapropism ("ludicrous misuse of words, esp. through confusion caused by resemblance in sound"); **concluded** ("decided by reasoning") fits the context. No commas are needed after **drivers** (1) or **city** (2), since both words are followed by essential prepositional phrases. **Successive** (3) contains double **c**'s and double **s**'s. (5) is incorrect.

51. **(2) Sentence 2**   The correct answer is choice (2). A semicolon needs to be placed after **signs** because the material before and after the punctuation mark contains an independent clause. The independent clauses have to be separated by a mark stronger than a comma (the error is a comma splice); a semicolon is used if the clauses are closely related. **Yield** (3) is the correct spelling. No comma is needed after **approached** (4) in compound parts. (5) is incorrect .

52. **(3) Sentence 3**   The correct answer is choice (3). Though **In fact** is conjunctive in nature, it is not a conjunction and cannot link independent clauses; the adverbial expression is preceded by a semicolon and followed by a comma when placed between independent clauses. **Impatient** (1) is the correct spelling. The comma is needed after **road** (2), since **while** means "whereas." No comma follows **stop** (4), since the adverb clause begins with **while** meaning "when." (5) is incorrect .

Note: Some grammar books discourage the use of the subordinate conjunction **while** meaning "whereas."

53. **(4) Sentence 4**   The correct answer is choice (4). **Made**, a past tense verb, is the correct choice, since the paragraph is written in the past tense. No comma is needed after **lady** because the participial phrase which follows is essential (1). **Traveling** (2) is the preferred spelling. No comma is needed after **boulevard** (3), since the participial phrase is essential. (5) is incorrect.

54. **(4) Sentence 5**   The correct answer is choice (4). The sentence contains two independent clauses with no coordinate conjunction; therefore, a semicolon is needed to separate the independent clauses. **Crept** (1) is the correct past tense form. A comma is needed after **along** (2) to set off the participial phrase which follows. **Posing** (3) is the correct spelling of the verbal. (5) is incorrect.

55. **(2) Sentence 6**   The correct answer is choice (2). The change in choice (2) is much more concise. The original sentence has redundancy ("needless repetition"), especially with the prepositional phrases that tell where the truck stopped—for instance, **On one street with two narrow lanes edged by deep ditches** and **right in the middle of the road**. No comma

is needed after **lanes** (1) because the participial phrase which follows is essential. A semicolon cannot be used after **ditches** because the material before the punctuation mark does not rank equally with that after the mark (3). No change is needed in **road, causing all traffic** because the participial phrase coming at the end of the sentence is set off by a comma; the change cannot be accurate because no comma is used in compound parts (4). Choice (5) is incorrect.

TEST 1: WRITING SKILLS, PART II

Sample Essay — Possible Score of 6 or 5

Occasionally, I feel that I need to escape the pressures of my job. The only way to relieve this stress is to go to a completely different location. My choice of site varies with the seasons and weather conditions.

Since I am not a lover of cold weather, the southern climate is better in late winter and early spring. Actually, the coastal beaches are my choice. There I can sit outside, listening to the waves while dreaming about faraway places. Usually in these reveries, the last thing I think about is my job.

In the summer I like to find a location where the weather is temperate. I like to feel a gentle breeze against my cheek, as well as to see lush foliage and flowers in full blossom; observing the beauty of nature is very relaxing to me. Some of the foothills of the Ozark Mountains and of the Rocky Mountains provide the serenity that I need. Compared to that of the city, the pace of life there seems so deliberate. At least, in such a locale, I can clear my mind for a few days before returning to my job.

Actually, in the fall I have difficulty in choosing among the places of escape. The foliage is so beautiful in many areas. Still, though, I think that the mountains provide some of the prettiest scenes; some are breathtakingly beautiful. I am entranced by the sights and spend little time worrying about my work.

When the pressures of my job weigh heavily, I am never in a quandary about what to do. I know that I need to escape my work environment. The only problem I have is in deciding at which beach or in which mountain area I want to while away my time. Somehow, I usually manage to make a choice, though.

Why this essay scores a 6 or 5

This essay is very well developed. It thoroughly addresses the topic of explaining how the essayist relieves job-related pressures. He/she provides many examples to support the main idea which makes for a more believable essay. In addition, his examples are presented in full detail.

There are no obvious errors in the use of standard written English which shows that the author has a good command of the English language. The essay is easy to follow and read, and also draws the reader through to the end of the essay. The conclusion nicely ties together the ideas presented, without merely reiterating the essay.

Sample Essay — Possible Score of 4 or 3

To relieve job-related pressure, I have to escape the hustle and bustle of the city. I can no longer be a part of the rat race if I want to maintain my sanity. I have to get away from it all.

My escape is not complete unless I can let my hair down. I try to find some place where I do not worry about my looks. If I want to be a slouch, I can. When I want to dress up, I do. I don't want anyone telling me how to act or look. I just do my own thing.

I want no one making any demands on me. Since I leave my alarm clock at home, I get up when I want to and sleep when I want to; I also eat when I get ready. Finally, I do no work—for myself or anyone else.

The main way I can escape stress associated with my work is to do the opposite of what I usually do. My looks do not concern me. I want neither demands made or me nor a schedule to meet. To put it simply, I want to be free as a bird.

Why this essay scores a 4 or 3

Although this essay is not extensively organized, it does present some effective points. However, the effectiveness of these points is minimized by the fact that the essayist does not present supporting examples. The essay is wordy, somewhat repetitive, and not well developed. The ideas that the essayist relieves job-related stress through escaping work, going someplace where he does not have to worry about his looks, and having no demands made upon him are repeated throughout the essay. It is apparent that some thought was put into the creation of this essay, but not enough.

The writing style of this essay is a bit too informal. Poor sentence structure and some spelling errors detract from the overall writing. A quick proofreading would have caught the incorrect word "or" in the third sentence of the last paragraph. The sentence should have read "…demands made **on** me…." Consistent with the essay, the conclusion is weak. It basically reiterates the points previously mentioned and does not tie-up the ideas presented.

Sample Essay — Possible Score of 2 or 1

During the summer, most of us who work look forward to weekends when we can find relief from job-related pressures. Some of my friends like to escape to the woods. Others trade the drudgery of their jobs for dangerous but exhilarating activities. Still others, including me, prefer relaxing in front of the television or out by the pool. All of us escapees have one thing in common—to forget our Monday-Friday activities.

The people who flee to the woods sometimes rest but sometimes encounter other kinds of problems. Tents are not good shelters during a three-day rainstorm. Despite advertising claims, insect repellents for the deep woods are ineffective against Texas-sized mosquitoes whose droning song lingers long after the lights have been snuffed out. Crawling things come to check you out. Someone tells a scary story or reminds you that you can get leeches on you when you are in some damp places. In the woods is no place for me!

Several of my co-workers like excitement. Hot-air ballooning, flying through the air with the greatest of ease, is a favorite activity of a few. It is said that some even wind-surfed last year. Let's not forget skydiving. The worst accident a skydiver had was getting tangled in his ropes and breaking his leg when he landed. Though many have tried, many have failed to entice me to engage in dangerous activities.

Other ways of relaxing include watching my favorite television shows and sitting out by the pool. Unless someone tells me to get up and get him a drink or a snack or something else. Then I go bananas! Anyway, back to my favorite escape. I like watching game shows—at least until I get depressed because I am not winning any money. I hate sports programs, especially boxing and wrestling, because most of them are just incediary anyways. And who can relax under those conditions? The soap operas are sickening; all of the characters have facades. They get on my nerves! Maybe, I'd better relax by the pool instead of in front of the television. I like the pool when the water is clear. I hate it when that yucky green stuff is floating in the pool or attaches itself to the sides. I guess I don't like the pool, either.

Well, I've just about concluded that relaxation anywhere is just not for me. Though I have no escape, I certainly won't try to mess up or begrudge the lives of others. I'll remain envious of those who blaze a path to the woods, leave old terra firma for excitement, or become couch potatoes or pool loungers every weekend. It would be a dull world if everyone was as unhappy as I am.

Why this essay scores a 2 or 1

This essay has a few very serious problems. First, it does not directly address the topic. The topic requires the essay writer to explain how he/she relieves job-related stress; however, this essayist puts more thought into describing how other people relieve their job-related stress. Less than one-third of the entire essay really deals with the topic.

Second, the essayist has a horrible habit of going off on a tangent. The second paragraph begins by going off the topic to describe how other people relax in the woods. Then, the essayist begins to describe some of the problems these people face such as rainstorms, which leads him to mention that tents are not good shelters during three-day rainstorms and that, "despite advertising claims, insect repellents for the deep woods are ineffective against Texas-sized mosquitoes...." All of this has absolutely noting to do with topic of relieving job-related stress.

Finally, this essay contains numerous errors in use of standard written English, such as incomplete sentences, "Unless someone tells me to get up and get him a drink or a snack or something else," and consistently employs bad sentence structure. All of the sentences are short and choppy which is monotonous to read. This essay consistently has no real structure or organization.

TEST 2: SOCIAL STUDIES

1.   **(5)**   is correct. The chart clearly lists "upbringing" as the cause of a person becoming criminal.

2.   **(2)**   seems to meet more of the higher percentage causes than any other, although the others would each meet a need. For example, social services could address bad environment, broken home problems, lack of money in home, and mental illness. (1) This is a solution to repeat offenders, but not to, "why do people become criminals?" in the first place, except for the fear factor. (3) Drugs and the money they generate are certainly causers of crime, but they are not the highest priority on the opinion poll. (4) Again, this is seen by many as a solution for the social causes, but the poll does not reflect this except in one item. (5) This may be attractive to those who see either genetic causes (born bad), or poverty caused by large families, but it doesn't relate to most of the poll.

3.   **(3)**   is most correct because environmental causes would blame the person's family upbringing, socioeconomic status, and stresses created by everyday life. Economic crises can cause all of these to malfunction. (1) may be a frustration once someone is already in the legal system, but shouldn't create original behavior. (2) The type and access to weapons may help dictate the type and degree of crime, but not the original motive. (4) This is a genetic theory that someone is born with a criminal mentality, regardless of environment. (5) This is too general and doesn't relate directly to the issue.

4.   **(3)**   is the least sociological. It is basically a historical study. All the others fit into the definition of sociology: (1) deals with groups of people, (2) discusses how several people interact, (4) deals with a specific type of group, and (5) studies several people comparing similarities and differences.

5.   **(1)**   is most correct. Scapegoating is the stage of prejudice that goes beyond feelings and translates hatred into action. (2) is the feeling of disliking a type of person or a group by pre-judging all members of that group. It does not necessarily lead to any actions. (3) Racism is a form of prejudice directed at a racial or ethnic group. Again, it does not necessarily have to lead to action. (4) Fascism is an economic/political form of dictatorship. Its practice in places like Nazi Germany has linked it to extreme scapegoating, but it is not inherent in the definition. (5) Hostility is one of the emotions that prejudice can trigger that can lead to scapegoating, but many known prejudice forms of hatred also exist.

6.   **(3)**   is correct. The reference to Ft. Sumter and Lincoln's call refer to the already seceded lower states. (1) is second in order of events and in fact was triggered by secession. (2) Lincoln's call for troops was made clear by the lower South's attack on Ft. Sumter. (4) The article states that the earlier

events, touched off a second secession in the border states. (5) The upper states joined the Confederacy after Lincoln's appeal for troops.

7.   **(3)**   The article quotes Southern enthusiasm as being in the same mood as in the Union states. (1) and (2) are incorrect because the mood was similar in both areas. (4) is wrong because, although fear was a natural and secondary reaction, the article does not emphasize it. (5) is not a logical reaction to such dramatic and exciting events.

8.   **(2)**   The war was fought between 1861–65. (1) and (3) are the wrong decades. (4) Lincoln's well-known views on slavery stated that slavery should not be extended, but he would not attempt to eliminate it in the existing slave states. (5) The cotton export trade to Europe was not restricted.

9.   **(1)**   is the correct answer because it is "industries managed by politicians, manned by government employees," that is called immune. The rest are all part of pro-capitalist arguments: (2) is the very definition of capitalism, creating investment money, (3) is seen as creating a greater "flow of goods." (4) The article talks about how abilities, talents, and skills will be developed. (5) Several areas refer to consumers who will get more and determine the products and services.

10.   **(3)**   is correct. Several key terms, like liberty, free, and democracy, are used to describe a capitalistic society. (1) is incorrect because there is no reference to any flaws of capitalism. (2) is wrong. The first sentence refers to "the struggle of socialism against capitalism...." (4) is wrong because there are several references to keeping business free from government rules. (5) The author emphasizes the historical influence of capitalism.

11.   **(4)**   "No work, no eat" was the famous rule of early struggling colonists and it expresses the idea that a person's economic fate is directly related to his or her own efforts. (1) is very socialistic, emphasizing the group rather than the individual. (2) President John Kennedy's famous appeal to patriotism has no relationship to capitalism. (3) This famous concept, tried in many socialist utopian experiments, is the opposite of capitalism. (5) This is also not an economic theory, but refers to emotional and spiritual needs.

12.   **(1)**   is most correct. Although the Canadian Shield and St. Lawrence Lowlands overlap north to south, the general trend is from the Atlantic Maritimes westward to the Rockies and Pacific.

13.   **(3)**   These two southern lakes empty the waters of the Great Lakes into the St. Lawrence River through Lake Ontario. (2) would be equally true if the question just said the Great Lakes in general, because they touch on Lakes Huron and Superior.

14.   **(4)**   All these are prairie provinces that are part of the same Great Plain ecosystem as the U.S. states to their south.

15. **(3)**   is not correct. Lake Michigan is entirely within the U.S.

16. **(3)**   Richard Nixon was president of the United States during the Watergate crisis. References to his administration are made in the passage. He held the office from 1969 until he resigned due to the crisis, on August 9, 1974. The other four people listed as choices were not presidents.

17. **(4)**   The passage clearly states that the break-in occurred "during the 1972 presidential campaign...early on the morning of June 17..." Answer choice (1) is the date of the so-called "Saturday Night Massacre." Choice (2) represents the correct month and day of the break-in, but cites the wrong year. Answer choice (3) is the date on which Nixon announced that his administration was in no way involved in the burglary attempt, and choice (5) is the date of this announcement with the incorrect year cited.

18. **(1)**   When stories of White House involvement in the Watergate break-in began surfacing in 1973, President Richard Nixon came under increasing pressure to formally investigate the entire affair. Nixon denied any involvement in the Watergate caper, but during the trial of one of the Watergate burglars, a White House aid revealed that Nixon had a taping system which had recorded virtually all conversations in the oval office during the period in question. Investigators demanded the tapes. Nixon refused on the grounds of "executive privilege." Investigators smelled a coverup.

To quiet his critics, Nixon appointed a special prosecutor, Archibald Cox, to investigate any White House involvement in Watergate. Cox also requested the tapes. When Nixon refused, Cox went to court to obtain a court order forcing Nixon to relinquish the tapes. When Nixon realized what Cox had done and also realized that Cox might succeed in getting the court order, he ordered Cox to be fired. Nixon's attorney general and his assistant both refused to carry out the order. Instead, they resigned in protest. Nixon finally got another Justice Department official to carry out the order. Cox and his staff were duly fired on Saturday night October 20, 1973, thus the name "Saturday Night Massacre."

The press, the public, and Nixon's political opposition (even some of his supporters) were outraged. The demand for continued investigation forced Nixon to name a new special prosecutor, Leon Jaworski. Jaworski also sought, and eventually got, custody of the complete tapes and those tapes proved to be the "smoking gun" which ruined the little credibility Nixon had left and finished his presidency.

19. **(4)**   Bob Woodward and Carl Bernstein were the two *Washington Post* reporters who painstakingly tracked down the Watergate scandal for the American public. Their investigative journalism eventually led to the resignation of President Nixon in 1974 and the criminal indictments for most of his top advisors owing to violations of various campaign laws and obstruction of justice charges. Gordon Liddy and John Dean were two of Nixon's indicted aides, while Sam Ervin and Howard Baker were the two U.S. Senators

heading the Senate Investigative Hearings into the Watergate affair. William Randolph Hearst and Joseph Pulitzer were New York newspaper editors in the late 19th century who created "yellow journalism." Walter Cronkite and Dan Rather were television media reporters.

20. **(1)** is correct. The reading states that the cultural achievements had been lost. (2) is incorrect because, although the Moslems lived better, they did not control Western Europe. (3) is wrong because the article refers to merchants trading with the Byzantine Empire. (4) Several near civilizations are mentioned: the Moslems and Byzantium. (5) Some nobles and church scholars were learned, as stated.

21. **(5)** is correct. The article says that these two Moslem cultures were much higher than the others. (1) is wrong. The whole purpose of the reading was to show how inferior Western Europe was at the time. (2) lists Byzantine culture as only "slightly higher" than Europe's. (3) and (4) are incorrect because they are no longer in existence during the Crusades, their cultures are referred to as "lost."

22. **(3)** is correct. Only the Holy Land and the Eastern Mediterranean were attacked. Other, closer areas such as Spain and North Africa were left alone. (1) is the main official Church reason for calling for Crusades. (2) Demand had been increasing for the new spices and silks that merchants had bought from Moslem traders. (4) One of the reasons for demanding Christian control of the Holy Land was the poor treatment that some pilgrims had received. (5) As a feudal society, nobles always sought new land wealth, merchants wanted expanded trade, and the Catholic Church wanted control over the Jerusalem area.

23. **(5)** is most correct as the two line graphs have met in the 1970's. (1) The opposite has been true as the GNP line was almost always below that of the labor force. (2) is incorrect as the difference between the two lines widened and narrowed in different areas. (3) Farming had declined to below 50% well before 1900. (4) Even though the graphs' curves became more level in the 1970's, they still reflected a declining influence.

24. **(4)** is most correct. The closing of the gap between GNP and labor force reflect the increasing efficiency of each farmer. (1) is not an accurate conclusion because, with fewer farmers growing the food supply, their importance is great. (2) is not addressed by the graph. The range of farm incomes is wide. (3) Automation might be an explanation for the increased efficiency, but the graphs do not supply that information. (5) There was at least one period on each graph when the line went upward.

25. **(3)** is the correct answer. Farming has become increasingly agri-business and the family farm has decreased in influence and number. (1) is a traditional problem as farmers have to borrow until crops are harvested and hope income is good. (2) The U.S. is usually a food exporter, using its

surpluses to sell crops abroad. (4) Several years of severe weather, such as drought, in the 1980's illustrated how dependent agriculture still is on nature. (5) Government farm programs have been very important for 70 years, helping by price supports, quotas, crop limits, and direct payments.

26. **(3)** is most correct. Efficiency is not necessarily a problem, but the reduction of workers reduces both the earning power of agricultural workers and the the political clout of agriculture as an occupation. (1) is the exact opposite of the trend which has continued for most of the 20th century. (2) World food demands, not supplies are increasing with population growth and all food exporters will be pressured to increase production. (4) Water supplies are decreasing in relation to the population worldwide. (5) Again, the world population growth will increase food needs.

27. **(2)** is the best choice because the excerpt limits itself to the topic of search law. (1) is not correct because the article refers to both citizen and police rights. (3) The article discusses how the Fourth Amendment works, not what limits it. (4) Evidence search is discussed, but other topics are also covered. (5) The article does not detail specific Court rulings on the Fourth Amendment.

28. **(5)** is correct. All of the other choices were listed as exceptions in the article. A person's property is protected from search unless probable cause convinces a court to issue a warrant. (1) The article uses several examples, such as a plain view car search, of non-warrant legal searches. (2) The article states that police may search a suspect during an arrest for their own protection. (3) That "a person may consent to a search" is stated in the article. (4) The search is legal to find evidence of a shooting whether or not the drugs can be used in a criminal charge is up to court.

29. **(4)** is the correct answer. Slavery was made illegal as part of the Constitution after the Civil War (Thirteenth Amendment), which is not part of the original Bill of Rights, the first 10 amendments. (1) is guaranteed under the Seventh Amendment. (2) is part of the First Amendment. (3) is the Third Amendment. It is little known now, but that's because the abuse by the British Army against the colonists was eliminated by the American Revolution and then by the Bill of Rights. (5) is the Second Amendment.

30. **(3)** is correct. The Department of State advises the President on foreign policy, maintains diplomatic relations with foreign nations, issues passports, and maintains embassies and consulates. (2) Defense may carry out a foreign policy goal, but does not make the policy. (3), (4) and (5) are not directly involved in foreign policy but may carry it out.

31. **(4)** The Justice Department is the federal law enforcement agency including the Federal Bureau of Investigation. The other agencies do not have any control over the FBI.

32. **(3)** Is the correct answer, the parks are under the Interior Department. All the others are part of HHS.

33. **(4)** is correct. The SEC is one of many independent agencies that is not part of any branch of government. It has a specific non-partisan role. (1) The Secret Service is under the Treasury Department. (2) The Pentagon is the headquarters of the Armed Forces under the Defense Department. (3) and (5) are part of the Executive Branch offices that advise the President.

34. **(1)** As the chart indicates, the voters elect a legislature and the legislators then choose a prime minister or premier. (2) is not correct because the legislature enacts laws, not the people. (3) This type of government gives the legislature more power than ours because Congress does not get to choose the government leader. (4) As answered in (2), only the legislature can create laws, the leader my propose legislation for them to consider. (5) There is a dual function, with the leader proposing laws and the legislature either passing or rejecting them.

35. **(3)** is correct. Many nations have copied the form and even the names of the British system, but historically, the British pioneered it and named their legislature Parliament . (1) Congress is the American legislature. (2) and (4) have their own parliaments elected by the people. (5) China has a communist system with the party leadership meeting to proclaim policy, and is not a true democratic legislature.

36. **(4)** is correct. Bicameral legislature has two houses, such as our Congress with the Senate and House of Representatives. The other terms may be characteristics of democracy, but bicameral does not define them.

37. **(4)** The theory of plate tectonics explains the areas around the edge of the Pacific plate being geologically active. (1) Geothermics is the study of using the energy released by hot spots around the world and why it exists. It fits into the theory of tectonics. (2) This is the general study of all ocean behavior, not just the Ring of Fire. (3) Any climate and the natural life forms it supports is an ecosystem. (5) All physical features of the surface of the Earth are landforms.

38. **(3)** These cyclonic storms may occur but are not common to the region or caused by tectonic activity. (1) Volcanoes occur where the Earth's crust is thin, such as where two plates come together. The Ring of Fire takes its name from their eruptions. (2) and (5) go together when tension builds up as two plates rub against each other on fault lines and the eventual slippage creates earthquakes. (4) Many islands in this ring are volcanic in origin or have been reshaped by Earthquakes.

39. **(2)** An archipelago is a chain of islands. In Asia, many such as Japan and Indonesia are united into nations. (1) An atoll is a coral reef surrounding

a lagoon. (3) A barrier reef is a coral formation offshore that protects the shore from wave action and storms. (4) A lagoon is a bay created by protective atolls. (5) The continental shelf is the shallow portion of the ocean offshore of a land mass.

40. **(1)** is most true. Besides AT&T, the various Bell companies are all on the list. (2) Obvious manufacturing companies, such as General Motors and General Electric, are outnumbered by service companies, such as utilities. (3) Retailers, such as Sears, appear toward the bottom of the list. (4) Bell Canada obviously does foreign business, as do most of the others with their international branches, such as IBM. (5) Exxon appears on the list, with over three-quarters of a million stockholders.

41. **(5)** is correct because it has the least number of stockholders on the list, so, therefore, the fewest number of votes is required to make decisions. All of the others have more stockholders, so each share of stock is less important in a total vote. The reality is that the number of shares in any large company is so great that influence at the annual stockholders meeting is minimal for any one share of stock.

42. **(4)** is correct. The stockholders elect a board of directors and give them direction at the annual meeting. The board then directs the company for the rest of the year, appointing a chairperson and setting policy. (1) The chief executive officer (CEO) is appointed or elected by the board of directors. (2) The board elects a chair, but controls its power. (3) The president (often the CEO) directs the day-to-day operations under board direction. (5) Stock options are opportunities for top employees to invest in the company, but do not give control unless the employees buy a large portion of the outstanding stock, thus gaining control.

43. **(3)** is the correct answer because East Germany's $31 billion is 10% of West Germany's $323 billion. (1) is incorrect because the U.S. was not the leading exporter ($322 billion v. $323 billion for West Germany). (2) is wrong because Britain's $145 billion is less than half of Germany's total of $354. (4) is not correct because with East Germany's $31 billion added to West Germany's $323 billion, the total gap will widen to $32 billion more than the U.S. (5) is wrong because the total will be almost $500 billion, not $600 billion.

44. **(1)** is correct. Per capita gross national product is one of the accepted economic figures to compare relative standards of living because it includes all (gross) goods and services produced by a nation. (2) relates to a nation's exporting production per capita only, not standard of living. (3) The annual exports alone do not show a relationship to the number of people who share those sales. (4) is incorrect because it compares an individual figure (per capita) with a total national figure. (5) creates the gross national product of a country, not individuals.

45. **(3)** is correct. The U.S., with a population of 248 million, produced $322 billion in exports. Not worrying about the zeroes, the 248 is less than double 322. West Germany produced over 5 times its population, East Germany nearly double, and the British nearly 3 times. (1) is incorrect because the graphs do not show total productivity, only the products exported. (2) is wrong. Britain was fourth. It will go to third and the unified Germany will be second behind the U.S. (4) is incorrect. As noted in explaining (3), the West Germans produced the most exports per capita. (5) is wrong. In a unified Germany, the East German lower GNP will temporarily create a figure for the total for the whole country somewhere between the two figures $12,480 and $14,260.

46. **(2)** is correct. It is mentioned the most often and called the "most continuous attraction." (1) is mentioned the second most often, but not in every example like soil. (3) is only mentioned in connection with its good soils. (4) is not specifically referred to. (5) is mentioned as one occupation that came from settlements by farmers and hunters/trappers.

47. **(5)** is correct. As stated in the last sentence, he learned the route from traders and led the first farmers there. (1) is wrong. Farming is mentioned as one of his occupations but nowhere does it say how good he was at it. (2) He learned the route to Kentucky from traders who had already been there. (3) is wrong for the same reason that (2) is, others were first to trade there. (4) is incorrect for the same reason as (1). Cattle-raising is listed only as one of his occupations.

48. **(3)** is true, after being persecuted in the Midwest, the Mormons sought religious freedom by choosing the isolated area between the mountains and the Great Salt Lake. (1) is wrong. Jefferson did purchase Louisiana, but it was from the French after Napoleon had taken it from Spain. (2) is not correct. California had been settled by native Americans, the Spanish, and even the Russians, as well as Americans before the Gold Rush. (4) is wrong. Hawaii was taken over and became a state and other Pacific possessions, such as Guam and the Philippines became colonies. (5) The Mexicans in the Mexican War, the British in the Canadian boundary disputes, and the Indians all opposed U.S. expansion.

49. **(4)** is most correct. All the items do mark a change. (1) not all are "normal," in the sense that they happen to nearly everyone. (2) Not all create a crisis; many are normal changes in routine. (3) Some may cause problems, but many may not. (5) Many are positive or should be.

50. **(2)** All the experiences, positive or negative, are stress creators. (1) Not all are universal in the sense of happening to everyone. (3) Many of these are normal and not necessarily linked to illness. (4) Some may turn to religion to solve problems, but a direct link is not suggested. (5) The intended use of the chart is to show how a combination of these factors may create a stress

overload and trigger stress-related illness, but there is no direct link to death rate.

51. **(3)** is the most useful in coping with the ups and downs of life, especially the variety listed. (1) Money is not the solution to many of the items listed and the recent history of lottery winners indicates it is not a substitute for good coping skills. (2) Assertive behavior, or taking action, is often helpful, but some of the situations do not lend themselves to this, or it may be the wrong approach in a given case. (4) This attempt to put the problem out of mind often makes it worse or delays a solution. (5) This means to try to blame something or someone else for a problem, which often makes things worse, not better.

52. **(4)** This is the expression made famous by Alvin Toffler's famous book to show how people have problems in a rapidly changing world. (2), (3) and (5) are all ways in which people may react to the changes of future shock.

53. **(2)** is correct. The key references are to leading an army, helping soldiers, and commander-in-chief. (1) is not correct because the article tells about the thirteen states, not colonies, and never mentions the British. The date, 1777, is during the American Revolution. (3) Washington did preside over the Constitutional Convention in Philadelphia, but not until 1787, after the Revolution was over. (4) is wrong because the references to his political leadership are not as president, but as military commander. (5) Thomas Jefferson wrote the Declaration of Independence.

54. **(5)** is correct. The example is given that some in government feared he would become a dictator while others (Lee, Lowell) talked about replacing him as unsuccessful. (1) is incorrect. The article gives several examples of officer discontent but only praise from the common troops. (2) There are several references to his character and justice. (3) Since he was the commander-in-chief this has to be incorrect. (4) The last part of the article discusses the "deep respect and affection" the people had for him.

55. **(2)** is the only choice not true about Washington. Although he presided over the Convention, James Madison is considered to be the author and "father" of the Constitution. All the other statements are true about Washington: (1) he was the first president, (3) he was nicknamed the "father of his country" for his role as a military and political leader, (4) he was the revolutionary army commander, and (5) he did own the plantation at Mt. Vernon.

56. **(5)** is correct. The lead sentence in each paragraph deals with projected water shortage. All the other topics such as (1) alternative water supplies, (2) poor nations, (3) famine, and (4) grain supplies are focused on fresh water shortages. (1) is mentioned only in the first paragraph as options to a global water shortage. (2) is incorrect because water problems in both rich and poor nations are discussed. (3) is not correct because starvation is

a sub-topic in the main discussion of fresh water for farming. (4) The statistics on world grain supplies are related back to lack of water. So, although all topics are mentioned, water resources is the one common main topic; the others are examples.

57. **(4)** is correct. The article states that irrigated land is being lost to improper watering. (1) is incorrect because the article does not discuss individual food consumption. (2) and (3) are wrong because, even though the producing nations are sharing their surpluses, the population growth has reduced the world surplus from a 101-day to a 54-day supply. (5) is wrong because only rich nations, like Saudi Arabia, can afford such projects.

58. **(2)** is correct because fresh water precipitation occurs in all temperature ranges, from rain forest heat to arctic snow. (1) is incorrect because annual rainfall is the measure used to tell a dry climate from a wet one. (3) Hydrologic cycle is the name for the constant pattern of precipitation and evaporation between the earth and atmosphere. (4) is wrong because how the soil absorbs and holds water does influence the supply of water available through rivers and wells for example. (5) is the theory that the warming of the atmosphere will create new climate regions, including shifting rainfall patterns.

59. **(2)** is correct. The main point is that despite different colors used in different cultures, the rule is always that the mourning costume must be different from the non-mourning costume. (1) is too general. It is an obvious statement, but ignores the point of the reading that the same custom can take different forms. (3) is wrong. The difference in colors, not the shade, is the point. (4) is not discussed in the reading. (5) The reading states that it is difficult to understand the point of seemingly different customs.

60. **(5)** is most correct. The opening statement declares the details are different, but the social customs are the same in most cultures. (1) refers to part of the article which uses examples to make the main point about similarities. (2) Again, is just the example used, not the main point. (3) is wrong; the point is the opposite. (4) is incorrect because the article compares cultures, not isolate them.

61. **(3)** is correct because anthropology is the study and comparison of different cultures, whether historical or present-day. (1) is too limited to past cultures. (2) deals with the physical characteristics of the Earth and man's impact on it. (4) is the study of individual, not group behavior. (5) economics studies how people make a living, not their social customs.

62. **(3)** is correct. Greenpeace is the only environmental group on the list. (1) The National Rifle Association has environmental concerns, but they are not the group's main concern. (2) The Commerce Department's goal is to encourage U.S. business and trade, not to protect the environment. (4) OPEC, the Organization of Petroleum Exporting Countries, is trying to increase the use of fossil fuels to keep demand and prices high. Several of

these problems, such as acid rain and the greenhouse effect, can be traced to burning petroleum. (5) The North Atlantic Treaty Organization was formed to defend Western Europe from Soviet aggression, not to deal with ecology.

63. **(5)** is correct. All of the world's major rain forests are in less developed areas. (1) Acid rain is primarily caused by industrial pollution created by the industrialized nations. (2) Underdeveloped nations generally do not have the technological ability to have large-scale nuclear facilities. (3) Most toxic waste is generated by developed nations' industries. (4) Again, developed nations' products seem to be depleting the ozone.

64. **(5)** is correct because the greenhouse effect would have the opposite effect and would raise radiation levels by depleting the ozone layer protecting the Earth. (1) is a predicted result of ozone damage that would create a world-wide warming trend. (2) Sea levels would rise as the rising temperatures helped to melt polar ice caps (4). (3) The increased radiation levels are predicted to increase the incidence of skin cancer.

TEST 3: SCIENCE

1. **(2)** If the car's speed is considered negative when backing up, then it must be going forward when it is positive. The graph shows positive speed for all times past approximately the 2.5 second mark. Since the total time is 30 seconds, the time it must be moving forward is 27.5 seconds. Note the car is backing up at 20 meters per second when the time starts and constantly slows down to a rest and increased in speed until it is going 60 meters per second, which is about 134 mph.

2. **(3)** The vertical axis represents the speed of the car. For it to be constant the vertical movement on the graph must be zero. That is, the curve must remain horizontal. This happens between the 10 and 20 second marks. Before that, the car is accelerating in the forward direction, and after that, the car is slowing down to rest.

3. **(5)** The vertical axis represents the speed of the car. The maximum speed it has backing up is 20 meters per second and the maximum speed it has going forward is 60 meters per second. It is the highest value reached on the vertical axis. The average speed of the car during the first 10 seconds is 20 meters per second and the distance covered during the first 10 seconds is 200 meters or 656 feet.

4. **(5)** Acceleration is change in velocity over change in time. During the first 2.5 seconds the acceleration is (20/2.5) 8 m/s^2. During the 2.5–10 second interval the acceleration is (60/7.5) 8 m/s^2. During the 15–20 second interval the acceleration is (0/5) 0 m/s^2. During the 20–25 second interval the acceleration is (10/5) 2 m/s^2. During the 25–30 second interval the acceleration, or actually, deceleration, is greatest. It's the steepest part of the graph. The brakes are being applied!

5. **(2)** Answer choice (2), phloem, is the correct answer since phloem conducts food to the storage areas of the plant. Xylem (1) cannot be the correct answer since xylem conducts water from the roots throughout the plant. Precambrium (3) cannot be the correct answer since this is a geologic age. Stomata (4) cannot be the correct answer since stomata are the openings on the underside of leaves. Cuticle (5) cannot be the correct answer since the cuticle is a thin, waxy covering that waterproofs the leaf.

6. **(5)** Answer choice (5), cuticle, is the correct answer since the cuticle is a thin waxy covering that waterproofs the leaf. Xylem (1) cannot be the correct answer since xylem conducts water from the roots throughout the plant. Phloem (2) cannot be the correct answer since phloem conducts food to the storage areas of the plant. Precambrium (3) cannot be the correct answer since this is a geologic age. Stomata, (4) cannot be the correct answer since stomata are the openings on the underside of leaves.

7. **(4)** Answer choice (4), stomata, is the correct answer since stomata are the openings on the underside of leaves. Xylem (1) cannot be the correct answer since xylem conducts water from the roots throughout the plant. Phloem (2) cannot be the correct answer since phloem conducts food to the storage areas of the plant. Precambrium (3) cannot be the correct answer since this is a geologic age. Cuticle (5) cannot be the correct answer since the cuticle is a thin, waxy covering that waterproofs the leaf.

8. **(4)** Answer choice (4), stomata, is the correct answer since stomata are the openings on the underside of leaves and the guard cells on either side of the opening swell and shrink to regulate the passage of air into and out of the leaf. Xylem (1) cannot be the correct answer since xylem conducts water from the roots throughout the plant. Phloem (2) cannot be the correct answer since phloem conducts food to the storage areas of the plant. Precambrium (3) cannot be the correct answer since this is a geologic age. Cuticle (5) cannot be the correct answer since the cuticle is a thin, waxy covering that waterproofs the leaf.

9. **(3)** Answer choice (3), vascular tissue, is the correct answer since the vascular tissue is a general term referring to the xylem and phloem together. Roots (1) cannot be the correct answer since the roots contain the vascular tissue. Stems (2) cannot be the correct answer since the stems also contain the vascular tissue. Muscular tissue (4) cannot be the correct answer since plants do not have muscular tissue.

10. **(2)** The correct answer is (2). For Na(s) and Cl_2(g) to react, they must each first become ions. Na will form Na_+ ions by losing an electron, while a Cl atom forms Cl_- ions by gaining an electron. Thus, the electron is removed from the sodium and transferred to the chlorine atom. This transfer shows that NaCl is an ionic compound. Na_+ is a cation since it carries a positive electric charge, and Cl_- is an anion since it has a negative electric charge (since it gained an additional electron).

11. **(5)** is correct. The bonds in H_2 (1) and Cl_2 are covalent because the two identical atoms share the electrons equally. Additionally, diamonds (4) are covalently bonded. To be so hard, a diamond cannot have any weak bonds. NaCl (3) is ionic because Na_+ and Cl_- are ions of opposite charge.

12. **(2)** is correct, because Wyoming is located in an area of predicted minor damage. (1), (3), (4), and (5) are all states that are predicted to have more serious Earthquakes.

13. **(5)** is correct. The map indicates that Earthquakes of varying degrees can occur in almost every state. (1) and (2) are incorrect because the map is making predictions about where Earthquakes might occur, rather than where Earthquakes will definitely occur. (3) is wrong because according to the map, Texas might suffer minor damage in the next 100 years. (4) is

incorrect, because many theories and conclusions can be drawn from the information given.

14. **(1)** is correct, because all of the gases listed are dangerous to life. (2) is wrong because volcanoes, according to the passage, do not always emit both lava and gas. (3) is incorrect, because "volcanic activity" is a term that relates to different types of events. (4) and (5) are wrong, and sentence 1 confirms this.

15. **(4)** is correct. In the above statement a list of gases emitted from volcanoes is given and oxygen is not listed. (1) and (2) are incorrect choices as stated in the paragraph. (3) is an incorrect choice since the volcanoes formed the early atmosphere, and the earth now has oxygen, the oxygen must have come from some other activity.

16. **(5)** is the only correct answer. "Pyroclastic" comes from the term "pyro," meaning fire. A "pyroclastic display" is a shower of fire and debris from a volcano.

17. **(3)** The water column is 34 feet high while the mercury column under the same conditions is only 2.5 feet high. Since the columns have the same cross-sectional area, the weight of the mercury must be 34/2.5 times that of water. This ratio is 13.6 to 1. Mercury is 13.6 times more dense than water. This is why air pressure was formerly measured with mercury barometers rather than water barometers. The latter would not fit in a normal classroom.

18. **(4)** The pressure is defined to be force per unit area. Weight is a force. The weight of the man divided by the area of the boots is 200 lb/70 square inches. This is a pressure of about 2.86 PSI. Notice that this is only about one-fifth of what the air applies to snow.

19. **(4)** The pressure is defined to be force per unit area. Weight is a force. The weight of the girl is 110 pounds. and the area of the skis is 330 square inches. This is a pressure of (110/330) 0.333 PSI. Since air applies a pressure of 14.7 PSI, it is greater by a factor of about 44. This explains why sleds and snowshoes are so useful in traveling great distances over snow-covered terrain.

20. **(1)** Since air exerts the same pressure whether it is viewed over one square inch or over one square mile, the one square foot column of water will be forced to the same 34-foot height. It is the total force that is greater on the larger area, but it is the ratio of force divided by area that is the same. The larger diameter column of fluid needs more force to reach the same height but the area is larger so that the pressure stays the same.

21. **(5)** Answer choice (5), cotyledon is the correct answer since it is a seed leaf that is found within the seed coat. Plumule (1) cannot be the correct

answer since it is a region of growth located between the first foliage leaves. Radical (2) cannot be the correct answer since it is a region of growth found at the opposite end of the plant from the plumule. Apical meristem (3) cannot be the correct answer since it is a generalized term for a growing region of a plant. Seed coat (4) cannot be the correct answer since it covers the seed and prevents mechanical injury.

22. **(3)** Answer choice (3), apical meristem, is the correct answer since it refers to an area where cells are actively dividing to produce growth. Plumule (1) cannot be the correct answer since it is a region of growth located between the first foliage leaves. Radical (2) cannot be the correct answer since it is a region of growth found at the opposite end of the plant from the plumule. Seed coat (4) cannot be the correct answer since it covers the seed and prevents mechanical injury. Cotyledon (5) cannot be the correct answer since it is a seed leaf that is found within the seed coat.

23. **(1)** Answer choice (1), plumule, is the correct answer since it is the growing region that is found between the first foliage leaves of the plant and will produce all of the shoot system. Radical (2) cannot be the correct answer since it is a region of growth found at the opposite end of the plant from the plumule. Apical meristem (3) cannot be the correct answer since it is a generalized term for a growing region of a plant. Seed coat (4) cannot be the correct answer since it covers the seed and prevents mechanical injury. Cotyledon (5) cannot be the correct answer since it is a seed leaf that is found within the seed coat.

24. **(2)** Answer choice (2), radical, is the correct answer since it is the region of growth found opposite the the plumule and will produce all of the root system. Plumule (1) cannot be the correct answer since it is a region of growth located between the first foliage leaves. Apical meristem (3) cannot be the correct answer since it is a generalized term for a growing region of a plant. Seed coat (4) cannot be the correct answer since it covers the seed and prevents mechanical injury. Cotyledon (5) cannot be the correct answer since it is a seed leaf that is found within the seed coat.

25. **(5)** Answer choice (5), cotyledons, is the correct answer since they are the leaves found inside the seed and the embryonic plant will use these for food until it can make its own food by photosynthesis. Plumule (1) cannot be the correct answer since it is a region of growth located between the first foliage leaves. Radical (2) cannot be the correct answer since it is a region of growth found at the opposite end of the plant from the radical. Apical meristem (3) cannot be the correct answer since it is a generalized term for a growing region of a plant. Seed coat (4) cannot be the correct answer since it covers the seed and prevents mechanical injury.

26. **(2)** is correct. Electrons will fill the 1s orbital first, then 2s, then 2p, then 3s, 3p, 4s, 3d, etc. Each electron is placed in the lowest-energy orbital available. Since hydrogen occupies 1s, the 1s orbital must be of lowest en-

ergy. Thus (1) and (3) can be excluded from consideration. (5) is wrong because a 1p orbital does not exist. (4) is wrong because an s orbital has lower energy than a p orbital.

27. **(1)**   The answer is (1). The spins of electrons are paired when they are spinning in opposite directions, or one has $m_s = +1/2$ and the other has $m_s = -1/2$. (2) and (3) are wrong because these electrons cannot occupy the same orbital if they have the same spin. Thus, (5) is also wrong. (4) is wrong because spin is designated by +1/2, not +1. Additionally, the spins shown here are the same (both positive) so the electrons could not both be present in the same orbital.

28. **(3)**   is correct. Two electrons fill the 1s orbital, two electrons fill the 2s orbital, which can hold six electrons. (2) shows the right energy levels but the superscripts are missing. (4) is wrong because 2s is not higher in energy than 2p. (1) is wrong because the 1s can only hold two electrons. (5) is wrong because the 1s orbital fills first, and all nine electrons cannot fit in the 2p orbital.

29. **(2)**   is correct. Only Well 2 breaks through the surface at a point below the artesian water table, causing water pressure to force water to the surface. (1) is incorrect because Well 1 would require a pump to bring water to the surface. (3) is incorrect; Well 3 does not extend into the aquifer. (4) is incorrect because Well 4 is in impermeable rock which does not contain water.

30. **(1)**   is correct; Well 1 reaches into the aquifer, yet it is above the water table and would need a pump. (2) is incorrect as this well would gush water due to the pressure of an artesian system. (3) and (4) are incorrect as neither reaches the aquifer.

31. **(3)**   is correct as Well 1 is the only well to be in the local water table. (1) and (2) are incorrect as they are aquifer wells. (4) is incorrect as this well is dry, being in the impermeable rock layer.

32. **(5)**   The cell membrane, which surrounds the outside of a cell, is the first barrier that a foreign molecule will meet. Nucleoplasm (1) is the substance inside the nucleus and is far from the outside of a cell. Cytoplasm (2) is immediately inside the cell membrane, so the foreign molecule must pass the cell membrane first before reaching the cytoplasm. Both the nuclear membrane (3) and the chromosomes (4) are inside the cell and will not be the first structure reached by an approaching foreign molecule.

33. **(4)**   There is a constant number of chromosomes for any somatic cell within an organism. Thus, choice (4) is correct. (1) is incorrect because the chromosomes do not assemble randomly. (2) is incorrect because it is the opposite of the correct answer. (3) is incorrect because the strength of the microscope will not change or affect the number of chromosomes. Also,

during cell division, all of the chromosomes should be easily visible. (5) is incorrect because there is no evidence for nucleoli interfering with chromosome coiling.

34. **(2)**   It is true that ribosomes function in protein synthesis, which occurs in the cytoplasm. Thus, the ribosomes must move from the site of their synthesis in the nucleus to the cytoplasm. Choice (2) is correct. (1) is incorrect because the ribosomes are located in the cytoplasm. (3) is incorrect because mitochondria, not ribosomes, produce the energy for a cell. (4) is wrong since there is no evidence that chromosome coiling interferes with ribosome formation. (5) is incorrect because one cannot assume that the product (the ribosome) of a dark staining organelle (the nucleolus) will also stain dark.

35. **(3)**   A selective membrane is considered semipermeable (3) because some things pass through while others do not. Thus, (1) and (2) are wrong. The terms opaque (4) and translucent (5) refer to the ability of light to pass through. These terms are unrelated to selective membranes.

36. **(3)**   Answer choice (3), nucleoli is the correct answer since nucleoli are dark staining spherical bodies found suspended within the nucleoplasm. Nucleoplasm (1) cannot be the correct answer since the nucleoplasm is the viscous matrix inside of the nuclear membrane. Cytoplasm (2) cannot be the correct answer since it is the viscous matrix outside of the nuclear membrane. Chromosomes (4) cannot be the correct answer since they are rod-shaped bodies found suspended within the nucleoplasm. Mitochondria (5) cannot be the correct answer since they are found suspended in the cytoplasm.

37. **(3)**   Answer choice (3), vacuoles, is the correct answer since vacuoles store either waste food, or water. Ribosomes (1) cannot be the correct answer since they are structures that function in protein synthesis and have nothing to do with storage. Mitochondria (2) cannot be the correct answer since they are the energy producers of the cell. Nucleoli (4) cannot be the correct answer since they are thought to produce the ribosomes. Chromosomes (5) cannot be the correct answer since they carry the genetic code.

38. **(2)**   Answer choice (2), nucleoli, is the correct answer since nucleoli, which are composed of RNA, are thought to produce ribosomes which function in protein synthesis. Chromosomes (1) cannot be the correct answer since they carry the genetic code. Vacuoles (3) cannot be the correct answer since they are storage structures. Mitochondria (4) cannot be the correct answer since they are the energy producers of the cell. Cytoplasm (5) cannot be the correct answer since the cytoplasm is the viscous matrix in which many of the organelles are suspended.

39. **(3)**   The right answer is (3). Rutherford concluded that the particles were colliding with the nucleus of the gold atom which is where most of the mass of the atom is concentrated. (1) is incorrect because the particles do

have enough velocity to pass through the empty space surrounding the nuclei. (2) is wrong because the electrons have a mass too small to repel alpha particles. (4) is wrong because although alpha rays and gold nuclei are both positively charged, this would not cause the large deflection. (5) is wrong because air cannot pull alpha particles in any way.

40. **(1)** is correct since it is true that most of the atom is empty space. (2) is wrong because the thickness of the gold foil does not affect the movement of the alpha particles. If a nucleus was in the path of the particle, the particle would then be deflected. (3) is wrong because the electrons are too small to influence the alpha particles. (4) is incorrect; atomic nuclei are not semi-permeable. They are dense and cause the alpha particles to be deflected. (5) is wrong because the nuclei will not be moved by the alpha particles. Instead, the alpha particles collide with the nuclei and bounce off at an angle.

41. **(5)** (5) Au is the correct answer. (4) Na is the chemical symbol for sodium. (3) He is the symbol for helium. Hg, answer choice (2), is mercury, and (1), Ga, is the symbol for Gallium.

42. **(3)** is correct. In reading the graph, the lowest numbers are located in the Northeast, and these numbers indicate the more concentrated acid. (1), (2), (4), and (5) are all incorrect as these areas all have higher readings, which indicate lower pH.

43. **(4)** is correct; both Lakes Erie and Ontario are located in the area of lowest pH reading. (1) is incorrect; not all lakes are located in areas of low pH. (2) Lake Superior is in the least danger from acid rain. (3) is incorrect as Lakes Huron and Michigan are not in areas of low pH.

44. **(5)** is correct. The amount of rainfall does not affect the pH of the rain. (1), (2), (3), and (4) are all factors that concentrate pH or direct the pattern of rainfall.

45. **(5)** Answer choice (5), internal, is the correct answer since sharks do not lay their eggs to be externally fertilized by the male shark. Denticle (1) cannot be the correct answer since denticles are the little toothlike appendages found on the skin of a shark. Viviparous (2) cannot be the correct answer since this term refers to how the embryos of some kinds of shark get their nourishment. Ovoviparous (3) cannot be the correct answer since this term refers to how the embryos of some kinds of shark get their nourishment. External (4) cannot be the correct answer since sharks do not lay eggs to be externally fertilized by the male shark.

46. **(5)** Answer choice (5), class Chondrichthyes, is the correct answer since sharks, rays, skates, and dogfishes are members of this class. Phylum Reptilia (1) cannot be the correct answer since there is no phylum Reptilia, and it is not mentioned in the paragraph. Class Aves (2) cannot be the correct answer since this is a class/group of birds, and it is not mentioned in the

paragraph. Class Vertebrata (3) cannot be the correct answer since there is no class Vertebrata, even though the shark is a vertebrate animal. Class Osteichthyes (4) cannot be the correct answer since this is the class of fish that have skeletons composed of bone.

47. **(5)** Answer choice (5), "as an embryo it gets its nourishment from the yolk's blood vessels which are close to the oviduct's blood vessels," is correct because this is the correct term referring to viviparous. "As an embryo it eats its brothers and sisters before they hatch" (1) cannot be the correct answer since viviparous refers to an embryo that gets its nourishment from the mother's blood supply by having the yolk's blood vessels close to the oviduct's blood vessels. "As an embryo it gets nourishment from the yolk" (2) cannot be the correct answer since viviparous refers to an embryo that gets its nourishment from the mother's blood supply by having the yolk's blood vessels close the the oviduct's blood vessels. "As an embryo it gets its nourishment directly from the mother's blood" (3) cannot be the correct answer since viviparous refers to an embryo that gets its nourishment from the mother's blood supply by having the yolk's blood vessels close to the oviduct's blood vessels. "As an embryo it gets its nourishment by eating the mother's oviduct" (4) cannot be the correct answer since viviparous refers to an embryo that gets its nourishment from the mother's blood supply by having the yolk's blood vessels close the oviduct's blood vessels.

48. **(1)** Answer choice (1), denticles is the correct answer since embedded in the shark's skin are little toothlike appendages called denticles. Yolks (2) cannot be the correct answer since yolks are not found in the skin. Oviducts (3) cannot be the correct answer since oviducts are part of the reproductive system and not a part of the skin. Embryos (4) cannot be the correct answer since embryos are, in this case, young sharks. Internal fertilization (5) cannot be the correct answer since this is a process and not a structure.

49. **(3)** An electroscope can measure whether electrons are added to it or taken away. It can also measure whether a charged object is brought near by either attracting electrons to its top knob or driving electrons down the rod and into the gold leaves. Choice (4) makes no sense. The source of the electrons is either from without by direct contact or from the knob above or from the gold itself. However, the electroscope does not indicate how many electrons the gold contains. Choice (5) is meaningless. The electroscope responds to the surplus or deficiency of electrons, not to the surplus or deficiency of protons.

50. **(2)** When a positively charged rod is brought near the top, electrons will be drawn from the gold up the internal rod to the knob. This leaves the gold leaves positively charged. If they are close to the same mass, they both will give up the same number of electrons and will result in the same positive charge. They then repel each other and separate. The knob has become negative but the entire electroscope is still neutral since no charge has been

added to it or taken away. All that has happened is that charge has been rearranged upon it due to the presence of an outside electrical field provided by the positively charged rod.

51. **(2)** If the gold leaves of an electroscope are separated before the vinyl is brought near, it must mean that some charge has been added to or taken from the electroscope. In this case electrons have been added to the electroscope so that it is charged negatively. When a negative vinyl is now brought near, electrons in the knob will be repelled down the internal rod to the gold leaves. They will now acquire a greater negative charge and tend to spread even further apart.

52. **(3)** Answer choice (3), vertebrates, is the correct answer since fish have a backbone (vertebrate). Filter feeders (1) cannot be the correct answer since these are animals like clams and oysters which have no backbones. Invertebrates (2) cannot be the correct answer since invertebrates do not have backbones. Zooplankton (4) are very small invertebrate animals that are carried by the currents and have no backbones. Phytoplankton (5) cannot be the correct answer since they are one- to few-celled plants and do not have backbones.

53. **(1)** Answer choice (1), invertebrates, is the correct answer since zooplankton are very small animals without backbones. Vertebrates (2) cannot be the correct answer since vertebrates have backbones and zooplankton are not vertebrates. Phytoplankton (3) cannot be the correct answer since they are plant-like organisms. Toxic mucus (4) cannot be the correct answer since it is not mentioned in relation to being a type of organisms, but it is a protective device. Toxic mobile predators (5) cannot be the correct answer since zooplankton are carried by the currents, they are not extremely mobile, and they are not toxic.

54. **(4)** Answer choice (4), filter feeders, is the correct answer since organisms like the clam, which filter their food by straining it from the water by passing it over their gills, would be called filter feeders. Fish (1) cannot be the correct answer since fish do not use any means of filtering the water for food. Vertebrates (2) cannot be the correct answer since no mention is made of vertebrates filtering the water. Phytoplankton (3) cannot be the correct answer since they are plantlike organisms and are not mentioned in the paragraph. Toxic mobile predators (5) cannot be the correct answer since no mention of these are made in the paragraph.

55. **(5)** Answer choice (5), be firmly attached, is the correct answer since being sessile is to be anchored or attached to something. Move around (1) cannot be the correct answer since sessile means to be attached or anchored to something. Swim freely (2) cannot be the correct answer since sessile means to be attached or anchored to something. Crawl along the sea floor (3) cannot be the correct answer since sessile means to be attached or anchored to something. Answer choice (4), float on the surface, is also wrong because something which floats is not sessile.

56. **(5)** Answer choice (5), tiny enough to float near the surface, is the correct answer since zooplankton are very small and they are easily buoyed up by the water. Voracious predators (1) cannot be the correct answer since nothing of this nature is mentioned in the paragraph. Powerful swimmers (2) cannot be the correct answer since zooplankton are invertebrates and it is mentioned that invertebrates are not powerful swimmers. Fish (3) cannot be the correct answer since fish are not invertebrates. Able to move from one ocean current to another (4) cannot be the correct answer since this implies being able to be a powerful swimmer, which zooplankton are not.

57. **(2)** is correct. The physical properties of the ground allow it to absorb heat. (1) is incorrect, because the troposphere is under the ozone layer. (3) is incorrect, because ice cover affects only the place it is covering, not the entire planet. (4) is incorrect, because land and water have different rates of heating and cooling.

58. **(2)** is correct, according to the chart the lowest temperatures are in the thermosphere, reaching −80°C. (1) and (4) are incorrect; they are boundaries, not layers. (3) and (5) are incorrect; they are layers, yet their temperatures are well above that of the thermosphere.

59. **(5)** is correct. Changes in composition would cause different rates of heating. (1) is incorrect, because change in distance is insignificant. (2) is incorrect, because weather is only found in the lowest atmospheric layer. (3) is incorrect, because ozone is only found in one layer. (4) is incorrect, because man does not affect the atmosphere.

60. **(3)** Answer choice (3), roots, is the correct answer since the main function of the root system is to absorb water and minerals, and to firmly anchor the plant in the ground. Flower (1) cannot be the correct answer since the main function of a flower is reproduction. Stem (2) cannot be the correct answer since the main function of the stem is the support of the leaves and flowers. Stomata (4) cannot be the correct answer since stomata are openings on the underside of leaves that aid in transpiration. Leaves (5) cannot be the correct answer since the main function of leaves is in the process of photosynthesis.

61. **(4)** Answer choice (4), flowers, is the correct answer since the seed is an embryonic plant that is produced by flowers. Nodes (1) cannot be the correct answer since nodes are regions from where leaves arise. Internodes (2) cannot be the correct answer since internodes are the regions between nodes. Stomata (3) cannot be the correct answer since stomata are openings on the underside of leaves that aid in transpiration. Tubers (5) cannot be the correct answer since tubers are formed in the roots of a plant.

62. **(3)** Answer choice (3), nodes, is the correct answer since nodes are the regions on the stem from which leaves arise. Stems (1) cannot be the correct answer since nodes is a more specific answer. Roots (2) cannot be

the correct answer since leaves do not arise from roots. Internodes (4) cannot be the correct answer since internodes are the regions between nodes. Stomata (5) cannot be the correct answer since stomata are openings found on the underside of leaves and function in the process of transpiration.

63. **(5)**   Answer choice (5), stomata, is the correct answer since guard cells make up the stomatum. Stems (1) cannot be the correct answer since there might be stomata on the stem, but the stem is not made of stomata. Roots (2) cannot be the correct answer since roots are located underground and are not known for their stomata or guard cells. Nodes (3) cannot be the correct answer since nodes are regions where leaves arise. Internodes (4) cannot be the correct answer since internodes are the regions between nodes.

64. **(3)**   Answer choice (3), nodes, is the correct answer since nodes are the regions from which leaves arise. Stems (1) cannot be the correct answer since nodes are regions on a stem. Roots (2) cannot be the correct answer since roots do not produce leaves. Internodes (4) cannot be the correct answer since internodes are regions between nodes. Seeds (5) cannot be the correct answer since seeds are reproductive structures produced by flowers.

65. **(4)**   Answer choice (4), flowers, is the correct answer since seeds are produced by the flowers. Stems (1) cannot be the correct answer since stems do not produce the embryonic plants (seeds). Roots (2) cannot be the correct answer since roots do not produce the embryonic plants (seeds). Leaves (3) cannot be the correct answer since leaves do not produce the embryonic plants (seeds). Fruits (5) cannot be the correct answer since fruits are the embryonic plants (seeds), and not the reproductive organ itself.

66. **(1)**   Desert areas increase evaporation of the water that is present, causing a concentration of salts. Therefore, the remaining answers are incorrect.

TEST 4: LITERATURE AND THE ARTS

1   **(2)**   This idea is explicit throughout the passage in such excerpts as "particularly happy in the smiles of all the county damsels." (1) "by all" is not expressed, (3) is incorrect as state above; (4) "country bumpkin" is far from the truth with such phrases as "vastly superior taste and accomplishments"; (5) is not a good choice since the schoolmaster was "inferior in learning only to the parson."

2.   **(4)**   That he thrives on all this attention is apparent since he gathered grapes and recited for them, excluding (1) shy and retiring and (2) modest as well as (3) humble, all this makes striving to keep out of the limelight (5) a poor choice.

3.   **(1)**   Taken figuratively the term means he wandered through the countryside a great deal. (2) is incorrect since the schoolmaster was "inferior in learning only to the parson." (3) All indications are that the schoolmaster's life was quite fulfilled. (4) There is no mention of his having two actual jobs; not even entertaining the ladies is considered a "job."

4.   **(2)**   That the schoolmaster "was a kind of travelling gazette," is a figurative expression for gossiping having nothing actually to do with (1) newspapers, (3) esteem, nor (5) economy.

5.   **(3)**   The author blatantly reveals to us that the schoolmaster is preoccupied with New England witchcraft. (1) Well read is not specific enough, and (2) well educated is not the point at hand. Neither (4) classical literature nor (5) fiction are mentioned.

6.   **(5)**   Tongue-in-cheek is the most apt description for this madcap prankster. (1) admiration would not account for the author's frequent recounting of Brom's mischievous deeds nor would (3) indifference account for the same repetition. (2) Hostility and (4) anger are entirely inappropriate choices.

7.   **(4)**   Physical skills and prowess is the best answer since the excerpt is full of complimentary phrases acknowledging his skill in horsemanship, excluding (1) intellectual since knowledge of horsemanship is the extent of it. (2) Family background and (3) formal education are not mentioned nor hinted at, and his "fur cap with flaunting fox tail" do not suggest that (5) love of nature is a particularly good answer.

8.   **(2)**   Sense of humor and high spirit is correct since phrases such as "strong dash of waggish good humor" proliferate, therefore (1) completely quarrelsome is incorrect, and since he was "umpire in all disputes" excludes (3) frivolous of nature. That "neighbors looked upon him with a mixture of awe, admiration, and good will" discounts (4) feared and (5) regarded lightly as good answers.

9. **(4)**   This simile suggests rowdiness although it is clear that the author treats Brom with a light touch, even as he recounts his numerous misdeeds. (1) School boys and (2) lovesick young men are not strong enough to identify this "troop"; neither is (5) horsemen—(3) and dignified gentlemen they clearly are not.

10. **(4)**   A mixture of awe, admiration, and good will is what the author tells us that neighbors of Brom Bones felt. Neither (1) terror, (3) honor, nor (5) as an intellectual appropriately describe their feelings.

11. **(3)**   is correct when using guidelines from the question itself; the "turn of events" is that the artist was initially "neglected," now considered by some as "America's first." Choices (1) modernists rejected him and (2) art resists easy classification do not present a "turn of events." (4) is also incorrect since it does not contain an incongruity of what is expected and what actually happens. (5) Combining richness and simplicity is simply a statement of style, not irony.

12. **(3)**   "Carefree" is the most accurate answer since lines 8 and 9 define him as an artist who has taken "all the work out and left only the joy." (1) Conservative is incorrect according to line 7, "vibrant images," and so is (4), ordinary, since lines 29 and 30 describe his work as "an explosion in a color factory." (5) Suggestive is a poor choice because nothing suggests that his work brings something else to mind.

13. **(1)**   The most apt and literal definition for pathfinder is "unlike any of his predecessors." All of the following are mentioned in the review, but they do not adequately define the term: (2) difficult to classify, (3) hard worker, (5) influenced by Impressionism. (4) is incorrect since nothing in the review states or suggests that Pendergast's successors were affected by his success.

14. **(4)**   Line 26 is clear as to what was revolutionary—"Above all, his color—or rather, the amount he used—was new." (1) Lines 20 and 21 state that he took his improvisational brushwork from the impressionists, making it anything but new—which is the same as his subjective, stylized view of reality (2) which is not new, patterned after the Postimpressionists, lines 21 and 22, additionally, (3) is incorrect since he borrowed his decorative expression of color from the Nabis.

15. **(5)**   Clearly, father refuses to talk to his wife because his farm business does not require his wife's opinion or deal with her sphere of the house to which he orders her to go back; the home is her affair, not the farm.

16. **(4)**   Words like "diggin'," "an'," and "ain't" portray a non-standard from of speaking particular to a certain section of the country or a certain type of person. (1) and (2) are poetic terms. There is no hint of irony or exaggeration.

17. **(2)** Mother's persistence and defiance make her quite strong willed; certainly none of the other choices would justify the fact that father sees her as "immovable."

18. **(1)** Mother blatantly says, "we was goin' to have a house." (2) Geography and (5) economics do not factor into their discussion. Mother does not sound (3) pleased or (4) willing to help out with the barn since she questions the idea in the first place.

19. **(2)** The poem tells a story, so it is narrative. It is too long for (1) a sonnet or (3) a limerick and too short for (5) an epic poem. (4) Although folk ballad is narrative also, the missing element is that this poem is not designed to be sung.

20. **(2)** The poet effectively uses metaphor in the first three lines which implicitly compare two objects (road and ribbon). (1) If like or as were used then the poetic technique would be simile. There is more rhythmic beat than (3) rhyme; neither (4) gross exaggeration nor (5) entertainment are apparent.

21. **(3)** From his claret velvet coat to his French cocked hat, there is no doubt that he is a romantic and dashing figure. No hint of any other possible choice is apparent in lines 6 through 15.

22. **(3)** In line 21, Bess is braiding a dark red "love-knot" in her long black hair; the symbolism is explicitly love, then.

23. **(2)** Since a metaphor, unlike a simile, does not employ the use of like or as, eyes were hollows of madness is the correct answer. (4) and (5) are similes.

24. **(3)** A close look at these lines reveal that he is "after a prize to-night," and he will be back with "the yellow gold" before daylight. Therefore, "planned a robbery" is the best answer.

25. **(4)** Since meter in poetry is its measure, a close look at these stanzas suggest horses' hoof beats due mainly to the number of monosyllable words.

26. **(3)** Although the narrator wishes us to believe that he is "nervous" we are led to believe that he is not "healthy" in mind, but crazy. He seems to be struggling to be (1) clever, and (4) intelligent, but he falls short. There is no hint of (2) anger or (5) suicidal tendencies.

27. **(2)** Since "gold" could be used synonymously with money, and since the old man has gold, it seems that the old man therefore has money.

28. **(4)** The speaker is quite clear that there was no passion, just the desire to be rid of "the eye."

29. **(2)** The desire to prove to the reader that he is not mad is evident when the speaker utters this phrase. To select (1) is mad or (3) is not mad would be too presumptive. He is too apparent in motive to be (4) clever; nor is he concerned about the old man since he plans to kill him.

30. **(4)** Line 32, "but I found the eye always closed," excludes all other possible answers.

31. **(1)** Lines 34–39 include "spoke courageously" and calling in a "hearty tone" while all the while plotting his demise indicate that the speaker is proud and self-serving rather than (2) sincere and (3) charitable. Since we are considering the speaker's intentions, (4) hesitant and (5) frivolous are poor choices.

32. **(5)** The general tone of the narration from the onset is anxious, as witnessed by statements as "—nervous—very dreadfully nervous—." (1) Tranquile and (3) reverent are entirely inappropriate responses. The narrator is neither (2) afraid of his crime, since he is so calculating, and neither is he (4) hostile, since he tells us that he has no passion for the old man.

33. **(4)** The narrator's increasing tiredness and unstable emotional state seem to be caused by an illness. She certainly does not mention (1) or (5) happiness, or (2) an accident she once had. She is relieved that her family has left, so (3) is incorrect .

34. **(3)** The narrator says, " I don't know why I should write this," therefore the passage is being written by her, and not (5) another.

35. **(4)** The narrator knows "John would think it absurd" if she confessed her weariness and yet her desire to write. This renders John an unsympathetic character (2) and not very (1) supportive. It seems that the narrator hides her writing from John, so (3) is incorrect. She does not mention John's health, so (5) is incorrect.

36. **(2)** The narrator spends a great deal of time discussing and following the design of the wallpaper while she seems happy to dismiss the other member of her family.

37. **(3)** Since the narrator cries, though "of course, I don't when John is here." and because she hides her writing from him and only reveals what she really feels and thinks in her writing, it seems that she fears her husband. There is no indication that she (2) feels sorry for him, or (5) is angry at him. Because she hides so much from him, (1) and (4) cannot be fully realized as they require more trust.

38. **(2)** "Desperate haste to succeed" as well as "keeping pace with companions" are but two of a number of phrases suggesting that society

does pressure man in a quest for achievement and success, excluding all other choices.

39. **(1)** These often-quoted lines have far-reaching implications when taken as intended as figures of speech. "Keeping pace" could mean trying to "keep up with," and "different drummer," as figurative language, could mean a man's inner drive or natural bent.

40. **(1)** Imagery of nature is present within this excerpt with references to apple and oak trees. By inference (2) material wealth is not held in high regard as suggested by such terms as "desperate enterprises."

41. **(4)** Humble is the closest synonym for mean in this particular context, since we are soon instructed not to "shun it and call it hard names," and that "It looks poorest when you are richest." There are no references to an (1) unkind, (2) benevolent, or (5) lonely life. Since (3) wealthy is an antonym for the intended meaning of the word, it is also incorrect.

42. **(4)** Mention is made of having "pleasant, thrilling glorious hours, even in a poorhouse," as well as other references suggesting that true happiness is not a result of material wealth. Since the question asks for the message of the excerpt, the reader must be careful not to make judgments based on personal beliefs concerning wealth and happiness as suggested in choices and (1), (2), and (3). Since (5) does not include wealth or the lack of wealth, it is a poor choice.

43. **(5)** Nonappreciative is the best description of material wealth as revealed in the comparison of the "alms-house" and the "rich man's abode." Since (1) sympathetic and (2) accepting are entirely opposite of the author's intended attitude, they are poor choices. Both (3) envious and (4) contemptuous are unsubstantiated.

44. **(1)** The third passage concentrates on truth and mentions sincerity. (5) Nature is forgotten momentarily. (2) Material wealth is opposite in the inherent intent of the line as well as (3) a rare, vintage wine. (4) Mankind and greed is a value judgment and not part of the general theme.

45. **(3)** Since this entire passage endorses truth, "rather than love, than money, than fame...," then (3) truth and sincerity is your best choice. (1) Nature, as in the preceding passage is momentarily put aside. (2) Material wealth is mentioned as lesser in importance than truth and sincerity; and since (4) a rare, vintage wine is symbolic of wealth, it is not endorsed. (5) Heaven is not referred to.

TEST 5: MATHEMATICS

1. **(2)** Subtracting 35 from each side of the equation gives x = 35.

2. **(3)** The two angles pictured form a linear pair, and together they form a straight angle. The sum of the measure of angle R and 59 is 180, the number of degrees in a straight angle. To obtain the answer, subtract 59 from 180.

3. **(3)** 2 times 17 is 34. The number of marbles Joe has is not known and is not needed.

4. **(3)** Dividing both sides of the equation by 12 yields x = 13.

5. **(1)** The sum of the measures of the angles of a triangle is 180 degrees. Angle U is marked as a right angle, which is 90 degrees. This leaves the other two angles to make up the other 90 degrees. So the correct answer is obtained by subtracting 47 from 90. Also you could add 90 and 47 to get 137 and subtract 137 from 180. The answer is the same.

6. **(4)** $15 times 10 is $150. Answers (1) and (3) have the decimal point in the wrong place. Answer (5) would be correct if he received $10.00 going and another $10.00 returning from the airport, but he returned to the hotel without fare.

7. **(5)** Multiplying x and 3x gives $3x^2$. Multiplying x and 4 gives 4x. Multiplying 1 and 3x gives 3x. Multiplying 1 and 4 gives 4, collecting like terms gives $3x^2 + 7x + 4$.

8. **(4)** Angle ACD is called an exterior angle of the triangle, and it is equal to the sum of the two remote interior angles. This means you add the two opposite angles inside the triangle and the answer is the measure of angle ACD.

Another way to obtain the answer is to find the measure of the interior angle of the triangle at C, by adding the other two angles and then subtracting from 180. Angle C is 72 degrees. Then the two angles at point C form a linear pair whose sum is 180. So subtract 72 from 180 and you have the measure of angle ACD.

9. **(4)** 98 divided by 2 gives the cost of one pound, which is $0.49. Then $0.49 times 5 is $2.45. Answer (1) incorrectly multiplies 2 times 98 times 5.

10. **(5)** Answer (5) is correct because 7 times (-4y) is (-28y), and 7 times 2 is 14.

11. **(3)** Angle BEF and angle CFE are alternate interior angles and are therefore congruent, or equal in measure. If we can find the measure of either one, we will know the measure of angle CFE. We know that angle GEB and angle BEF form a linear pair, and we know angle GEB measures 40 degrees. Subtracting 40 from 180 we find that angle BEF is 140 degrees. Since CFE is an alternate interior angle and congruent to angle BEF, the measure of angle CFE is 140 degrees.

12. **(3)** To get to work it takes $2.50 ($0.50 for the bus plus $2.00 for the train). Then it takes another $2.50 to get home. That totals $5.00 each day. There are 5 work days in a week, so 5 days times $5.00 equals $25.00 for each week.

13. **(2)** The correct solution may be obtained by substituting each ordered pair in both equations. If both equations are then true, that ordered pair is the true solution. The correct solution may also be obtained by solving the system by the substitution or addition methods. To use the substitution method, solve the first equation for x by transposing the (-3y) to the right side of the equation, thus $x = 9 + 3y$. Substitute this expression in the second equation, which gives $3(9 + 3y) + y = 7$ and solve for y. Use of the addition method employs the addition property of equality, which says that if equals are added to equals, then the results are equal. First multiply the second equation by 3. This gives $9x + 3y = 21$. If this new equation is added to the first equation, the result is $10x = 30$. The terms containing the y variable disappeared. Now if both sides are divided by 10, $x = 3$. Now substitute 3 for x in the first equation: $3 - 3y = 9$ and solve for y; $y = -2$.

14. **(4)** The problem is asking, "20 times what equals 220." You must know that the length times the width of a rectangle is the area, and then use algebra to solve for the unknown. $20x = 220$. Divide both sides by 20 to find $x = 11$. Also, for a problem like this, you may try each answer to find the one which gives 220.

15. **(5)** Two tickets times $400 equals $800, plus $210 equals $1,010. Multiplying by 0.1 (for 10%) the answer is $101.

16. **(1)** The easiest way to solve this is with a chart. The chart below represents the trip going and the trip returning. The distance is the same for both trips. The trip going has the speed of the airplane plus the tail wind. The trip returning has the speed of the airplane minus the tail wind. The times are as stated.

	D =	r	t
going ⟹	D	r + 60	6
returning ⟸	D	r − 60	8

Since the distance equals the rate times the time and the distances are equal, set up an equation of representations of the equal distances and solve: 6(r + 60) = 8(r – 60). 6r + 360 = 8r – 480. Then r = 420.

17. **(2)** All sides of an equilateral triangle are congruent, or have the same measure. The altitude is the perpendicular bisector of the base and the bisector of the vertex angle. So the altitude divides the triangle into two triangles that have angles of 30° -60° -90°. The sides of this kind of triangle have the special relationship $1: \sqrt{3}:2$. This makes the length of the altitude of our triangle $3\sqrt{3}$.

18. **(1)** This is simply a subtraction problem. The arrival time, 7:32, minus the departure time, 7:09, equals 23, and these are minutes.

19. **(4)** Let n represent the number of nickels and q represent the number of quarters, then n = q + 3. The value of the nickels is 5 cents and the value of the quarters is 25 cents and the total value of the coins she has is 465 cents or $4.65. The equation for this is 5n + 25q = 465. If (q + 3) is substituted in the second equation for n, we get 5(q + 3) + 25q = 465. Distribute the 5 and get 5q + 15 + 25q = 465. Collect like terms 30q + 15 = 465. Subtract 15 from both sides 30q = 450, then divide both sides by 30 to find q = 15. She has three more nickels than that or 15 + 3 = 18. She has 18 nickels and 15 quarters for a total of 33 coins.

20. **(4)** The hypotenuse is the longest side of the triangle. It is the side opposite of the right angle. A special relationship exists between the lengths of sides of a 45-45-90, or isosceles right, triangle. The hypotenuse is always $\sqrt{2}$ times the length of a leg. So this one is $\sqrt{2}$ times 4 or $4\sqrt{2}$. Another method may be used to find this. The Pythagorean Formula for right triangles is a2 + b2 = c2, where a and b are legs and c is the hypotenuse. $4^2 + 4^2 = c^2$ or $32^2 = c^2$ or $\sqrt{32} = c$. $\sqrt{16}$ times $\sqrt{2} = c$. Therefore $4\sqrt{2} = c$.

21. **(4)** This multi-step problem requires multiplication and then addition. Two times $4.19 is $8.38 plus two times $0.69 ($1.38) plus three times $1.15 ($3.45) equals $13.21. Multiplying $13.21 by 0.05 to find the tax is $0.66. Adding the tax to the total of merchandise gives $13.87.

22. **(5)** To find the f(-3) simply substitute (-3) for x. This gives f(-3) = -(-3) + 4, which is 7, because -(-3) = +3.

23. **(2)** The area of a parallelogram is A = bh. We know the base is 8, but we must find the height. That is possible because we are given the measure of the angle. When the height is drawn in, we have a triangle with angles 30-60-90. The hypotenuse of this is 4. Remember the relationship of the sides of a 30-60-90 is $1: \sqrt{3}:2$. Since the hypotenuse is 4, the side opposite the 30

degree angle is 2. This is the height of the triangle and of the parallelogram. Now put this in the formula and get A = (8) (2) or the area is 16cm².

24. **(3)** The tax rate is $2.10 for each $100 in value. There are 550 100's in 55,000. Therefore the tax is $2.10 times 550, or $1,155.

25. **(1)** This may be solved by "translating" the problem directly into algebraic symbols. "What" = x, percent = 0.01, "of" = multiply or times, and "in" = equals. Put this together and you have an equation, x (0.01) (80) = 32. Solve for x and x = 40. This is the percent. Another way to work this problem is to divide 32 by 80 and multiply by 100. A third way to work percent problems is by setting up a proportion, with the "parts" on top and the "wholes" on the bottom.

$$\frac{\text{percent}}{100} \quad \frac{\text{quantity}}{} $$

$$\frac{x}{100} = \frac{32}{80}$$

By solving the proportion, you find the answer to the problem. You may use a proportion to solve any percent problem by letting X fill in the unknown place in the proportion.

26. **(4)** The tank is a rectangular solid with length = 48 cm, width = 35 cm, and height = 52 cm. 2 cm at the top will be without water, so the actual height of the water will be only 50 cm. The formula for the area of a solid is A = Length x Width x Height. So, multiply 48 times 35 times 50.

27. **(1)** The cost of the drill is $5; the cost of the mixer is $20, so it costs $25 for each day, and the real answer is $25 times 3 or $75.

28. **(5)** To solve this, simply divide both sides of the equation by r.

29. **(5)** The formula usually used to find the area of any polygon is A = 1/2 ap, where a is the apothem and p is the perimeter. Since the side is known and the number of sides is known, the perimeter can be found. It is 8 times 6 or 48. The apothem is the segment from the center of the figure perpendicular to one of the sides (see figure below). The radius (the segment from the center of the figure to a vertex) is 8, the same length as a side, and forms a

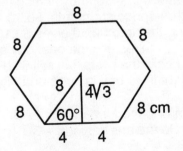

triangle with the apothem and a side. This triangle is 30-60-90. The side opposite the 30 angle is 4, therefore the apothem is $4\sqrt{3}$.

30. **(5)** The correct answer is found by adding together the costs of the items, which is $33.36, and multiplying this by 0.06 to find the tax of $2.00, and adding the two totals together.

31. **(3)** The rule for multiplying variables with exponents is $a^N \cdot a^M = a^{N+M}$. So the exponents are just added together.

32. **(4)** Completing the formula A = 1/2 ($4\sqrt{3}$) (48). The formula for the area of a circle is $A = \pi r^2$. Since the diameter is 10, the radius is 5. Completing the formula: A = 3.14 times 25.

33. **(3)** There are 52 weeks in a year, therefore multiply the weekly cost of $26.03 by 52.

34. **(5)** When a fraction is raised to a power, both the numerator and the denominator is raised to that power. So, x^2 taken as a factor 5 times is x^{10}, and y taken as a factor 5 times is y^5.

35. **(5)** The correct answer is found by multiplying 300 by 3.5.

36. **(2)** The rule for dividing variables with exponents is a^N divided by a^M = a^{N-M}. So the exponents are just subtracted—the one in the denominator subtracted from the one in the numerator.

37. **(2)** The best answer given is not exact, but it is an estimate. 76 rounds to 80, which goes into 4,000,000 exactly 50,000 times. Answer (1) is 76 times 4. Answer (3) is produced by incorrectly rounding 76 to 70 and dividing that into the 4,000,000. Answer (4) is 76 times 4, and answer (5) is 4,000,000 divided by 100.

38. **(4)** We want to find what binomials multiplied together would give $(x^4 - 1)$. $(x^2 + 1)$ and $(x^2 - 1)$ would give the results, but $(x^2 - 1)$ can also be factored into $(x + 1)$ and $(x - 1)$.

39. **(4)** The correct answer is found by finding the unit cost (cost for one pencil) in each of the three price structures. $0.10 each is $0.10 for one. 2 dozen is 24 and dividing that into $2.50 gives $0.10416666 as the cost for one. $0.99 divided by 10 makes this the best buy at $0.099 for one pencil. There is a slight difference in the costs, but still $0.099 is the smallest value. (The difference is evident if we buy in large quantity).

40. **(3)** This problem is in the form of $A^2 + 2AB + B^2$, which is the square of a binomial $(A + B)^2$. So the answer is $(x + 3)^2$.

41. **(1)** Her chances are 8 out of 1600 or 8/1600. This is one out of 200 or 0.5%.

42. **(1)** This problem requires a system of equations. Let A represent the number of adult tickets and S represent the number of student tickets, then A + S = 350. The value of the adult tickets is $5 and the value of the Student tickets is $3.50 and the total value of all of the tickets is $1,306. The equation for this is 5A + 3.5S = 1306. If A + S = 350, then A = 350 - S. This can be substituted in the second equation for A and get 5(350 - S) + 3.5S = 1306. Distribute the 5 and get 1750 - 5S + 3.5S = 1306. Collect like terms and solve for S to find 54 is the number of adult tickets. Subtract this from 350 to get 296 student tickets.

43. **(3)** If one integer is represented by x the the next consecutive integer is (x + 1). The product is represented by x (x + 1).

44. **(1)** To read the graph properly, notice that the columns represent millions of dollars, so locate 1.5 for the $1,500,000. Then look down to the bottom of the column to read the name of the salesperson. It is J. Johns.

45. **(1)** First find the amount sold by P. Sellers. Look to the top of the column above his name and read the amount to the left. It is 0.5 or one half of a million dollars. Three times that would be 1.5 million. The person selling 1.5 million is J. Johns. C. Chan did not sell that much, and S. Smith sold more.

46. **(3)** The formula for simple interest is I = PRT, where I is the interest, P is the principle, R is the rate of interest, and T is the amount of time in years. So the correct answer is obtained by multiplying 2,000 times 0.105 times 2.

47. **(4)** Her annual benefit is the amount she receives as her discount. It is 20% of the amount she spends at that store. It is found by multiplying $592.86 by 0.2.

48. **(3)** To compare these two jobs, you must compare equal pay periods. The easiest way is to multiply the weekly amount by 52 to give the annual amount. $298 times 52 is $15,496. When $14,900 is subtracted from that, you know that Job A pays $596 more in a year.

49. **(5)** The correct answer is obtained by multiplying 367 miles times 50 weeks times $0.19.

50. **(2)** They will have the $550 plus the interest. The interest is 0.082 times the $550, or $45.10. So they will have $550 plus $45.10 or $595.10.

51. **(4)** 12 times 1/3 or 12 divided by 3 is 4. Each person would get 4 pieces.

52. **(4)** There are two easy ways to solve this. First, if there are 36 girls, then there are 90 – 36 or 54 boys. 54 divided by 90 times 100 gives the percent of boys. Another way is to divide 36 by 90 then multiply by 100 to give 40% girls. If there are 40% girls, then 100% – 40% = 60% boys.

53. **(5)** To find the correct answer the common denominator must be determined and all fractions changed to that denominator. The common denominator of 6 and 3 is 6. 1/3 = 2/6. Add all of the numerators 5 + 2 + 7 = 14. 14/6 = 2 and 2/6 or 2 and 1/3. 3 + 2 and 1/3 is the correct answer of 5 and 1/3. Answer (1) adds the 3 in with the numerators. Answer (2) changes 1/3 to 2/6 and adds the 3 in with the numerators. Answer(3) and (4) are distractors.

54. **(1)** This is found by taking 25%, or 1/4, of $2,500 and then multiplying by 12 months.

55. **(2)** The correct answer is written on the graph.

56. **(2)** She saves 12% of $2,500, or $300.

▼ APPENDIX

PERIODIC TABLE OF THE ELEMENTS

Legend:

ATOMIC NUMBER ▶ 46	+2 ◄ OXIDATION STATES
SYMBOL ▶ Pd	+4
ATOMIC WEIGHT ▶ 106.4	
-18-18-0 ◄ ELECTRON CONFIGURATION	

TRANSITION ELEMENTS — GROUP 8

NOBLE GASES

Numbers in parentheses are mass numbers of most stable isotope of that element

Main Table

1a	2a	3b	4b	5b	6b	7b	8	8	8	1b	2b	3a	4a	5a	6a	7a	0	Orbit
1 H +1,-1 1.0079 / 1																	2 He 0 4.00260 / 2	K
3 Li +1 6.94 / 2-1	4 Be +2 9.01218 / 2-2											5 B +3 10.81 / 2-3	6 C +2,+4,-4 12.011 / 2-4	7 N +1,+2,+3,+4,+5,-1,-3 14.0067 / 2-5	8 O -2 15.9994 / 2-6	9 F -1 18.998403 / 2-7	10 Ne 0 20.179 / 2-8	K-L
11 Na +1 22.98977 / 2-8-1	12 Mg +2 24.305 / 2-8-2											13 Al +3 26.98154 / 2-8-3	14 Si +2,+4,-4 28.0855 / 2-8-4	15 P +3,+5,-3 30.97376 / 2-8-5	16 S +4,+6,-2 32.06 / 2-8-6	17 Cl +1,+5,+7,-1 35.453 / 2-8-7	18 Ar 0 39.948 / 2-8-8	K-L-M
19 K +1 39.0983 / -8-8-1	20 Ca +2 40.08 / -8-8-2	21 Sc +3 44.9559 / -8-9-2	22 Ti +2,+3,+4 47.90 / -8-10-2	23 V +2,+3,+4,+5 50.9415 / -8-11-2	24 Cr +2,+3,+6 51.996 / -8-13-1	25 Mn +2,+3,+4,+7 54.9380 / -8-13-2	26 Fe +2,+3 55.847 / -8-14-2	27 Co +2,+3 58.9332 / -8-15-2	28 Ni +2,+3 58.71 / -8-16-2	29 Cu +1,+2 63.546 / -8-18-1	30 Zn +2 65.38 / -8-18-2	31 Ga +3 69.735 / -8-18-3	32 Ge +2,+4 72.59 / -8-18-4	33 As +3,+5,-3 74.9216 / -8-18-5	34 Se +4,+6,-2 78.96 / -8-18-6	35 Br +1,+5,-1 79.904 / -8-18-7	36 Kr 0 83.80 / -8-18-8	-L-M-N
37 Rb +1 85.4678 / -18-8-1	38 Sr +2 87.62 / -18-8-2	39 Y +3 88.9059 / -18-9-2	40 Zr +4 91.22 / -18-10-2	41 Nb +3,+5 92.9064 / -18-12-1	42 Mo +6 95.94 / -18-13-1	43 Tc +4,+6,+7 98.9062 / -18-13-2	44 Ru +3 101.07 / -18-15-1	45 Rh +3 102.9055 / -18-16-1	46 Pd +2,+3 106.4 / -18-18-0	47 Ag +1 107.868 / -18-18-1	48 Cd +2 112.41 / -18-18-2	49 In +3 114.82 / -18-18-3	50 Sn +2,+4 118.69 / -18-18-4	51 Sb +3,+5,-3 121.75 / -18-18-5	52 Te +4,+6,-2 127.60 / -18-18-6	53 I +1,+5,+7,-1 126.9045 / -18-18-7	54 Xe 0 131.30 / -18-18-8	-M-N-O
55 Cs +1 132.9054 / -18-8-1	56 Ba +2 137.33 / -18-8-2	57 La +3 138.9055 / -18-9-2	72 Hf +4 178.49 / -32-10-2	73 Ta +5 180.9479 / -32-11-2	74 W +6 183.85 / -32-12-2	75 Re +4,+6,+7 186.207 / -32-13-2	76 Os +3,+4 190.2 / -32-14-2	77 Ir +3,+4 192.22 / -32-15-2	78 Pt +2,+4 195.09 / -32-16-2	79 Au +1,+3 196.9665 / -32-18-1	80 Hg +1,+2 200.59 / -32-18-2	81 Tl +1,+3 204.37 / -32-18-3	82 Pb +2,+4 207.2 / -32-18-4	83 Bi +3,+5 208.9804 / -32-18-5	84 Po +2,+4 (209) / -32-18-6	85 At +3,+5,-1 (210) / -32-18-7	86 Rn 0 (222) / -32-18-8	-N-O-P
87 Fr +1 (223) / -18-8-1	88 Ra +2 226.0254 / -18-8-2	89 Ac +3 (227) / -18-9-2	104 Rf +4 (260) / -32-10-2	105 Ha (260) / -32-11-2	106 (263) / -32-12-2													O P Q

Lanthanides

3b	4b	5b	6b	7b	8	8	8	1b	2b	3a	4a	5a	6a	7a	Orbit
58 Ce +3,+4 140.12 / -20-8-2	59 Pr +3,+4 140.9077 / -21-8-2	60 Nd +3 144.24 / -22-8-2	61 Pm +3 (145) / -23-8-2	62 Sm +2,+3 150.4 / -24-8-2	63 Eu +2,+3 151.96 / -25-8-2	64 Gd +2,+3 157.25 / -25-9-2	65 Tb +3 158.9254 / -27-8-2	66 Dy +3 162.50 / -28-8-2	67 Ho +3 164.9304 / -29-8-2	68 Er +3 167.26 / -30-8-2	69 Tm +3 168.9342 / -31-8-2	70 Yb +2,+3 173.04 / -32-8-2	71 Lu +3 174.967 ± 0.003 / -32-9-2		N O P

Actinides

3b	4b	5b	6b	7b	8	8	8	1b	2b	3a	4a	5a	6a	7a	Orbit
90 Th +4 232.0381 / -18-10-2	91 Pa +4,+5 231.0359 / -20-9-2	92 U +3,+4,+5,+6 238.029 / -21-9-2	93 Np +3,+4,+5,+6 237.0482 / -22-9-2	94 Pu +3,+4,+5,+6 (244) / -24-8-2	95 Am +3,+4,+5,+6 (243) / -25-8-2	96 Cm +3 (247) / -25-9-2	97 Bk +3,+4 (247) / -27-8-2	98 Cf +3,+4 (251) / -28-8-2	99 Es (254) / -29-8-2	100 Fm (257) / -30-8-2	101 Md (258) / -31-8-2	102 No (259) / -32-8-2	103 Lr (260) / -32-9-2		O P Q

REFERENCE TABLE

SYMBOLS AND THEIR MEANINGS

=	is equal to	≤	is less than or equal to
≠	is unequal to	≥	is greater than or equal to
<	is less than	‖	is parallel to
>	is greater than	⊥	is perpendicular to

FORMULAS

DESCRIPTION	FORUMLA

AREA (A) of a:
square $A = s^2$; where s = side
rectangle $A = lw$; where l = length, w = width
parallelogram $A = bh$; where b = base, h = height
triangle $A = \frac{1}{2} bh$; where b = base, h = height
circle $A = \pi r^2$; where π = 3.14, r = radius

PERIMETER (P) of a:
square $P = 4s$; where s = side
rectangle $P = 2l + 2w$; where l = length, w = width
triangle $P = a + b + c$; where a, b, and c are the sides
circumference (C) of a circle $C = \pi d$, where π = 3.14, d = diameter

VOLUME (V) of a:
cube $V = s^2$; where s = side
rectangular container $V = lwh$; where l = length, w = width, h = height
Pythagorean relationship $c^2 = a^2 + b^2$; where c = hypotenuse, a and b are legs of a right triangle

distance (d) between two points in a plane $d = \sqrt{(x_2 - x_1)^2 + (y_2 - y_1)^2}$
where (x_1, y_1) and (x_2, y_2) are two points in a plane

mean $\text{mean} = \frac{x_1 + x_2 + \ldots + x_n}{n}$;
where the x's are the values for which a mean is desired, and n = number of values in the series

median   **median** = the point in an ordered set of numbers at which half of the numbers are above and half of the numbers are below this value

simple interest (i) $i = prt$; where p = principal, r = rate, t = time
distance (d) as function of rate and time $d = rt$; where r = rate, t = time
total cost (c) $c = nr$; where n = number of units, r = cost per unit

INDEX

Acceleration (physics), **313**
Acids, 238
Acute angles, 466
Addition
  in algebra, 430
  of decimals, 408
  of fractions, 400
  of positive and negative numbers,
  396-97
  of radicals, 419
  in solving equations, 439
Adjectives, in sentences, 31-32
Air, 271-72
Algebra, 430-48
Amendments, of the Constitution,
  124-141
Amplitude (physics), **328**
Analysis, of literature, 344-84
Anatomy, 177
Angles (geometric), **451**-59
Area
  of geometric figures, 463
  of quadrilaterals, 472
  of triangles, 465-69
Arithmetic, 393-426
Astronomy, 248-51
Atmosphere, 271-72
Atoms, 221
Averages, finding, 424

Bacteriology, 177
Banks, deregulation of, 138
Bases, chemical, **238**
Behavioral science, 164-70
Bill of Rights, 141
Bills, legislature, 143-44
Biology, 177-216
  of human systems, 209-12
Bisectors, of triangles, **467**
Botany, 177

Business
  factors, 132
  types, 132-33

Canada, 157
Capital, 132
Capitalization, 43-47
Cells (biological), 178-90
Central America, 160-61
Characters
  in drama, 370
  in fiction, 348-49
Chemical
  elements, 221-22, 235, **242**
  formulas, 238
  properties, of earth, 260
Chemistry, 221-43
Chromosomes, 189
Circles, 479-82
City government, 144
Civil War, 123-24
Classical literature, 345
Classification, scientific, 203-6
Clauses, in sentences, 55, 57
Climate, 161, 273-74
Commas, 53, 55, 57, 61-67
Commentary, 346, 383-84
Compounds, chemical, **242**
Congress, 142-44
Conjunctions, in sentences, 34-35
Constitution, 124, 141
Coordinate geometry, 487-89
County government, 144
Court system, 144
Cytology, 177

Decimals, 407-10
Deflation, economic, **137**
Denominators, 399-400
Density (physics), 311
Depression, the Great, 125-26

Distances, measurement of, **488**
Division
   in algebra, 431-32
   of decimals, 408-9
   of fractions, 401
   of positive and negative numbers,
     396
   of radicals, 418
   in solving equations, 439
DNA, 184-85, 199
Drama, 367-81

Earth
   chemical properties of, 260
   evolution of, 265-69
   physical properties of, 259-61,
     271-74
Earth science, 248-84
Earthquakes, as natural disasters, 280
Ecology, 177, 215-16
Economic systems, 132
Economics, 130-38
Ego, 170
Election of 1912, 125
Electricity, 336-37
Elements, chemical, 221-22, 235-**242**
Embryology, 177
Energy, 226, 274, **318**-20
Energy sources, 151
Entrepreneurship, 132
Equations, mathematical, 439-43
Equilateral triangle, 466
Erosion, 273
Essay test, 94
Essays
   conclusion in, 101, 110, 112-13
   development in, 101, 109-11, 113
   introduction in, 100, 109, 111, 113
   reading of, 354-57
   types of, 347, 354-55
   writing of, 96-104
Evolution, 200-201, 265-69
Executive branch (government),
   141-42
Exponents, 421-23

Factoring, 435-37
Family sociological, 164-65, 168
Farce, 371
Federal government
   agencies, 125-26, 134
   branches of, 141
   court system, 144
Fiction, 347-54
Force (physics), **316**
Formulas, chemical, 238
Fractions, 399-402

Galaxies, 251
GED Exam
   facts about, 2-3
   preparation for, 3-7
   scoring of, 7-20
   study schedule, viii-ix
   tips for passing, 21-24
Genetics, 188-90
Geography, 150-61
Geological
   evolution, 201
   properties of earth, 260
Geometry, 451-89
Government, 143. *See also* Federal
   government
   and economy, 130
   local and state, 144
   types of, 144-45
Gravity, 296, 299
Graying of America, 165
Greatest common factors (algebraic),
   435

Heat, as energy, 323-24
Heredity, 170
History, U.S. 119-27
Homophone, 85
House of Representatives, 143-44
Hurricanes, as natural disasters, 283
Hypothesis, 177

Id, 170
Industrial Revolution, 121-22
Improper fractions, 399

Inequalities, (algebraic), **443**-46
Inertia, (physics), **313**
Inflation, economic, **137**
Inorganic chemistry, 221
Insurance, 134-35
Integers, mathematical, **393**

Judicial branch (government), 141, 144

Labor, 132
Laissez-faire, 130
Least common multiple, 435
Legislative branch (government), 141, 143
Light, properties of, 330-31
Lines
  on coordinate grids, 487-89
  geometric, **451**-59
Literature
  classical, **345**
  interpreting, 344-84
  popular, **345**
Local government, 144
Lowest common denominator, 400

Magnetism, 339
Market systems, 130, **132**
Mass, 311
Mathematics, 388-489
Matter, chemical, **226**-28, 234, 237-39, 311
Mean (mathematical), **424**-26
Median (mathematical), **424**-26
Meteors, 250
Methods, scientific, 301
Mexico, 156
Midpoint, calculation of, 489
Migration, 281
Minerals, 157, 260
Mixtures, chemical, **226**-27
Modifiers, in sentences, 35-36
Momentum (physics), **313**
Monogamy, 168
Motifs, in literature, **350**

Multiplication
  in algebra, 431
  of decimals, 408
  of fractions, 401
  of positive and negative numbers, 397
  of radicals, 418
  in solving equations, 439
Municipal government, 144

Narrator, 355
Natural resources, 156-57, 216
  in economics, 132
  in geography, 151-52
New Deal, 126
New World, the, 119
Newton's laws, 298
Nonfiction, 347, 354-57
Nouns, possessive, 32-33
Numbers
  mixed, 399
  positive and negative, 396
  real, 393
Numerators, 399

Obtuse triangle, 466
Oceans, natural disasters, 281
Organic chemistry, 221

Paragraphs, 100-103
Parallel lines (geometric), **455**-59
Parallelogram, 471-72
Percents, 413-14
Perimeter, of triangle, **465**
Phonic, 347
Photosynthesis, 186
Physics, 296-339
Physiology, 177
Planes (geometric), 451-59
Plot, 347-48
  in drama, 368-70
  in literature, 347, 354
Poetry, 359-64
Point of view, in literature, 352-53
Points (geometric), 451-59

Polarization, 330-31
Political science, 141-45
Pollution, 216
Polygamy, 168
Polygons (geometrical), **462**-64
Polynomials, 430-32
Popular literature, 345
Population, 150-52, 156-57, 160, 165, 216
 change in, 121
 distribution of, 127
Power (physics), **320**
Powers (mathematical), 421
Prepositions, in sentences, 33
President, 142
Pressure, air, **273**
Prime factor (algebraic), **435**
Production, factors of, 132
Progressive Party, 125
Proofreading, 104
Proportions (algebraic), 447-48
Prose, 347-56
Psychology, 170
Punctuation, 49-67. *See also* Commas
Purpose, in essays, 354-55

Quadrilaterals, 471-76

Radicals, in mathematics, 418-19
Radius, of a circle, **479**
Ratios, 447-48
Reactions, chemical, 237-39
Reading skills
 in commentary, 383-84
 in drama, 367-81
 in poetry, 359-64
 in prose, 347-56
Rectangles, 472
Rectangular solids, 485
Reflection (physics), 300, 330
Refraction (physics), 300, **330**
Relativity, theory of, 300-301
Resources, 151-52, 156-57, 216, 280-84
Rhombus, 473

Right angles, 466

Salts, chemical, 238-39
Satire, 371
Science, 174-339
Scientific
 classification, 203-206
 method, 301
Senate, 143-44
Sentences, 36-38
 compound, 58, 63-64
 editing, 103-104
 fragments, 37-38
 modifiers in, 65-66
 run-on, 37
 structure, 36, 61, 63
Setting
 in drama, 368
 in fiction, 351
Social status, 165
Social studies, 117-170
Sociology, 164-65
Solar system, 248-51
Solid geometry, 485-87
Solution sets (algebraic), 439
Solutions, chemical, 242-43
Sound energy, 334-35
South America, 160
Speed (physics), **313**
Spelling
 of frequently misspelled words, 75-83
 list, 75-83
 of sound-alike (homophones) words, 85
Square root, 418
Squares, 473-74
Stars, formation of, 250
State government, 144
Status, social, 165
Style, in literature, **351**
Subjects
 agreement of, 30-31
 combining two, 58, 63-64
 in sentences, 36, 61, 63

Subtraction
  in algebra, 430-31
  of decimals, 408
  of fractions, 400
  of positive and negative numbers,
    396
  of radicals, 419
  in solving equations, 439
Superego, 170
Supreme Court, 144

Taxation, 136
Technology, 132
Temperature, 273
Theme
  in literature, 349
  in science, 177
Theory, of relativity, 300-301
Tides, behavior of, 282
Topics
  in drama, 370-77
  in literature, 349
Transitions, in writing, 101-102
Trapezoids, 474-75
Triangles (geometrical), **465**-69

United States
  geography, 151-52
  history, 119-27

Value, sociological, 164, 167-**68**
Velocity (physics), **312**
Verbs
  agreement of, 30-31
  in sentences, 63
  tense, of 38
Veto, 144
Vocabulary, in science, 177
Volcanoes, as natural disasters,
  280-81

Water, 272
Water formations, 282-83
Waves, behavior of, 282
Wavelengths, 327-28
Weather, 161
Weathering, in erosion, **273**
Writing skills, 26-42, 95-104

Zoology, 177